John

THE CROSSWAY CLASSIC COMMENTARIES

John

by
John Calvin

Series Editors
Alister McGrath and J. I. Packer

CROSSWAY BOOKS

A PUBLISHING MINISTRY OF GOOD NEWS PUBLISHERS

WHEATON, ILLINOIS • NOTTINGHAM, ENGLAND

John

Copyright © 1994 by Watermark

Published by Crossway
        1300 Crescent Street
        Wheaton, Illinois 60187

Art Direction: Mark Schramm

First printing, 1994

Printed in the United States of America

Library of Congress Cataloging-in-Publication Data
Calvin, John. 1509-1565
   John / by John Calvin.
     p.   cm. — (Crossway classic commentaries)
   1. Bible. N.T. John—Commentaries. I. Title. III. Series.
BS2615.C326 1994   226.5'07—dc20   94-2284
ISBN 13: 978-0-89107-778-7
ISBN 10: 0-89107-778-2

Crossway is a publishing ministry of Good News Publishers.

CH		21	20	19	18	17	16	15	14	13	12
21	20	19	18	17	16	15	14	13	12	11	10

First British edition 1994

ISBN 1 85684 095-6

Contents

Series Preface

The purpose of the Crossway Classic Commentaries is to make some of the most valuable commentaries on the books of the Bible, by some of the greatest Bible teachers and theologians in the last five hundred years, available to a new generation. These books will help today's readers learn truth, wisdom, and devotion from such authors as J. C. Ryle, Martin Luther, John Calvin, J. B. Lightfoot, John Owen, Charles Spurgeon, Charles Hodge, and Matthew Henry.

We do not apologize for the age of some of the items chosen. In the realm of practical exposition promoting godliness, the old is often better than the new. Spiritual vision and authority, based on an accurate handling of the biblical text, are the qualities that have been primarily sought in deciding what to include.

So far as is possible, everything is tailored to the needs and enrichment of thoughtful readers — lay Christians, students, and those in the ministry. The originals, some of which were written at a high technical level, have been abridged as needed, simplified stylistically, and unburdened of foreign words. However, the intention of this series is never to change any thoughts of the original authors, but to faithfully convey them in an understandable fashion.

The publishers are grateful to Dr. Alister McGrath of Wycliffe Hall, Oxford, Dr. J. I. Packer of Regent College, Vancouver, and Watermark of Norfolk, England, for the work of selecting and editing that now brings this project to fruition.

THE PUBLISHERS
Crossway Books
Wheaton, Illinois

Introduction

"The chief excellence of a commentator lies in lucid brevity," wrote Calvin; and following his own precept, he created the modern expository commentary, where the goal is to bring out the sense and thought-flow of the text as it applies to the readers. A tireless worker who for years kept four secretaries busy, Calvin wrote landmark expositions of most of the Old Testament and all the New Testament except Revelation. They remain standard resources for scholars and students today.

With his cool clarity of mind, Calvin was a typical French scholar, while his ardent zeal for God's honor and praise marks him out as a model for every disciple of Christ. He had wanted to be an aristocrat of letters like Erasmus, but the outstanding impact of his *Institutes of the Christian Religion*, published in 1536, followed by his call to church leadership in Geneva later that year, pitchforked him into high exposure and an international role as the Everest among Reformational theologians. Luther's junior colleague Melanchthon, himself no mean exponent of divine things, always spoke of Calvin simply as "the theologian." In Geneva, where at first Calvin was slightingly referred to as "the Frenchman" and constantly demeaned and opposed by the top townspeople, he received great honor during the latter years of his life, as the Grand Old Man of the Reformation. Worn out by long-term ill health, he died in Geneva in 1564, having accomplished in his fifty-four years the work of two or three ordinary lifetimes.

Basic to Calvin's commenting was his view of the Bible as essentially written communication of the mind of God, given (sometimes, he says, dictated) by the Holy Spirit using chosen human agents. The Spirit now authenticates and applies it to God's people by opening minds and hearts to its self-attesting impact. It is true, and well known, that *sola Scriptura* — "by Scripture alone" — was the Reformers' slogan about the knowledge of God; but "alone" there is only excluding tradition as a second source of revealed truth, not discounting the Spirit as the illuminator of our hearts. Without the personal ministration of the Spirit, Calvin believed, we shall not learn from Scripture as we should, however much exegetical brainwork we do. Calvin's reverence for the God-given written Word — that is, for God, whose didactic utterance the written Word is — comes out in all his commentaries: nowhere, however, more plainly than in his exposition of John.

John's Gospel — "the spiritual gospel," as it has been called from very early times — is among the profoundest books of the New Testament, and Calvin matches its profundity in a way that few can rival. Published in 1553, this commentary is one of Calvin's best pieces of work, and one of the best elucidations of the evangelist's text ever achieved.

When Calvin began his commenting career he explained that he took as read the full treatment of theological themes offered in the *Institutes*, so that the commentaries would contain no elaborate discussion of these themes, but just a brief indication of what each particular text actually meant. The reader will find, therefore, in the pages that follow no plugging of any form of the system called Calvinism, but simply some top-class spelling out of key truths about Jesus Christ, whom Calvin hailed as the central focus of all Scripture and whom John in his Gospel exalts stupendously. So read, learn Christ, and be blessed!

J. I. PACKER

Preface

The meaning of the Greek word translated "Gospel" is well known. In Scripture it means, above all, the glad and delightful message of the grace shown to us in Christ. It teaches us to despise the world and its riches and pleasures, which do not last, and wholeheartedly to desire this invaluable blessing, and to embrace it when it is offered to us. We see unbelievers take extreme delight in the empty enjoyments of the world, while they have little if any taste for spiritual blessings. Such conduct is natural to us all. To correct this fault, God calls "Gospel" the message about Christ which he orders to be proclaimed. So he reminds us that nowhere else can true and solid happiness be obtained, and that in him we have all that is needed for a perfect, happy life.

Some people think the word *Gospel* covers all God's gracious promises, even the ones scattered in the Law and the Prophets. Certainly, whenever God declares that he will be reconciled to men and women, he shows Christ at the same time. It is Christ's special role to shed the light of joy wherever he shines. I admit, then, that the patriarchs had the same Gospel of free salvation that we have. But since the Holy Spirit declares in the Scriptures that the Gospel was first proclaimed when Christ came, let us keep to this way of speaking too; and let us keep to this definition of "Gospel": it is a solemn announcement of the grace revealed in Christ. Thus the Gospel is called "the power of God for the salvation of everyone who believes" (Romans 1:16) because in it God displays his righteousness. It is also said that we are "Christ's ambassadors," imploring people to "be reconciled to God" (2 Corinthians 5:20). As Christ is the pledge of God's mercy, and of his fatherly love to us, so he is especially the subject of the Gospel.

That is why the stories of Christ's appearing in the flesh, dying, and at length being taken up into heaven have become known particularly as Gospels. Although the word means the whole of the New Covenant, it has come to mean that part of it which declares that Christ appeared to us in the flesh, and died, and rose from the dead. Merely telling this story would not be enough for salvation — indeed, it would not help at all; so the evangelists also explain *why* he was born, died and rose again, and what benefit we derive from those events.

The other three Gospels give a fuller narrative of the life and death of Christ, but John dwells at greater length on the teaching about the role of Christ and the power of his death and resurrection. The others certainly say that Christ came to bring salvation to the world, to atone for the sins of the world by the sacrifice of his death, and, in short, to do everything that was required from the Mediator. John, likewise, devotes a portion of his work to historical details. But the teaching which points out to us the power and benefit of the coming of Christ is far more clearly shown by him than by the rest. They all had the same purpose: to point out Christ. The first three Gospels show his body, so to speak, but John shows his soul. For this reason I usually say that this Gospel is a key to understanding the rest; for whoever understands the power of Christ strikingly pictured here will then profit by reading what the others tell about the Redeemer who appeared.

John is believed to have written chiefly in order to emphasize that Christ was God, as against the wicked blasphemies of Ebion and Cerinthus. This is what Eusebius and Jerome say, as did most of their contemporaries. But whatever his motive for writing at the time, there can be no doubt whatever that God intended something far greater for his church. He therefore dictated to the four evangelists what they should write, in such a way that while each had his own part, the whole might be collected into one. It is now our duty to blend the four together so that we may learn from all of them as if by one teacher. As for John being placed fourth, it was done because of when he wrote; but it would be better to read the Gospels in a different order: when we wish to read in Matthew and the others that Christ was given to us by the Father, we should first learn from John the purpose for which he appeared.

John
Chapter 1

Verses 1–5

1. In the beginning was the Word. In this introduction the evangelist asserts the eternal divinity of Christ, telling us that he is the eternal God who "appeared in a body" (1 Timothy 3:16). The intention is to show that mankind's restoration had to be accomplished by the Son of God, since by his power all things were created, and he alone breathes life and energy into all creatures so that they remain as they are, and since in mankind he has uniquely shown both his power and his grace. Even after the fall of Adam he has not stopped being generous and kind to Adam's descendants.

This teaching is very necessary. Since we should only seek life and salvation in God, how can we put our trust in Christ if we are not sure of what is taught here? The evangelist therefore assures us that when we believe in Christ we are not moving away from the one eternal God, and also that life is now restored to the dead through the kindness of Christ, who was the source and cause of life when mankind was still sinless.

The evangelist calls the Son of God **the Word** simply because, first, he is the eternal wisdom and will of God; and secondly, because he is the exact image of God's purpose. Just as men's speech is called the expression of their thoughts, so it is not inappropriate to say that God expresses himself to us by his speech or **Word.**

The other meanings of **the Word** are not so appropriate. The Greek certainly means "definition" or "reason" or "calculation"; but I do not wish to enter into philosophical discussion beyond the limits of my faith. And we see that the Spirit of God is so far from approving such subtleties that in talking with us his very silence proclaims how sober we should be in our intellectual approach to such high mysteries.

Now, since God in creating the world revealed himself by **the Word,** he had previously had Christ hidden in himself. Thus **the Word** has a double relationship, to God and to men. Servetus, that most arrogant and worthless Spaniard, imagines that the eternal **Word** came into being

13

only when Christ was active in the creation of the world. As if he had not been active before his power was made known by his visible work!

The evangelist teaches something quite different here, for he does not ascribe a temporal beginning to **the Word** but says that he was from **the beginning** and thus transcends all times. I am fully aware how this dog barks against us and what quibbles were once raised by the Arians — that "In the beginning God created the heavens and the earth" (Genesis 1:1), but they are not eternal, for "beginning" refers to order and does not indicate eternity. The evangelist, however, forestalls this calumny when he says **and the Word was with God.** If **the Word** had a beginning in time, they must find some time sequence in God.

There is no doubt that by this clause John intended to distinguish Christ from all other created things. Many questions could arise: Where actually was this **Word?** How did he exercise his power? What was his nature? How could he be known? Therefore the evangelist declares that we must not limit our views to the world and created things, for Christ was always united with God before the world existed. Now, when men make **the beginning** refer to the creation of heaven and earth, do they not reduce Christ to the ordinary order of the world, from which this passage specifically excludes him? By doing this they dreadfully insult not only the Son of God but also his eternal Father, whom they deprive of his Wisdom. If we are not free to think of God without his Wisdom, we are not free to look for the origin of **the Word** anywhere else but in the eternal Wisdom of God.

Servetus objects that **the Word** cannot have existed before Moses refers to God as speaking. As if, because he was not yet openly seen, Christ did not exist in God! As if he had no inner existence before he began to show himself outwardly! But the evangelist destroys every excuse for such outrageous rubbish when he affirms, unconditionally, that **the Word was with God.** Here he expressly calls us away from all events in time. Those who infer a continuing existence from the imperfect tense of the verb are in a weak position. They say that "was being" expresses continuity better than if John had said "he was." But such important matters demand more solid arguments. What I have suggested should suffice — that the evangelist sends us to God's eternal sanctuary and teaches us that **the Word** was, as it were, hidden there before he revealed himself outwardly in the world. Augustine is therefore right when he reminds us that **the beginning** mentioned here has no beginning. For although in a natural sequence the Father is before his Wisdom, yet those who imagine any point of time when he preceded his Wisdom deprive Christ of his glory. And this is the eternal Son who, extending back for an infinite time before the foundation of the world, lay hidden in God (if I may put it like that) and who, after being dimly outlined to the patriarchs under the law for a long succession of years, was at length shown more fully in a human body.

I am surprised that the Latin versions translate the Greek word for **the Word** (*logos*) with the Latin word *verbum*, which translates a different Greek word. But even if we allow that translation as a possibility, it cannot be denied that the word "speech" would have been far more appropriate. This shows up the barbarous tyranny of those theologians who harassed Erasmus so fiercely because he changed a single word for the better.

And the Word was with God. We have already said that the Son of God is thus placed above the world and all creatures and before all ages. But at the same time this expression attributes to him a personality distinct from the Father. For it would have been absurd if the evangelist had said that **the Word** was always **with God** or in God's presence unless he had a certain subsistence of his own in God. This verse, therefore, refutes the error of Sabellius, since it shows the Son is distinct from the Father. I have already said that such profound mysteries demand sober thinking. But the early church writers can be excused when, because they could not in any other way defend true and pure doctrine against the ambiguous quibbles of the heretics, they were forced to coin certain words which still said nothing but what is taught in the Scriptures in another way. They said that there are three *hypostases* or Persons in the one, simple essence of God. The Greek word *hypostasis* has this sense in Hebrews 1:3 and corresponds to the Latin for "substance," as it is used by Hilary. They called distinct properties in God which present themselves for our contemplation Persons. As Gregory of Nazianzus says: "I cannot think of the One (God) without having the Three (Persons) shining around me."

And the Word was God. In case any doubt should remain about Christ's divine essence, the evangelist clearly declares that he is **God.** Now, since **God** is one, it follows that Christ is of the same essence as the Father, and yet in some way different. But we have already spoken about the second clause. Arius was extremely wicked about the unity of the essence. To avoid being compelled to confess the eternal divinity of Christ, he prattled on about God being some kind of creature. But when we hear that **the Word was God,** what right have we any longer to question his eternal essence?

2. He was with God in the beginning. In order to impress more deeply into our minds what had already been said, the evangelist condenses the two preceding clauses into a short summary: **the Word** always was, and **the Word *was with God*** — so that you may understand that this beginning was before all time.

3. Through him all things were made. Having declared that **the Word** is God and having asserted his divine essence, John goes on to prove his divinity from his works. And it is in this practical knowledge that we ought especially to be trained. Just attributing the name of God to Christ will leave us cold unless our faith feels this to be the case. But the evangelist correctly declares about the Son of God what strictly applies to the person of God. Sometimes, indeed, Paul simply says that "to him [God] are all things" (Romans 11:36). But when the Son is compared with the Father he is usually distinguished in the ordinary way of speaking used here: the Father made all things by the Son, and all things are made by God through the Son. Now as I have said, the evangelist's purpose is to show that immediately after the creation of the world **the Word** of God was seen to be at work. Having previously been incomprehensible in his essence, he was then openly known by the effect of his power. Even some philosophers say God is the architect of the world in a way that makes him the intelligence behind the building of this work. In this they are right, for they agree with Scripture; but as they immediately degenerate into trivial meditations, there is no reason why we should desire their witness eagerly; instead we should be satisfied with this heavenly oracle, knowing that it says much more than our minds can absorb.

Without him nothing was made that has been made. Although this verse has been interpreted in a variety of ways, I have no hesitation in taking it as a single thought: **nothing was made that has been made.** Nearly all the Greek manuscripts (or at least those with the best authority) agree here. Moreover, the sense undoubtedly demands it. Those who separate the phrase **that has been made** from the preceding clause, linking it to the following sentence, make it mean, "that which has been made was life in him" — i.e., "lived" or "was sustained in life." But they cannot show that this expression is ever applied to creatures. Augustine, being an extreme Platonist, is addicted to the teaching of the ideas that before God built the world he had the form of the whole work as a concept in his mind, and since the creation of the world was ordered in Christ, the life of those things which did not yet exist was in him. But this is far from the evangelist's thinking, as we will now see.

I return now to the former clause. This is no superfluous phrase, as it seems to be at first sight. For since Satan exerts all his strength to detract from Christ, the evangelist wished to declare specifically that there are no exceptions at all, since **without him nothing was made that has been made.**

4. In him was life. So far he has taught us that **all things were made by the Word** of God. He now attributes to him in the same way the preservation of what had been created, as if he were saying that in the creation of the world the Word's power did not simply suddenly appear only to pass quickly away, but that it is seen in the permanence of the stable and settled order of nature. Hebrews 1:3 says he is "sustaining all things by his powerful word." Moreover, this **life** may either include inanimate creations in general, which do live in their own way though they lack feeling, or **life** may just refer to living creatures. It is of little consequence which you choose, for the simple meaning is that **the Word**

of God was not only the source of life for all creatures, so that those which had not yet existed began to be, but that his life-giving power makes them remain in their state. For if his continuing inspiration did not give life to the world, everything that lives would immediately decay or be reduced to nothing. In summary, what Paul ascribes to God, that "in him we live and move and have our being" (Acts 17:28), John declares is accomplished through the gracious agency of **the Word.** So it is God who gives us **life;** but he does so through the eternal **Word.**

That life was the light of men. I deliberately disregard some other interpretations which disagree with the evangelist's meaning. In my opinion he refers here to that part of life in which men surpass the other animate creatures. It is as if he were saying that the life given to men was not life in general but life united with the light of reason. Moreover, he separates men from the ranks of other creatures, as we are more aware of God's power by feeling it in us than by viewing it from a distance. Thus in Acts 17:27 Paul tells us to "seek [God] . . . [as] he is not far from each one of us." And so, when the evangelist has presented a general consideration of the grace of Christ, to persuade men to give it closer attention he shows what was given especially to them; that is, that they were not created in the likeness of the beasts, but, endowed with reason, they had reached a higher rank. Furthermore, since God effectually illuminates their minds with his **light,** it follows that they were created so that they might know that he is the author of such a special blessing. And since this **light** beamed on us from its source, **the Word,** it should be like a mirror in which we may see clearly the divine power of **the Word.**

5. The light shines in the darkness. It might be objected that because men are called blind in many passages of Scripture, the blindness for which they are condemned is already too well-known. For in all their reasoning powers they collapse miserably. How is it that there are so many labyrinths of errors in the world except that men are always led by their own understanding only into vanity and error? Yet if no **light** is visible in men, the evangelist's witness to the divinity of Christ is destroyed. For, as I have said, in the **life** of men (verse 4) there is something far more excellent than movement and breathing. The evangelist anticipates this question by first of all warning us that **the light** which was originally given to men must not be assessed by their present state, since in this marred and degenerate nature **light** has been turned to **darkness.** And yet he denies that the light of reason is completely put out; for in **the darkness** of the human mind there still shine some sparks of that brightness.

Readers will now understand that there are two ideas in this sentence. He says that men now greatly differ from that perfectly holy nature with which they were originally endowed, because their mind, which should have been completely radiant, has been plunged into darkness and is unhappy in this blindness. And so this corrupt nature shrouds the glory of Christ, as it were, in darkness. But on the other hand, the evangelist maintains that in the middle of the darkness certain remnants still exist which show to a certain extent Christ's divine power. Therefore the evangelist shows that man's mind is quite blinded, so that it may reasonably be seen as overwhelmed with darkness. He could have used a weaker word and said that the light was dark or murky; but he wanted to state more clearly how wretched our condition is since the fall of the first man. His statement that **the light shines in the darkness** is not at all meant to praise corrupt nature but rather to deprive ignorance of any excuse.

But the darkness has not understood it. Although the Son of God has always called people to himself through this poor light still left in us, the evangelist says that it did not succeed, because "Though seeing, they do not see" (Matthew 13:13). After man was alienated from God, his mind was so overwhelmed by ignorance that whatever light remains in it is choked and made ineffectual. Experience proves this daily. Even people who are not born again by God's Spirit still possess some reason, so that we are clearly taught that man was made not only to breathe but to have understanding. Yet, led by their reason they do not reach or even approach God; and so all their understanding is nothing but vanity. So it follows that there is no hope for men's salvation unless God steps in with a new help. For though the Son of God sheds his light on them, they are so dull that they do not understand the source of that light. They are carried away by foolish and perverse fancies into madness.

There are two main parts to the **light** which still remains in corrupt nature. First, some seed of religion is sown in everyone; and second, the distinction between good and evil is etched on their consciences. But what are the fruits that eventually come from this, except that religion degenerates to a thousand superstitions, and conscience corrupts all judgment, confusing vice with virtue? In summary, natural reason will never direct men to Christ. The fact that they are endued with wisdom to live their lives by or are born for the humanities and sciences disappears without having any effect.

We must remember that the evangelist is speaking only about natural gifts and is not yet saying anything about the grace of regeneration. For there are two distinct powers which belong to the Son of God. The first appears in the structure of the world and in the order of nature. In the second he renews and restores fallen nature. He is the eternal **Word** of God, and so by him the world was made; by his power all things keep the life they once received; in particular, man was endued with the unique gift of understanding, and though through his rebellion he lost the light of understanding, he still sees and understands, since what he naturally possesses from the grace of the Son of God is not entirely destroyed. But because of his stupidity and perversity he darkens the light he still has, and so the Son of God has to assume a new office, the role of Mediator,

18

and renew fallen man by the Spirit of regeneration. People who say the **light** which the evangelist mentions refers to the Gospel and the preaching of salvation are arguing in an absurd and inconclusive way.

Verses 6–13

6. There came a man. The evangelist now begins to discuss the way in which **the Word** of God was revealed in the flesh. In case anyone doubts that Christ is the eternal Son of God, he tells how he was publicly heralded by John the Baptist. For Christ did not only show himself to men, but he also wanted to be made known by the witness and preaching of John. Or rather, God the Father sent this witness before his Christ that men might all the more readily receive the salvation he offered.

But at first sight it might appear absurd that anyone should bear witness to Christ, as if he needed it. For, on the contrary, he declares, "Not that I accept human testimony" (5:34). The answer is easy and obvious: this witness was appointed not for Christ's sake but for ours. If anyone objects that man's testimony is too weak to prove that Christ is the Son of God, the answer is again easy: the Baptist is not cited as a private witness, but as one who, endowed with divine authority, appeared in the role of an angel rather than of a man. So he is not praised for his own abilities, but just because he was the ambassador of God. Nor does it contradict the self-witness of Christ in the preaching of the Gospel committed to him. The purpose of John's preaching was to draw his readers' attention to Christ's teaching and miracles.

Sent from God. The evangelist does not confirm John's calling but only mentions it in passing. This assurance is not sufficient for many people who push themselves forward and boast that they are sent by God. But the evangelist, intending to say more later about this witness, thought the one word was enough for now: John had come at God's commission. We shall see later how John claims that God is the author of his ministry. What we have to grasp now is (as I mentioned before) that what is said about John is required in all church teachers: they must be called by God, so that the authority of teaching may have no other basis than God alone.

He gives him the name **John** not only to identify the man, but because the meaning of the name showed who he really was. For there is no doubt that the Lord was referring to the office for which he appointed John when through his angel he commanded that he should be called John. In this way everyone might recognize from this that he was the herald and ambassador of divine grace. Although the name **John** signifies grace which would be pleasing to God, yet I unhesitatingly extend it to the benefit which others ought to derive from it.

7. He came as a witness. The purpose of John's calling is briefly noted: that he should prepare the church for Christ. For when he invites everyone to Christ, he shows plainly enough that he did not come on his own account.

8. He himself was not the light. John had so little need of being commended that the evangelist emphasizes that he **was not the light,** in case an excessive brightness ascribed to him should obscure Christ's glory. For some clung so tightly to John that they neglected Christ, like a man who is overcome at the sight of dawn and does not deign to look at the sun. Now we will see the meaning the evangelist gives to the word **light.** All the godly are "light in the Lord" (Ephesians 5:8) in that, enlightened by his Spirit, not only do they themselves see, but also by their example they direct others to the way of salvation. The apostles are called "light" (Matthew 5:14) because they are the special Gospel torch-bearers, scattering the world's darkness. But here the evangelist is discussing the unique and eternal source of illumination, as he at once shows more clearly.

9. The true light that gives light. The evangelist was not contrasting **the true light** with a false light; he wanted to differentiate Christ from all others in case anyone should think that Christ's **light** is the same as the light of angels or men. The difference is that heavenly and earthly light has only a derived brightness; but Christ is **light** shining from himself and through himself and so shining brightly on the whole world. There is no other source of its brightness anywhere. And so the evangelist calls Christ **the true light** whose own nature is to be **light.**

Gives light to every man. The evangelist emphasizes this so that we may learn that Christ is the **light** from the effect which each of us feels in himself. He could have argued more subtly that since Christ is eternal **light,** he has a natural and underived brightness. But instead, he sends us back to the experience we all have. For since Christ makes us all share in his brightness, it must be acknowledged that to him alone strictly belongs the honor of being called **light.**

This verse is often explained in one of two ways. Some limit the universal phrase **every man** to those who, born again by the Spirit of God, are made to share in the life-giving **light.** Augustine uses the simile of a schoolmaster who, if his is the only school in the town, will be called the master of everyone, even of those who do not attend his school. Therefore they understand this phrase in a comparative sense: all are enlightened by Christ, since no one can boast that he has obtained the **light** of life in any other way than through his grace. But as the evangelist uses the general phrase **light to every man was coming into the world,** I prefer the other meaning, which is that beams from this **light** are shed over all mankind, as I said before. For we know that men have this special quality which raises them above the other animals, that they are endowed with reason and intelligence, and that they bear the distinction between right and wrong engraved on their conscience. Thus there is no man to whom some awareness of the eternal **light** does not penetrate.

But since fanatics eagerly seize on this verse and twist it into saying that the grace of illumination is offered equally to everyone, let us remember that it is only referring to the common **light** of nature, which is far inferior to faith. No man will penetrate into the kingdom of God through the cleverness and perspicuity of his own mind. Only the Spirit of God opens heaven to his elect. We must also remember that the light of reason which God imparted to men has been so darkened by sin that scarcely a few meager sparks still shine unquenched in this thick darkness or rather dreadful ignorance and abyss of errors.

10. He was in the world. He accuses men of ingratitude, in that they were, as it were, voluntarily blinded — blinded in such a way that they did not know how the **light** they enjoyed was caused. And this is true of every age. Even before Christ was manifest in the flesh he displayed his power everywhere. Therefore those daily effects ought to correct men's stupidity, for what could be more unreasonable than to draw water from a running stream and never think of the spring it flows from? It follows that the world cannot plead ignorance as a legitimate excuse for not knowing Christ before he was manifest in the flesh. For it arose out of slackness and wicked stupidity in those who always had opportunities of seeing him present in his power. The summary is this: Christ was never so absent from the world that men ought not to have been aroused by his rays and to have looked up to him. So it follows that they are guilty.

11. He came to that which was his own. Here he displays man's absolutely desperate wickedness and malice, their accursed ungodliness, in that when the Son of God revealed himself in the flesh to the Jews, whom God had separated to himself from the other nations as his own, he was not acknowledged or received. This verse, too, is interpreted in different ways. Some think the evangelist is speaking of the whole world in general, for there is certainly no part of the world which the Son of God may not rightly claim as his own. Thus, according to them, the meaning is: "When Christ came to earth, he did not enter a foreign country, for the whole human race was his own inheritance." But I prefer the view of those who refer Christ's coming to the Jews only. The evangelist heightens men's ingratitude by an implied comparison. The Son of God had chosen a dwelling-place for himself in one nation; when he appeared there, he was rejected, and this shows clearly how wicked men's blindness is. But the evangelist must have said this simply to remove the offense which the Jews' unbelief might put in many people's way. For who would believe that he was the Redeemer of the whole world when he was despised and rejected by that nation to which he had been especially promised? We see what extraordinary care the apostle Paul took in handling this subject.

The emphasis is on both the verb and the noun. The evangelist says the Son of God **came** to where he was formerly. Therefore by this expression he must mean a new and extraordinary kind of presence by which the Son of God manifested himself so that men might see him closer at hand. When he says **to that which was his own** he is comparing the Jews with other nations; for by a unique privilege they had been elected into the family of God. Christ therefore first offered himself to them as if they were his own family and belonged to his kingdom in their own right. God's complaint in Isaiah 1:3 has the same intention: "The ox knows his master, the donkey his owner's manger, but Israel does not know, my people do not understand." For although he has dominion over the whole world, he becomes the Lord especially to Israel, whom he had gathered, as it were, into a sacred fold.

12. Yet to all who received him. In case anyone should be hindered by the stumbling block that the Jews despised and rejected Christ, the evangelist exalts above heaven the godly who believe in him. He says that the result of their faith is the glory of being counted as **children of God.** The universal term **all** implies an antithesis: the Jews were carried away by a blind glorying, as if God belonged exclusively to them. So the evangelist declares that their condition has changed; the Gentiles have succeeded to the place left empty by the disinherited Jews. It is just as if he transferred the rights of adoption to strangers. As Paul says, the downfall of one nation was the life of the whole world (Romans 11:12); for when the Gospel was, as it were, driven out from them, it began to be dispersed far and wide throughout the whole world. Thus they were deprived of their special privilege. But their ungodliness did Christ no harm; for he set up the throne of his kingdom elsewhere and without discrimination called to the hope of salvation all peoples who formerly seemed to be rejected by God.

He gave the right (KJV, "power"). The Greek word translated **right** here means an honor, and it would be better to translate it so, to refute the Roman Catholics' false interpretation. Their corruption of this verse is that we are given only a freedom of choice, a privilege we may see fit to make use of. To read free will from this word, as they do, is like extracting fire out of water. At first sight there is some excuse for it, for the evangelist does not say that Christ makes them **children of God** but gives them the **right** to become so. Hence they infer that this grace is only offered to us and that the capacity to make use of it or reject it lies with us. But the context overthrows this paltry quibbling over one word, for the evangelist goes on to say that they **become children of God — children born not . . . of human decision . . . but born of God.** For if faith regenerates us so that we are the **children of God,** and if God breathes faith into us from heaven, the grace of adoption offered to us by Christ is obviously not only potential but actual, as they say.

And, indeed, the Greek word for **right** does occasionally mean "being reckoned worthy"; this meaning suits this passage best.

The circumlocution which the evangelist has used commends the excellence of grace better than if he had said in a single word that all who believe in Christ are made **children of God** by him. For here he is speaking of the unclean and profane who, condemned to perpetual disgrace, lie in death's darkness. And so Christ revealed a wonderful example of his grace by conferring this honor on such people, so that they suddenly began to be **children of God.** The evangelist rightly exalts the greatness of this blessing, and so does Paul in Ephesians 2:4-5: "because of his great love for us, God, who is rich in mercy, made us alive with Christ." But even if anyone prefers the usual meaning of the word **right**, yet as used the way the evangelist uses it here, it does not stand for any sort of halfway faculty which does not include the full and complete effect. Rather, it means that Christ gave what seemed to be impossible to the unclean and uncircumcised. For this was an incredible change — that Christ raised up children to God out of stones (see Matthew 3:9). **Right** is therefore what Paul speaks of in Colossians 1:12 when he gives thanks to God "who has qualified you to share in the inheritance of the saints."

Who believed in his name. He indicates briefly how Christ is to be received — that is, by "believing" in him. Implanted into Christ by faith, we obtain the right of adoption as the **children of God.** And because he is the one and only Son of God, this honor does not belong to us at all except insofar as we are part of him. This again refutes the false Roman Catholic interpretation about the word **right.** The evangelist declares that this **right** is given to those who already believe, and it is certain that they are indeed already the **children of God.** Those who say that by believing, a person becomes nothing more than a son of God if he chooses to, greatly underestimate the value of faith. They replace a present result by an uncertain possibility.

The contradiction is shown to be even more mistaken by what follows. The evangelist says (verse 13) that those who believe are already **born of God.** It is not, therefore, merely the liberty of choice that is offered, for they obtain the very privilege itself. Although in Hebrew **name** is often used for "power," it is here a reference to the preaching of the Gospel. For we believe in Christ when he is preached to us. I speak of the usual way by which the Lord leads us to faith. And this must be carefully noted, since many foolishly invent for themselves a faith confused and without any understanding of the Gospel. Christ offers himself to us through the Gospel, and we receive him by faith.

13. Children born not of natural descent (KJV, "blood"). I readily agree with those who think that this refers indirectly to the wicked presumption of the Jews. The worthiness of their line was always on their lips, as if they were naturally holy because they were born of a holy descent. They might justly have been proud that they were descended from Abraham if they had been true sons and not degenerate sons; but the glorying of faith claims nothing at all for human procreation, but declares that it has received all that is good from the grace of God alone. John therefore says that those previously unclean Gentiles who believe in Christ are not sons of God from the womb but are born again by God, that they may start to be his children. **Blood** (literally, "bloods") seems to have been put in the plural to bring out the idea of the long succession of the line. For a part of the Jews' boasting was that they could trace their descendants along an uninterrupted line back to the patriarchs.

Nor of human decision or a husband's will. I think these two phrases mean the same thing, for I do not see why **human decision** should signify "woman" (as many, following Augustine, suppose). The evangelist is rather repeating the same thing in different words, so as to impress and fix it more deeply on our minds. And although he is thinking specifically of the Jews, who gloried in the flesh, a general doctrine can be learned from this verse: we are reckoned the children of God not on account of our own nature, nor from our initiative, but because "he chose to give us birth" (James 1:18), from undeserved love. Hence it follows, first, that faith is not produced by us but is the fruit of spiritual new birth. For the evangelist says that no one can believe except he who is born of God. Therefore faith is a heavenly gift. Moreover, faith is not cold and bare knowledge, for no one can believe unless he is born again by the Spirit of God.

It seems as if the evangelist puts things back to front by making regeneration prior to faith, since it is rather the result of faith and therefore follows it. I reply that both statements are in perfect agreement: by faith we receive the imperishable seed by which we are born again to new and divine life; and also, faith is itself the work of the Holy Spirit, who dwells in no one except the children of God. Thus, in many respects faith is a part of our new birth, the entry point into the kingdom of God, that he may count us among his children. The enlightening of our minds by the Holy Spirit belongs to our renewal. So faith flows from its source: new birth. But since by this same faith we receive Christ, who sanctifies us by his Spirit, it is called the beginning of our adoption.

Another solution can be advanced which is clearer and easier. When the Lord breathes faith into us, he gives us new birth in a hidden and secret way that is unknown to us. But when faith has been given, we grasp with a living awareness not only the grace of adoption but also newness of life and the other gifts of the Holy Spirit. For since, as we have said, faith receives Christ, it leads us in a sense to the possession of all his blessings. Thus, so far as our attitude is concerned, we begin to be the children of God only after we believe. For since the inheritance of eternal life is the result of adoption, we see that the evangelist ascribes the whole of our salvation to the grace of Christ alone. And, indeed, however closely people examine themselves, they will find nothing worthy of the children of God except what Christ has given them.

Verse 14

14. The Word became flesh. The evangelist now teaches the nature of the coming of Christ which he had spoken of — that, clothed in our flesh, he showed himself openly to the world. Although he touches only briefly on the indescribable mystery of the Son of God being clothed in human nature, this brief statement is wonderfully clear. Here some madmen fool about with paltriest sophistries, such as saying that **the Word became flesh** in that God sent his Son as a mental concept into the world to become man — as if **the Word** were I know not what kind of shadowy idea. But we have shown that this expresses a genuine personality in the essence of God.

Flesh. This word expresses his meaning more forcibly than if the evangelist had said that Christ was made man. He wanted to show to what a low and abject state the Son of God descended from the height of his heavenly glory, for our sake. When Scripture speaks of man derogatorily it calls him "flesh." How great is the distance between the spiritual glory of **the Word** of God and the stinking filth of our flesh! Yet the Son of God stooped so low that he took on himself that flesh which is subject to so many miseries. Here **flesh** is not used for corrupt nature (as is often the case in Paul), but for mortal man. It denotes derogatorily his frail and almost transient nature: "All men (KJV, "flesh") are like grass" (Isaiah 40:6 and similar verses). But we must note at the same time that this is a figure of speech, for in the word **flesh** the whole man is included. Apollo was therefore foolish to imagine that Christ was clothed with a human body without a soul. It is easy to prove from innumerable statements that he had a soul as well as a body. When Scripture calls men "flesh," it does not thereby make them soulless.

Therefore the plain sense is that **the Word** born of God before all ages, and always dwelling with the Father, became man. Here are two main articles of belief: first, in Christ two natures were united in one person in such as way that one and the same Christ is true God and man. Secondly, the unity of his person does not prevent his natures from remaining distinct, so that the divinity retains whatever is special to it, and similarly the humanity has separately what belongs to it. And so, when Satan has tried through heretics to overturn sane theology with this or that madness, he has always dragged in one or other of these two errors: either that Christ was the Son of God and son of man in a confused way, so that neither his divinity remained intact, nor did he have the true nature of man; or that he was so clothed with flesh as to be, as it were, double and have two distinct persons. Thus Nestorius specifically acknowledged each nature but imagined one Christ who was God and another who was man. Eutyches, on the other hand, acknowledged that the one Christ is the Son of God and the Son of man, but left him neither of the two natures, as he imagined that they were mingled. Today, Servetus and the Anabaptists invent a Christ who is a confused mixture of the two natures, as if he were a divine man. He certainly declares in words that Christ is God, but if you follow his insane imaginations, at one moment the Divinity was temporarily changed into human nature and at another moment the human nature has been absorbed into the Divinity.

The evangelist's words are apposite for refuting both these blasphemies. When he says that **the Word became flesh**, we can plainly infer the unity of his person. For it does not make sense that he who is now man should be other than him who was always truly God, since it is God who is said to have become man. Again, since he distinctly attributes the name **the Word** to the man Christ, it follows that when he became man Christ did not cease to be what he was before and that nothing was changed in that eternal essence of God which assumed flesh. In summary, the Son of God began to be man in such a way that he is still that eternal **Word** who had no temporal beginning.

. . . **lived for a while among us.** Those who say that **flesh** was like a home to Christ have not grasped the evangelist's thought. He does not ascribe a permanent residence among us to Christ, but says that he stayed for a time, as a guest. The Greek word he uses for **dwelt** (KJV) is derived from "tabernacle." So he simply means that on earth Christ carried out his appointed office; in other words, he did not only appear for one moment but lived among men while he was fulfilling his office. It is doubtful whether the phrase **among us** refers to men in general or only to John himself and the other disciples who were eyewitnesses of the events he narrates. I prefer the latter explanation, for the evangelist immediately adds:

We have seen his glory. Though the **glory** of Christ could have been seen by all, it was unknown to most people because of their blindness; only a few, whose eyes the Holy Spirit had opened, saw this manifestation of **glory**. In a word, Christ was recognized as a man who showed in himself something far greater and more sublime. Hence it follows that the majesty of God was not annihilated though it was clothed in flesh. It was indeed hidden under the lowliness of the flesh, but its **glory** was still seen.

. . . **the glory of . . .** This does not denote an improper comparison but rather a true and strong assertion. Similarly, when Paul says in Ephesians 5:8, "Live as children of light," he wants us really to bear witness by our works to this very thing that we are — "children of light." The evangelist therefore means that in Christ there was to be seen a **glory** consistent with the Son of God and witnessing certainly to his divinity.

One and only ("the Only Begotten," NIV footnote — Ed.). He calls Christ this because he is by nature the **only** Son of God. It is as if he wants to place him above men and angels and claim for him alone that which belongs to no creature.

Full of grace. This confirms the last clause. The majesty of Christ certainly also appeared in other respects, but the evangelist chose this example instead of others to train us in the practical rather than the speculative knowledge of him, and this must be carefully observed. When Christ walked with dry feet on the waters (see 6:19), when he expelled devils and revealed his power in other miracles, he could indeed be recognized as the only begotten Son of God. But the evangelist puts at the center that part of the proof from which faith receives the sweet fruit of Christ, declaring that he is in very truth the inexhaustible source of **grace and truth.** Stephen also was said to have been "full of grace" (Acts 7:55), but in another sense. [This must have been a slip of memory on Calvin's part as the phrases applied to Stephen are different, though parallel; see Acts 6:5; 6:8; 7:55 — Pringle.] For the fullness of grace in Christ is the well from which we all must draw, as we will shortly explain more fully.

Full of grace and truth. This can be taken as a figure of speech for "true grace," or it may be an explanation: "He was full of grace, which is truth of perfection." But since he immediately repeats the same form of words (verse 17), I consider the meaning to be the same in both passages. This **grace and truth** he later contrasts with the law; and so I simply understand it to mean that Christ was to be acknowledged the Son of God by the apostles because he had in himself the fullness of all things belonging to the spiritual kingdom of God. In summary, he truly showed himself to be the Redeemer and Messiah in all things, which is the most important characteristic by which he ought to be distinguished from all others.

Verses 15–18

15. John testifies concerning him . . . He now describes John's proclamation. By using the present tense of the verb **testifies**, he denotes a continuous activity, and indeed this preaching must always flourish, as if John's voice was continually sounding in men's ears. For the same reason, he then uses the word **cries out** to indicate that John's preaching was not at all obscure or involved in ambiguities or murmured among the few. He preached Christ publicly in a loud voice. The first sentence refers to his being sent on Christ's account, so that it would have been senseless for him to be exalted while Christ was humbled.

"This was he of whom I said . . ." By these words he means that from the very first his purpose was to make Christ known, and this was the aim of his preaching; in no other way could he carry out his duties as ambassador than by calling his disciples to Christ.

"'He who comes after me.'" It is true he was some months older than Christ, but age is not what he is speaking about now. As he had performed the office of prophet for some time before Christ appeared in public, he puts himself first in time. Therefore Christ **comes after** John so far as public appearance goes.

The words that follow might literally read: "He became before me, for he was my chief." But the meaning is that Christ was correctly preferred to John because he was more excellent. Therefore John yields to Christ and, as the proverb puts it, hands the torch on to him, or gives way to him as his successor. But as Christ came later in time, John warns us that this is one reason for his being preferred as his rank deserved. Thus, all who excel either in the gifts of God or in any degree of honor must remain in their own position, below Christ.

16. From the fullness . . . He now begins to preach about Christ's office, which contains such an abundance of all blessings that no part of salvation is to be sought elsewhere. In God, indeed, is the fountain of life, righteousness, power, and wisdom; but this fountain is hidden and inaccessible to us. Yet in Christ the wealth of all these things is laid before us so that we may seek them in him. Of his own will he is ready to flow to us, provided we open up a channel by faith.

He declares briefly that we should not seek any blessing at all outside Christ. But this sentence is composed of several clauses. First, he shows that we are all utterly destitute and empty of spiritual blessings. Christ's riches are intended to help our failure, support our poverty, and satisfy our hunger and thirst. Secondly, he warns us that as soon as we forsake Christ we seek in vain a single drop of happiness, since God has willed that whatever is good will live in him alone. Therefore, we shall find angels and men arid, heaven empty, the earth barren, and all things worthless if we want to share God's gifts other than through Christ. Thirdly, he reminds us that we do not need to fear that we will lack anything if only we draw from the **fullness** of Christ, which is in every way so perfect that we will find it to be an inexhaustible fountain indeed. John classifies himself with the rest, not out of modesty, but to make it plainer that there are no exceptions.

It is uncertain whether he is speaking about the whole human race in general or only about those who, since Christ has been shown in the flesh, have shared more fully in his blessings. It is true that all the godly who lived under the law drew from this same **fullness**; but since John immediately distinguishes between the different periods, it is more probable that he is here especially praising that plentiful wealth of blessings which Christ revealed when he came. We know that under the law they had experienced God's benefits more infrequently; and when Christ was revealed in the flesh the blessings were poured out, as it were, with a full hand, so that they even overflowed. Not that any of us has received more grace from the Spirit than Abraham did, as I am speaking about God's ordinary dispensation and the way it was given. Therefore John the Baptist, in order to attract his disciples to Christ better, declares that in him everyone is offered the wealth of the blessings which they lack. But it would not be absurd if anyone chose to press the meaning further — or rather, it is not at all against the drift of the argument. From the beginning of the world all the patriarchs drew whatever gifts they had from Christ. Although the law was given by Moses, it was not from him that they obtained grace. But I have already shown what explanation I prefer — that John here compares us with the patriarchs that he may thereby bring into prominence what has been given to us.

We have all received one blessing after another (KJV, "grace for grace"). Augustine's interpretation of this verse is well-known: all the blessings continually given to us by God, and at length everlasting life, are not a payment for our merits, as if they were wages owing to us, but are from the pure kindness of God, who rewards prior grace and crowns his own gifts in us. This is a godly and wise observation, but it does not fit this verse. The meaning would be easier if you took the preposition **for** comparatively, as if he said that whatever graces God heaps on us flow equally from this source. It could also be taken to indicate the final purpose: we receive grace now so that God may at last finish the work of our salvation, which will be the completion of grace. But I subscribe rather to the opinion of those who say that we are watered with the graces which were poured out on Christ. For not only as God does Christ bestow on us what we receive from him, but the Father conferred on him what would flow to us through him, that he might anoint us all along with him. It is for this reason, too, that he is called Christ, and we, Christians.

17. For the law was given through Moses. He anticipates a hostile objection, and so sets out to forestall it. Moses was so highly esteemed by the Jews that they would hardly allow anything that differed from him. Therefore the evangelist teaches us how inferior Moses' ministry was compared with the power of Christ's. The evangelist warns the Jews, who paid the utmost deference to Moses, that Moses' contribution was extremely scanty compared to the grace of Christ. It would have been a great stumbling block to expect from the law what we can only obtain through Christ.

Grace and truth came through Jesus Christ. We must note the antithesis as he contrasts **the law** to **grace and truth**, for he means that **the law** lacked both of these. To my mind, the word **truth** denotes a firm and fixed state of things. But by the word **grace** I understand the spiritual fulfillment of those things of which the bare letter was contained in **the law.** The two expressions can refer to the same thing, as if he had said that **grace,** in which the **truth** of **the law** consists, was at last revealed in Christ. But as the sense remains the same, it does not matter whether you connect or distinguish them. What is certain is that the evangelist means that in **the law** there was merely the outlined image of spiritual blessings, which are actually found in Christ. So it follows that if you separate **the law** from Christ, nothing remains in it except empty shapes. This is why Paul says in Colossians 2:17 that in **the law** is the "shadow," but the "reality" is in Christ. But it must not be supposed that anything false was shown in **the law,** for Christ is the soul who gives life to what would otherwise have been dead in **the law.**

But here we are dealing with a different question — the validity of **the law** in itself and apart from Christ. And the evangelist denies that anything permanently valuable is to be found in it until we come to Christ. Moreover, **truth** consists in our obtaining through Christ the **grace** which **the law** could not give. Therefore I take the word **grace** generally, as both the free forgiveness of sins and the renewal of the heart. For when the evangelist briefly indicates the difference between the Old and New Testaments (which is more fully described in Jeremiah 31:31), he includes in this word everything that relates to spiritual righteousness. Now, there are two parts to this: God freely reconciles himself to us by not imputing our sins; and also, he has engraved his **law** in our hearts and renews people inwardly by his Spirit to obey it. It is clear from this that **the law** is expounded incorrectly and falsely if it holds people to itself or prevents them from coming to Christ.

18. No one has ever seen God. This addition confirms very aptly what went before, for the knowledge of God is the door through which we enter into the enjoyment of all blessings. Therefore, since God reveals himself to us through Christ alone, it follows that we should seek all things from Christ. This doctrinal sequence should be carefully observed. Nothing seems more obvious than that we each take what God offers us according to the measure of our faith. But only a few realize that the vessel of faith and of the knowledge of God has to be brought to draw with.

When he says that **no one has ever seen God,** he is not referring to sight with the physical eye. He means generally that, since God "lives in unapproachable light" (1 Timothy 6:16), he cannot be known except in Christ, his living image. Moreover, commentators usually expound this verse thus: "Since the naked majesty of God is hidden within himself, he could never be understood except in the way he has revealed himself in Christ. Hence God was known to the patriarchs of old only in Christ." But I think that the evangelist is here dwelling on the comparison already made — how much better our state is than the patriarchs', in that God, who was then concealed in his secret glory, has now in a sense made himself visible. For certainly, when Christ is called "the exact representation of his being" (Hebrews 1:3) it refers to the special blessing of the New Testament. So also in this verse the evangelist points to something new and strange when he says (verse 14) that **the one and only Son, who came from the Father** has made known to us what was previously hidden. Therefore he praises the revelation of God, brought to us through the Gospel, in which he distinguishes us from the patriarchs and shows that we are superior to them. Paul treats this more fully in 2 Corinthians 3 and 4, declaring that there is no longer any veil, as under the law, but that God is openly seen in the face of Christ.

If it seems ridiculous that the fathers should be deprived of the knowledge of God, when their prophets hand on the torch to us today, I reply that what is allotted to us is not simply or absolutely denied to them, but (as they say) a comparison is made between the minor and major; for they had nothing more than little sparks of that light of life whose full brightness brings us light today. If any object that even then God was seen face to face (see Genesis 32:30; Deuteronomy 34:10), I say that that sight cannot be compared with what we see; but since God showed himself obscurely and, as it were, from afar, those to whom he appeared more clearly said that they saw him face to face. They speak with reference to their own time. They only saw God wrapped up in many coverings. The vision that Moses received on the mountain (Exodus 33:23) was remarkable and excelled almost all the others; and yet God expressly declares: "you will see my back; but my face must not be seen." With this metaphor he shows that the time for the full and clear revelation had not yet come.

We must also note that when even the fathers wanted to behold God, they always turned their eyes to Christ. I do not only mean that they beheld God in his eternal **Word**, but also that they longed single-mindedly and wholeheartedly for the promised manifestation of Christ. For this reason Christ said, "Abraham rejoiced at the thought of seeing my day; he saw it" (John 8:56). And what is subordinate is not contradictory. Therefore this is certain — that God, who was formerly invisible, has now appeared in Christ.

When he says that the Son was **at the Father's side** (KJV, "in the bosom of the Father"), he uses a human metaphor. Men are said to receive into their bosom those to whom they communicate all their secrets. The breast is the seat of counsel. Therefore he teaches that the Son knew the most hidden secrets of his Father, so that we may know that we have, so to say, the breast of God laid open to us in the Gospel.

Verses 19–23

19. Now this was John's testimony . . . The evangelist has related John's preaching about Christ. He now comes down to a more outstanding example of this, which was delivered to the ambassadors of the priests to take back to Jerusalem. So he says that John openly confessed why he was sent by God. But we may first ask what the priests' purpose was in questioning him. The common supposition is that they pretended to give John honor because of their hatred for Christ. But this could not be the reason since at that time Christ was not yet known to them. Others say that John would have been in favor with the priests because he came from the priestly line and order. But this is also improbable; for why should they invent a false Christ for themselves when they expected everything to come from Christ? I think that they were moved by another reason. For a long time they had been without prophets. John suddenly and unexpectedly appeared, and everyone's mind was excited and expectant. Besides, they all believed the Messiah's coming was imminent.

Lest they should seem careless about their duty by neglecting or disguising such an important matter, the priests ask John who he is. At first, then, they do not act from malice, but on the contrary, moved by a desire for redemption, they want to know whether John is the Christ, for he is beginning to change the usual order of the church. And yet I do not deny that a desire to cling to their rights was powerful in them; but nothing was farther from their minds than to transfer Christ's honor to another. Nor are they acting inconsistently with their office. Since they held the government of the church of God they had to take care that no one should rashly put himself forward, that no founder of a new sect should arise, that the unity of the faith should not be broken among the people, and that no one should introduce new and foreign ceremonies. It is evident, therefore, that talk about John was common and aroused everybody's mind. But this was ordered by the wonderful providence of God, that the testimony might be the more conspicuous.

20. He did not fail to confess. That is, he confessed openly and without any evasion or hypocrisy. The first **confess** means in general that he stated the fact as it was. The second, **confessed,** is a repetition to express the form of the confession. So he replied definitely that he was not the Christ.

21. "Are you Elijah?" Why do they mention Elijah rather than Moses? Because they learned from the prophecy in Malachi 4:5 that when the Messiah came, Elijah would be the morning star to announce his arrival. But they ask this from a false presupposition, for, believing as they did in the transmigration of souls, they imagined that when the prophet Malachi announced that Elijah would be sent, he meant the same Elijah who lived under Ahab (1 Kings 17:1). Therefore John replies fairly and properly that he is not Elijah, using the word in their sense. But Christ affirms that John *is* Elijah, giving a true interpretation of the prophet (Matthew 11:14).

"Are you the Prophet?" Erasmus incorrectly restricts this to Christ, for the addition of the article (*"the* **Prophet"**) has no weight in this verse; and the messengers afterwards declare plainly enough that they meant a different prophet than Christ, when they summarize it all by saying, **"If you are not the Christ, nor Elijah, nor the Prophet . . ."** (verse 25). Thus we see that different people are meant. Others think that they were asking whether he was one of the prophets of old. But I do not like that exposition either. Rather, by this term they are referring to John's office, as to whether he was a prophet appointed by God. When he denies this, he is not lying out of modesty, but is honestly and sincerely separating himself from the company of the prophets. And yet this reply is not contrary to Christ's description of him. Christ bestows on John the title of prophet and even adds that he is "more than a prophet" (Matthew 11:9). But by these words he only adds weight and authority to John's teaching, while at the same time extolling the excellence of the office committed to him. But in this passage John has a different aim. He wants to show that he has no personal commission, as was usual with the prophets, but was appointed only to be the herald of Christ.

This will become clearer by a metaphor. Even ambassadors who are not sent on matters of great importance receive the name and authority of ambassadors, if indeed they hold personal commissions. Such were all the prophets who, provided with definite prophecies, discharged the prophetic office. But suppose a matter of great weight comes up and two ambassadors are sent, one of whom announces that another will soon come to negotiate the whole affair and with a commission to carry the business through. Will not the former be thought of as a part and appendix of the principal one? So it was with John, to whom God had entrusted nothing more than the preparation of disciples for Christ. And this meaning is easily drawn out from the whole context of the passage; for we must consider the contrasting clause immediately following. He says: "I am not a prophet. **'I am the voice of one calling in the desert'"** (verse 23). The distinction lies in the fact that the voice calling, **"Make straight the way for the Lord"** is not a prophet with a distinct function special to himself, but only, as it were, an assistant minister, and his preaching only a sort of preparation for listening to another teacher. In this way John, though more excellent than all the prophets, is nevertheless not a prophet himself.

23. "'The voice of one calling.'" Since he would have been rash in assuming the teaching office unless he had been given a ministry, he shows what his function was and confirms it with a quotation from Isaiah 40:3. So it follows that he did nothing except what God commanded. Isaiah is not there speaking only of John, but, promising the restoration of the church, he foretells that joyful voices will be heard commanding a way to be leveled for the Lord. Now although he means God's coming in bringing back the people from the Babylonian captivity, yet the true fulfillment was the manifestation of Christ in the flesh. Therefore, among the heralds who announced that the Lord was close at hand, John was chief.

It would be a waste of time to embark upon abstruse questions, as some do, about the word **"voice."** John is called a **"voice"** because his duty was to call out. Isaiah allegorically calls the miserable desolation of the church a desert which seemed to preclude the people's return; as if he said that the way out for the captive people was blocked, but that the Lord would find a way through the trackless land. But that visible wilderness in which John preached was a figure or image of the lonely desolation where there was no hope of deliverance. If you think about this comparison, you will soon see that the prophet's words have not been twisted. God arranged everything as if he was putting a mirror of this prophecy in front of the eyes of his people, bewildered by their miseries.

Verses 24–28

24. Now some Pharisees . . . He says that they were **Pharisees**, who held then the highest office in the church, in order to teach us that they were not some minor figures of the Levitical order but men endowed with authority. This is why they ask about his baptism. Ordinary ministers would have been satisfied with any kind of answer; but these men, because they cannot get the reply they want, accuse John of rashness for daring to introduce a new ceremony.

25. "Why then do you baptize?" They seem to argue conclusively when they lay down these three possibilities — **"if you are not the Christ, nor Elijah, nor the Prophet"** — for not everyone would institute the practice of baptism. The Messiah would possess all authority. Of the Elijah who was to come they had formed the opinion that he would begin the restoration of both the kingdom and the church. They also agreed that God's prophets ought to discharge the office committed to them. Therefore they conclude that for John to baptize is an unlawful innovation, since he had received no public office from God. But even though he denies that he is the Elijah of whom they were dreaming, they are at fault in that they do not acknowledge him to be the Elijah mentioned in Malachi 4:5.

26. "I baptize with water." This should have been sufficient to correct their mistake; but however clear teaching may be, it is of no use to the deaf. When he sends them to Christ and declares that he is already present, it is plain, not only that he was divinely appointed to be Christ's minister, but that he was the true Elijah sent to testify to the restoration of the church. The full antithesis is not expressed here, for the spiritual baptism of Christ is not distinctly contrasted with the external baptism of John, but that latter clause about the baptism of the Spirit might well be supplied. Indeed, shortly afterwards the evangelist puts them both down.

There are two points in this answer: John claims nothing beyond what is right for him, for the author of his baptism is Christ, in whom exists the truth of the sign. Secondly, he does no more than administer the outward sign, while all the power and efficacy is in the hands of Christ alone. So he defends his baptism because its truth depends on another. But yet, by disclaiming the power of the Spirit, he praises the worthiness of Christ, that men may look to him alone. The best self-restraint is when a minister so borrows from Christ whatever authority he claims for himself that he gives him the credit, ascribing it all to him alone.

But a very silly mistake has been made in supposing that John's baptism was different from ours. John is not here arguing about the advantage and profitableness of his baptism, but is merely comparing his role with that of Christ. Just as today, if it were asked what is our part in baptism and what is Christ's, we have to acknowledge that Christ alone performs what baptism represents, and we have nothing beyond the bare administration of the sign. Scripture speaks in a twofold way about the sacraments. Sometimes it tells us that they are "the washing of rebirth" (Titus 3:5), that "this water symbolizes baptism that now saves you" (1 Peter 3:21), that we are grafted into the body of Christ, that our old man is crucified and that we rise again in newness of life (see Romans 6:4-6). And in these instances Scripture unites the power of Christ with the ministry of man, so that the minister is nothing but the hand of Christ. Such expressions show not what the man can accomplish by himself, but what Christ brings about through the man and through the sign, as his instruments. But since men tend to fall into superstition and from their innate pride snatch from God his honor and keep it for themselves, Scripture, to curb this blasphemous arrogance, occasionally distinguishes the ministers from Christ, as in this passage, so that we may learn that ministers are nothing and can do nothing.

"But among you stands one you do not know." He indirectly censures their stupidity for not knowing Christ, of whom they ought to have been taking particular notice. And he always carefully insists that nothing can be known of his ministry until men have come to its author. He says that Christ stands in their midst, so that he may make them eager to know him. In summary, he wants to abase himself as much as he can in case any honor is mistakenly given to him which would obscure the superiority of Christ. It is probable that these sentences were frequently on his tongue when he saw himself praised too much by the perverse opinions of men.

27. "He is the one who comes after me." Here he says two things: that Christ followed him in time, but that in rank and dignity he was far ahead of him, for the Father preferred him to everybody else. Soon after he will add a third point — that Christ was preferred to all others because he excelled all others by right.

28. This all happened at Bethany (KJV, "Bethabara"). The place is mentioned not only to authenticate the account, but also to inform us that this reply was given in a crowd of people. Many flocked to John's baptism, and this was his ordinary place for baptizing. It is also thought to have been a crossing place of the Jordan; and commentators derive the name from this, for they interpret it as "the house of crossing." Some, perhaps, may prefer the opinion of those who refer it to the memorable passage of the people, when God opened up a way for them through the midst of the waters, under Joshua (Joshua 3:13). Others consider it should be read "Bethabara." The name **Bethany**, put here by some, is a mistake; for we shall see later how close Bethany was to Jerusalem. The site of Bethabara which the topographers describe agrees best with the evangelist's words.

Verses 29–34

29. The next day . . . There is no doubt that John had previously spoken about the manifestation of the Messiah; but when Christ came, he wanted his proclamation to be known quickly; and the time was now at hand when Christ would bring John's ministry to an end, just as the dawn suddenly disappears at sunrise. Therefore, when he had borne witness to the priests who were sent to him that they ought to seek the truth and power about his baptism from Christ who was already present and living in the middle of the people, **the next day** John makes Christ known openly. These two acts, following each other in close succession, must have powerfully affected their minds. This is the reason why Christ showed himself in John's presence.

"Look, the Lamb of God." The principal office of Christ is explained briefly but clearly. By taking away the sins of the world through the sacrifice of his death, he reconciles men to God. Christ certainly bestows other blessings on us, but the chief one, on which all the others depend, is that by appeasing the wrath of God he brings it about that we are reckoned righteous and pure. From this source flow all the streams of blessings: by not imputing our sins, God receives us into favor. Accordingly, John, in order that he may lead us to Christ, begins with the free pardon of sins which we obtain through him.

The Lamb is an allusion to the ancient sacrifices of the law. He was dealing with the Jews, who were used to sacrifices and could not be taught about atonement for their sins in any other way than in terms of sacrifice. But as there were various kinds of sacrifice, he makes one sacrifice stand for all types of sacrifices. Probably John is thinking of the paschal lamb. The main point is that John used an expression which was suitable for teaching the Jews. In the same way today, because of the ceremony of baptism, we have a better understanding about what the forgiveness of sins through the blood of Christ means when we hear that we are washed and cleansed by it from our sins. At the same time, as the Jews commonly held superstitious ideas about sacrifices, he corrects this fault in passing by reminding them of the object to which all the sacrifices pointed. It was a very wicked abuse of the institution of sacrifice to fix their trust on its outward signs. Therefore John, as he points to Christ, bears witness that he is **the Lamb of God,** by which he means that whatever sacrificial victims the Jews used to offer under the law had no power at all to atone for sins, but were only figures whose reality was revealed in Christ himself.

". . . who takes away the sin of the world!" He uses the word **sin** in the singular, for any kind of iniquity, as if he said that every sort of unrighteousness which alienates God from men is taken away by Christ. And when he says **the sin of the world** he extends this kindness indiscriminately to the whole human race, so that the Jews might not think the Redeemer had been sent to them alone. From this we infer that the whole world is bound in the same condemnation, and that since all men without exception are guilty of unrighteousness before God, they have need of reconciliation. John the Baptist, therefore, by speaking about **the sin of the world** in general wanted to make us feel our own misery and exhort us to seek the remedy. Now it is for us to embrace the blessing offered to all, that each may make up his mind that there is nothing to hinder him from finding reconciliation in Christ if only, led by faith, he comes to him.

Besides, he proclaims one way only of taking away sins. We know that at the beginning of the world, when their consciences convicted them, all men labored anxiously to procure forgiveness. Hence the vast number of propitiatory offerings, by which they wrongly imagined they appeased God. I confess, indeed, that all the spurious propitiatory rites originated in a holy way, as God had ordained the sacrifices which directed men to Christ. But yet everyone continued for himself his own way of appeasing God. But John leads us back to Christ alone and teaches us that God is only reconciled to us through his blessing, since he alone takes away sins. He therefore leaves no other course for sinners than to flee to Christ. In this way he excludes all human satisfactions, expiations, and redemptions, since they are nothing but ungodly inventions framed by the craft of the devil.

The verb "to take away" can be expounded in two ways: either that Christ took upon himself the burden under which we were crushed, as it is said in 1 Peter 2:24 that he "bore our sins . . . on the tree," and in Isaiah 53:5 that "the punishment that brought us peace was upon him"; or that he blots out our transgressions (Psalm 51:1). But since the latter depends on the former, I willingly accept both — that Christ, by bearing our sins, takes them away. Although, therefore, sin continually stays in us, yet in the judgment of God it is nothing, for as it is abolished by the grace of Christ, it is not imputed to us. Nor do I dislike Chrysostom's point that the present tense of the verb (**"who takes away"**) denotes a continuing action; for the satisfaction which was once completed flourishes forever. But he tells us not merely that Christ **"takes away . . . sin,"** but also indicates the method — that he has reconciled the Father to us by means of his death; for this is what he means by the word **Lamb.** Let us therefore learn that we are reconciled to God by the grace of Christ if we go straight to his death and believe that he who was nailed to the cross is the only propitiatory sacrifice through whom all our guilt is removed.

30. "This is the one I meant when I said . . ." He embraces everything in a summary when he declares that it is Christ who he had said would be preferred before him. For it follows that John is nothing but a herald sent on Christ's behalf. And from this again it is established that Christ is the Messiah. Three things are mentioned here. When he says that a man is coming after him, he means that he himself was before Christ in time, to prepare the way for him, according to the testimony of Malachi 3:1 — "See, I will send my messenger, who will prepare the way." When he says that **"he surpassed me,"** this refers to the glory with which God adorned his Son when he came into the world to perform the office of Redeemer. Thirdly, the reason is added — that Christ is far above John the Baptist in position. The honor, therefore, which the Father bestowed on him was not accidental but was due to his eternal majesty. But I have already touched on this expression, **"has surpassed me because he was before me"** (see my commentary on 1:15).

31. "I myself did not know him." That his testimony may not be suspected of having been given from friendship or favor, he anticipates such a doubt, denying that he had any other knowledge of Christ than what had been obtained by divine inspiration. Therefore the summary of it is that John does not speak from his own understanding, nor in order to please man, but at the inspiration of the Spirit and by the command of God.

"I came baptizing with water" — that is, "I was called and ordained to this office" — **"that he might be revealed to Israel."** John the Baptist afterwards explains this more fully and confirms it when he represents himself as testifying that he had known Christ by a divine oracle — that is, through information or revelation from God. In place of what we have here ("I came to baptize"), he there declares expressly that he was **"sent"** (verse 33). It is only God's calling that makes lawful ministers. Whoever pushes himself forward unasked, whatever learning or eloquence he may possess, is not entitled to any authority, for he is not authorized by God. Now since John, to baptize regularly, had to be **"sent"** by God, you must understand that no man has any right to institute sacraments. This right belongs to God alone. Christ, on another occasion, to prove the baptism of John, asks, "Was it from heaven, or from men?" (Matthew 21:25).

32. "I saw the Spirit come down from heaven as a dove." This is not a literal but a figurative expression, for with what eyes could he see the Spirit? But as the dove was a sure and infallible sign of the presence of the Spirit, it is called **the Spirit** by a figure of speech in which one name is substituted for another; not that it is really the Spirit, but it shows him in a way man can grasp. And this metaphorical language is usual in the sacraments; for why does Christ call the bread his body but because the name of the thing is suitably transferred to the sign — especially when the sign is at the same time a true and efficacious pledge by which we are assured that the thing itself which is signified is bestowed on us? Yet you must not think that **the Spirit** who fills heaven and earth (see Jeremiah 23:24) was contained in **a dove**, but that he was present by his power, so that John might know that such a sight was not put in front of his eyes in vain. Similarly, we know that the body of Christ is not bound to the bread, and yet we share in his body.

So why did **the Spirit** appear under the form of **a dove**? We must always hold that here is an analogy between the sign and the reality. When the Spirit was given to the apostles, they saw "tongues of fire" (Acts 2:3) because the preaching of the Gospel was to be spread abroad through all tongues and was to have the power of fire. But in this verse God wished to represent openly that gentleness of Christ which Isaiah 42:3 praises: "a bruised reed he will not break, and a smoldering wick he will not snuff out." This was the first time that the Spirit was seen coming **down from heaven** on him. Not that before this he had been empty of the Spirit, but now he is, as it were, consecrated with a solemn ceremony. We know that he remained hidden like a private individual for thirty years, because the time of his manifestation had not yet come. But when he wished to make himself known to the world, he began with his baptism. He therefore received the Spirit on that occasion not so much for himself as for his people. And the Spirit descended visibly that we may know that in Christ dwells the abundance of all gifts of which we are destitute and empty. This may easily be gathered from the words of John the Baptist. When he says God told him, **"The man on whom you see the Spirit come down and remain is he who will baptize with the Holy Spirit"** (verse 33), it is as if he had said that the Spirit was seen in a visible way and remained on Christ to the end, that he might water all his people with his fullness. What it is to "baptize with the Spirit" I have briefly touched on above — that Christ gives baptism its effect, so that it will not be vain and invalid, and this he does by the power of his Spirit.

33. "... on whom you see the Spirit come down." Here a difficult question arises: if John did not know Christ, why did he refuse to admit him to baptism? He would certainly not say to someone he did not know, "I need to be baptized by you" (Matthew 3:14). Some reply that he knew him in a limited way, so that although he reverenced him as a distinguished prophet, he did not know that he was the Son of God. But this is a poor solution, for everyone should obey God's calling regardless of what other people think. No rank or excellence of man ought to stop us from doing our duty. Therefore John would have shown disrespect for God and his baptism if he had spoken like this to anyone else but the Son of God. Therefore he must have known Christ previously.

First, we must note that this refers to a knowledge arising from intimate acquaintance. Although he recognizes Christ as soon as he sees him, it is still true that they were not known to each other in the ordinary way of human friendship, for the beginning of his knowledge came from God. But the question is not yet fully resolved, for he says that the sight of the Holy Spirit was the mark of recognition. But he had not yet seen the Spirit when he addressed Christ as the Son of God. I willingly agree with the opinion of those who think that this sign was added for confirmation, and that it was not so much for John's sake as for us all. Certainly John alone saw it, but for others rather than for himself. Bucer aptly quotes Moses in Exodus 3:12 —"This will be the sign to you that it is I who have sent you: When you have brought the people out of Egypt, you will worship God on this mountain." Undoubtedly, when they were going out they already knew that God would lead them and watch over their deliverance, but this was a confirmation, from the event, after it had taken place. Similarly, this came as an addition to the former revelation which had been given to John.

34. "I have seen and I testify that this is the Son of God." He means that he is not declaring anything uncertain, for God was pleased to give him thorough and profound knowledge about those things of which he was to be a witness to the world. And it is noteworthy that he testified that Christ was the Son of God, for the giver of the Holy Spirit must be the Christ, since the honor and office of reconciling men to God belongs to no one else.

Verses 35–39

35. "Look, the Lamb of God!" In this appears more clearly what I have already stated, that when John felt that he was reaching the end of his course, he worked incessantly to hand on his office to Christ. His persistence gives greater weight to his witness. But by insisting so earnestly day after day on repeating his praise of Christ, he shows that his own ministry was now finished. Moreover, we see here how weak and low the beginning of the church was. John indeed had prepared disciples for Christ, but not until now had Christ begun to collect a church. John has just the two obscure and insignificant men, but even this makes his glory shine, so that within a short time, unaided by man's power or a strong company, he extends God's kingdom in a wonderful and unbelievable way. We ought also to observe where especially he leads men to. It is to find in Christ the forgiveness of sins. And as Christ had specifically presented himself to the disciples that they might come to him, so now, when they do come, he gently encourages and exhorts them; for he does not wait for them to speak first, but asks them, **"What do you want?"** (verse 38). This kind and friendly invitation, once made to two men, now belongs to everyone. Therefore, we must not be afraid that Christ will hold back from us or deny us easy access, provided that he sees us striving towards him. No, indeed! He will stretch out his hand to help our efforts. And will he not meet those who come to him, he who seeks from a distance those who are wandering and straying, that he may bring them back onto the right road?

38. "Rabbi." This name was often given to men of high rank or honor. But here the evangelist records another contemporary use of it. "Rabbi" was used to address teachers and expounders of the Word of God. Although, therefore, they do not yet know that Christ is the only teacher of the church, nevertheless, moved by John's recommendation of him, they regard him as a prophet and teacher, which is the first step towards receiving instruction.

"Where are you staying?" From this example we are taught by the very beginnings of the church that we ought to acquire a taste for Christ that will kindle our desire to progress. Nor should we be satisfied with a mere passing look, but we must seek out where he lives, that he may receive us as his guests. There are very many who merely sniff at the Gospel from a distance, and thus let Christ suddenly disappear, and all they have learned about him slips away. Although they did not then become his full-time disciples, there is no doubt that he taught them more fully that night, that he might have them entirely devoted to him soon afterwards.

39. It was about the tenth hour. That is, the evening was approaching, for it was only two hours to sunset. In those days the days, which were longer in summer and shorter in winter, were divided into twelve hours. And from this mention of the time we gather that those two disciples were so eager to hear Christ and to know him more intimately that they were not concerned about their night's lodging. But we, for the most part, are very different from them, for we procrastinate endlessly because it is never convenient for us to follow Christ.

Verses 40–42

40. Andrew, Simon Peter's brother, was one of the two. The evangelist's aim, up to the end of this chapter, is to inform us how the disciples were gradually led to Christ. Here he talks about Peter, and later he will mention Philip and Nathanael. That Andrew immediately brings his brother expresses the nature of faith, which does not conceal the light or quench it, but rather spreads it in every direction. Andrew has scarcely one spark, and yet through it he enlightens his brother. Woe to our apathy if we, who are more fully enlightened than he, do not try to make others share in the same grace! We may observe two things in Andrew that Isaiah requires of the children of God — that each should take his neighbor by the hand, and also that he should say, "Come, let us go up to the mountain of the Lord . . . he will teach us his ways" (Isaiah 2:3). For Andrew holds out his hand to his brother with just this object, that he may become a fellow-disciple with him in the school of Christ. Moreover, we ought to notice God's purpose. He wanted Peter, who was to be far the more eminent, to be brought to the knowledge of Christ by Andrew's agency and ministry, so that none of us, however excellent, may refuse to be taught by an inferior. For he will severely punish that fastidious, or rather arrogant, person who, through this contempt of a man, will not deign to come to Christ.

41. "We have found the Messiah." The evangelist has translated the Hebrew word for **Messiah** ("anointed") into the Greek word *Christ* in order to tell the whole world what had been a Jewish mystery. This was the ordinary title of kings, as anointing was observed by them as a solemn ceremony. But yet they were aware that one King would be anointed by God, under whom they hoped for perfect and eternal happiness, especially when they learned that David's earthly kingdom would not be permanent. Then as God stirred them up, overcome and burdened with various tribulations, to look for the Messiah, he revealed to them more clearly that his coming was close at hand. Daniel's prophecy is clearer than all the rest, insofar as it relates to the name of *Christ*. For he does not, like the earlier prophets, ascribe it to kings but applies it exclusively to the Redeemer (Daniel 9:25-26). Thus, this way of speaking became prevalent, that whenever **the Messiah** or **Christ** was mentioned they understood by it none other than the Redeemer. And so the woman of Samaria says, "Messiah . . . is coming" (John 4:25), which makes it the more amazing that he who was so eagerly longed for and spoken about by everyone should be accepted by so few.

42. "You are Simon." Christ gives Simon a name, not, as is usual, because of some past event, or from what he now sees in him, but because he was going to make him **Peter.** First he says, **"You are Simon son of John."** He puts his father's name in its abridged form, a common enough custom when names are translated into foreign languages. It will be clear from the final chapter (see 21:15) that he was the son of Johanna or John. But all this amounts to nothing more than that he will be a very different person from what he is now. For Christ does not mention his father because he was of high repute; rather, since Peter was born of an obscure family and of no esteem among men, Christ declares that this will not prevent him from making Simon a man of unconquerable courage. The evangelist therefore records it as a prediction, not only in that Christ foresaw the future steadfastness of faith in Peter, but also that he foretold what he was going to give him. So now he praises the grace which he had determined to give him later on; and therefore he does not say that this is his present name but postpones it to a future time.

"You will be called Cephas." Indeed, all godly people may be correctly called Peters (stones) if they build their foundation on Christ, so that they may be suitable for building the temple of God. But Peter alone is called **Cephas** because of his particular excellence. The Roman Catholics are ridiculous when they put him in Christ's place as the foundation of the church, as if he too were not founded on Christ like the others. And they are doubly ridiculous when they make him a head. A silly canon under the name of Anacletus, among Gratian's rhapsodies, changes a Hebrew word for a Greek and so muddles up the Greek word *kephale* with Cephas, suggesting that by this name Peter was appointed head of the church. Moreover, Cephas is Aramaic rather than Hebrew, but that was the usual post-exilic pronunciation of it. There is, then, no ambiguity in Christ's words. Christ promises Peter what he would never have expected and thus exemplifies in him his own grace to all ages, that his former state may not tell against him, since this remarkable title proclaims that he has been made a new man.

Verses 43–46

43. "Follow me." Philip's mind was set on fire to follow Christ by this one word; and hence we infer how great is the efficacy of the Word, though it is not evident in everyone indiscriminately. For God urges many without any effect, just as if he beat their ears with an empty sound. Therefore, the external preaching of the Word is of itself unfruitful, except that it mortally wounds reprobates, so that they have no excuse before God. But when the secret grace of the Spirit brings us to life, all the senses will inevitably be so affected that men will be prepared to **follow** God wherever he calls them. We must therefore pray that Christ will put the same power of the Gospel in us. It is true that Philip's following of Christ was special, for he was commanded to follow, not only like any of us, but as an intimate companion and an inseparable comrade. All the same, everyone's calling is illustrated in Philip's calling.

44. . . . was from the town of Bethsaida. The name of the city seems to have been mentioned deliberately to show more clearly God's goodness to the three apostles. We learn from other passages how sternly Christ threatens and curses that city (Matthew 11:21; Luke 10:13). Accordingly, that some from such an ungodly and wicked race should be received into God's favor ought to be viewed as if they were brought out of hell. When Christ decided to rescue them from the bottomless abyss and make them worthy of the honor of being appointed apostles, it was a magnificent and memorable blessing.

45. Philip found Nathanael. Though proud people despise these feeble beginnings of the church, we ought to see in them a greater glory of God than if the condition of the kingdom of Christ had been noble from the start and grand in every way. For we know how this little seed eventually grew into a great harvest. Again, we see the same desire to build which was seen in Andrew. Philip's modesty, too, is remarkable, in desiring and caring only to have others to learn along with him from the common Teacher of everyone.

"We have found . . . Jesus." How small Philip's faith was is clear because he cannot say four things about Christ without including two huge mistakes. He calls him **"the son of Joseph,"** and he incorrectly states that Nazareth is his native town. And yet, because he really wants to help his brother and make Christ known, God approves his earnestness and makes it successful. Indeed, everyone needs to keep soberly within his own limits; and the evangelist certainly does not mention it as being worthy of commendation in Philip to dishonor Christ twice, but just relates that his teaching, though faulty and full of error, was useful because in spite of everything it aimed to make Christ truly known. He foolishly calls Jesus **"the son of Joseph"** and out of ignorance calls him a Nazarene, but all the same, he leads Nathanael to none other than the Son of God who was born in Bethlehem (see Matthew 2:1). He does not forge a counterfeit Christ but only wants him to be known as he was shown by Moses and the prophets. Thus we see that the main aim of preaching is that those who hear us should somehow or other come to Christ.

Many engage in abstruse arguments about Christ and so cloak him with their subtleties that he can never be found. The Roman Catholics, for example, will not say that Christ is **the son of Joseph,** for they know precisely what his name is; and yet they empty him of his power and so exhibit a phantom in his place. Would it not be better to stammer ridiculously with Philip and still keep the true Christ than to introduce a false Christ in clever and impressive language? On the other hand, there are many ordinary people today, ignorant and unskilled in speaking, who proclaim Christ more faithfully than all the Pope's theologians with their lofty speculations. This passage, therefore, warns us not to reject disdainfully anything about Christ put badly by the simple and unlearned, provided they do direct us to Christ. But in case we should be drawn away from Christ by the false thoughts of men, let us always keep the remedy at hand and seek the pure knowledge about him from **the Law** and **the prophets.**

46. "Nazareth! Can anything good come from there?" At first Nathanael, put off by Christ's birthplace as described by Philip, refuses the invitation. But he is deceived by Philip's thoughtless word. What Philip foolishly believed, Nathanael took as certain. To this is added an unreasonable criticism arising from hatred or contempt of the place. We should note both these points carefully. This holy man was not far from cutting himself off from all approaches to Christ. Why was this? Because he rashly believed Philip's incorrect statement about Christ, and also because his mind was full of the preconceived idea that nothing **good** could come from **Nazareth.** Unless we are on our guard, we will be liable to the same danger.

With similar obstacles Satan strives daily to prevent us from coming to Christ. He carefully spreads very many falsehoods which make us detest or suspicious of the Gospel, so that we do not venture to taste it. Moreover, there is another stone he does not leave unturned as he tries to make Christ contemptible to us, for we know how many people take offense at the degradation of the cross as they view Christ the head and his followers. But as we can hardly avoid being tempted by those tricks of Satan, let us at least remember the words **"Come and see."** Nathanael allowed his double error to be corrected by what Philip said. And so, following his example, let us first show ourselves teachable and obedient; and second, let us not shrink from seeking when Christ himself is ready to remove the doubts which harass us. Those who take this sentence not as a question but as an affirmation are greatly mistaken: "Nazareth! Some good may come from there." How trite this would be! And again, we know that the city of Nazareth was not thought much of then; and Philip's reply shows clearly hesitation and mistrust.

Verses 47-51

47. "Here is a true Israelite." Christ does not praise Nathanael on his own account but through him gives a general lesson. For since many who call themselves believers are anything but believers in fact, it is very important to have some yardstick to distinguish the true and genuine from the false. We know how proudly the Jews gloried in their father Abraham, and how boldly they boasted about the holiness of their ancestry. And yet hardly one in a hundred was not utterly degenerate and estranged from the faith of the patriarchs. Therefore Christ, to tear the mask away from hypocrites, gives a brief definition of what **"a true Israelite"** is and at the same time removes the offense which would later arise from the ungodly obstinacy of the nation. For those who wished to be counted as the children of Abraham and the holy people of God soon became the deadly enemies of the Gospel. But to prevent the ungodliness common in nearly all ranks from discouraging or alarming anyone, he gives a timely warning that there are only a few **true** Israelites among those who claim the name of Israelite.

Moreover, since this passage also contains a definition of Christianity, we must not pass it by hastily. Now, to sum up Christ's meaning in a few words, we must observe that deceit is contrasted with sincerity. Hence he calls those deceitful who elsewhere in Scripture are said to have a double heart (see Psalm 12:2, KJV). Nor does this refer only to that total hypocrisy when those who know they are wicked pretend to be good, but also to an inner hypocrisy when men are so blinded by their vices that they deceive not only others but themselves as well. Integrity of heart in the eyes of God and uprightness before men make a Christian. What Christ is mainly pointing to is the deceit that Psalm 32:2 speaks of.

48. "How do you know me?" Although Christ did not intend to flatter Nathanael, he wanted to gain a hearing to elicit a new question, which he would reply to in such a way as to prove himself to be the Son of God. Nor is it without good reason that Nathanael asks, **"How do you know me?"** For a person to be so sincere as to be free from all deceit is very rare, and the knowledge of that purity of heart belongs to God alone. Christ's reply, however, seems to be inappropriate. For though he **"saw [Nathanael] while . . . still under the fig tree,"** it does not follow from this that he could penetrate into the deep secrets of the heart. But there is another reason. As it belongs to God to know men when they are never seen, so also God is able to see what is not visible to human eyes. Nathanael knew that Christ saw with divine eyes, which is different from the way humans perceive, and so he could understand that Christ did not now speak as a man. Therefore the proof is taken from things that are alike; for God is no less qualified to see what lies out of our sight than to judge about purity of heart. We should also learn a useful lesson from this passage, that when we are not even thinking of Christ we are observed by him, and that this must be the case, so that he can bring us back when we have wandered from the right path.

49. "You are the Son of God." That he acknowledges him to be **"the Son of God"** because of his divine power is not surprising. But why does he call Christ **"King of Israel"**? The two things do not seem to be necessarily connected. But Nathanael takes a loftier view. He had already heard that Jesus is the Messiah, and to this belief he adds the confirmation which he had been given. He also holds another principle: **the Son of God** will not come without showing himself as **King** over the people of God. Therefore he correctly acknowledges **the Son of God** to be also **the King of Israel**. And, indeed, faith should not cling only to the essence of Christ but should pay attention to his power and office. For it would be of little advantage to know who Christ is unless this second point is added about what he wishes to be towards us and for what purpose he was sent by the Father. Hence it has come about that the Roman Catholics have nothing but a shadow of Christ, for all their attention has been to understand his mere essence; but they have neglected his kingdom, which consists in the power to save.

Again, when Nathanael declares Christ is **"King of Israel,"** it is a confession limited to the measure of his faith, for Christ's kingdom extends to the remotest parts of the earth. Nathanael did not yet realize that Christ was appointed to be **King** over the whole world; or rather, that from every corner the children of Abraham would be gathered in, so that the whole world would be the Israel of God. We to whom the extent of Christ's kingdom has been revealed should exceed those narrow limits. But all the same, let us follow Nathanael's example and exercise our faith in hearing the Word and strengthen it by whatever means we can, allowing it not to stay buried but to break out into confession.

50. Jesus said . . . Jesus does not reprove Nathanael as if he had been too credulous, but rather approves his faith and promises him and all others that he will confirm it by stronger arguments. Besides, it was special to one man that he was seen under a fig tree by Christ when absent and at a distance, but now Christ brings a proof which would be for everyone, and thus, as if breaking off his discourse, he turns from talking to one man to speak to everyone.

51. "You shall see heaven open." To my way of thinking, those who anxiously inquire into the place where and the time when Nathanael and the others see heaven open are greatly mistaken. Rather, Christ is pointing to something continuous which was always to exist in his kingdom. I acknowledge, of course, that the disciples sometimes saw angels. I acknowledge that the manifestation of the heavenly glory, when Christ ascended to heaven, was different from what we now see. But if we think it over carefully, we see that what happened then is of perpetual duration. For the kingdom of God, once closed to us, has in Christ indeed been opened. A visible example of this was shown to Stephen (Acts 7:55) and also to the other disciples at Christ's ascension (Luke 24:51; Acts 1:9). But all the signs by which God shows himself present with us depend on this opening of heaven, especially when God communicates himself to us to be our life.

"... ascending and descending on the Son of Man." In this second statement angels are said to "ascend and descend" that they may be ministers of God's kindness towards us. By this expression the reciprocal communication between God and men is noted. Now we must acknowledge that this benefit was received in Christ, because without him the angels are our deadly enemies rather than offering us caring friendship. They are said to "ascend and descend" on him not because they minister to him alone, but because for his sake and in honor of him they include the whole body of the church in their care. Nor do I doubt that he alludes to the ladder which was shown to the patriarch Jacob in a dream (Genesis 28:12), for what that vision sketched out is really fulfilled in Christ. Finally, the summary of this passage is that though the whole human race was outside the kingdom of God, the gate of heaven is now open to us, so that we are "fellow citizens with God's people" (Ephesians 2:19) and companions of the angels, and that they, the appointed guardians of our salvation, descend from that blessed calm to relieve our miseries.

John
Chapter 2

Verses 1–11

1. A wedding took place at Cana in Galilee. The fact that this story relates the first miracle performed by Christ is sufficient reason to consider it extremely carefully, though, as we shall see later, there are other reasons which compel our attention. But its manifold usefulness will be shown more clearly as we go along. The evangelist first mentions the place, **Cana in Galilee**; not the one situated towards Sarepta, between Tyre and Sidon, and called "the greater" in comparison with this other Cana, which some place in the country of the tribe of Zebulon and others assign to the tribe of Asher. For Jerome also declares that it was near the town of Nazareth, since the mother of Jesus went to the marriage. From chapter 4 it will be seen that it was within a day's journey of Capernaum. Its proximity also to the city of Bethsaida can be inferred from the fact that the evangelist tells us the marriage was celebrated three days after Christ had been in that district. It is possible there was also a third Cana, not far from Jerusalem, though outside Galilee; but I leave this undetermined, because I do not know.

Jesus' mother was there. It was probably some relative of Christ who was being married, for Jesus is mentioned as having accompanied his **mother.** From the fact that the disciples are also invited we can gather how simple and frugal his way of living was, since he lived in common with them. It might be thought incongruous that a man not at all rich or having plenty of provisions (as will appear from the failure of the wine) invites four or five others for Christ's sake. But the poor are readier and more open in their invitations; for unlike the rich, they are not afraid of being a disgrace if they do not treat their guests sumptuously and magnificently. It is the poor who keep up the old custom of generous hospitality.

Again, it seems uncivil that the bridegroom should let his guests go short of wine in the middle of the celebration; he is an inconsiderate man who does not have enough wine for his feast. I reply, what is related here often happens, especially when wine is not in daily use. Besides, the context shows that **the wine was gone** towards the end of the banquet when it is usual to have had enough already. The master of the banquet says as much: **"Everyone brings out the choice wine first and then the cheaper wine after the guests have had too much to drink; but you have saved the best till now"** (verse 10). Moreover, I have no doubt that all this was arranged by divine providence, so that there might be an opportunity for the miracle.

3. Jesus' mother said to him . . . It may be doubted whether she hoped or asked anything from her son, since he had not yet performed any miracle. And it is possible that without expecting any such help, she advised him to allay the guests' annoyance with some godly exhortations, at the same time relieving the embarrassment of the bridegroom. Moreover, I consider her words as expressing sympathy or compassion. When the holy woman saw that the feast might be disturbed from the guests' thinking that they were being treated with discourtesy or that they might grumble at the bridegroom, she wanted to find some way of solving the problem. Chrysostom suspects her of being moved by her feminine instincts to seek after some sort of favor for herself and her Son. This conjecture is baseless.

4. "Dear woman, why do you involve me?" But why does Christ rebuff her so sternly? I reply that although neither ambition nor any other human affection motivated her, she nevertheless did wrong by going beyond her proper bounds. Her solicitude about the inconvenience of others and her desire to remedy it in some way came from kindness and should receive credit; all the same, by intruding she could have obscured the glory of Christ. But we also ought to notice that Christ spoke like this not so much for her sake as for the sake of others. Her modesty and goodness were too great to need so severe a reproof. Again, she was not sinning knowingly and willingly; but Christ just meets the danger of his mother's words being misconstrued, as if it were at her behest that he afterwards performed the miracle.

"Why do you involve me?" The Greek literally means, "What to me and to you?" But this Greek expression comes to the same thing as the Latin phrase rendered, "What hast thou to do with me?" The old translator led many astray by saying that Christ regarded the failure of the wine as no concern of his or of his mother. But from the second clause we may easily conclude how far this is from Christ's meaning, for he takes upon himself this care and declares it is his concern when he adds, **"My time has not yet come."** These two things should be linked to each other — that Christ understands what he must do, and yet that he will do nothing in this matter at his mother's suggestion.

This is indeed a remarkable passage. Why does he positively refuse to his mother what he afterwards freely granted so often to all sorts of people? Again, why is he not satisfied with a bare refusal, but puts her in the common order of "women," not even honoring her with the name of "mother"? It is certain that this saying of Christ openly warns men not to transfer to Mary what belongs to God by superstitiously exalting the honor of the maternal name in Mary. Christ therefore addresses his mother like this so as to transmit a perpetual and general lesson to all ages, lest any excessive honor paid to his mother should obscure his divine glory.

How necessary this warning became in consequence of the enormous and abominable superstitions which followed is known well enough. For Mary has been made Queen of Heaven, the Hope, the Life and Salvation of the world; and in fact, some went so far that they just about stripped Christ naked and adorned Mary with his spoils. When we condemn those accursed blasphemies against the Son of God, the Roman Catholics call us malicious and envious. What is more, they spread the wicked slander that we are deadly enemies of the honor of the holy Virgin. As if she had not all the honor that belongs to her without being made a goddess! As if it were honoring her to adorn her with sacrilegious titles and put her in Christ's place! The Roman Catholics, therefore, do Mary a cruel injury when they snatch from God what belongs to him that they may disfigure her with false praises.

"My time has not yet come." He means that he has not been inactive from carelessness or laziness, and at the same time hints that he will take care of the matter when the right time comes. And so he not only charges his mother with untimely zeal, but also gives her hope of a miracle. The holy virgin recognizes both these thoughts, for she does not press him further. And when she tells the servants to **"do whatever he tells you"** (verse 5), she shows that she is expecting something new to happen. But this lesson has a wider application: whenever the Lord keeps us in suspense and delays his help, it does not mean that he is inactive, but rather that he regulates his works so that he acts only at the right time. Those who have applied this passage to prove that the timing of events is governed by Fate are too ridiculous to need a single word wasted in refuting them.

The **"time"** of Christ sometimes means the hour appointed for him by the Father; and he will afterwards call his **"time"** what was convenient and suitable for carrying out the Father's commands. But in this place he claims the right of taking and choosing the **"time"** to work.

5. His mother said to the servants . . . Here the holy virgin shows an example of the true obedience she owed to her Son in matters not of human duties but of his divine power. Therefore she modestly acquiesces to Christ's reply and exhorts others to obey his will. I acknowledge that the virgin spoke about that present situation as if she were denying to herself any jurisdiction in the matter and saying that Christ would follow his own will and do whatever he pleased. But if you look into her intention, her statement has a wider application. For she first disclaims and lays aside the power she might seem to have usurped, and then she ascribes all power to Christ alone when she tells them, **"Do whatever he tells you."** Hence we are taught here, in general, that if we desire anything from Christ we shall not obtain our prayers unless we depend entirely on him, look to him, and, in short, do whatever he tells us. But he does not send us away to his mother but invites us to himself.

6. Nearby stood six stone water jars. We gather that these **water jars** were very large. Christ supplied them therefore with a great abundance of wine — enough indeed for more than a hundred and fifty people at a banquet. Besides, both the number and the size of the **water jars** serve to confirm the truth of the miracle. If they held only a small amount, many might have suspected that the wine had been brought from elsewhere. If the water had been changed into wine in one vessel only, the certainty of the miracle would not have been so clear and indisputable. It is not, therefore, without a good reason that the evangelist mentioned their number and says how much they held.

The presence of so many large vessels came from superstition. They received the ceremony of cleansing from the law of God; but just as the world is prone to excess in externals, the Jews, not satisfied with the simplicity God had ordered, amused themselves with continual washing; and since superstition is ambitious, it undoubtedly led to ostentation. In the same way, we see in Catholicism today that everything said to belong to the worship of God is arranged for mere display. There was, then, a double error: without any command from God they engaged rashly in an unnecessary ceremony of their own invention; and also, under the guise of religion, ambition ruled in that ostentatious display.

Now, certain scoundrels in the Papacy had the astounding wickedness to dare to put forward some water jars as being these actual jars; but, first, they were too small, and also they were unequal in size. Even today they are not ashamed in the broad light of the Gospel to practice these tricks. This is certainly not deception by juggling but insolently making fun of the blind. The world must be bewitched by Satan not to perceive such obvious derision.

7. "Fill the jars with water." The command may have seemed absurd to the servants, for they already had more than enough water. But this is the way the Lord often acts towards us, so that an unexpected result may make his power shine out more brightly. This detail is put in to emphasize the nature of the miracle, for when the servants drew wine from jars that had been filled with water, no suspicion can remain.

8. "Take it to the master of the banquet." For the same reason as before, Christ wanted the wine to be tasted by **"the master of the banquet"** before he himself or any other of the guests drank any. The quiet way that the servants obey him in everything shows us the great reverence and respect in which he was held by them. The man whom the evangelist calls **"the master of the banquet"** oversaw the preparation of the feast and the arrangement of the tables — not that the feast was very grand and magnificent, but because poor weddings borrowed high-flown ways from the grandeur and luxury of the rich. But it is surprising that Christ, a teacher of self-control, should supply a large quantity of wine and that it should be the very best wine. I reply that when God daily provides us with plenty of wine it is our own fault if his kindness is an incitement to luxury; but it is an undoubted proof of our temperance if we are sparing and moderate in the midst of plenty. In the same way Paul could say, "I know what it is to be in need, and I know what it is to have plenty" (Philippians 4:12).

11. This, the first of his miraculous signs. The meaning is that this was Christ's first miracle. Although the angel's announcement to the shepherds that he was born in Bethlehem and the star appearing to the Magi and the Holy Spirit descending on him in the likeness of a dove were miracles, they were not performed by Christ himself. It is here talking about miracles of which Christ himself was the author. It is a frivolous and ridiculous interpretation which some give that this is numbered first among the miracles which Christ did in Cana of Galilee, as if he chose a place to display his power where we read he only went twice. Rather, the evangelist's purpose was to note the order which Christ followed in exercising his power. For until he was thirty he stayed at home like anyone holding no public office. He was consecrated at his baptism for the exercise of his duties, after which he began to appear in public and show openly by clear proofs why he had been sent by the Father. We need not be surprised, therefore, if he delayed the first proof of his divinity until now.

Marriage is greatly glorified that Christ not only honored a wedding banquet with his presence but also adorned it with his first miracle. Certain ancient canons exist in which the clergy are forbidden to attend weddings. The reason for the prohibition was that their being spectators of the customary licentiousness might perhaps be construed as approval. But it would have been far better for them to have taken with them a seriousness that would curb the wantonness which shameless and disso-lute men indulge in when there is no one to keep an eye on them. Rather, let Christ's example be our rule; and let us not suppose that anything can be more profitable for us than what we read that he did.

He thus revealed his glory — by giving this remarkable and glorious evidence from which it could be established that he was the Son of God. All the miracles which he showed to the world were so many testimonies to his divine power. And now the proper time for manifesting his glory had come, when at the Father's command Christ wished to make himself known. Moreover, from this we learn the purpose of miracles, for the expression amounts to a declaration that Christ performed this miracle to reveal his glory.

His disciples put their faith in him. If they were **disciples** they must have already possessed some faith. But whereas they had hitherto followed him with an uncertain and cloudy faith, they now began to dedicate themselves to him, acknowledging him to be the Messiah, as he had already been proclaimed to them. But Christ is very kind to accept as his **disciples** those whose faith was so weak. And, indeed, this teaching has a universal application. For any adult faith was once in its infancy; nor is it so perfect in any man that he does not need to progress in believing. So those who were already believers began to believe inasmuch as they daily made further progress towards the end of their faith. Therefore those who have arrived at the beginnings of faith strive always to make progress. Here is shown also the fruit of miracles — that they ought to be related to the confirmation and progress of faith. Whoever twists them to any other purpose corrupts and debases the whole use of them, just as we see the Roman Catholics boasting of their fictitious miracles for no other purpose than to bury faith and turn men's minds away from Christ to creatures.

Verses 12–17

12. After this he went down to Capernaum. The evangelist moves on to a new narrative. He had resolved to collect a few things worthy of remembrance which the other three evangelists had omitted, and he states the time when what he is about to tell us took place. The other evangelists also relate what we read about Christ doing here, but the difference of time shows it was a similar but not the same event. Christ therefore twice cleansed the temple from base and secular financial business: first, near the beginning of his mission and the other time when he was about to leave the world and go back to his Father (Matthew 21:12; Mark 11:15; Luke 29:45; John 16:28).

To get a general view of the passage we must examine the details in order. There was a good reason for oxen, sheep, and doves being offered for sale in the temple and for money-changers sitting there. They could claim that their transactions were not at all secular, but on the contrary were connected with the sacred worship of God, so that anyone could easily obtain something to offer to the Lord. And certainly it was very convenient for religious people to find the various oblations on the spot and so be spared the trouble of looking for them. Therefore we may be surprised that Christ should be so angry. But two reasons must be noted. First, the priests misused this merchandise for their own gain and avarice, and such a mockery of God was unendurable. Second, whatever excuse men may plead, as soon as they stray, however slightly, from God's command, they need correcting. And this is the main reason why

Christ cleansed the temple, for he clearly declares that the temple of God is not a place of merchandise.

But it may be asked why he did not begin by teaching them. It seems a disorderly and improper procedure to use force to correct abuses before the remedy of teaching has been tried. But Christ had a different aim. Since the time had come for him to discharge in public the office committed to him by the Father, he wanted in some way to enter into possession of the temple and give proof of his divine authority. So that everyone should pay attention to his teaching, their sluggish and drowsy minds had to be aroused by something new and startling. The temple was the shrine of heavenly teaching and religion. Since Christ wanted to restore purity of teaching, it was of great importance to establish himself as the Lord of the temple. Besides, there was no other way to bring the sacrifices and other religious exercises back to their spiritual purpose than to stop their being abused. What he did at that time was therefore a sort of prelude to the reformation the Father had sent him to carry out. In a word, it was right that the Jews should be aroused by this example to expect something unusual from Christ; and it was also necessary to remind them about the corrupt and perverse way that God was worshiped, so that they might not object to its correction.

With his mother and brothers. Why Christ's brothers accompanied him is uncertain, unless they intended to go along with him to Jerusalem. Further, the word **brothers** in the Hebrew language, as is well-known, signifies all sorts of male relatives.

13. When it was almost time for the Jewish Passover, Jesus went up to Jerusalem. Christ had a twofold object: since the Son of God was subject to the law for our sake, he wished, by observing precisely all the law's commands, to show in himself a pattern of complete submission and obedience. Again, as he could do more good among a multitude of people, he almost always made use of such an opportunity. Whenever, therefore, it is said afterwards that Christ came to Jerusalem for the feast days, let the reader observe that he did so, first, so that along with the rest he might perform religious duties instituted by God, and, next, so that he might proclaim his teaching to a larger group of people.

16. ". . . turn my Father's house into a market." At the second cleansing of the temple the other evangelists mention his harsher and severer language — that they had made the temple of God a "den of robbers" (Matthew 21:13), and this was appropriate when a milder reproof was of no avail. He simply warns them now not to profane the temple of God by using it improperly. The temple was called the **"house"** of God because God willed to be invoked there in particular, because there he exercised his power, and because he had set it apart for spiritual and holy ceremonies.

"My Father's house." Christ declares that he is the Son of God so as to claim the right and authority to cleanse the temple. Moreover, since he here gives a reason for what he did, anyone who wishes to derive any advantage from it must concentrate mainly on this sentence. Why then does he cast the buyers and sellers out of the temple? To restore the original purity of the worship of God, which had been corrupted by the wickedness of men, and in this way to renew and defend the holiness of the temple. Now that temple, as we know, was made to be the shadow of those things whose living image is in Christ. That it might remain sacred to God, it had to be applied exclusively to spiritual uses. For this reason he declares it unlawful that it should be turned into a marketplace. He founds his statement on God's institution, which we ought always to hold. By whatever illusions Satan may deceive, we know that whatever (no matter how small it is) turns us aside from God's command is perverse. It was a specious and misleading deceit that the worship of God was helped and promoted, as if sacrifices were not conveniently at hand for believers. But since God had ordained his temple for different uses, Christ disregards the objections that could be offered against the order set up by God.

This cannot be applied to our church buildings today, but what is said of the ancient temple applies justly and properly to the church, which is the heavenly shrine of God on earth. Therefore the majesty of God which dwells in the church should always be set before our eyes, that it may not be defiled by any impurities. But its holiness will remain sound only if nothing at variance with the Word of God is admitted into it.

17. His disciples remembered . . . Some people waste their time asking how the disciples remembered Scripture which was hitherto unknown and strange to them. We must not think that this passage of Scripture came into their minds at this time; but afterwards, when, taught by God, they considered among themselves what this action of Christ's might mean, this passage of Scripture occurred to them under the direction of the Holy Spirit. And, indeed, the reason for God's works is not always plain to us at once; but afterwards in the course of time he makes his purpose known to us. And this is a bridle well fitted to restrain our presumption in case we should complain against God when our judgment does not approve his actions. We are reminded at the same time that when God keeps us in suspense we must wait patiently for the time of fuller knowledge and curb our excessive haste. God delays the full manifestation of his works to keep us humble.

"Zeal for your house will consume me." This means that the disciples at length grasped that Christ was impelled by a burning **"zeal"** for God's house to drive these acts of profanity out of it. Without doubt, by a figure of speech in which a part is taken for the whole, David uses the name for the temple to denote the whole worship of God. For the complete verse runs like this: "For zeal for your house consumes me, and the insults of those who insult you fall on me" (Psalm 69:9). The second clause balances the first, or rather is simply an explanatory repetition. The meaning of both clauses is that David was so anxious to defend God's glory that he willingly accepted on his own head all the reproaches that the wicked threw at God, and that he burned with such zeal that this one feeling swallowed up all others. He tells us that he himself felt like this; but there can be no doubt that in his own person he was describing what strictly belonged to the Messiah.

Accordingly the evangelist says that this was one of the marks by which Jesus was known to the disciples as the protector and restorer of the kingdom of God. Now observe that they followed the guidance of Scripture to understand Christ properly. Indeed, no one will ever learn who Christ is, or the purpose of his actions and sufferings, except through the guidance and teaching of the Scriptures. So far, then, as each of us desires to advance in the knowledge of Christ we shall need to meditate diligently and continually on Scripture. Nor does David mention the "house" of God without good reason when he speaks of his glory. For although God is sufficient for himself and can be satisfied with himself alone, yet he wishes his glory to be revealed in the church. In this he shows a remarkable example of his love towards us, because he joins, as if by an indissoluble bond, his glory with our salvation. Each individual should imitate Christ, since the example of the head gives a general lesson for the whole body, as Paul teaches in Romans 15:3. So far as we can, let us not allow the sacred temple of God to be polluted in any way. At the same time we must all beware of transgressing the bounds of our calling. In common with the Son of God we should all be zealous; but it is not for all of us to take a whip and correct vices with our hands. For the same power has not been given to us, nor have we been entrusted with the same office.

Verses 18–22

18. "What miraculous sign can you show us?" From the fact that in such a big crowd no one laid hands on Christ and none of the cattle dealers or money-changers drove him away by violence we may conclude that they were all beaten down and stunned by God and were just petrified. Hence, if they had not been utterly blind, this miracle would have been obvious enough, that one man should dare so much, one man against many, an unarmed man against the strong, an unknown man against great rulers. Since they were far the stronger, why did they not oppose him, unless their strength was weakened and, as it were, broken?

Yet they have some reason for questioning him; for it is not for everyone to change at once anything faulty or displeasing in God's temple. All are certainly at liberty to condemn corruptions; but if a private individual sets out to remove them, he will be accused of being rash. As the custom of selling in the temple was accepted, Christ undertook something new and unusual; and so they quite rightly ask him to prove that he was sent by God, for they base their argument on the principle that in public administration it is not lawful to change anything without a definite calling and command of God. But where they went wrong was in refusing to admit the calling of Christ unless he performed a miracle, for it was not a general principle that the prophets and other ministers of God had to perform miracles, nor had God limited himself to this necessity. They were therefore wrong to impose a law on God by demanding a sign. When the evangelist says that the Jews **demanded of him,** he undoubtedly means the multitude standing by and, as it were, the whole body of the church, as if he were saying that it was not the word of one or two but of the people.

19. "Destroy this temple." This is an allegorical expression. Christ deliberately spoke in this obscure way because he thought that they were not worthy of a direct reply — just as elsewhere he declares that he speaks to them in parables because they cannot grasp the mysteries of the kingdom of heaven (see Matthew 13:13). But, first, he refuses to show them the sign they asked for, either because it would have done no good or because he knew it was not the right time. He occasionally made some concessions even to their unreasonable requests; so there must have been some good reason why he refused now. But in case they seize on this as an excuse for themselves, he declares that his power will be proved and confirmed by a special sign. No greater proof of Christ's divine power could be desired than his resurrection from the dead. But he gives this information in a figurative way because he does not judge them worthy of an explicit promise. In short, he treats them as unbelievers as they deserve and at the same time protects himself from all contempt. It is not yet clear that they are obstinate, but Christ knew well what their attitude was.

But since he performed so many miracles and so many different kinds of miracles, it may be asked why he now mentions only one. First, he was silent about all the other miracles because his resurrection alone was sufficient to shut their mouths. Secondly, he did not want to expose the power of God to their ridicule. For he spoke allegorically even about the glory of his resurrection. Thirdly, he mentioned what was appropriate to the case in hand. By these words he shows that all authority over the temple belongs to him, since his power is so great in building the true temple of God.

"This temple." Although he uses the word **"temple"** in accommodation to the present situation, the body of Christ is rightly and fittingly called a temple. Each of our bodies is called a tent (2 Corinthians 5:4; 2 Peter 1:13) because the soul dwells in it; but the body of Christ was the home of his divinity. We know that the Son of God so clothed himself with our nature that in the flesh, which he assumed, the eternal majesty of God dwelt as in his sanctuary.

Nestorius' misuse of this passage to prove that one and the same Christ is not both God and man is easily refuted. He reasoned thus: the Son of God dwelt in the flesh, as in a temple; therefore the natures are divided, so that the same person was not God and man. But this argument might also be applied to men; for it will follow that it is not one man whose soul dwells in the body as in a tent; and therefore it is folly to twist this form of expression to take away the unity of person in Christ. Moreover, it ought to be observed that our bodies also are called temples of God (1 Corinthians 3:16; 6:19; 2 Corinthians 6:16), but in a different sense, simply because God dwells in us by the power and grace of his Spirit; but in Christ the fullness of the Godhead dwells bodily, so that he is truly God appearing in the flesh (see 1 Timothy 3:16).

"I will raise it again." Here Christ claims for himself the glory of his resurrection, though usually in Scripture it is declared to be the work of God the Father. But these two statements are thoroughly compatible. To commend God's power to us, Scripture expressly ascribes to the Father the resurrection of his Son from the dead; but here Christ particularly proclaims his own divinity. And Paul reconciles the two in Romans 8:11: "And if the Spirit of him who raised Jesus from the dead is living in you, he who raised Christ from the dead will also give life to your mortal bodies through his Spirit, who lives in you." While Paul makes the Spirit the author of the resurrection, sometimes he calls him the Spirit of Christ and sometimes the Spirit of the Father.

20. "Forty-six years." Daniel's calculation agrees with this passage (Daniel 9:25), for he calls it seven weeks, which makes forty-nine years; but before the last of these weeks had ended, the **"temple"** was finished. It seems contradictory that the time mentioned in the history of Ezra is far shorter, but in fact it does not conflict with the prophet's words. For when the sanctuary had been erected, before the building of the temple was complete, they began to offer sacrifices. Afterwards there was a long interruption in the work due to the people's laziness, as is clear from the complaints of the prophet Haggai (1:4), who reproved the Jews severely for being too busy building their private houses while they left the temple of God unfinished.

But why does he mention the temple that had been demolished by Herod forty years or so earlier? The present temple, though built very magnificently and at vast expense, had been completed by Herod in eight years, contrary to expectation, as Josephus relates (*Antiquities*, 15.11). I think it likely that this new building of the temple was regarded as if the ancient temple had always remained in its original condition, so that it might be held in greater veneration. And so speaking in the common and usual way they said that the temple had hardly been built, with the greatest difficulty, by the fathers in forty-six years.

Their reply shows plainly in what spirit they sought a sign, for if they had been ready to obey reverently a prophet sent by God, they would not have rejected so arrogantly what he had said in confirmation of his office. They want some testimony of divine power, and yet they will not receive anything that does not correspond to the feeble capacity of man. In the same way the Roman Catholics today demand miracles, not that they would give way to the power of God (for they are determined to prefer men to God and not to shift a hair's breadth from what they have received by usage and custom); but so that they may not appear to rebel against God without a cause, they make this excuse a cloak for their obstinacy. So do the minds of unbelievers rage blindly and desire to have the hand of God exhibited to them and yet do not want it to be divine.

22. After he was raised from the dead ... This reflection was similar to the other that the evangelist has just mentioned (verse 17). The disciples did not understand Christ's saying; but the teaching which seemed to have vanished uselessly into thin air later produced fruit in its own time. Therefore although many of our Lord's actions and sayings are obscure at the time, we must not give up in despair or despise what we do not understand at once. The context should be noted here: **they believed the Scripture and the words that Jesus had spoken.** By comparing **the Scripture** with the **words** of Christ they were helped to progress in faith.

Verses 23–25

23. Many ... believed ... The evangelist appropriately connects this narrative with the former. Christ had not given the sign which the Jews had demanded. Now, since he had made no progress among them by many miracles, except that they conceived a cold and abstract faith, the present event shows that they did not deserve him to fall in with their wishes. There was indeed some result of the signs in that many believed in Christ and in his name so as to profess their readiness to follow his teaching — for **name** is used here for "authority." This appearance of faith, which was up to now fruitless, might ultimately become true faith and be a useful preparation for proclaiming the faith of Christ to others. Yet what we have said is true, that they were far from having the right attitude to profit from the divine works as they should have done.

Theirs was not, however, a phony faith by which they commended themselves to men. For they were convinced that Christ was some great prophet, and perhaps they even ascribed to him the office of Messiah, who was then widely expected. But since they did not grasp the Messiah's special office, their faith was ridiculous, clinging as it did to the world and earthly things. It was also a cold belief, a persuasion empty of any serious attitude of heart. Hypocrites assent to the Gospel, not that they may devote themselves to the allegiance of Christ, nor that with sincere religion they may follow God's call, but because they do not dare to reject entirely the truth they have known, especially when there is no reason to oppose it. For just as they do not voluntarily or gratuitously wage war against God, so also when they see that his teaching is against their flesh and their perverse desires they are immediately offended or at least withdraw from the faith which they had embraced.

So when the evangelist says that those men **believed**, I do not take it as a counterfeit and non-existent faith, but that they were in some way constrained to enlist on Christ's side; and yet that it was not a true and genuine faith is shown by Christ's excluding them from the number of those whose conviction could be relied on. Besides, their faith depended solely on miracles and had no root in the Gospel, and therefore could not be steady and permanent. Miracles do indeed help God's children to arrive at the truth, but it does not amount to actual believing when they are amazed at God's power in such a way as merely to believe that the teaching is true without subjecting themselves to it wholly. And therefore, when we speak about faith in general, let us realize that there is a certain faith which is perceived by the understanding only, and afterwards quickly disappears because it is not fixed in the heart; that is the faith which James calls "dead," whereas true faith always depends on the Spirit of regeneration (James 2:17, 20, 26). Observe that all do not derive equal profit from the works of God; for by them some are led to God, while others are only driven by a blind impulse, so that although they perceive the power of God they do not cease to wander in their own imaginations.

24. But Jesus would not entrust himself ... Those who expound this as Christ being on his guard against them because he knew they were not honest and faithful do not seem to me to express sufficiently well the true meaning of the evangelist. Still less do I agree with what Augustine says about recent converts. The evangelist means rather, in my opinion, that they were not thought of by Christ as genuine disciples, but he despised them as unsteady and trifling. This passage should be observed carefully; not all who profess to be Christ's are such in his estimation. But the reason which immediately follows must be added.

For he knew all men. Nothing is more dangerous than hypocrisy; for this reason, among others, it is an exceedingly common fault. There is scarcely a man who is not pleased with himself; and while we deceive ourselves with empty flatteries, we think God is blind like ourselves. But here we are warned how much his judgment differs from ours. He sees clearly the things that escape our notice because they are concealed by some disguise; and he estimates according to their hidden source — that is, according to the most secret attitude of the heart — the things which dazzle our eyes with their false brilliance. This is the same as Solomon says in Proverbs 21:2 — "All a man's ways seem right to him, but the Lord weighs the heart." Let us remember, therefore, that the only true disciples of Christ are those who are approved by him, because he alone is the proper arbiter and judge of this matter.

Where the evangelist says that Christ **knew all men**, it may be asked whether he means only those of whom he had just spoken or whether it refers to the whole human race. Many extend it to man's common nature and think that the whole world is here condemned for ungodly and faithless hypocrisy. And it is certainly true that nothing can be found in men which makes Christ accept them in the company of his own followers. But I do not see that this agrees with the context, and therefore I limit it to those who had been mentioned.

25. As it might be doubted where Christ obtained this knowledge, the evangelist anticipates the question and replies that everything in men concealed from us is seen by Christ, so that he could of his own authority distinguish between men. Therefore Christ, who knows the hearts, **did not need man's testimony about man** to inform him what sort of men they were. But he knew them to be imbued with such a nature and attitude that he justly regarded them as people who did not belong to him.

Some ask whether we too, after Christ's example, may suspect those who have not given us proof of their sincerity; but this has nothing to do with the present passage. Our judgment is far different from his. Christ knew the very roots of the trees; but we can only know the nature of any individual tree from the outward fruits. Besides, as Paul says, "[Love] keeps no record of wrongs" (1 Corinthians 13:5), and we have no right to entertain unfavorable suspicions about men who are unknown to us. But that we may not always be deceived by hypocrites and that the church may not be too much exposed to their wicked frauds, Christ can furnish us with the Spirit of discretion.

John
Chapter 3

Verses 1–6

1. Now there was a man . . . In the person of Nicodemus, the evangelist now shows us how transient and vain was the faith of those who had been moved by Christ's miracles and hastily joined his side. For this man was of the order of the Pharisees and held the rank of a ruler in his nation and should therefore have been much more advanced than the others. The common people are, for the most part, lightweight and unsteady. But who would not have thought that a man so learned and experienced was also prudent and wise? Yet from Christ's reply it is plain that nothing was further from his purpose in coming than a desire to learn the first principles of religion. If a member of the Jewish ruling council is less than a child, what are we to think of the public in general?

Now, although the evangelist's aim was to show us, as in a mirror, how few in Jerusalem were properly disposed to receive the Gospel, yet this story is extremely useful for other reasons as well — particularly because in it we are taught about the corrupt nature of mankind and what is the right entrance into the school of Christ. This must be the start of our training for making progress in heavenly doctrine, for the sum of Christ's discourse is that to be his true disciples we must become new people. But before we go any further we must, from the details narrated by the evangelist, consider the obstacles which kept Nicodemus from giving himself unreservedly to Christ.

Of the Pharisees. This was, of course, a title of honor for Nicodemus among his countrymen, but the evangelist does not give it to him for the sake of honor, but on the contrary marks it out as an obstacle to his coming boldly and freely to Christ. Hence we are reminded that the elevated people of this earth are most frequently caught in the worst snares; indeed we see many of them so firmly bound that not even the slightest wish or prayer to heaven comes from them in their whole lives. We have explained elsewhere why they were called **Pharisees**, for they boasted that they were the only interpreters of the law, as if they possessed the marrow and hidden meaning of Scripture; and for that reason they called themselves *Perishim*. Although the Essenes won a reputation for holiness by their more austere life, they were like hermits and forsook the ordinary life and custom of men; and therefore the sect of **the Pharisees** was held in the higher estimation. Besides, the evangelist mentions not only that Nicodemus was of the order of **the Pharisees** but that he was **a member of the Jewish ruling council.**

2. He came to Jesus at night. From his coming at night we infer that he was very fainthearted; his eyes were dazzled, as it were, by the splendor of his own greatness and reputation. Perhaps, too, he was hindered by shame, for ambitious men think that their reputation is ruined if they once descend from the rank of teacher to the rank of pupil. There is no doubt he was puffed up with a foolish opinion of his learning. In short, as he had a high idea of himself, he did not want to let go of any part of it. And yet there appears in him some seed of piety; for hearing that a prophet of God had come, he does not despise or neglect the teaching brought from heaven and is moved by a certain desire for it — a desire which sprang from nothing else but fear and reverence of God. Many are titillated by an idle curiosity to inquire eagerly after novelties, but there is no doubt that religion and a perception of conscience impelled Nicodemus to desire to know the teaching of Christ more intimately. And although that seed long lay hidden and dead, after the death of Christ it yielded fruit no one would ever have expected (see 19:39).

"Rabbi, we know . . ." These words amount to his saying, "Master, we know that you have come as a teacher." But as learned men were then commonly called "Master," Nicodemus first greets Christ in the usual way, giving him the ordinary title **"Rabbi"** (which means "Master") and afterwards declares that he who performs the office of a master was sent **"from God."** And on this principle depends all the authority of teachers in the church. For from the Word of God alone must we learn wisdom, and therefore no other should be listened to except those through whose mouth God speaks. We must observe that although religion was greatly corrupted and almost overthrown among the Jews, they always kept to the principle that no man was a lawful teacher unless he had come from God. But since none boast more arrogantly and definitely of being sent **"from God"** than the false prophets, they need to be tried by the spirit of discernment. Accordingly Nicodemus adds, **"For no one could perform the marvelous signs you are doing if God were not with him."** It is evident that Christ has been sent **"from God,"** for God displays his power in him so strongly that it cannot be denied that God is with him. Nicodemus takes it for granted that God is not accustomed to work except through his ministers, that thus he may set his seal to the office he has entrusted to them. And he is right, for God always intended miracles to be the seals of his teaching.

He is also right in making God the sole author of miracles when he says that no man can do these signs unless God is with him. It is as if he said that they are not human acts, but that the power of God reigns and stands out plainly in them. In a word, miracles have the twofold result of preparing us for faith and then of further strengthening what has been formed by the Word; and so Nicodemus profited aright in the former part, since from the miracles he recognized Christ as a true prophet of God.

Yet his argument appears to be inconclusive. For since fake prophets may completely deceive the ignorant with their deceits as if they had through signs proved themselves to be the ministers of God, what difference will there be between truth and falsehood if faith depends on miracles? Indeed Moses expressly declares that in this way: "the Lord your God is testing you to find out whether you love him" (Deuteronomy 13:3). We know also Christ's warning (Matthew 24:24), and Paul's (2 Thessalonians 2:9), that believers should beware of "counterfeit miracles" by which Antichrist dazzles many eyes. I answer, this is done by the righteous permission of God, that those who deserve it may be deceived by the trickery of Satan. But I say that this does not stop the power of God from being manifested to the elect in miracles, which may be a valuable confirmation of true and sound doctrine to them. Thus Paul boasts that his apostleship was confirmed by "signs, wonders and miracles" (2 Corinthians 12:12). Therefore, no matter how much Satan may strut about aping God in the dark, when the eyes are opened and the light of spiritual wisdom shines, miracles are a strong enough attestation of the presence of God, as Nicodemus here declares.

3. "I tell you the truth" (RSV, "Truly, truly, I say to you"). Christ repeats the word **"truly"** (*"amen"*) to catch his attention. For when he was going to speak about the most important and weighty of all subjects, he needed to make Nicodemus more attentive; otherwise he might have passed over this whole discourse carelessly and lightly. Such then is the purpose of the double affirmation.

Although this discourse seems far-fetched and almost inappropriate, yet it was most apt for Christ to begin like this. For as it is useless to sow seed in an uncultivated field, so the teaching of the Gospel is thrown away heedlessly unless the hearer has first been broken in and duly prepared to be obedient and teachable. Christ saw that Nicodemus' mind was so full of thorns and choked with so many poisonous weeds that there was scarcely room for spiritual teaching. Therefore this exhortation was like a plowing to purify him, that nothing should prevent him from benefitting from the teaching. Let us, therefore, remember that this was spoken to just one individual, so that the Son of God may address us all daily in the same tenor. For which of us will say that he is so free from sinful desires that he does not need such a purification? If therefore we want to make good and useful progress in the school of Christ, let us learn to begin at this point.

"Unless a man is born again." In other words, "So long as you lack the most important thing in the kingdom of God I do not think much of your acknowledging me as Master, for your first step into the kingdom of God is to become a new man." But as this is an outstanding passage, every part of it must be examined in detail.

"He cannot see the kingdom of God" means the same thing as entering into the kingdom of God, as the context soon indicates. But people who think "the kingdom of God" means "heaven" are mistaken. It is rather the spiritual life, which is begun by faith in this world and daily increases according to the continual progress of faith. So the meaning is that no one can be truly united to the church and be reckoned among the children of God until he has first been renewed. And thus this shows briefly what the beginning of the Christian life is. At the same time we are taught that we were born exiles and complete strangers to the kingdom of God, and that there is perpetual opposition between God and us until he changes us by a second birth. For the statement is general and includes the whole human race. If Christ had said just to one man or to a few that they could not enter into heaven unless they had first been "born again," we might have thought that it was only certain sorts of people who were meant; but he is speaking of all without exception. For the language has no boundary and has the same meaning as the universal expression, "No one can see the kingdom of God unless he is born again."

Moreover, by the term "born again" he means not the amendment of a part but the renewal of the whole nature. Hence it follows that there is nothing in us that is not sinful; for if reformation is necessary in the whole and in each part, corruption must have spread everywhere. We will soon speak about this more fully. Erasmus, following Cyril's opinion, has incorrectly translated the adverb "from above" [NIV footnote, "born from above"]. I agree that the meaning is ambiguous in Greek, but we know that Christ spoke to Nicodemus in Hebrew. In that case there would have been no ambiguity to mislead Nicodemus into his childish hesitation over a second birth of the flesh. Hence he took Christ's words in no other sense than that a man must be born "again" before he is admitted into the kingdom of God.

4. "How can a man be born . . . ?" Although Christ's form of speech does not expressly occur in the Law and the Prophets, yet as renewal is everywhere mentioned in Scripture and is one of the first principles of the faith, it is evident how imperfectly learned the Scribes at that time were in the reading of the Scriptures. This man was certainly not the only one at fault in not knowing what the grace of regeneration was. The most important thing about the teaching of godliness was neglected because almost all of them were preoccupied with useless subtleties. The

Roman Catholic Church today shows us a similar instance in her theologians. They spend their whole lives in profound speculations but know no more about all that belongs to the worship of God, to the confident hope of our salvation, or to the practice of godliness than a cobbler or a plowman knows about astronomy. And what is more, delighting in exotic mysteries, they openly despise the true teaching of Scripture as unworthy of the rank of teachers. We need not be surprised, then, that Nicodemus trips over a straw; for it is a just vengeance of God that those who think themselves the most excellent and eminent teachers and to whom the ordinary simplicity of doctrine is vile and despicable stand amazed at little things.

5. "Unless a man is born of water . . ." This passage has been explained in various ways. Some have thought that two parts of regeneration are distinctly referred to and that the word **"water"** means the denial of the old man, while they take **"Spirit"** to refer to the new life. Others think there is an implied antithesis, as if Christ contrasted **"water"** and **"Spirit"** — i.e., pure and liquid elements — with man's earthly and gross nature. Thus they take this saying as allegorical, that Christ was commanding us to put off our heavy and burdensome mass of flesh and become like water and air so as to move upwards or at least not be so much weighed down to earth. But both opinions seem to be at variance with Christ's meaning.

Chrysostom, with whom most expositors agree, relates the word **"water"** to baptism. The meaning would then be that by baptism we enter into the kingdom of God because God's Spirit regenerates us then. Henceforth arose the belief in the absolute necessity of baptism for the hope of eternal life. But even were we to grant that Christ is speaking of baptism here, we ought not to press his words so as to make him confine salvation to the outward sign. On the contrary, he links **"water"** with **"the Spirit"** because under that visible sign he testifies and seals the newness of life which by his Spirit God alone produces in us. It is absurd to confine hope of salvation to the sign. So far as this passage is concerned, I cannot at all bring myself to believe that Christ is speaking of baptism, for it would have been inappropriate.

We must always keep Christ's purpose in mind, which we have already explained. He intended to urge Nicodemus to newness of life, because he was not capable of receiving the Gospel until he began to be another man. That to be the children of God we must be born anew and that the Holy Spirit is the author of this second birth is therefore one single and simple statement. Nicodemus was dreaming of some regeneration or transmigration taught by Pythagoras (who imagined that souls, after the death of their bodies, passed into other bodies); but Christ, to liberate him from this error, added by way of explanation that it does not happen naturally that men are born a second time and that they do not have to put on a new body, but they are born when they are renewed in mind and heart by the grace of the Spirit.

Accordingly he used the words **"Spirit"** and **"water"** to mean the same thing, and this ought not to be thought of as a harsh or forced interpretation. It is a frequent and common way of speaking in Scripture, when "the Spirit" is mentioned, to add the word "water" or "fire" to express his power. We sometimes hear of Christ baptizing with the Holy Spirit and with fire (Matthew 3:11; Luke 3:16), where "fire" does not mean something different from the Spirit but only shows what is his power in us. It matters little that he puts the word **"water"** first. This phrase just flows more easily than the other, since a plain and straight-forward statement follows the metaphor. It is as if Christ had said that no one is a son of God until he has been renewed by **"water"** and that this **"water"** is **"the Spirit"** who cleanses us anew and who, by his power poured on us, imparts to us the energy of the heavenly life when by nature we are utterly dry. To reprove Nicodemus for his ignorance Christ very properly uses a form of speech common in Scripture, for Nicodemus ought at length to have acknowledged that what Christ had said was taken from the ordinary teaching of the prophets.

By **"water,"** therefore, is meant simply the inner purification and quickening of the Holy Spirit. Nor is it unusual to employ the word "and" instead of "that is" when the latter clause is intended to explain the former. And the context supports this view of mine; for when Christ at once adds the reason why we must be **"born again"** he shows without mentioning **"water"** how the newness of life which he requires comes from **"the Spirit"** alone. So it follows that **"water"** must not be separated from **"the Spirit."**

6. "Flesh gives birth to flesh." He shows, by using a contrast, that the kingdom of God is closed to us unless an entrance is opened to us by a new **birth,** for he takes it for granted that we cannot enter into the kingdom of God unless we are spiritual. But we bring nothing from the womb except a carnal nature. Therefore it follows that we are all naturally banished from the kingdom of God, deprived of heavenly life and remaining in slavery to death. Besides, when Christ argues here that men must be **"born again"** because they are only **"flesh,"** he definitely includes all mankind under the word **"flesh."** Here, "flesh" means not the body but the soul, and consequently every part of it. The Roman Catholic theologians are mistaken to restrict it to that part which they call sensual, for Christ's argument must in that case have been inconclusive — that we need a second birth because part of us is corrupt. But if **"flesh"** is contrasted to **"the Spirit,"** as something corrupt is contrasted with what is uncorrupt, the crooked thing with what is straight, the defiled thing with what is holy, the polluted thing with what is pure, we may readily conclude that the whole of man's nature is condemned by a single word. Christ is therefore saying that our understanding and reason are corrupted because they are carnal and that all the affections of the heart are depraved and wicked because they too are carnal.

But here it may be objected that since the soul is not born through human effort, the greater part of our nature is not born of the **flesh.** This has led many to think that not only does our body derive its origin from our parents, but that our souls are also passed on from them. For it was thought absurd that original sin, which is correctly centered in the soul, should be spread from one man to all his descendants unless all souls flowed from his soul as from a spring. And certainly at first sight Christ's words seem to suggest that we are **"flesh"** just because we are born of **"flesh."** I answer that Christ's words mean nothing else but that we are all unspiritual when we are born, and in that we come into this world as mortals our nature has no appetite for anything but what is **"flesh."** He is simply distinguishing here between nature and a supernatural gift. For the corruption of all mankind in the person of Adam alone did not come as a result of human birth but from the ordinance of God. As through one man God gave gifts to all of us, so he has also in him deprived us of his gifts. Therefore, we do not draw our individual vice and corruption from our parents but are all alike corrupted in Adam alone, because immediately after his fall God took away from human nature what he had given to it.

Here another question arises. It is certain that in this degenerate and vitiated nature some remnant of God's gifts still remains, and so it follows that we are not corrupt in every respect. The answer is easy: the gifts which the Lord left to us since the Fall, if they are judged by themselves, are indeed worthy of praise. But since the contagion of evil has spread through every part, nothing pure and free from all defilement will be found in us. That we naturally possess some knowledge of God, that some distinction between good and evil is engraved on our consciences, that we have the capacity to cope with supporting our present life, that, in short, we excel the brute beasts in so many ways is excellent in itself, so far as it proceeds from God. But all these things are polluted in us, just as wine which has been completely spoiled and tainted by the stench of its leather bottle loses its pleasant flavor and has a bitter and horrible taste. The knowledge of God as it now remains in us is nothing but a dreadful fountain of idolatry and all superstitions; the judgment of choosing and distinguishing things is partly blind and foolish, partly imperfect and confused; whatever industry we have is wasted on vanity and trifles; and the will itself rushes with raging impetus headlong into evil. Thus in the whole of our nature there remains not a speck of uprightness. And so it is plain that we must be formed for the kingdom of God by a second birth. And the meaning of Christ's words is that since a man is born from his mother's womb only carnal, he must be fashioned anew by **the Spirit** so that he may begin to be spiritual. And the word **Spirit** is used here in two senses — for grace, and for the effect of grace. In the first place Christ is teaching us that the Spirit of God is the only author of a pure and upright nature, and afterwards he says that we are spiritual because we are renewed by his power.

Verses 7–12

7. **"You should not be surprised . . ."** This passage has been twisted by commentators in various ways. Some think that Christ reproves the gross ignorance of Nicodemus and others like him, as if Christ were saying that it is nothing surprising if they do not understand the heavenly mystery of regeneration, since even in nature they fail to understand the things which are brought to their attention. Other commentators give an ingenious but forced interpretation: "as **the wind blows wherever it pleases** (verse 8), so we are set free by the new birth of the Spirit, and, once we are freed from the grip of sin, we run voluntarily to God." Augustine's interpretation of this passage is equally far from Christ's meaning, for Augustine asserted that God's Spirit exerted his power just as he pleased. Chrysostom and Cyril give a better interpretation when they say that the comparison is taken from the wind and apply it to the present passage like this: "Though its power is felt, we do not know its source and cause." While I almost agree with this view, I will endeavor to explain Christ's meaning more clearly and precisely.

I believe that Christ is using a comparison from nature. Nicodemus thought that what he had heard about new birth and new life was unbelievable because this new birth was beyond his comprehension. To remove this difficulty Christ told him that even in the earthly life God's amazing power is displayed, even though it remains concealed. Everyone takes in their crucial breath from the air. We observe the movement of the air but **"cannot tell where it comes from or where it is going"** (verse 8). If during this frail and transitory life God acts so powerfully that we have to wonder at his power, how foolish it is to try to measure, by the observation of our own minds, God's secret work in the heavenly and supernatural life, as if there was no more to believe than what we could observe. Thus Paul, when he is indignant with the people who reject his teaching about the resurrection on the grounds that this is impossible for a body that is decaying into dust and then into nothing, says that the body will be clothed in a blessed immortality. He rebukes them for their stupidity for not thinking that a similar display of God's power is seen in a grain of wheat where the seed does not come to life until it has decayed (see 1 Corinthians 15:36-

37). This is the amazing wisdom David speaks about when he says, "How many are your works, O Lord! In wisdom you made them all" (Psalm 104:24).

So people who have observed the natural order and who do not go beyond this to acknowledge that God's hand is far more powerful in the spiritual kingdom of Christ are extremely stupid. When Christ tells Nicodemus that he should not be surprised, we must not think that Christ intended us to despise God's work, which is so illustrious and worthy of the highest admiration. Rather, Christ means that we should not be so surprised that our faith is harmed. After all, many people reject as fanciful anything they think is too lofty or difficult. In a word, we must not doubt that through God's Spirit we are made anew and made new people even though the way this is done is hidden from us.

8. "The wind blows wherever it pleases." Strictly speaking, the blowing of the wind has no will of its own. But the wind is said to blow wherever it pleases because the movement of the wind is free, variable, and unpredictable, and because it is sometimes carried along in one direction and sometimes in another direction. This is relevant to the matter in hand, because if the wind flowed in a uniform way like water it would be less miraculous.

"So it is with everyone born of the Spirit." Christ means that the movement and working of God's **Spirit** is no less visible in the renewal of a man than the movement of the wind is in this earthly and outer life, even though its method of moving is concealed. So we are ungrateful and malicious if we do not worship God's unbelievable power in the heavenly life, where we observe such a striking example of this in the world. We must not give Christ less honor for restoring salvation to our souls than we do for Christ preserving our human lives. This lesson becomes clear when you read the sentence as follows: "Such is the power and efficacy of the Holy Spirit in the renewed man."

9. "How can this be?" We observe what is the main difficulty in Nicodemus' way. Everything that he hears seems to be impossible because he does not understand how it works. Our biggest difficulty is our pride, as we always want to know more than we should and therefore we reject with devilish pride everything that we cannot understand, as if it is right to limit God's infinite power by our tiny understanding. We are indeed permitted, to a limited extent, to inquire into the manner and reason of God's deeds, so long as we do this soberly and humbly. But Nicodemus rejects what he hears because he does not believe that it is possible. We shall treat this subject more fully in chapter 6.

10. "You are Israel's teacher." Christ sees that he is wasting his time and effort in trying to teach such a proud man, so he begins to rebuke him sharply. It is certain that such people will never make any progress until their wicked confidence, which puffs them up, is removed.

Quite correctly, this is placed first as, on the very subject in which Nicodemus applauds himself for being acute and wise, Christ exposes his ignorance. Nicodemus thought that not admitting that something was possible would be considered proof of his intelligence, since a person is thought to be foolishly credulous if he agrees to what he is told by someone else before he has fully gone into it. But Nicodemus, with all his magisterial haughtiness, exposes himself to ridicule because he is more at a loss over the first principles than a schoolboy. This kind of doubt is certainly shameful and wicked. For what religion, what knowledge of God, what rule about living correctly, what hope of eternal life do we have if we do not believe that a person is renewed by God's **Spirit**? So the word **these** is emphasized in the sentence **"do you not understand these things?"** Since Scripture frequently repeats this part of the teaching, it should be known about even by the humblest beginner. It is quite unendurable that anyone should be ignorant and untaught about this if he professes to be a teacher in God's church.

11. "We speak of what we know." Some commentators refer this to Christ and to John the Baptist, while other commentators say that the plural is used for the singular. For myself, I am certain that Christ mentions himself together with all of God's prophets and is speaking in general terms for them all. Philosophers and other conceited teachers frequently propose trifles which they themselves have invented, but Christ claims that it is unique to him and to God's servants to deliver only teaching that is certain. God does not send ministers to chat about unknown or uncertain things, because he trains them in his own school so that they are able to deliver later to others what they have learned from Christ himself. Again, as Christ, by this testimony, commends to us the certainty of his teaching, so he makes it a rule for all his ministers to be humble and not to propose their own dreams and suppositions, nor to preach about any human inventions which have no foundation to them, but to give faithful and pure witness to God. So everyone should see what the Lord has revealed to them, so that no one exceeds the limits of his faith. Finally, no one should speak about anything except what he has heard from the Lord. It should be noted that Christ here confirms his teaching with an oath so that it may have complete authority over us.

"Still you people do not accept our testimony." This is added so that the Gospel may not lose anything because of man's ingratitude. Since so few people exercise faith in the truth of God, and since the truth is rejected everywhere by the world, we must defend it against contempt, that its majesty may not be held in less esteem because the whole world despises it and obscures it by its impiety. Although the meaning of these words is simple enough, there is still a double lesson to be drawn from this passage. The first is that our faith in the Gospel should not be weakened just because there are only a few disciples on the earth. Rather, it is as if Christ had said, "Though you do not receive my teaching, it nevertheless remains certain and lasting, for man's unbelief will never stop God from always remaining true." The other lesson is that people who disbelieve the Gospel today will not escape with impunity, as God's truth is holy and sacred. We should be strengthened with this shield so that we persevere in obeying the Gospel and oppose man's obstinacy. We must keep to the principle that our faith is based on God. When we do have God as our foundation, we should be like people who are raised above the heavens, boldly treading the whole world under our feet, treating it with disdain, and not allow any unbelievers to make us afraid. From Christ's complaint that his witness was rejected we learn that the Word of God has at all times been especially characterized by being believed by only a few people. For the expression **"do not accept our testimony"** refers to the majority of people — in fact, to almost all people. So there is no reason for us to be discouraged if only a small number of people believe.

12. "I have spoken to you of earthly things." Christ concludes that Nicodemus and others are to blame if they do not make progress in the teaching of the Gospel. Christ explains that he is not to blame that everyone is not better instructed, since he came down to earth so that he might raise us up to heaven. All too often people desire to be taught in an ingenious and amusing way. For this reason most people are delighted with lofty and abstruse speculations. For this reason many people have a low estimate of the Gospel, because no grand language fills their ears, and so they do not deign to give their attention to such a mean and common teaching. But it reveals an extraordinary degree of wickedness that we give less reverence to God speaking to us just because he condescends to speak to us in ways we can understand. So when God speaks to us in Scripture in a simple, rough-and-ready way, we must note that he does so out of his love for us. Anyone who says he is offended by such simple language and uses this as an excuse for not submitting himself to the Word of God is lying. Anyone who is unable to embrace God as he approaches God on this earth will be even less likely to rush up to meet him above the clouds.

"Earthly things." Some expositors explain this as meaning the basics of spiritual teaching, since self-denial can be said to be the beginning of piety. I prefer to agree with those who refer it to the type of instruction. Although all of Christ's teaching was heavenly, he spoke in such a homely way that his style itself seemed to be **"earthly."** In any case, these words do not exclusively refer to any one sermon. Christ's normal method of teaching was popular and simple and contrasts with the pompous, high-sounding language which ambitious people are so strongly addicted to.

Verses 13–18

13. **"No one has ever gone into heaven."** Christ again exhorts Nicodemus not to trust himself and his own wisdom because no mortal man can through his own unaided strength enter into heaven, since he can only go there under the guidance of the Son of God. **"Gone into heaven"** here means "to have a pure knowledge of the mysteries of God and the light of spiritual understanding." Christ is giving here the same instructions as Paul did when he wrote, "The man without the Spirit does not accept the things that come from the Spirit of God" (1 Corinthians 2:14). So Christ excludes from divine things all clever human understanding because it is far inferior to God.

So we must concentrate on the truth that Christ alone, who is heavenly, has **gone into heaven** and that this entrance is closed to everyone else. For in the previous clause Christ humbles us when he excludes the whole world from heaven. Paul teaches, "If any one of you thinks he is wise by the standards of this age, he should become a 'fool' so that he may become wise" (1 Corinthians 3:18). There is nothing we do with greater reluctance. For this reason we should remember that all our senses fail and collapse when we come to God. Christ shuts us out of heaven, but then quickly supplies a solution when he adds that what was denied to everyone is granted to the Son of God. This is also why he called himself the Son of Man. We can now have no doubt that we have an entrance into heaven in common with Christ who clothed himself with our flesh so that he might make us share in all the blessings. Since he is the Father's only "Counselor" (Isaiah 9:6), he reveals to us those secrets which otherwise would have remained hidden.

"Who came from heaven" (KJV, "which is in heaven"). It may seem absurd to say that he **"is in heaven"** while he still lives on earth. If it is answered that this is true about his divine nature, then this expression would mean something else — namely, that while he was man he was **"in heaven."** I could point out that no place is mentioned here and that only Christ is distinguished from everybody else as far as his state is concerned, since he is the heir of the kingdom of God, from which the whole human race is banished. However, as very frequently happens, because of the unity of the person of Christ, what correctly applies to one of his natures is applied to another of his natures, and so we need seek no other solution. So Christ, who **"is in heaven,"** has clothed himself in our flesh, so that by stretching out his brotherly hand to us he may raise us to heaven with himself.

14. **"Just as Moses . . ."** Christ explains more clearly why heaven is only open to him: he brings to heaven everyone who is willing to follow him as their guide. Christ testifies that he will be openly and publicly

seen by everyone so that he may pour out his power over every kind of person.

"Lifted up." To be **"lifted up"** means to be placed in an elevated position so that everyone can see you. This was done by the preaching of the Gospel. The explanation of this which some people put forward, that it refers to the cross, does not fit the context or match his present argument. So the straightforward meaning of the words is that by the preaching of the Gospel Christ was raised up like a standard so that everybody's eyes would be directed to him, just as Isaiah had predicted (Isaiah 2:2). As a type of this lifting up he refers to the snake which was erected by Moses. People who had been harmed by the fatal bite of snakes were healed when they looked at the elevated bronze serpent. The detail of this story is well-known from Numbers 21:9. Christ introduces this here to show that he has to be viewed by everyone through the teaching of the Gospel, so that everyone who looks at him with faith may receive salvation. So it should be inferred that Christ is clearly shown to us in the Gospel — so that nobody can complain that he cannot see Christ, that this revelation is available to everyone, and that as faith looks to him Christ is present. When Christ is faithfully preached, Paul says, Christ becomes a living portrait: "Before your very eyes Jesus Christ was clearly portrayed as crucified" (Galatians 3:1).

This metaphor is neither inappropriate nor far-fetched. Just as it was only a snake in appearance and possessed no venom or poison, so Christ clothed himself in the form of sinful flesh, which was pure and free from all sin, so that he might cure in us the deadly wound of sin. It was not in vain that the Lord previously supplied this kind of antidote for the Jews when they were bitten by snakes, as this only confirmed the teaching Christ gives here. Christ saw that he was despised as a lowly and unknown person. So he could produce nothing more appropriate than the snake being **"lifted up"** to inform these people that they should not think it strange if Christ was, contrary to men's expectation, **"lifted up"** on high from the most low condition, since this had already been foreshadowed under the law by the type of the snake.

So this question arises: does Christ compare himself to **the snake,** since there are some similarities; or does he say that it was a sacrament, as the manna was? For although the manna was bodily food, intended to be consumed, Paul declares that it was a "spiritual" mystery (1 Corinthians 10:3). I am inclined to think that this was also the case with the bronze snake, both on account of this passage and because it was preserved for posterity until it was made into an idol through superstition (2 Kings 18:4).

16. "For God so loved the world." Christ reveals the first cause and, as it were, the source of our salvation in a way that leaves no room for uncertainty, for our minds cannot find rest until we embrace God's unmerited love. Just as the entire basis of our salvation must not be looked for anywhere other than in Christ, so we must see where Christ came from and why he was offered to be our Saviour. Both these points are distinctly stated here. For faith in Christ brings life to everyone; and Christ brought life because the Heavenly Father loves the human race and wishes that they should not perish. This order should be noted carefully, for our nature is so wickedly ambitious that when the question about the origin of our salvation arises, we quickly imagine diabolical things about our own merits. So we imagine that God is reconciled to us because he has thought that we are worthy to be looked on by him. But everywhere in Scripture God's pure and simple mercy is extolled, which sets to one side all merits.

Christ's words mean nothing else when he declares God's love to be the basis for our salvation. If we want to go any higher, the Spirit stops us through Paul's writing when he tells us that this love was founded "in accordance with his pleasure and will" (Ephesians 1:5). Indeed, it is clear that Christ spoke like this in order to stop people from thinking about themselves, in favor of looking to God's mercy alone. The evangelist does not say that God was moved to deliver us because he saw something in us which deserved such an excellent blessing; rather, he ascribes the glory of our deliverance entirely to his love. This is even clearer from what follows; for he adds that God **"gave his one and only Son, that whoever believes in him shall not perish but have eternal life."** So it follows that until Christ set about rescuing the lost, everyone was destined for eternal destruction. Paul also declares this by pointing out the order in which the events happened: "God demonstrates his own love for us in this: While we were still sinners, Christ died for us" (Romans 5:8; see also Romans 5:10). For where sin reigns, we find nothing other than God's wrath, which brings death in its train. Therefore, it is mercy that reconciles us to God, so that he may also restore us to life.

This way of speaking, however, may seem to be different from many passages of Scripture which attribute to Christ the first foundation of God's love for us and show that outside Christ we are detested by God. But we ought to remember, as I have already said, that the Heavenly Father's secret love which embraced us is the first love given to us. However, the grace which he desires us to know, and through which we are stirred up to know the hope of our salvation, begins with the reconciliation which was won through Christ. Since Christ must hate sin, how can we believe that we are loved by him until atonement has been made for those sins which rightly cause offense in Christ's sight? So Christ's love must intervene in order to reconcile us to God before we can experience God's fatherly kindness. Just as we are told, first of all, that God gave his Son to die for us because he loved us, so it is immediately added that our faith should, strictly speaking, look on Christ alone.

"He gave his one and only Son, that whoever believes in him

shall not perish but have eternal life." The correct direction in which faith should be fixed, says the evangelist, is on Christ, where it views God's heart filled with love. Our firm and constant support is to rely on Christ's death as the only pledge of that love. The Greek word for **"one and only"** is emphatic, to emphasize the fervor of the love God has for us. Since people are not easily convinced that God loves them, and to remove all doubt about this, Christ has specifically stated that we are so very dear to God that on our account he did not even spare his **"one and only Son."** Since God has most abundantly shown his love for us, anyone who is not satisfied or remains doubtful about this demonstration of love is being most insulting to Christ, as if he were an ordinary man going to his death accidentally. We should rather consider that God's love for his **"one and only Son"** is a measure of how much more precious our salvation was to him, which he ransomed by choosing that his **"one and only Son"** should die. Christ is correctly called the **"one and only"** Son of God because he is this by nature, and he bestows this honor on us by adoption when we are grafted into his body.

"That whoever believes in him should not perish." One remarkable aspect of faith is that it delivers us from eternal destruction. God specifically states that although we appear to have been born for death, certain deliverance is offered to us through faith in Christ. So we should not fear death, which would otherwise hang over us. He used the broad word **"whoever"** to invite everyone, indiscriminately, to share this life, and also to leave unbelievers with no excuse. This is the significance of the word **"world,"** which is used earlier in this verse. For although there is nothing in the **"world"** which deserves God's favor, God shows that he himself is reconciled to the whole **"world"** as he invites everyone, without any exceptions, to have faith in Christ, which is no less than entry into life.

On the other hand, we must remember that while **"life"** is promised to everyone, to **"whoever believes"** in Christ, faith is nevertheless not common to everyone. Christ is made known to everyone and seen by everyone, but only the elect have their eyes opened by God to seek him by faith. In this the wonderful effect of faith is seen. Through faith we receive Christ as he is given to us by the Father. In this way we are freed from the condemnation of eternal death and made heirs of **eternal life,** because through the sacrifice of his death he has atoned for our sins so that nothing will prevent God from acknowledging us as his sons. Therefore, as faith embraces Christ with the efficacy of his death and the fruit of his resurrection, we will not be surprised to obtain Christ's life in the same way.

However, it is still not very clear how faith gives us life. Is it through Christ renewing us by his Spirit, so that God's righteousness may live and be strong in us? Or is it because once we are cleansed by his blood we are indeed counted as righteous before God through a free pardon? It is true that these two things are always linked together, but since the certainty of salvation is the subject in hand, we ought to mainly emphasize that we live because God loves us freely by not holding our sins against us. So sacrifice is specifically mentioned through which, along with our sins, the curse and death are destroyed. I have already explained that the reason for these two clauses is that they explain that in Christ we regain the life we lack in ourselves, for because of the wretched state of mankind, redemption precedes salvation.

17. "For God did not send his Son into the world to condemn the world." This confirms the preceding statement, for it was not in vain that God sent his own Son to us. He did not come to destroy us, and so it follows that the Son of God's special office is that **"whoever believes"** (verse 16) may obtain salvation through him. So no one should hesitate or be in an anxious state about how to escape from death when we believe that it was God's purpose that Christ should deliver us from it. The word **"world"** is repeated again so that nobody can think that he is excluded so long as he keeps on the road of faith.

The Greek word for "judge" is used here for **"condemn,"** as in many other passages. When God says that he **did not send his Son into the world to condemn the world,"** he states the reason for his coming. For why should Christ come to destroy people who were already completely destroyed? So we should not look for anything else in Christ other than that God, out of his limitless goodness, chose to give us his help as he saved us who were lost. So whenever our sins press in on us, as Satan seeks to drive us to despair, we should hold up this shield, knowing that God is unwilling that we should be overwhelmed with everlasting destruction since he has appointed Christ to be the salvation of the **"world."**

In another passage Christ says, "For judgment I have come into this world" (9:39). Christ is called "the stone the builders rejected"; and Christ is said to be "destined to cause the falling and rising of many" (Luke 2:34). These statements may be discounted since they are given for a different reason, since people who do reject the grace offered in Christ do deserve to have him as their Judge and the avenger of such unworthy and evil contempt. A striking example of this is seen in the Gospel: although it is strictly speaking "for the salvation of everyone who believes" (Romans 1:16), many people's ingratitude turns this into a death sentence for them. Paul expressed both sides of this well when he wrote, "We will be ready to punish every act of disobedience, once your obedience is complete" (2 Corinthians 10:6). What this amounts to is this: the Gospel, in the first instance, is intended for believers, to give them salvation; but those will not escape unpunished who despise Christ and choose him as the author of death rather than of life.

18. "Whoever believes in him is not condemned." Since he so frequently and earnestly repeats that all believers are beyond the danger of death, we may infer from this that there is a great need for firm and definite confidence so that the conscience may not be in a perpetual state of anxiety and fear. God again declares that when we **"believe in him"** we are no longer **"condemned,"** which is explained more fully in chapter 5. The present tense — **"is not condemned"** — is used here instead of the future tense — "will not be condemned" — as is usual in Hebrew, since it means that believers are safe from the fear of condemnation.

"But whoever does not believe stands condemned already." This means that there is no other way by which any human being can escape death. So in other words, everyone who rejects the life Christ offers remains in death, since life is nothing other than faith. The past tense, **"stands condemned already,"** is used emphatically to express more strongly the idea that all unbelievers are completely ruined. It should, however, be noted that Christ is especially speaking about people whose wickedness is seen as an open contempt for the Gospel. While it is true that there is no other way of escaping death than by going to Christ, yet since Christ is referring to the preaching of the Gospel here, which would be spread throughout the world, he aims his teaching against people who deliberately and maliciously put out the light which God had lit.

Verses 19–21

19. "This is the verdict . . ." Christ meets the murmurs and complaints of wicked people who censure what they think is God's excessive harshness when God acts towards them with more severity than they expected. All who do not believe in Christ think it harsh that they should be turned over to destruction. To prevent anyone from ascribing his condemnation to Christ, Christ shows that everyone ought to put the blame on himself. The reason for this is that unbelief witnesses to a bad conscience, which shows that it is their own wickedness which hinders unbelievers from coming to Christ. Some people think that he is pointing out here nothing more than the sign of condemnation. However, Christ's purpose is to restrain man's wickedness, so that they may not, as they always do, argue and dispute with God, as if he treats them unfairly when he punishes unbelief with eternal death. He shows that this condemnation is fair and beyond reproach not only because these men behave wickedly, preferring **"darkness"** instead of **"light,"** and refusing the **"light"** which is offered to them, but also because their hatred of **"the light"** (see verse 20) only stems from a mind that is wicked and conscious of its guilt.

Many people appear to be beautiful and to have an aura of holiness about them but are, all the time, opposing the Gospel. While they appear to be holier than the angels, they are definitely hypocrites who reject Christ's teaching for no other reason than that they love the secret places in which they conceal their wickedness. Since only hypocrisy makes people offensive in God's sight, they are all convicted because without their blinding pride they would not indulge in their crimes, and they would readily and willingly receive the Gospel's teaching.

20. "Everyone who does evil hates the light." This means that they hate **"the light"** just because they are wicked and want to conceal their sins as much as they can. So it follows that when they reject the remedy, they are deliberately inviting the basis for their condemnation. So we make a great mistake if we think that the people who rage against the Gospel are motived by godly zeal; on the contrary, they reject and shun the light so that they may be even freer to indulge themselves in the **darkness.**

21. "But everyone who lives by the truth . . ." This appears to be a wrong and absurd statement unless you say that some people are upright and true before they have been renewed by God's Spirit, which is not at all in line with the overall teaching of Scripture. We know that faith is the fruit from which spring the further fruits of good deeds. To resolve this difficulty, Augustine says that **"lives by the truth"** means "to acknowledge that we are miserable and destitute of all power to do good." It is a good preparation for faith: we are compelled to flee to God's grace under the conviction of our own poverty. But all this is a long way from Christ's meaning, as he intended simply to say that people who act sincerely desire nothing more earnestly than **"light, so that it may be seen plainly"** that they are seeking God. Then, after this trial, it becomes even clearer in God's sight that they are speaking **"the truth"** and are free from all deceit. It would be a wrong deduction to infer from this that people have a clear conscience before they have faith. Christ does not say that the elect believe, as if they deserve the praise of good deeds, but only what unbelievers would do if they did not have a bad conscience.

Christ used the word **"truth"** because when we are deceived by the outward dazzle of deeds, we do not think about what is hidden inside. So he says that people who are upright and free from hypocrisy go into God's presence willingly, for they know that God can judge their deeds correctly. For what he has done is said to have been done **"through God"** or "according to God," as God approves of these deeds and as they are done in line with his directions. So we must learn that we are not to judge anybody else's deeds except in the light of the Gospel, since our reasoning is completely blind.

Verses 22–28

22-23. After this, Jesus and his disciples went out into the Judean countryside. It is likely that, after the feast, Christ went into the area of Judea which is near to the town of **Aenon**, which was in the territory of the tribe of Manasseh. The evangelist says that **there was plenty of water** there, which was not so plentiful in Judea. Geographers tell us that these two towns of **Aenon** and **Salim** were near to the confluence of the river Jordan and the brook Jabbok. They also add that Scythopolis was nearby. From this we infer that John and Jesus totally immersed people's bodies in the water when they baptized them. However, we ourselves should not be uneasy about this outward ceremony, provided that its spiritual truth is in line with the Lord's instructions. Insofar as we can tell, the proximity of these places caused various reports to circulate and many debates to arise about the law, about worshiping God, and about the state of the church because two new people started to baptize at the same time. When the evangelist says that Jesus **baptized** (verse 22), I take this to refer to the beginning of his ministry. He started to publicly exercise the office to which his Father had appointed him. Even though Christ baptized through his disciples, he is here named as the person who did the baptizing. His ministers are not mentioned, although they did not do anything except in his name and by his command. We shall have more to say on this subject in the next chapter.

25. An argument developed. The evangelist has good reason to note that **an argument** arose between some of John's disciples. Ignorance always makes people bold and presumptuous. John's disciples were ignorant about doctrine, and they loved to argue in their ignorance. Had other people accused them, they might be excused. But they were rash and foolish to make unprovoked accusations against Jews when they were so unfit themselves to pass such comments. The verse means that the Jews started the discussion. So they were responsible for embarking on a discussion they did not understand and for speaking in a rash way beyond their own understanding. They were equally at fault because they intended to defend their leader so that his authority would remain intact, rather than defending the reason for baptism. They deserved to be told off on both these counts. Because they did not understand the real nature of baptism they exposed God's holy ordinance to public ridicule, and through their own ambition they set up their master's cause in opposition to Christ.

Clearly, they were amazed and confused by a single word when they were told that Christ was also baptizing. They had devoted all their attention to a person and his outward appearance and were much less concerned about doctrine. These men teach us how mistaken it is to be motivated by a sinful desire to please men rather than to be zealous for

God. We are also reminded to be single-minded by all the means we have, ensuring that Christ alone is preeminent.

The **argument** was **over the matter of ceremonial washing**, as the law laid down for the Jews how baptisms and ceremonial washings should be carried out. Not content with the directions God had given them, they carefully observed many other rules which their ancestors had handed down to them. When they discovered, in addition to the numerous and varied methods of **ceremonial washing** they knew about, that Christ and John were introducing a new ceremony for purification, they thought it was absurd.

26. "The one you testified about." Through this argument they try to make Christ either inferior to John, or to show that John, through conferring honor on him, had put Christ under obligation to him. For they thought that John was doing Christ a favor by giving him such honorable titles. In reality it was John's duty to make this proclamation, as it was his greatest privilege to be the Son of God's herald. Nothing could have been been more absurd than to make Christ inferior to John, as John's witness to Jesus had been so strong, and we know what this testimony was. The expression **"everyone is going to him"** is used by envious people and is motivated by sinful ambition. They fear that the crowd will immediately stop following their master.

27. "A man can receive only what is given him from heaven." Some people think these words refer to Christ, as if John accused the disciples of wicked presumption against God, through trying to deprive Christ of what the Father had given him. They think the meaning would then be, "Since he has risen to such great honor so quickly, it must be God's doing; so it is pointless for you to try to degrade the person God has raised so high by his own hand." Other people think these words are an exclamation which he voices about the little progress his disciples had made. Certainly it was completely absurd that they should still try to reduce the person who they had often heard was the Christ to the rank of an ordinary person, as if he should not rise above his own servants. So John could be saying that it is useless to spend time teaching people who are dull and stupid, until their minds are renewed.

I tend to agree with the view that these words refer to John, who asserts that it is not in his power, or in theirs, to make him great, because the standard for us all is to be what God intended us to be. For if even the Son of God did not take "this honor upon himself" (Hebrews 5:4), which ordinary person would dare desire more than what the Lord has given him? If this one thought was sufficiently impressed on all our minds, it would be more than enough to curb our ambition. Once ambition is held in check and destroyed, the plagues of contentious arguments would also be removed. So anyone who is exalting himself more than he should is not trusting in the Lord and so is not content with the station in life he has been given.

28. "You yourselves can testify that I said . . ." John complains to his disciples that they did not believe his words. He had often warned them that he was not the Christ, and so it was only right that he should be a servant and a subject of the Son of God, along with other people. This passage is noteworthy, for by affirming **"I am not the Christ"** it only remains for John to be subject to the head and to be just another servant in the church, and not to be so highly exalted as to obscure the honor of the head. He says that he is **"sent ahead of him"** to prepare the way for Christ, as kings have heralds or forerunners.

Verses 29–34

29. "The bride belongs to the bridegroom." Through this comparison John emphasizes that only Christ is elevated above the rank of ordinary people. A person who is about to marry does not call and invite his friends to the marriage so that they can make his wife a prostitute or, through giving up his own rights, allow them to share the bridal bed. Rather, the bridegroom invites his friends to the marriage so that it is honored by them and made more sacred. In the same way, Christ does not call his ministers to the teaching office so that by conquering the church they dominate it, but rather that Christ may use their faithful labors and unite them to himself. It is an important and splendid distinction that people are appointed to positions in the church where they can represent the person of the Son of God. So they are like the friends whom the **"bridegroom"** brings with him so that they can be with him in celebrating the marriage. We must observe this distinction carefully: ministers must remember their position and not take to themselves what belongs to the **"bridegroom."** It all amounts to this: however eminent teachers may be, they should not hamper Christ from alone ruling his church, or from ruling it through his Word alone.

This comparison often occurs in Scripture when the Lord wants to show the holy bond of adoption through which he binds us to himself. Just as he offers himself to be truly enjoyed by us, so that he may be ours, so he correctly claims from us the mutual faithfulness and love which a wife owes to her husband. This marriage is completely fulfilled in Christ, for "we are members of his body" (Ephesians 5:30), according to Paul. The chastity which he demands is mainly concerned with the obedience to the Gospel, so that our minds may not be led astray from our sincere and pure devotion to Christ (see 2 Corinthians 11:2-3). We must be subject to Christ alone; only he is to be our head; we must not turn away by a hair's breadth from the simple teaching of the Gospel.

Only Christ must have the highest glory, so that he may keep the right and authority of a **"bridegroom"** over us.

So what should ministers do? Certainly the Son of God calls them to carry out their duties in conducting the holy wedding. So it is their duty to take care, in every way, that the bride who is in their charge should be presented by them as a chaste virgin to her husband, which Paul, in the passage already quoted, boasts that he has done. People who draw the church to themselves rather than to Christ are guilty of badly violating the marriage which they should have honored. And the greater the honor that Christ confers on us by making us guardians of his bride, the more evil our lack of faithfulness is if we do not endeavor to keep and defend his rights.

"That joy is mine, and it is now complete." He means that he has succeeded in fulfilling all his wishes, and that he has no further desires when he sees Christ reigning and people listening to him as he deserves. Whoever has these desires and can so disregard themselves that they extol Christ and are satisfied to see Christ honored will be faithful and successful in ruling the church. But anyone who deviates from this goal in the slightest degree is a wicked adulterer and will only corrupt the bride of Christ.

30. **"He must become greater."** John the Baptist goes further. He had been raised by the Lord to the highest honor, but he shows that this was only temporary, and now that "the sun of righteousness" (Malachi 4:2) has risen, he must give way to him. So he not only scatters and drives away the empty trappings of honor which had been rashly and ignorantly heaped on him by men, but he is also very careful that the genuine and rightful honor which the Lord had bestowed on him should not obscure the glory of Christ. So John the Baptist tells us that the reason why he had up to that time been counted as a great prophet was that he should only be placed in this elevated position temporarily, until Christ came, to whom he must surrender his office. In the meantime, he says that he is most willing to be reduced to nothing, so long as Christ occupies and fills the whole world with his beams. All pastors in the church should imitate John's zeal in lowering his head and shoulders so that Christ is elevated.

31. **"The one who comes from above."** Through another comparison he shows how different and superior Christ is to everyone else. He compares Christ with a king or a distinguished general whom everyone should listen to with reverence because of his authority as he speaks from his high throne. But for John the Baptist it is sufficient for him to speak from Christ's lowest footstool. In the Latin translation of the second part of this verse the phrase **"from the earth"** only occurs once, while the Greek manuscripts repeat the phrase so that it occurs twice. I assume that ignorant people thought that the repetition was superfluous, and so they cut the second phrase out. However, the meaning is

this: **"the one who is from the earth"** reveals his own ancestry and remains on his earthly plane according to his nature. John asserts that you can only refer to Christ as coming **"from heaven"** because he is **"above all."**

But you may ask: "Did not John also come **from heaven** as far as his calling and office are concerned? So, men should have listened to the Lord speaking through him. Or else it seems that John is contradicting the heavenly doctrine he is teaching." But I reply that this is not an absolute statement but a comparison. If you consider ministers on their own, they do speak **from heaven**, as they do so with the highest authority about what God has commanded. However, as soon as they are compared with Christ, they must be nothing. Thus the apostle Paul compares the law with the Gospel: "If they did not escape when they refused him who warned them on earth, how much less will we, if we turn away from him who warns us from heaven?" (Hebrews 12:25). So Christ does want to be acknowledged in his ministers, but in such a way that he stays the only Lord and they are content with being servants. When comparisons are made, Christ wants to be so differentiated from them that he alone is exalted.

32. "He testifies to what he has seen." John continues to carry out his duty. In order to obtain disciples for Christ, he commends Christ's teaching as being certain since he says nothing that he has not received from the Father. **"Seen and heard"** are contrasted with uncertain opinions, unsubstantiated rumors, and all kinds of lies. John means that Christ does not preach anything except what has been fully accredited. Some may argue that little credence can be given to anyone who only knows **"what he has ... heard."** I answer that this word **"heard"** shows that Christ has been taught by the Father, so that he only says what is divine — that is, what has been revealed to him by God.

This is true of the whole person of Christ as the Father sent him into the world as his ambassador and interpreter. Later he accuses the world of being ungrateful, rebelliously and wickedly rejecting such a certain and faithful witness to God. As he does this, he answers an objection which might cause many people to reject the faith and which might hinder and slow down the progress of others in their faith. For since we are so used to being overdependent on the opinions of the world, many people judge the Gospel with the same contempt that the world does. At least they are prejudiced because they see the Gospel being rejected everywhere and so are even more reluctant and more slow to believe. As we view such obstinacy in the world, let this warning keep us in continuous obedience to the Gospel: Christ is the truth who came from God. When he says that **"no one accepts his testimony,"** he means that there are very few believers, almost no believers, when they are compared with the huge crowd of unbelievers.

33. "The man who has accepted it." Here he encourages and exhorts godly people to fully accept the teaching of the Gospel, as if he had said that there is no reason why they should be ashamed or uncomfortable about the small number of believers. For they do have God as the author of their faith who abundantly supplies us with everything. So even if the whole world rejected or refused to have faith in the Gospel, this should not stop good people from giving their assent to God. They have something they can be certain about when they know that to believe the Gospel is nothing less than assenting to the truths which God has revealed. Moreover, we learn that it is unique to faith to rely on God and to have this confirmed by his words, as there can be no assent unless God, in the first place, had come and spoken. This teaching differentiates faith from all human ideas as well as from uncertain and doubtful opinions. For it must correspond to the truth of God, which is free from all doubt, and therefore, since God cannot lie, it would be impossible for faith to waver. Armed with this defense, whatever tactics Satan may use in his attempts to disturb and shake us, we will always remain victorious.

So we are also reminded how acceptable and precious a sacrifice faith is in God's sight. Since nothing is dearer to him than his truth, we cannot give him more acceptable worship than when we acknowledge through our faith that he is true, as we are then giving that which correctly belongs to him. On the other hand, we cannot offer a bigger insult to God than not to believe his Gospel, since he cannot be deprived of his truth without all his majesty and glory being taken away. His truth is closely linked with the Gospel, and it is his will that this should be recognized. So unbelievers, insofar as they have power, leave God with nothing. They do not hesitate to accuse God of lying, but their wickedness does not eclipse God's faithfulness. Unless we are harder than stones, this noble truth which adorns faith should set our minds on fire with the strongest love for it. God confers great honor on poor, worthless men, who, although they are by nature nothing other than vain and false, are thought worthy of approving, through their assent, the sacred truth of God.

34. "For the one whom God has sent speaks the words of God." He confirms his preceding statement as he shows that we are really concerned with God when we receive Christ's teaching, since Christ came from no one other than the Heavenly Father. So it is God alone who speaks to us through him, and we do not give to Christ's teaching all it deserves unless we acknowledge that it is divine.

"God gives the Spirit without limit." There are two ways of looking at this passage. Some people think it refers to the ordinary dispensation in this way: "God, who is the inexhaustible fountain of all his blessings, does not in the least degree diminish his resources when he liberally pours his gifts on men. People who give to other people liquid they draw from a container eventually reach the bottom of the container.

But there is no danger that anything like this can happen with God, nor will his abundant gifts be so big that he cannot surpass them whenever he wishes to shower even more blessings on us." This interpretation is plausible as the sentence is indefinite; it does not specifically point to any individual.

However, I incline to Augustine's view that this verse refers to Christ. It is no good objecting that Christ is not named in this clause, since all ambiguity is removed in the next clause where what might appear to refer to many different people is limited to Christ. **"The Father loves the Son and has placed everything in his hands"** (verse 35) should be read along with verse 34. In verse 34 the verb **"gives"** is in the present tense and denotes, as it were, a continuous act. For although Christ received the Holy Spirit in complete perfection at one moment, yet, as the Holy Spirit flows, as it were, from a source, and is widely disseminated, it is not wrong to say that Christ now receives the Spirit from the Father. If anyone wishes to interpret this more simply, it is not unusual for tenses of verbs to change and for "give" to be substituted for "has given."

But the meaning is clear. **"The Spirit"** was given to Christ **"without limit"** since the power of grace which he possesses knows no limits. As Paul teaches, "to each one of us grace has been given as Christ apportioned it" (Ephesians 4:7), so that nobody possesses the fullness on his own. Between us there is a mutual bond of brotherly fellowship, and no individual has all he needs, since everyone needs help from somebody else. But Christ differs from us in this respect because the Father has poured out on him an unlimited supply of his Spirit. It is certainly right that the Spirit should live **without limit** in him, so that we may all draw on his fullness, as we saw in chapter 1. This relates to verse 35: **"the Father loves the Son and has placed everything in his hands."** Through these words John the Baptist not only declares Christ's excellence but at the same time shows the purpose and use of the riches with which Christ is endued. Christ, who has been appointed by the Father to administer these gifts, distributes them to everyone as he chooses and as he thinks fit, which Paul explains more fully in Ephesians 4, as I have just quoted. While God enriches his own people in various ways, it is unique to Christ that he has **"everything in his hands"** (see verse 35).

Verses 35–36

35. "The Father loves the Son." What is the significance of this statement? Does it mean that the Father hates everyone else? The answer is simple: he is not referring to the normal love which God has for everyone he has created, or for his other works, but he is referring to that special love which, beginning with the Son, flows from him to all creatures. For with this love, which includes the Son, God embraces us also with Christ, and this leads God on to give us all his blessings through Christ's hand.

36. "Whoever believes in the Son . . ." This was added not only to inform us that we ought to ask for all good things from Christ, but also so that we might know the way in which they are enjoyed. He shows us that this enjoyment is made up of faith, and not without reason, since we possess Christ through faith, who brings with him both righteousness and **"life,"** which is the fruit of righteousness. As faith is declared to be the cause of **"life,"** we realize that **"life"** is only found in Christ, and that there is no other way we can share in this **"life"** than through the grace of Christ himself. However, not everybody agrees about how Christ's **"life"** comes to us. Some people understand it in the following way: "We receive the Spirit through believing, and the Spirit gives us new life so we can be justified, but through this actual new life we receive salvation." As far as I am concerned, I acknowledge that it is true that we are given new life through faith, so that the Spirit of Christ rules us; but I also believe that we should, first of all, take into account the free forgiveness of sins through which we are accepted by God. It is on this that all our confidence for salvation is based and consists. We cannot be counted as justified before God in any other way than that God does not impute to us our sins.

"Whoever rejects the Son . . ." Just as John the Baptist proclaimed "life" in Christ, through whose sweetness we might be wooed to God, so he now consigns to eternal death everybody who does not believe in Christ. In doing this, he exalts God's kindness as he warns us that there is no other way of escaping death unless Christ delivers us. This sentence stems from everyone being accursed in Adam. So if Christ's office is to save people who are lost, anyone who rejects this offer of salvation deserves to remain in death. We have just said that this especially applies to people who reject the Gospel which has been revealed to them. Everyone is involved in this destruction, but a heavier and double vengeance is in store for those who refuse to have the Son of God as their deliverer. Clearly, it was the Baptist's aim in proclaiming death to the unbelievers that we should be aroused through the fear of this and put our faith in Christ. It is also plain that all the righteousness which the world thinks that it has outside of Christ is condemned and reduced to nothing. Nor can anyone say that it is unjust that people who are devout and holy in every way, except for belief in Christ, should perish. For it is foolish to imagine that there is any holiness in people unless it has been given to them by Christ.

"See life" means "enjoy life." To state more clearly that we have no hope unless we are rescued by Christ, John says that **"God's wrath**

remains" on unbelievers. I am not dissatisfied with Augustine's view that John the Baptist used the word **"remains"** to explain to us that from the womb we were destined to death, because "we were by nature objects of wrath" (Ephesians 2:3). I can readily agree to this kind of allusion, so long as we hold on to the simple and true meaning about what I have said about death hanging over all unbelievers, which keeps them oppressed and overwhelmed so that they can never escape. Although the reprobate are already condemned, yet through their unbelief they bring down on their heads a new death. This is why the power of binding was given to ministers of the Gospel. For it is a just punishment on man's obstinacy that people who manage to shake off the saving yoke of God should bind themselves with the chains of death.

John
Chapter 4

Verses 1–9

1. When the Lord learned of this . . . [verse 3 in NIV, verse 1 in Calvin's edition]. The evangelist now intends to give an account of the conversation between Christ and **a Samaritan woman** (verse 7), and he begins by explaining the reason for his journey. Christ knew that **the Pharisees** were ill-disposed towards him, and so he did not want to expose himself to their anger before the correct time. This is why he left Judea. The evangelist tells us that Christ did not go into Samaria hoping to stay there but because he had to pass through it on his way from Judea to Galilee. For until his resurrection opened up the way for the Gospel, Christ had to spend his time in collecting the sheep of Israel, to whom he had been sent. It was an extraordinary and accidental, if we may use the word, event by which Christ now favored the Samaritans with his teaching.

So why does Christ seek the quiet life in the hidden places of Galilee, as if he did not want to be known, which was most desirable? I answer that Christ was fully aware of the correct way to behave and that he used his opportunities so that he did not waste a moment. He wanted to live methodically and in the way he knew to be right. So our minds, too, should be so ordered that on the one hand no fear deters us from performing our duty and that on the other hand we may not throw ourselves rashly into dangers. Everybody who really wants to follow their calling will take care to keep this balance. They will follow the Lord steadfastly even through the middle of deaths, but they will not rush recklessly into such situations but will walk in God's paths. Therefore, let us remember not to go further than our calling demands.

The Pharisees heard. The evangelist mentions that **the Pharisees** were hostile to Christ not because the Scribes were friendly, but because the Pharisees were then in the ascendancy and were filled with rage under the guise of godly zeal. It may be asked if they envied Christ because he had more disciples, since their stronger leanings to John made them promote his honor and reputation. These words mean something different. Although they had been annoyed to find John making disciples, they were even more exasperated when they saw that even **more disciples** went to Christ. From the time that John vowed to be nothing more than the Son of God's herald, people began to flock in greater numbers to Christ, as John had almost finished his ministry. So John handed over the office of teaching and baptizing to Christ.

2. Although in fact it was not Jesus who baptized. The evangelist refers to Christ "baptizing" when in fact the baptism was carried out by other people, so that we understand that baptism is not to be judged according to who baptizes. The power in baptism depends on its author, in whose name and by whose authority it is administered. So we take amazing comfort when we appreciate that our baptism has no less power to wash and renew us than if it had been performed by the hand of the Son of God. We can be sure that for as long as he lived on earth Christ abstained from administering the outward sign of baptism, for the express purpose of witnessing to all ages that baptism is no less efficacious when it is administered by a mortal man. In summary, Christ not only baptizes us inwardly by his Spirit, but the actual symbol which we receive from mortal man ought to be thought of in the same way as if Christ himself revealed his hand from heaven and stretched it out to us. So if the baptism administered by a man is Christ's baptism it will not stop being Christ's baptism, no matter who actually baptizes. This is sufficient reason for refuting the Anabaptists who argue that when the minister is an evil man the baptism is invalid. Through this absurd reasoning they upset the church. Augustine rightly used this same argument against the Donatists.

5. A town in Samaria called Sychar. Jerome in his epitaph on Paula believes that this is a wrong reading and that it ought to be "Sichem." This latter name was indeed a true name in ancient times. However, it is probable that in the evangelist's time **Sychar** was already in common use. As to the place, it is generally agreed that it was a city near Mount Gerizim, whose inhabitants were treacherously killed by Simeon and Levi (Genesis 34:25), and which Abimelech, a native of the place, later razed to the ground (Judges 9:45). Its location was so convenient that a city was built there for a third time which in Jerome's time was called Neapolis. By giving all these details the apostle John makes the town's identity certain. Moses definitely tells us where the field was which Jacob gave to the children of Joseph (Genesis 48:22). It is universally agreed that Mount Gerizim was near Shechem. Later we will see that a temple was built there; also, it is certain that Jacob lived a long time there with his family.

6. Jesus, tired as he was from the journey . . . Jesus did not pretend to be weary but was actually tired. Jesus took on himself our weaknesses so that he could be better prepared to have sympathy and compassion on us, as the apostle Paul states: "We do not have a high priest who is unable to sympathize with our weaknesses" (Hebrews 4:15). All this agrees with the time factor. For it was not surprising that since he was thirsty and **tired** he rested at the well at about noon. **The sixth hour** was noon, as they timed their twelve-hour day from sunrise to sunset. When the evangelist says that Jesus sat down by the well, he is describing the attitude of a **tired** man.

7. A Samaritan woman. When Jesus asked the woman for water, he did so not merely with the intention to make this an opportunity to teach her, but because he was genuinely thirsty. However, this did not prevent him from taking this opportunity to teach her, since Jesus put the woman's salvation above his own needs. He forgets about his own thirst as if he were satisfied with being at leisure and having the opportunity for conversation. In order to teach her about true godliness, he draws a comparison between the visible water and the spiritual water, and with the heavenly teaching he waters the mind of the woman who had refused him a drink.

9. "You are a Jew and I am a Samaritan woman. How can you ask me for a drink?" She uses this reproach against Jesus because of the general contempt shown by his nation. Samaritans were known as the scum of the earth collected from foreign peoples. The Jews detested them because they had corrupted the worship of God and had introduced many spurious and wicked ceremonies. However, it is certain that most of the Jews used their zeal for the law as a cloak for their own human hatred. Many Jews were motivated more by ambition and envy, and by the displeasing sight of their country being lived in by the Samaritans, than by unease and sadness about the corruption of their worship of God. There were just grounds for their separation if their feelings had been pure and restrained. This is why when Christ first sent the apostles out to proclaim the Gospel, he forbade them to go to the Samaritans (Matthew 10:5).

This woman does what is natural to most of us. We take exception to being despised and want to be thought well of. This disease of human nature is so widespread that everyone wants his vices to be approved of. If anyone disapproves of us or of anything we do or say, we immediately take offense for no reason at all. Any person who examines himself will find this seed of pride in his mind until God's Spirit eradicates it. This woman knew that the superstitions of her nation were condemned by the Jews, so she now insults the nation in the person of Christ.

(For the Jews do not associate with the Samaritans.) I believe that these words were said by the woman. Other people think that the evangelist added them, by way of an explanation. It hardly matters which view you take. But I think that it is more natural to see the woman taunting Christ in this way: "What? Is it lawful for you to ask me for a drink when you think of me as being so unholy?" But if you take the other interpretation I do not mind. In any case, it is possible that the Jews extended their hatred of the Samaritans beyond proper bounds. As we have said, they used their feigned zeal in a wrong way, and so they would naturally go to extremes, as nearly always happens to people who give in to their evil desires.

Verses 10–15

10. Jesus answered her. Christ now takes the opportunity to start preaching about the grace and power of his Spirit, even though the woman did not at all deserve that he should say anything to her. This is clearly an example of his amazing goodness. For what was there in this wretched woman that she should suddenly become a disciple of the Son of God rather than being a prostitute? But we know that in all of us Christ has shown the same compassion. All women are not prostitutes, and all men are not stained by some heinous crime. However, what excellence can any of us plead as a reason for Christ to give us his heavenly teaching and the honor of being allowed into his family?

This conversation did not take place by accident. For the Lord shows us a model example that people to whom he gives the teaching of salvation are not selected on the basis of merit. At first sight it seems amazing that Jesus ignored so many great men in Judea and yet had this friendly conversation with this woman. But it was necessary so that it could be explained how truly Isaiah's prophecy was fulfilled in the person of Christ: "'I revealed myself to to those who did not ask for me; I was found by those who did not seek me. To a nation that did not call on my name, I said, "Here am I, here am I"'" (Isaiah 65:1).

"If you knew the gift of God . . ." The two clauses **"If you knew the gift of God"** and **"who it is that asks you for a drink"** I take as separate sentences and view the latter as an interpretation of the former. For it is through God's wonderful kindness that she had Christ present with her who also brought eternal life. The meaning becomes clearer if we replace **and** with "namely" or some similar word, in this way: "If you knew the gift of God — namely, who it is that asks you for a drink . . ." These words teach us that we only know who Christ is when we understand what the Father has given us in him and what blessings he brings us. The starting point of this is being convicted by our poverty; nobody seeks a solution unless he believes that there is a problem. So the Lord does not invite those who have quenched their thirst, but the thirsty, not those who are satiated, but the hungry, to eat and drink. For why would Christ be sent with the fullness of the Spirit unless we were empty?

Moreover, the person who has made good progress and who is aware of his deficiency already acknowledges how much he needs another person's help. It would not be enough for him to moan in his distress if he did not also hope that help was ready and waiting. If we just moaned expecting no help, we would be just wallowing in our sorrow, or we might be like the Roman Catholics who run about in every direction, burdening ourselves with useless and unprofitable weariness. But when Christ appears, we no longer wander around in vain seeking a remedy where one cannot be found, but we go straight to Christ. The only genuine and profitable knowledge of God's grace is when we know that it is shown to us in Christ and that it is given to us by his hand. In the same way, Christ reminds us how efficacious knowledge of his blessings is, since it stirs us up to seek them and warms our hearts. **"If you knew,"** he says, **"you would have asked."** These words are easy to understand. Christ uses them to whet the woman's appetite so that she would not despise or reject life when it was offered to her.

". . . he would have given you . . ." Through these words Christ testifies that our prayers are not fruitless when they are addressed to him. Indeed, without this expectation our desire to pray would certainly cool. But when Christ meets those who come to him and is ready to satisfy their desires, there is no more room for procrastination or sloth. It is only a person's unbelief that would prevent him from feeling that this applies to everyone.

10. **"Living water."** Christ uses the word **"water"** in this situation and applies it to the Spirit. This metaphor is frequently used in Scripture, for we are like dry and barren soil, and there is no sap or activity in us until the Lord waters us with his Spirit. In another passage the Spirit is called "pure water" (Hebrews 10:22), but in the different sense that he washes and cleanses us from pollution which completely covers us. But in this passage and in similar passages the word speaks of secret energy through which God restores life in us, maintaining it and bringing it to perfection. Some people think that this refers to the teaching of the Gospel, which I agree is quite appropriate. But I think that Christ includes here the whole grace of our renewal, for we know that he was sent to bring us a new life. Therefore, in my opinion, he contrasts **"water"** with the emptiness of all the blessings which men groan and labor under. Again, **"living water"** is not called this because it gives life; the allusion is to different kinds of waters. It is called **"living"** because it flows from a **"living"** fountain.

11. **"Sir," the woman said, "you have nothing to draw with."** Just as the Samaritans were despised by the Jews, so the Samaritans also held the Jews in contempt. So this woman at first not only despises Christ but even mocks him. She fully understands that Christ is speaking figuratively, but she throws out a jibe, using a different metaphor, meaning that Christ promises more than he can deliver.

12. **"Are you greater than our father Jacob?"** She goes on to accuse him of arrogantly exalting himself above the holy patriarch **Jacob.**

"Jacob," she says, "was satisfied with this well which he used for himself and his whole family, but do you have better water?" It is clear enough that she is making a false comparison as she compares a servant with a master and a dead man with the living God. And yet how many people today fall into this same error. So we ought to be even more careful not to extol the virtues of men if this obscures God's glory. Indeed, we should reverently acknowledge God's deeds wherever they appear. Therefore, it is right that we should honor men who are outstanding in piety or who are endowed with unusual gifts. However, this should be done in such a way that God stands out above them all and that Christ, with his Gospel, shines clearly, since all the world's splendor must bow to him.

It should also be noted that the Samaritans falsely boasted that they were descended from the holy fathers. In the same way, the Roman Catholics arrogantly boast about the Fathers, despising God's true children. Even if the Samaritans were descended from Jacob in a human way, yet because they had completely degenerated and had abandoned true godliness, their boasts were ridiculous. As it is, they are descended from the people of Cuthah (2 Kings 17:24), or at least gathered from the unholy Gentiles, and yet they still continue to make these false claims about being descended from the holy patriarch. But this does not do them any good. This is the case with everyone who wickedly exults in the light of men and so deprives himself of the light of God, and who has nothing in common with the holy fathers whose name he has misused.

13. "Everyone who drinks this water . . ." Even though Christ realizes that he is making little headway and that his teaching is even being mocked, he continues and explains more clearly what he has said. He makes a distinction between two ways in which water is used. Some water is used by the body, just for a specific time; other water has the power to give the soul continuous strength. Just as the body is liable to decay, so the means by which it is supported must be weak and temporary. But that which gives life to the soul has to be eternal. Again Christ's words are in line with the experience of believers, who right to the end of their lives burn with desire for more abundant grace. Christ does not say that from the very first day we will be completely satisfied as we drink, but rather that the Holy Spirit is a fountain that flows continuously. So there is no danger that people who are renewed through spiritual grace will ever dry up. Therefore, although we are thirsty throughout our lives, it is nevertheless certain that we have not received the Holy Spirit for a single day or for any short time but as a constantly flowing fountain which will never let us down. Thus believers thirst and thirst throughout their lives, and yet they have plenty of life-giving water. No matter how small the amount of grace which may have been received, it provides them with continuous strength so that they never entirely dry out. So when Christ says that they will be satisfied, he is making a contrast with dryness and not with desire.

14. ". . . will become in him a spring of water welling up to eternal life." These words explain the last statement even more clearly. They indicate a constant watering which sustains in believers a heavenly eternity during this mortal and perishing life. Therefore, Christ's grace does not flow to us just for a short time, but it overflows into a blessed immortality, since it does not stop flowing until the incorruptible life which is started has been perfected.

15. "Sir, give me this water." Clearly, this woman knows perfectly well that Christ is speaking about spiritual **"water."** However, she discounts all his promises, for she despises him. As long as we do not acknowledge the authority of the person speaking to us, we set up a barrier to his teaching. So indirectly the woman taunts Christ, saying, "You boast a lot, but I see nothing; prove it to me, if you can."

Verses 16–21

16. "Call your husband." This appears to have no links with the subject. Indeed, one might suppose that Christ, annoyed and put to shame by the impudence of the woman, changes the subject. But this is not the case. When Christ saw that the only reply the woman made to what he said was jeering and scoffing, he applied the appropriate remedy to this disease and struck the woman's conscience with a conviction of her sin. This is further remarkable evidence of Christ's compassion, that when the woman was unwilling to come to him of her own accord, he drew her to him, as it were, against her will. However, we should note most of all what I have said, that people who are completely careless and almost stupid must be deeply wounded through conviction of sin. For such people will think of the teaching of Christ as a fable until they are summoned to God's judgment-seat, where they are forced to face him as their dreaded Judge whom they had previously despised. Everybody who has no scruples about opposing Christ's teaching with their scoffing humor must be treated in this way, so that they are made to feel that they will not pass unpunished.

Some people are so obstinate that they will never listen to Christ until they are forced to. So whenever we see that the oil of Christ is flavorless, more wine should be mixed in so that its flavor can be tasted again. Indeed, this is necessary for all of us, as we are not seriously affected by what Christ says unless we are moved to repentance. So if anyone wants to derive any benefit from Christ's school, his hardness must be subdued by the demonstration of his wretchedness, just as the earth needs to be broken up through plowing. This knowledge alone removes all our delight in ourselves so that we no longer dare to mock God. So when-ever neglect of God's Word overtakes us, the best remedy is that each of us should sit up to our sins, so that we become ashamed of ourselves and, trembling before God's judgment-seat, may be humbled so we will obey him whom we had deliberately despised.

17. "I have no husband." We have yet to fully see the fruit of Christ's advice, which was intended to pierce the woman's heart in order to lead her to repentance. Indeed, we are so intoxicated, or rather stupefied, by our love of ourselves that we are left unmoved by the first wounds that are inflicted. But Christ applies the appropriate cure for this sluggish-ness, as he presses the ulcer more forcibly by openly accusing her about her wickedness. However, I do not think that this is a simple case of fornication here, for when Christ says, **"You have had five husbands"** (verse 18), this was probably because she had been such a stubborn and disobedient wife that she forced her husbands to divorce her. This is how I interpret these words: "Although God joined you to lawful husbands, you did not stop sinning, and as you were made infamous by your numerous divorces, you turned to prostitution."

19. "Sir," the woman said, "I can see that you are a prophet." Now the fruit of the reproof becomes evident. The woman humbly acknowl-edges her fault. She is ready and willing to listen to Christ's teaching, which she had previously rejected, and now desires and asks for it of her own accord. Therefore, repentance is the beginning of being genuinely teachable, as I have already said, and it opens the gate for entering into Christ's school. The woman teaches us through her example that when we meet any teacher, we should avail ourselves of this opportunity. Then we will not be ungrateful to God, who never sends us his prophets without, as it were, stretching out his hand to invite us to himself. And we must remember what Paul teaches, that those who have been given grace to be good teachers are sent to us by God, for "How can they preach unless they are sent?" (Romans 10:15).

20. "Our fathers . . ." Some people interpret this wrongly to mean that the woman, finding the rebuke disagreeable and hateful, cleverly changes the subject. On the contrary, she moves on from what is par-ticular to what is general and, having been informed about her sin, wants to be taught generally about the pure worship of God. She acts properly and regularly in consulting a prophet, so that she may not make mistakes about worshiping God. It is as if she asked God himself about how he wanted to be worshiped. Nothing is more wicked than to make up vari-ous ways of worship which do not have the authority of God's Word.

It is well known that there was a constant dispute between the Jews and the Samaritans about the true pattern of worshiping God. Even though the Cutheans, and other foreigners who had been brought into Samaria when the ten tribes were taken into captivity, were forced through the plagues and punishments of God to adopt the ceremonies of the law and to profess the worship of the God of Israel (as we read in 2 Kings 17:27), yet their religion was imperfect and corrupt in many ways. All this the Jews could not tolerate. But the dispute became even more inflamed after Manasseh, the son of the high priest John, the brother of Jaddus, had built the temple on Mount Gerizim. This happened when Darius, the last king of the Persians, governed Judea through Sanballat, whom he had installed as his governor. For Manasseh, who had married a daughter of the governor so that he might not be inferior to his brother, made himself a priest there and through bribery gathered round him as many followers as he could, as Josephus recounts in the *Antiquities of the Jews*, XI.

"Our fathers worshiped on this mountain." The words of this woman tell us that the Samaritans did, at this time, what was usual for people who have rejected true godliness who try to appeal to the **"fathers"** as precedents. It is certain that this was not the reason which caused them to offer sacrifices there; but once they had set up false and perverse worship, they obstinately invented ingenious excuses. I agree that thoughtless people are sometimes aroused by foolish zeal, as if they had been bitten by a gadfly. When such people hear about anything that has been done by the saints, they latch on to it immediately without exercising any judgment.

A second fault is even more common, in that they steal the deeds of the **"fathers"** as a cloak for their own errors, just as is easily observable in the Papacy. But this passage is a remarkable warning of how absurd they are who neglect God's command in order to conform to the examples of the **"fathers,"** and we should note how often the world sins in this respect. It frequently happens that the majority uncritically follow such people as **"fathers,"** people who have the least right to be called **"fathers."** In our day we observe that the Roman Catholics, while they openly talk about the Fathers, give no place to the prophets and apostles. When they have mentioned a few people who deserve to be honored, they collect a large group of people like themselves, or at least go to the more corrupt times when, although gross barbarism did not exist as it does now, yet religion and purity of teaching had greatly declined. We should carefully note the difference, so that nobody can be counted a father except those who are clearly sons of God and whose outstanding piety entitles them to this honorable rank. All too often we make mistakes in this respect because we rashly establish a common law as a result of the actions of the **"fathers."** For most people do not think that they are conferring sufficient honor on the **"fathers"** unless they make them superhumans. When we forget that they were fallible, we indiscriminately mix their vices with their virtues, and so the worst kind of confusion about their lives arises. While all men's behavior should be tried by the rule of the law, we can subordinate the scales of justice themselves to what ought to be tried by it. In summary, while there is great importance attached to imitating the **"fathers,"** the world thinks that there can be no danger in sinning if they follow their example.

A third fault is thoughtless and perverted imitation. This occurs when we who are not endued with the same spirit or authorized with the same command give as a precedent anything that the **"fathers"** did. It is as if any private individual who wanted to avenge injuries done to his family could cite the example of Moses (Exodus 2:12), or that one can put fornicators to death just because Phinehas did (Numbers 25:7). Many believe that the savage practice of child sacrifice originated in the Jews wanting to copy their father Abraham. It is as if they took the command "Take your son . . . sacrifice him" (Genesis 22:2) to be a general command, rather than the remarkable test of one man. This kind of false imitation is usually produced through pride and excessive confidence, when men claim more for themselves than they have a right to and when they are not content with their own limits. So none of these people are genuine imitators of the **"fathers"**; they only ape them. People who study the writings of the ancients carefully will acknowledge that a great deal of old monarchism flowed from the same source. So if we do not want to deliberately make the same mistakes, we should always observe what spirit each person has received, what his calling requires, what is appropriate for him, and what he is commanded to do.

Closely linked to this third fault is another — namely, the confusing of different times. In later times men devoted themselves to the examples of the **"fathers"** without thinking that the Lord had given a different way of behavior which they ought to follow. The huge mass of ceremonies which Popery has buried the church under exemplifies this kind of ignorance.

So that we do not make this mistake, we should always be careful to keep to the following rule: previously incense, candles, sacred vestments, an altar, vessels, and certain kinds of ceremonies pleased God. This was because nothing is more precious and acceptable to him than our obedience. But since Christ has come, everything has completely changed. So we should find out what pleases Christ under the Gospel dispensation so that we do not unthinkingly follow what the **"fathers"** did under the law. What was then a sacred observation in worshiping God would now be a wicked sacrilege.

The Samaritans went wrong because they did not realize how different their own time was from Jacob's. The patriarchs were allowed to put up altars everywhere because the place which the Lord later chose had not yet been appointed. From the time that God ordered the temple to be built on Mount Zion, the freedom which they had previously enjoyed ceased. So Moses said, "You are not to do as we do here today, everyone as he sees fit. . . . Offer them only at the place the Lord will choose" (Deuteronomy 12:8, 14). From the time that the Lord gave the law, he restricted the true worship of himself to the requirements of the law, even though previously greater liberty had been enjoyed. A similar excuse was put forward by those who worshiped in Bethel. There Jacob had offered a solemn sacrifice to God, but later the Lord had chosen the place of sacrifice to be in Jerusalem. It was no longer Bethel, "the house of God," but Bethaven, "the house of wickedness."

Now we understand the question in hand. The Samaritans followed the example of the "fathers," while the Jews followed God's commandment. Up to now this woman had followed the practice of her nation, but this no longer satisfied her. By "worship," we should understand here not any kind of "worship" (such as daily prayers which might be prayed in any place), but the "worship" that was linked to sacrifices and which constituted a public and solemn profession of religion.

21. "Believe me, woman." In the first part of this reply Christ quickly dispenses with the ceremonial worship which had been appointed under the law. For when he says, **"a time is coming"** when there will be no special and fixed place for **"worship,"** he is declaring that Moses' instructions were only meant for a limited time, and that the time was now close when the "the dividing wall of hostility" (Ephesians 2:14) would be destroyed. In this way he extends the worship of God far beyond its former narrow limits, so that the Samaritans can share in it.

"A time is coming." Christ uses the present tense and not the future tense here. But this means that the reform of the law is imminent, insofar as it relates to the temple, the priesthood, and other outward ceremonies. When Christ calls God **"Father,"** he appears to be contrasting him indirectly with **"our fathers"** (verse 20) mentioned by the woman. Christ is also teaching that God will be everyone's **"Father,"** so that he can be universally worshiped, irrespective of location or nationality.

Verses 22–26

22. He now begins to explain in more detail about what he had briefly said about the abolition of the law. He divides his main teaching into two parts. First, he accuses the Samaritans of worshiping God superstitiously and erroneously. He states that the genuine and lawful way to worship was observed by the Jews. He attributes the reason for this difference to the Jews receiving definite instructions about worship from the Word of God, while the Samaritans received nothing of certainty from God's mouth. Second, he declares that the ceremonies which the Jews had observed so far would soon come to an end.

"You Samaritans worship what you do not know; we worship what we do know." This sentence should be noted very carefully. It teaches us that we should not do anything religious in a rash or haphazard way. If we do not know what we are doing, we will be worshiping an idol or a ghost rather than God. Like a thunderbolt, this sentence strikes down all good intentions, as they are called. It teaches us that everybody must go wrong if they are guided by their own opinion rather than by the Word or command of God. For Christ, supporting his own nation, shows how very different the Samaritans are from the Jews. And why?

"For salvation is from the Jews." These words explain that God has made a covenant of eternal salvation with the Jews, and in this respect they are superior to the Samaritans. Some people would restrict this reference to Christ, who was descended from the Jews, and it is indeed the case that "no matter how many promises God has made, they are 'Yes' in Christ" (2 Corinthians 1:20), since there is no salvation outside Christ. Undoubtedly Christ shows preference to the Jews since they do not worship some unknown deity, but only God, who revealed himself to them and by whom they were adopted as his people. We should understand from the word **"salvation"** the saving manifestation which they had received about the heavenly doctrine.

So why does he say, **"from the Jews,"** when it was given *to* them that they might enjoy it? In my opinion, he alludes to what had been predicted by the prophets: "The law will go out from Zion" (Isaiah 2:3; see Micah 4:2). For a time the Jews were separated from other nations, for the specific reason that the pure knowledge of God should flow from them to the whole world. It amounts to this: God cannot be properly worshiped except by the certainty of faith, which cannot be born in any way other than by the Word of God. So it follows that everyone who forsakes the Word of God falls into idolatry, for Christ declares plainly that an idol or a thought from their own minds takes God's place when people are ignorant about the true God. He accuses everyone of being ignorant who has not had God revealed to them. As soon as we are deprived of the light of his Word, darkness and blindness reign.

It should be noted that the Jews, when they had faithlessly rejected the covenant of eternal life which God had made with their fathers, were not deprived of the treasure which they had enjoyed until then, as they had not yet then been driven out of God's church. But now that they deny the Son, they have nothing in common with the Father, for "No one who denies the Son has the Father" (1 John 2:23). We must reach the same conclusion about everyone who turns away from the pure faith of the Gospel to their own ideas and to men's traditions. Everyone who worships God as he sees fit or according to men's traditions only flatters and applauds himself in his obstinacy. This single phrase, **"You Samaritans worship what you do not know,"** comes thundering from heaven and flattens everybody who imagines that they are holy or godly. So it follows on from this that if we want God's approval of our religion, it must rest on knowledge derived from God's Word.

23. "Yet a time is coming." Now follows the latter clause, about reforming the worship or ceremonies which was prescribed by the law.

When he says, **"Yet a time is coming and has now come,"** he indicates that Moses' ordinances were not meant to be forever. When he says that **"a time is coming,"** ceremonies are abolished, and he declares that the "external regulations" (spoken of by the apostle Paul in Hebrews 9:10) are now fulfilled. Even so, he approves of the temple, the priesthood, and all the ceremonies linked to them, so far as they are related to the past. Again, to show that God does not choose to be worshiped either in Jerusalem or on Mount Gerizim, he moves on to a higher principle, that true worship of God is **"in spirit."** From this it follows that God can be properly worshiped anywhere.

But the first question raised here is, "Why, and in what sense, is the worship of God called spiritual?" To understand this, we must note the contrast between the spirit and outward signs, which correspond to the shadow and the substance. The worship of God is said to be **"in spirit"** since nothing but the inner faith of the heart produces prayer, and then clear consciences and self-denial, so that we may be dedicated to obeying God as holy sacrifices.

This gives rise to another question: did not the fathers worship God spiritually under the law? My reply is that because God never changes, from the beginning he only approved of spiritual worship, since this is in line with his own nature. This is abundantly attested to by Moses himself, who declares in many passages that the law has no other purpose than that people may cling to God in faith and with a pure conscience. But the prophets declare this even more plainly when they attack with severity people's hypocrisy when they thought that they had satisfied God through their sacrifices and by their outward display. It is not necessary to quote here the many testimonies which can be found everywhere, although the following are the most striking: Psalm 1; Isaiah 1 and 58; Micah 5; and Amos 7.

While under the law the worship of God was spiritual, it was overlaid with so many outward ceremonies that it seemed to be earthly and carnal. This is why Paul calls the ceremonies "weak and miserable principles" (Galatians 4:9). In the same way, the author of the letter to the Hebrews says that the ancient "sanctuary," with its appendages, was "earthly" (Hebrews 9:1). So we may correctly say that the worship of the law was spiritual in its substance, but in its form it was rather earthly and unspiritual, for that whole economy whose reality was not fully manifested was shadowy.

Now we can see how much the Jews differed from us and how much they had in common with us. In every age God wanted to be worshiped by faith, prayer, thanksgiving, purity of heart, and innocence of life. Never did he delight in any other sacrifices. However, under the law there were various additions so that **"spirit"** and **"truth"** were concealed by the forms and shadows. But now that "the curtain of the temple" has been "torn in two from top to bottom" (Matthew 27:51), nothing is hidden or obscure.

There are indeed among us today some outward exercises of godliness which are necessary because of our weakness. But they are moderate and sober, and so they do not hide Christ's plain truth. In summary, what was revealed to the fathers in types and in a shadowy way is now openly displayed.

But under the Papacy this distinction is not only confused but is completely overturned. There the shadows are as dark as they were under Judaism. It is undeniable that Christ is here laying down an obvious distinction between us and the Jews. Whatever deceptions the Roman Catholics use to try and escape from this accusation, it is clear that we only differ from the fathers in matters of outward form, since as they worshiped God spiritually, they were bound to perform ceremonies which were abolished with Christ's coming. So all those who burden the church with an excessive number of ceremonies are using their own power to deprive the church of Christ's presence. I will not pause to examine the feeble excuses they make — for example, that people today are as much in need of these props as the Jews were in ancient times. It is always our duty to find out how our Lord wishes to govern his church, since only he knows what is expedient for us. Certainly nothing is further from God's ordinance than the gross and especially carnal show which prevails in Roman Catholicism. The **"spirit"** was indeed concealed under the shadow of the law, but the hypocrisy of Papacy completely disfigures it. So we must not entertain any such gross and shameful corruptions. No matter what arguments are used by clever men, or by those who do not have enough courage to correct vices, saying that these are indifferent things which are of questionable importance, it certainly cannot be allowed that Christ's ordinances should be violated.

". . . the true worshipers . . ." Christ appears to indirectly reprove the obstinacy of many people, which later became evident. For we know how obstinate and contentious the Jews were when the Gospel was revealed, as they defended the ceremonies which they had become used to. But this statement has a wider application. Christ knew that the world would never be completely free from superstitions, and so he separates the devout and upright **"worshipers"** from the false and hypocritical **"worshipers."** Armed with this testimony, we should not hesitate to condemn Roman Catholics and all their inventions and to boldly despise their reproaches. Why should we be afraid when we see that God is pleased with this plain and simple worship, which the Roman Catholics disdain because it is not encumbered with numerous ceremonies? And of what use is the empty show of the flesh to them, through which, Christ says, the Spirit is quenched?

It is clear from what has already been said what the meaning of **"worship the Father in spirit and truth"** is. It is to set aside the entanglements of the ancient ceremonies and just keep what is spiritual in the worship of God. The **"truth"** of the **"worship"** is in the **"spirit,"** and the ceremonies are a mere appendage. Once more it must be noted that "truth" is not contrasted with falsehood, but with the outward additions of the figures of the law. For the "truth," to use a simple expression, is the pure and simple substance of spiritual "worship."

24. "God is spirit." Here is a confirmation drawn from God's actual nature. Since men are flesh, we should not be surprised if they delight in those things which correspond to their own disposition. So it happens that they invent many things in worshiping God which are full of show and are insubstantial. In the first place they should remember that they are dealing with God, who can have as much to do with the flesh as fire can mix with water. When this single consideration is made in relation to the worship of God, it ought to be enough to restrain our rebellious minds. For God is so different from us that the things that delight us most are most loathsome and abhorrent in God's sight. Hypocrites are so blinded by their own pride that they do not fear to subject God to their own will, or rather to their own sinful desires. We know that this kind of modesty does not hold the lowest place in the true worship of God, as we are suspicious of whatever pleases the flesh.

In addition to this, since we cannot climb up to God's height, we should remember that we should seek from his Word the rule by which we are governed. This passage is often quoted by the Fathers against the Arians, to prove the divinity of the Holy Spirit, but it is not correct to twist it in this way. Christ is simply stating here that his Father has a spiritual nature and is therefore unmoved by the frivolous matters which influence the unsteady and superficial characters of men.

25. "I know that Messiah" (called Christ) "is coming." Although the Samaritan religion was corrupt and mixed up with many errors, some of the principles from the law impressed themselves on their minds, such as those which related to the Messiah. Most probably, when the woman realized from her conversation with Christ that a very unusual change was about to take place in God's church, her mind instantly recalled the **Christ** under whom she hoped that everything would be fully restored. When she says, **"I know that Messiah is coming,"** she seems to be speaking about an imminent happening. Indeed, it is sufficiently clear for many reasons that men's minds everywhere were excited about the expectation of the Messiah. He would restore the badly decayed, or rather the utterly ruined, state of affairs.

At least it is beyond question that the woman prefers **Christ** as teacher to Moses and all the prophets. In a few words she understands three things. First, the teaching of the law was not absolutely perfect, and nothing more than first principles were delivered in it. For if the law was to make further progress she would not have said, **"When he comes, he will explain everything to us."** Here is an implied contrast between him and the prophets — that it is his special function to lead the disciples to the goal, when the prophets had just given them the initial instructions and, as it were, showed them which direction to take. Second, the woman declares that she expects this **Christ** to be the interpreter of his Father and the teacher and instructor of all the ungodly. Third, she shows that she believes that we should not desire anything better or superior than Christ's teaching, but that, on the contrary, this is the height of wisdom, beyond which it is not lawful to proceed.

I wish that people who boast that they are the pillars of the Christian church would at least imitate this poor woman. They should be satisfied with the simple teachings of Christ, rather than claim I know not what authority for introducing these inventions. Was not the religion of the Pope and Mohammed composed of the evil additions through which they imagined that they had enhanced the teaching of the Gospel into a perfect state? As if it would have been incomplete without such foolishness! Anybody who is instructed properly in the school of Christ will seek no other teachers and, indeed, will not accept them.

26. "I who speak to you am he." When Christ acknowledges to the woman that he is the Messiah, he unquestionably presents himself to her as her teacher, in line with the expectation she had. So I think that it is probable that he went on to give further instruction to quench her thirst. Christ intended that this sign of grace, given in this instance to this poor woman, should be a witness to everyone that he always fulfills his office when we want him as our teacher. So there is no danger that he will disappoint anyone who readily becomes one of his disciples. But people who refuse to submit to him, as we see is the case with many haughty and irreligious people or with those people who try to find a more perfect wisdom elsewhere, as the Muslims and Roman Catholics do, deserve to be haunted by innumerable delusions until they are plunged into the abyss of errors. By using these words **"I who speak to you am he,"** the Messiah, the Son of God, Christ, takes the name **"Messiah"** (verse 25) as a seal to ratify the teaching of his Gospel. For we must remember that Christ was anointed by the Father and that "The Spirit of the Sovereign Lord is on me" (Isaiah 61:1), to bring us the message of salvation.

Verses 27–34

27. Just then his disciples returned and were surprised. The disciples' surprise, which the evangelist records, might stem from one of two reasons. Either they were offended by the woman's bad condition, or they thought that the Jews would be defiled if they talked with the Samaritans. Although both these thoughts came from a devout reverence for their Master, it was still wrong for them to be **surprised**, as if Christ was doing something wrong by bestowing such a great honor on a woman who was totally despised. Should they not rather look to themselves? They would have found no less reason to be **surprised,** for they were not men of note and were almost the dregs of society who had been raised up to the highest honor. But it is useful to note what the evangelist says: they did not dare to ask Christ a question. Their example teaches us that if there is anything in the deeds or words of God or Christ which we find unpalatable, we should not allow ourselves a free rein so that we have the audacity to grumble. Rather, we should keep humbly silent, until what is hidden from us is revealed from heaven. The basis of this modesty lies in the fear of God and in reverence for Christ.

28. Then, leaving her water jar . . . The evangelist notes this detail to show the strength of the woman's zeal. She leaves her jar behind as she returns to the city, indicating what a hurry she is in. This is the nature of faith, that when we have shared in eternal life we want to bring other people to share it with us. It is impossible that a knowledge of God should lie buried and inactive in our hearts and not show in front of men. The psalmist's saying is true: "I believed; therefore I said . . ." (116:10). The earnestness and prompt action of the woman are the more notable because they were set off by such a small spark of faith. She had scarcely tasted Christ before she told the whole city about him. People who have made reasonable progress in the school of Christ and who remain sluggish will be greatly disgraced. This woman may be accused of overstepping the bounds of her faith as she is still so ignorant and partially taught. But I reply, she would have acted improperly if she had assumed the role of teacher, but when she wants nothing more than to enthuse her fellow-citizens to hear Christ speaking, we will not say that she forgot who she was or went further than she had a right to do. She just acts as a trumpet or a bell, inviting others to come to Christ.

29. "Come, see a man . . ." Since she speaks here with uncertainty, it might seem that she had not been greatly affected by Christ's authority. But I reply: since she was not qualified to discuss such high mysteries, she tries, with her feeble power, to bring her fellow-citizens so they can be taught by Christ. She uses a very powerful stimulus to engage their interest, since she knew through a clear and certain sign that he was a **"prophet"** (verse 19). As they were not able to judge Christ's teaching, this inferior preparation was useful and appropriate for them. Once they had found out that Christ had revealed to the woman things which were hidden, they infer from this that he is God's **"prophet."** Once this has been established, they begin to listen to his teaching. But the woman goes further: she asks them to ask if he is indeed the Messiah. She would be satisfied if she could just persuade them to seek for themselves what she had already found in Christ, for she knew that they would find more than she had promised.

". . . who told me everything I ever did." Why does she lie in saying that Christ told her **"everything"** she had done? I have already said that Christ did not rebuke her for a single instance of fornication, but he set before her, in a few words, the many sins of her whole life. For the evangelist has not recorded every sentence but states in broad terms that Christ, in order to stop the woman from incessantly talking, brought her past and present life before her. But we see that the woman, fired by holy zeal, does not spare herself, or her reputation, to magnify Christ's name. She does not hesitate to relate the disgraceful parts of her life.

32. "I have food to eat that you know nothing about." It is amazing that when Christ is tired and hungry he refuses to eat. If it is thought that he does this to teach us through this example to endure hunger, then why does he not always do this? Christ has a different purpose in mind from saying that we should simply refuse food. We must pay attention to this particular situation: Christ is absorbed about the matter in hand, and this holds him so strongly and fills his whole mind that it is nothing for him to ignore food. But he does not say that he is so keen to obey his Father's commands that he will neither eat nor drink. He is just indicating the order in which he will do things. So, by his example he shows us that the kingdom of God should have priority over all bodily comforts. God allows us to eat and to drink so long as we are not distracted from what is of the greatest importance; everyone should attend to his own calling.

Perhaps it will be said that eating and drinking must be distractions and that we could make better use of our time. While I agree with this, the Lord does graciously allow us to look after the necessities of our bodies. People who try to nourish their bodies soberly and in moderation are not failing to give the priority they owe to obeying God. But we must be careful not to stick so closely to our set hours that we are not prepared to go without food when God gives us some opportunity and, as it were, arranges the time. Christ has this fleeting opportunity and embraces it with open arms and holds on to it. When the duty in hand, given to him by the Father, is so urgent that he has to drop everything else, he does not worry about eating later. Indeed, it would have been wrong for Christ to show less zeal than the woman did in leaving her jar behind while she runs to invite the people. In summary, if we are determined not to lose the purpose for living for the sake of life, it will be hard to keep everything in proportion. Anybody who has as his goal in life to serve the Lord, and who will not deviate from this even in times of mortal danger, will certainly not think that eating and drinking are more important than this. The metaphor of eating and drinking is the more appropriate as it was taken from this present conversation.

34. "My food . . . is to do the will of him who sent me." Christ means that he not only thinks of this very highly, but that he takes no greater delight in anything else and is not more happily and eagerly engaged in anything else. As David said, when he wanted to praise the law of God he not only valued it highly but saw it as "sweeter than honey" (Psalm 19:10). So if we want to follow Christ, we should not only devote ourselves diligently to God's service, but we should cheerfully carry out his commands so that we do not find this work to be at all burdensome or objectionable.

"**. . . to finish his work.**" Christ adds these words to explain more fully what his Father's "**will**" is, to which he is devoted: it is to fulfill the commission which has been given to him. Everyone should think about his own vocation, so that he does not think that God has ordered him to carry out his own rash activities which he thought up himself. Christ's office is well-known. It was to advance God's kingdom, to restore lost souls to life, to spread the light of the Gospel, and, in summary, to bring salvation to the world. The importance of these things made him, when tired and hungry, forget about eating and drinking. Yet we derive from this no ordinary comfort, as we see that Christ was so concerned about man's salvation that it gave him the greatest delight to bring it about. We cannot doubt that he has similar feelings towards us now.

Verses 35–38

35. "Do you not say . . . ?" Christ follows on from the previous statement. He has said that nothing is closer to his heart than finishing his Father's work, and now he shows how ripe it is, as he uses an illustration from "**the harvest.**" When the corn is ripe the harvest cannot be delayed, or else the grain drops to the ground and is lost. Similarly, the spiritual corn is ripe, and Christ declares that there should be no delay because delay is harmful. We understand why this comparison is made, since it explains why Christ hurries to do his work. By using the expression, "**Do you not say . . . ?**" Christ meant to point out obliquely how men's minds are more preoccupied with earthly things than with heavenly things. They are so consumed about the harvest that they calculate the months and the days, but it is amazing how sleepy and lazy they are about harvesting the heavenly wheat. Daily experience proves that this evil not only comes to us naturally, but that we can hardly tear it out of our hearts. Everyone provides for their earthly future, but how lazy we are about thinking about heavenly things! On another occasion Christ said, "Hypocrites! You know how to interpret the appearance of the earth and the sky. How is it that you don't know how to interpret this present time?" (Luke 12:56).

36. "Even now the reaper draws his wages." Christ uses a further argument to show how diligently we should devote ourselves to God's work — namely, that a large and wonderful reward is in store for our labor. Christ promises that there will be fruit (the crop), a kind that is imperishable and everlasting. What Christ says about the fruit can be understood in two ways. It is either an announcement about the wages (but this supposes that Christ is saying the same thing in two different ways), or Christ is approving the work of those who enrich God's kingdom, since we later find him saying these words: "I chose you to go and bear fruit — fruit that will last" (15:16). Both of these explanations should greatly encourage ministers of the Word, so that they never sink under their work, as they consider that a crown of glory is prepared for them in heaven, and since they know that the fruit of their harvest will not only be precious in God's sight but will be eternal. This is why the Scriptures mention the *reward* everywhere, and not because we measure against it the merits of good deeds. For who among us, if it came to a reckoning, would not be found more worthy of being punished for sloth than being rewarded for diligence? Even the best workers could do nothing other than humbly go to God begging for his forgiveness. But the Lord treats us with a father's kindness, to correct our sloth and to encourage us who would otherwise be dismayed, and deigns to give us an undeserved reward.

Rather than overturning justification by faith, this confirms it. First, how can God find anything in us that deserves a reward unless he has bestowed it on us by his Spirit? We know that the Spirit is the down payment and pledge of adoption (Ephesians 1:14). Second, how can God confer so great honor on imperfect and sinful deeds unless, after he has reconciled us to himself by free grace, he accepts our deeds without any reference to merit, by not imputing the sins which cling to them? The conclusion of this passage is that the labors which the apostles expend on teaching should not be onerous and unpleasant, since they know how useful and helpful it is to Christ and to the church.

"The sower and the reaper may be glad together." Through these words Christ shows that the fruit which the apostles derive from other people's labors can give no grounds for complaint. This extra statement should be carefully noted. In the world the moans of those who complain that the fruit of their labor has been given to another do not stop the new owner from happily reaping what someone else has sown. So, the reapers should be even happier when there is mutual consent, mutual joy, and thanksgiving.

To understand this passage properly we must see the contrast between sowing and reaping. The sowing was the teaching of the Law and the Prophets. During that time, the seed was sown in the ground where it remained, as it were, a shoot. But the teaching of the Gospel, which brings people to full maturity, is correctly compared with the harvest. For the law is far from the perfection which was eventually seen by us in Christ. Paul uses the well-known comparison between childhood and manhood in the same way. He says, "What I am saying is that as long as the heir is a child, he is no different from a slave, although he owns the whole estate. He is subject to guardians and trustees until the time set by his father" (Galatians 4:1-2). To sum up, since Christ's coming brought with it present salvation, we should not be surprised if the Gospel, through which the door of the heavenly kingdom is opened, is called the harvest of the teaching of the prophets. And this is not at all inconsistent with the statement that the fathers under the law were gathered into God's barn. But this comparison must refer to the type of teaching. The childhood of the church carried on until the end of the law. But as soon as the Gospel was preached, the church reached manhood, and salvation then began to ripen.

Since Christ gave this teaching in Samaria, he appears to apply the sowing more widely than to just the Law and the Prophets. Some people relate these words to Jews and Gentiles equally. I do agree that some grains of piety were always scattered throughout the world, and there can be no doubt, if we are permitted to use the expression, that God "sowed," through the hands of the philosophers and secular writers, the excellent thoughts which are found in their writings. But since the seed was defiled from the very root, its corn was neither good nor natural, but was choked by a great number of errors; so it is not reasonable to think that such destructive corruption can be compared with sowing. Besides, what is said here about people uniting in joy cannot be applied to philosophers or anybody like them.

However, the problem is still unresolved because Christ does make special mention of the Samaritans. My answer is that although everything about them was corrupt, some hidden seed of piety still remained. How can it be that as soon as they hear a word about Christ they are so keen to find him, unless they had learned from the Law and the Prophets that the Redeemer would come? Judea was indeed the Lord's special field which he had cultivated through the prophets. However, a small part of this seed had gone into Samaria, and so there is good reason for Christ to say that it had also reached maturity there. If it is objected that the apostles were chosen to proclaim the Gospel throughout the whole world, the answer is simple. Christ spoke in a way that suited the time, except that, because of the hope of the fruit which was already nearly ripe, he commends in the Samaritans the seed of prophetic teaching, even though it was mixed up with many weeds and corruptions.

37. "The saying . . . is true." This is a common saying, through which Christ explains that many people often receive the fruit of other people's labors. But there was this difference: people who see the fruit of their labors taken over by somebody else are displeased, whereas the apostles are glad to have the prophets as their friends. However, it cannot be inferred from this that the prophets themselves are witnesses to, or are aware of, what is going on in the church now. Christ just means that the prophets, so long as they were alive, taught under the influence of such feelings, that they already rejoiced because of the fruit which they were not allowed to harvest. Peter makes a similar comparison (see 1 Peter 1:12), except that he directs his exhortation to all the believers, while here Christ is just speaking to the disciples and, through them, to the ministers of the Gospel. Through these words Christ tells them to throw their labors into a common pool, so that there is no evil envy among them. The people who were sent into the work first of all ought to so concentrate on the cultivation in hand that they would not be jealous about the greater blessing received by those who came after them. The people who were sent, as it were, to harvest the ripe fruit should do their work just as cheerfully. For the comparison which is made here between the teachers of the law and the teachers of the Gospel may also be applied to the teachers of the Gospel when seen in relationship to one another.

Verses 39–45

39. Many of the Samaritans from that town believed. The evangelist records here how successful the woman's proclamation to her fellow-citizens was. From this it is clear that the expectation and desire for the promised Messiah was powerful among them. The word **believed** is not used here with great accuracy, for it means that they were persuaded by the woman's words to acknowledge that Christ was a **"prophet."** In some ways faith begins when minds are prepared to receive teaching. This commencement of faith is honored with being called faith to teach us how much store God places on reverence for his Word, as he confers such great honor on the docility of those who had not yet been taught. Their faith is seen as they are gripped with a desire to make progress, and so they urge Christ to stay with them (see verse 40).

41. Many more became believers. It is clear from what followed that Christ's consent to their wish was justified. He granted their request and stayed for **two days** (verse 40), and we see how much fruit was harvested. This example teaches us that we should never stop working when we have it within our power to advance God's kingdom. If we are frightened that our readiness to help may be open to unfavorable reports or may often turn out to be useless, we should ask Christ for the Spirit of counsel to direct us. Now the word "believe" is used in a different way. Not only does it mean that they were prepared for faith, but that they actually had a true faith.

42. ". . . because of what you said." I have followed Erasmus' translation of the word **said** because the word the old translators used, *loquela*, is so barbaric. However, I want to warn my readers that the Greek word is equivalent to the Latin word *loquentia*, which means "talk" or "gossip." The Samaritans seem to be boasting that they now have a stronger support than a woman's tongue, which is mostly superficial and trivial.

"We . . . believe." This expresses more fully the nature of their faith, which was derived from the Word of God itself, so that they can boast about having the Son of God as their teacher. And, indeed, it is on his authority alone that it is safe to rely. Of course, his presence is no longer visible so that we can speak to him face to face, but no matter through whom we happen to hear him, our faith can only remain on Christ himself. The knowledge which is referred to here comes from no other source. Words which come from the mouth of a mortal man may be able to fill and please our ears, but they will never be able to strengthen the soul in the calm confidence of salvation, so that the person who has heard is entitled to boast that he knows. So the first thing that is necessary for faith is to know that Christ is speaking to you through his ministers. The second thing that is necessary is to give him his due honor. We do this by not doubting that he is true and faithful, and by relying on this certain guarantee, so that we may safely trust his teaching.

Again, when they affirm that Jesus is the Christ and **"the Savior of the world,"** they have clearly discovered this from listening to him. So we infer that in the space of **two days** (verse 40) the whole Gospel had been more clearly taught by Christ than he had taught it up to that point in Jerusalem. Christ proclaimed that the salvation he brought was for the whole world, so that they would more clearly understand that it also belonged to them. For Christ did not say that they were heirs according to law, as was the case with the Jews, but he taught them that he had come to admit strangers into God's family and to bring peace to those "who were far away" (Ephesians 2:17).

44. Now Jesus himself had pointed out . . . The apparent contradiction which faces us here, at first sight, has been explained in various ways. Augustine's explanation is too clever as he states that Christ had **no honor in his own country** because he had done more good in just **two days** (verse 40) among the Samaritans than he had done over a long period of time among the Galileans. Also, without doing any miracles, Christ had won more disciples in Samaria than he did in Galilee where he performed numerous miracles. I am not happy with Chrysostom's interpretation either. He believed Christ's **country** was Capernaum because he lived there more than anywhere else.

I incline towards Cyril's view that Christ lived in the city of Nazareth and traveled to different parts of Galilee, as the other three evangelists mention Nazareth when they recount this testimony of Christ. Then it could mean that while the time for Christ's full manifestation had not yet come, he chose to stay hidden in his home country since he would be less conspicuous. Others also explain the meaning of staying in Samaria for **two days** (verse 40) by saying that he had no reason to hurry away to a place where contempt awaited him. Other people think that he went straight to Nazareth and then immediately left there. I do not agree with this speculation since John does not say anything like this. A better view is that when Christ saw himself despised in his home city of Nazareth he withdrew to another place. So it immediately follows (verse 46) that

he visited Cana. What is recorded next — that the Galileans received him — was a sign of their respect, not of their contempt.

A prophet has no honor in his own country. Doubtless this was a common proverb, and we know that proverbs are intended to be graceful expressions of what usually and most often happens. Therefore, in these instances we do not have to rigidly demand uniform accuracy, as if what the proverb states is always true. Certainly prophets are usually appreciated more in countries other than their own. It also may happen, and sometimes does, that **a prophet** is not less honored by his countrymen than by strangers. However, this proverb states what normally happens, that prophets receive **honor** more readily in any place other than from their own people.

This proverb may have originated in two ways. It is a worldwide mistake that we despise people throughout their lives whom we have known as crying babies and foolish boys, as if they had never grown up. A further evil can be added to this: jealousy, which is more prevalent among acquaintances. However, I think that it likely that this proverb stems from the ill-treatment of prophets by their own countrymen. For good, holy people, when they saw that there was such ingratitude towards God in Judea, such great contempt for God's Word, and such great obstinacy, were right to complain that God's prophets are nowhere honored less than in their own country. If the first interpretation is preferred, then the word **prophet** should be understood in a general way, just as Paul calls Epimenides "one of their own prophets" (Titus 1:12).

45. The Galileans welcomed him. We have no way of saying whether or not they welcomed Christ for a long time, for there is nothing people forget about more than God's gifts. John does not record this incident for any other reason than to inform us that Christ performed miracles in the presence of many witnesses, so that this news would spread everywhere. This highlights one reason for miracles, that they prepare the way for teaching, since they encourage reverence for Christ.

Verses 46–54

46. And there was a certain royal official. This is more accurate than Erasmus' version, which translates the Greek word by the Latin word *regulus*, which means "little king." I agree that at that time they gave the title "little kings" to people we now call dukes, barons, or earls. However, nobody of that rank would have lived in Capernaum at that time. I think that he was someone in Herod's court, as it is possible that he was sent by Caesar, as some people think. The evangelist specifically mentions this because the position this man held made the miracle the more notable.

47. When this man heard that Jesus had arrived . . . He showed some degree of faith by asking for Christ's help, but he reveals his own ignorance by placing limits on the way Christ might assist. He thought that Christ's power was inseparably linked to his bodily presence, as it is clear that he had no other view about Christ than this. He thought that Christ was a prophet sent by God and that his authority and power, demonstrated by his miracles, showed that he was God's minister. Christ overlooks this wrong idea, even though it deserved censure. But Christ told him and the Jews off very strongly for something else — that they were too eager to see miracles.

Why is Christ now so harsh when he usually warmly welcomed other people who asked for miracles? There must have been a specific reason for this which remains unknown to us for him to treat this man so severely, which he did not usually do. Perhaps Christ was thinking more of the whole nation than of this one man. He realized that his teaching carried no great authority and was not only neglected but completely despised. But on the other hand, they all had their eyes fixed on miracles, and their whole beings were consumed with stupidity rather than with admiration. So their evil contempt for God's Word, which was so prevalent then, caused Christ to accuse them in this way.

It is true that sometimes the saints have wanted miracles to confirm their faith so that they do not doubt the truth of the promises. When God graciously granted their requests we see that he was not offended by them. But Christ is describing a far greater evil here. The Jews were so consumed by the miracles that they had no time for the Word. First, it was extremely wicked for them to be so stupid and unspiritual to have no reverence for teaching unless this was brought to life by miracles. They would have been well versed in God's Word, which they had been taught from childhood. Second, when miracles were performed, they did not benefit from them properly but remained in a state of stupidity and amazement. So they had no religion, no knowledge of God, no practice of godliness except for that which came through miracles.

Paul makes the same criticism of them: "Jews demand miraculous signs" (1 Corinthians 1:22). Paul says that they were irrationally and immoderately attached to signs, while they had little time for Christ's grace, the promises of eternal life, or the secret power of the Spirit. They rejected the Gospel with proud disdain because they had no appetite for anything but miracles. I wish that there were few people today infected with this same disease. However, nothing is more common than the saying, "Let them first perform miracles, and then we will listen to their teaching." This would mean that we should despise and disdain the truth of Christ unless it is corroborated from another source. But even if God overwhelmed them with masses of miracles, they would still speak incorrectly when they said that they believed. Some outward surprise would be produced, but they would not be the least bit more interested in the teaching.

49. "Sir, come down before my child dies." The royal official persists in asking for Christ's help and at length obtains his request. From this we may conclude that Christ did not tell him off in such a way that he intended to totally reject him or refuse his prayers, but he told him off in order to correct his mistaken idea which was blocking his way to true faith. And we should remember, as I have said before, that this was a general telling off to the whole people rather than being specifically directed at one individual. Similarly, whatever is wrong, distorted, or superfluous in our prayers must be corrected and removed so that harmful obstructions can be taken out of the way. Courtiers are usually fastidious and haughty and do not willingly submit to being treated harshly. But it is worth noting that this man was humbled by his need and by his fear of losing his son; so he does not burst out in anger or grumble when Christ talks to him roughly, but allows the reproof to pass, keeping humbly silent. It is the same with us. We are amazingly spoiled, impatient, and fretful until we are subdued by adversities which force us to dispense with our pride and disdain.

50. "Your son will live." Christ's amazing kindness and humility, in bearing the man's ignorance and extending his power beyond what the man had expected, is the first thing that hits us. The man asked that Christ would come and heal his son. He had thought that his son might be healed of his sickness and disease, but not that he could be brought back to life after he had died. So he pleads with Christ to go quickly before his son dies. Christ pardons both these errors, and we may conclude from this how much he values even the smallest amount of faith. It is worth noting that Christ, while he does not comply with the man's request, gives him much more than he had asked for. For Christ assures the man that his son is now healthy. If often happens that while our Heavenly Father may not grant our desires in every particular, he nevertheless helps us in unexpected ways, so that we may learn not to dictate to him in anything. When Christ says, **"Your son will live,"** he means that he is no longer in danger of dying.

The man took Jesus at his word. The man arrived convinced that Christ was God's prophet, and so he was well disposed to believe. So as soon as he heard one word, he latched on to it and kept it in his heart. Even though he did not have all the respect for Christ's power that he should have had, one small promise suddenly brought new confidence in his mind, so that he believed that his son's life was enclosed in a single word of Christ. We should be just as ready to receive God's Word, although it is far from producing such an immediate effect on its hearers. For how many people do you know who have benefited from listening to many sermons as this half-pagan man benefitted from hearing a single word? So we should work even more zealously to wake up from our sluggishness and above all to pray that God would so touch our hearts that we may be as willing to believe as he is willing and gracious to promise.

51. While he was still on the way . . . Here is a description of the effect of faith together with the efficacy of the Word. For just as Christ, through a word, restores this child to life who was at the point of death, so in one moment the father, through his faith, regains his son, safe and sound. So we should know that whenever the Lord offers his blessings to us, his power is always ready to fulfill what he has promised, so long as we have not closed the door through our unbelief. I agree that God does not always, or even frequently or usually, instantly display his hand in helping us. However, whenever he delays in helping us, he always has a good reason for doing so which is to our great benefit. At least we know this for certain, that God never unnecessarily delays, but rather he deals with the obstacles we throw in the way. So when we do not immediately see him helping us, let us consider how much secret distrust there is in us, or at least how small and limited our faith is. And we should not be surprised if he does not want his blessings to be lost or thrown randomly on the ground, but that he prefers to give them to people who, through opening the heart of their faith, are prepared to receive them. God does not help everyone in the same way. But he will never let anyone's faith go unrewarded or prevent us from experiencing the truth of what the prophet says — that the promises of God, even when they seem to delay, are in reality making great haste. "Though it linger, wait for it; it will certainly come and will not delay" (Habakkuk 2:3).

52. He inquired as to the time . . . The royal official asked his servants what time his son started to recover through a secret impulse from God, so that the truth of the miracle could be seen more openly. For by nature we have an exceedingly evil disposition to put out the light of God's power, while Satan labors, through various ways, to hide God's deeds from our sight. To make sure that God's deeds receive from us the praise they deserve, they have to be so clear that there is no room for doubt left. So no matter how ungrateful men may be, this detail will not allow such a remarkable deed of Christ to be put down to luck.

53. So he and all his household believed. It may seem absurd for the evangelist to mention that this man started to have faith now, when he had already commended him for his faith. We should not suppose that the word **believed**, at least in this passage, relates to the progress of faith. We have to understand that this man, being a Jew and educated in the teaching of the law, had already been given some taste of faith when he came to Christ. Later he believed what Christ told him, and this was special faith with particular reference to his son's recovery. Now he starts to believe in a different way. Now that he has welcomed the teaching of

Christ, he publicly professes to be one of his disciples. So he now not only believes that his son will be cured through Christ's kindness, but he acknowledges Christ to be the Son of God and makes a profession of faith in his Gospel. His complete family joins him, which backs up the miracle. It cannot be doubted that he did his best to bring other people with him to welcome Christianity.

John
Chapter 5

Verses 1–9

1. A feast of the Jews. Even though the evangelist does not specifically state what this feast is, it most probably refers to Pentecost, so long as what is related here took place immediately after Christ came to Galilee. Immediately after the Passover Christ set out from Jerusalem, and as he passed through Samaria he thought there were still four months to the harvest. Once he came into Galilee he cured the royal official's son. The evangelist adds that the feast came later, and so from this sequence of events we are to understand that the feast refers to Pentecost, although I will not argue the point. Christ **went up to Jerusalem for a feast of the Jews** partly because there were so many people gathered there at that time, giving him the opportunity to proclaim his teaching more fully, and partly because he had to be subject to the law, so that he might redeem us from the bondage of the law, as we have already explained elsewhere.

2. Now there is in Jerusalem near the Sheep Gate a pool. From the additional detail about the pool we know that the miracle was not hidden or known by only a few people. The five covered colonnades indicate that the place was well-known, as many people went there, and this is also supported by its closeness to the temple. Besides, the evangelist specifically states that **a great number of disabled people used to lie** there (verse 3). As far as the meaning of the name is concerned, the learned correctly reject Jerome's fanciful opinion (he replaces **Bethesda** with "Betheder," meaning "the house of the flock," because a pool is mentioned here which was near the sheep market). People who read the name as **Bethesda**, meaning "a place of fishing," have no evidence on their side. There is more evidence for those who believe it means "a place for pouring out," since the Hebrew word *eshed* signified "flowing out." But the evangelist uses the normal way of speaking and pronounces it *esda*. I believe that water flowed into it via conduits so that priests could draw water from it, unless perhaps the place was named after the pipes which poured into it. In my opinion it was called the **Sheep Gate** because the animals used in sacrifice were taken there.

3. Here a great number of disabled people . . . Possibly, ill people lay in the colonnades to beg for money from people who were on their way into the temple to worship. There they also usually bought the animals for the sacrificial offerings. God cured some people at every feast so that he might commend both the worship prescribed in the law and the holiness of the temple. This might appear to be questionable since we do not read about anything like this being done then, when religion was at its best. Even in the time of the prophets, miracles were not normally performed except on exceptional occasions; so God's power and grace were displayed with greater brilliance, as the state of the nation was so decayed and almost ruined.

I answer that there were two reasons for this, in my opinion. First, since the Holy Spirit lived in the prophets, this was sufficient witness to the divine presence, and so religion needed no additional corroboration then. The law had been supported with enough miracles, and God continued to give his approval of the worship he had commanded through countless testimonies. However, at about the time of Christ's coming, since there were no prophets and because the condition of the people was terrible, with various temptations pressing on them from every side, they were in need of some very special assistance, so that they would not think that God had completely deserted them and so be discouraged and fall away. We know that Malachi, the last of the prophets, ends his teaching with the admonition that the Jews should "remember the law of my servant Moses" (Malachi 4:4) until Christ appears. God could see the advantages in depriving them of the prophets. He kept them in suspense for a time so that their desire for Christ might burn more strongly and that they might welcome him more reverently when he was shown to them. But as a witness to the temple and its sacrifices and to all the worship through which salvation would be known to the world, the Lord kept the gift of healing among the Jews. In this way they knew that there was a good reason for God separating them from the other nations. Through healing, like an outstretched arm from heaven, God clearly showed people that he approved of this kind of worship, which they had derived from the commands of the law.

Second, God undoubtedly intended to remind them through these signs that the time of redemption was approaching, and that Christ, the author of salvation, was already close at hand, so that everybody's minds might be aroused. I think that signs had two purposes in that age: first, so that the Jews might know that God was with them, which would help to make them constant in obeying the law; and second, so that they might earnestly long for a new and unusual condition.

The blind, the lame, the paralyzed. The evangelist lists the diseases so that we realize that the Lord cured unusual ailments. Human remedies could not help the blind, the lame, and the paralyzed. It was a dreadful spectacle to see so many people with so many different kinds of disabilities. However, God's glory shone more brightly there than in the sight of the biggest and best disciplined army. For there is nothing more magnificent than God's unusual power correcting and restoring the defects of nature. Nothing is more beautiful and delightful than when God relieves men's afflictions through his infinite goodness. This is why the Lord intended that this should be a wonderful sight. The local inhabitants, as well as foreigners, could see and meditate on God's majesty. In addition to this, as I have already suggested, it was no small ornament and glory for the temple when God stretched out his hand and showed clearly that he was present.

4. An angel of the Lord would come down. Healing the sick was undoubtedly God's special work. He often used the ministry of angels in his work, so he commanded an **angel** to perform this duty. This is why the angels are called "powers or rulers" (Colossians 1:16). It is not that God gave over his power to them and so has nothing to do in heaven, but since he acts powerfully through them he shows and displays his power magnificently. So it is evil and shameful to think that anything belongs to the angels or to imagine that they are the mediators between us and God. This would obscure God's glory, as if it was a long way away from us, when the opposite is the case, as God uses them to manifest his presence. We should be on our guard against Plato's foolish speculations, since the gap between us and God is too big to allow us to go to the angels so that they may gain favor on our behalf. On the contrary, we should come straight to Christ, so that through his guidance, protection, and command we may have the angels to assist and minister our salvation.

From time to time. God could have cured everyone in a single moment, but since his miracles had a purpose, they should also have a limit. Christ reminds them that although there were so many people who died in Elisha's time, only one child was raised from the dead (2 Kings 4:32-35), and that although there were so many starving widows during the time of the drought, Elijah only helped one poor widow (1 Kings 17:9-15; Luke 4:25-26). So the Lord thought that it was sufficient to demonstrate his presence through a few ill people. The way in which people were cured, which is described here, shows clearly enough that nothing is so unreasonable as subjecting God's deed to our own judgment. After all, what help or relief could be expected to come from waters that had been disturbed? The Lord deprives us of our own senses in this way and makes us used to the obedience of faith. Although it is against God's Word, we are all too eager to follow what appeals to our minds. So, to make us more obedient to him, he often confronts us with things which contradict our minds. This is the only way we demonstrate our humble obedience, as we close our eyes and follow the plain

Word even though we think that what we are doing will be useless. The Syrian Naaman is an example of this. He is sent to the river Jordan by the prophet so he can be cured of his leprosy (2 Kings 5:10). Doubtless, he starts off by despising this as a bit of mockery, but later he actually comes to realize that although God does act contrary to human reason, he never mocks or disappoints us.

. . . and stir up the waters. This stirring up of the waters shows that God is free to use the elements as he wishes and then claim the result as his own handiwork. It is a very common mistake to ascribe to creatures what belongs to God alone, for it would be the height of foolishness to look for the reason for the cure in the stirring of the waters. Therefore, God points to the outward symbol in such a way that, by looking at the symbol, the ill people are made to raise their eyes to the One who alone is the author of grace.

5. One who was there . . . The evangelist draws on various details which show that the miracle is reliable. The many years' duration of the disease had taken away all hope of being cured. The man grumbles that he is deprived of the cure of the water. Often he had tried to get into the water without success. Nobody was there to help him, and this highlights Christ's power more strikingly. Christ's command, **"Pick up your mat"** (verse 8), is important because through it everyone could clearly see that he was better and that Christ has been responsible for this. When he suddenly stood up, healthy and strong in all his limbs which had been previously disabled, the speed of the cure hit home to the minds of everybody who saw it.

6. "Do you want to get well?" Christ did not ask this as if there was any uncertainty about the matter, but partly to stir up in the man a desire for the offer that was being made to him, and partly to attract the attention of everyone who was watching. These people might have missed the miracle, as does often happen with sudden miracles, if their minds had been elsewhere. So for these two reasons, this preparation was necessary.

7. "I have no one." The ill man does what we nearly all do: he limits God to what he thought was possible and does not dare promise himself anything more than his mind can envisage. As Christ forgives this man's weakness, we have a picture of the patience he has with us every day. On the one hand, we train our minds on what is within our experience; but on the other hand, God shows his hand in unexpected places, quite against our expectation, and so shows how his goodness extends beyond the narrow confines of our faith. In addition, this example should teach us to be patient. **Thirty-eight years** (verse 5) was a long time for God to delay giving to this poor man the cure which, from the beginning, he had set out to confer on him. So no matter how long we may be held in suspense, and even when we grumble in our afflictions, we should never be discouraged or annoyed by the lengthy wait. When we are afflicted for a long time, and we find no relief, we should still believe that God is a wonderful deliverer who through his power can easily remove any obstacle out of the way.

9. The day on which this took place was a Sabbath. Christ was fully aware what offense people would immediately take if they saw a man walking along carrying a burden. The law specifically forbids this: "Be careful not to carry a load on the Sabbath day" (Jeremiah 17:21). There were two reasons why Christ ignored this danger and chose to make such a spectacle. First, this would make the miracle more widely known; second, it gave Christ the opportunity, as it were, for the wonderful teaching he gave immediately after this. Knowledge about that miracle became so important that Christ found that he had to boldly challenge people who took offense, especially as he had such a good defense with which, although it did not pacify the ungodly people, he abundantly refuted their slanders. So we should take notice of this principle: even if the whole world is angry with us, we should proclaim God's glory and celebrate his deeds to the extent that his glory requires that they should be made known. We should not be worried or discouraged if our efforts are not immediately successful, so long as we keep in mind the goal I have stated and do not go beyond the limits of our office.

Verses 10–16

10. "It is the Sabbath." Everyone had to keep the Sabbath holy, and so they are right in accusing the man. However, when the explanation the man gives them does not satisfy them, they are already beginning to be at fault. Once the reason he gave was known, he should have been acquitted. As we have said, to carry a burden broke the Sabbath. However, since Christ took this responsibility on his shoulders, the man is excused by Christ's authority. From this example we should be careful to avoid all rash judgment until we know in full the reason for each action. Anything that is against God's Word deserves to be condemned without hesitation. But since we often make mistakes here, we should first of all make calm and humble enquiries, so that we can make sound and sober judgments. The Jews, who were prejudiced through their evil outlook, had no patience to make inquiries, and they closed the door to moderation and fair judgments. However, if they had allowed themselves to know the facts, not only would their reason for taking offense be removed, but they would have made more progress, to their great advantage, in knowing the Gospel.

We can see just how wrong the Jews were — and all because they would not allow a reasonable defense to be made. The defense is made by the cured man who says that he is not doing anything except by the command of the person who had the power and authority to command. For although he was not yet aware of who Christ was, he was convinced that Christ had been sent by God, as the man had received proof of Christ's divine power. From this he learns that Christ is endued with authority, and so it must be the man's duty to obey him. However, a rebuke does seem to be justified if a miracle makes him disobey the law. I agree that the argument which this man uses against them is not strong enough, although the other arguments are faulty for two reasons: they neither take into account God's extraordinary work, nor do they suspend their judgment until they have heard God's prophet who is equipped with the Word.

13. The man who had been healed had no idea who it was. Christ certainly did not want the glory of so great a work to fade away, since he planned that it should become generally known before he acknowledged that he was the author of it. So for a little time he withdrew, so that the Jews could have the opportunity to judge the facts without reference to any person. So we learn that this man's cure cannot be ascribed to his faith, since even after he was cured he does not acknowledge his doctor. However, when he was told to pick up his mat and walk, he seems to have done so out of faith. For myself, I agree that he had some secret glimmer of faith, though I will say that it is clear from what follows that he had no firm teaching or clear light to rely on.

14. Later Jesus found him. These words show even more clearly that Christ did not hide himself so that the memory of his miracle might vanish, as he now appears in public of his own accord. He wanted the miracle to be known about first of all, and then later he declared that he was the author of it. This passage contains some very important teaching. When Christ says, **"See, you are well again,"** he is saying that we misuse God's gifts if we are not stirred to gratitude. Christ does not reproach the man with what he had given him, but just reminds him that he had been cured so that he could remember the favor he had received, and so serve God, his rescuer, all his life. As God instructs and spurs us on to repentance through wounds, so he invites us to it by his goodness and patience. Indeed, it is the whole purpose both of our redemption and of all God's gifts that we should be completely devoted to him. But this cannot be done unless the memory of the past punishment is impressed on our minds and unless the pardoned person meditates on this throughout all of his life.

This rebuke also teaches us that all the evils we endure should be imputed to our sins, for men's afflictions are not accidental, but are so many wounds to chastise us. First of all, we should acknowledge God's hand when he strikes us and not imagine that our afflictions come from blind fortune. Next, we should ascribe this honor to God, because since he is a good Father, he does not take pleasure in our sufferings, and so he does not treat us more harshly than our sins deserve. When Christ tells the man, **"Stop sinning,"** he is not commanding him to be free from all sin, but is speaking in a comparative way about his former life. Christ exhorts him to repent and not to do as he had done previously.

"Or something worse may happen to you." If God is unsuccessful in changing us through the wounds with which he gently chastises us, like the kindest father chastises his tender and delicate children, he is forced to take a different stance and a character which, as it were, is unnatural to him. So, as he threatens to do in the law, he seizes the whip to subdue our obstinacy (Leviticus 26:14ff.; Deuteronomy 28:15; Psalm 32:9). Indeed, there are similar passages throughout the Scriptures. So, when we are incessantly attacked with new afflictions, we should trace these back to our obstinacy. We are not only like obstinate horses or mules, but we are like wild beasts which cannot be tamed. So there is no reason to be surprised if God uses severer punishments to grind us into the dust, as it were, when reasonable punishment has no effect. It is right for people who refuse to be corrected to be bruised. In summary, the purpose of punishment is to make us more careful about the future. If after the first two strokes we continue to be obstinate and hard-hearted, he will strike us seven times more severely. If after we have begun to show signs of repentance for a time we immediately relapse to our old nature, he punishes our forgetful levity and slothfulness more severely.

Further, we should note carefully how gentle and patient the Lord is with this man. If we imagine that this man was approaching old age now, he must have been afflicted with this disease in his prime of life, if not as a young child. We can imagine how terrible it must have been for him to suffer in this way for so many years. We certainly should not blame God for being too severe in making this man languish, half-dead, for such a long time. So when we receive less severe punishment, we must learn that it is because the Lord, in his infinite goodness, tempers the full effects of his punishments which we really deserve. We must also learn that no punishments exist which are so rigorous or severe that the Lord could not make them worse whenever he wants to. We cannot doubt that wretched men, through their evil grumbling, often bring down on themselves dreadful and shocking tortures and assert that they could not endure any worse distress and that God could not send them anything worse to endure. "Have I not kept this in reserve and sealed it in my vaults?" (Deuteronomy 32:34).

We should also note how slow we are to benefit from God's punishments. For unless Christ's exhortation is valueless, we may learn from it that this man's soul was not yet fully purified from every sin. Indeed the roots of sins are so deep within us that they cannot be pulled up in one day, or even in a few days. The diseases of the soul are so serious that they cannot be remedied quickly.

15. The man went away. Nothing was further from this man's mind than that the Jews should hate Christ, and nothing was further from his thoughts than that they would accuse Christ so furiously. This man's motives were holy, as he wanted to give to his doctor the honor he justly deserved. However, the Jews had poisonous intentions, as they not only accused him of breaking the Sabbath, but burst out into extreme cruelty.

Verses 17–19

17. "My Father is always at his work to this very day." We note the defense Christ used. He did not answer that keeping the Sabbath was a temporary law and that it was now abolished. On the contrary, he insists that he did not break the law since this was divine work. It is true that Christ put an end to those shadowy ceremonies by his coming, as Paul points out (see Colossians 2:17), but the question before us does not hinge on this. For people are only commanded to cease from their own deeds, so that anything which is God's work and not man's work — for example, circumcision — is not breaking the Sabbath.

So Christ insists that the holy rest which is commanded in the law of Moses is not broken when God's work is done. On this ground, Christ excuses his own actions and those of the man who carried his bed, since this was linked to the miracle, as it demonstrated that a miracle had taken place. In addition to this, if giving thanks to God and preaching God's glory are to be included among God's deeds, the Sabbath is not broken when hands and feet testify to God's grace. Christ is mostly referring to himself, as the Jews were more hostile to him than to the healed man. Christ declares that the healthy body which he had restored to the sick man was an example of his divine power. Christ asserts that he is the Son of God and that he acts in the same way as his Father.

The purpose of the Sabbath and why it was given, I will not expand on now. For the present passage it is enough to say that keeping the Sabbath, far from interrupting or hampering God's deeds, actually gives priority to them alone. For the law commands men to cease from their own work, so that their faculties are free to be given over to thinking about God's deeds. So anyone who does not allow, on the Sabbath, free rein to God's deeds is not only explaining the law incorrectly but is wickedly overturning it.

If you raise the objection that God gave men the seventh day for rest, the answer is straightforward. Men are not like God in the way in which he ceased from work, but as men cease from their labors in the world they aspire to heavenly rest. So the Sabbath, or rest, of God is not idleness but true perfection, which brings a calm state of peace with it. This is consistent with Moses' saying, "God . . . finished the work he had been doing" (Genesis 2:2). After God had finished creating the world, he consecrated that day so that men might make use of it to reflect on his deeds. But God did not stop upholding his world with his power or ruling it with his wisdom or supporting it with his goodness, so that everything on earth and heaven is done according to his will. In six days the world was created, but it continued to be governed, and God never stopped working and upholding it. Paul says this: "'For in him we live and move and have our being'" (Acts 17:28). David says that all things exist so long as God's Spirit upholds them and that they collapse as soon as he withdraws his support (see Psalm 104:29). Nor is it only by a general providence that the Lord upholds the world which he has created, for he organizes and rules every part of it; in particular, he protects and keeps watch over believers, who are under his protective care.

"I, too, am working." Christ moves on from defending this present case and explains the purpose of the miracle — namely, that through it he would be acknowledged as the Son of God. The aim he had in mind in all his words and actions was that he was the author of salvation. What he now claims for himself belongs to his divinity. As the apostle says, "The Son . . . sustaining all things by his powerful word" (Hebrews 1:3). Christ testifies that he is God, as he is manifested in the body, so that he may carry out the office of Christ. When Christ declares that he came from heaven, it is mainly so that we will know why he came down to earth.

18. For this reason the Jews tried all the harder to kill him. This defense did not allay their anger but enraged them all the more. Christ was used to their malign and evil ways and their hard obstinacy. Christ wanted a few of his disciples who were there to benefit from this, and he also wanted to make a public example of their incurable malice. Through Christ's example he teaches us never to give way to the anger of evil men, but rather always to uphold God's truth insofar as this is necessary, even if the world is opposed to us and objects. Christ's servants should not worry that everyone does not benefit from what they do, as what Christ himself did was not always a success. We should not be surprised that the more Satan vents his wrath violently among those in his grip, the more God's glory is clearly seen.

Not only was he breaking the Sabbath . . . When the evangelist says that the Jews were hostile to Christ because he was breaking the Sabbath, he is speaking from their point of view. I have already shown that the truth of the matter is quite the reverse. The main reason why they were angry was that **he was even calling God his own Father.** Christ certainly intended that it should be understood that God was his **Father** in a special sense, so that he could be differentiated from the ordinary rank of other people. **Making himself equal with God.** Christ did this when he claimed to be carrying on God's work, and, rather than denying this, Christ now affirms it more strongly. This refutes the crazy teaching of the Arians, who acknowledge that Christ is God but do not think that he was equal to the Father, as if there could be any inequality in the one and simple essence of God.

19. Jesus gave them this answer . . . As I have said, we see that Christ, so far from clearing himself of the Jews' accusations, although they were meant maliciously, maintains more openly that his statement is true. He starts by insisting that the deed which the Jews complained about was divine work, so that they would understand that they would have to oppose God himself if they continued to condemn what had to be ascribed to him. This passage has been interpreted in different ways by the Arians and the orthodox Fathers. Arius inferred from it that the Son is inferior to the Father because Christ could do nothing by himself. The Fathers replied that these words only denote a distinction of the person, so that it is known that Christ comes from the Father, although Christ is not deprived of intrinsic power of action. Both these arguments were wrong. This discourse does not relate to the simple divinity of Christ, and the next statements do not of themselves relate to the eternal Word of God, but only apply to the Son of God insofar as he is manifested in the body.

So we must keep Christ in our sights, as he was sent into the world by the Father to be a Redeemer. The Jews could see in him nothing more than a human being. So Christ argues that when he cured an ill man, he was not using his human power but his divine power, which was concealed by his visible body. This is the principle at stake. The Jews focused their attention on what the body did, and so they despised Christ. Christ encourages them to raise their sights and to look at God. The whole discourse must be viewed in this light. People who think that they are dealing with a human being are making a flagrant mistake when they blame Christ for doing truly divine work. This is why Christ insists so strongly that in this work there is no difference between him and his Father.

Verses 20–24

20. "For the Father loves the Son." Everybody can see how harsh and far-fetched the Fathers' interpretation of this passage is. They say, "God loves himself in the Son." But this statement applies beautifully to Christ as he is in the human body, that he is loved by **the Father.** Further, we know that he is distinguished both from men and from angels by this wonderful title: "This is my Son, whom I love" (Matthew 3:17). We know that Christ was chosen so that the complete love of God might live in him and that this love might flow, like an overflowing fountain, from him to us. Christ is loved by **the Father,** since he is the head of the church. He shows that this love is the reason why **the Father** does everything through his hand. When Christ says that **"the Father show[ed] him,"** this means that communication is taking place. It is as if he said, "As **the Father** has given me his heart, so he has poured out his power on me, so that the divine glory may shine in my deeds, and, what is more, so that men cannot seek anything divine except what they find in me." Indeed, outside Christ it is useless to seek God's power.

"He will show him even greater things than these." Here Christ means that the miracle he had performed in healing this man was not the greatest deed that his **Father** had told him to do. For Christ had only given it as a small foretaste of the grace which he is well-equipped to minister and of which he is also the author — namely, to restore life to the world.

"Yes, to your amazement . . ." Through these words Christ is obliquely accusing them of ingratitude when they despised such an illustrious demonstration of God's power. It is as if he had said, "Even though you are dull and stupid, the deeds which God will do through me later will attract you, no matter now reluctant you are." However, this does not appear to have been fulfilled, since we know, as Isaiah says about the reprobate who are blind in God's light, that they were like people "seeing, but never perceiving" (Isaiah 6:9). In answer to this, I say that Christ is not speaking about their attitude but only throws out a suggestion about the splendor of the proof which he would later give about being the Son of God.

21. "For just as the Father raises the dead . . ." Christ now summarizes the nature of the office **the Father** has given him. For although Christ seems to specify one aspect of this teaching, it is in fact a general teaching, in which he declares that he is the author of life. Not only is righteousness contained in life, but all the gifts of the Holy Spirit and every part of salvation is also contained there. This miracle must have been such a remarkable demonstration of Christ's power that it yielded this general fruit; that is, it opened the door to the Gospel. We should also take note how Christ gives us life, for he found us when we were all dead, and so it was necessary to start with a resurrection. When the two phrases **"raises the dead"** and **"gives life"** are linked, Christ is not using exaggerated language. For it would not have been enough for Christ to rescue us from death if he had not completely and perfectly restored life in us. Again, Christ does not say that this life is given to everyone indiscriminately, for he says that **"the Son gives life to whom he is pleased to give it."** This means that Christ specially confers his life only on certain people, his elect.

22. "Moreover, the Father judges no one." Now Christ is stating more clearly the general truth that the Father rules the world through the person of his Son and exercises control through his hand. The evangelist uses the word **"judgment"** in line with the Hebraic idiom meaning authority and power. We can now see what is meant here. The Father gave a kingdom to the Son so that he might rule heaven and earth according to his will. It might seem completely absurd for the Father to surrender his right to rule and stay in heaven like an ordinary person having nothing to do. The solution is easy. This is said both in regard to God and to men. The Father did not change when he appointed Christ as supreme King and Lord of heaven and earth, for the Father is in the Son and works in him. But since our senses fail us when we want to picture God, Christ is put in front of our eyes as the living image of the invisible God. So we have no reason for fruitlessly working at exploring the secrets of heaven, since God has provided for our weakness as he shows himself near in the person of Christ. However, whenever we are concerned about the government of the world, our own condition, the heavenly protection of our salvation, we must learn to train our eyes on Christ alone, since all power has been entrusted to him (see Matthew 28:18). In Christ's face God the Father, who would otherwise have been hidden and distant from us, is seen by us, so that the exposed majesty of God does now swallow us up in its unimaginable brightness.

23. ". . . that all may honor the Son." This phrase confirms my earlier suggestion that when it says God rules in the person of Christ, it does not mean that the Father is resting in heaven, like lazy monarchs do, but that in Christ he shows his power and reveals his presence. What else can the words **"that all may honor the Son"** mean other than that the Father wants to be acknowledged and worshiped in the Son? So our duty is to seek God the Father in the Son, to view his power in Christ, and to worship him in Christ. For as is immediately stated, **"he who does not honor the Son"** deprives God of his deserved honor. Everybody agrees that we should worship God, and this thought, which comes naturally to us, is deeply rooted in our hearts, so that no one dares to completely refuse God the honor which he deserves. Yet men's minds go all over the place as they seek God. That is the reason for so many supposed deities and so many perverse ways of worship. We can only find the true God in Christ, and we will only worship him properly as we "kiss the Son," as David puts it (see Psalm 2:12), for, as John declares elsewhere, "whoever acknowledges the Son has the Father also" (1 John 2:23).

Muslims and Jews give the God they worship beautiful and magnificent titles. However, we should remember that whenever God's name is separated from Christ, it is nothing more than empty imagination. So everyone who wants the true God to approve his worship must never turn away from Christ. It was the same for the fathers under the law. Even though they only had a shadowy perception of Christ, God never revealed himself without Christ. But now that Christ has been manifested in the body and has been appointed to rule over us as King, the whole world must bend the knee to him, so that God may be obeyed.

The Father has made Christ sit at his right hand; so anybody who thinks of God without Christ takes away half of him.

24. "Whoever hears my word . . ." Here is a description about how to honor God, so that no one thinks that it involves only rites or superficial ceremonies. The Gospel's teaching is like Christ's scepter, with which he rules believers whom the Father has made his subjects. This definition is worth paying careful attention to. Nothing is more common than a false profession of Christianity. But here Christ demands no other honor than that we obey his Gospel. So it follows that all the honor which hypocrites lavish on Christ is like Judas' kiss, which betrayed his Lord. Even if they call him King a hundred times over, they are depriving him of his kingdom and of all power when they do not exercise faith in the Gospel.

". . . has eternal life." Christ also commends the fruit of obedience, so that we are more willing to produce it. Who can be so hard as not to want to submit willingly to Christ when the reward of eternal life is offered? And yet we see how few people Christ won over to himself by such great goodness. We are so depraved that we prefer to die voluntarily rather than hand ourselves over in obedience to the Son of God so that we may be saved by his grace. So Christ includes here both the life of devout and sincere worship which he requires of us, and the way in which he restores us to life. It is not enough just to understand what he had previously taught about coming to raise the dead (verse 21) unless we also know how he restores this life to us. Christ now states that this life is received by **"whoever hears"** his **"word."** By "hearing" he means faith, as he immediately declares. But faith has its center in the heart, not in the ears.

We have already explained how faith receives this great power. We should always think about what the Gospel offers us. We should not be surprised that the person who receives Christ, with all his merits, is reconciled to God and acquitted from the condemnation of death. Also, the person who has received the gift of the Holy Spirit is clothed with heavenly righteousness so that he "may live a new life" (Romans 6:4). The additional clause **"believes him who sent me"** only confirms the Gospel's authority. For Christ testifies that it came from God rather than being man's invention, since he says elsewhere that what he says is not from himself (see 7:16; 14:10), but was given to him by the Father.

". . . and will not be condemned." There is an implied contrast here between the guilt which we all have by nature and the unconditional acquittal which we receive through Christ. If everyone did not deserve to be condemned, what would be the point of rescuing from this condemnation those who believed in Christ? It must mean that we are out of danger from death because we are acquitted through Christ's grace. So although Christ sanctifies us and regenerates us to new life through his Spirit, he specially mentions here the unconditional forgiveness of sins, in which alone consists man's happiness. For once a person is reconciled to God, he starts to live. How could he love us if he had not pardoned our sins?

"He has crossed over . . ." Some Latin editions put this word into the future tense, "will pass from death to life." This has come about through some people's ignorance and rashness, who did not understand the evangelist's meaning and have taken more liberty than they should have. For there is no ambiguity at all with the Greek word translated **"has crossed over."** There is nothing wrong in saying that we have **"crossed over from death to life."** The "imperishable" seed (1 Peter 1:23) lives in the children of God, and they already sit in the heavenly glory with Christ through hope (see Colossians 3:3), and they already have the "kingdom of God . . . within" them (Luke 17:21). Just because their life is hidden, this does not prevent them from possessing it by faith. Just because they are attacked on all sides by death, they still remain calm, as they know that they are perfectly safe because of Christ's protection. But we must remember that believers are now alive in such a way that they always have with them the death sentence. However, the indwelling Spirit is **"life"** and will eventually destroy the remnants of death. Paul states the truth: "The last enemy to be destroyed is death" (1 Corinthians 15:26). This passage says nothing about the complete destruction of death, or the entire manifestation of life. Even though life has only begun in us, Christ declares that believers are so sure to receive it that they should not be frightened about death. We should not be surprised about this since we are united to the One who is the inexhaustible source of **life.**

Verses 25–29

25. "I tell you the truth." The evangelist shows the Son of God very often solemnly swearing in reference to our salvation. From this we can see, first, how much he cares about our welfare, and, second, how very important it is that the faith of the Gospel should be deeply fixed and thoroughly confirmed. On the face of it, this statement seems incredible, since we are told that it applies to the faith Christ is speaking about. So he confirms with an oath that the voice of the Gospel has power to bring **"the dead"** back to life. It is generally agreed that Christ is referring to spiritual death here, since those who want to link it to Lazarus (11:44) and to the son of the widow of Nain (Luke 7:15) and other similar instances are refuted by what follows. First of all, Christ shows that we are all **"dead"** before he gives us life. This makes clear what man contributes towards his salvation.

When the Roman Catholics want to emphasize their free will, they compare it to the Samaritan who was left half-dead on the roadside by the robbers (Luke 10:30). They use the smoke-screen of an allegory to obscure Christ's clear statement which declares that we are totally condemned to death. Since we have been separated from God by the rebellion of the first man, anybody who does not acknowledge being overwhelmed with eternal destruction is only deceiving himself with vain flattery. I am happy to agree that man's soul does contain some remnant of life, since our understanding, judgment, will, and senses are all part of this life. However, no part of us aspires to the heavenly life, and so we are hardly surprised if the complete person, as far as the kingdom of God is concerned, is accounted "dead." Paul explains in more detail what this death means: "You were dead in your transgressions and sins" (Ephesians 2:1); and, "You must no longer live as the Gentiles do, in the futility of their thinking. They are darkened in their understanding and separated from the life of God because of the ignorance that is in them due to the hardening of their hearts. Having lost all sensitivity, they have given themselves over to sensuality so as to indulge in every kind of impurity, with a continual lust for more" (Ephesians 4:17-19). If such a corrupt nature does not have the strength to seek righteousness, it follows that God's life is extinguished in us.

So Christ's grace is a true resurrection from "the dead." This grace is conferred on us by the Gospel. However, the external voice does not possess this kind of power, as it so often strikes the ear in vain. But Christ speaks to our inner hearts by his Spirit, so that by faith we can receive the life he offers us. Christ does not refer indiscriminately to all "the dead," but only to the elect, whose ears God pierces and opens so that they can receive the voice of his Son, which brings them back to life. Indeed, Christ specifically refers to this twofold grace when he says, **"The dead will hear the voice of the Son of God and those who hear will live."** It is just as unnatural for the "dead to hear" as it is for the dead to be brought back to life. Both come from the secret power of God.

"A time is coming and has now come." Christ refers to this event as if it had never happened, since the proclamation of the Gospel was a new and sudden resurrection of the world. But did not the Word of God always give life to men? There is an easy answer to this question. The teaching of the Law and the Prophets was addressed to God's people, and so must have been intended to preserve life in God's children, rather than bring them back from death. But it was different with the Gospel. Through the Gospel, nations which had been previously separated from God and his kingdom and who had no hope of salvation were invited to share God's life.

26. "For as the Father has life in himself . . ." Christ shows the source of the efficacy of his voice: namely, that he is the source of **"life"** and through his voice gives **"life"** to men; for **"life"** would not come to us from his mouth if he did not have in himself the cause of and source of it. God is said to **"have life in himself,"** not just because he is the only

One to live by his own inherent power, but because he has this fullness of **"life"** in himself and passes on **"life"** to everything. This belongs especially to God; "for with you is the fountain of life" (Psalm 36:9). Because God's majesty is so far from us and would remain unknown and hidden from us, it was necessary for it to be openly manifested in Christ. So we have an open fountain, close at hand, to draw from. These words mean that "God did not choose to hide **life** — as it were, buried within himself; so he poured this life into his Son, that it might flow onto us." So we conclude that this title is correctly applied to Christ inasmuch as he was manifested in the flesh.

27. "And he has given him authority." Christ repeats that the Father has given him authority to be in total charge of everything in heaven and on earth. The Greek word used here is rightly translated **"authority."** The word **"judge"** here refers to the rule of a government, as if Christ had said that the Father had made him a King to govern the world and to exercise the authority of the Father himself.

"Because he is the Son of Man." This explanation, which is immediately given, deserves special attention. It shows that Christ came to men, clothed in such magnificent power, so that he could give them what he had received from the Father. Some people think that this passage expresses nothing else but Paul's writing — that Christ "made himself nothing, taking the very nature of a servant, being made in human likeness. And being found in appearance as a man, he humbled himself and became obedient to death — even death on a cross! Therefore God exalted him to the highest place and gave him the name that is above every name, that at the name of Jesus every knee should bow . . ." (Philippians 2:7-10). But I think that this passage has a broader meaning: that Christ, insofar as he was a man, was appointed by the Father to be the author of life, so that we would not have far to go to seek it; for Christ did not have this life for his own benefit, as if he was in need of it, but in order to enrich us through his wealth. We can sum it up in this way: "What had been hidden in God is revealed to us in Christ; and **life**, which was previously inaccessible, is now in front of our eyes." Some people want to remove this argument from its context and link it with the next clause, but this is forcing the interpretation and is against Christ's meaning.

28. "Do not be amazed at this." We may be tempted to think that Christ is not using a strong argument by taking the last resurrection as confirmation of what he had said, for raising bodies is no greater than raising souls. My reply is that Christ's comparison between the greater and the lesser is not about the real state of things, but about what men think they are. Since they are unspiritual, they only appreciate the outward and visible. So they give very little attention to the resurrection of the soul, while they become very excited about the resurrection of the body. Another result of this gross stupidity of ours is that what we see with our eyes is more likely to produce faith than the things which we only perceive by faith. Christ mentions the last day but does not add the limitation "and now is," but simply declares that the time will one day come.

There is a further objection. Although believers are looking forward to the resurrection of the body, they cannot know for certain that their souls are delivered from death just because their bodies will one day rise from their graves. What could be more ridiculous, in the eyes of ungodly people, than to demonstrate the truth of something that is uncertain by using an even less certain thing? My answer is that Christ is asserting his power over the reprobate in order to show that the Father has put into his power the restoration of everything. It is as if he said: "What I am now telling you I have already started, and one day you will see that it is finished." So when Christ brings to life souls which had been buried in hell, through the sound of the Gospel, this is a kind of preparation for the final resurrection. Again, although he includes the whole human race, he distinguishes between the elect and the reprobate. This distinction shows that the reprobate, as they are now summoned to judgment by Christ's voice, will also, through the same voice, be dragged in front of his judgment-seat.

So why does he only mention the people who are enclosed in "**graves**," as if others, who might have been drowned, killed by wild beasts, or burned to death, will not share in the resurrection? The answer is that the burying of the dead is a figure of speech in which a part is taken for the whole; so all the dead are included here. But this is a more emphatic expression than just saying "the dead." Those whom death has already deprived of life and light, the grave, as it were, takes away from the world.

"**. . . will hear his voice.**" The "**voice**" of the Son means the sound of the trumpet (see Matthew 24:31; 1 Corinthians 15:52), which will sound out through the command and power of Christ. While an "angel" will be its herald or forerunner (see 1 Thessalonians 4:16), this does not prevent what is being done by the authority of the Judge, as it were in his own person, being ascribed to himself.

29. "Those who have done good . . ." Christ marks out believers by their good deeds, as he teaches elsewhere by implication that "By their fruit you will recognize them" (Matthew 7:16). Christ praises their "**good**" deeds, which they have devoted themselves to since they were called. Even the thief who was promised life by Christ on the cross (see Luke 23:42-43), who had spent his whole life in criminal activity, says with his last breath that he wants to do good. Since he is born again and becomes a new person and changes from being the servant of sin to a servant of righteousness, his whole past life is not taken into account by God. Moreover, the sins which condemn all believers are not imputed to them. Without God's pardon, which God gives to believers, we can never say that anybody has lived a good life. Also, not one deed can be thought of as being good unless God pardons its sinfulness, for everyone is imperfect and corrupt. These people are here called those who have "**done good,**" and Paul refers to them as people who are "eager to do what is good" (Titus 2:14). However, this assessment of them depends on God's fatherly kindness, who through his free grace approves of people who deserve to be rejected.

The inference which Roman Catholics draw from these passages — that eternal life is dependent on the merits of good deeds — can be easily refuted. Christ is not here talking about the basis of salvation, but is distinguishing between the elect and the reprobate by their own actions. He does this in order to encourage and exhort his own followers to lead a holy and blameless life. We are not denying that the faith which justifies us comes with an earnest desire to live a good and righteous life. However, we assert that our confidence lies in nothing other than God's mercy alone.

Verses 30–32

30. "By myself I can do nothing." It is pointless to engage in abstruse arguments here about whether the Son of God can do anything by himself or not insofar as this refers to his eternal divinity. He never meant our minds to be occupied with such trifles. So the old writers should not have been so upset as they refuted the malicious teaching of Arius. This evil man taught that the Son is not equal to the Father, because he said, **"By myself I can do nothing."** The holy men reply that everything that can be ascribed to the Father, the Son correctly claims for himself. Christ takes his beginning from the Father, in being a person. But, firstly, Christ does not only refer to his divinity but warns that, insofar as he is clothed with our flesh, we should not judge him according to outward appearances, because he possesses something higher than man. Again, we must remember whom he was dealing with. Christ was refuting the Jews who were trying to compare him with God. So Christ affirms that he does not do anything through human power because God, who lives in him, is his guide and leader.

We should always remember that whenever Christ speaks about himself, he claims only what is proper to man. He is keeping one eye on the Jews who wrongly said that he was just like any other man. It is for this same reason that Christ ascribes to the Father whatever is higher than man.

"I judge." This word "**judge,**" strictly speaking, refers to Christ's teaching. But it also applies to his whole life. It is as if he is saying that he lives according to his Father's directions in everything and that his Father's will governs him, and so he will defend him from all his attackers.

"And my judgment is just." Christ concludes by saying that his actions and teaching are blameless, because he never tries to do or say anything that is not commanded or directed by his Father. It is beyond question that everything that comes from God must be right. This humility ought to be held up by us as the first principle of godliness. We should have such reverence for the words and the deeds of God that God's name alone would be enough to demonstrate their justice and rightness. But how few people are willing to acknowledge God's justice unless they are forced to! I do agree that God shows us his righteousness by experience. But to restrict this to the understanding of our flesh, so that we will only think about it in the way our minds suggest, is evil and flagrantly unholy. So we must say for certain and beyond question that whatever comes from God is right and true, that it is impossible for God to be wrong about anything that he says, and that he is just and right in all his actions. We are also reminded that the only principle for good behavior is to do nothing except by God's direction and command. Even if the whole world is against us, we still have this invisible defense, that God's followers cannot go astray.

"For I seek not to please myself." Christ's will and his Father's will are not opposing each other here, as if they were saying different things. Christ is only refuting what they were accusing him of, that he was motivated by human aspirations rather than by the guidance and authority of God. Therefore, Christ affirms that he has no disposition which is special to or which separates him from his Father's commands.

31. "If I testify about myself . . ." Christ does not detract from the authority of his witness, which he elsewhere strongly asserts, but is just making a concession. Although Christ had been most amply supported in other ways, he now says that they should not believe what he says. He says, "If my witness about myself is suspected by you, as is the custom of men, then let it go for nothing." We know that nothing anybody says about himself can be thought of as being true or authentic, even if he says the truth in everything else, because no one can testify about himself. Although it would be wrong to reduce the Son of God to this level, Christ is prepared to give over his rights so that he may convince his enemies by God's authority.

Verses 33–36

33. "You have sent to John." Before putting forward God's witness, Christ gives them John's testimony, which they could not honorably disbelieve, for why should they have sent for John if they did not intend to abide by what he said? They "sent to John" because he was God's prophet, and so they pretend that they will accept what he says as an oracle. Now, although this implies conceding to them, Christ openly accuses them that only their own malice stops them from believing. So we see that this detail of sending to John is very relevant, because it was as if they really wanted to learn from him when they asked him who the Messiah was, and yet disregarded his reply.

34. "Not that I accept human testimony." However, God did not choose John to be his witness for nothing, as on another occasion Christ tells his disciples that they will be his witnesses: "And you will be my witnesses in Jerusalem, and in all Judea and Samaria, and to the ends of the earth" (Acts 1:8). I answer that Christ uses John's witness not because he needs to, but because it does us good to receive confirmation from it. Men accept testimony from each other because they cannot exist without it. But it is different with God and Christ. If philosophers assert that virtue does not need outside corroboration, what is there in man that can confirm the truth about God? Christ immediately says that he put forward John's testimony on their account: **"I mention it that you may be saved."** Christ is not saying this for his own benefit, but for man's benefit as he lifts up the herald of the Gospel, through whom he witnesses to us about his will. From this we also see striking proof of his wonderful goodness, through which he orders everything for our salvation. So after all the great care he has lavished on us, it is incumbent on us to be fruitful.

35. "John was a lamp that burned and gave light." When Christ calls John **"a lamp"** he emphasizes their ingratitude. It follows from this that they are blind from deliberate choice, since God's **"lamp"** was in front of their eyes. So these words mean, "God never wanted you to go astray: he appointed John to be a **lamp**, to guide you with God's brightness; so when you do not acknowledge me to be the Son of God, you are deliberately choosing wrong." Christ also accuses them of something else. Not only did they reject the light they were offered, by closing their eyes, but they deliberately perverted it so they could attack Christ. They were prepared to support John more than was necessary, because this came from an evil and treacherous plan to ignore the Son of God.

Christ gracefully compares this evil abuse of the heavenly **"light"** to foolish actions. It is as if the head of the household would light a lamp for his servants at night so that they could carry out the duties he had given them, but they use it for revelry and every kind of immorality. Christ accuses the Jews with these words and at the same time warns us all that when God sends us faithful teachers to guide us in the right way, we should not ignore them by wandering off in every direction. Every age knows from experience how useful this warning is. God arranges to direct people throughout their lives, up to the final goal, and he sends his prophets to guide them. But men are so stupid that instead of making progress they prefer to stay where they are, indulging in worthless dancing. They are so superficial and frivolous that they despise and reject God's continual guidance and are carried away by their sudden passions.

". . . for a time," or "for an hour." Christ uses this phrase to rebuke their foolishness in thinking that transient and short-lived evil can extinguish God's **"light."** So, in our own day the Roman Catholics misuse all the faithful teachers he has given his church to be burning lamps. It is as if they wanted to dazzle their eyes by looking at the **"light."** Not only do they misuse the lamps to put out God's **"light,"** but they often rejoice in the darkness as they revel in the foolish teaching of those who oppose the pure teaching of the Gospel. What Christ says here about John, Paul says should be true of all believers, who should "shine like stars in the universe" (Philippians 2:15). Christ says that apostles and ministers of the Gospel are the right people to lead others and show them the way. While we are all blind and in the middle of darkness, God shines on us through the **"light"** of his Word. Here Christ specifically gives this title to John because God shone on his church with great brightness through that man's ministry.

36. "I have testimony weightier than that of John." After Christ had shown that in the person of John the Jews had evilly corrupted God's gift, he now repeats for the second time that he does not need the **"testimony"** of man, as if he did not have enough of his own. However, because Christ saw that they were contemptuous of him, he directed them to his Father, as he always did.

"For the very work that the Father has given me to finish . . ." Christ sets out two things which show that he was the Son of God. "My **Father**," he says, "attests by miracles that I am his Son; and before I came into the world, he gave abundant witness to me in the sacred writings." We must always remember what Christ is aiming to do. He wants to be recognized as the Messiah whom God had promised, so that people would listen to him. Therefore, he insists that he is now revealed to be this person whom the Scriptures describe. You may ask: are miracles enough proof of this, since the prophets had already performed similar miracles? My answer is that the miracles performed by the prophets did not extend beyond their original purpose — namely, to show that they were God's ministers, as they could not gain authority for their office in any other way. God wanted to exalt his Son more highly, and this is the reason why God used miracles. So if the Jews had not been maliciously prejudiced and had not decided to shut their eyes, Christ could have easily shown them through his miracles who he was.

Verses 37–40

37. "And the Father who sent me . . ." It is wrong to limit this statement, as some people have done, to Christ's baptism (see Matthew 3:17). For Christ says, using the past tense, that the Father **"sent"** him, to show that he did not arrive as an unknown person. Long ago his Father had earmarked him in the Law and the Prophets, so that he would be recognized when he came with the Father. My explanation is that God witnessed to his Son whenever he offered to the ancient people the hope of salvation or promised that the kingdom of Israel would be completely restored. This is how the Jews would have gained an idea about Christ from the prophets before he was manifested in the flesh. When Christ was in front of their eyes, they despised and rejected him, thus showing their disdain for the law; and Christ reproaches them for this. Yet they boasted about their knowledge of the law, as if they had been educated on God's lap.

"You have never heard his voice." Following his complaint about not being received by them, Christ uses even stronger language against their blindness. He uses the metaphorical expression **"You have never heard his voice nor seen his form"** to make the general statement that they are completely cut off from the knowledge of God. Just as men are known through their appearance and their speech, so God uses **"his voice"** when he speaks to us through the voice of the prophets; and in the sacraments God's voice takes, as it were, a visible **"form"** in which he can be known according to our small capacity. But anyone who does not recognize God in his living image clearly shows that he only worships the deity of his own imagination. This is why Paul says of the Jews, "a veil covers their hearts" (2 Corinthians 3:15), so that they cannot perceive the glory of God in the face of Christ.

38. "Nor does his word dwell in you." We really benefit when God's Word takes root in us, so that it is engraved on our hearts as it takes a firm hold there. Christ says that the heavenly teaching has no place among the Jews because they do not receive the Son of God, whom it proclaims everywhere; and so his reproach on them is just. God did not speak through Moses and the prophets for nothing. All that Moses wanted to do was to invite everyone to go straight to Christ. So, clearly everyone who rejects Christ is no follower of Moses. Moreover, how can people have God's Word living in them when they drive away life itself? How can anyone obey the law's teaching when he destroys the soul of the law as much as he can? Without Christ the law is empty and feeble. So people know Christ depending on their progress in the Word of God.

39. "You diligently study the Scriptures." We have said that Christ's previous statement, about the Father being his witness in heaven, refers to Moses and the prophets. Here is a clearer explanation: Christ says that this witness is found in **"the Scriptures."** Christ again reproves their foolish boasting. While they acknowledged that **"the Scriptures"** possessed eternal life, they only concentrated on the dead letter. Christ does not actually blame them for seeking life in **"the Scriptures,"** for this was the reason why they were given to us. But Christ does blame the Jews for thinking that **"the Scriptures"** gave them **"eternal life,"** while they were so against their real meaning; and, even worse, because they quenched the light of **"life"** which **"the Scriptures"** contained. For how can the law give **"life"** without Christ, who alone can give **"life"**?

This passage also teaches us that if we want to know Christ, we must find out about him from **"the Scriptures."** Those who imagine whatever they want to about Christ end up with nothing other than a shadowy ghost. So first of all, we should believe that Christ cannot be properly known in any way except through **"the Scriptures."** If this is the case, it follows that we should read **"the Scriptures"** with the specific purpose of finding Christ in them. Whoever neglects to do this, even if he wears himself out through a lifetime of learning, will never reach the knowledge of the truth. For what wisdom can we have if it is not God's wisdom?

After telling us to seek Christ in **"the Scriptures,"** he assures us in this passage that our labors will bear fruit. The Father bears witness to his Son in **"the Scriptures"** in such a way that he manifests him to us and leaves no room for doubt. Most people are hampered from benefitting from this because they give this idea no more than superficial thought or cursory attention. But it requires the most careful attention, and for this reason Christ says we must **"diligently study"** for this hidden treasure. Hence the deep abhorrence the Jews have for Christ must be due to their laziness, since they have the law in their hands all the time. The brightness of the glory of God shines brightly in Moses, but the Jews choose to put a veil over this to obscure this brightness. It is well known that **"the Scriptures"** here refer to the Old Testament. For Christ was not manifested first of all in the Gospels; after he had received testimony from the Law and the Prophets, he was openly revealed in the Gospel.

"Yet you refuse to come to me." Christ reproaches them again that nothing but their malice stops them from sharing in the **"life"** which is offered in **"the Scriptures."** When Christ says that they **"refuse"** to come to him, he imputes the reason for their ignorance and blindness to wickedness and obstinacy. They must have been deliberately blind, because Christ offered himself to them so graciously. When they intentionally turned away from the **"light,"** and even tried to put it out with their dark unbelief, Christ properly reproved them more severely.

Verses 41–47

41. "I do not accept praise from men." Christ continues his rebuke. To make sure that he is not accused of pleading his own cause, Christ starts by saying that he does not care about **"praise from men"** and that he is not at all worried or unhappy about being despised himself. Indeed, Christ is too great a person to be dependent on men's opinions, since the malignity of the whole world can take nothing away from him or have the slightest effect on his elevated position. So Christ is keen to refute their malicious attacks in which they say he exalts himself above men. After this Christ attacks them quite openly and charges them with having contempt and hatred towards God. Although we are far less honorable than Christ, we should still courageously despise men's opinions. We should particularly be on our guard against being driven to anger when we are despised. In fact, we should never become indignant except when men do not give God the honor he deserves. This holy jealousy should burn and torture us whenever we see the world ungratefully rejecting God.

42. "You do not have the love of God in your hearts." All religious feelings are included in **"the love of God,"** for nobody can love God without respecting him and entirely submitting to his authority. This is why Moses gives us a summary or recapitulation of the law: "Love the Lord your God with all your heart and with all your soul and with all your strength" (Deuteronomy 6:5).

43. "I have come in my Father's name." False prophets certainly claim this title. Today the Pope loudly boasts that he is Christ's Deputy or Vicar. In this disguise Satan has deceived many unhappy people from the beginning. But here Christ is referring to the real and not to the phony. When Christ testifies that he has come in his **"Father's name,"** he not only means that the **"Father"** has sent him, but that he faithfully carries out the commission he has received. In this way he distinguishes the lawful teachers of the church from the spurious and phony teachers. So this passage teaches us to reject boldly all those who lift themselves up and who in their own name claim to have authority over souls. Anybody who wants to be thought of as God's servant should keep nothing back from God. But if all the papal teaching is examined, even a blind person will see that the Pope has come in his own name.

"If someone else comes in his own name, you will accept him." Because the Jews are eager to welcome false prophets, and yet refuse to obey God, Christ demonstrates that the Jews neither love nor reverence God. For Christ knows that it is a certain sign of evil and ungodly thinking when people ignore the truth and embrace false teaching. There is a simple answer to the argument that this is done through ignorance rather than through malice. No one is exposed to Satan's attacks except that he prefers false teaching to the truth, due to some evil disposition. For how can we be deaf to God's voice and be so ready and willing to follow Satan unless we are opposed to righteousness and personally desire evil?

It should be noted that Christ is mainly referring to people God has specially enlightened, just as he gave this privilege to the Jews, who should have kept to the true way of salvation because they had been taught by the law. The only reason these people listen to false teachers is because they want to be deceived. Moses says that when false teachers appear, God will test the people to see if they love him with all their heart (see Deuteronomy 13:3). Doubtless, many people appear to be guileless and innocent, but their eyes are definitely blinded by the hypocrisy which lurks in their minds. It is certainly true that God never shuts the door on those who knock (see Matthew 7:8) and never lets anyone down who sincerely prays to him (see Isaiah 45:19). So Paul is right in ascribing this acceptance of one who comes in his own name to God's wrath, for power to deceive is given to Satan so "that all will be condemned who have not believed the truth but have delighted in wickedness," and so that "they perish because they refused to love the truth and so be saved" (2 Thessalonians 2:12, 10). Many people who have given themselves over to the false and wicked superstitions of the Pope, and who rant and rage with venom against the Gospel, have their hypocrisy exposed in this way. If their hearts were devoted to living in awe of God, they would have been obedient to him.

44. "How can you believe . . . ?" It might seem harsh to say that people who have been brought up since their childhood as disciples of the Law and the Prophets could be accused of such great ignorance and declared to be enemies of the truth. Because this might seem to be so impossible, Christ explains what stops them from believing. Their ambition has deprived them of sound judgment. For Christ speaks in a special way to the priests and the teachers of the law, who disobey God because they are so inflated with pride. This is a remarkable passage since it teaches that the doorway to faith is shut against all those who are preoccupied with a vain desire for worldly glory. Anybody who wants to become somebody in this world becomes feeble and wanders away from God. Until a person is convinced that the main aim of his whole life should be approved by God, he will never be prepared to obey the heavenly teaching.

It might be thought that the hypocrites' evil assurance, through which they elevate themselves in God's presence, is more of a stumbling block than their worldly ambition. We know that this disease was deeply ingrained in the teachers of the law. But the simple answer is that Christ wanted to expose their false piety, which deceived the ignorant crowds. So Christ points his finger at their greater sin so that everybody could clearly see that what they wanted to be known as could not have been further from who they really were. Moreover, although hypocrisy exalts itself against God, it remains ambitious in the eyes of men and of the world. It is precisely this pride that fills us with false presumption, so that we choose our own judgments and other people's judgments in preference to God's judgments. Anybody who comes into God's presence knowing that God is his Judge has to humbly bow down before God, as he has nothing in himself that he can trust. Anybody who wants to seek God's glory alone is overcome with his own shame and runs to God for his undeserved mercy. Indeed, all those who turn to God realize that they are condemned and lost and that they have nothing to boast about except for Christ's grace. The desire for such glory will always be accompanied by humility.

So far as the present passage is concerned, Christ is saying that there is no other way for people to receive the teaching of the Gospel than by withdrawing all their senses from the world and turning them to God alone. They have to take seriously that they have to deal with God, dispense with their usual flatteries which only deceive them, and go down into their own consciences. So we need not be surprised that the Gospel today finds so few people who are prepared to be taught, since everyone is carried away by ambition. Nor should we be surprised if many people fall away from following the Gospel, as such people are carried away by their own vanity and fly off. So we should seek this one thing even more earnestly, so that while we may be despised in the eyes of the world, and even overwhelmed within ourselves, we may be reckoned among God's children.

45. "But do not think that I will accuse you before the Father." This is how obstinate and hardened people should be dealt with, since they learn nothing from teaching and friendly warnings. They must be brought before God's judgment-seat. Few people may publicly mock God, but many people think that God's favor rests on them while they treat him as their enemy and leisurely amuse themselves with empty, flattering thoughts. In the same way, today's Titans walk all over Christ's teaching and yet proudly go about as if they are God's close friends. For who can persuade the Roman Catholics that Christianity exists anywhere other than with them? The teachers of the law whom Christ was arguing with were just like this. While they despised the law so much, they still proudly boasted about Moses and never hesitated to use him in their arguments against Christ. If Christ had threatened them with being a powerful and strong opponent, he knew that they would have despised this out of hand. So Christ tells them that he will charge them with an accusation that Moses has against them.

"Moses, on whom your hopes are set." Some people think that Christ is here making a distinction between his own office and Moses', since the law convinces people that they are unbelievers. This, however, is wrong. Christ did not mean this, because he only wanted to shake the hypocrites out of their confidence, as they pretended to have such great reverence for Moses. We must also note from this that we should not glory in the Scriptures without having a good reason. For if we do not honor God's Son through the true obedience of faith, everybody whom God has elevated to his witnesses will be against us on the last day. When Christ says, **"Moses, on whom your hopes are set,"** he is not accusing them of trusting Moses in some superstitious way, as if they went to Moses for their salvation, but of wrongly relying on Moses' protection, as if he was their defense for their evil obstinacy.

46. "If you believed Moses, you would believe me." Christ shows that Moses will accuse them, because they rejected his teaching. We know that no greater insult to God's servants can be given than to despise and defame their teaching. Moreover, people who have been appointed by the Lord to be ministers of his Word should be prepared to defend it against those who despise it. So Christ gave a double commission to all his prophets: that they should teach and instruct for the salvation of the believers, and that one day they would defeat the reprobate with their testimony.

"For he wrote about me." Christ's saying that Moses "wrote about me" needs no drawn-out proof for people who acknowledge that Christ is the end and soul of the law. However, if someone is not satisfied with this and wants the passages pointed out to him, I would suggest that he read carefully the Letter to the Hebrews, with which Stephen's sermon in Acts 7 agrees. Then I suggest that he note the quotations which Paul uses in this connection. I agree that there are few quotations of Moses in which Christ is specifically mentioned. But what was the purpose of the tent, the sacrifices, and all the ceremonies if they did not serve as a "copy and shadow of what is in heaven" (Hebrews 8:5; see Exodus 25:40)? So without Christ, the whole ministry of Moses disappears. Again, we note how Moses is always reminding the people about the covenant of the fathers, which had been ratified in Christ, and even how he makes Christ the basis and central theme of the covenant. This was not unknown to the fathers, as they always fixed their eyes on the Mediator. To deal with this subject in more detail would be inconsistent with the brevity which is my aim.

47. "But since you do not believe what he wrote . . ." Christ seems to be claiming less authority for himself than for Moses, even though we know that at that time heaven and earth had been shaken (see Hebrews 12:26) by the voice of the Gospel. But Christ is accommodating his teaching to his listeners. For the authority of the law was, beyond question, held sacred by the Jews. So it was impossible that Christ could be inferior to Moses. The contrast between "what he wrote" and "what I say" is given for the same reason. Christ emphasizes their unbelief in that the truth of God, recorded in an authentic way, had no authority with them.

John
Chapter 6

Verses 1–13

1. Some time after this, Jesus crossed . . . Although John usually recorded the deeds and sayings of Christ which the other three evangelists left out, in this passage, contrary to his custom, he repeats the story of a miracle which the others told. But John does this for the specific reason of moving on to the sermon which Christ preached the next day in Capernaum, as the two events are linked. So this narrative, though common to the other three evangelists, is special because of the different way it is used, as we will see. The other evangelists (see Matthew 14:13; Mark 6:32; Luke 9:10) state that this happened shortly after the death of John the Baptist, by which detail of time they indicate the reason for Christ's leaving. Once tyrants have stained their hand with the blood of godly people, they become even more cruel, just as intemperate drinking intensifies the thirst of drunkards. So Christ wanted to cool Herod's rage by his absence. **The Sea of Galilee** refers to the Sea of Gennesaret. When John adds that it was called **the Sea of Tiberias**, he is explaining in more detail where Christ went, for the whole lake was not called **Tiberias**, but just the part of the lake adjacent to the town of Tiberias.

2. And a great crowd of people followed him. When they saw the power of Christ's miracles, they followed Christ most enthusiastically, as they were sure that he was some great prophet who had been sent from God. The evangelist leaves out here what the other three evangelists record, that Christ used some of the day to teach and heal the sick, and that at sunset his disciples asked him to send the crowds away (see Matthew 14:13-15; Mark 6:34-36; Luke 9:11-12). John thought that it would be enough to give the substance of what happened in a few words, so that he could take this opportunity to lead us on to the rest of the story which followed.

First of all, we see how keen people were to hear Christ, as they were all unconcerned about themselves and quite prepared to spend the night in the desert. So our indifference, or rather sloth, is the more inexcusable when we give way to hunger pangs in preference to heavenly teaching, so that the slightest interruption immediately stops us meditating on the heavenly life. It is very rare for Christ to find us free and disentangled from the world. We are all very far from being prepared to follow Christ to a desert mountain. In fact, hardly one in ten of us could bear to welcome him into the comforts of our homes when he comes. Even though this is a worldwide disease, it is certain that no one is fit for the kingdom of God until he has put aside such indulgence and has learned to desire the food of the soul so much that he is not hampered by his human appetite.

Just as the body demands attention, so we should note that Christ, of his own accord, takes care of those who neglect themselves in order to follow him. Christ does not wait until they are starving and crying out for food because they have nothing to eat, since he provides food for them before they even ask for it. We might be told that this is not always the case, as we often see godly people, who have been completely devoted to the kingdom of God, exhausted and almost faint with hunger. My answer is that even though Christ may be glad to test our faith and patience in this way, he still sees our needs from heaven and is careful to provide for them as far as is expedient for us. When help is not immediately forthcoming, it happens for the best of reasons, even though that reason may be hidden from us.

3. Then Jesus went up on the hillside. Christ undoubtedly sought a place to retreat to until **the Jewish Passover Feast** came. So it is said that he **sat down with his disciples** on the mountainside. This was his purpose, in that he was a man; but God had a different purpose, which Christ was glad to follow. So although he managed to be out of the sight of people, Christ still allowed himself to be led by God's hand into a crowded place. For there were more people on the **hillside** than in any crowded town, and the miracle became better known than if it had been performed in the open market in Tiberias. So this example teaches us to shape our plans in line with the course of events, but after that, if the result is different from what we had expected, not to be angry that God is in control and organizes everything according to his will.

5. He said to Philip . . . What we read here as being said just to Philip, the other evangelists tell us was said to all the disciples. There is no inconsistency here, for Philip probably spoke on behalf of the rest, and so Christ replies to him in particular. In the same way, immediately after this, Andrew is introduced as being the speaker, while the other evangelists attribute these words to all the disciples. Christ sees that the disciples have no thoughts about a miraculous solution, so he wakes up their sleepy minds so that they at least have their eyes open to see what is immediately shown them. Everything that the disciples say is designed to make Christ dismiss the people. Perhaps they are thinking about themselves and do not want to be inconvenienced in this matter. So Christ ignores their objections and proceeds with his plan.

7. "Eight months' wages . . ." [KJV, "two hundred pennyworth (denarii)"]. According to Budaeus' calculations a denarius is worth four *caroli* or two *deniers* of Tours, and so is equivalent to thirty-five francs. If you divided this between five thousand people, each hundred would have seventeen pence. If you add in about one thousand women and children, Philip is allocating to each person about one-sixth of an English penny to buy bread with. **"Not enough bread for each one to have a bite!"** But as is usually the case in a great crowd, he probably overestimated the size of the crowd. Nevertheless, the disciples were poor and ill equipped to supply the money. Andrew wanted to draw Christ's attention to the great sum of money needed, because they did not have the means to entertain so many people.

10. "Have the people sit down." The disciples were stupid and to blame for not being more quick to entertain the hope which their Master gave, and because they did not think of ascribing to his power all that they should have. But they deserve no small praise for cheerfully obeying in carrying out Christ's orders, even though they do not know his intention or how they would benefit from what they were doing. The crowd of people was just as willing to obey, for they all sat down at the single word of command, even though they did not know what would happen. This is the test of genuine faith — when God commands people to walk, as it were, in the darkness. From this we learn not to be wise in ourselves but, in the middle of great confusion, still hope for a happy outcome as we follow God, our guide who never lets his own people down.

11. Gave thanks. More than once, Christ sets us the example of praying before we eat. The things which God has given us to use are evidence of his goodness and his fatherly love for us, and they summon us to praise God. Thanksgiving is a kind of solemn consecration through which what we are given becomes pure to us (see 1 Timothy 4:3-5). So people who eat without giving thanks to God are guilty of sacrilege and of profaning God's gifts. This instruction is worthy of special note since we daily see most of the world eating like brute beasts. Christ was determined that the bread given to the disciples should multiply in their hands, and from this we learn that God blesses our efforts when we serve one another.

We now summarize the meaning of the whole miracle. In common with other miracles, Christ displays his divine power together with his kindness. It also confirms for us Christ's statement when he exhorts us to "seek . . . his kingdom," promising that "all these things will be given to you as well" (Matthew 6:33). If Christ looked after the people who only came to him by a sudden impulse, how can he fail us who seek him with a firm and steady purpose? While it is true, as I have said, that

Christ will sometimes allow his own people to suffer hunger, he will never withhold his help from them. Meanwhile, he has very good reasons for not helping us until the matter becomes desperate.

Moreover, Christ clearly showed that he not only gives spiritual life to the world, but that his Father commanded him to feed the body. Abundance of all blessings is committed to his hand, which, as a channel, he gives to us. I actually speak inaccurately by calling Christ a "channel," as he is rather a living fountain flowing from the eternal Father. In the same way, Paul prays that all blessings may come to us "from God our Father and the Lord Jesus Christ" (1 Corinthians 1:3). And in another passage Paul shows that we should be "always giving thanks to God the Father for everything, in the name of our Lord Jesus Christ" (Ephesians 5:20). This office does not just belong to his eternal divinity, but also to his human nature; and to the extent that he has taken on himself our humanity, the Father has appointed him to dispense food to us through his hands. Although we do not see miracles every day in front of our eyes, God no less generously reveals his power in feeding us. Also, we do not read that Christ used any special means when he wanted to supply supper to his people. So it would be inappropriate for anyone to pray that Christ should use any unusual method to give him food and drink.

Again, Christ did not supply great delicacies for people, but those who witnessed his amazing power in that meal had to be satisfied with barley-bread and fish without any sauce. Although Christ satisfies the hunger of five thousand people with five loaves, he nevertheless continues to feed the whole world in a wonderful way. To us, it seems like a paradox that "man does not live on bread alone but on every word that comes from the mouth of the Lord" (Deuteronomy 8:3). We are so firmly attached to outward means that nothing is as difficult as to depend on God's provision. As soon as we have no bread at hand we start trembling. If we think correctly about it, we are forced to see God's blessing in all food. However, frequent use and familiarity make us undervalue the miracles of nature. However, in this respect it is not so much our stupidity as our malignity which hinders us. For who can find the person who does not prefer to let his mind wander over heaven and earth a hundred times rather than to look at God who offers himself?

13. And filled twelve baskets. When four thousand men were fed through seven loaves, Matthew says that there were the same number of baskets filled with leftovers as there were loaves (see Matthew 15:37). So, if a smaller quantity is enough for more people, and since nearly twice as much is left over, we can clearly see how beneficial God's blessing is against which we deliberately close our eyes. We should also note, in passing, that while Christ commands them to fill **twelve baskets** in order to show that the miracle has taken place, Christ also tells the disciples not to be wasteful when he says, **"Gather the pieces that are left over.**

Let nothing be wasted" (verse 12). God's increased generosity should not lead us into luxury. So people who have plenty should remember that they will have to account for their huge wealth if they do not carefully and faithfully use their abundance for good purposes of which God would approve.

Verses 14–21

14. After the people saw the miraculous sign . . . The miracle appears to have done some good, as they acknowledge that the Messiah is its author; Christ had nothing else in mind than this. But then they immediately go on to use the knowledge which they have just received about Christ to a wrong end. This mistake is very common among men, as they corrupt and pervert Christ's truth by their own lies just as soon as Christ has revealed himself to them. Even when they seem to have started along the correct path, they immediately fall away.

15. Make him king. These men did have some reason for wanting to give Christ the title and honor of king. But they made a flagrant mistake in giving themselves the freedom to **make him king.** Scripture ascribes this to God alone, as it is said, "I have installed my King on Zion, my holy hill" (Psalm 2:6). Again, what kind of kingdom do they imagine he will have? It is an earthly one, which is wholly inconsistent with who he is. So we see how dangerous it is in divine matters to neglect God's Word and to invent anything that comes from our own minds. The perverted cunning of our minds corrupts everything. What good is a show of zeal when through our perverted worship we are insulting God more than if someone were specifically and deliberately attacking his glory?

We are aware how Christ's detractors attempted to smother his glory. Indeed, this violent attack reached its climax when Christ was crucified. However, through Christ's crucifixion the world received salvation, and Christ himself triumphed magnificently over death and Satan. If Christ had allowed them to **make him king** then, his spiritual kingdom would have been ruined, the Gospel would have been stamped with everlasting infamy, and the hope of salvation would have been completely destroyed. Worship and ceremonies made up by the whim of men only serve to rob God of his true honor and heap reproach on him.

By force. We should note this phrase. The evangelist says that **they intended to come and make him king by force.** With impetuous violence they wanted to force him to become **king** against his will. If we want Christ to approve the honor we give him, we should always remember what he desires. Indeed, people who presume to offer God their own made-up honors are guilty of doing him violence. Obedience is the foundation of true worship. We should also learn from this how reverently we should live by the pure and simple Word of God. As soon as we turn away from it in the smallest way, the truth itself is polluted by our leaven, so that it ceases to be itself. From the Word of God they learned that the promised Redeemer would be a **king.** But from their own minds they imagined an earthly kingdom, and so they gave Christ a kingdom that was contrary to the Word of God. Whenever we mix our own thoughts with the Word of God, faith degenerates into superficial conjecture. So believers should cultivate the habit of being humble, in case Satan rushes them into thoughtless and rash zeal so that, like the Titans, they fall headlong against God. God cannot ever be worshiped properly unless we receive him as he presents himself to us.

It is amazing that five thousand men should have been overtaken with the reckless audacity to make Christ **king,** without any hesitation, and so provoke Pilate's army and the vast strength of the Roman empire to be against them. Certainly they would not have gone so far if they had not relied on the predictions of the prophets, hoping that God would be on their side and that, as a result, they would win. But they still went wrong because they were thinking of a kingdom which the prophets never spoke about. So they are far from having God's hand of favor to help them in their quest; on the contrary, Christ withdraws from them. This is also why unhappy men under Roman Catholicism wandered around for so long in deep darkness while God appeared to be absent, because they had dared to pollute all of his worship with their foolish inventions.

16. His disciples went down . . . Clearly, Christ wanted to hide himself until the crowd had dispersed. We know how difficult it is to calm a turbulent crowd. If they had now tried to carry out their intentions openly, it would have been very hard to remove the stain this would have made on Christ. Meanwhile, Christ spent all his time in prayer, as the other evangelists relate (Matthew 14:23; Mark 6:46). Christ was probably asking God the Father to restrain the foolishness of the people. Christ's miraculous crossing of the lake is meant to strengthen his disciples' faith. In addition to this, everyone would readily realize, on the following day, that Christ had not come there by boat or ship but through his own power. For they had blocked the shore from which he would have set out and would hardly have been drawn away from it if they had not seen the disciples cross over at a different point.

17. Now it was dark. John passes over many of the details which the other evangelists include, such as their several hours' struggle against the wind, for this storm probably arose after nightfall. The other evangelists tell us that Christ did not appear until about the fourth watch of the night (Matthew 14:25; Mark 6:48). People who think that the disciples were still in the middle of the lake when Christ appeared to them, because John says that **they had rowed three or three and a half miles** (verse 19), are mistaken if they think this refers to their sailing to the further or opposite shore. For Bethsaida, close to the town where Luke tells us the miracle took place (Luke 9:10), and Capernaum, to which the boat crossed (verse 17), were both sited on the same coastline.

In Pliny's fifth book, he says that this lake was six miles wide and sixteen miles long. In Josephus' third book of the *Jewish Wars*, he says the lake is one hundred furlongs long and forty furlongs wide. Since there are eight furlongs in a mile, we may conclude that these two descriptions are in agreement with each other. As far as this present boat trip is concerned, I believe that they did not sail such a great distance by going directly across the lake but were driven along by the wind. Whatever actually happened, the evangelist wants to show that when Christ showed himself to them, they were in the height of danger. It might seem surprising that the disciples were distressed in this way when the others had a calm trip. But it is often the Lord's way to lead his followers into great danger so that they will recognize him as their deliverer more clearly and intimately.

19. They were terrified. The other evangelists explain that the disciples were afraid because they thought, "It's a ghost!" (Matthew 14:26; see Mark 6:49). People will always be overwhelmed with fear and worry if a ghost appears in front of them. We conclude that this is either a Satanic deception or a bad omen sent by God. John is showing us here, in a mirror, the kind of knowledge about Christ we may receive without sound, and how we may benefit from this knowledge. When Christ presents himself in a straightforward demonstration of his divinity, we immediately go into our imagination, and everyone makes an idol for himself which replaces Christ. Once we have wandered off in our minds, a shaking and confused state of heart immediately follows. But when Christ starts to speak, we immediately receive from his voice clear and dependable knowledge, as well as joy and pleasing peace of mind.

20. "It is I; don't be afraid." There is great weight in these words. From them we learn that it is in Christ's presence alone that we have sufficient grounds for confidence, so that we can be calm and relaxed. This belongs exclusively to Christ's disciples. Later (see 18:6) we will see that basically these same words, **"It is I,"** bowl over wicked men. The reason for this difference is that Christ is sent to be a Judge to the reprobate and unbelievers for their destruction; and therefore they cannot stand in his presence without being completely overwhelmed. But believers, who know that Christ has been given to them for their propitiation, take courage as soon as they hear his name. To them this is a firm pledge both of God's love and of their salvation. It is as if they had been raised from the dead to life, and so they calmly look at the clear sky, live quietly on earth, win over every disaster, and take Christ as their shield in every danger. Christ not only comforts and encourages them by his Word, but he also actually removes the reason for their fear by calming the storm.

Verses 22–25

22. **The next day . . .** The evangelist gives details which would lead the crowds to conclude that Christ had crossed over the lake through his divine power. There had been only one boat, which they had seen leave without Christ. The next day, ships from other places take them to Capernaum, where they find Christ. So it follows that Christ must have arrived there in a miraculous way. There appears to be confusion in what they say, but their meaning is clear enough. In this verse John says that **only one boat had been there**, which everyone had seen set sail from the shore, without Christ on board. In verse 23 John adds that **some boats from Tiberias**, in which the crowds had crossed over, had remained on the shore, blockading, as it were, all exits, so that Christ could not escape.

23. **Near the place where the people had eaten bread.** It is not clear what is meant here. The words could mean that Tiberias was **near the place** where Christ had fed them with five loaves, or it could mean that the boats reached the shore which was near to and below that place. I incline to the latter explanation, since Bethsaida, which was close to where Luke said the miracle took place, is halfway between Tiberias and Capernaum. So boats which sailed down from there sailed along the shore where the crowds were standing. Clearly they landed in order to take passengers on board.

After the Lord had given thanks . . . When John says that Christ gave thanks, he is making an unnecessary repetition. John is stating that as a result of prayer the few loaves were enough to feed the crowd of people, and as we are dull and lazy in prayer, John emphasizes the same thing for a second time.

25. **. . . on the other side of the lake . . .** We have already said that Capernaum was not on the facing shore. Tiberias is sited on the broadest part of the lake, then Bethsaida comes next, and Capernaum lies at the lowest part, not far from where the river Jordan flows into the lake. So when John identifies Capernaum as being **on the other side of the lake**, we should not think that he means directly across the lake; rather, because the lowest part of the lake winds in and out, and because of the bay in between, it was impossible to travel by land except by a very circuitous route. So the evangelist says **on the other side of the lake**, using a normal turn of phrase, because the only direct and normal way to travel was by boat.

Verses 26–29

26. **Jesus answered . . .** Christ does not answer their question in order to show them his power in having arrived there miraculously. On the

contrary, Christ rebukes them for diving in thoughtlessly. They did not know the real reason behind what he did since they looked to Christ for something other than Christ himself. Christ accuses them of seeking him to satisfy their bodily hunger and not because they saw miraculous signs. However, it is undeniable that they had the miracle in mind, and furthermore the evangelist had already said that they had their interest aroused to follow Christ by miracles. But because they used the miracles for the wrong reason, Christ quite rightly accuses them of caring more about their bodily hunger than about miracles. Christ meant that they did not benefit from God's deeds in the way they should have done. If they had benefitted from the miracles correctly, they would have acknowledged Christ as Messiah by surrendering themselves to him to be taught and ruled by him. Under Christ's direction they would have gone into God's heavenly kingdom. But they expected nothing from Christ other than to live happily and comfortably in this world. This robs Christ of his most important power. Christ was given to us by the Father and revealed himself to men so that he could remake them in God's image by giving them his Holy Spirit, and so he could lead them to eternal life, dressed in his righteousness.

So what we see in Christ's miracles is most important. People who do not long for the kingdom of God but are satisfied with the pleasures of this present life seek nothing beyond their bodily appetite. This is how many people today would like to embrace the Gospel, so long as it is free from the bitterness of the cross and only brings human pleasure with it. Indeed, we see many people make a profession of being Christians hoping to live a happier and freer life. So some people claim to be Christ's disciples because they hope to derive benefit from this; others do so out of a sense of fear; and others for the sake of those they want to please. The main reason for seeking Christ is to despise the world and "seek . . . his kingdom and his righteousness" (Matthew 6:33). Moreover, most people persuade themselves that they are seeking Christ from the best of motives while all the time they are debasing his power. So Christ, as he often did, uses the words, **"I tell you the truth,"** as if he were on oath, so he can expose the evil which hides under our hypocrisy.

27. "Do not work for food that spoils." Christ points to eternal life as the goal of our lives. But because the dullness of our understanding keeps us devoted to worldly things, Christ cures this innate disease before he goes on to tell us what to do. The simple teaching would have been, "Work for food that does not spoil." But Christ knew that men's senses are locked into worldly concerns, so he first of all commands them to be untied and freed from these ties so they can ascend to heaven. However, Christ does not forbid his followers from working for their daily food, but he does show that the heavenly life ought to be preferred to this worldly life. The godly have no reason for living here other than that they may travel quickly towards the heavenly country.

Next, we should understand what the point of this is. Since Christ's power is defiled by people who are given over to worldly appetites and worldly things, Christ explains what we should seek from him, and why we should seek it. Christ uses metaphors which are suitable for the situation. If food had not been mentioned, he would have said, without using any metaphor, "You should never be worried about the world, but work to obtain the heavenly life." But because men were rushing to their food like cattle, seeking nothing better than this, Christ delivers his sermon in a metaphorical way and calls everything to do with newness of life "food." We know that our souls are fed by the teaching of the Gospel, as it becomes effective in us through the power of the Spirit. So, as faith is the life of the soul, everything that feeds and promotes faith is likened to "food."

"... that endures to eternal life." Christ says that this kind of food is imperishable and says that it "endures to eternal life," thus telling us that our souls are not given food for just one day but are nourished in the expectation of blessed immortality. For the Lord "who began a good work in you will carry it on to completion until the day of Christ Jesus" (Philippians 1:6). This is why we must receive the gifts of the Spirit, so that they can be down-payments and pledges of eternal life. The reprobate often reject the food they have tasted, so that it does not stay permanently with them, but believing people experience lasting power as they share in the power of the Holy Spirit in God's gifts, which are not temporary but, on the contrary, never fail.

It is a waste of time to infer, as some people do, from the word "work" that we can earn eternal life through our deeds. For as we have said, Christ is using metaphors to encourage people to apply their minds earnestly to meditate on the heavenly life instead of clinging to the world as they usually do. Christ puts this question beyond doubt when he says that he is the one who gives the "food." What we receive as a gift can hardly be won through our own efforts. Although there appears to be real contradiction in these words, the two statements can be easily reconciled. The soul's spiritual food is Christ's free gift, and we must try with all the strength of our heart to share in this great blessing.

"On him God the Father has placed his seal of approval." Here Christ confirms the preceding statement by saying that the Father gave him to us for this reason. The older writers have twisted this passage by insisting that Christ is said to be "sealed" because he bears the stamp and living image of the Father. Christ does not go into abstruse discussions about his eternal being here but explains what he has been commissioned and commanded to do, what his office is in relation to us, and what we should seek and expect from him. Through using an appropriate metaphor, Christ alludes to an old custom. They used to seal with signet rings things they wanted to sanction with their own authority. So, Christ — so that it may not look as if he claimed anything for himself or on account of his own authority — declares that his office was laid on him by the Father and that this decree of the Father was seen, as if a seal had been pressed on him. We can summarize it in this way: not everyone has the ability or right to feed souls with imperishable **"food."** But when Christ appears in public, he not only promises that he will be the author of a great blessing, but that he is approved by God, and that he has been sent to men with God's seal; the mark made by a signet ring is on him.

So it follows that people who want to present their souls to Christ so that they can be fed will not be disappointed. We must realize that life is shown to us in Christ so that we can each aspire to it, not aimlessly but with the knowledge of certain success. At the same time, we are taught that everybody who gives this praise to anyone other than Christ is guilty of doing wrong in God's sight. So it is clear that Roman Catholics are in error in their teaching. As soon as they substitute any way of salvation in Christ's place, which they often do by rubbing out, as it were, Christ's authentic seal, they deface his image. We must learn to preserve for Christ, in purity and in its entirety, everything the Father has given to him, so that we do not fall into such a terrible condemnation.

28. "What must we do to do the works God requires?" The crowd understood well enough that Christ had exhorted them to aim at something higher than the comforts of this present life and that they should not restrict their attention to this world, since God calls them to more worthwhile blessings. But they are partially mistaken in their question because they do not understand what is meant by **"works."** They do not take into account that God gives us, through his Son's hand, everything that is necessary for spiritual life. First of all, they ask what **"must we do"**; then, when they use the expression **"the works God requires,"** they do not understand what they are saying. In this way they show great ignorance about God's grace. And yet they appear to be grumbling about Christ, as if he accused them without reason. "Do you think," they say, "that we do not care about eternal life? Why, then, do you tell us to do what is beyond our ability?" By **"the works God requires,"** we have to understand the deeds God demands and approves of.

29. "The work of God is this . . ." They had spoken about **"works."** Christ reminds them about one **"work"** — that is, faith, by which he means that everything that men do without faith is in vain and useless. Only faith is enough, because God requires that we **"believe."** There is an implied contrast here between "faith" and the **"works"** and efforts of men. It is as if Christ had said, "Men work to no purpose when they try to please God without faith, because they are running off-course and do not go towards the finishing post." This is a remarkable passage, since it shows that even if men strain themselves throughout their lives, they achieve nothing if they do not have faith in Christ as the rule of their life. People who infer from this passage that faith is God's gift are mistaken, for Christ does not show here what God produces in us, but what God wants and requires from us.

We may think it odd that God approves of nothing other than faith; after all, we should not overlook loving our neighbor, and other religious duties should not lose their place and honor. So even if faith heads the list, the other deeds are not superfluous. The answer to this is easy. Faith does not exclude either loving our neighbor or any other good deed, because they are all included within faith itself. Faith is called the only **"work of God,"** because this means that we possess Christ and so become the sons of God in order that he may rule us by his Spirit. So, because Christ does not separate faith from the fruits of faith, we should not be surprised that faith is all that God requires.

". . . to believe in the one he has sent." In chapter 3 we explained the meaning of the word **"believe."** We should always remember, if we are completely to understand the power of faith, who Christ is, in whom we **"believe,"** and why he was given to us by the Father. It is useless to argue from this passage that we are justified by deeds if faith justifies, because faith is called a work. First, it is clear enough that Christ is not speaking literally when he calls faith a **"work,"** in the same way that Paul compares the *law of faith* with the *law of works* (see Romans 3:27). Second, when we affirm that people are not justified by works, we are referring to meritorious works through which people gain God's favor. But faith brings nothing to God. On the contrary, faith places people in God's presence in their poverty and emptiness, so that they can be filled with Christ and his grace. So this is, if we may use the expression, a passive work, for which no reward is given, and it gives people no other righteousness than what they receive from Christ.

Verses 30–33

30. **"What miraculous sign . . . ?"** This wicked question clearly shows the truth of what is said elsewhere: "A wicked and adulterous generation asks for a miraculous sign" (Matthew 12:39). They had been drawn to Christ in the first place through observing his miracles or **"miraculous sign."** Later, because they were amazed at a new **"sign,"** they acknowledged that Christ was the Messiah, and they were determined to make him king. But now they were demanding a **sign** from him as if he were an unknown man. Their ingratitude to God makes them forgetful, and because of their malice they are blind to his power, which they saw in front of their eyes. Clearly they treat with disdain all the miracles they had already seen because Christ does not come up to their expectations or meet their wishes. If Christ had led them to expect worldly happiness, they would have praised him loudly. Doubtless, they would have

hailed him as a prophet, the Messiah, and the Son of God. But because Christ now accuses them of being so addicted to the flesh, they prefer not to listen to him anymore. How many people are like them today! To start with, they assure themselves that Christ will encourage their vices, so they eagerly embrace the Gospel and do not ask for any proof of it. But when they are called on to deny the flesh and to take up the cross, they begin to desert Christ and ask where this Gospel came from. In summary, as soon as Christ does not answer their prayers, he ceases to be their Master.

31. "Our forefathers ate the manna in the desert." From this we see that Christ put his finger on a sore point. He told them that they were like wild animals stuffing their stomachs. They show this evil disposition when they demand that the Messiah feed them. They use wonderful words to praise God for his grace in giving them **"manna,"** but only as a ploy to hide Christ's teaching, in which Christ condemned them for their hunger for perishable food. They contrast this with the wonderful title given to the **"manna"** when it is called **"bread of heaven."** But when the Holy Spirit calls the **"manna"** this (also see Psalm 78:24), it is not with the idea that God fed his people like a herd of cattle and gave them nothing more valuable. So they have no excuse when they wickedly reject the soul's spiritual food which God now offers to them.

32. "I tell you the truth, it is not Moses who has given you the bread from heaven." Christ appears to contradict this quotation from the Psalm, but he is only speaking comparatively. The **"manna"** is called **"the bread from heaven,"** although it is for feeding the body. But the bread which they should really have seen as **"from heaven"** is the bread which feeds the soul. So Christ is contrasting heaven with the world here, because we should only be seeking the imperishable life of the kingdom of heaven. In this passage **"truth"** is contrasted with fiction, as is often done elsewhere. But Christ is considering man's true life or, in other words, what makes him different from brute beasts and the first among his creatures.

"It is my Father who gives you the true bread from heaven." By adding these words, Christ means, "The manna which Moses gave to your fathers did not bring heavenly life, but now heavenly life is really shown you." While it is true that Christ says that it is the **"Father"** who gives **"the true bread,"** Christ actually means that the bread is given by his own hand. So the contrast is not between Moses and God, but between Moses and Christ. Christ says that it is his **"Father,"** rather than himself, who is the author of this gift so that he can win deeper reverence for himself. It is as if he said, "Recognize me as God's minister, through whose hand God wants to feed your souls to eternal life." However, this again appears to contradict Paul's teaching when he calls the manna "spiritual food" (1 Corinthians 10:3). My answer to this is that Christ is speaking in a way his hearers can understand, which often happens in Scripture. We can see, for example, that Paul speaks about circumcision in a variety of ways. When he writes about this ordinance he calls it, "a seal . . . of faith" (Romans 4:11); but when he has to argue with false apostles, he calls it a seal of cursing. When Christ did a similar thing here, he was using his hearers' own ideas. We will now consider the objection leveled against Christ: he would not be considered to be the Messiah if he did not supply his followers with bodily food. So Christ does not ask what the **"manna"** represented but insists that the bread which Moses fed the stomachs with was not **"true bread."**

33. "For the bread of God . . ." Christ reasons negatively from the definition to the thing defined in the following way: "The heavenly bread is what comes down from heaven to give life to the world. The manna did not possess anything like this. Therefore, the manna was not heavenly bread." But simultaneously Christ confirms what he had already said — namely, that he was sent by the Father so that he may feed men in a way that is superior to Moses. While it is true that the **"manna"** did come down from the visible heaven — that is, from the clouds, it did not come from the eternal kingdom of God, from where life flows to us. And the Jews Christ was talking with looked no further than their forefathers' stomachs which were stuffed and fattened in the desert.

What he had previously called **"the bread from heaven"** he now calls **"the bread of God."** This is not because the bread which sustains us in this life comes from anywhere but God, but because what gives life to the soul for blessed immortality can alone be thought of as **"the bread of God."** This passage teaches that the whole world is dead to God except where Christ gives it life, because life can be found nowhere apart from Christ.

". . . who comes down from heaven." There are two things to note about **"comes down from heaven."** First, our divine life is in Christ, because he has come from God in order to be the author of life in us; second, the heavenly life is close to us, so that we do not need to travel beyond the skies or across the sea (see Deuteronomy 30:12-13; Romans 10:6-8). Christ **"comes down"** to us because we cannot go up to him.

Verses 34–40

34. "From now on give us this bread." Undoubtedly they are speaking in a sarcastic way, accusing Christ of making empty boasts when he says that he can give them **the bread of life.** These miserable people reject God's promises, and, not content with this evil alone, they even accuse Christ with their own unbelief.

35. "I am the bread of life." First, Christ shows that **"the bread"**

which they ask about in mocking tones is in front of their eyes. Next, Christ rebukes them. Christ starts teaching them, in order to make it clear that they are ungrateful. This teaching has two parts to it. Christ explains where we should seek this **"life"** and also how we can enjoy this **"life."** We know that Christ used these metaphors because **"manna"** and daily **"food"** had been mentioned. This metaphor is even more apt to teach ignorant people than straightforward speech. When we eat bread to nourish our bodies, we can clearly see not only our own weakness but also the power of divine grace, which we would not be so aware of without the bread — that is, if God decided to feed our bodies miraculously. So the analogy taken from the body and the soul clearly shows us Christ's grace. As we learn that Christ is **"the bread"** which feeds our souls, this penetrates more deeply into our hearts than if Christ had just said that he is our **"life."**

However, we should note that the word **"bread"** does not express Christ's power to bring us alive as much as we experience it. Bread does not give life but sustains life which already exists. Through Christ's kindness we not only continue to possess life but have been given life itself, and so this comparison is not entirely appropriate. However, it is not inconsistent, because Christ adapts his method to suit the details of the teaching he has already given. The question has been raised: out of Moses and Christ, who is the most important in feeding men? This is why Christ only calls it **"bread,"** because they only objected to the **"manna"**; so Christ thought that it would be sufficient to contrast it with another kind of bread. The straightforward teaching is: "our souls do not live by what can be called an intrinsic power, by a power which is innate in our souls, but from life taken from Christ."

"He who comes to me . . ." Christ now explains how to eat this food. It is as we receive Christ by faith. Just because Christ is **"the bread of life"** does not in itself help unbelievers, because they still remain empty. But Christ does become our **"bread"** when we come to him as hungry people so that he may fill us. "To come to Christ" and "to believe" mean the same thing here. The former phrase expresses the effect of faith — namely, that we run to Christ for life out of a sense of hunger.

People who infer from this passage that eating Christ is the same as faith, rather than anything else, are not thinking straight. I readily agree that there is no other way to "eat" Christ than to believe, but the eating is the effect and fruit of faith, and not faith itself. Faith does not just look at Christ from a distance but embraces him, so that he becomes ours and lives in us. This makes us united with him, and we share a common life and, in summary, are one with him (see 17:21). So it is true that by faith alone we eat Christ, so long as we understand how faith unites us to him.

". . . will never be thirsty." This seems to be added for no apparent reason, since bread does not quench thirst but satisfies hunger. So Christ is giving a wider meaning to bread than nature permits. I have already mentioned that he only uses the word **"bread"** because the comparison between **"manna"** and the heavenly power of Christ, which sustains our souls, demands this. At the same time, Christ uses the word **"bread"** to refer to everything that nourishes us, as was normally used by his nation. The Hebrews, through the figure of speech in which a part is taken for the whole, use the word "bread" to include "dinner" or "supper." When we pray to God for "our daily bread" (see Matthew 6:11), we include drink and everything else that sustains life. So the meaning is: "whoever comes to Christ for life will not lack anything, but will have plenty of everything that sustains life."

36. "But as I told you . . ." Christ now rebukes them for rejecting God's gift, which is an offer to them. Anybody who rejects what he knows to be given him by God is accused of holding God in wicked contempt. Their guilt might have been mitigated by a plea of ignorance if Christ had not made known his power and clearly shown that he had come from God. But when they reject the teaching of the One they had previously acknowledged to be the Lord's Messiah, their plea is completely groundless. It is undoubtedly true that men never deliberately and purposely reject Christ. As Paul says, "None of the rulers of this age understood it, for if they had, they would not have crucified the Lord of glory" (1 Corinthians 2:8). But unbelievers voluntarily close their eyes to the light and are justly said to see what immediately vanishes from their sight because Satan darkens their minds. At least this is beyond dispute: when Christ said that **"you have seen me,"** he was not referring to his physical body, but he was describing their deliberate blindness, because they could have known who he was if their malice had not stopped them.

37. "All that the Father gives me . . ." To make sure that their unbelief does not take anything away from his teaching, Christ says that the reason for their obstinacy is that they are reprobate and do not belong to God's flock. So Christ is here distinguishing between the elect and the reprobate, so that his authoritative teaching is not undermined even though many people do not believe it. On the one hand, ungodly men may malign and utterly despise the Word of God because they have no reverence for it; and on the other hand, many feeble and ignorant people doubt whether what is rejected by a large part of the world is actually the Word of God. Christ deals with this objection when he affirms that everyone who does not believe does not belong to him, and we should not be surprised that these kind of people have no appetite for the Word of God, although it is embraced by the children of God. In the first place, Christ says, **"All that the Father gives me will come to me."** By this Christ means that faith is not dependent on man's will, as if this man or that man may believe indiscriminately, as if by chance, because he elects those people he gives, as it were, to his Son. When Christ says, **"All that**

the Father gives me will come to me," we conclude that everyone will not come. We also infer from this that God works so effectively in his elect that none of them fall away. For the word **"gives"** has the same meaning as if Christ had said, "People whom the Father has chosen he regenerates and gives to me, so that they may obey the Gospel."

"And whoever comes to me I will never drive away." This is added to comfort the godly, so that they can be completely sure that they have free access to Christ by faith, and that as soon as they have placed themselves under his protection and care, they will be graciously received by him. So it follows that the teaching of the Gospel is a salutary lesson to all believers, because no one becomes Christ's disciple who does not feel and experience Christ as his true and faithful teacher.

38. **"For I have come down from heaven."** This confirms the previous statement that we do not seek Christ in vain. Faith is God's work, through which he shows that we are his people and appoints his Son to protect our salvation. The Son has no other mission than to fulfill his Father's commands. So Christ never rejects those whom his Father has sent. In conclusion, it follows that faith is never useless. The distinction which Christ makes between his own will and his Father's will in this respect is made as an accommodation to his hearers. Since man's mind is naturally distrustful, we are prone to invent something that causes us to doubt. To take away all excuse for such wicked thoughts, Christ declares that he has been shown to the world so that he may actually ratify what the Father has decreed about our salvation.

39. **"And this is the will of him who sent me . . ."** Christ now testifies that this is his Father's **"will"**: that believers may find salvation securely in Christ. Again, it follows from this that everyone who does not benefit from the teaching of the Gospel is a reprobate. So if we see that this causes the destruction of many people, we should not be despondent, because such people voluntarily bring this evil down on themselves. We should remain satisfied that the Gospel always has the power to draw the elect to salvation.

". . . that I shall lose none of all that he has given me." This means, ". . . that I should not allow anyone to be taken away from me or perish." So Christ is not the guardian of our salvation for just one day, or even for a few days, but he will take care of our salvation to the end. He will accompany us, as it were, from the start to the finish of our journey, and so he mentions here the final resurrection. This promise is most necessary for us, as we labor wretchedly under the great weakness of the flesh, about which we are all fully aware. Indeed, the salvation of the whole world might be in jeopardy at any time if believers were not supported by Christ's hand and so able to boldly advance to the day of resurrection. So let this become fixed in our minds, that Christ has stretched out his hands to us, that he will not desert us in mid-stream, but that as we rely on his goodness we may confidently raise our eyes to the final day.

Christ also mentions the final resurrection for another reason. It is because so long as our life is hidden (see Colossians 3:3) we are like dead people. For how do believers differ from wicked people except that they are overwhelmed with affliction and are like sheep ready for the slaughter (see Romans 8:36) and always have one foot in the grave and, indeed, are never far from being swallowed up by death? Nothing else can support our faith and patience than this: we do not look at the state of this present life but concentrate our minds and senses on the final day and pass through the world's distractions until the fruit of our faith finally appears.

40. "For my Father's will is . . ." Christ had said that the Father had entrusted him with the work of protecting our salvation, and now he describes how this is done. Therefore, the way to obtain salvation is to obey the Gospel of Christ. He had briefly made this point before, but now he goes into more detail about what he had only touched on. If it is God's will that the people he has elected should be saved, and if he ratifies and carries out his eternal wish in this way, anybody who is not content with Christ but goes into strange questions about eternal predestination is trying to be saved, insofar as he has power to do this, in a different way from what God desires. God's election is itself hidden and secret. The Lord reveals it through calling us to receive this blessing.

So people who seek their own salvation, and other people's salvation, in the whirlpool of predestination and do not keep to the way of salvation which is shown to them are mad. What is more, through this foolish speculation they try to neutralize the power of predestination. For if God has elected that we might believe, to take away faith and election would be imperfect. But it is wrong to break the unbroken and ordained order of the beginning and the end of God's decrees. Moreover, since the election of God brings his calling with it as an inseparable bond, it is the same when God has effectually called us to faith in Christ. It should have as much force with us as if he had ratified his decree about our salvation with an engraved seal. The witness of the Holy Spirit is nothing other than the sealing of our adoption (see Romans 8:15). So each person's faith is enough attestation to the eternal predestination of God, and it would be an impertinent sacrilege to delve deeper. Anybody who refuses to assent to the Holy Spirit's straightforward testimony is doing him a serious injury.

"Everyone who looks to the Son and believes in him . . ." Christ uses the words "look" and "believe" to contrast with what he had said before. He had told the Jews off for not believing even though they had seen him (verse 36). But now, referring to the sons of God, he links the obedience of faith to their sense of divine power in Christ. Moreover, these words show that faith comes from the knowledge of Christ. It does not want anything more than the simple Word of God; but when we trust Christ, we must see who he is and what he brings us.

Verses 41–45

41. The Jews began to grumble about him. The evangelist says that the Jews murmured because they took offense at Christ's lowly human form and so did not see anything divine or heavenly about him. Christ shows that they had two problems. They had made up a wrong idea when they said, **"Is this not Jesus, the son of Joseph, whose father and mother we know?"** (verse 42). Their other mistake came from an evil thought — they did not believe that Christ was the Son of God, because he came down to men clothed in our flesh. But we are guilty of being excessively malign if we despise the Lord of glory, because it was on our account that he "made himself nothing, taking the very nature of a servant, being made in human likeness" (Philippians 2:7). In reality this was a vivid demonstration of his boundless love for us and of his wonderful grace. Moreover, Christ's divine majesty was not so concealed under the lowly and contemptible appearance of the flesh that it failed to shine out rays of his brightness in a variety of ways. But those evil and stupid men did not have the sight to see his obvious glory.

We, also, sin, every day in both of these ways. First, it greatly handicaps us that we only view Christ with our physical eyes. This is why we see nothing wonderful in him, since through our sinful outlook we pervert everything that belongs to him and to his teaching, and so we derive no benefit from this, and we view nothing in the correct way. Second, not content with this, we adopt many false ideas which make us contemptuous of the Gospel. Some people even imagine monstrous ideas about the Gospel just in order to give them a reason for rejecting the Gospel. This is how the world deliberately drives away God's grace. The evangelist especially mentions the Jews, so that we might know that this grumbling came from the people who boasted that they had faith and were the church. From this we can all learn to receive Christ reverently when he comes down to us and can learn that the closer he comes to us, the more happily we approach him, so that he may raise us to his heavenly glory.

43. "Stop grumbling among yourselves." Christ puts the blame for **"grumbling"** on them, as if he had said, "My teaching contains nothing that gives offense, but because you are reprobate, it irritates your poisonous hearts, and you do not like this because you have a warped taste."

44. "No one can come to me unless the Father who sent me draws him." Christ does not just accuse them of wickedness, but also reminds them that the embracing of this special teaching which they have seen in him is also a gift of God. Christ does this so that their unbelief may not disturb weak minds. Some people are so ignorant about the things concerning God that they depend on other people's opinions. Consequently, they have doubts about the Gospel as soon as they see that it is not received by the world. Unbelievers, on the other hand, flatter themselves about their obstinacy and have the audacity to condemn the Gospel because it does not appeal to them. In contrast with this, Christ declares that the teaching of the Gospel, although it is preached to everyone without exception, cannot be embraced by everyone, but that a new understanding and new perception is needed. Therefore, faith is not dependent on man's will, since it is a gift from God.

"Unless the Father . . . draws him." "Coming to Christ" is here used metaphorically for believing. So that the evangelist can apply this metaphor to the opposite clause, he says that people are "drawn" when their minds are enlightened by God and when their hearts bend in obedience to Christ. What this statement amounts to is this: we should not be surprised if many people refuse to embrace the Gospel, since no one is ever able of himself to come to Christ unless God first comes to him by his Spirit. So it follows from this that not everyone is drawn, but that God gives this grace to those whom he has elected. This is not the kind of drawing that is violent, as if it were compelling men through external force. However, it is a powerful impulse of the Holy Spirit which enables men to be willing to follow Christ, men who had been unwilling and reluctant previously. Therefore, it is a false and ungodly assertion that nobody is drawn unless they are prepared to be drawn, as if a person could make himself obey God through his own efforts. Men's willingness to follow God has already been given to them by God, who made their hearts to obey him.

45. "It is written in the Prophets . . ." Through Isaiah's witness Christ confirms that "No one can come to me unless the Father who sent me draws him" (verse 44). Christ refers to "the Prophets" in the plural, since all their prophecies had been put into one volume, so that all "the Prophets" could be correctly thought of as being just one book. The passage quoted here is from Isaiah 54:13, where, speaking about the restoration of the church, God promises her, "your sons will be taught by the Lord." So it can be easily inferred that the church can only be restored when God becomes its teacher, thus bringing believers to himself. The kind of teaching which the prophet is referring to is not just an external voice, but rather the secret work of the Holy Spirit. In summary, this teaching of God is the inner illumination of the heart.

"They will all be taught by God." The word "all" must be limited to the elect, as only they are the true children of the church. It is not hard to see how Christ applies this prediction to the matter in hand. Isaiah says that the church is only truly edified when her children are taught by God. Therefore, Christ correctly concludes that men do not have eyes to see the light of life until God opens them. But at the same time he attaches the word **"all"** to the general term. He does this because he argues that **"all"** who are **"taught by God"** are effectually drawn, so that they come. This links up with what he says next.

"Everyone who listens to the Father . . ." What this amounts to is that everyone who does not believe is reprobate and doomed to destruction, for all the sons of the church and heirs of life are made by God to be his obedient disciples. From this it follows that not one of God's elect will not share faith in Christ. Again, just as Christ previously said that not everyone is suitable for believing until they have been drawn, so he now declares that the grace of Christ by which they are drawn is effective, so that they necessarily believe.

These two clauses completely overturn the whole ideal of free will, about which the Roman Catholics dream. If we do not start to come to Christ until we have been drawn by the Father, neither the beginning of faith nor the preparation of faith lies in us. But if everyone comes whom the Father has taught, Christ gives them both the choice to believe and to have faith itself. When we willingly yield to the guidance of the Spirit, this is a part and, as it were, a sealing of grace. For God would not draw us if he just stretched out his hand and left our will suspended in the air. But he is properly said to draw us when he extends the power of his Spirit to the full effect of faith. People are said to hear God who willingly assent to God's speaking within them, because the Holy Spirit reigns in their hearts.

". . . comes to me." Christ shows that he and the Father are inseparably linked. This means that it is impossible for God's disciples not to obey Christ and that those who refuse Christ refuse to be **"taught by God."** The only wisdom that all the elect learn in the school of God is to come to Christ, for the Father, who sent Christ, cannot deny himself.

Verses 46–51

46. "No one has seen the Father." As Christ had previously magnified the grace of his Father, so now he earnestly points believers to himself alone, for these two things must be joined. Knowledge of Christ cannot be received until the Father enlightens by his Spirit those who are blind by nature. However, it is pointless to seek God unless Christ leads the way, for God's majesty is so much higher than any of man's senses can reach. What is more, all the knowledge about God which men think that they have acquired outside Christ will be a deadly abyss. When Christ says that he alone has known the Father, he means that his office is special to himself: to show God to people, for God would otherwise have been concealed.

47. ". . . he who believes . . ." This explains the previous sentence. These words teach us that when we believe in Christ, God is made known to us. From then on we begin to see, as in a mirror or as in a bright and living image, God who has been previously invisible. So everything that is said to us about God is cursed if it does not lead us to Christ. I have already explained who should believe in Christ. We must not think of a confused and hollow faith which deprives Christ of his power, as the Roman Catholics do, who believe in Christ in the way that suits them. The reason we obtain life by faith is that we know that every part of our lives is contained in Christ.

The inference which some draw from this passage — that to believe in Christ is the same thing as to eat Christ or his flesh — is not well-founded. These two things are as different as the beginning is different from the end. In the same way, to come to Christ and to drink Christ differ from each other, because coming to Christ must happen first. I agree that Christ cannot be eaten except by faith. But the reason for this is that we receive him by faith, that he may live in us and that we may be made to share in him and thus be united to him. Therefore, to eat Christ is the effect or work of faith.

48. "I am the bread of life." In addition to what Christ has already said, that he is the life-giving **"bread"** through which our souls are nourished, he now goes on to explain this more fully and repeats the contrast between this "bread" and the ancient **"manna,"** as well as comparing the men concerned.

49. "Your fathers ate the manna in the desert, yet they died." Christ says that the **"manna"** which their **"fathers"** ate was a physical food which did not save them from death. So it follows that souls find in Christ alone the food which gives them spiritual life. Moreover, we must bear in mind what I have already said, that what is said here does not relate to the **"manna"** as a secret reference to Christ. For in that respect Paul calls it "spiritual food" (1 Corinthians 10:3). We have said that Christ accommodates himself to his hearers, who are only concerned about feeding their stomachs and look for nothing else in the **"manna."** So Christ is right to say that their fathers are dead — that is, those who were obsessed in the same way by their stomachs or, in other words, whose thoughts never went higher than this world. And yet Christ invites them to eat when he says that he has come so that any man can eat. It is as if he said that he is prepared to give himself to everyone so long as they are willing to believe. That none of the people who have once eaten Christ shall die must mean that the life which Christ gives us is never put out, as we said in chapter 5.

51. "I am the living bread." Christ often repeats the same thing, as nothing needs to be known as much as this. Everyone experiences for himself how difficult it is to believe, and how quickly it passes away and is forgotten. We all want life; but as we seek it, we foolishly and wrongly wander around circuitous routes. When life is offered, most people disdainfully reject it. Who does not try to lead a life for himself outside Christ? And how few people are satisfied with Christ alone! So it is not mere repetition when Christ so often asserts that he alone can give life. He claims for himself the name **"bread"** in order to rip out from our hearts all false hopes about living. Having previously called himself **"the bread of life"** (verse 35), he now calls himself **"the living bread that came down from heaven."** Christ often mentioned "coming down from heaven," because spiritual and imperishable life cannot be found in this world, where life passes away and vanishes; it can only be found in God's heavenly kingdom.

"If a man eats of this bread . . ." Whenever Christ uses this word "eat," he exhorts us to have faith, which alone enables us to enjoy this **"bread"** and so have life from it. Christ has a good reason for doing this, as only a few people deign to stretch out their hand to put this **"bread"** into their mouth. And even when the Lord puts it into their mouth, few people relish its taste, as some are filled with wind, and others, like Tantalus, die of hunger through their own folly, even while the food is next to them.

"This bread is my flesh, which I give." Since this secret power to give life, which he has spoken about, might be referred to his divine essence, he now comes to the second step and shows that this life lives in his **"flesh,"** so that it may be drawn from it. Without doubt it is God's wonderful purpose that he has shown life to us in this **"flesh,"** which beforehand had been the cause of death. In this way he makes allowances for our weakness, as he does not call us beyond the clouds to enjoy life, but displays it on earth, in the same way as if he were raising us to the secrets of his kingdom. While Christ tries to correct our proud minds, he tests the humility and obedience of our faith when he orders those who want to seek life to place their trust in his **"flesh,"** which has a contemptible appearance.

But it is objected that Christ's **"flesh"** cannot give life because it was liable to death, and because even now it is not immortal in itself. In addition to this, it does not belong in any way to the nature of flesh to give life to souls. My reply to this is that although this power comes from a source other than the flesh, there is no reason why this name should not be given to it. Just as the eternal Word of God is the fountain of "life" (see 1:4), so Christ's **"flesh"** is a channel which brings us that life which resides intrinsically, as we say, in his divinity. This is the sense in which it is called life-giving, because it brings us that life which it borrows from another source. This is not hard to understand if we recall what is the reason for life — namely, righteousness. Although righteousness flows from God alone, we will never receive its complete manifestation anywhere outside the **"flesh"** of Christ. In it man's redemption was accomplished, in it a sacrifice for sins was offered, and in it an obedience was given to God to reconcile him to us. This righteousness was also filled with the sanctification of the Spirit, and finally, after it had defeated death, it was received into the heavenly glory. So it follows that every part of life is placed in it and that no one has any reason for complaining that he is deprived of life because it is hidden and far off.

"... which I give for the life of the world." The word "give" is used in different ways. The first giving, which Christ previously spoke about, is made daily, whenever Christ offers himself to us. Secondly, it denotes that singular giving which happened on the cross, when Christ offered himself as a sacrifice to his Father. There he delivered himself up to death for the life of men, and now he invites us to enjoy the fruit of his death. For we would derive no benefit from that sacrifice, which was offered once, if we did not now feast on that sacred banquet. It should be noted that Christ claims for himself the role of sacrificing his **"flesh."** This shows up the evil sacrilege that the Roman Catholics defile themselves with when they take on themselves in the Mass what belongs exclusively to that one High Priest.

Verses 52–58

52. Then the Jews began to argue sharply among themselves. Christ mentions the Jews again, not to honor them but to reproach them for their unbelief. They did not accept the well-known teaching about eternal life, or at least did not look into it carefully, if it was at all obscure or uncertain. When it says that they **began to argue sharply,** it shows obstinacy and contempt. People who argue so sharply do indeed divert themselves from the road to the knowledge of the truth. But they are not blamed for looking into the matter, or else Abraham and the blessed Virgin would also be guilty (see Genesis 15:2; Luke 1:34). So these people are either led astray through ignorance or are lacking in frankness as they overlook the passion and frankness of the argument, which is all that the evangelist condemns; they put all their effort into attacking the word **"how,"** as if it had been unlawful for the Jews to ask about the way to eat the flesh of Christ.

If we deliberately and knowingly leave unresolved the doubts and difficulties which are taken away by the Word of the Lord, we are being lazy, rather than showing the obedience of faith. Not only is it lawful to ask about the way of eating the **"flesh"** of Christ, but it is very important to understand it, insofar as the Scriptures make it known. Let us move away from the fierce and obstinate pretense of humility which says, "For my part I am satisfied with Christ's Word alone when he declares that his **flesh is real food** (verse 55). I will happily close my eyes to everything else" — as if heretics would not have the same excuse when they are deliberately ignorant about Christ being conceived by the Holy Spirit because they believe that he was from the seed of Abraham and make no more inquiry. We must show caution about these secret deeds of God and not wish to know more than God's Word allows.

53. "I tell you the truth . . ." When Christ saw his grace rejected with such high-handed disdain, he was right to use this solemn oath. Christ is not just using straightforward teaching but mingles threats with it to terrify them. He pronounces eternal perdition on everyone who refuses to seek life from his **"flesh."** It is as if he said: "If you hold my flesh in contempt, you can be sure that you have no other hope of life." The judgment which is in store for everyone who despises Christ's grace is that they will perish in their pride. They are severely and roundly rebuked so that they will not continue to flatter themselves. If we say to ill people that they will die if they do not take their medicine, what can we do with evil people when they work with all their might to destroy life itself?

"Unless you eat the flesh of the Son of Man . . ." Christ emphasizes the phrase **"the flesh of the Son of Man"** so that he can reprove them for their contempt, because they thought Christ was just like everyone else. So the meaning here is: "You can despise me as much as you like on the grounds of the lowly and despicable appearance of my flesh, but that flesh that you despise contains life. If you do not have this life, you will not find anything else to give you life."

The ancients made the serious mistake of believing that small children were deprived of eternal life if they were not given the Eucharist — that is, the Lord's Supper. However, this discussion is not about the Lord's Supper but about uninterrupted communion from the **"flesh"** of Christ, which we receive apart from reception at the Lord's Supper. The Hussites were not correct when they used this passage to prove that everyone without exception should be allowed to receive the cup. As far as young children are concerned, Christ's ordinance forbids them to share in the Lord's Supper, because they are not yet able to know or to celebrate the remembrance of the death of Christ.

54. "Whoever eats my flesh . . ." This is a repetition, but it is not superfluous, because it confirms what is hard to believe — that souls feed on his **"flesh"** and **"blood"** in exactly the same way as the body is sustained by eating and drinking. So, as he recently stated that nothing but death remains for everyone who seeks life anywhere else than in his **"flesh,"** so now he encourages all believers to a good hope, as he promises them **"life"** in the same **"flesh."**

"And I will raise him up at the last day." It should be noted that Christ often links the resurrection with eternal life, because our salvation will be hidden until that day. So, we cannot understand what Christ gives us unless we rise above the world and train our eyes on the last resurrection. These words show us that it is a false interpretation to apply this passage to the Lord's Supper. If it was true that everyone who attended the Lord's holy table shared his body and **"blood,"** then, in the same way, everyone would receive life. But we know that many people who take part in the Lord's Supper are condemned. Indeed, it would have been stupid and senseless to talk about the Lord's Supper before it had been instituted. Clearly, Christ is speaking here about the constant and ordinary eating of the **"flesh"** of Christ, which is done only by faith.

However, I do agree that everything that is said here can be figuratively applied to the Lord's Supper, where believers can receive such blessings. Christ wanted the holy Supper to be, as it were, a seal and confirmation of this teaching. This is why the evangelist John does not mention the Lord's Supper. And so Augustine follows the correct order as he explains this chapter and does not mention the Lord's Supper until the end. He then shows that this mystery is represented symbolically whenever the churches celebrate the Lord's Supper — in some places daily, and in other places only on the Lord's day.

55. "My flesh is real food." Christ is saying, "As the body is weakened and consumed by lack of food, so the soul, if it is not fed with heavenly bread, will soon die of hunger." When Christ declares that his **"flesh is real food,"** he means that souls are starving if they do not have this **"food."** Thus you will only find life in Christ when you seek the **"food"** of **"life"** in his **"flesh."** So with Paul we should glory in nothing except "Christ and him crucified" (1 Corinthians 2:2). As soon as we move away from Christ's sacrificial death, we are faced with nothing other than death. There is no other way to understand his divine power than through his death and resurrection. Therefore, embrace Christ as a "servant" (Isaiah 42:1) of the Father, so that he may reveal himself to you as "the author of life" (Acts 3:15). For when Christ "made himself nothing" (Philippians 2:7), we were enriched with the abundance of all his blessings. Christ's humiliation and going down to hell raised us up to heaven. Because Christ endured the curse of his cross, he lifted up the banner of our righteousness as a splendid memorial of his victory. So people who misinterpret the mystery of the Lord's Supper draw souls away from Christ's **"flesh."**

"My blood is real drink." Why does Christ mention his **"blood"** separately though it is included in his **"flesh"**? My answer is that he did so to help us in our weakness. When he specifically mentions **"food"** and **"drink,"** Christ is declaring that the **"life"** he gives is complete in every way, and so we are not to envisage an imperfect or incomplete life. It is as if Christ says that we will not lack anything in life so long as we eat his **"flesh"** and drink his **"blood."** In the same way, in the Lord's Supper, which corresponds to this teaching, Christ is not content with the symbol of the bread, and so he adds the cup. So in Christ we have this double pledge, and we must learn to be satisfied with him alone, for only a person who has his complete and entire life in Christ will find life in him.

56. "Whoever eats my flesh . . ." Here is another confirmation. While Christ alone has life in himself, he shows us how we may enjoy it by eating his **"flesh."** It is as if he is saying that he can only become our life when our faith is directed to his **"flesh."** Nobody will ever go to Christ as God who despises Christ as a man. So if you want to be united with Christ, you must be careful, above everything else, that you do not despise his **"flesh."**

". . . remains in me, and I in him." When we say that he **remains** in us, we are saying that we are united to Christ. We become one with Christ when our faith relies on his death. Similarly, we infer that Christ is not speaking here about an outward symbol, which many unbelievers receive alongside believers even though they continue to be separated from Christ. So we can refute the mistaken idea of those who say that Judas received the body of Christ along with the other disciples when Christ gave bread to them all. It reveals a lack of understanding to limit this teaching to an outward sign, and so we must remember what I have already said, that this teaching is sealed in the Lord's Supper. We note, firstly, that Judas was never a member of Christ. Secondly, it is totally wrong to imagine that the **"flesh"** of Christ is dead and devoid of the Holy Spirit. Lastly, it is a ridiculous dream to eat the **"flesh"** of Christ without faith, since faith alone is, as it were, the mouth and the stomach of the soul.

57. "Just as the living Father sent me . . ." Up to now Christ has explained how we must become sharers in life. Now he moves on to the principal cause, since the beginning of life is the **"Father."** But he meets the objection that this might imply that Christ is taking away from God something that belonged to him when he made himself the cause of life. So he makes himself the author of life in such a way that it is clear that what he administers to others he had himself received.

We note that Christ adapts his sermon to the limits of his hearers, for Christ only compares himself with the **"Father"** as far as his **"flesh"** is concerned. Though the **"Father"** is the beginning of life, the eternal Word himself is actually life. But the external divinity of Christ is not under discussion here, for Christ shows himself to the world, clothed in our flesh.

"I live because of the Father." This does not apply just to his divinity or to his human nature, but to the Son of God as manifested in the flesh. Moreover, we know that it is not unusual for Christ to ascribe to **"the Father"** everything divine which he himself had. We should note that he lists three degrees of life. In the first place he is **"the living Father,"** who is the source, although he is far away and hidden. Next comes the Son, who is shown to us as an open fountain from whom life flows to us. Thirdly, there is the life which we draw from him. Now we understand what is being said: God the **"Father,"** in whom life lives, is a long way away from us, and Christ, the second cause of life, has been placed between him and us, so that what would otherwise be hidden in God may flow from him to us.

58. "This is the bread that came down from heaven." Christ returns to the comparison between the **"manna"** and his **"flesh,"** which is where he started. He had to end his sermon like this: "There is no reason why you should prefer Moses to me because he fed your fathers in the desert. I give you far better food, for I bring heavenly life with me." As has already been said, the **"bread"** is said to come down **"from heaven,"** because it has nothing perishable or earthly about it but breathes the immortality of God's kingdom. People who only cared about feeding their human stomachs did not discover this virtue in the manna. For although the manna had a twofold use, the Jews who were arguing with Christ saw nothing else in it other than bodily food. But the life of the soul is not transitory, for it continues to progress until the whole person is renewed.

Verses 59–64

59. He said this while teaching in the synagogue. John mentions the place to show that many people were present, and also that a sermon was preached on a weighty and important subject. But it is quickly seen that very few people in the large crowd benefitted from it. And what is worse, it became the occasion for many people who professed discipleship to desert Christ. If the evangelist had just said that some of them had been offended, that would have been dreadful enough. But when they rise up in crowds and conspire together against him, what name do we give to such an action? We must take this passage deep into our hearts, to make sure that we never murmur against Christ's words. If we note that other people are doing this today, we must not allow their pride to rock our faith.

60. "This is a hard teaching." In reality, it was not the saying that was **"hard,"** but their hearts. But the reprobate often collect stones from God's Word and cut themselves on them. In their hard obstinacy they rushed against Christ, complaining that his teaching was **"hard,"** when it could have softened them. Anybody who humbly submits to Christ's teaching will not find anything **"hard"** or rough in it. But to unbelievers, who obstinately oppose it, it is "like a hammer that breaks a rock in pieces" (Jeremiah 23:29). But the same hardness is innate in all of us, and if we judge Christ's teaching according to our feelings his words will seem to be full of paradoxes. So all we have to do is to commit ourselves to the guidance of the Holy Spirit, that he may write on our hearts what our ears would never have listened to.

"Who can accept it?" We see here the dreadful evil of unbelief. Those who wickedly and profanely reject the teaching of salvation are not content to excuse themselves, but deliberately make the Son of God guilty in their place and say that he is not worth hearing. So today Roman Catholics not only boldly reject the Gospel but indulge in similar terrible blasphemies, so that everyone will think that they have good reasons for opposing God. And, indeed, since they want darkness it is hardly surprising if Satan deceives them with fictitious portents. But what they refuse to accept because of their anger and hatred will not only be seen to be reasonable to moderate and teachable people, but will also support and comfort them. But the reprobate, through their obstinate outcries, will do nothing more than bring down dreadful condemnation on themselves.

61. Aware that his disciples were grumbling . . . Christ knew that there was no way to remove the stumbling block from the reprobate. For if the truth is told, this teaching does not so much wound them, but exposes their rotten ulcer which they nourished in their hearts. But Christ wanted to use every method to find out if any of these people who had been offended might still be curable, and to curb the voices of the others. The question Christ put to them shows that they had no reason to be offended by him, or at least that the basis of the offense did not lie in the teaching itself. So we should restrain the wickedness of those who slander God's Word as if they were fighting dogs out of control. In the same way we should attack the foolishness of those who attack the truth rashly.

John says that Christ was **aware** that the disciples were quietly **grumbling** among themselves, because they had not as yet said openly what was upsetting them. So Christ anticipated their complaints. If anyone objects that the nature of their complaints is clear, since they rejected Christ's teaching in plain words, I agree that the words which John had previously related were clear enough, but they still muttered and grumbled among themselves. If they had spoken to Christ, there would have been more grounds for hope, because then Christ could have taught them. But since they now indulge in secret grumbling, they put up barriers to profiting from any teaching. So whenever we do not immediately understand the Lord's teaching, we can do no better than go straight to him, so that he may resolve all our problems.

"Does this offend you?" Christ seems to be increasing the problem here, rather than solving it. But if you examine the reason for the complaint carefully, Christ's statement will be seen to satisfy their minds.

62. "What if you see the Son of Man ascend to where he was before!" The lowly and despicable condition of Christ which they saw when he was clothed in the flesh made him look like everyone else, and this prevented them from submitting to his divine power. Now Christ removes the veil, as it were, and invites them to view his heavenly glory. It is as if he said, "Because I live without honor among men, you despise me, and you can see nothing divine in me. But soon God will clothe me in splendid power and remove the contemptible state of mortal life from me and raise me above the heavens." In the resurrection of Christ, the power of the Holy Spirit that was displayed was so great that it clearly showed Christ to be the Son of God (see Romans 1:4). And when the Scripture says, "You are my Son; today I have become your Father" (Psalm 2:7), the resurrection is shown to be a proof for the acknowledgment of Christ's glory. And his ascension to heaven was the completion of this glory. When Christ says that he was previously in heaven, this does not, strictly speaking, apply to his human nature, and yet he is here speaking about **"the Son of Man."** But since the two natures in Christ constitute one person, it is not an unusual way of speaking to transfer what is special from one nature to the other.

63. "The Spirit gives life." Christ tells us through these words why the Jews derived no benefit from his teaching, because it was spiritual and gave life and did not fall on well-prepared ears. Because this passage has been interpreted in different ways, it is important, first of all, to understand the real meaning of Christ's words, and then it will be easy to see what Christ is teaching. When Christ affirms that **"the flesh counts for nothing,"** Chrysostom, wrongly to my mind, refers his statement to the Jews, who were unspiritual. I readily agree that in heavenly mysteries the whole power of the human mind can achieve nothing. Christ's words do not have this meaning, unless they are twisted. In my opinion, it is equally wrong to apply them to the other clause, as if they shed light on the phrase **"The Spirit gives life."** I do not go along with the view of those who say that Christ's flesh is beneficial because of the crucifixion, although when we eat it, it is of no benefit to us. On the contrary, it is necessary to eat the crucified flesh for it to benefit us.

Augustine thinks that we should add the word "only" or "by itself," as if Christ had said, "The flesh alone, and by itself, counts for nothing because it must be accompanied by the Spirit." This fits in well with the argument, for Christ is referring simply to the matter of eating. So he does not exclude every kind of usefulness, as if none at all could be derived from his flesh, but says that it will be useless if it is separated from the Spirit. For where does the flesh derive its power to give life except that it is spiritual? So anyone who merely concentrates on the earthly nature of the flesh will only find that it is dead. But those who raise their eyes to the power of the Spirit with which the flesh is imbued will learn from the actual experience of faith and from the effect itself that it is called "life-giving" for good reason.

We now understand how the flesh is meat indeed and yet **"counts for nothing."** It is meat in that, through it, life is procured for us, in it God is reconciled to us, and in it we have all the parts of salvation accomplished. It **"counts for nothing"** if considered in its origin and nature, for the descendant of Abraham, which in itself is subject to death, does not give life but receives its power of feeding us from the Spirit. So we must also bring the spiritual mouth of faith that we may be truly nourished by it.

The sentence breaks off here probably because Christ saw that he had to act in this way for the sake of the unbelievers. So he ends his sermon with this clause, because they did not deserve to hear any more from him. But Christ did not neglect the godly and the teachable, for these few words are enough to completely satisfy them.

"The words I have spoken to you . . ." This is an allusion to the previous statement, for Christ now uses the word **"spirit"** in a different sense. He had spoken about the secret power of **"the Spirit,"** and now he aptly applies it to his teaching, since it is spiritual. Here the word **"spirit"** is used as an adjective. Now the Word is called spiritual because it calls us upward to seek Christ in his heavenly glory through the guidance of the Spirit, by faith and not by our unspiritual understanding. We know that what was said can only be understood by faith. We also note that Christ links **"life"** with the Spirit. He calls his Word **"life"** because of its effect, as if he had called it life-giving. But he says that it will only be life-giving to people who receive it spiritually; others will derive death from it. For the godly, this is a most delightful commendation of the Gospel, because they are assured that it is appointed for their eternal salvation. Yet at the same time they are reminded to work hard to show that they are genuine disciples.

64. "Yet there are some of you who do not believe." Again Christ blames them. They wickedly corrupt and debase his teaching because they are devoid of the Spirit and so turn it to their destruction. Otherwise they would have objected, "You claim that you speak about bringing life, but we experience nothing like that." Therefore, Christ says that they are a stumbling block to themselves, for unbelief is always proud and will never understand anything about Christ's words, which it despises and disdains. Therefore, if we want to benefit at all from this Master, we must bring minds that are well disposed to listen to him. For if his teaching is not opened up with humility and reverence, our understanding will be harder than stones and will not agree with any part of the teaching. Therefore, today when we see so few people in the world benefitting from the Gospel we must remember that this comes about because of men's depravity. For how many people deny themselves and truly devote themselves to Christ? As for Christ merely saying that there were some unbelievers when the accusation fit almost all of them, he seems to have done it in case any who might be cured should become depressed.

For Jesus had known from the beginning . . . The evangelist added this in case anyone should think that Christ had made a hasty opinion about his hearers. Many professed to belong to his flock, but their sudden apostasy laid bare their hypocrisy. But the evangelist says that Christ knew their treachery, even when it was not seen by others. And he said this not so much on his own account, but to teach us not to make judgments until we know about the matter. That Christ knew them **from the beginning** was special to his divinity. But it is different with us. Because we cannot read other people's hearts, we should suspend our judgment until ungodliness reveals itself in outward signs, and thus the tree will be judged by its fruits (see Matthew 7:16).

Verses 65–71

65. "This is why I told you . . ." He says again that faith is a rare and special gift of God's Spirit, so that we will not be surprised if the Gospel is not welcomed by everyone everywhere. We may misunderstand things badly and think less highly of the Gospel if the whole world does not assent to it. We think to ourselves, "How can it be that most people deliberately reject their salvation?" Christ explains why there are so few believers. It is because no one can attain faith by his own cleverness. Everyone is blind until they are enlightened by God's Spirit. So they can only share this great blessing as the Father decides to include them. If this grace was for everyone indiscriminately, it would be inopportune and inappropriate to mention it in this passage. We have to understand Christ's aim — that not many people believe the Gospel, because faith comes only from the sacred revelation of the Spirit. **"Unless the Father has enabled him."**

The evangelist now relates (verse 66) how much disturbance this sermon caused. It is dreadful and monstrous that so kind and friendly an invitation from Christ should have alienated so many minds, especially of those who had previously been on his side and were even his close disciples. But this example is placed before us like a mirror so we can see how great the world's depravity and ingratitude is, as it heaps up material to stumble over even on the smooth way to life, that it may not come to Christ. Many might say that it would have been better if this kind of sermon had never been preached, as it caused so many people to fall away. But we should view this very differently. It was necessary then, as it is necessary every day now, that what had been foretold about Christ should be seen in his teaching — namely, that "he will be a stone that causes men to stumble" (Isaiah 8:14).

Of course, we should moderate our preaching so that no one will be offended by it through our fault. We should take care that we do not, by inconsiderate speech, upset ignorant or weak minds. But it will never be possible to be so careful that Christ's teaching will not cause offense to many. For the reprobate, who are given over to destruction, such poison comes from the most wholesome food and gall from honey. Undoubtedly, the Son of God knew best what was useful. And yet we see that he does not escape from offending many of his own followers. So although many people object to pure teaching, we are not at liberty to change it. The teachers of the church should remember Paul's instruction that the word of truth should be handled "correctly" (see 2 Timothy 2:15) and then advance boldly through every kind of offense. If many people fall away, we should not blame the Word of God because it does not please the reprobate. They are too dainty and soft who are so shaken by some people's apostasy that as soon as such people fall away, they become discouraged.

. . . no longer followed him. By adding this, the evangelist means that it was not a complete apostasy, but that they only withdrew from close companionship with Christ; and yet he does condemn them as apostates. From this we see that we cannot retreat one step without falling into the possibility of a treacherous denial.

67. Jesus asked the Twelve. Since the apostles' faith might be seriously shaken when they saw that they, only a few, remained out of a large crowd, Christ directs his words to them and tells them that there is no reason for them to allow themselves to be carried away by the lightness and fickleness of the others. When Christ asks them if they also want to go away, he does it to strengthen their faith. Presenting himself to them as the one they may stay with, he also exhorts them not to become the companions of apostates. Indeed, if faith is to be founded on Christ, it will not depend on men and will never waver even though it might see chaos in heaven and earth. We should also note that when Christ is deprived of nearly all of his disciples, he keeps only the Twelve. In the same way Isaiah had been commanded to "bind up the testimony and seal up the law among my disciples" (Isaiah 8:16). From examples such as these, every believer is taught to follow God even if he has no companions.

68. Simon Peter answered him. Here, as elsewhere, Peter is their spokesman, as they were all of the same mind, except that no sincerity existed in Judas. This reply has two parts. First, Peter says why he and his brothers are glad to remain with Christ, because they see that his teaching is wholesome and brings life; and secondly, he confesses that if they left him, nothing but death awaited them, whomever they went to.

"You have the words of eternal life." When he says, **"the words of eternal life,"** he uses the genitive for an adjective, which was common among the Hebrews. It is a remarkable commendation of the Gospel that it gives **"eternal life"** to us; Paul testifies, "It is the power of God for the salvation of everyone who believes" (Romans 1:16). The law does, indeed, also contain life; but because it pronounces the sentence of eternal death against transgressors, it can do nothing but kill. But life is offered to us in the Gospel, for "God was reconciling the world to himself in Christ, not counting men's sins against them" (2 Corinthians 5:19). Moreover, Peter is saying no ordinary thing about Christ when he declares that he has **"words of eternal life."** But Peter ascribes this to Christ, as being special to him alone. Hence the second statement follows, which I pointed out above, that as soon as they have gone away from Christ, nothing remains for them but death, wherever they go. Certain destruction awaits everyone who is not satisfied with that Master but runs off to men's inventions.

69. "We believe." The verbs here are in the past tense, but they can be changed into the present tense, and it makes very little difference to the meaning. In these words Peter gives a short summary of faith. But the confession does not seem to relate to the subject in hand, for the question concerned the eating of the flesh of Christ. My reply is that although the Twelve did not at once understand all that Christ was teaching, it was enough for them, according to the strength of their faith, to confess him as the author of their salvation and to submit to him in everything. The word **"believe"** comes first because the obedience of faith is the beginning of true understanding. But at once knowledge is added, which distinguishes faith from erroneous and false opinions. Turks and Jews and Papists believe, but without knowing or understanding anything. Knowledge is linked to faith because we have a sure and certain conviction about God's truth, not in the same way as human sciences are understood, but when the Spirit seals it in our hearts.

70. Then Jesus replied . . . Because Christ replied to them all, we may infer that everyone agreed with what Peter said. And now Christ prepares and arms the eleven apostles against a fresh offense which was already threatening. That they were already reduced to such a small number was a powerful instrument of Satan to shake their faith. But the fall of Judas might discourage them altogether, for since Christ had chosen this sacred number, who would ever have thought that any part of it could be taken away. So Christ's admonition may be interpreted in this way: "Out of a large group of people, you twelve alone are left. If your faith has not been shaken by the unbelief of many, prepare for a new trial. This group, small as it is, will be further diminished by one person."

"Have I not chosen you, the Twelve?" When Christ says that he has chosen **"the Twelve,"** he is not referring to the eternal purpose of God, for it is impossible that any of those who have been predestinated to life could fall away. But they who had been chosen to the apostolic office ought to have surpassed all others in godliness and holiness. So Christ used the word **"chosen"** for those who were selected and separated from the common rank.

"Yet one of you is a devil!" There is no doubt that by using this name Christ wanted to make Judas utterly abominable. People who water down this word are making a mistake. We cannot pronounce a severe enough curse on those who dishonor such a sacred office. Teachers who faithfully discharge their office are called angels. "From his mouth men should seek instruction — because he is the messenger of the Lord Almighty" (Malachi 2:7). He is justly accounted a devil, therefore, who falls away through his treachery and wickedness when he had been admitted to so honorable an order. There is an additional reason. God allows more power and freedom to Satan over wicked and ungodly ministers than over more ordinary people. So, if those who were chosen to be pastors are driven by such devilish madness that they are like wild and monstrous beasts, we should not despise the dignity of their order, but rather honor it the more when its profanation is followed by such fearful punishment.

71. He meant Judas. Although Judas had a bad conscience, we do not read that he was moved. So numbed are hypocrites that they do not feel their own wounds, and before men they are so hardened that they do not scruple to prefer themselves to the very best of men.

John
Chapter 7

Verses 1–8

1. Jesus went around in Galilee. The evangelist does not seem to be compiling a continuous narrative, but selects events worth telling from what occurred at different times. He says that Christ lived in Galilee for a time because nowhere among the Jews was it safe for him. If anyone thinks it strange that Christ sought a hiding-place when at his will he could break and incapacitate all the efforts of his enemies, the answer is easy. Christ remembered the commission he was given by the Father and wanted to confine himself within the limits of humanity. He took the form of a servant and emptied himself until the Father exalted him (see Philippians 2:6-9).

If you object that Christ knew that the time of his death was fore-ordained and therefore he had no reason to avoid it, the same answer applies here also, for he behaved as a man who was at the mercy of danger, and it was not right that he should rush headlong into danger. In meeting perils, it is not for us to ask what God has determined about us, but what he commands and enjoins on us, what our office requires and demands, and what is the correct way to order our life. Besides, although Christ avoided dangers, he did not turn aside a hair's breadth from the course of his duty. For what is the point of a safe life except to serve the Lord? We must always beware that we do not for the sake of life lose the purpose of living. When a despised corner of Galilee gives Christ a place to stay, while Judea will not, we learn that piety and fear of God are not always outstanding in the most important places of the church.

2. The Jewish Feast of Tabernacles was near. Although I am not certain, this probably took place in the second year after Christ's baptism. At the moment we do not need to say much about this feast day mentioned by the evangelist. Moses tells us about its purpose and use (see Leviticus 23:33-36). Through this unusual ceremony the Jews were to remember how their fathers had lived for forty years in tents when they had no houses, so that they might be thankful for their deliverance.

We have already mentioned that Christ came to Jerusalem for the feast for two reasons. One was that as he was subject to the law to redeem us all from its bondage, he did not want to leave out any part of its observance. The other was that he had a better opportunity to spread the Gospel among a crowd and an unusual mix of people. The evangelist now relates that Christ stayed quietly in Galilee, as if he were not going up to Jerusalem.

3. Jesus' brothers said to him . . . Under this name, **brothers**, the Jews embraced all members of the family and blood relations. John says that they mocked Christ because he escaped from the public eye and hid in the obscure and despised district of Galilee. They were doubtless impelled by ambition to want Christ to become famous. But even allowing for this, it is still clear that they despised and ridiculed him because they thought he was acting unwisely and injudiciously. They even reproached him for foolishly wanting to be something but lacking the self-confidence to appear openly among people. When they say, "**that your disciples may see the miracles you do,**" they are not just referring to his inner circle of disciples but to everyone he wanted to win from the whole nation, for they add, "You want to be known by everyone, and yet you hide yourself away."

4. "Since you are doing these things . . ." That is, "If you aspire to such greatness that all will talk of you, make sure that everyone can see you." Then they contrast the world with those few people among whom he was now living without being held in honor. A further meaning can be drawn from this: "If you do these things (that is, with the power to win fame through miracles), do not waste these miracles. You are wasting everything God has given you here, where there is no one to witness and esteem you as you deserve." Here we see how lazy men are in thinking about God's deeds. For Christ's family would never have spoken in this way if they had not trodden underfoot, as it were, the shining proofs of his divine power which they ought to have seen and revered with the highest admiration. What we see happened to Christ happens every day. The children of God suffer more at the hands of their families than they do from outsiders, for they are Satan's instruments to tempt either to ambition or to avarice those who desire to serve God purely and faithfully. But Christ repels such satans sharply and warns us, through his example, not to give in to the foolish wishes of our families.

5. For even his own brothers . . . From this we deduce how worthless human relationships are. For the Spirit brands Christ's relations with an everlasting mark of infamy because even when they were proved wrong by the witness of so many works, they did not believe. "Therefore, if anyone is in Christ, he is a new creation," says Paul (2 Corinthians 5:17; see Galatians 6:15). People who give themselves over entirely to God are in the position of being father and mother and brothers and sisters to Christ, but other people Christ completely disowns. The more ridiculous is the Roman Catholic superstition about ignoring everything else in the Virgin Mary and giving her only the honor of a relationship, as if Christ himself had not reproved the woman who called out from the crowd, "Blessed is the mother who gave you birth and nursed you" by replying, "Blessed rather are those who hear the word of God and obey it" (Luke 11:27-28).

6. "The right time for me has not yet come." Some people think that this refers to the time of Christ's death. But they are wrong because it refers to the time when he would set out on his journey. Christ is telling them that in this he is different from his relations. They may freely and safely go about at all hours before the world, because the world is friendly and on their side. But he rightly fears for himself, because the world hates him. Through these words Christ is saying that they were wrong to give advice on something they did not understand.

7. "The world cannot hate you." When Christ says this he is reproving them for their complete worldliness, for peace with the world can only be bought by an ungodly assent to vices and every kind of evil.

"The world . . . hates me because I testify . . ." The word **"world"** here refers to people who are not born again but retain their own nature. So Christ says that everyone who has not yet been born again by the Spirit is his enemy. Why? Because Christ condemns their deeds. If we agree with Christ, we have to acknowledge that man's whole nature is so corrupt and perverse that nothing right, nothing sincere, nothing good can come from it.

"Because I testify that what it does is evil." When Christ says that the world **"hates"** him because of this, he is saying that the Gospel cannot be preached faithfully without summoning the whole world as guilty to the judgment-seat of God, that flesh and blood may thus be crushed and reduced in this way, in line with the saying, "When he [the Spirit] comes, he will convict the world of guilt" (16:8). From this we see that man's innate pride is so strong that he flatters and congratulates himself about his vices. For men would not object to being reproved if their self-love did not blind them, so that they flatter themselves about their own sins. Haughtiness and arrogance are the leading and most destructive of all men's vices. Only the Spirit can break us down to bear reproofs patiently and so offer ourselves willingly to be killed by the sword of the Gospel.

Verses 9–13

9. He stayed in Galilee. The evangelist sets before us, on the one hand, Christ's family members, who in the normal way pretend to worship God but remain friends with unbelievers and so walk around safely;

and, on the other hand, Christ himself, who was hated by the world and comes in secret into the city until the work he has to do forces him to show himself openly. But if there is nothing worse than to be separated from Christ, cursed is the high price we pay for peace by renouncing Christ.

11. The Jews were watching for him. Here we should think about the state of the church. At that time the Jews were longing for the promised redemption like hungry men. However, when Christ does show himself to them, they remain doubtful about him. This accounts for the confused murmuring and the differences of opinion about Christ. The secret whispering of some indicates the tyranny of the priests and the teachers of the law. Indeed, it is a dreadful example that this church, at that time the only church on earth, is seen here in a confused and chaotic state. Their leaders, far from being shepherds, hold the people in fear and terror, and throughout the whole body there is a shameful desolation and lamentable disorder. By **the Jews** the evangelist means the common people, who for two years had been used to listening to Christ and who now look for him because he does not arrive as he normally did. When they say, **"Where is that man?"** they are referring to somebody they already knew. However, this also shows that they had not yet been deeply moved and always remained in doubt.

12. There was widespread whispering. The evangelist means that they were holding private conversations about Christ, as people in large crowds do. The arguments described here show that it is nothing novel for evil people to hold different opinions about Christ, even in the very heart of the church. Although we should not hesitate to welcome Christ even though he was condemned by the majority of his own people, we should still be on our guard against upsetting, everyday disagreements. Again we can see man's dreadful arrogance about divine matters. In many unimportant matters people would not be so high-handed, but where the Son of God and his most holy teaching is concerned, they immediately make rash judgments. We should be the more careful not to condemn our lives in the light of God's eternal truth. If the world thinks that we are imposters, we must remember that this is a sign of being Christ's, so long as we show that we are being genuine at this moment. This passage also shows that among a large crowd, most of whom are confused in their thinking, there are always some people who think correctly. But the well-disposed minority are overwhelmed by the bewildered majority.

13. But no one would say anything publicly. The reference to **the Jews** here is to the people who ruled and had the power of government in their hands. They fumed with hatred against Christ so much that they would not allow anyone to speak. This was not because they minded Christ being slandered with all kinds of malice, but because they thought it would be better if his name was buried in oblivion. So when those who are opposed to truth find that there is nothing to be gained from their cruelty, their great longing is to eradicate Christ's memory, and this alone they seek to achieve. The fact that everyone was silent and subdued through **fear** was proof enough of the great tyranny the Jews imposed. Just as unbridled license has no place in a well-ordered church, so when all freedom is repressed by fear so that no one dares to speak, it is a wretched situation. But Christ's power shone more clearly and wonderfully when he gained a hearing for himself from the armed enemies, and in the middle of this furious hatred a terrifying government publicly proclaimed the truth about God.

Verses 14–19

14. . . . to the temple. We now see that Christ was not worried about failing to do his duty, but he waited so that he could preach to a large crowd. So, while we may sometimes retreat from danger, we should never neglect or miss any opportunity to do good. Christ teaches in the temple in line with the ancient traditions and customs. For although God had commanded all these ceremonies, he did not want people to be taken up with useless and cold spectacles. To make them understandable, they had to be accompanied by teaching. This is how external ceremonies become living images of spiritual things, when they take their form from the Word of God. But because the priests then almost said nothing, and the teachers of the law adulterated pure teaching with their leaven and false notions, Christ took on the role of teacher. As High Priest, Christ was right to take on this office, as he was soon to confirm that he did nothing except at the Father's command.

15. The Jews were amazed. People are wrong to think that Christ's word was so welcomed that it was esteemed and honored, for the Jews' amazement meant that they used it as an excuse to show contempt. Men's ingratitude reveals itself when they deliberately make wrong assessments about God's deeds. If God acts through the usual means and in the ordinary way, as they say, these visible means are like veils which stop us from seeing God's hand at work, so that we only acknowledge what is human about them. But if some extraordinary power of God shines out way beyond what is natural and what is generally known, we are paralyzed, and what should have deeply moved us disappears like a dream. We are so proud that we take no notice of anything we do not understand.

It is a wonderful demonstration of God's power and grace that Christ, even though he had not studied under any great teacher, had exceptional understanding of the Scriptures, and that even though he had never been a pupil he was such an excellent teacher and Master. For the Jews despised God's grace just because it was beyond their understanding. This should warn us, therefore, and teach us to show more reverence for God than we usually do about his deeds.

16. "My teaching is not my own." Christ tells the Jews that what they took offense at should have been a ladder for them to climb higher on, to see God's glory. It is as if Christ had said, "When you see a teacher who has not been taught in human schools, tell people that he has been taught in God's school." The Heavenly Father chose his Son to come from a laborer's workshop rather than from the schools of the teachers of the law, so that the origin of the Gospel would be even clearer for all to see, and so that no one could think that it had been devised on earth through some human being. Christ chose ignorant and uneducated men to be his apostles for the same reason. For three years he withdrew them from human influences, so that once he had taught them just for a moment, he could send them out as new people, like angels coming down from heaven.

Meanwhile, Christ points us in the direction of the authority of spiritual teaching — God alone. When Christ insists that the teaching of his Father is not his, he is thinking about how much his hearers can understand — they thought that he was just a man. So as a concession he allows himself to be thought of as being different from his Father, and yet at the same time he did not teach anything he had not been told to. In summary, Christ teaches in the name of his Father and not in the name of men, or from men, so that his teaching could be despised with impunity. We can see the argument he used to procure authority for his teaching. He says God is its author. We also see by what right and for what reason Christ demands to be heard. It is because the Father sent him to teach. Everyone who takes on the office of teacher and wants to be believed should have these two divine gifts.

17. "If any one chooses . . ." Christ anticipates objections against this teaching. He had many opponents there, and one of them might have been prepared to grumble, "Why do you boast about God's name? We do not acknowledge that you come from him. So why do you lay it down as a principle, which we do not accept, that you teach nothing except by God's command?" So Christ replies that correct judgment stems from the fear and reverence of God. If their minds are inclined to fear God they will quickly see whether his preaching is true or not. Christ also rebukes them indirectly. How is it that they are unable to make this judgment unless it is because they lack the basis for a sound understanding — namely, godliness and a strong desire to obey God?

This statement should be carefully noted. Satan is always waiting to catch us in his nets, through his deceit. So here Christ is giving us good warning not to lay ourselves open to any of his tricks. If we are prepared to obey God, he will always give us the light of his Spirit so we can distinguish truth from falsehood. Only our obstinacy and unwillingness to be taught stop us from making correct judgments, and whenever Satan deceives us we are rightly punished for our hypocrisy. Moses tells us that when false prophets come, "The Lord your God is testing you to find out whether you love him with all your heart and with all your soul" (Deuteronomy 13:3). Upright people will never be deceived. So it is clear how wickedly and foolishly many people behave in our own day who, fearing the danger of falling into error, allow that fear to stifle all desire to learn, as if it was said in vain, "Knock and the door will be opened to you" (Matthew 7:7).

We must not doubt that God will give us the Spirit of discernment to be our constant guide and director, so long as we are completely given over to obeying him. People who waver in this will eventually discover how hollow their excuses for their ignorance are. Indeed, we will see that everyone who hesitates now and prefers to nurse their doubt rather than make serious inquiries by reading and hearing God's truth are being bold enough to defy God on a major matter of principle. One person might say that he prays for the dead because he is uncertain in his own mind and dares not condemn what perverse people have invented about purgatory — and yet he will freely allow himself to commit fornication. Another person will say that he is not clever enough to distinguish between Christ's pure teaching and the spurious inventions of men — but he will be clever enough to steal or perjure himself.

In summary, all the skeptics who hide behind a veil of doubt in our present controversies are showing a public contempt for God in matters which are not at all obscure. So we should not be surprised that the Gospel is welcomed by so few people today, since a fear of God is so uncommon in the world. These words of Christ also have a definition of true religion: it is when we are wholeheartedly prepared to follow God's will. The only person who can do this is he who has renounced his own point of view.

"Or whether I speak on my own." We must notice how Christ wants us to make judgments about any teaching. He wants us to receive, without arguing, what is from God, but to reject what comes from man. This is the only way he gives us to distinguish the teachings from each other.

18. "He who speaks on his own . . ." Up to now Christ has shown that the only reason for men's blindness lies in their not being ruled by God's fear. Christ now places a distinctive mark on the teaching itself by which it may be known whether it is from God or from man. Everything that displays God's glory is holy and divine; but everything that serves man's ambition, thus obscuring God's glory by exalting men, not only does not deserve to be believed but ought to be rejected outright. Everyone who makes God's glory his goal will never go wrong, and everyone who uses this as the touchstone to test what comes in God's name will never be deceived by what appears to be right. This also warns us that no one can carry out the office of teacher in the church faithfully except he who is devoid of ambition and who undertakes, with all his strength, as his one overriding concern, the promotion of God's glory. When Christ says, "There is nothing false about him," he means that

there is nothing wicked or false about himself, but that he acts as an upright and sincere minister of God should.

19. "Has not Moses . . . ?" The evangelist does not record all of Christ's sermon but just selects the principal points which summarize the rest. The priests and the teachers of the law had become angry with Christ because he had healed the paralytic, though they maintained that it was because they were being zealous for the law. To refute their hypocrisy Christ does not argue about the matter in hand but about their characters. For they indulged in their vices without restraint, as if they had never known any law. Therefore, Christ concludes that they are unaffected by any love or care for the law. This argument, on its own, would not have been enough to prove Christ's case, for even allowing for their wicked and unjust hatred being cloaked in false motives, it does not follow that Christ acted correctly by breaking the law's commands. We should not blame others in our quest to prove our own innocence.

In fact, Christ links two clauses here. In the first he appeals to his enemies' consciences. They proudly boasted that they were guardians of the law, but Christ unmasks them as he rebukes them for allowing themselves to break the law whenever they wished and for not caring about the law. Then, as we will see later, Christ tackles the question itself. So Christ's defense is complete and strong in every respect. The summary of this clause is that people who despise the law have no zeal for it. So Christ concludes that the great anger the Jews had in wanting to kill him came from another source. This is how we should drag the wicked from their hiding-places when they oppose God and sound teaching and pretend to act from godly motives.

Today's fiercest enemies of the Gospel have nothing more praiseworthy on their side than their burning zeal. When their lives are looked into, they are all seen to conceal ugly shame, so that they openly mock God. Are bishops and abbots modest enough to hide their uncleanness, so even a semblance of religion may be apparent? Are not monks, also, and other rowdy people, completely given over to wickedness, lust, avarice, and every kind of sin against nature, so that their lives cry out that they have forgotten God? And if they boast unashamedly about their zeal for God and the church, should not this reply from Christ restrain them?

Verses 20–24

20. "You are demon-possessed." This is another way of saying, "You are mad." It was a common phrase among the Jews, who had been brought up to believe that when people were overtaken by anger or had lost their mind and reason they were under the devil's attack. God's fatherly rebukes are so soft and gentle that when he treats us with greater harshness and severity, it feels as if he is not hitting us with his own hand, but that the devil is administering and venting his anger on us. The crowd, in their ignorance, reproach Christ, for the ordinary people were unaware of the priests' intentions. So these foolish men often said that Christ was acting like a madman when they sought to kill him. From this we see that we should be very cautious about making up our minds about subjects we know nothing about. If we are ever condemned without reason by the ignorant, we should follow Christ's example and humbly accept the insult.

21. "I did one miracle." Christ now moves on from discussing their characters to the matter in hand. He shows how the **"miracle"** he performed was in no way against God's law. When Christ says that he did **"one miracle"** he means that he is being blamed for just one crime, that of miraculously healing a man on the Sabbath, whereas his accusers do many deeds of a similar kind on the Sabbath without thinking that they are wrong. A Sabbath never passed without many infants being circumcised in Judea (verses 22-23). Christ defends his action by this example, although he does not just base his argument on a similar case, but compares the greater with the lesser. Circumcision and healing a paralytic were similar in that each was a divine work. But Christ insists that the latter was superior since it benefitted the whole person. Now, if Christ had only healed the man's physical disease, the comparison would have been invalid, as circumcision would then have been superior, as it affected the health of the soul. So Christ links the spiritual result of the **"miracle"** with the outward benefit given to the body. Thus, Christ correctly prefers the entire healing of a man to circumcision.

There may be another reason for this comparison. The sacraments are not always accompanied by power and efficacy, whereas Christ worked efficaciously in healing the paralytic. However, I prefer the former exposition, that the Jews are maliciously and slanderously blaming a **"miracle"** in which God's grace shines more brightly than in circumcision, which they honor so much that they do not think that the Sabbath has been broken by it. The "astonishment" Christ is referring to is the grumbling which met what he had done because they believed that Christ dared to do more than was lawful.

22. "Yet, because Moses . . ." (KJV, "Moses therefore"). The introductory particle **"therefore"** seems unsuitable. Some take "on this account" or **"therefore"** in the sense of "because," although the Greek is against this. I have a simpler explanation: circumcision was commanded in such a way that the sign had to be performed even **"on the Sabbath."** So Christ says, **"therefore,"** as if he were saying that it has already been demonstrated that the worship of the Sabbath is not broken by the deeds of God. Christ allows the example of circumcision to fall into this category, but he then immediately corrects what he is saying by pointing out that Moses was not the first minister of circumcision. It was not enough that Moses, who so strictly insisted on the Sabbath, should have commanded these infants to be circumcised on the eighth day, even though it should fall **"on the Sabbath."**

24. "Stop judging." After finishing his defense Christ rebukes them for being carried away with their perverse inclinations rather than making judgments from the facts of the case. They rightly had a high regard for circumcision, and when it took place on the Sabbath they knew that the law was not being broken, because God's deeds are in harmony with one another. So why did they not think in the same way about Christ's deed, unless their minds were full of preconceived prejudices against him? Correct judgments can never be made unless they are based on the truth of reality. As soon as personalities are allowed to intrude, eyes and senses are focussed on them, and the truth immediately disappears. This warning applies to all kinds of situations, but it is particularly applicable to Christian teaching. For we are always prone to being put off by Christian teaching on account of the hatred and contempt of men.

Verses 25–30

25. Some of the people of Jerusalem . . . This means that some people knew about the plots the rulers had laid and how much they hated Christ. Ordinary people, as we saw above, thought that this was a dream or madness. Those who knew how wholeheartedly their nation's rulers hated Christ were surprised that while Christ not only openly walked in the temple but preached freely, they left him alone. But they were mistaken in this, because they did not take into account God's providence in such a divine miracle. Whenever unspiritual people see any unusual work of God, they are indeed surprised, although no thought about God's power ever enters their mind. But it is our duty to ponder the works of God more wisely. In particular, when the ungodly do not stop the progress of the Gospel as they want to, we should be sure that their attempts are ineffective because God has set his hand against them and scattered them.

27. "But we know where this man is from." Here we see not only men's great blindness in making judgments about divine things, but their almost innate vice at being gifted at constructing stumbling blocks which prevent them from arriving at the knowledge of the truth. Offense is often given by Satan's deceits, and this alienates many from Christ. But even if the path was flat and smooth, everyone would make his own stumbling block to fall over. So long as the rulers were against Christ, their unbelief alone would have been an obstacle to this crowd of people. Now that this obstacle has been removed, they make up for themselves a new reason for not coming to the faith. Even though it was right for them to be influenced by their rulers' example, they are so far away from following the right path that they fall over the first step if they are left to themselves. So people who start well often quickly fall away, unless the Lord directs their steps to the end of their journey.

The reasoning which causes them to stumble is as follows: "The prophets witnessed that Christ's origin would be unknown. But we know where this man comes from. So he cannot possibly be the Christ." From this we are reminded how dangerous it is to twist the Scriptures, and how it is even more dangerous to attack Christ by saying that he is only half the person he really is. God promised that the Redeemer would be a descendant of David, but he also often reserves this position for himself. Thus Micah points out the future birthplace of Christ: "But you, Bethlehem Ephrathah . . . out of you will come for me one who will be ruler over Israel" (Micah 5:2). But straight afterwards he talks about another person going out who is far higher, and who is thus hidden and secret. But when those sad people could only express contempt for Christ, they thoughtlessly concluded that he was not the promised one. Therefore, we must learn to look on Christ's lowliness, as far as his flesh is concerned, in such a way that this humility, despised by the wicked, may raise us to his heavenly glory. So Bethlehem, where the man had to be born, will be a doorway to the eternal God for us.

28. Then Jesus . . . cried out. Christ used bitter words as he attacked their rashness, but they arrogantly flattered themselves as they held the wrong view and shut themselves off from the knowledge of the truth. It is as if he had said, "You know everything, and yet you know nothing." Indeed, there is no worse plague than when people are so drunk with confidence in their own tiny learning that they boldly reject every opposing opinion.

Christ is speaking ironically when he says, **"Yes, you know me, and you know where I am from. I am not here on my own."** Christ compares the truth with the false opinion they held, as if he were saying, "You have your eyes fixed on the earth, and you think that you see all of me, and therefore you despise me as an unknown son of the earth. But God will testify that I come from heaven. While I may be rejected by you, God will testify that I am in reality his."

"He who sent me is true." Christ calls God **"true"** in the same way that Paul calls him "faithful": "If we are faithless, he will remain faithful, for he cannot disown himself" (2 Timothy 2:13). His argument is that the faith of the Gospel is not reduced at all by all the attacks of the world against it. Even when the wicked take from Christ what belongs to him, Christ remains complete, because God's truth is strong and never changes. Christ realizes that he is despised. But he is such a long way from giving in that he triumphs splendidly over the mad arrogance of those who think that he is a nobody. All believers should be endued with such unconquerable and heroic greatness. Indeed, our faith will never be strong and firm unless it derides the presumption of wicked people when they rise up against Christ.

Above everything else, godly teachers should rely on this support — namely, to persevere in maintaining godly teaching even if the whole world opposes it. Thus Isaiah, overwhelmed on all sides by slanders and reproaches, runs to the refuge that God will approve his cause (see Isaiah 50:8). Thus Paul, when he is oppressed by unjust judgments, appeals against them all "till the Lord comes" (1 Corinthians 4:5), thinking that it is enough to have God alone to set against the whole raging world.

"You do not know him." Christ means that it is not surprising if the Jews **"do not know him,"** for they do not know God. True wisdom starts in looking at God.

29. "But I know him." When Christ says that he knows God, he means that he does not have such great confidence without good reason. Through his example, he warns us not to take the name of God lightly and boast of him as the patron and defender of our cause. Many people are over-presumptuous in boasting that they possess God's authority. Indeed, no greater readiness and boldness in rejecting everyone's judgments can be imagined than that of the fanatics who claim that their own ideas are the oracles of God. These words of Christ teach us to be especially on our guard against being puffed up and foolishly confident, and to resist people strongly only after we have discovered God's truth. Anyone who really knows that God is on his side has no reason to fear the accusation of arrogance in trampling down all the world's haughtiness.

". . . because I am from him." Some people make a distinction between these two clauses, so that the former refers to the divine essence of Christ, while the latter refers to the office given him by the Father, to carry out which he took on human nature and flesh. While I do not reject this, I am not sure that Christ wanted to speak so subtly. I agree that Christ's descent from heaven may be inferred from this, but it would not be a strong enough proof of his eternal divinity against the Arians.

30. At this they tried to seize him. They did not lack the will to hurt Christ. They even made the attempt, and they had the power to do it. Why then, with so much enthusiasm, are they paralyzed, as if their hands and feet were tied? The evangelist replies that **his time had not yet come.** He means by this that Christ was protected against their violence and their furious attacks by God. At the same time he anticipates the stumbling block of the cross. We have no reason to be upset when we hear that Christ was dragged to death not through men's wishes but because the Father's decree appointed him to be such a sacrifice. From this a general teaching may be deduced. While we live from day to day, the moment of everyone's death has been fixed by God. It is hard to believe that, subject as we are to so many accidents, exposed to so many injuries and dangers from man and beast, and liable to so many diseases, we are safe from all dangers until God wishes to call us away. But we must fight against our own lack of trust. First, we should cling to the teaching given here, and then to its purpose and the exhortation drawn from it — namely, that each of us should "cast all your anxiety on him" (1 Peter 5:7). Each should serve in his own calling and not be led away from his duty by any fears. But no one should exceed his own limitations. Confidence in God's providence should go no further than God himself commands.

Verses 31–36

31. Still, many in the crowd . . . It might appear that Christ was preaching to the deaf and utterly obstinate, and yet the evangelist says that some fruit followed. So while some people may grumble, others smile, and others slander; and though many differences may arise, the preaching of the Gospel will not be without effect. So we must sow the seed and wait patiently, until eventually the fruit appears. The words **put their faith in him** are used here in an imprecise way, for they relied more on the miracles than on teaching and were not convinced that Jesus was the Christ. But as they were ready to listen to him and allowed themselves to be taught by him, such a preparation for faith is called **faith.** So when the Holy Spirit gives to a small spark of the right attitude such an honorable title, it should encourage us not to doubt that **faith,** however small, will be accepted by God.

32. The Pharisees heard . . . It is clear from this that **the Pharisees** were on the lookout and were always set on preventing Christ from being known. To start with, the evangelist only mentions **the Pharisees,** but he then links the priests with them, of whom **the Pharisees** were a part. There is no doubt that because they wanted to be thought the most zealous enthusiasts for the law, they opposed Christ more bitterly than everyone else. But they could not topple Christ on their own, so they delegated the matter to the whole priestly order. So those who had differences on other matters now united under the guidance of Satan against God's Son. Meanwhile, since **the Pharisees** were so zealous and careful to defend their tyranny and the corrupt state of the church, how much more fervent should we be to maintain Christ's kingdom. The Roman Catholics' desire to extinguish the Gospel today is no less furious. But it is dreadful that our desires are not at least whetted by their example to work more courageously in the defense of true and sound teaching.

33. "I am with you for only a short time." Some people think that this sermon was given to the assembly, while other people think that it was addressed to the officers who were sent to arrest Christ. For myself, I have no doubt that Christ is speaking especially to his enemies, who had laid plans to kill him. He laughs at their efforts, for they will all work in vain until the time set by the Father comes. He also rebukes their obstinacy in not only rejecting but furiously opposing the grace that is offered to them, while at the same time he threatens that it will soon be taken from them.

When he says, **"I am with you,"** he is telling them off for their ingratitude. For although he had been given to them by the Father, although he had come down to them from his heavenly glory, although by lovingly inviting them to him he wanted nothing more than to be with them, only a few people received him. When he says, **"only a short time"** he is warning them that God will not endure for long his grace being exposed to such shameful contempt. He also means that neither his life nor his death is given over to their power, but that a time has been fixed by his Father which must be fulfilled.

"I go to the one who sent me." By these words he declares that he will not be destroyed by death but will, when he has put off his mortal body, be declared the Son of God by the magnificent victory of his resurrection. It is as if he had said, "Work as hard as you like — you will never stop my Father from receiving me into his heavenly glory when I have discharged the ambassadorship committed to me. Thus, not only will my rank remain undiminished after my death, but a more excellent one will then be provided for me." A general warning should also be drawn from this. As often as Christ calls us to the hope of salvation through the preaching of the Gospel, he is present with us. There is a good reason for the preaching of the Gospel to be called a descent of Christ to us (see Ephesians 2:17). If we take Christ's outstretched hand, he will lead us to the Father. As long as we have to live in this world, he will not only show himself to be near us but will continually live in us. If we ignore his presence, he loses nothing; but if he leaves us, we become strangers to God and life.

34. "You will look for me." They tried to kill Christ. Here Christ makes a play on the word "seek" (KJV). Soon they were going to **"seek"** Christ for another reason — namely, to find help and comfort in their wretchedness and lost state. It was as if Christ had said, "My presence, which you find so irksome and unpleasant now, will only last for a short time. Soon you will try to find me in vain. For I will be distant from you not only physically but also in power, and from heaven I will observe your destruction." So we may inquire here about the nature of this seeking of Christ. Quite clearly Christ is referring to the reprobate, who were extremely obstinate in rejecting the Gospel. Some people think it refers to teaching because the Jews, through wrongly pursuing the righteousness of deeds, did not obtain what they wanted. Many people think it refers to the Messiah himself, because the Jews in vain begged for a Redeemer when they were in extreme difficulties. But I think it simply denotes the distressed groans of the wicked when necessity forces them to look in some sense towards God.

"But you will not find me." Even as they **"seek"** him they are not really seeking him, since unbelief and obstinacy shut up their hearts, as it were, and so alienate them from God. They really do want God to be with them as their Redeemer, but through impenitence and hardness of heart they obstruct the path. Esau is an example of this. When his birthright is taken away from him, he is not only full of grief, but he groans and grinds his teeth and bursts into furious indignation (see Genesis 27:38; Hebrews 12:17). But even then, he is so far away from seeking God's blessing that he is not worthy to receive it. This is how God usually punishes the contempt of his grace in the reprobate, so that, afflicted by severe punishments or oppressed by a conviction of their misery or reduced to other extremities, they complain or cry or howl, but all to no advantage. Because they always act in character, they inwardly feed the same cruelty as before and are brought no closer to God. Instead, since they are unable to destroy God, they wish that God was different.

From this we learn that Christ must be received with no delay, while he is still with us, in case we lose the opportunity to enjoy him. Once the door is closed it is no good trying to enter (Isaiah 55). Therefore, we must be diligent in going to God while it is open (Isaiah 55:6). We do not know how long God will tolerate our negligence. In the words **"where I am, you cannot come,"** he uses the present tense instead of the future.

35. "Where does this man intend to go?" The evangelist adds this to highlight the people's stupidity. The ungodly are not only deaf to God's teaching, but they even make mock threats, as if they were listening to a story. Christ speaks about the Father by name, but they remain earthbound and only think about a journey to distant lands.

"Will he go where our people live scattered among the Greeks?" It is well-known that the Jews called any foreigner a "Greek." But they did not mean that Christ would go to people who had not been circumcised, but to the Jews dispersed throughout the various regions of the world. For the word "Dispersion" does not apply to the native inhabitants of a place, but to the Jews who were exiles and fugitives there. Thus, in his first letter Peter writes "to God's elect, strangers in the world" — that is, "scattered throughout Pontus, Galatia, Cappadocia, Asia and Bithynia" (1 Peter 1:1). Also James greets "the twelve tribes scattered among the nations," which is an expression taken from Moses and the prophets. So these words mean, "Will Christ go overseas to the Jews who live in lands we do not know?" Perhaps they wanted to upset Christ with this kind of mockery. "If this man is the Messiah, is he going to become king of Greece, when God has already given him Canaan to live in?" However that may be, we see that they were not at all affected by Christ's severe threats.

Verses 37–39

37. On the last and greatest day . . . The first thing to note here is that none of the plots and intrigues of Christ's enemies frightened Christ from doing his duty. On the contrary, his courage rose with danger, and he carried on more bravely. This is seen in the details about the time and the crowd and in Christ's freedom in calling out when he knew that they were close at hand to arrest him, for the officers were probably then ready to carry out their orders.

Next, we notice that, relying on nothing but God's protection, Christ could stand firm against the violent efforts of those people who had everything in their control. For what other explanation can there be for Christ preaching on the great day in the middle of the temple, which they ruled completely and where they had already prepared a group of soldiers, except that God restrained their anger? But we also derive great benefit from the evangelist introducing Christ's cry: **"If a man is thirsty, let him come to me and drink."** From this we may infer that more than just a few people were invited in a quiet, gentle whisper, but that the teaching was proclaimed to everyone in such a way that it was hidden only from those who deliberately closed their ears and refused to hear this loud, resounding cry.

"If a man is thirsty . . ." Through this clause Christ exhorts everyone to share his blessings, so long as they are aware of their own poverty and want to be helped. Indeed, we are all poor, empty, and destitute of all blessings, although a sense of poverty does not convict everyone to search for the remedy. This is why many people do not make any move but waste away in a wretched decline. There are also many people who even remain unaffected by their own emptiness until the fire of God's Spirit kindles hunger and thirst in their hearts. Therefore, it is the work of the Spirit to give us an appetite for his grace.

As far as the present passage is concerned, the first thing to be understood is that no one is called to receive the riches of the Spirit except he who burns with a desire for them. We know how acutely painful thirst can be. It can make the strongest of men, who can endure any amount of labor, feel faint. Christ invites the thirsty, rather than the hungry, so that he can keep this metaphor when later on he uses the words **"water"** and **"drink."** In this way the different parts of his teaching are consistent with each other. I am sure that Christ is alluding to the passage in Isaiah which says, "Come, all you who are thirsty, come to the waters" (Isaiah 55:1), for what the prophet there attributes to God had eventually to be fulfilled in Christ. It is also like the blessed Virgin Mary's song: "He has . . . sent the rich away empty" (Luke 1:53). Therefore, Christ tells us to go straight to him, as if he is saying that only he can fully satisfy everyone's thirst and that everyone who seeks even the slightest relief from their thirst elsewhere is cheated and works in vain.

"Let him come to me and drink." A promise is added to the exhortation. Christ declares that he is not a dry and empty cistern but an inexhaustible spring plentifully and abundantly supplying everyone who comes to drink. From this it follows that if we ask Christ for what we want, our wishes will not be disappointed.

38. "Whoever believes in me . . ." Christ now points out how we come. We come not on foot but by faith. Or rather, to come is simply to believe — that is, if you define the word "believe" properly. As we have already said, we believe in Christ when we welcome him as he is shown to us in the Gospel — full of power, wisdom, righteousness, purity, life, and all the gifts of the Spirit. Further, Christ emphasizes here even more clearly the promise we have just spoken about, for he says that he has a rich abundance with which he will fully satisfy us.

"Streams of living water will flow from within him." At first sight the metaphor that "streams of living water will flow from within" believers seems definitely uncouth. But Christ's meaning is quite straightforward. People who believe in him will never lack any spiritual blessings. Christ calls it "living water" whose spring never grows dry and whose flow never ceases. "Streams," in the plural, I interpret as the many diverse graces of the Spirit which are necessary for the spiritual life of the soul. In summary, there are promised here, forever, the abundance of the gifts of the Spirit. Some people interpret the saying that "water will flow" from believers to mean that he to whom the Spirit has been given passes on some of the "water" to his brothers, since we should give to each other. But the meaning seems simpler than this to me. Whoever believes in Christ will have a spring of life welling up in him, as it were. This will be as Christ said before: "Whoever drinks the water I give him will never thirst" (4:14). For whereas ordinary drinking only quenches the thirst for a short time, Christ says that by faith we draw on the Spirit, who is the spring of water, welling up to eternal life.

However, he does not say that believers are so filled with Christ on the first day that they neither hunger nor thirst afterwards, but rather that the enjoyment of Christ kindles a new desire for him. This means that the Holy Spirit is like a living and constantly flowing spring in believers, just as Paul says that he "lives in you" (Romans 8:11), although we still carry about the cause of death in the remnants of sin. And, indeed, just as everyone shares the gifts of the Spirit according to the amount of faith they have, so there cannot be complete fullness in them in this life. But as believers progress in the faith, they continually aspire to new increases of the Spirit, so that the firstfruits which they have tasted are enough for the continuance of eternal life. This is also a warning for us about the small capacity of our faith, since the graces of the Spirit come to us by drops, whereas they would flow like rivers if we gave due place to Christ — that is, if faith made us capable of receiving him.

"As the Scripture has said . . ." Some commentators restrict this to the former clause, others to the latter. I extend it to cover the whole discourse. Indeed, I think that Christ is not referring to any one scriptural passage but takes a testimony from the common teaching of the prophets. For whenever the Lord promises an abundance of his Spirit, he refers mainly to Christ's kingdom and focuses the minds of the believers on that. Therefore all the predictions about living waters are fulfilled in Christ, who alone has opened and revealed God's hidden treasures. The graces of the Spirit are poured out on him, so that we may all draw from his fullness. Therefore people who are so kindly and graciously called by Christ and yet wander off in every direction deserve to perish miserably.

39. By this he meant the Spirit. The word "water" is sometimes used for **the Spirit** because of its purity, for it is his role to cleanse away our pollutions. But in this and similar passages the expression has a different meaning, which is that we are destitute of all the sap and moisture of life except when **the Spirit** of God gives us life and waters us, as it were, by a secret power. This is an expression in which one part is included under the whole, for under the one word "water" he includes all the parts of life. From this we also infer that everyone who has not been brought to life by Christ's **Spirit** is to be thought of as being dead, no matter how much they pretend to be alive.

Up to that time the Spirit had not been given. As we know, **the Spirit** is eternal. But the evangelist is saying that so long as Christ lives in the world in the humble form of a servant, that grace of **the Spirit** which was poured out on mankind after Christ's resurrection had not yet come about openly. Christ is speaking comparatively, just as when the New Testament is compared with the Old. God promises his **Spirit** to believers as if he had never given him to the fathers. By that time the disciples had undoubtedly already received the firstfruits of **the Spirit**, for where does faith come from if it does not come from **the Spirit?** So the evangelist is not just denying that the grace of **the Spirit** was revealed to believers before Christ's death, but that it was not yet so bright and illustrious as it would be later. The main glory of Christ's kingdom is that he governs the church by his **Spirit.** But he entered into the lawful and, as it were, ceremonial possession of his kingdom when he was exalted to the right hand of the Father. So there is nothing surprising in his delaying the full manifestation of **the Spirit** until then.

There is one outstanding question. Is Christ referring here to the visible graces of **the Spirit**, or to being given new life, which is the fruit of adoption? My reply is: **the Spirit**, who had been promised at the coming of Christ, appeared in those visible gifts like mirrors. Here, however, Christ is just referring to the power of **the Spirit**, through whom we are born again in Christ and become new creatures. That we lie on earth poor and hungry and almost destitute of spiritual blessings, while Christ sits in glory at the right hand of the Father, clothed with the highest majesty, must be put down to our slothfulness and to our tiny faith.

Verses 40–44

40. Some of the people . . . The evangelist now recounts the result of this latest discourse of our Lord Jesus Christ. The differing opinions caused a division among **the people.** It should be noted here that John is not referring to Christ's avowed enemies, or to **the people** who already hated his teaching, but to the ordinary people, who should have shown the greatest integrity. He enumerates three classes of such people.

"Surely this man is the Prophet." The first group of people acknowledged that Jesus really was a prophet, and from this we can conclude that they were not against his teaching. However, the light-heartedness and carelessness of this confession is clear from the fact that although they approve the teacher, they neither understand what he means nor are happy with what he says. They could not really embrace Christ as a prophet without also confessing him to be the Son of God and the author of their salvation. But we can say this for them, that they did see something divine in Christ which led them to reverence him, for this willingness to learn might lead on to faith.

41. Others said, "He is the Christ." The second have a better opinion than the first. They clearly confess that he is **"the Christ."** But people oppose them, and this causes the division of opinion. This warns us not to think it strange if in our own day people are divided over various controversies. We see that Christ's sermon caused a division not among Gentiles who were outside the faith, but in the middle of the church of Christ and even in the chief seat of the church. Should Christ's teaching be blamed for this as the cause of the disturbance? No. Even if the whole world was up in arms, the Word of God is so precious that we should want it to be received, by a few people at least. So we should not have a guilty conscience about people who think they are among God's people arguing and debating among themselves.

However, we should note that the divisions do not really originate in the Gospel, for there can be no strong agreement among people except in undoubted truth. The peace enjoyed by those who do not know God stems from stupidity rather than from true agreement. In summary, the reason and seed of all the differences that spring up when the Gospel is preached is already latent in men. When these are, as it were, woken up, they start to move, just as mists produced by something other than the sun do not become apparent until the sun rises.

"How can the Christ come from Galilee?" They arm themselves with the testimony of Scripture in case they appear to reject Christ without thought. Although they use this against Christ, they do have some semblance of truth. They are only wrong in thinking that Christ was a Galilean. But what is the cause of this ignorance if it is not contempt? If it had not been too much to find out, they would have seen that Christ was honored with both titles — that he was born in Bethlehem and was the son of David. But our nature is such that in small things we are ashamed of our laziness, but with the mysteries of the kingdom of heaven we sleep on unconcerned. It is worth noting how they are keen and industrious to find an excuse to turn away from Christ, yet are surprisingly slow and dull to receive sound teaching. People often erect obstacles for themselves like this against coming to Christ out of the very Scriptures which lead us to Christ by the hand.

44. Some wanted to seize him. The evangelist means by this that they not only despised Christ, but that their wicked rejection of him was joined with cruelty and a desire to hurt him; for superstition is always cruel. The ineffectiveness of their efforts was due to God's providence. For as we said earlier, since Christ's hour had not yet come, he relied on and was guarded by his Father's protection and so overcame all dangers.

Verses 45–53

45. The temple guards went back. Here we can see how blind is the arrogance of ungodly people. They worship and admire their greatness in the world so much that they do not hesitate to trample down human and divine law. If anything happens against their wishes, they happily throw everything into confusion. When these haughty and wicked priests ask why Christ was not brought to them, they elevate their own position as if nothing should oppose their command.

46. "No one ever spoke the way this man does." The officers acknowledge that they are subdued and overcome by Christ's word alone; and yet it does not make them repent or give due honor to that word. If it was true that **"no one ever spoke the way this man does,"** why did not the divine power which they were forced to feel so touch their hearts that they really devoted themselves to God? But Isaiah's words had to be fulfilled in this way: "with the breath of his lips he will slay the wicked" (Isaiah 11:4). Moreover, we shall see later on how those who were seeking Christ's death were overwhelmed by Christ's voice alone and fell backwards, as if felled by a hammer blow. From this we learn that Christ's teaching has so much power that it can even frighten the wicked; but as this results in their destruction, we must be careful to be softened rather than to be broken.

There are still many people around today who are very similar to these officers. Reluctantly they are drawn to admire the Gospel's teaching and yet are so far from yielding to Christ that they stay in the enemy's camp. Some other people are even worse, and in order to curry favor with the wicked they defame that teaching with all the slander they can muster, even though they are inwardly convinced it is from God.

47. "You mean he has deceived you also?" They tell their officers off in such a way as to keep them subject to them. Through these words they mean that it would be unreasonable and out of place for them to be unsteady, even if everyone else fell away. But we must examine the basis of their argument when they insult Christ haughtily.

48. "Has any of the rulers or of the Pharisees believed in him?" "Only the common people and the ignorant," they say, "are on his side; the rulers and notables are against him." They single out the Pharisees, because they had a higher reputation than the others, both for learning and for holiness, and were like the princes of the rulers. This objection seems quite plausible, for if the rulers and governors of the church do not hold on to their authority, nothing can ever be well-ordered, nor can the church long continue in a well-ordered condition. We know the desires of ordinary people, and the most anarchical disorder that would soon follow if every person was allowed to do as he liked. Therefore, the authority of rulers is a necessary bridle to keep order in the church, and it was accordingly provided by God's law that if any question or controversy arose, it should be submitted to the decision of the high priest (see Deuteronomy 17:8).

But they sinned because they were unwilling to submit to God, and because they claimed for themselves the highest authority. It is true that God conferred the power of judgment on the high priest, but God only intended him to decide in accordance with the law. Therefore, whatever authority pastors possess is subject to God's Word, so that everyone may be kept in their own order, from the highest to the lowest, and God alone exalted. If pastors who honestly and sincerely do their duty claim authority for themselves, it is a holy and legitimate claim. But when the mere authority of men is exalted apart from God's Word, it is vain and useless boasting. However, it often happens that the wicked dominate the church, and therefore we must beware of attributing anything to men once they depart from God's Word.

We see that nearly all the prophets were troubled with this nuisance, for, to bury their teaching, men continually conferred on them the lofty titles of "princes," "priests," and "the church." The Roman Catholics today, armed with the same weapons, are not less fierce than were the opponents of Christ and the prophets. It is indeed a fearful blindness when mortal man is not ashamed to set himself against God. But Satan drives them to this state of madness, so that they love their own ambition more than God's truth. But we for our part must so revere the Word of God that all the splendor of the world is put out and its empty mists scattered. For we would be in a bad way if our salvation depended on the will of princes, and our faith would be most unstable if it were to stand or fall at their pleasure.

49. "But this mob . . ." Their pride consisted, first, in relying on the title of priest and desiring that everyone should submit to them. Next, their pride made them despise everyone else as being worthless. People who are too pleased with themselves are always showing contempt for others; disdain of Christian brothers and sisters always follows love of ourselves. They pronounce that everyone is accursed. Why? They doubtless say that people do not know the law, but they kept the other reason quiet — that they thought there was no holiness except in their own order. In the same way today, Roman Catholic priests claim that they alone are the church, and they despise the laity, as they call them, as if they were heathen. But God throws down such arrogant madness by preferring the lowly and despised to the highest and most powerful.

We note that the knowledge of the law which they are boasting about here is not that which teaches men religion and the fear of God, but such as they possessed when, with professional superciliousness, they gave their replies as if they alone were the proper interpreters of the law. It is quite true that everyone who has not been taught by God's law is accursed, because through its knowledge we are truly made holy. However, knowledge about this is not confined to only a few people, who would then be swollen with perverted confidence and excuse themselves from the ranks of the rest. This knowledge belongs to all of God's children, so that everyone, from the least to the greatest, may be gathered together in the same obedience of faith.

50. Nicodemus . . . The evangelist shows Nicodemus' neutrality as he does not attempt to put up any good defense on behalf of sound teaching, although he cannot bear to have the truth opposed.

. . . who had gone to Jesus earlier. This detail which the evangelist includes is partly to Nicodemus' shame and partly to his credit. Had he not loved Christ's teaching, he would never have dared go against the wrath of the ungodly, for he knew that if anyone only opened his mouth, he would immediately be exposed to their dislike and to danger. Therefore, when he dares to say a word, however feeble it may have been, it is a small spark of godliness shining from his heart. But he does not defend Christ more strongly because he is over-timid. So the evangelist is saying that Nicodemus still hankers after the concealment of the night and is not Christ's true disciple. He says that Nicodemus once came to Christ by night, but remained openly among the enemy and kept his place in their camp.

This should be carefully noted because many people today pretend that they are like Nicodemus and hope to escape punishment as they mock God in their hypocrisy. Granting their point that there is no difference between them and Nicodemus, how, pray, does such an example help them? Nicodemus says that Christ should not be condemned unheard. Exactly the same could be said of a robber or murderer, for it is well-known and proverbial that it is better to acquit the guilty than to condemn the innocent. Moreover, in his desire to clear Christ's character, he leaves and abandons the teaching itself. What is there here worthy of a godly and believing person? In this way the seed of the Gospel, which later bore fruit, still lay dormant in him. It is more beneficial if we apply this example in another way. The Lord often makes the teaching which seemed to have perished gradually take root secretly and after a long time grow some buds, at first apparently abortively, but then, later, with life and vigor. This is just what happened to Nicodemus' faith which came to life in a new and vigorous way after Christ's death.

52. "Are you from Galilee, too?" They say that everyone who is in favor of Christ comes from Galilee, but this is said scornfully, as if Christ could only have on his side people from the despised corner of Galilee. The way they turn on Nicodemus shows what furious hatred burned in their hearts against Christ. Nicodemus had not openly undertaken to defend Christ, but had only said that he should not be condemned unheard. In the same way today among the Roman Catholics, no one can show the slightest sign of impartiality about the oppression of the Gospel without the enemy at once flying into a passion and labeling him a heretic.

53. Then each went to his own home. The scene ends in an amazing way. If anyone considers the way the priests ruled, and their rage and the power at their command, and, on the other side, Christ bare and unarmed without an armed bodyguard, he was bound to be finished. When so formidable a conspiracy dissolves of its own accord and all these men break themselves with their own violence like waves of the sea, who will not acknowledge that they are scattered by God's hand?

But God always continues to be like himself. Therefore he will, whenever he pleases, break up all the plans of his enemies, so that when they have everything in their power and are ready and prepared to carry out their plans, they will leave without doing their work. We have often found that whatever schemes the enemy has made to extinguish the Gospel, they soon failed by the amazing grace of God.

John
Chapter 8

Verses 1–11

3. The teachers of the law and the Pharisees brought . . . It is quite clear that this story was unknown to the ancient Greek churches. Hence some conjecture that it was inserted from another place. But it has always been received by the Latin churches and is found in many Greek manuscripts and contains nothing unworthy of an apostolic spirit; so there is no reason why we should refuse to make use of it. When the evangelist says that **the teachers of the law** brought a woman to him, he means that they were acting in concert to lay a trap for Christ. He mentions **the Pharisees** in particular because they were paramount in the hierarchy of the teachers of the law. They were extremely wicked to use this pretext for slander, and their very words gave them away, for they do not disguise the fact that they have a clear commandment of the law in mind. Hence it follows that they act maliciously in asking a question as if they were in doubt. But their intention was to force Christ to give up his office of preaching grace, so that he might seem fickle and unsteady. They say plainly that adulteresses are condemned by Moses, in order to hold Christ bound by the decision of the law, for it was not right to acquit those whom the law condemned. But it would be uncharacteristic of Christ to agree with this law.

6. Jesus bent down. This gesture showed that Christ despised them. Those who suppose that he wrote something or other are mistaken, in my opinion. Nor do I agree with Augustine's ingenious idea (he thinks that this indicates the distinction between the law and the Gospel, in that Christ wrote not on tables of stone, but on man who is dust and earth). Rather, Christ intended, by doing nothing, to show that they were not worth listening to — just as if anyone, while another was speaking to him, were to trace lines on the wall with his finger or turn his back or show by some other sign that he was not listening to what was being said. Thus today when Satan tries in various ways to distract us from the right path of the Gospel, we should with contempt pass by the many things he sets against us. The Roman Catholics worry as much as they can with many trifling cavils, like clouds scattered in the air. If godly teachers laboriously examine each one of their cavils, they will be starting on a Penelope's web. Therefore hindrances of this kind, which merely impede the progress of the Gospel, are wisely disregarded.

7. **"If any one of you is without sin . . ."** This was in line with the normal law, for God commanded that the witnesses should put law-breakers and evil-doers to death with their own hands, so that very great care would be shown in bearing witness (Deuteronomy 17:7). There are many who rush thoughtlessly into overwhelming their brother with perjury because they do not consider the fact that they inflict a deadly wound with their tongue. And this argument had weight with those slanderers, wicked as they were; and when it is put to them, they calm down. Yet Christ's words are different from what the law commanded. In the law, God merely warned them not to condemn a man with words except for the person whom they were allowed to put to death with their own hands. But Christ is demanding perfect innocence from the witnesses, so that no man may take it upon himself to avenge a crime in another unless he himself is pure and free from all guilt. Now what Christ then said to a few we should apply to everyone, so that whoever accuses another should himself be innocent. Otherwise, we are not attacking wicked deeds but are against people.

In this way, however, he seems to be taking justice out of the world, so that no one will dare to say that he punishes crimes. Is there one single judge who is not aware of something wrong in himself? Can a single witness be called on who is not guilty of some fault? So he seems to be driving all witnesses away from the witness box and all judges from their bench. I reply: this is not an absolute and straightforward prohibition in which Christ forbids sinners to do their duty in correcting other people's sins. But through these words Christ only reproves hypocrites, who gently flatter themselves and their own vices but are excessively severe and even savage rulers of other people. So no one must allow his own sins to stop him from correcting other people's sins and even punishing them when necessary, so long as he hates, both in himself and in others, what is to be condemned. Moreover, everyone should start by interrogating his own conscience and be both witness and judge against himself before he judges others. In this way we shall wage war on sins without hating people.

9. **Those who heard began to go away.** Here we see the great power of an evil conscience. Though these wicked hypocrites meant to get the better of Christ with their cavils, their shame puts them to flight as soon as he pierces their consciences with a single word. This hammer breaks the pride of hypocrites. They must be summoned to the judgment-seat of God. It may be, however, that they were more influenced by their shame before men than by their fear of God. Yet at least of themselves they con-

fess they are guilty and flee away confounded. The detail to note is that their conviction of guilt was in proportion to their status. Would that our present-day teachers of the law, who oppose Christ, had at least as much shame. But they are so shameless that, notorious for all wickedness, they glory that they can be shameless with impunity. We should also observe how much this feeling of sin, with which the teachers of the law were touched, differs from true penitence. We should be so affected by God's judgment that we shall not look for hiding-places to flee from the presence of the Judge but will go straight to him to ask his forgiveness.

Only Jesus was left. The Spirit of wisdom arranged it so that those wicked men went away when they had tempted Christ in vain. And there is no reason to doubt that we shall be superior to all the schemes of our enemies if only we will let ourselves be ruled by the same Spirit. But it often happens that they defeat us because we do not notice their interests and do not trouble to take advice, or, trusting in our own wisdom, we do not think how much we need the rule of the Holy Spirit. **Only Jesus was left.** This does not mean that the people whom he had been teaching had left him, but that all **the teachers of the law** who had brought the adulteress troubled him no more. When it says that **the woman** stayed with Christ, we learn that there is nothing better for us than to be brought guilty before him and judged, so long as we submit ourselves calmly and obediently to it.

11. "Neither do I condemn you." It does not say that Christ only absolved the woman, but that he let her go free. And this is not surprising, for he did not want to do anything that was inappropriate for him. He had been sent by the Father to gather the lost sheep, and so, mindful of his calling, he exhorts the woman to repentance and comforts her with a promise of grace. Those who deduce from this that adultery should not be punished by death must on the same reasoning admit that inheritances should not be divided, since Christ refused to arbitrate between two brothers. Indeed, every crime will be exempt from the penalties of the law if the punishment of adultery is remitted, for the door will then be thrown open to any kind of treachery and to poisoning, murder, and robbery. Moreover, when an adulteress brings an illegitimate child into a family, she not only steals the family name but robs the legitimate issue of the right of inheritance and transfers it to strangers. But the chief evil is that the wife disgraces the husband to whom she had been joined, by indulging in a shameful deed and violating the sacred covenant of God, without which no sound holiness can continue to exist in the world.

"Leave your life of sin." From this we deduce what the aim of Christ's grace is: when the sinner is reconciled to God, he may honor the author of his salvation through a godly and holy life. In summary, the same Word of God that offers us pardon calls us at the same time to repentance. Besides, although this exhortation looks forward to the future, it nevertheless humbles sinners with the memory of their past life.

Verses 12–14

12. "I am the light of the world." Those who omit the foregoing narrative join this discourse of Christ to the sermon he preached on the last day of the assembly. It is a most beautiful title of Christ when he is called **"the light of the world."** We are all blind by nature, but a remedy is offered to rescue and free us from darkness and make us share in the true light. And this blessing is not offered just to one person, here or there, for Christ says that he is the **"light"** of the whole **world.** By this general statement he wanted to remove the distinction both between Jews and Gentiles, between the learned and ignorant, and between exceptional people and ordinary people.

First of all, we must see the need for seeking this **"light."** For no one will ever present themselves to Christ to be enlightened except those who have known both that this world is darkness and that they themselves are altogether blind. We must realize, then, that when the means of obtaining light is shown us in Christ, we are all condemned for blindness, and everything that we think is light is compared to darkness and thick night. For Christ is not speaking of what he has in common with others, but he claims it as uniquely his own. Hence it follows that outside him there is not even a spark of true light. There may be some semblance of brightness, but it is like lightning, which only dazzles the eyes. We must also notice that the power and function of enlightening is not confined to the physical presence of Christ, for although he is far from us bodily, he nevertheless daily sheds his **"light"** on us in the teaching of the Gospel and by the secret power of his Spirit. But we do not have a total picture of this **"light"** until we learn that we are enlightened by the Gospel and the Spirit of Christ, so that we may know that the fountain of all knowledge and wisdom is hidden in him.

"Whoever follows me . . ." To this teaching Christ adds an exhortation, which he immediately confirms with a promise. For when we hear that everyone who allows himself to be ruled by Christ is out of danger of straying, we should be stirred up to follow him. Indeed, Christ draws us to himself with an outstretched hand, as it were. So great and magnificent a promise must also be full of power, so that those who look to Christ are certain that they will have a sure way, even through the midst of darkness, and not just for a little while, but until they have reached their goal. That is the significance of the words being put in the future tense, **"he will never walk in darkness, but will have the light of life."** This is also the meaning of the latter clause, which expressly states the everlasting nature of this **"light."** We must not be afraid, then, that this **"light"** will fail in the middle of our journey, for it leads us right up to **"life."** The genitive is used, in the Hebrew manner, instead of the adjective, to denote the effect, as if he had said, "the life-giving light." It is no wonder that such deep darkness of errors and superstitions reigns in the world when so few look to Christ.

13. The Pharisees challenged him. They protest that, as was generally agreed, no one can give testimony on behalf of himself. A genuine witness consists in what is lawful and worthy of belief. In summary, they mean that Christ's words are powerless unless he brings proof from elsewhere.

14. "Even if I testify . . ." Christ replies that his witness has sufficient credit and authority because he is not a private person among the great mass of men, but holds a very different rank. For when he says that he knows where he came from and where he is going to, he is separating himself from ordinary people. So this means that everyone is suspect in his own cause, and the laws provide that no one is to be believed when he speaks on his own behalf. This does not apply to the Son of God, however, who stands outside the whole world. For he is not to be thought of as belonging to the category of human beings, but has been honored by his Father with the privilege of bringing all men to order by his Word alone.

"I know where I came from." By these words he declares that his origin is not from the world, but that he came from God. Hence it would be unjust and unreasonable for his teaching, which is divine, to be subjected to men's laws. But because they despised him, who was then clothed with the form of a servant in the lowliness of the flesh, he reminds them about the future glory of his resurrection, which was a clear proof of his hitherto hidden and unknown divinity. Therefore, this temporary state should not have stopped the Jews from submitting to God's only ambassador, who had been promised beforehand to them in the law.

When Christ says that he knows but that they do not know, he means that his glory is not diminished at all by their unbelief. And as he has given us the same testimony, our faith ought to despise all the contradictions and murmurings of the ungodly; for if it is founded on God, it will be far above the most elevated thing in the world. But in order that his majesty in the Gospel may stand firm in us, we must always concentrate on the heavenly glory of Christ and hear him speaking in the world, so that we remember where he came from and what authority he has now that he has completed the work he came to do. As he humbled himself for a season, so he now sits at the right hand of the Father, that every knee may bow to him.

Verses 15–20

15. "You judge by human standards." This can be expounded in two ways — either that they judge according to depraved human standards, or from the appearance of the person. For the expression **"human stan-**

dards" is sometimes used of the outward appearance of a man. Both meanings fit in well with this passage, since neither truth nor justice has any place where **"human standards"** hold sway or where a respect for people overrides justice. But it seems to me that the meaning will be clearer if you contrast **"human standards"** with those of the Spirit, so that Christ denies that they are lawful and competent judges because they are not guided by the Spirit.

"I pass judgment on no one." Commentators differ here also. Some make the distinction that Christ does not judge as man does. Others refer it to the time — that is, he had not yet undertaken the office of Judge while he was on earth. Augustine gives both expositions but does not decide between them. But the former distinction does not apply at all. The sentence contains two clauses — that Christ does not judge, and that if he judges, his judgment is firm and authoritative because it is divine (verse 16). And so I restrict the former clause, in which he says that he does not judge, to the circumstances of the present passage. To convict his enemies more deeply of pride, Christ uses the comparison that they unlawfully assume the license to judge and yet cannot condemn him when he only teaches and refrains from executing the office of judge.

16. "But if I do judge . . ." Christ adds this correction lest he should seem to be giving up his right entirely. **"If I do judge, my decisions are right,"** he says; that is, they deserve to be authoritative. The authority arises from his doing nothing that is not in line with his Father's commandment.

The phrase **"I am not alone"** adds weight to the affirmation that he is not like any other ordinary person, but must be seen in the light of the office placed upon him by the Father. But why does he not assert his divinity more clearly, as he might truly and fairly have done? Because, as his divinity was hidden under the veil of the human body, he sets before them his Father, in whom it was more conspicuous. Nevertheless, the tenor of the discourse is that all he does and teaches should be taken as divine.

17. "In your own Law . . ." At first sight the argument might seem weak, in that no man is accepted as a witness in his own case. But we must remember what I have already said, that Christ is not to be viewed as any ordinary person, since he is neither a private man, nor does he transact his own private business. By distinguishing himself from the Father, he accommodates himself to what his hearers can cope with. He does this for the sake of his office; for at that time he was the Father's minister, and so he asserts that the Father is the author of all his teaching.

19. "Where is your Father?" Without doubt they inquired in a sarcastic way about his **"Father."** For they not only, with their usual pride, treat what Christ said about the Father contemptuously, but also ridicule him for highly exalting his Father, as if he himself traced his origin from heaven. Hence these words affirm that they do not value Christ's "Father" so highly as to ascribe to his Son anything on his account. The reason why there is such bold contempt of Christ everywhere today is that few believe that Christ was sent by God.

"You do not know me . . ." He does not condescend to give them a straight answer, but curtly reproaches the ignorance within which they flattered themselves. They asked about the "Father," and yet with the Son present before their eyes, seeing they did not see. Therefore it was a just punishment of their pride and wicked ingratitude that those who despised the Son of God, who was exhibited so closely to them, never approached the "Father." For how can any mortal man ascend to the height of God unless he is raised on high by his hand? God in Christ descended to the lowliness of men to stretch out his hand to them. So do not those who reject God when he approaches them like this deserve to be excluded from heaven?

We must realize that the same thing is addressed to us all. Whoever aspires to know God without beginning with Christ must wander in a labyrinth, so to speak, for it is not for nothing that he is called the image of the "Father," as has been said already. Again, because everyone is deprived of all right knowledge of God who leaves Christ and strives like a Titan after heaven, so whoever directs his mind and all his sense to Christ will be led straight to the "Father." For the apostle Paul truly declares that by the mirror of the Gospel we clearly behold God in the person of Christ (see 2 Corinthians 3:18). And it is indeed an incomparable reward for the obedience of faith that he who humbles himself before Christ penetrates beyond all the heavens, even to those mysteries which the angels behold and adore.

20. He spoke these words . . . The treasury was the part of the temple where the sacred offerings were stored. It was a very busy place, and so we infer that Christ preached this sermon to a large group of people, and thus the people had even less excuse for not believing Christ. The evangelist also shows us the astonishing power of God, in that they were forced to put up with Christ's public teaching in the temple even though, shortly before, they had tried to put him to death. For their rule in the temple was undisputed, so that they domineered there with a tyrannical fierceness and could have banished Christ at a word. When he dared to take upon himself the office of teacher, why did they not immediately seize him? So we see that God made them hear and kept Christ safe with God's protection, so that those savage beasts did not touch him, though their jaws were open wide. John again mentions Christ's time, to teach us that it is not by men's will but God's that we live and die.

Verses 21–24

21. "I am going away." When Christ sees that he is doing no good among these obstinate men, he threatens their destruction. And this is the end of all who reject the Gospel, for it is not sown uselessly in the air, but has to result in either life or death. The meaning of the words, however, is this: in the end, the wicked will feel how great an evil it was that they rejected Christ, when he freely offered himself to them; but it will be too late, and there will be no more time for repentance. To frighten them still more with the closeness of their judgment, Christ first says that he will soon go away, meaning that the Gospel is preached to them only for a little while, and, if they let this opportunity pass, the accepted time and days of salvation will not last forever. In the same way today, we must go at once to meet Christ when he knocks at our door, in case he becomes impatient with our laziness and goes away from us. Indeed, it is well-known from many examples in every age how much Christ's departure is to be feared.

But we must first discover how these people who are now spoken about sought Christ. For if there had been a real change, they would not have sought him in vain, since Christ has rightly promised that as soon as a sinner mourns for his sins, Christ will be present to help. Therefore, Christ did not mean that they sought him with genuine faith but were like men in desperate trouble, looking everywhere for help. Unbelievers would like God to be reconciled to them but do not stop running away from him. God calls them. The way to him is by faith and repentance. But they oppose God by hardness of heart, and when they are overwhelmed by despair they murmur against him. In summary, they are so far from aspiring to God that they do not give him an opportunity to help them unless he denies himself, which he will never do.

In this way, however wicked the teachers of the law were, they would gladly have applied to themselves the redemption promised by the hand of the Messiah, if only Christ had transfigured himself according to their wishes. Therefore, through these words Christ warns all unbelievers that when they have despised the teaching of the Gospel, they will be brought to such straits that they will be forced to cry to God. But their wailing will be useless because, as we have already said, seeking, they do not seek. This is expressed plainly enough in the next clause, where he says, **"You will die in your sin."** Christ is telling them that the reason for their destruction will be their disobedience and rebellion against God to the very end. We will soon see the nature of their sin.

22. "Will he kill himself?" The teachers of the law continue boldly to scorn and to be impudent. They ridicule Christ, saying that they cannot follow where he is going. It is as if they said, "We acknowledge that we cannot accompany him if he kills himself, for we do not choose to do that." They do not think anything about Christ's departure and imagine that they will defeat him in every respect; and so they tell him to go where he likes. Shocking stupidity! But this is how Satan bewitches the reprobate, so that, drunk with worse than madness, they may throw themselves into the middle of the flame of God's wrath. Do we not today see the same rage in many who stifle their consciences and with their jests and insolent jeering mock at everything they hear about the fearful judgment of God? Yet this is certainly a sardonic smile, for inwardly they are pierced with unseen wounds; but all of a sudden, as if bereft of their senses, they burst out into furious guffaws.

23. "You are from below." Since they did not deserve to have Christ teach them, he only wanted to hit them with curt reproofs. So in this passage Christ says that they do not receive his teaching because the kingdom of God is utterly abhorrent to them. He includes in the words **"world"** and **"below"** all that men have by nature, and so indicates the difference between his Gospel and the acuteness and perspicacity of the human mind; for the Gospel is heavenly wisdom, but our mind is earthbound. So only the person whom Christ has made by his Spirit will ever be a proper disciple. And this is why faith is so rare in the world, because the whole human race is naturally opposed and averse to Christ — except for those whom he raises on high through the special grace of his Spirit.

24. "You would die in your sins." First Christ had used the singular, and now he puts it in the plural, though with the same meaning, except that in the former passage he wanted to point out that unbelief is the source and cause of all evils. Not that unbelief alone is sin, or that it alone makes us guilty of eternal death before God, as some exaggerate. But it alienates us from Christ and deprives us of his grace, by which we should seek deliverance from all our sins. The deadly disease of the Jews is that they reject the medicine with obstinate malice. Hence also the slaves of Satan do not stop heaping up sin on sin and continually bring fresh guilt on themselves. Therefore, Christ adds the next sentence.

"If you do not believe that I am . . ." There is no other way for the lost to recover salvation than by running to Christ. The emphasis is on the phrase **"that I am."** We must understand by it all that the Scripture ascribes to the Messiah and all that it tells us to expect from him. But the sum and substance is the restoration of the church, of which the beginning is the light of faith, from which spring righteousness and a new life. Some of the earlier commentators have misapplied this to the divine essence of Christ. He is in fact speaking about his office in relation to us. The statement is noteworthy, for men never consider enough the evils in which they are plunged; and although they are constrained to acknowledge their destruction, they neglect Christ and grope around for useless remedies. Hence we must believe that until the grace of Christ is seen to save us, there reigns a boundless mixture of all kinds of evil.

Verses 25–29

25. "From the beginning" (KJV). They are very mistaken who take **"all along"** (NIV) in the nominative, as if Christ was here asserting his eternal divinity. There can be no ambiguity of this sort in the Greek, but the Greek commentators also differ among themselves. They are indeed all agreed that a preposition is to be supplied, but many expound it as an adverb, as if Christ were saying, "This is the first thing to be observed." Some, too, like Chrysostom, make it read continuously: "The beginning, which also speaks to you, I have many things to say and judge of you." This sense has been put into verse by Nonnus. But a different reading is more generally adopted and seems the true one to me. I interpret the Greek to mean **"all along,"** so that, to my mind, the meaning is this: "I did not arise suddenly, but I now arrive publicly, just as I was formerly promised."

He adds, **"just what I have been claiming."** By this Christ means that he is declaring plainly enough who he is, if only they had ears for it. **"Just"** is not used merely to give a reason, as if Christ wanted to prove that he was from the beginning. Rather, he asserts that the links between his teaching and the eternity he has spoken about are such that they ought to be taken as a definite confirmation. The words may be explained thus: "As it was in the beginning — that is, he whom I confirmed in time past — I now reaffirm"; or, "And, indeed, what I now speak is in line with the prophecies of all ages as firm proof of them."

In summary, this reply consists of two clauses. In the phrase **"all along,"** he includes a continuous series of ages, from the time when God made his covenant with the fathers. When Christ says that he also speaks, he joins his present teaching to the ancient prophecies and shows that it depends on them. It follows that the only reason for the ignorance of the Jews was that they believed neither the prophets nor the Gospel, for the same Christ is on view in them all. They pretended to be the prophets' disciples and to look to the eternal covenant of God, but they still rejected Christ, who had been promised from the beginning and now presented himself before them.

26. "I have much to say . . ." Seeing that Christ is preaching to the deaf, he does not go on with his sermon, but only declares that God will vindicate the teaching that he is author of, and which they despise. "If I wanted to accuse you," he says, "your malice and wickedness give me reason enough. But I leave you for the present. My Father, who has committed to me the office of teaching, will not neglect his part. He will always justify his Word against the ungodly and sacrilegious contempt of men." This saying of Christ's is similar to Paul's: "If we are faithless, he will remain faithful, for he cannot disown himself" (2 Timothy 2:13). In summary, Christ threatens the judgment of God against unbelievers who refuse to believe his Word, because God will defend his truth. Now this is the true anchor of our faith: when we believe that God is sufficient of himself to establish the authority of his teaching, even if the whole world should reject it. All who rely on this teaching and serve Christ faithfully may fearlessly accuse the whole world of falsehood.

"**And what I have heard . . .**" He says that he is proposing nothing that he has not received from the Father. The only confirmation of teaching is when the minister shows that what he says has come from God. Now we know that Christ undertook then the role of a minister, and so it is not surprising if he demands a hearing, since he brings God's commands to men. Moreover, by his example he lays down a general principle for the whole church: no one is to be listened to unless he speaks from the mouth of God. But while he knocks down the perverse arrogance of those who put themselves forward without God's Word, faithful teachers who are well aware of their calling are fortified and armed by him with unconquerable firmness, and thus they may, under God's guidance, boldly defy all mortals.

27. They did not understand. From this it is clear how stupid people are whose minds are possessed by Satan. Nothing could be plainer than that they were summoned to the judgment-seat of God; but they are altogether blind to this, just as other enemies of the Gospel are every day. Their blindness should teach us to fear.

28. "When you have lifted up . . ." Displeased at the dullness that the evangelist had described, Christ again declares that they are not worthy of hearing any more from him. "All your senses," he says, "are, as it were, bewitched, and therefore you understand nothing that I say. But the time will yet come when you will realize that God's prophet has lived among you and spoken to you." This is the way we should deal with the ungodly; we should summon them positively to the judgment-seat of the supreme Judge. But the knowledge that Christ speaks of comes too late when the ungodly are dragged to punishment and reluctantly confess that the God they should have calmly revered is their Judge. Christ does not promise them repentance but says that, when they have been struck with new and unexpected horror at God's wrath, they will be aroused from their state of numbness.

Adam's eyes were opened like this, so that he was overwhelmed with shame and in vain sought for hiding-places and at last saw that he was lost. Yet this knowledge that Adam had, although useless in itself, was turned to his advantage through God's grace. But when the reprobate are overwhelmed with despair, their eyes are only opened to see their destruction. God leads them to this kind of knowledge in a variety of ways. Often they are forced through afflictions to realize that God is angry with them. Sometimes he tortures them inwardly without any outer punishment. And sometimes he lets them go on sleeping until he calls them out of this world.

By the words **"lifted up"** Christ refers to his own death. He mentions his death to warn them that they will gain nothing by destroying his body. It is as if he said, "You now haughtily mock my words. But your wickedness will soon extend to killing me. Then you will triumph, as if your wish had come true; but it will not be long before you feel, to your utter ruin, how little my death is my destruction." He uses the words **"lifted up"** to make a deeper impact on them. They wanted to take Christ down to the lowest depths. He tells them they will be totally disappointed and that the outcome will be the exact opposite. It may be, indeed, that he was alluding to the outward form of his death, that he was to be **"lifted up"** on the cross. But he was chiefly looking to its glorious result, which followed soon after, contrary to all expectation.

It is true that even through the cross Christ triumphed magnificently over Satan, in front of God and the angels, blotting out the handwriting of sin and canceling the condemnation of death. But it was only after the Gospel had been preached that this triumph began to be apparent to men. The same thing that happened soon after — that Christ rose from the grave and ascended to heaven — is what we should expect daily; for no matter how the ungodly may scheme to oppress Christ in his teaching and his church, he will not only rise above them, but will turn their wicked efforts to advance his kingdom the more.

". . . that I am" (KJV). I have already said that this does not refer to Christ's divine essence but to his office. This is even more apparent from the context, where he affirms that he does nothing except at the command of his Father. This was as good as saying that he was sent by God and carries out his office faithfully.

"I do nothing on my own." That is, "I do not put myself forward and undertake anything rashly." The word **"speak"** refers to the same thing — that is, the teaching office. When Christ wants to prove that he does nothing without the Father's command, he says that he speaks as he has been taught by him. And so the meaning of these words is: "In all my activity, which you condemn, no part is my own; I am simply executing what God has commanded me. The words you hear from my mouth are his, and my calling is governed by him alone, who is its author." But we must remember that these words are, as I have mentioned before, said in such a way that his hearers can cope with them. Since they viewed Christ merely as an ordinary person, he asserts that whatever is divine in him is not his own — as if he were saying that it is not of man or by man, because the Father teaches us by him and appoints him to be the only teacher in the church. This is why he says that he has been taught by the Father.

29. "The one who sent me . . ." Christ again proclaims that God, under whose guidance and authority he does everything, will help him, and therefore he will not work in vain and uselessly. It is as if he said that the power of God's Spirit is joined to his ministry. All faithful teachers should have the same confidence and not doubt that God's hand will be near them when they carry out, with a clear conscience, the ministry that he demands. For God does not equip them with his Word in order to punch the air with a cold and empty sound. He gives success to his Word by the hidden efficacy of his Spirit, and at the same time protects them, so that their enemies may be vanquished and they are left standing invincible against the whole world. If they use their own judgment and strength, they will be overturned all the time. Therefore the only way for them to stand is for them to be convinced that they are upheld by God's hand.

But we must note why Christ says that God is on his side and why he will never be without his help. It is because he depends entirely on his will and serves him sincerely. For this is what the adverb **"always"** means — that he does not just partially obey God, but is entirely and without exception devoted to his obedience. So if we want to enjoy this same presence of God, our whole being must be subjected to his rule. If our senses rule us in any way, all our endeavors will be fruitless, since God's blessing will be absent. Although for a time the happy semblance of success may please us, the final result will be unhappy.

When Christ says, **"he has not left me alone,"** he is obliquely attacking the treachery of his nation, where he found practically no support. Yet Christ shows that it is quite enough for him to have God's protection. This is the spirit we should have today, so that we may not be discouraged by the small number of believers. Even if the whole world is opposed to our teaching, we are not alone.

Verses 30-38

30. Even as he spoke . . . Although the Jews were then not unlike a dry and barren soil, God did not allow the seed of his Word to be lost completely. Against all hope and in the middle of many obstructions, some fruit appears. But the evangelist imprecisely calls **faith** what was only a sort of preparation for faith. For he is saying no more about them than that they were inclined to receive Christ's teaching. The next warning also refers to this.

31. "If you hold to my teaching . . ." Here Christ, first of all, warns them that it is not enough for anyone to begin well if he does not continue to progress to the end. This is why he exhorts those who have tasted his teaching to persevere in the faith; he says that those who are so firmly rooted in his Word, if they continue in it, will truly be his disciples. Christ means that many people profess to be disciples who are not really and do not deserve to be thought of as such. He distinguishes his followers from the hypocrites in that those who falsely proclaim they believe fall away from the very start, or at least in the middle of the race, whereas believers persevere to the winning-post. Therefore, if Christ is to view us as his disciples, we must endeavor to persevere.

32. "Then you will know the truth . . ." Christ says that those who have attained some knowledge of the truth will know it. It is true that those whom Christ was addressing were as yet untaught and had barely had their first lessons, so that it is not surprising if he promises them a fuller understanding of his teaching. But the statement is general. Whatever progress anyone has made in the Gospel, let him know that he needs to make further advances. The reward that Christ bestows on such perseverance is to make a man more familiar with himself. But by doing so, he merely adds another gift to the former, so that no one may think that he is paid anything by way of reward. For he who puts his Word in our hearts by his Spirit is the same who daily drives from our minds the clouds of ignorance which obscure the brightness of the Gospel. We should strive after the truth sincerely and earnestly, that it may be fully revealed to us. It is the same unvarying truth which Christ teaches his own from first to last; but first he enlightens them with small sparks, as it were, and finally pours out a full light upon them. Thus, until they have been fully strengthened, believers are in a sense ignorant about what they know. Yet this knowledge of faith is not so small and obscure that it is not efficacious for salvation.

"The truth will set you free." Christ commends the knowledge of the Gospel from the fruit we receive from it, or, which is just the same, from its effect; namely, it restores us to freedom. This is an incomparable blessing. Hence it follows that there is nothing more excellent or desirable than the knowledge of the Gospel. All feel and acknowledge that slavery is a most wretched thing. Since the Gospel delivers us from this, it follows that the treasure of the blessed life comes from the Gospel.

We must now find out what kind of freedom Christ is describing here. It is that which sets us free from the tyranny of Satan, sin, and death. And if we obtain it by means of the Gospel, it is clear that by nature we are the slaves of sin. Next, we must find out the method of our deliverance, for so long as we are ruled by our own sense and nature, we are in bondage to sin. But when the Lord brings us to life by his Spirit he also makes us free, so that we are released from the snares of Satan and willingly obey righteousness. But new birth comes from faith. Hence it is evident that freedom comes from the Gospel.

We who are aware of our own slavery glory in no one other than Christ our Liberator. For the reason why we must regard the Gospel as having achieved our deliverance is that it offers and gives us Christ so we will be freed from the yoke of sin.

Lastly, we should observe that freedom has its degrees according to the measure of faith. This is why Paul, although already set free, still groaned and sighed for perfect freedom.

33. "We are Abraham's descendants." It is uncertain whether the evangelist is here introducing the same people speaking or others. I think they replied to Christ in a confused way, as usually happens in a mixed crowd, and that they were despisers rather than believers. It is a customary way of speaking in Scripture, when a group of people is mentioned, to ascribe generally to all what belongs only to a part.

Now those who object that they are **"Abraham's descendants"** and have always been free easily gather from Christ's words that freedom was promised to them as slaves. But people who are a holy and elect people cannot bear being called slaves. For what was the use of being adopted and having the covenant, by which they were separated from other nations, unless they were counted the children of God? So they think they are being insulted when freedom is offered to them as a blessing which is foreign to them. But it might be thought strange that they should deny they were ever enslaved when they had been so often oppressed by various tyrants and were even then subject to the Roman yoke and groaned under the heaviest burden of slavery. From this we can easily see how foolish their boasting was. Yet they had a partial excuse, in that the unjust domination of their enemies did not prevent them from continuing to be free by right. But they were wrong, first, in not considering that the right of adoption was founded on the Mediator alone. For how is it that **"Abraham's descendants"** are free but because by the unique grace of the Redeemer they are exempt from the bondage common to the human race? But there was another and less tolerable error. Although they were altogether degenerate, they wanted to be reckoned among Abraham's children and did not consider that it is only the new birth of the Spirit that makes them legitimate children of Abraham.

And, indeed, it has been a vice too common in almost all ages to refer the extraordinary gifts of God to a carnal origin and to ascribe to nature those remedies that God bestows for correcting nature. Moreover, we see how all who are swollen with a false confidence and flatter themselves about their state drive away the grace of Christ. Yet this pride is spread over the whole world, so that there is hardly one person in a hundred who feels he needs God's grace.

34. "Everyone who sins . . ." This is arguing from opposites. They boasted that they were free. Christ proves that they are the slaves of sin because, enslaved by the desires of human nature, they continually sin. It is astonishing how men are not convinced by their own experience and do not learn to be humble and put away their pride. And this is more than common today; the greater the mass of vices anyone is buried under, the more fiercely and bombastically does he extol free will.

It seems as if Christ is saying here nothing more than was earlier discussed by the philosophers: that the people who are devoted to their lusts are in the worst slavery. But there is a deeper and more hidden meaning.

He is not only speaking about the evil that men bring on themselves, but about the state of human nature. The philosophers thought that any man by his own decision becomes a slave and returns to freedom. But here Christ declares that all who are not freed by him are in slavery, and that all who derive the contagion of sin from corrupted nature are slaves from birth. We must grasp this comparison between grace and nature which Christ emphasizes here and from which we can easily see that men forfeit freedom unless they acquire it from somewhere else. Yet this slavery is voluntary, so that those who sin deliberately are not forced to sin.

35. "Now a slave . . ." He adds a simile from common and civil law. A slave, though he has power for a while, is not the heir of the house. From this Christ deduces that there is no perfect and permanent freedom except what is obtained through the Son. In this way he accuses the Jews of vanity, in that they put a mask in place of the reality. They occupied a place in the church of God, but such a place as Ishmael the slave, triumphing over his free-born brother, usurped for a little while. The conclusion is that all who boast of being Abraham's children have nothing but a false and transient appearance.

36. "So if the Son sets you free . . ." By these words Christ means that the right of freedom belongs only to himself, and that all others are born slaves and can be delivered only by his grace. What Christ has because of his own nature he gives to us through adoption, when we are engrafted by faith into his body and made part of him. Therefore we should remember what I said before — that Christ sets us free by the signed deed of liberation. Hence our freedom is a gift from Christ, but we obtain it by faith, through which Christ also gives us new faith by his Spirit.

When Christ says that they will be **"free indeed,"** the emphasis is on the word **"indeed."** We must supply the contrast to the foolish conviction with which the Jews were swollen, just as most people imagine that they possess a kingdom when they are in the most wretched slavery.

37. "I know you are Abraham's descendants." I explain this, as I said, by way of concession. Yet at the same time Christ laughs at their folly in glorifying in such a worthless title, as if he said, "Even allowing for what you flatter yourselves about so much, what is the point of being called Abraham's descendants who angrily attack God and his ministers and are moved by such wicked and horrible hatred of the truth that they rush headlong into shedding innocent blood?" So it follows that nothing is further from the truth than what they wanted to be called, for they were totally unlike Abraham.

"You are ready to kill me, because you have no room for my word." By this Christ means that they were not merely murderers, but were driven into a rage in their hatred for God and his truth; and what is worse, this rage is not just against men, but it also dishonors God.

Christ says they have no room for his words, for their minds are filled with malice, and they cannot let in anything wholesome.

38. "I am telling you what I have seen in the Father's presence." Christ had already mentioned his Father frequently, and now, using an argument from opposites, he infers that they are God's enemies and the devil's children because they oppose his teaching. "I bring forward nothing," he says, "except what I have learned from my Father. So why are you so upset by the Word of God, unless you have a totally opposite father?" Christ says he *tells* and they **do** because he carried out the office of teacher, whereas they had worked hard to destroy his teaching. At the same time, Christ protects the Gospel from contempt by showing that it is nothing to be surprised at if the Gospel is opposed by the devil's children. Some people interpret this as, "*Do* what you have seen in your father's presence," as if Christ were saying, "Come on now, prove that you are the devil's children by opposing me, for I only speak what God has commanded me."

Verses 39–42

39. "Abraham is our father." This argument shows quite clearly how proudly and fiercely they despised all of Christ's reproofs. They keep on claiming to be Abraham's children, not just meaning that they are descended from Abraham, but that they are a holy race, God's heritage and children. And yet they are still placing their confidence in human nature. But unspiritual descent without faith is mere hypocrisy. We can now see what blinded them and made Christ of no interest to them, even though he was armed with deadly thunder. In the same way the Word of God, which should move stones, is today ridiculed by Roman Catholics as if it were a story. They only do this because they trust in the false title of the Church. In summary, as soon as hypocrites have a plausible pretext, they oppose God with iron obstinacy, as if he could not pierce into their hearts.

"If you were Abraham's children . . . then you would do the things Abraham did." Christ now distinguishes more clearly between illegitimate and legitimate children of Abraham and takes away the name from all who are unlike Abraham. It is true that children often do not reflect in their behavior the father they have sprung from. But Christ is not discussing physical descent here, but only affirms that people who do not by faith keep the grace of adoption are not to be reckoned among Abraham's children before God. Since the Lord promised to Abraham's descendants that he would be their God (Genesis 17:7), all unbelievers exclude themselves from Abraham's family when they reject this promise.

Should those who reject the blessing offered to them in the Word be accounted Abraham's children and therefore a holy nation, God's special people, and a royal priesthood (Exodus 19:6; Joel 3:2)? Quite rightly Christ denies this. Those who are the children of the promise must be born again by the Spirit, and everyone who wants to obtain a place in God's kingdom must be a new creature. Human descent from Abraham was indeed useless and unimportant so long as the truth was not added to it. Election resides in the seed of Abraham, but it is free, so that those who are accounted heirs of life are those whom God sanctifies with his Spirit.

40. "As it is, you are determined to kill me." Christ proves from the effect that they are not, as they boasted, Abraham's children, since they opposed God. For what is more highly commended than the obedience of faith? And this is the distinguishing mark whenever we have to differentiate his children from strangers. Empty titles, however much they are esteemed by the world, are nothing to God. Therefore, Christ again concludes that they are the devil's children, because they are deadly enemies of true and sound teaching.

41. "We are not illegitimate children." They claim no more for themselves than before, for it meant the same thing to them to be Abraham's children or God's. But they were greatly at fault in thinking that God was bound to all the descendants of Abraham. This is how they reason: "God adopted the family of Abraham for himself. Therefore, because we are Abraham's descendants, we must be the children of God." We now see that they believed that they had holiness from the womb, because they sprang from a holy root. In summary, they maintain that they are the church of God because they trace their origin from the holy patriarchs. An uninterrupted line of succession from the Fathers puffs up the Roman Catholics today and makes them swollen-headed. Satan deceives them with tricks like this, so that they separate God from his Word, the church from faith, and the kingdom of heaven from the Spirit.

So we must realize, then, that people who have corrupted the seed of life are anything but God's children, even though, according to human descent, they are not illegitimate but make a plausible claim to being the church. They can beat about the bush as much as they like, but they can never avoid the fact that their only boast is, "We are in the line of succession from the holy Fathers, and therefore we are the church." If Christ's reply was good enough to refute the Jews, it is good enough to expose the Roman Catholics. Hypocrites will always falsely claim God's name with a most wicked boldness. But the false grounds of boasting which they babble about will never fail to be ridiculous to everyone who abides by Christ's decision.

42. "If God were your Father, you would love me." This is Christ's argument: "Everyone who is God's child will acknowledge God's first-born Son. But you hate me. Therefore, you have no reason to claim that you are the sons of God." We should pay particular attention to this passage, for where Christ is rejected there is no piety or fear of God. Feigned religion certainly hides boldly behind God; but what agreement can they have with the Father who disagree with his only Son? What kind of knowledge of God is it where his living image is rejected? This is what Christ means when he testifies that he came from the Father.

"**For I came from God.**" Christ means that all that he has is divine, and therefore it is completely inconsistent for God's true worshipers to run away from his truth and righteousness. Christ says, "I did not come **on my own.** You cannot discover anything in me that opposes God. In summary, you will find nothing earthly or human in my teaching or in the whole of my ministry." He is not speaking of his essence but of his office.

Verses 43–45

43. "Why is my language not clear to you?" In this passage Christ reproaches the Jews for their obstinacy, which was so great that they could not even bear to hear Christ speak. From this Christ infers that they are motivated and carried away by a devilish rage. Some people make a distinction here between "**language**" and speech ("**what I say**"), as if speech had a greater meaning; but I do not see it. Also, the lesser word would not be placed first. Many people divide this verse as if it consisted only of the words, "Why do you not understand my language?" And then the reason is immediately given: "Because you cannot hear my word." But I think that it should be read all together, as if Christ said, "For what reason is my speech barbarous and unknown to you, so that I do no good by speaking to you, and you do not even trouble to open your ears to what I say?" In the first clause Christ rebukes their stupidity, in the second their obstinate and unbridled hatred of his teaching. Afterwards Christ gives a reason for both by saying that they come from the devil. By questioning them, Christ wanted to take away their continual boast that they were led by reason and judgment to oppose him.

44. "You belong to your father, the devil." Christ now expresses more fully what he had twice hinted at, that they are the devil's children. We have to supply the antithesis, that they could not hate the Son of God so much were it not that their father was the perpetual enemy of God. Moreover, he calls them children of "**the devil**" not only because they imitate him, but because they are led by his prompting to fight against Christ. We are called God's children not only because we are like him, but because he governs us by his Spirit, and Christ lives in us and is strong in us, transforming us into the image of his Father. In the same way, "**the devil**" is said to be the "**father**" of those whose minds he blinds, whose hearts he stirs up to all unrighteousness, and, in summary, on whom he acts powerfully and exercises his tyranny (see 2 Corinthians 4:4; Ephesians 2:2, and other places).

The Manicheans vainly and foolishly misused this passage to prove their absurd tenets. When Scripture calls us the children of God, it is not referring to the transmission or origin of substance, but to the grace of the Spirit regenerating us to newness of life. Thus, Christ's saying is not concerned with transmission of substance but with the corruption of nature, of which man's fall was the cause and origin. When people, therefore, are born children of **"the devil,"** it must not be imputed to creation, but sin must bear the blame. And Christ now proves this from the result, in that they willingly and of their own accord are disposed to follow **"the devil."**

"He was a murderer from the beginning." Christ explains what those desires are and mentions two instances, cruelty and falsehood, in which the Jews greatly resembled Satan. When Christ says that the devil was **"a murderer,"** he means that he plotted man's destruction. For as soon as man was created, Satan was impelled by a wicked desire to hurt, and so directed his strength to destroying him. Again, Christ does not mean the beginning of the creation, as if it were God who had planted in the devil a desire to hurt; but he is condemning in Satan the corruption of nature which he brought upon himself.

This comes out more clearly in the second clause, where he says, **"not holding to the truth,"** for although those who imagine the devil was wicked by nature try to escape from this, these words clearly express a change for the worse and say that Satan was a liar, in that he deserted the truth. His being a liar does not arise from his nature having always been against the truth, but from his defection by a voluntary fall. This description of Satan is very helpful for us, because everyone can be on guard against his snares and also to repel his power and force; he "prowls around like a roaring lion, looking for someone to devour" (1 Peter 5:8) and is equipped with a thousand deceiving tricks. This is even more reason why believers should be armed with spiritual weapons for the fight and earnestly watch with vigilance and prudence. If Satan is unable to throw off this disposition, we must not be alarmed, as if it were a new and unusual happening, when various errors spring up. For Satan stirs up his followers like agitators to distract the world with their impostures. It is hardly surprising that Satan tries so hard to extinguish the light of truth, for it is the only life of the soul. Hence, the chief and most deadly weapon for killing the soul is falsehood. As anybody with eyes can see such a picture of Satan in the Papacy today, they should first of all consider the enemy they are fighting against, and next take refuge in the command of Christ their captain, under whose banner they fight.

"For there is no truth in him." This statement, which immediately follows, is a confirmation from the result, *a posteriori* as they say. Satan hates the truth and cannot bear it but is utterly filled with falsehoods. Hence Christ infers that he is completely fallen and turned away from the truth. So we must not be surprised if he daily shows the fruits of his apostasy.

"When he lies . . ." These words are usually explained as referring to Christ's denial that the blame for lies belongs to God, who is the author of nature, and his affirmation that it proceeds rather from corruption. But I explain it more simply; it is usual for the devil to lie, and he thinks of nothing but contriving frauds, deceits, and tricks. And yet we correctly infer from these words that the devil has this vice from himself, and that it is unique to him but may also be said to be accidental. For although Christ calls the devil the maker of lying, he clearly separates him from God and even declares him to be contrary to God. The word "father," which he now adds, has the same object as the preceding statement. Satan is said to be "the father of lies" because he is estranged from God, in whom alone dwells the truth and from whom it flows as a unique fountain.

45. "Yet because I tell the truth . . ." Christ confirms the above statement, for since they have no other reason for opposing him than that the truth is hateful and unbearable to them, they show openly that they are Satan's children.

Verses 46–50

46. "Can any of you . . . ?" The question arises out of complete confidence. Christ knows that they are unable to justly accuse him and that he is victorious over his enemies. However, Christ does not say that he is free from their slanders; for although there is no substance in their accusations, they continue to attack Christ with their abuse. What Christ means is that he is not guilty. This is the significance of the words "prove me guilty." People who think that Christ is here asserting his perfect innocence, in that he alone was perfect among men since he was the Son of God, are wrong. Christ's defense is limited to the details of the passage. Here Christ shows that nothing can be deduced to show that he was not a faithful minister of God. In the same way Paul also was not aware of anything against him (see 1 Corinthians 4:4). This is not referring to his whole life, but just to the defense of his teaching and apostleship. So it is irrelevant to speculate, as some do, about the perfect righteousness which belongs to the Son of God alone. His only purpose is to gain credit for his ministry, which becomes clear in what follows, when he again immediately adds, "If I am telling the truth, why don't you believe me?" From this we can infer that Christ is defending his teaching rather than his person.

47. "He who belongs to God . . ." Christ has a right to take it for granted that he is his Heavenly Father's ambassador and that he is faithfully carrying out the special work committed to him. So Christ speaks against them more vehemently, because their ungodliness was no longer hidden now that they were so obstinate in rejecting God's Word. Christ shows them that they were unable to pinpoint anything which he said that did not come from God's mouth. So Christ concludes that they have nothing in common with God, as they do not listen to him; and so without saying anything about himself, he accuses them of fighting against God. Further, this passage shows that there is no clearer sign of a reprobate mind than when a person cannot stand Christ's teaching, even though in other respects he has an outer glow of angelic sanctity. In the same way, if we embrace this happily we have, as it were, a visible seal of our election. Anyone who has God's Word enjoys God himself, but anyone who rejects God's Word is depriving himself of righteousness and life. There is nothing we should fear more than falling under that awful sentence.

48. "Aren't we right in saying . . . ?" More and more they show how they are stupefied by Satan, for although they are quite convicted, they rush shamelessly into the middle of despair. Although they bring two accusations against Christ, all they want to do is to say in a few words that he is a detestable man who is motivated by an evil spirit. Because the Jews thought of the Samaritans as apostates who perverted the law, they called a person **"a Samaritan"** when they wanted to vilify him. So, as they did not have any worse accusation to attack Christ with, they seize this common taunt at random, without thinking. In summary, we see that they curse Christ as men usually do when they are enraged like mad dogs and cannot find anything to say.

49. "I am not possessed by a demon." Because Christ passes over the first charge and clears himself only of the second, some people think that he is overlooking the insult against his person and just defends his teaching. But I believe that they are mistaken, because the Jews would not be making such a subtle distinction between his life and teaching. In addition to this, they hated his name, as we have said, because the Samaritans, who observed the law perversely and degenerately, had debased it with many superstitions and corruptions and had polluted the whole worship of God with foreign ideas. Augustine finds an allegory here and says that Christ did not refuse to be called **"a Samaritan"** because he is a true guardian of the flock. But I think that Christ meant something different here. The two accusations leveled at him have the same aim, and as Christ refutes one, he is refuting the other. Indeed, if we think about it carefully, being called **"a Samaritan"** was worse than being called a demoniac. But as I have said, Christ is content with a simple rebuttal, drawn from the opposite, asserting that he works to uphold his Father's honor. Whoever properly and sincerely honors him must be guided by God's Spirit and be his faithful servant.

"You dishonor me." This clause can be explained as if Christ were complaining that he does not receive the honor due to him as he promotes God's glory. But I think that he is looking higher and links God's glory with his own, as if he said, "I claim for myself nothing that does not result in the glory of the Father. His majesty shines in me, and his power and authority live in me. So when you receive me with no honor, you are insulting God himself." Therefore, Christ immediately adds that God will avenge this insult. They could have accused him of being ambitious if he had not said that he was unconcerned personally or humanly about the honor or contempt shown to him, but only insofar as it showed disrespect and contempt of God. Even though we are far removed from Christ, every one should be fully convinced that if he sincerely desires to seek God's glory, a great deal of praise will be stored up for him with God. We will always find the saying true, "Those who honor me I will honor" (1 Samuel 2:30). If people despise you and weigh you down with accusations, calmly wait for the day of the Lord to dawn.

Verses 51–55

51. "I tell you the truth . . ." Christ undoubtedly knew that some people in the crowd could be won over and that others were hostile to his teaching. Therefore, Christ wanted to frighten the maliciously wicked, and yet still give grounds for comfort for good people and to attract to himself those who were not yet lost. However much most people reject God's Word, the godly teacher must not give all his time to reproving the wicked, but should also teach the doctrine of salvation to God's children and attempt to influence the thinking of anyone who is not totally incurable. So in this passage Christ offers eternal life to his disciples, but insists that these disciples should not merely nod like donkeys, agreeing with his teaching, or say with their lips that they approve of his teaching, but should treat this teaching as a prized treasure. Christ says, **"He will never see death"**; for when faith brings life to a man's soul, the sting of death is already lessened and its poison removed, so that it cannot inflict a fatal wound.

52. "Now we know . . ." The reprobate persist in their stupidity and are unmoved by promises as well as by threats, so that they can neither be led nor drawn to Christ. Some people think that some are twisting and misusing his words because they say **"taste death,"** which Christ did not say. But I think that this is groundless. The phrases "to taste of death" and "to see death" were synonymous in Hebrew and meant "to die." But it is a false interpretation to transfer the spiritual teaching of Christ to the body. No believers will see death, because they have been born again of incorruptible seed and so will live even when they die. They are united to Christ, their head, and cannot be extinguished by death. Believers will also not see death because "Your spirit is alive because of righteousness" (Romans 8:10), until Christ swallows up the residue of death. But those other people are unspiritual and know nothing about being delivered from death unless it becomes very apparent in the body. It is an all too common disease in the world that most people care almost nothing about the grace of Christ, since they only view it in an unspiritual way. To avoid the same thing happening to us, we must alert our minds to discern spiritual life in the middle of death.

53. **"Are you greater than our father Abraham?"** Here is another offense they commit as they try to obscure Christ's glory by the splendor of **"Abraham"** and the saints. But just as the brightness of the sun obscures all the stars, so all the glory that is to be found in the saints must fade away before the immeasurable brightness of Christ. So they are acting unjustly and absurdly as they contrast the servants with the Lord. They are doing **"Abraham"** and **"the prophets"** a disservice when they use their names to attack Christ. But this wickedness has prevailed in almost every age and has spread to our own day, so that the ungodly tear up God's deeds and make him look different from who he is. God made his name shine out through the apostles and martyrs. The Roman Catholics make the apostles and martyrs idols for themselves, to take God's place. As they do this, are they not taking ammunition from God's actual kindness in order to destroy his power? How little remains for God or for Christ if the saints possess what the Roman Catholics so lavishly bestow on them! Therefore, we must know that the whole order of God's kingdom is confounded unless prophets, apostles, and all real saints are relegated to a much lower place than Christ, that he alone may be exalted. Indeed, we cannot honor the saints more than by subjecting them to Christ. But the Roman Catholics, although they may deceive the ignorant by boasting that they are honest worshipers of the saints, harm both God and the saints; for as they elevate the saints to a very high position, they reduce Christ to the same level. They are wrong for two reasons: because they prefer the saints to Christ in teaching, and because by clothing them with what they have taken from Christ, they strip Christ of almost all his power.

54. **"If I glorify myself . . ."** Before replying to their unfair comparison, Christ begins by saying that he does not seek his own glory, and so replies to their slanderous attack. If anyone objects that Christ did also glorify himself, the answer is easy. Christ did so not as a human being, but under the direction and authority of God. For here, as in many other passages, Christ makes a concession to them by distinguishing between himself and God. In summary, he says that he is not seeking his glory except for what had been been given him by the Father. From these

words we learn that when God glorifies his Son, he will not allow the world to despise him with impunity.

Meanwhile, those voices sounding from heaven — "Kiss the Son" (Psalm 2:12); "Let all God's angels worship him" (Hebrews 1:6); "at the name of Jesus every knee should bow" (Philippians 2:10); "Listen to him!" (Matthew 17:5); "Praise the Lord, all you Gentiles" (Romans 15:11) — should greatly encourage believers to give honor and reverence to Christ. These words also remind us that all the glory men gain for themselves is trivial and worthless. How blind ambition is, working so hard for nothing! We must always bear in mind Paul's saying, "For it is not the one who commends himself who is approved, but the man whom the Lord commends" (2 Corinthians 10:18). Moreover, as we are all destitute of God's glory, we must learn to glory in Christ alone, since it is through his grace that he makes us share in his glory.

". . . whom you claim as your God." Christ snatches away from them the false pretense of the name of God, which they were accustomed to use. "I know," he says, "how audaciously you boast that you are God's people, but this is a false claim, for you do not know God." From this we also learn the genuine profession of faith as that which comes from true knowledge. And from where does that knowledge arise but from the Word? Hence everyone who boasts in God's name without God's Word are only liars. Christ counters their impudence with the assurance of his conscience. So all of God's servants should be prepared in their hearts to be satisfied with having God alone on their side, even if the whole world opposes them. From of old the prophets and apostles had invincible courage and magnanimity which stood firm against the fearful attacks of the world, because they knew who had sent them. But when this substantial knowledge of God is lacking, we have nothing to uphold us.

55. "If I said I did not . . ." By this phrase Christ declares that the needs of his office force him to speak, and silence would be a betrayal of the truth. In this statement we note that God reveals himself to us so that we may profess with our mouths before men the faith of our hearts. For it should make us terrified that those who act hypocritically to please men and either deny God's truth or distort it with ungodly ideas are not just told off lightly, but are banished to be the children of the devil.

Verses 56–59

56. "Your father Abraham . . ." He grants them, in words only, what he previously took from them, that Abraham is their father. But he shows how idle is the objection based on the name of "Abraham." "He had no other aim," he says, "during his whole life than to see my kingdom

flourish. He longed for me when I was absent, but you despise me when I am present." What Christ here asserts simply about **"Abraham"** applies to all the saints. But this doctrine has greater weight concerning **"Abraham"** because he is the father of the whole church. So whoever wants to be among the godly should rejoice in the presence of Christ, which **"Abraham"** longed for.

"... rejoiced at the thought of seeing my day." The word "rejoiced" expresses a vehement zeal and ardent affection. We must now supply the contrast. Though the knowledge of Christ was still so obscure, Abraham was inflamed by so strong a desire that he preferred the enjoyment of it to everything that was reckoned desirable. How mean, then, is the ingratitude of those who despise and reject him when he is plainly offered to them! The word **"day"** does not in this passage mean eternity (as Augustine thought) but the time of Christ's kingdom, when he appeared in the world clothed with a human body to do the work of a Redeemer.

But a question now arises: how did Abraham see, even with the eyes of faith, the manifestation of Christ? This seems to conflict with another of Christ's statements, that "Many prophets and kings wanted to see what you see" (Luke 10:24). I reply that faith has various stages in seeing Christ. The ancient prophets saw Christ at a distance, as he had been promised to them, and yet were not permitted to see him close, as he made himself familiarly and completely visible when he came down from heaven to men.

Again, we are taught by these words that as God did not disappoint Abraham's desire, he will not now permit anyone to sigh after Christ without obtaining some good fruit which will correspond to his holy desire. The reason he does not grant the enjoyment of himself to many is human wickedness, for few people desire him. Abraham's joy shows that he regarded the knowledge of the kingdom of Christ as an incomparable treasure; and the reason why we are told that **"Abraham rejoiced at the thought of seeing my day"** is so we may know that there was nothing he valued more highly. But all believers receive this fruit from their faith — namely, that, being satisfied with Christ alone, in whom they are fully and completely happy and blessed, their consciences are calm and cheerful. And, indeed, no one knows Christ properly unless he gives him this honor of relying entirely on him.

Others explain this to mean that Abraham, being already dead, enjoyed the presence of Christ when he appeared to the world; and so they make the time of *desiring* and the time of *seeing* different. And, indeed, it is true that Christ's coming was manifested to holy spirits after death — the coming for which they had waited during their lifetime; but I do not know if so refined an exposition agrees with Christ's words.

57. "You are not yet fifty years old." They try to refute what Christ says by showing that he had asserted what was impossible: he was "not yet fifty," yet he makes himself equal to Abraham, who had died many centuries before. Though Christ was not yet thirty-four, they allow him to be a little older so that they would not appear to be too rigid and exact in dealing with him — as if they had said, "You will certainly not make yourself out to be so old, even if you were to boast that you are already **fifty years old.**" Consequently, to conjecture that he looked older than he actually was, or that the years mentioned in this passage are not calendar years, is pointless. The idea of Papias, who says that Christ lived more than forty years, cannot be accepted at all.

58. "Before Abraham was . . ." As unbelievers only judge by appearances, Christ reminds them that he has something greater and higher than human appearance, something which is hidden from physical senses and is perceived only by the eyes of faith, and that in this respect he could be seen by the patriarchs before he was revealed in the world. But he uses different verbs: **"Before Abraham was born, I am!"** By these words he excludes himself from ordinary human beings and claims superhuman power for himself, a heavenly and divine power, the perception of which reached from the beginning of the world through all ages.

Yet these words may be explained in two ways. Some think that this applies simply to the eternal Deity of Christ and compare it with that passage in the writings of Moses, "I am who I am" (Exodus 3:14). But I extend it much farther, because the power and grace of Christ, so far as he is the Redeemer of the world, was common to all ages. It agrees therefore with what the apostle said: "Jesus Christ is the same yesterday and today and forever" (Hebrews 13:8). The context appears to demand this interpretation. He had previously said that Abraham longed for his day with vehement desire; and as this seemed incredible to the Jews, he adds that he himself also existed at that time. The reason will not seem strong enough if we do not understand that he was even then acknowledged to be the Mediator by whom God was to be appeased. And yet the efficacy which belonged in all ages to the grace of the Mediator depended on his eternal Deity; so this saying of Christ's contains a remarkable witness of his divine essence.

We should also note the solemn form of an oath: **"I tell you the truth."** I do not disapprove of Chrysostom's opinion that there is great weight in the present tense of the verb; for he does not say, "I used to be," or "I was," but **"I am,"** indicating a condition uniformly the same from the beginning to the end. And he does not say, "before Abraham was," but **"before Abraham was born,"** thus attributing a beginning to him.

59. At this, they picked up stones to stone him. It is possible that they did this thinking that Christ had to be stoned according to the command of the law. Hence we infer the great madness of thoughtless zeal. They have no ears to learn the real state of the case, but they have hands ready for murder. I do not doubt that Christ delivered himself by his secret power, though under the guise of a lowly condition, for he did not want to display his divinity plainly without leaving room for human weakness. Some copies have the words, "He walked right through the crowd and went on his way," which Erasmus judiciously considers to have been borrowed from Luke 4. It also deserves notice that the wicked priests and teachers of the law retain possession of the outward temple only when they have banished Christ, "for in Christ all the fullness of the only Deity lives" (Colossians 2:9). But they are very mistaken in thinking that they have a temple when it is empty of God. Thus the Pope and his followers today, when they have driven Christ away and so profaned the church, foolishly glory in the false mask of a church.

John
Chapter 9

Verses 1–5

1. He saw a man blind from birth. In this chapter the evangelist describes a blind man receiving his sight, at the same time combining teaching with it which explains the purpose of the miracle. **From birth.** This detail amplifies Christ's power, for being blind from birth until manhood could not be cured by human remedies. This was the reason why the disciples asked a question.

2. "Rabbi, who sinned, this man or his parents?" In the first place, since the Scripture declares that all mankind's troubles come from sin, whenever we see anyone in a bad state we cannot help thinking that the distresses are punishments inflicted by God's hand. But here we generally err in three ways:

Since everyone is a sharp critic of others, few apply the same severity to themselves as they should. If things go badly with my brother, I at once acknowledge the judgment of God. But if God chastises me with a heavier blow, I overlook my sins. In thinking about punishments, everyone should begin with himself and spare no one less than himself. And so, if we want to judge fairly in this matter, we must learn to be perspicacious about our own evils rather than about other people's.

The second error lies in being unduly severe. No sooner is a man touched by the hand of God than we interpret it as deadly hatred and make crimes out of faults and almost despair of his salvation. On the other hand, we excuse our sins and are hardly conscious of faults when we have committed most serious crimes.

Thirdly, we are wrong to condemn everyone without any exception whom God exercises with the cross. What we have said just now is undoubtedly true, that all our distresses arise from sin. But God afflicts his people for various reasons. Just as there are some whose crimes he does not avenge in this world, but whose punishment he delays to the future life, to try them the harder, so he often treats his faithful more severely, not because they have sinned more, but that he may put to death the sins of the flesh for the future. Sometimes, too, he is not concerned about their sins but only with testing their obedience or training them to be patient. We see that the holy Job — a righteous man, and one who fears God — is the most miserable person on earth, and yet not on account of his sins. For God's purpose was quite different: it was that his godliness might be the more fully testified in adversity. So it is a wrong interpretation to attribute all afflictions, without distinction, to sins, as if the measure of punishments were equal, or as if God had no other purpose in punishing men than what every man deserves.

There are therefore two things to be observed here: judgment begins, for the most part, "with the family of God" (1 Peter 4:17); and consequently, whereas he passes over the ungodly, he punishes his own people severely when they have sinned, and in correcting the sinful actions of the church his wounds are far more severe. Secondly, there are different reasons why he afflicts men, for he allowed Peter and Paul to be executed just like the most wicked thieves. Hence we infer that we cannot always put our finger on the reasons for men's punishments.

When the disciples follow the common view and ask what kind of sin it was that God in heaven punished as soon as this man was born, they do not speak so stupidly as when they ask whether he sinned before he was born. Yet this silly question was derived from a common and prevalent opinion. It is quite plain from other passages of Scripture that they believed in the transmigration of souls which Pythagoras dreamed about. From this we see the deep labyrinth people are in because of their curiosity, especially when presumption is added to it. They say that some were born lame, some cross-eyed, some completely blind, and some with a deformed body. But instead of revering the secret judgments of God, as they should have done, they wanted to have a clear reason for his actions. Through their rashness they fell into those childish ways of thinking, that when a soul has finished one life it migrates into a new body and there undergoes the punishments due to the past life.

We are taught by this example that we ought to take care that our mind does not wander and err and so quickly plunge us into dreadful abysses if we inquire into God's judgments beyond what is reasonable. It was truly dreadful that such a great error should have found a place among God's elect, in whom the light of heavenly wisdom had been kindled by the Law and the Prophets. But if God avenged their presumption so severely, the best thing for us to do as we humbly consider the works of God, when the reason for them is concealed from us, is for our minds to burst out in admiration and our tongues to cry out, "You are righteous, O Lord, and your judgments are right, even though they are beyond our understanding."

The disciples' question about the sin of the parents is not irrelevant. For although the innocent son is not punished for his father's fault, and "the soul who sins is the one who will die" (Ezekiel 18:20), yet it is not an empty threat that the Lord puts the parents' crimes into the hearts of the children and punishes sin to "the third and fourth generation" (Exodus 20:5). Thus God's anger often rests on one family for many generations; and as he blesses the children of believers for their sake, so he also rejects an ungodly offspring, determining the children to the same ruin as their fathers by a fair punishment. And no one can complain that in this way he is unfairly punished for the sin of another. Concerning where the grace of the Spirit is lacking, as the proverb says, from bad crows must come bad eggs. This was the reason for the apostles wondering whether the Lord punished in the son some crime committed by the parents.

3. "Neither this man nor his parents." Christ does not free the blind man and his parents absolutely from all blame, but says that the reason for the blindness is not to be found in sin. This is what I have already said: God sometimes has a purpose in mind other than punishing men's sins when he sends them afflictions. Consequently, when the reasons for affliction are hidden, our curiosity must be restrained, so that we may neither dishonor God nor be malicious to our brothers.

And so Christ adduces another reason why this man was born blind: **"this happened so that the work"** (KJV, "works") **"of God might be displayed in his life."** He does not say, "one work," but **"works,"** in the plural; for so long as he was blind, there was seen in him an example of the divine severity, from which others might learn to fear and to humble themselves. This was followed by the benefit of his deliverance, in which the wonderful goodness of God was reflected. So Christ meant through these words to heighten his disciples' expectation for a miracle. But at the same time he reminds them in general that this reason must be abundantly seen as true and lawful in the theater of the world when God glorifies his name. Nor have people any right to argue with God when he makes them the instruments of his glory in both ways, whether he appears to be merciful or severe.

4. "We must do the work." Christ now testifies that he has been sent to show God's grace in bringing sight to the blind. He also borrows a comparison from ordinary life. "The sun rises. . . . Then man goes out to his work, to his labor until evening" (Psalm 104:22-23). He therefore calls the time fixed by the Father the **"day,"** in which he must finish the work commanded him, just as every man called to some public office has to be employed in his daily task to do what the nature of his office demands. From this we should also deduce a universal rule, that the course of a man's life is as it were his **"day."** Therefore, as the shortness of daylight stirs laborers to industry and toil, that they may not be overtaken by the darkness of **"night"** in the middle of their work, so when we see that a short life is allotted to us, we should be ashamed of idleness. In summary, as soon as God enlightens us by calling us, we must not delay, in case the opportunity is lost.

5. "While I am in the world . . ." I interpret this as having been added by way of anticipation. For it might have seemed absurd that Christ should fix his time of working in advance, as if there were danger that he, like others, would be overtaken by the **"night."** Thus he makes this distinction between himself and others, to say that his time for work also is limited. For he compares himself with the sun, which gives light to the earth with its brightness, but when it sets, takes the day away with it. In this way Christ means that his death will be like the setting of the sun; not that it will extinguish or obscure his light, but that it takes away its sight from the world. At the same time Christ shows that when he came in the flesh, it was then truly the daylight of the world. For though God enlightened all ages, yet Christ brought a new and special brightness by his coming. Hence he infers that this was a very fit and proper time, the brightest day, so to speak, for making clear the Father's glory, when God wanted to show himself more plainly in his wonderful deeds.

But this poses a problem; after Christ's death, a greater power of God shone out, both as a result of the teaching and in miracles. And Paul applies this, rightly, to the time of his own preaching: "For God, who said, 'Let light shine out of darkness,' made his light shine in our hearts to give us the light of the knowledge of the glory of God in the face of Christ" (2 Corinthians 4:6). And Christ irradiates the world no less now than when he lived on earth. I reply: when Christ had fulfilled the work of his office, he labored no less powerfully through his ministers than he had through himself when he was in the world. This I confess to be true; but, first, it is not inconsistent with his being bound to perform through himself what had been commanded him by the Father when he was manifested in the flesh for that purpose. Secondly, it is not inconsistent with his bodily presence being the true and wonderful **"day"** of the world, whose brightness was spread over all ages. For whence came **"light"** and **"day"** to the holy fathers in old times, or to us now, but because the manifestation of Christ always sent out its rays far and wide, so as to form one continual **"day"**? From this it follows that everyone who does not name Christ as their guide gropes in the dark like the blind and wanders in confusion and disorder. Yet we must understand from this that as the sun brings to our eyes the most beautiful theater of earth and heaven and the whole order of nature, so God has visibly displayed the chief glory of his work in his Son.

Verses 6–12

6. He spit on the ground. Christ's purpose was to restore sight to the blind man; but he starts the work in what seems to be a very strange way, for by anointing his eyes with **mud** he, as it were, doubles the blindness. Anyone would have thought he was mocking the poor man or carrying on senselessly like a madman. But by doing this Christ intended to test the faith and obedience of the blind man, so that he might be an example to everyone. It is certainly no normal proof of faith that the blind man embraces just Christ's word and is quite convinced that his sight will be restored and with this trust goes quickly to where he was told. It is also a wonderful commendation of his obedience that he simply obeys Christ, though many things pulled against him. It is the test of true faith when the godly mind is satisfied with the simple Word of God and is confident, in advance, of what otherwise appears incredible. A readiness to obey instantly follows faith, so that whoever is convinced that God will be his faithful guide calmly yields himself to his ruling.

There can be no doubt that a suspicion and fear that he was being mocked crossed the blind man's mind. But he found it easy to break through every obstruction when he decided it was safe to follow Christ. If anyone objects that the blind man did not know what Christ was and could not give him the honor due to him as the Son of God, I acknowledge that this is so; but since he believed that Christ had been sent by God, he submitted to him and, without doubting that he was true, saw in him nothing but the divine. Moreover, his faith deserves to be praised the more because with such little knowledge he devoted himself completely to Christ.

7. "Wash in the pool of Siloam." There was certainly no virtue for healing the eyes either in the **mud** or in the water of **Siloam**, but Christ freely and often added outward symbols to his miracles, either to make believers used to the use of signs, or to show that everything was under his control, or to show that each of his creatures has just as much power as he chooses to give them. But some people ask what the **mud**, made of earth and **saliva**, signifies and explain it as a figure of Christ, in that the earth denotes the earthly nature of his flesh, and the **saliva**, coming from his mouth, the divine essence of the Word. But I dispense with this allegory as it is more ingenious than true and am content with the simple view that just as man was at first made out of mud, so Christ used **mud** in restoring his eyes, to show that he had the same power over a part of the body that the Father had exercised in creating the whole man. Or perhaps Christ wanted through this sign to declare that it was no more difficult for him to remove the obstruction and open the blind man's eyes than for anyone to wash the **mud** away. Or maybe Christ's power could control the man's sight just as another person could daub his eyes with **mud**. I prefer this latter interpretation.

Christ told him to **"wash in the pool of Siloam,"** perhaps to show the Jews that it was their own fault that they could not discern the present power of God. Similarly, Isaiah reproaches his contemporaries that "this people has rejected the gently flowing water of Shiloah" (Isaiah 8:6). This, I think, was also why Elisha ordered Naaman the Syrian to wash in

Jordan (see 2 Kings 5:10). If we may believe Jerome, the pool was formed by waters springing out of Mount Zion at certain hours.

This word means Sent. The evangelist deliberately adds the interpretation of the word **Siloam.** The fountain, which was near the temple, daily reminded the Jews of the Christ who was to come, yet whom they despised when he was shown to them. So the evangelist is commending Christ's grace, since he alone lightens our darkness and restores sight to the blind. In the case of this one man, there is depicted the state of our nature: we are all from birth deprived of light and understanding and should seek the cure for this illness in Christ alone.

Observe that even though Christ was then present, he did not wish to neglect symbols for reproving the dullness of the nation, which abolished the substance and kept only the empty shadow of the signs. Moreover, his wonderful goodness shines in his coming of his own will to heal the blind, without waiting for prayers for his help. Indeed, since by nature we are turned away from him, unless he meets us before we call on him and in his mercy goes ahead of us who are drowned in forgetfulness of the light and life, it is all over for us.

8. His neighbors and those who had formerly seen him . . . The blind man was known not only to the **neighbors** but to all the inhabitants of the city, since he used to sit and beg at the gate of the temple, and the ordinary people take more notice of people like him. Since people knew this man, news about the miracle became widespread. But ungodliness is clever at obscuring God's deeds and so many people thought it was not the same man, since a new power from God appeared in him. The brighter God's majesty is in his works, the less credit men give to him. But their doubts helped to prove the miracle, for they made the blind man praise Christ's grace the more through his testimony. So the evangelist collects all the details which demonstrated the truth of the miracle more clearly.

11. "So I went and washed." This happy outcome of obedience summons us to surmount all obstacles and proceed courageously wherever the Lord calls us and to never doubt that whatever we do at his leading and authority will turn out well.

Verses 13–17

13. They brought to the Pharisees the man . . . The narrative which follows shows that the ungodly are so far from benefitting from the works of God that the more they are influenced by their power, the more they give out the poison conceived within them. The restoration of sight to the blind should have softened even minds made of stone. **The Pharisees** should have been struck with the uniqueness and greatness of the miracle, and at least hesitated a little while they found out whether it was a divine work or not. But hatred for Christ drives them rushing into such unreasonableness that out of hand they condemn what they hear he has done.

The evangelist names **the Pharisees** not because the other parties were on Christ's side, but because this sect was more zealous than the others to maintain the status quo. Hypocrisy is always cruel and proud. Therefore, swollen with a false idea about their own holiness, they were seriously wounded by the teaching of the Gospel, which condemned all their fake righteousness. Above all, they were fighting for their own power and authority under the guise of defending the law.

When the evangelist says that the crowd brought the blind man to **the Pharisees**, their motivation is unclear. Nearly everyone knew how much the Pharisees hated Christ; and it is therefore possible that many flatterers, to curry favor with them, deliberately tried to hide the glory of the miracle. But I think that most of them, as usually happens, wanted to make their rulers the arbiters and judges. But being willfully blind in the sunlight, they brought on themselves a darkness which obscures its light. The ordinary people have a perverted religion. Under the cloak of reverence towards God, they praise the ungodly tyrants of the church and despise God himself in his Word and works, or at least do not trouble to consider him.

14. . . . a Sabbath. Christ deliberately chose **a Sabbath**, which would offend the Jews. He had already found, with the paralytic, that even this work was open to misrepresentation. Why then does he not avoid giving offense, as he could easily have done, unless the malignant reaction of his enemies would magnify the power of God? The **Sabbath** is like a whetstone that sharpens them to inquire more eagerly into the whole affair. And yet what good does a careful and earnest examination of this question do except to make the truth of the miracle shine more brightly? Moreover, we see in this example that if we want to follow Christ we have to frustrate the enemies of the Gospel, and that those who compromise between the world and Christ, so as to condone every kind of scandal, are utterly mad, since Christ, on the contrary, knowingly and deliberately provoked the ungodly. So we should heed the rule that he lays down elsewhere — that the blind and the leaders of the blind are to be ignored (see Matthew 15:14).

15. The Pharisees also asked him . . . The people had heard this confession from the mouth of the blind man already. Now **the Pharisees** become witnesses to it. They might have objected that a baseless rumor had been thoughtlessly circulated by the ordinary people and mindlessly believed. First of all, leaving aside the question of the facts, they say, they argue only about the law of the case. They do not deny that Christ restored sight to the blind man, but they find fault about the time that it was done and deny it was a work of God, since it broke the Sabbath.

First of all, they should have found out if a divine work was a violation of the Sabbath. What hinders them from seeing this unless they are blinded by a depraved attitude and malice and see nothing? Besides, they had already been abundantly taught by Christ that the benefits which God gives to people no more break the Sabbath than circumcision does. For the words of the law command people to rest only from their own works and not from the works of God (see Exodus 20:8; 23:12). When they agree with an error which has so often been refuted, they do so out of obstinate malice; or at least there is no other reason why they go wrong except that they choose to.

In the same way, the Roman Catholics never cease to advance, with hardened impudence, their empty and foolish slanders which have been answered a hundred times. So what are we to do with them? When the opportunity arises, so far as we are able, we must oppose the wickedness of those who reproach and slander the Gospel out of a false prejudice. And if no defense, however just, silences them, we have no need to be discouraged but should trample down, with a great and bold spirit, that obstinate eagerness to slander, through which they oppress us. We readily agree with their principle that we ought not to listen to those who secede from the church and break the unity of the faith. But they cunningly pass over what should be the main topic of discussion and which we have explained clearly in a thousand places: that nothing could be less like the church than the Pope and his gang — that mixture of corrupt ideas infected by so many superstitious fictions which are far from the genuine faith. But with all their furious impudence they will never stop the truth, which we have so often and firmly maintained, from prevailing in the end. Similarly **the Pharisees** accused Christ with the plausible argument that he who breaks the Sabbath is not from God. But they were unjust and wrong in asserting that the work of God is a violation of the Sabbath.

16. "How can a sinner . . . ?" As in many other places, **"sinner"** is used here for a very wicked person who despises God. "Why does he eat with tax collectors and 'sinners'?" (Mark 2:16) — that is, with ungodly and wicked men who are notorious for their evil. Christ's enemies inferred from his breaking the Sabbath that he was a pagan man and irreligious. Those who are neutral and judge more fairly, however, decide that he is a godly and religious man who is equipped with a remarkable power from God to work miracles. And yet the argument does not seem strong enough. For God sometimes allows false prophets to perform miracles, and we know that Satan, like an ape, imitates the works of God to deceive the unwary.

Suetonius relates that when Vespasian was in Alexandria and was on his judgment-seat dispensing justice in the open court, he was asked by a blind man to anoint his eyes with spittle — this remedy having been revealed to him in a dream by Serapis. Vespasian was unwilling to expose himself to contempt and was reluctant and slow to agree. But when the friends all around him urged him on, he granted the blind man's request, and in this way his eyes were at once opened. Who would number Vespasian among God's servants for this reason or give him praise for being pious? I reply, among good men and God-fearers miracles are definite pledges of the power of the Holy Spirit; but by a just judgment of God it also happens that Satan deceives unbelievers with false miracles, as well as by witchcraft. I do not think that what I have just quoted from Suetonius is a fable, but I ascribe it to the righteous vengeance of God, that the Jews who had despised so many clear miracles of Christ were at last handed over to Satan as they deserved. They should have benefitted from Christ's miracles in their pure worship of God; they should have been confirmed in the teaching of the law and should have gone closer to the Messiah, who was the end of the law. There is no doubt that by giving sight to the blind, Christ had clearly proved that he was the Messiah.

Now, although these men act uprightly, in that they speak with reverence about the miracles in which God's power is displayed, they do not give a valid reason why Christ should not be reckoned a prophet of God. Nor did the evangelist mean that their answer should be treated as an oracle. He is only showing the ungodly obstinacy of Christ's enemies in maliciously carping at the manifest works of God and not even pausing at all when they are warned.

So they were divided. Division is the worst and most harmful evil in the church of God. Why then does Christ give reason for discord among the very teachers of the church? The answer is easy. Christ's only aim was to bring with outstretched hand, as it were, all men to God the Father. The division arose from the malice of those who had no wish to go to God. Therefore, it is those who will not obey the truth of God who tear the church by schism. Yet, it is preferable that men should disagree rather than that they should all agree to move away from godliness. Therefore, whenever differences arise we should always consider their origin.

17. Finally they turned again to the blind man. The more diligently they inquire, the more powerfully God's truth is seen, for they act like someone trying to blow out a flame with his breath. So when we see the wicked endeavoring in every way to overwhelm God's truth, we need not be afraid or be overanxious about the result, for in this way they will only make it burn more fiercely.

"What have you to say about him?" Moreover, when they ask the blind man for his opinion, it is not because they want to abide by his judgment or think it has the slightest value, but because they hope the man will be frightened and give them the answer they want. In this the Lord disappoints them — for when a poor man disregards their threats and boldly maintains that Christ is a prophet, we must ascribe it to

God's grace. So this confidence is another miracle. And if he who did not yet know that Christ was the Son of God courageously and freely confessed he was a prophet, how shameful is the treachery of those who out of fear either deny him or are silent, though they know that he sits at the right hand of the Father and from there will come to be the Judge of the whole earth! If this blind man did not quench his tiny spark of knowledge, we should endeavor that a frank and full confession should blaze forth from the full brightness which has shone in our hearts.

Verses 18–23

18. The Jews still did not believe . . . There are two things to be noticed here. They do not believe a miracle has been performed; and because they are willfully blinded by a perverse hatred of Christ, they do not see what is clear. The evangelist relates that they **did not believe.** If the reason is asked, there is no doubt that their blindness was voluntary. What stops them from seeing a clear work of God set before their eyes? Or when they have been completely refuted, what prevents them from believing what they already know, except that the inward malice of their hearts keeps their eyes shut? Paul tells us that the same thing happens in the preaching of the Gospel. He says that it is "veiled" and hidden only to the reprobate, as "the god of this age has blinded the minds of unbelievers" (2 Corinthians 4:3-4). We must be warned by such examples not to put obstacles in our own way, which keep us from the faith. By **the Jews** the evangelist means those who were the rulers of the people.

19. "Is this your son?" Having failed at their first attempt, they now try another way. But the Lord not only upsets their efforts in a wonderful way, but even turns them to an opposite end. They do not just ask one straightforward question but cunningly wrap up several questions together, to prevent a reply. But out of these entwined questions the parents of the blind man only choose to answer one.

20. "We know he is our son . . . and we know he was born blind." From this it follows that he does not see naturally, but that his eyes have been opened by a miracle. But they pass over the latter point, since it was unacceptable. By this silence they show their ingratitude. For when they had received such a shining gift from God, they should have longed to celebrate his name. But they are terror-struck and bury God's grace as much as they can, except that they put their son in their place as witness to explain the whole affair as it happened. He will be heard with less prejudice and will be more readily believed. But though they prudently avoid danger by taking this middle path of testifying indirectly to Christ through the mouth of their son, it does not prevent the Spirit from condemning their cowardice through the evangelist because they failed in their duty. How much less excuse will those people have who through a treacherous denial completely hide Christ, his teaching, his miracles, and his power and grace?

22. The Jews had decided . . . This passage shows that the custom of excommunication is ancient and has been exercised in all ages. Excommunication was not a new invention then, but was a punishment which had been used in ancient times against apostates and despisers of the law and was used against Christ's disciples. So we learn that the rite of excommunication arose out of the most ancient discipline of the church. Also, that vice is not of recent origin and is not confined to one age whereby ungodly men corrupt God's holy ordinances by their sacrilege. God determined from the beginning that there should be some form of correction to restrain rebels. The priests and teachers of the law not only misused their power tyrannically to harass the innocent, but impiously attacked God himself and his doctrine. Christ's truth was so powerful that they could not resist it with laws and regulations, and therefore they brandished the thunders of excommunication to crush it.

The same thing has been done to Christian people. It is impossible to express the barbarous tyranny which the pseudo-bishops have exercised in subduing the people, so that no one dared to object. And now we see how cruelly they turn this weapon of excommunication against everyone who worships God. But we should insist that when excommunication is indulged in for a different end, by men's passions, it can safely be treated with contempt. When God committed the right to excommunicate to his church, he was not arming tyrants with a sword or executioners to murder poor souls, but was laying down a rule for governing his people, on the condition that he should hold supreme sway and have men of God for his ministers. Let the pseudo-bishops thunder as they wish. They will not terrify anyone with their empty noises except those who wander about in uncertainty and doubt, not yet taught by the voice of the Good Shepherd what is the true fold.

In summary, nothing is more certain than that people we see insubordinate to Christ are deprived of the lawful power of excommunicating. Nor should we fear to be shut out of their gatherings, from which Christ, our life and salvation, is also banished. We have no reason at all to worry about being thrown out. Although the ordinance of excommunication was so wickedly corrupted in the ancient church, Christ did not mean it to be abolished by his coming but restored it to purity, so that it might flourish properly among us. Although a filthy profanation of this holy discipline prevails today, we should, instead of abolishing it, rather use the utmost diligence to restore it to its former integrity. Things will never be so well ordered in the world that even the holiest laws of God will not degenerate into corruption, through men's vice. It would certainly give too much power to Satan if he could annihilate everything he corrupts. We would then have no baptism, no Lord's

Supper, and, in short, no religion; for he has left no part of it unaffected by his pollutions.

Verses 24–33

24. A second time they summoned the man. It was without doubt shame that made them again call the blind man, whom they had at first found too firm and steadfast. And so the more they struggle against God, the more nooses they wind around themselves, and the faster they tie themselves up. Moreover, they interrogate him in such a way that they try to make him say what they want. It is indeed a specious start when they tell him to give the glory to God. Immediately, they strictly forbid him from replying according to his convictions. Hence, by claiming the authority of God, they demand servile obedience from him.

"Give glory to God." This exhortation may refer to the details of the case, in that the blind man was not to obscure God's **"glory"** by ascribing to man the benefit he had received. But I prefer the view which says it was a solemn formula which was used when an oath was demanded from anyone. Joshua demands an oath from Achan with the same words when he wants him to own up honestly to having taken the accursed thing (see Joshua 7:19). And with these words they remind the healed man that no light insult is offered to God if a man lies in his name. Indeed, if we are required to take an oath, we should remember this, so that the truth may be no less precious to us than God's **"glory."** If this were done, the sacredness of an oath would be looked at very differently. Most people, however, thoughtlessly and contemptuously rush into swearing an oath without thinking that they deny God when they invoke his name to perpetuate a lie, and so situations everywhere are full of perjuries. We can also see how hypocrites pretend to have the greatest reverence for God but are not only deceitful, but also mock him insolently. For at the same time they add that the blind man should irreligiously swear what they want, and so openly insult God. Thus God drags their wicked plans into the light, however much they try to put a plausible appearance on them or conceal them by hypocritical pretenses.

25. "Whether he is a sinner or not, I don't know." The blind man does not seem to have been deterred by fear from his frank witness. It is improbable that he had any doubts about Christ, as his words seem to imply. I think that he was speaking ironically to wound them more deeply. He had confessed that Christ was **"a prophet"** a little earlier (verse 17). Seeing that he is no farther forward, he suspends his judgment about the man and puts forward the fact itself. While he says this in their favor, he is not free from also mocking them.

26. Then they asked him . . . When we see the ungodly so busy with their own depraved actions, we should be ashamed of our laziness in acting with such coolness in Christ's work. Although they look for grounds for slander to obscure the miracle, the Lord defeats their efforts remarkably by the unshaken firmness of the blind man. Not only does he persist in his opinion, but he freely and severely reproaches them for trying to bury the truth with their continual investigations after they had learned and known it well enough. He also accuses them of a perverted hatred of Christ when he says, **"Do you want to become his disciples, too?"** (verse 27). He means that if they are refuted a hundred times they will never give way, so seized are they by a malicious and hostile attitude. It is indeed a wonderful liberty that a lowly and obscure man, one almost shameful because of his begging, fearlessly provokes the rage of all the priests against himself. If nothing more than a slight preparation for faith made him so confident when he came to the struggle, what excuse can be put forward for those who are great preachers of the church when they are out of range of the darts but are silent in danger? Moreover, this question is ironical. He means that in pressing this question so urgently they are motivated by malevolence and not for a sincere desire for the truth.

28. Then they hurled insults at him. They probably called him everything that in the violence of their fury they could lay their tongues to. But in particular they called him an apostate from the law. To their mind he could not be Christ's disciple without defecting from the law of Moses. And they expressly represent these two things as contraries. It seems a most beautiful excuse, that they are afraid of falling away from the teaching of Moses. For a true rule of godliness is that we should listen to the prophets, by whom it is certain that God spoke, so that our faith may not be carried about by any ideas of men. They deduce their certainty as to the law of Moses from this true principle. Where they lie is that they say they are Moses' disciples, for they had turned aside from the end of the law. This is how hypocrites are accustomed to tear God asunder when they want to shelter under his name. If Christ is the soul of the law, as Paul teaches in Romans 10:4, how can the law be anything but a dead body when it is separated from him? By this example we are taught that only he truly hears God who hears so as to understand what he wishes and says, he who listens attentively to his voice.

29. They are not here referring to Christ's country or birthplace but to the prophetic office. They claim that they have no knowledge of his calling, so that they should receive him as having come from God.

30. "Now that is remarkable!" Indirectly Christ reproves them for being quite unmoved by such a striking miracle as they pretend to be unaware of Christ's calling. It is as if he were saying that it was altogether wrong that such an example of divine power should be seen as nothing and that Christ's calling, proved and testified through it, should gain no credit among them. To highlight their stupidity or malice even more clearly, Christ emphasizes the wonder of the miracle by saying that from man's earliest recollection it has never been heard that such a thing could be performed by man. From this it follows that those who deliberately close their eyes to an obvious work of God are malicious and ungrateful. So Christ infers that he was sent from God since he is endued with the mighty power of God's Spirit and so wins credit for himself and his teaching.

31. **"We know that God does not listen to sinners."** People who think that this was said in line with the prevailing opinions are wrong. Here, as in a recent passage, **"sinners"** means ungodly and immoral men. It is the consistent teaching of Scripture that God only listens to those who call on him from a true and sincere heart. Since only faith opens for us the door to God, it is certain that all the ungodly are barred from approaching him. God even says that he detests their prayers (see Proverbs 28:9) and abhors their sacrifices (see Proverbs 15:8). It is a unique privilege that God invites his children to come to him; and it is the Spirit of adoption alone that cries in our hearts, *"Abba*, Father" (Romans 8:15). In summary, no one is properly prepared to pray to God unless his heart is purified by faith. But because wicked men profane God's sacred name through their prayers, they deserve to be punished for the sacrilege rather than obtain anything for salvation. Consequently, the blind man does not reason wrongly that Christ has come from God, because he hears his prayers favorably.

Verses 34–41

34. **"You were steeped in sin at birth."** They were undoubtedly referring to his blindness, in the way proud men tease the unhappy and unfortunate. They insult him as if he had been born with the mark of his sins. All the teachers of the law believed that when souls ended one life, they migrated into new bodies and then suffered punishment for their previous sins. So they conclude that this blind man was covered with the pollution of his sins.

This undeserved blame teaches us to be very careful about identifying anybody else's sin as the judgment of God. As we have already seen, the Lord has different reasons for inflicting calamities on people. But these hypocrites not only insult this unhappy man but also reject his holy and good warnings. Most often people cannot bear to be taught by those whom they despise. Now, since God must always be listened to, we should not despise anyone through whom he talks to us, so that God will always find us teachable and submissive, even if he uses an altogether contemptible person, of no account, to instruct us. There is no more dangerous plague than when pride stops our ears and we refuse to listen to those who are warning us for our good. God often chooses worthless and base men to teach and warn us, that he may humble our pride.

And they threw him out. Though it is possible that they threw him out of the temple with physical violence, it seems to me that the evangelist actually means that they excommunicated him, and so his ejection would have the appearance of legality. This also fits the context better, for if they had only thrown him out physically, it would not have been important enough to reach Christ.

35. Jesus heard that they had thrown him out. From this detail I conjecture that they did it as if they were enacting a solemn rite of great importance. This teaches us how trivial and how little to be feared are the anathemas of Christ's enemies. If we are ejected from the congregation where Christ reigns, it is a fearful judgment on us as we are being handed over to Satan (see 1 Corinthians 5:5) and are banished from the kingdom of God's Son. But whenever Christ's Word and Spirit do not hold sway, we should run away voluntarily, without needing to be expelled. We definitely have no reason to fear that tyrannical judgment by which the ungodly insult Christ's servants.

When he found him . . . If he had been kept in the synagogue, he would have run the risk of becoming gradually alienated from Christ and plunged into the same destruction as the ungodly. Christ meets him wandering about outside the temple. Christ embraces this person who has been thrown out by the priests, lifts him up, and offers life to him who was under the death sentence. In our own time we have experienced the same thing. For when Luther and other people began to attack the worst abuses of the Pope, they had little appetite for pure Christianity. But after the Pope had thundered against them and thrown them out of the Roman synagogue through terrifying bulls, Christ stretched out his hand and made himself fully known to them. So there is nothing better for us than to be distant from the enemies of the Gospel, so that Christ may come close to us.

"Do you believe in the Son of Man?" Christ is speaking to a Jew who had been instructed in the teaching of the law from his childhood and had learned that God had promised the Messiah. Therefore, this question is tantamount to Christ exhorting him to follow the Messiah and give himself up to him. However, he uses a more honorable name than was usual, for the Messiah was only thought of as being David's son (see Matthew 22:42).

36. "Tell me so that I may believe." From the blind man's answer it is clear that although he did not yet know anything for certain about Christ, he was nevertheless ready to be taught. For these words mean, "I am ready to embrace him as soon as he is pointed out to me." But it should be noted that the blind man wants to be taught by Christ the prophet. He was already convinced that Christ had been sent by God, and therefore he is not thoughtlessly putting his trust in his teaching.

37. "You have now seen him." These words of Christ would not take the blind man beyond a small amount of frozen faith, for Christ did not mention his power, or why he was sent by the Father, or what he brought to mankind. But the main thing in faith is to know that Christ's sacrificial death has made atonement for our sins and that we are reconciled to God, that his resurrection triumphed over defeated death, that we are renewed by his Spirit so that we are dead to the flesh and to sin so that we may live righteous lives. For Christ is the only Mediator, and the Spirit is the pledge of our adoption. In summary, we find in Christ everything that belongs to eternal life. But the evangelist either does not relate the whole of Christ's conversation with him, or he just means that the blind man joined Christ's side and became one of his disciples. I am sure that Jesus wanted to be acknowledged by him as the Christ, so that from this initial faith Christ might lead him on to a fuller knowledge of himself.

38. And he worshiped him. It may be asked why he gave divine honor to Christ. The word which the evangelist uses simply means to show respect and veneration by bending the knee or in some other way. For myself, I think that it signifies something rare and unusual; the blind man gave far more honor to Christ than to an ordinary man or prophet. But I do not think that at that time he had made enough progress to know that Christ was God manifested in the flesh. What does **worshiped** mean then? The blind man was convinced that Jesus was the Son of God and prostrated himself before him, carried away in wonder as if he were out of his mind.

39. "For judgment I have come." The word **"judgment"** cannot be taken in this passage to mean just the punishment inflicted on the ungodly and the despisers of God, for it is broadened to include the grace of illumination. Christ calls it **"judgment"** in that he restores to its true order what was confused and disordered. But Christ means that this is done through a wonderful plan of God and contrary to the ordinary opinions of men. And, indeed, human reason thinks that nothing is more unreasonable than that people who see should be blinded by the light of the world. Therefore, this is one of the hidden judgments of God through which he throws down mankind's pride. Moreover, it should be noticed that the blindness mentioned here is due to man and not to Christ. By its own nature this light does not really blind anyone. But since the strongest desire of the reprobate is to extinguish the light, the eyes of their minds, which are diseased through malice and depravity, must be dazzled by the light shown to them. In summary, since Christ is by nature "the light of the world" (see 8:12), it is an accidental result that some people are blinded by his coming.

But another question may arise. Since everyone is accused of blindness, who are able to see? My answer is that Christ is here speaking in an ironic way to help his hearers understand. Although unbelievers are blind, they believe themselves to be very aware and perspicacious. They will not bother to listen to God, as they are so puffed up with their own self-confidence. Moreover, outside Christ the wisdom of the flesh looks very fine, because the world does not understand what it is to be really wise. So then, Christ says that people who see, deceiving themselves through a foolish confidence in their own wisdom, are guided by their own opinion and think their empty thoughts are wisdom. As soon as Christ appears in the brightness of his Gospel, they are blinded; not only because their foolishness, which had been hidden in the darkness of unbelief, is now exposed, but because they are plunged into a deeper darkness by God's righteous vengeance and lose that small remnant of I know not what light which has been theirs.

We are all born blind, but in the middle of the darkness of corrupted and vitiated nature some small sparks still shine, so that men are different from brute beasts. Now if anyone is puffed up and proudly confident in his own reason and refuses to submit to God, he may appear, apart from Christ, to be wise; but Christ's brightness will make him foolish. The vanity of the human mind only begins to appear when heavenly wisdom is brought into view. But as I have already said, Christ says something more than that here. For before Christ shines, hypocrites do not resist God so obstinately. But as soon as the light is brought close to them, they rise up against God in open warfare. On account of this depravity and ingratitude they become doubly blind, and God, in righteous vengeance, puts out their eyes completely, which were formerly destitute of the true light.

We can now see what this passage is saying. Christ came into the world to give light to the blind and to make insane those who think they are wise. In the first place Christ mentions illumination, which is the real reason for his coming. He did not come to judge the world but rather to save those who were lost (see Matthew 18:11). So when Paul declares that vengeance awaits the rebellious, he also adds that this punishment will take place after the obedience of the godly has been fulfilled (see 2 Corinthians 10:6). This vengeance should not be limited to Christ's physical presence, as if he did not perform the same thing daily through the ministers of his Gospel.

We should all be the more careful that we do not bring this dreadful punishment on ourselves through a foolish opinion of our own wisdom. Experience teaches us just how true this statement of Christ is. We observe many people who rant and rage just because they cannot endure the rising of the sun of righteousness. Adam lived and was endowed with the true light of understanding; but he lost that divine blessing by wanting to see more than was lawful. Now if we are plunged into blindness and are humbled by the Lord but are still pleased with ourselves in our darkness and set our mad ideas against the heavenly wisdom, we must not be surprised if God's vengeance falls heavily on us and we are made doubly blind. In earlier times this same punishment was inflicted on the ungodly under the law. Isaiah was sent to blind the ancient people, that seeing they may not see — to blind the heart of his people and to close their ears (see Isaiah 6:9-10). But the brightness of the divine light is displayed more fully in Christ than in the prophets. So this example of blindness must have been shown and seen more clearly. Similarly, today the midday light of the Gospel drives hypocrites into extreme rage.

40. Some Pharisees who were with him heard . . . They felt at once that they were wounded by Christ's saying; but they do not appear to have been the worst, for Christ's open enemies abhorred him so much that they had nothing to do with him. But those former men submitted to listening to Christ, although it did them no good. No one is a suitable disciple of Christ until he has put himself to one side, and they were very far from doing that.

Moreover, their question arose out of indignation. They considered that they were insulted by being classified with the blind. It also reveals a proud and derisive contempt of Christ's grace, as if they were saying, "You cannot become famous without disgrace. Are we going to put up with you getting honor from our shame? As for your promise to give new light to the blind, clear off and take your blessing with you! We do not want to be enlightened by you at the price of admitting that we have been blind." From this we observe that hypocrisy has always been full of pride and poison. Their pride is in self-satisfaction and a refusal to part with anything; and their poison lies in their rage against Christ, so that they argue with him as if he had seriously wounded them when he pointed out their disease. Hence their contempt of Christ and the grace he offered them.

The emphasis is on the word **"too."** It means that even if all the rest were blind, they should not be numbered with the ordinary people. People who hold superior positions are far too often drunk with pride and almost forget that they are people.

41. "If you were blind . . ." These words can be taken in two ways. Either that ignorance would to a certain extent excuse them of their guilt if they were not quite set in their ways and were not deliberately fighting against the truth; or that their disease of ignorance would be curable if only they would acknowledge it. The former is confirmed by Christ's words, "If I had not come and spoken to them, they would not be guilty of sin" (15:22). But as in this passage it is added, **"but now that you claim you can see,"** it seems more consistent to explain that a blind person is the person who is aware of his blindness and seeks a remedy for his disease. This seems to be the consistent explanation. So the meaning is, "If you acknowledged your disease, it would not be entirely incurable. But because you think you are healthy, you remain in a desperate state." When Christ says that those who are blind have no sin, it does not excuse their ignorance as being harmless and inculpable. He only means that the disease can be cured easily when it is really felt; for when a blind person seeks deliverance, God is ready to help him. But those who are unaware of their diseases and despise God's grace are incurable.

John
Chapter 10

Verses 1–6

1. "I tell you the truth . . ." Christ was dealing with teachers of the law and priests, who were regarded as the shepherds of the church. He had therefore to take the honor of this title away from them if he wanted his teaching to be received. The small number of believers might also lessen the authority of his teaching. So Christ insists that we must not reckon as shepherds or sheep everyone who outwardly claims a place in the church. The mark to distinguish lawful shepherds from the reprobate, and true sheep from the false, is if Christ himself is the object and the beginning and end of everything.

Every age has found this to be a useful warning, and it is especially needed today. There is no plague more destructive to the church than when wolves go around disguised as shepherds. We know what a serious offense it is when illegitimate or degenerate Israelites claim to be the sons of the church and triumph over believers. Throughout nearly every age the church has been subject to both these evils. But today there is nothing which alarms the ignorant and weak more than seeing God's sanctuary occupied by the church's greatest enemies. For it is hard to make them see that it is Christ's teaching which the shepherds of the church resist so fiercely. Moreover, since most people are led into error through false teaching, each person looks and waits for others, and hardly anyone lets himself be led along the right path.

Therefore, if we do not voluntarily lay ourselves open to wolves and thieves, we must especially guard against being deceived by false shepherds or sheep. The name "church" is rightly honorable; but the greater the reverence it deserves, the more careful and attentive should we be in observing the distinction between the true church and the false. Christ says here, quite clearly, that we should not regard as shepherds everyone who claims the title, nor reckon as sheep everyone who boasts the outward marks. Christ is referring to the Jewish church, but ours is similar in this respect. We should also ponder the reason behind these words, so that weak consciences may not be alarmed or discouraged when they see that those who govern the church in the place of the shepherds are hostile and opposed to the Gospel. They should not turn away from the faith because among those who are called Christians there are few fellow-disciples who listen to Christ's teaching.

"**The man who does not enter . . .**" In my opinion, those who scrutinize every part of this parable very closely are wasting their time. We should be content with the main point that Christ likens the church to a "**sheep pen**" in which God gathers his people, and compares himself to the "**gate**," since he is the only entrance into the church. It follows from this that they alone are good shepherds who lead men straight to Christ, and that they are truly gathered into God's fold and reckoned his flock who give themselves over to Christ alone.

All this refers to his teaching. Since "all the treasures of wisdom and knowledge" (Colossians 2:3) are hidden in Christ, anyone who turns away from Christ to go in another direction does not enter through the gate. The person who does not despise Christ as his teacher will easily overcome the hesitation which perplexes many people as to what the church is and who are to be listened to as shepherds. If the so-called shepherds try to lead us away from Christ, we should run away from them, as Christ tells us to, as if they were wolves or thieves. Also, we should not join or stay with any people except those who agree about the pure faith of the Gospel. This is why Christ tells his disciples to separate from the unbelieving crowd of the whole nation and not allow themselves to be ruled by ungodly priests or be imposed on by proud and empty names.

3. "The watchman opens the gate." If you wish to take this to refer to God I will not object. Christ even seems to be specifically contrasting God's judgment with men's false opinions in the approving of shepherds, as if he were saying, "There are some whom the world in general applauds and willingly honors. But God, who holds the reins of government, acknowledges and approves only those who lead the sheep along this path."

"**He calls his own sheep by name.**" This refers to the mutual consent of faith. The disciple and the teacher are united by the one Spirit of God, so that the one goes before and the other follows. Some think that this expresses the intimate knowledge which a shepherd should have for each sheep, but I think this is too weak.

4. "Because they know his voice." Although Christ is referring here to ministers, he does not so much want them to be heard, as God speaking through them to be heard. For we must notice the exception he has laid down, that the only faithful shepherd of the church is the person who governs his sheep under the guidance and authority of Christ. We should note the reason given why the sheep "**follow.**" It is because they can distinguish the shepherds from wolves through their voice. This is the spirit of discernment, through which the elect discriminate between God's truth and men's false inventions. So, in Christ's sheep there is first a knowledge of the truth, and then a strong desire to obey, so that they not only understand what is true, but gladly receive it. Nor does Christ commend the obedience of faith only because the sheep come submissively on hearing the shepherd's voice, but also because they pay no attention to the voice of strangers and do not scatter when anyone shouts at them.

6. This figure of speech. This is why, proud of their own wisdom, the Pharisees (9:40) rejected Christ's light. In quite an obvious matter they were very dull.

But they did not understand what he was telling them. There are variant readings in the Greek for these words. Some manuscripts have, "They did not understand what he said." Another, which I have followed, is fuller, though it comes to the same thing. A third says, "they did not know that he spoke about himself as the Son of God," but this one has received little approval.

Verses 7–10

7. "I am the gate." Without this explanation, the whole discourse would have been allegorical. But Christ now expounds more clearly the main point of the parable as he declares that he is **"the gate."** This means that the most important part of all spiritual teaching, which souls are fed on, consists in Christ. So Paul, one of the shepherds, also said, "I resolved to know nothing while I was with you except Jesus Christ" (1 Corinthians 2:2). This expression is equivalent to Christ saying that it is to him alone that we must all be gathered together. Therefore, he invites and exhorts everyone who seeks salvation to come to him. By these words he means that those who have left him and still strive after God wander about in vain, since only one door lies open and every other approach is barred.

8. "All who ever came before me ..." Literally, this means, "all — as many as." I think that those who restrict it to Judas the Galilean and his like are far from Christ's meaning. Christ is contrasting all false teaching in general to the Gospel and all false prophets to faithful teachers. It would not, in fact, be unreasonable to extend the statement to the Gentiles, in that everyone who from the beginning of the world has professed to be a teacher, without trying to gather sheep for Christ, has abused his title and destroyed souls. But this does not apply at all to Moses and the prophets. They only wanted to establish Christ's kingdom. We must note that Christ's words are contrasted with those things which oppose them. But we find no contradiction between the law and the teaching of the Gospel.

In summary, Christ says that all the doctrines which have led the world away from him are deadly plagues, since apart from him there is nothing but destruction and a dreadful confusion. We can also see how much importance antiquity has with God and should have with us when it enters, so to speak, into contest with Christ. In case anyone should be swayed by the fact that there have in all ages been teachers who cared nothing about directing men to Christ, Christ himself specifically declares that it does not matter how many people there have been or how soon they began to appear. What we should note is that there is only one **"gate,"** and those who miss it and make openings or breaches in the walls are thieves.

"But the sheep did not listen to them." Christ now clearly confirms what he said less distinctly in allegory. People who are led astray by imposters do not belong to the church of God. He said this, first, in case when we see a great crowd of people going astray we should decide to follow their example and so perish, and next, in case we should waver when God lets imposters loose to deceive many. It is a great comfort and reason for confidence when we know that Christ has always guarded his sheep under his faithful protection, in the middle of numerous attacks and crafty devices of wolves and robbers, so that no one should leave him.

But a question arises here. When does a person begin to belong to Christ's flock? We see many who are straying and wandering through the deserts for most of their lives and then, at last, are gathered into Christ's fold. My reply is that the word **"sheep"** can be taken in two ways here. When Christ says later that he has **"other sheep,"** he includes all God's elect, who were then nothing like his **"sheep."** Here Christ means sheep branded with the shepherd's mark. By nature we are not his **"sheep"** at all. Rather, we are born bears, lions, and tigers until Christ's Spirit tames us and out of wild and savage beasts forms us into a meek flock. According to God's secret election, we are already **"sheep"** in his heart, before we are born; and we begin to be **"sheep"** in ourselves through the calling by which Christ gathers us into his fold. Christ says that those who are called into the order of believers cleave to him too firmly to wander or be carried about by any wind of new teaching.

If anyone raises the objection that even those who have given themselves to Christ sometimes go astray, and that this is proved frequently in experience, and that Ezekiel is right to ascribe it to a good shepherd that he gathers "the scattered flock" (see 34:12), I quite agree that it is not a rare occurrence for those who are of the household of faith to be estranged for a time. But this does not contradict Christ's statement, for inasmuch as they go astray, they cease in a sense to be **"sheep."** Christ simply means that all God's elect, even though they are tempted into many errors, are kept in the obedience of pure faith and not exposed as prey to Satan and his ministers. But this work of God is no less wonderful when he brings back the **"sheep"** who had wandered for a little, as if they had all along been kept in the fold. It is always and without exception true that "they went out from us, but they did not really belong to us. For if they had belonged to us, they would have remained with us" (1 John 2:19).

This passage should make us deeply ashamed. First, because we are so unused to the voice of our Shepherd that hardly anyone listens to it without indifference. And then because we are so slow and lazy to follow him. I am speaking of the good, or at least of the passable, for most of those who claim to be Christ's disciples openly rebel against him. Lastly, as soon as we hear the voice of any stranger, we are carried unstably here and there, and this unsteadiness and levity shows just how little we have advanced in the faith so far. But although the number of believers is less than we would want, and many of this small number continually fall away, faithful teachers have the consolation of knowing that they are heard by God's elect, who are Christ's **"sheep."** It is our job to work hard and to strive in every way to bring, if possible, the whole world to agreement in the unity of the faith. Meanwhile, we must be content with our number.

9. "Whoever enters through me . . ." It is the highest consolation for the godly that they hear that they are out of danger once they have embraced Christ. Christ promises them salvation and a happy state. Later he divides this into two parts. First, they will go safely wherever they need to; and, next, they will be fed well.

"He will come in and go out, and find pasture." Scripture often denotes all the actions of life; as we say in French, *aller et venir* ("to go and come"), which means "to dwell." So according to these words, the Gospel is of service to us in two ways: in it our souls find nourishment, while they otherwise languish with hunger and are fed only with wind; and also Christ will be a faithful protector and defense against the attacks of wolves and robbers.

10. "The thief comes only to steal." In saying this, Christ, as it were, pulls our ear, in case Satan's ministers should surprise us when we are tired and careless. For our excessive indifference exposes us on every side to false teachings. Where does such credulity arise from, that those who should have stayed in Christ run about in a host of errors, except that they do not have sufficient fear and defense against the many false teachers? Not only that, but our uncontrollable curiosity is so happy with the novel and strange ideas of men that we rush headlong to meet thieves and wolves voluntarily. So it is with good reason that Christ says that false teachers, however smoothly they may conduct themselves, carry a deadly poison around with them. So we must be even more careful to drive them away. Paul gives a similar warning: "see to it that no one takes you captive through hollow and deceptive philosophy" (Colossians 2:8).

"**I have come . . .**" This is a different comparison. Christ had earlier called himself "**the gate**" (verse 7) and said that those who brought "**sheep**" to this "**gate**" were true shepherds. Now Christ himself assumes the role of shepherd, and, indeed, affirms that he is the only shepherd, for to no one else does the honor and title correctly belong. Because Christ raises up faithful shepherds for the church, equips them with the necessary gifts, governs them by his Spirit, and works through them, they do not stop him from being the only governor of his church or from ruling as the only shepherd. For although Christ uses their ministry, he does not cease to fulfill and discharge the office of a shepherd by his own power. They are masters and teachers in such a way as not to interfere with Christ's Mastership. In summary, when the word "shepherd" is applied to men, it is used, as they say, in a subordinate sense; and Christ communicates his honor to his ministers in such a way that he still remains the only shepherd of them and of the whole flock.

"**. . . that they may have life.**" Now, when Christ says that he came that the sheep might have life, he means that it is only those who do not submit to his shepherd's "rod and . . . staff" (Psalm 23:4) who are exposed to the attacks of wolves and thieves; and, to give them added confidence, he says that life is continually increased and strengthened in those who do not depart from him. And, indeed, the greater progress anyone makes in faith, the closer he comes to fullness of life, because the Spirit, who is life, increases in him.

Verses 11–15

11. "The good shepherd lays down his life." From his unique love for "**the sheep**," Christ shows that he really acts as a "**shepherd**" towards them, for he is so anxious for their salvation that he does not even spare his own life. From this it follows that those who reject the protection of such a kind and lovable "**shepherd**" are quite ungrateful and deserve to perish a hundred times over and are open to every kind of harm. What Augustine says is very true, that we are here shown what we should desire, what we should avoid, and what we should endure in the government of the church. Nothing is wanted more than that the church should be governed by good and diligent shepherds. Christ says that he is the one "**good shepherd**," who keeps his church safe and sound by himself in the first place and then also by his agents. Whenever there is good order, and suitable men rule, Christ is in fact acting as the "**shepherd**." But there are many wolves and thieves who, under the guise of shepherds, wickedly scatter the church. Christ denounces them as men to be avoided, whatever name they may assume. If the church could be purged of hired hands, so much the better; but because the Lord exercises the patience of believers in this way, and also because we are unworthy of such a wonderful blessing as Christ appearing to us in true shepherds, they are to be tolerated, however much they may be disapproved and disliked.

12. "The hired hand." I understand **"hired hand"** as referring to those who keep the pure doctrine but proclaim the truth, as Paul says, as time-servers rather than out of pure zeal. Such men, though they do not serve Christ faithfully, ought to be heard. Just as Christ wanted the Pharisees to be listened to because they sat "in Moses' seat" (see Matthew 23:2), we should also give the same kind of honor to the Gospel and not despise its less good ministers. Since even the slightest offense makes the Gospel offensive to us, we must always remember, as I previously hinted, that if Christ's Spirit does not work so powerfully in ministers as to clearly show in them that he is their **"shepherd,"** we are suffering the punishment of our sins, and also our obedience is being tested.

"The hired hand is not the shepherd." Although Christ claims the name **"shepherd"** for himself alone, he indirectly states that in certain respects he has it in common with the agents through whom he acts. We know how many there have been since Christ's time who have not hesitated to shed their blood for the salvation of the church. Even the prophets before his coming did not spare their own lives. But in himself he offers a perfect example to serve as a model for his ministers. How vile and shameful is our laziness when our lives mean more to us than the salvation of the church, which Christ put before his own life.

What is said here about laying down his life for the sheep is the main and sure mark of fatherly love. Christ wanted first to testify to the remarkable example of his love towards us which he showed in his death, and then to stir up all his ministers to imitate his example. However, we must note the difference between him and them. He laid down his life as the price of satisfaction, shed his blood to cleanse our souls, and offered his body as a propitiatory sacrifice to reconcile the Father to us. There can be none of this in the ministers of the Gospel, who all need cleansing and receive atonement and reconciliation to God by Christ's unique sacrifice. But Christ is not discussing the efficacy or fruit of his death and comparing himself with others, but is proving what kind of love he had towards us and invites others to follow his example. In summary, inasmuch as it is unique to Christ to win for us life by his death and to execute all that is in the Gospel, so it is the common duty of all pastors to defend the teaching which they proclaim, even if it means laying down their lives and sealing the teaching of the Gospel with their blood in order to testify that it is not in vain that Christ has won salvation for themselves and for others.

But this raises a question. Should we think a **"hired hand"** is a person who, for any reason, shrinks from encountering wolves? In past days this was a burning question when tyrants viciously attacked the church.

Tertullian and like-minded people were, in my opinion, too rigid on this point. I much prefer Augustine's moderation. He allowed pastors to flee, so long as by doing so they were contributing to the public safety rather than betraying the flock committed to their charge by forsaking it. He shows that this is the case where the church is not deprived of proper ministers, and when the life of the pastor personally is so eagerly sought by the enemy that his absence mitigates their rage. But if everyone is in danger, and if there is reason to believe that the pastor is fleeing more from a fear of death than out of desire for everyone's good, Augustine contends that this is not at all right, since the example of his flight will do more harm than his life can do good in the future. This may be read in the letter to Bishop Honoratus (Letter 108). For this reason it was right for Cyprian to flee, who was so far from fearing death that he bravely refused life offered at the price of a treacherous denial of his Master. Only we must insist that a shepherd should put his flock, or even a single sheep, before his own life.

". . . who owns the sheep." Here Christ seems to make everyone, without exception, apart from himself, to be hired hands. Since he alone is "the shepherd," none of us has a right to call "the sheep" he feeds his own. But we must remember that those who are guided by God's Spirit look on what belongs to their head as their own, not to claim power for themselves, but faithfully to look after what has been committed to their charge. People who are really united to Christ will never regard as alien to them those who were so dear to Christ. This is what Christ says next.

13. "The man runs away." He does this because he does not care about the sheep, because he is not touched by the scattering of the flock, since he thinks it is not his concern. The person who is concerned about his wages, and not about the flock, may deceive people when the church is at peace, but when the fight is on he will soon reveal his treachery.

14. "I know my sheep." In the first clause Christ pledges his love for us again, for knowledge is born of love and is accompanied by care. But it also means that Christ thinks nothing of those who do not obey the Gospel; for in the second clause he repeats and confirms what he had said before — that he is also known by "the sheep" in return.

15. ". . . just as the Father knows me." It is unnecessary and inexpedient to enter into thorny speculation about how the Father knows him. Christ simply says that inasmuch as he is the bond of our union with God, he is set between God and us. It is as if he had said that it is no more possible for him to be oblivious of us than for the Father to reject or neglect him. At the same time Christ demands the duty which we owe him. As he uses for our protection all the power he has received from the Father, so he wants us to be obedient and devoted to him, just as he is completely devoted to the Father and refers everything to him.

Verses 16–18

16. "I have other sheep." Although some people think this applies to everyone indiscriminately, whether Jews or Gentiles, who were not yet Christ's disciples, I am sure that Christ was thinking about the calling of the Gentiles. For Christ calls the congregation of the ancient people **"this sheep pen"** in which they were separated from the other nations of the world and united into one body as God's heritage. God had adopted the Jews in such a way as to surround them with, as it were, boundaries of rites and ceremonies, that they might not have to mix with unbelievers; yet the gate of the fold was the gracious covenant of eternal life confirmed in Christ. This is why Christ called all others **"other sheep"**; they did not have the same mark but were a different kind. In summary, this means that Christ's office as a **"shepherd"** is not restricted to the confines of Judea but is far wider.

Augustine's observation on this passage is indeed true. Even as there are many wolves within the church, so there are many **"sheep"** outside the church. But it is not wholly applicable to this passage, which refers to the outer aspect of the church, in that the Gentiles, who had been temporarily strangers, were later taken into the kingdom of God along with the Jews. Yet I agree that it applies in the sense that Christ calls unbelievers **"sheep"** who in themselves could not be thought of as **"sheep"** at all. Through this word Christ not only shows what they will be but, even more, refers it to God's secret election, in that we are already God's **"sheep"** before we are aware that Christ is our **"shepherd,"** just as elsewhere we are called **"enemies"** (see Romans 5:10), even when Christ loved us. This is why Paul also says that we were known by God before we knew him (see Galatians 4:9).

"I must bring them also." Christ means that God's election will be certain, and no one will perish whom he wishes to be saved. The hidden purpose of God, by which men were ordained to life, is at length manifested in his own time by the calling. And that calling is effectual, for Christ regenerates by his Spirit, to be his sons, those who were previously born of flesh and blood.

But it may be asked how the Gentiles became linked with the Jews, for the Jews did not have to reject the covenant that God made with their fathers before they could become Christ's disciples. Nor did the Gentiles, for their part, have to submit to the law's yoke in order to be grafted into Christ and allied to the Jews. Here we must note the distinction between the substance of the covenant and its appendages. The Gentiles could only consent to the faith of Christ by embracing that everlasting covenant on which the salvation of the world was founded. Thus the prophecies were fulfilled: "Five cities in Egypt will speak the language of Canaan" (Isaiah 19:18). Again, "ten men from all languages and nations will take firm hold of one Jew by the edge of his robe and say, 'Let us go with you'" (Zechariah 8:23). Again, "Many nations will come and say, 'Come, let us go up to the mountain of the Lord'" (Micah 4:2). Abraham was also called "the father of many nations" (Genesis 17:5), because "many will come from the east and the west, and will take their places at the feast with Abraham, Isaac and Jacob in the kingdom of heaven" (Matthew 8:11). As for the ceremonies, they are "the dividing wall" which Paul tells us has been "destroyed" (see Ephesians 2:14). Thus we have been joined by the Jews in the unity of the faith as far as the substance is concerned. But the ceremonies were abolished, so that nothing might prevent them from stretching out their hand to us.

"And there will be one flock." That is, he desires that all the children of God be gathered into one body, even as we confess that there is one holy catholic church; there must be one body with one head. Paul says that there is one God, one faith, one baptism, so that we should be one, just as we are called into one hope (see Ephesians 4:4-5). Now, although the flock seems to be divided into different folds, yet believers who are scattered throughout the world are encircled in common bonds, in that the same Word is preached to everyone and the same sacraments are used, and they have the same order of prayer and everything necessary for the profession of faith.

"They too will listen to my voice." Note how God's flock is collected. It happens when there is one shepherd of everyone and when his voice is heard. These words mean that only when the church submits to Christ alone, obeys his commands, and listens to his teaching is she in a state of good order. If Roman Catholics can show us anything like this among themselves, they can enjoy the title of church, which they boast so much about. But if Christ is silent there, his majesty trodden under foot and his sacred ordinances ridiculed, what is their unity but a devilish conspiracy, worse and far more abhorrent than any scattering? Therefore we must remember that our starting point must always be at the head. In this way the prophets, in describing the restoration of the church, always link King David to God, as if they were saying that there is no church if God does not reign there, and no Kingdom of God except where the title of shepherd is given to Christ.

17. "The reason my Father loves me . . ." There is, of course, another loftier reason why the Father loves the Son, for the voice from heaven was not meaningless: "This is my Son, whom I love; with him I am well pleased" (Matthew 3:17). But as Christ became man for our sake, and the Father loved him to the end, that he might reconcile us to himself, it is not surprising that Christ says that he is loved, since our salvation is dearer to him than his own life. Here is a wonderful commendation of the divine goodness to us which should bring our whole souls into rapturous admiration — that God not only extends to us the love due to the one and only Son, but ascribes it to us as the final cause. Indeed, there was no reason for Christ to put on our flesh, in which he was loved so much, except that it might be the pledge of his fatherly mercy in redeeming us.

"... only to take it up again." Because Christ's death would make the disciples very sad when they heard about it, so that their faith might even be greatly shaken, Christ comforts them with the hope of his resurrection, which would soon take place. It is as if he said that he would not just die and be swallowed up by death, but would quickly rise again as conqueror. Today we should always remember the resurrection when we think about Christ's death. So we know that Christ is life because in his contest with death he won a great victory and achieved a noble triumph.

18. "No one takes it from me." Here is a further consolation to encourage the disciples at the death of Christ: he is not forced to die, but offers himself willingly for the salvation of his flock. He not only denies that men have power to kill him without his consent, but he declares that there is no reason in him why he should be killed. This is not the case with us. We have to die because of our sins. It is true that Christ himself was born a mortal man, but this was a voluntary submission and not a bondage imposed by someone else.

Christ wanted to strengthen his disciples in case they became brokenhearted when they later saw him being dragged off to death as if he had been defeated by his enemies. Christ wanted them to know that his dying for his flock was under the control of God's wonderful providence. This teaching remains beneficial, for Christ's death is an expiation for our sins in that it was a voluntary sacrifice. As Paul said, "Through the obedience of the one man the many will be made righteous" (Romans 5:19).

"But I lay it down of my own accord." These words may be explained in two ways. Either that Christ divests himself of life but still remains complete, just as a person takes off some clothing; or that he dies through his own choice.

"This command . . ." Christ draws our attention to the eternal counsel of the Father to teach us that the Father cared so much about our salvation that he handed over to us his one and only Son, great as he is. Christ himself, who came into the world to be totally obedient to his Father, confirms that in everything his only aim is to think of us.

Verses 19–30

19. The Jews were again divided. Christ's sermon won over some disciples. But many were opposed to his teaching, and so a division arises, so that what seemed until then to be the one body of the church now splits up. Previously they were all agreed about worshiping the God of Abraham and following the law of Moses. But now that Christ comes, he causes them to be divided. If their Christian profession had been genuine, Christ would not have made them disagree, for he is the strongest bond of love, and his role is to gather together what is scattered. But through the light of the Gospel Christ unmasks the hypocrisy of many people who falsely claim to be God's people.

Because many people are sinful today, the church is troubled by divisions, and controversies arise. The disturbers of the peace blame us for this and call us schismatics — for the main accusation the Roman Catholics bring against us is that our teaching upsets the peace of the church. But if they gave way to Christ and upheld the truth, all the trouble would be over immediately. When they murmur and complain against Christ and will not allow us to agree to anything other than that God's truth be extinguished and that Christ be banished from his kingdom, they have no right to accuse us of schism. Everyone can see that it is they who are guilty. We should be greatly upset that the church is torn in two by internal divisions. But it is preferable that some people should separate themselves from the ungodly and be united to Christ their head than that everyone should agree to despise God. So the point about schism is that the people who rebel against God and his pure teaching should be noted.

20. **"He is demon-possessed."** They slander Christ in the most offensive way possible, so that everyone will be frightened to listen to him. In case they should be forced to give in to God, the ungodly close their eyes and burst into a furious rage and in their pride vilify Christ, whipping up other people into anger, so that nobody can hear Christ's words. But Christ's teaching is powerful enough in itself to overcome these slanders. This is what the believers mean in the next verse.

"These are not the sayings of a man possessed by a demon." It is as if they are asking that people should judge from the fact itself. The truth, as has been said, is quite capable of looking after itself. The one thing that strengthens our faith is that the ungodly will never be able to stop God's power and wisdom from shining in the Gospel.

22. **Then came the Feast of Dedication.** The Greek word here for **Dedication** really means "renewal." The temple, which had been polluted, was reconsecrated under Judas Maccabeus, and it was then decided that the new dedication would be an annual feast and celebration to remember God's grace which had ended Antiochus' reign of terror. In Christ's day, he appeared in the temple at that time, according to the custom, so that his preaching might bear fruit among a large crowd of people.

23. **In Solomon's Colonnade.** The evangelist calls **Solomon's Colonnade** the temple itself when, in fact, it was only an annex to the temple. Christ is not referring to the old porch which had been built by Solomon, as that had been completely destroyed by the Chaldeans, but

to that which the Jews, perhaps immediately after their return from the Babylonian captivity, built according to the plans of the old porch. They gave it the same name, so that it might be more highly honored. Herod later built the new temple.

24. The Jews gathered around him. This was undoubtedly a cunning attack on Christ by those who originated the plot. The ordinary people were sincere in their desire to see Jesus reveal himself as the one God had sent to be a deliverer. But just a few people, through craftiness and trickery, wanted to draw this word from him in the crowd, so that he might be lynched by the mob and arrested by the Romans.

"How long will you keep us in suspense?" By complaining that they were kept **"in suspense,"** they pretend to be so ardent for the promised redemption that their minds are incessantly taken up with the expected coming of Christ. Genuine godliness only finds its fulfillment in Christ. As Christ himself said, "Come to me, all you who are weary and burdened, and I will give you rest. . . . You will find rest for your souls" (Matthew 11:28-29). So the people who do come to Christ should do so in the way in which these people pretended to. But they accuse Christ unfairly, as if he had not up to then been responsible for their faith; for it was completely their own fault that their knowledge of Christ was partial and imperfect. But this is always the case with unbelievers. They would prefer to remain in a state of doubt rather than build on the solid foundation of the Word of God. Today we see many people voluntarily closing their eyes and spreading the clouds of doubt, so that the clear light of the Gospel is obscured. We also see many flighty spirits fluttering around in idle speculation and never finding, throughout their whole life, a fixed position.

"Tell us plainly." When they demand that Christ should declare himself **"plainly"** or freely and confidently, they mean that he should no longer be evasive and give indirect hints. They say that his teaching is obscure when in fact it is abundantly clear and distinct to everyone except when it falls on deaf ears. From this story we take the warning that we cannot escape from the tricks and slanders of the wicked if we are called to preach the Gospel. So we must be on our guard and not be caught unawares if the same thing happens to us as happened to our Master.

25. "I did tell you." The Lord does not conceal that he is the Christ; but neither does he teach them as if they were keen to learn. Instead, Christ rebukes them for their obstinate malice in that, although they had been taught by the Word and by the deeds of God, it had not benefitted them. So Christ blames them for not knowing him. It is as if he said, "My teaching is easy to understand, and it is you who are to blame, because you maliciously resist God."

"The miracles I do . . ." Christ speaks about his **"miracles"** to doubly convict them of their obstinacy. They had, as well as the teaching, a striking testimony in Christ's **"miracles,"** if they had not been ungrateful to God. Twice Christ says that they do not believe, showing that they were deaf to teaching and blind to deeds. This was a sign of extreme and desperate malice. Christ says that he did **"the miracles"** in his **"Father's name,"** because he wanted to testify to the power of God in them, which would clearly prove that he was from God.

26. ". . . because you are not my sheep." He gives a more profound reason for their not believing in either his miracles or teaching — it is because they are reprobate. We must take note of Christ's claim. Since they boasted that they were God's church, Christ affirms that believing is a special gift, in case their unbelief should detract from the Gospel. Indeed, for men to know God, they must be known first by God (see Galatians 4:9). But people for whom God has no regard have to always remain turned away from him. If anyone blames God for causing unbelief, since only he can make them his **"sheep,"** I answer that Christ is totally innocent here, because people only reject God's grace out of their own voluntary malice. God does everything necessary to bring about faith in himself, but wild beasts will never be tamed until they are changed into **"sheep"** by God's Spirit. Wild people will never succeed in blaming God for their wild state, because this is how they are by nature.

To sum up, Christ means that it is hardly surprising if only a few obey his Gospel, because all who are not subdued to the obedience of faith by God's Spirit remain fierce and untamable beasts. So it is even more unreasonable and absurd that the Gospel's authority should depend on man's assent. Rather, believers should realize that they are the more firmly bound to God because while others remain blind, they are drawn to Christ by the enlightening of the Spirit. This also is a comfort to ministers of the Gospel if their labor is wholly unproductive.

27. "My sheep listen to my voice." Christ uses two contrasting arguments to show that they are not his **"sheep"** because they do not obey the Gospel. For God effectually calls those whom he has elected, so that Christ's **"sheep"** are proved by their faith. Indeed, believers are called **"sheep"** because they surrender themselves to God to be ruled by the hand of the head Shepherd and, putting away their original fierceness, become meek and teachable. It is a great comfort to godly teachers that although most people in the world do not listen to Christ, he has his **"sheep"** whom he knows and by whom he is also known. They must do their utmost to bring the whole world into Christ's fold, but when they do not succeed as they aim to, they must be satisfied with this one thought, that those who are **"sheep"** will be gathered together through their agency. The rest has already been explained.

28. "They shall never perish." It is the incomparable fruit of faith that Christ invites us to be sure and untroubled when we are brought by faith into his fold. But we must also see what basis this assurance rests on. It is that Christ will be the faithful guardian of our salvation, for he says that it is in his **"hand."** And as if this were not enough, he says that they will be kept safe by his Father's power. This is a remarkable passage, teaching us that the salvation of all the elect is as certain as God's power is invincible. And Christ was not just tossing this word thoughtlessly into the air, but was giving a promise which should remain deeply fixed in our minds. Therefore, we deduce that Christ's saying indicates that the elect are firmly assured in their salvation. We are surrounded by powerful enemies, and our weakness is so great that we are not far from death every moment. But everyone who keeps what we **"have entrusted to him"** is greater and more powerful than everybody else (see 2 Timothy 1:12); and so we need not be afraid, as if our life were in danger.

From this, too, we see how foolhardy is the Roman Catholics' confidence in relying on free will, their own strength, and the merits of their deeds. Christ teaches his disciples to remember that in this world they are, so to speak, in the middle of a forest among countless robbers. What is more, they are not only unarmed and exposed as prey, but they know that the reason for death lies within themselves, so that they can only go about safely when they rely on God's protection. In summary, our salvation is certain because it is in God's **"hand."** Our faith is weak, and we are prone to wavering; but God has taken us in his **"hand"** and is powerful enough to scatter with one breath all the efforts of our enemies. It is very important for us to note this, so that fear of temptations do not overwhelm us. For Christ also wanted to show how the sheep live quietly even as they are surrounded by wolves.

29. "No one can snatch them out of my Father's hand." From the invincible power of God, Christ infers that the salvation of the godly is not exposed to their enemies' desires because God, who has taken them under his protecting **"hand,"** would first of all have to be overcome.

30. "I and the Father are one." Christ wanted to answer the jeers of the wicked. The ungodly might have objected that God's power did not belong to Christ, so that he would not be able to promise his disciples his unfailing help. Therefore, Christ declares that his affairs are so totally **"one"** with the Father's that the Father's help will never fail him or his **"sheep."** The ancients misused this passage to prove that Christ has the same essence as the Father. Christ is not discussing the unity of substance but the concord he has with the Father, so that whatever Christ does will be confirmed by his Father's power.

Verses 31–36

31. The Jews picked up stones to stone him. When godliness upholds God's glory, it burns with a zeal directed by God's Spirit. In the same way, unbelief is the mother of fury, and the devil stirs up the ungodly in such a way that they breathe nothing but slaughter. The result reveals their motive in questioning Christ, for his public confession, which they pretended to seek, at once drives them to madness. Even though they are carried away to attack Christ so violently, they undoubtedly tried to hide behind a pretense of legality, as if they were behaving according to the law's commands which prescribed that false prophets should be stoned (see Deuteronomy 13:5).

32. ". . . many great miracles." Here Christ is saying that they not only have no reason to be cruel, but he also accuses them of ingratitude in repaying God's blessings so inequitably. Christ does not say that he has done a service to them through one or two deeds, but that he has been kind to them in many ways. Christ then reproves them for being ungrateful not only to himself, but even more to God. Christ says that he is the Father's minister, openly manifesting his power so that it might be known and attested to them. For when Christ says **"from the Father,"** he means that God was their author. Here is the summary of this: "God wanted to tell you through me the excellent benefits bestowed on you by my hand. Examine me as much as you want to, for I have done nothing among you except what is worthy of praise and thanks. Therefore, in persecuting me you reveal your rage against the gifts of God." But put as a question it has greater force to pierce their consciences than if he had made a direct assertion.

33. "We are not stoning you for any of these." Although the ungodly wage open war on God, they never want to sin without a semblance of honesty. Therefore, when they rage against the Son of God, they are not satisfied with this cruelty but accuse him without provocation and make themselves advocates and avengers of God's glory. A good conscience should be like a brass wall for us as it boldly repels the reproaches and slanders which attack us. However plausible their malice may appear to be, and whatever ignominy they may bring on us for a time, if we are fighting for God's cause he will not refuse to uphold his truth. But the ungodly never lack excuses for oppressing God's servants, and they have such hardened impudence that they do not stop reviling even when they are overcome. Therefore we need patience and meekness to support us to the end.

". . . but for blasphemy." The word **"blasphemy,"** which secular authors generally use for any kind of reproach, the Scriptures apply to God when his majesty is wounded and insulted.

". . . because you, a mere man . . ." There are two kinds of **"blasphemy."** One is when God is robbed of his due honor. The other is when anything unworthy of or foreign to his nature is ascribed to him. So they argue that Christ is a blasphemer and sacrilegious because as a mortal man he usurps divine honor. This would be a correct definition of **"blasphemy"** if Christ were nothing more than **"a mere man."**

Where they go wrong is in not troubling to contemplate his divinity, which was conspicuous in his miracles.

34. "Is it not written in your Law . . . ?" Christ acquits himself of the charge against him, not by denying that he is the Son of God, but by maintaining that he had been right to say that he was (verse 36). Yet he adapts his reply to the people instead of explaining it fully, for he thought that it was enough for the present to refute their malice. When he says that he is the **"Son"** of God he does so indirectly rather than with a full explanation. The argument which he uses is not taken from equals, but from the less to the greater.

"'I have said you are gods.'" Scripture calls **"gods"** those on whom God has bestowed an honorable position. But the person God separated to be eminent above everyone else is far more worthy of this noble title. From this it follows that there are malignant and false expositors who agree with the first but take offense at the second. The passage which Christ quotes, "I said, 'You are "gods"; you are all sons of the Most High'" (Psalm 82:6), is where God expostulates with the kings and the judges of the earth who tyrannically abuse their authority and power for their own sinful desires and for oppressing the poor and for every kind of evil. He reproaches them for not thinking about the One from whom they received so much honor and for dishonoring God's name. Christ applies this to the present case. They have received the name of **"gods"** because they are God's ministers who should govern the world. Scripture calls the angels **"gods"** for the same reason, in that through them God's glory shines out on the world.

35. ". . . to whom the word of God came." Christ means that they were given a definite command from God. From this we infer that empires did not spring up by chance or from man's mistakes, but were appointed by the will of God, who wishes political order to flourish among people so that we may be governed by right and by law. This is why Paul says that everyone who resists the power over us is a rebel against God, because there is no power but what is ordained by God (see Romans 13:1-2). If anyone objects that other callings are also from God and are approved by him, and yet we do not call farmers, farmworkers, or cobblers "gods," my answer is that not all people who are called by God to any particular way of life are called "gods." Christ is speaking about kings, whom God has elevated to a higher rank so that they may rule and be above the rest.

In summary, we must realize that magistrates are called **"gods"** because God has given authority to them. Under the word **"Law"** (verse 34) Christ embraces the whole teaching by which God governed his ancient people. Since the prophets were simply expounders of the law, the Psalms were also thought of as an appendage to the law. **"The Scripture cannot be broken"** means that the teaching of Scripture is inviolable.

36. "... whom the Father set apart." There is a sanctification which is common to all godly people. But here Christ is claiming something far better for himself — namely, that he was separated from everyone else so that the power of the Spirit and God's majesty might be displayed in him. As he said earlier, "On him God the Father has placed his seal of approval" (6:27). But this rightly refers to the person of Christ as he is manifested in the flesh. Therefore, these two things are linked, that he was **"set apart"** and that he was **"sent into the world."** But we must also understand for what reason and on what condition Christ was **"sent."** It was to bring salvation from God and to prove and to show himself in every way to be **"God's Son."**

"Why then do you accuse me of blasphemy?" The Arians twisted this passage to prove that Christ is not God by nature but has a kind of secondary divinity. But this error is easily refuted, for Christ is not discussing here what he is in himself, but what we should acknowledge him to be from his miracles in human flesh. We can never understand his eternal divinity until we embrace him as the Redeemer revealed to us by the Father. Moreover, we should remember what I suggested before, that in this passage Christ is not openly and distinctly explaining what he is, as he would have done to his disciples; rather, he is concentrating on refuting the slander of his enemies.

Verses 37–42

37. "... unless I do what my Father does." Christ emphasizes his miracles again, in case the Jews should answer that he was boasting about sanctification which has nothing to support it. For Christ's miracles clearly demonstrated his divinity. Christ says this by way of concession, as if he were saying, "I do not want you to feel bound to believe in me for any other reason than that the fact itself is plain to see. You can reject me with impunity if God has not given public witness to me." Christ refers to his miracles as **"what my Father does"** because they were truly divine and because so great a power shone in them that they could not be ascribed to a man.

38. "But if I do it ..." Christ shows that they are clearly guilty of ungodly and sacrilegious contempt because they give no honor to the undoubted deeds of God. By way of a second concession Christ says, "Although I could allow you to doubt my teaching, you cannot deny, at any rate, that the miracles I have done are from God. Therefore, you are openly rejecting God and not a man."

"... that you may learn and understand ..." Although Christ puts faith after knowledge, as if it were inferior, he does so because he is dealing with unbelieving and perverse people who will never yield to

God until they are overcome and forced by experience. Rebels want to know before they will believe. So God indulges us and prepares us for faith through a knowledge of his deeds. But knowledge of God and of his secret wisdom follows after faith, because obedience of faith opens to us the door of the kingdom of heaven.

". . . that the Father is in me . . ." Christ repeats again what he has already said, but in different words: "the Father is in me, and I in the Father." It all comes down to this: in the conduct of his ministry there is nothing that contradicts his "Father." Here "the Father is in me," says Christ. That is, "divine power is manifested in me."

". . . and I in the Father." That is, "I do nothing but by God's authority, so that there is a mutual connection between me and my Father." This saying is not referring to the unity of his essence, but to the manifestation of divine power in Christ's person, which showed that he was sent from God.

39. Again they tried to seize him. This was undoubtedly so that they might drag him out of the temple and stone him to death, for their rage was not appeased by Christ's words. As for the saying, **escaped their grasp**, this could only have happened through God's wonderful power. It reminds us that we are not exposed to the passions of the ungodly, for God bridles them whenever he wishes.

40. Jesus went back across the Jordan. Christ passed **across the Jordan** so that he would not always be fighting at such a disadvantage. Therefore, he teaches us through this to make good use of opportunities. Concerning the place he went back to, you can read my comments on 1:28.

41. And many people came to him. The large crowd shows that Christ was not seeking solitude in order to escape from doing his duty, but so he could set up God's sanctuary in the wilderness after his own place, Jerusalem, had obstinately driven him out. Indeed, this was God's dreadful vengeance, that the temple which had been chosen by God was a "den of robbers" (see Jeremiah 7:11; Matthew 21:13), so that God's church gathered together in a despised place.

"**John never performed a miraculous sign.**" Here they infer that Christ is superior to John because Christ's miracles were so remarkable, whereas "**John never performed a miraculous sign.**" Not that we should always judge from miracles; but when they are linked with teaching, they have no small weight, as has often been pointed out. Moreover, the argument is defective. They compare Christ with John, but they mention only one part of the comparison. They take it for granted that John was an outstanding prophet from God and was endued with a unique grace from the Spirit. Therefore, they correctly reason that Christ is to be preferred to John because it was only through the definite providence of God that John, who in other respects was a very great prophet, was not given the honor of performing a miracle. So they conclude that this was for Christ's sake, so that he might be held in greater respect.

"All that John said about this man . . ." This appears not to have been said by them, but was added by the evangelist to show that there were two reasons which encouraged them to believe in Christ: they saw that the witness which John had given to Christ was true, and that the miracles brought Christ greater honor.

John
Chapter 11

Verses 1–10

1. Now a man named Lazarus was sick. The evangelist moves on to another story which contains an especially remarkable miracle. In addition to giving us a wonderful example of his divine power through the raising of Lazarus, Christ also shows us a living image of our future resurrection. This was nearly his last act, as the time of his death was approaching; so it is not surprising that he showed his glory particularly in this deed, as he wanted it printed in the minds of his followers, that it might act as a kind of seal on everything that had already happened. Christ had brought other people back from the dead, but here he demonstrates his power on a rotting corpse. In their correct place, we will note the details that bring praise to God's glory in this miracle.

He was from Bethany, the village of Mary and her sister Martha. This detail is probably mentioned because Lazarus was less well-known than his two faithful sisters, for Luke 10:38-39 mentions that these holy women used to welcome Christ into their home.

2. This Mary ... was the same one who poured perfume on the Lord. A similar display of ignorance is displayed by people who think that this Mary, Lazarus' sister, was the woman with the immoral reputation and life mentioned in Luke 7:37. The mistake arose because of Christ's anointing, as if he were not anointed on several occasions and at different places. According to Luke, the woman who anointed Jesus lived in Jerusalem. However, Mary of Bethany **poured perfume on** him later on in her village. The perfect tense used by the evangelist does not refer to the time when these things happened, but to the time when they were written down. It is as if he were saying, "This is Mary, who later poured on Christ the ointment and made the disciples indignant" (see Matthew 26:7).

3. "Lord, the one you love is sick." Although the message was short, Christ could readily tell what the two sisters wanted. In their sadness they humbly ask Christ to help them. While we are not forbidden to make longer prayers, the most important thing is to throw all our cares and troubles into God's heart, so that he might provide the answer. This is how these women behaved towards Christ. They immediately explain their trouble to him and look to him for help. It will be noted that because of Christ's love, they hope to receive help. This is a constant rule of true prayer; for where God's love is, there is certain and present salvation. He does not love us and then forsake us.

4. **"This sickness will not end in death."** Through this reply, Christ wanted to set his disciples' minds at ease and free them from worry when they see him being unconcerned about his friend's welfare. In case they fear for Lazarus' life, Christ says that the **"sickness"** will not be fatal and promises that it will bring **"glory"** to God. Even though Lazarus did die, because Christ would bring him back to life again soon afterwards, Christ knew what the outcome would be about Lazarus' sickness.

"It is for God's glory." We know that although the reprobate perish, **"God's glory"** shines no less clearly in their destruction than in the salvation of the godly. But here Christ is correctly pointing to **"God's glory"** which was linked to his office. Moreover, the power Christ demonstrated in his miracles was not threatening, but was gentle and kind. So when he says that Lazarus was in no danger of death, he wanted to show his own and his Father's **"glory."** We should think why and for what purpose Christ was sent by the Father: it was to save, not to destroy.

". . . so that God's Son may be glorified through it." This expression is most important. From it we gather that God wants to be known in the person of his Son in such a way that whatever honor he demands for himself may be bestowed on his Son. This is why we have already been told, "He who does not honor the Son does not honor the Father" (5:23). The Turks and the Jews pretend to worship God, but their insolence towards Christ means that they are trying to rob God of himself.

5. **Jesus loved Martha and her sister and Lazarus.** At first it seems inconsistent that Christ should stay for **two more days** (verse 6) on the other side of the Jordan if he cares about Lazarus' life. But the evangelist does say that **Jesus loved Martha and her sister and Lazarus.** Love gives birth to care, and so Christ should have rushed to Lazarus at once. But as Christ is the unique mirror of divine grace, his delay teaches us that we should not judge God's love through present circumstances. Christ often delays helping us after he has been asked — sometimes so that he may increase our devotion in praying to him, and at other times so that he may test our patience and make us more obedient. So believers should pray for God's help in such a way that they learn to put aside their own wants if Christ agrees to help them more slowly than the situation seems to demand. Although Christ may delay, he never sleeps or forgets his own people. We can be certain that he desires the salvation of everyone he loves.

7. **Then he said to his disciples . . .** At last, after the disciples thought that Christ had forgotten Lazarus, or at least was putting other things which seemed to be more important before him, Christ now shows his

concern for Lazarus. So Christ orders them to cross over the Jordan and to head for **Judea.**

8. "The Jews tried to stone you." The disciples try to deter Christ, not for his sake, but for their own. Everyone is afraid, sensing a common danger. When they are avoiding the cross and are ashamed to confess it, they offer the more specious excuse that they are concerned for their Master. This happens every day with many people. People who avoid doing their duty out of fear of the cross look for excuses everywhere to hide their laziness, in case they should be seen to be defrauding God of due obedience without just cause.

9. "Are there not twelve hours of daylight?" There are different ways to explain this verse. People who think that our minds can be changeable, so that each hour they have a new and different purpose, are far from Christ's meaning. I would not have bothered to mention this unless it had become a common idea. I content myself with the true meaning.

First, Christ takes a metaphor from day and night. If anyone travels in the dark, it is hardly surprising if he bumps into things or becomes lost or falls down. But during the day the sunlight shows the way, and there is no danger. God's calling is very similar to **"daylight,"** as it does not allow us to make mistakes or stumble. So whoever obeys God's Word and does nothing that is not commanded by God will have a heavenly leader and guide and in this confidence can go safely and boldly on his way. For as Psalm 91:11-12 says, "He will command his angels concerning you to guard you in all your ways; they will lift you up in their hands, so that you will not strike your foot against a stone." Relying on this protection, Christ advances boldly into Judea, not fearing that he will be stoned. There is no danger of becoming lost when God, like the sun, shines on us and shows us the way.

These words also teach us that whenever anyone follows his own ideas without consulting God, his whole life is spent wandering around lost. People who are very wise in their own estimation, and who do not ask for help from God's mouth and do not have his Spirit ruling all they do, are just blind people wandering around in the dark. The correct way is to be aware of God's call and always have God going on in front of us. Sure confidence in a successful outcome will follow the rule of ordering our lives aright, because God cannot but govern us well. We need to know about this, because believers can hardly make one step in following Christ without Satan at the same time putting thousands of obstacles in our way. But when the Lord, as it were, kindles his light and invites us to advance, we must move forward with a strong heart, though we are surrounded by death on every side. God never orders us to advance without encouraging us with a promise, so that we may be convinced that whatever we do at his command will turn out well and happily for us. This is our chariot. Whoever goes into it will never faint from tiredness. Indeed, if the obstacles are too difficult for us to travel by chariot, we will be given wings so that we can always reach our destination. However, believers will always encounter opposition, but adverse occurrences help us in our salvation.

In summary, God's eyes are always watching over those who are attentive to his will. Once again we see that whenever people allow themselves to neglect and overlook God's Word and do what they please, their whole lives are cursed by God, and vengeance on their rashness and blind passion is always imminent. Here again Christ divides the day into twelve hours, as the ancients did. Although the days are longer in summer and shorter in winter, there are always "**twelve hours of daylight**" and twelve at night.

Verses 11–16

11. "Our friend Lazarus has fallen asleep." Christ had already said that this was not a fatal illness. But now, in case the disciples are too upset at the unexpected, Christ informs them that Lazarus is dead, but gives them hope about his coming back to life. They show just how ignorant they are when they mistakenly believe that Christ is referring to "**sleep.**" For while this is an unusual metaphor, it is such a common one in Scripture that it should have been well-known to all the Jews.

12. "If he sleeps, he will get better." When the disciples say that sleep will be good for Lazarus, they are attempting to dissuade Christ from going there. But it is not as if they try and turn Christ's words to their own ends, for when they think that he spoke about "**sleep,**" they gladly seize the opportunity to run from danger. Augustine, and many other people after him, have speculated about the meaning of the word "**sleep.**" They say that it refers to death because it is easy for God to raise the dead to life, just as it is easy for us to wake up the sleeping. But because of its constant use in Scripture, we can deduce that Christ did not mean anything like this. Indeed, since even in secular writers "sleep" so often refers to death, it is certain that it was used just because a lifeless corpse lies insensible, exactly like the body of a person who is asleep. This is why sleep is quite appropriately called "the image of death," and Homer calls it "death's brother." Further, the word denotes only the sleep of the body, and it is too absurd for some fanatics to apply this to the soul, as if they too were subject to death by being deprived of understanding.

"**I am going there to wake him up**" (verse 11). Christ now asserts his own power when he says that he will "**wake him.**" For though, as has been said, the word "**sleep**" does not express the facility of the resurrection, Christ shows that he is Lord of death by saying that he wakes up those whom he restores to life.

14. "Lazarus is dead." Christ was remarkably kind in putting up with such stupidity from the disciples. Indeed, the reason why he temporarily delayed giving them the fuller grace of the Spirit was to heighten the miracle of restoring them in a moment.

15. "For your sake I am glad I was not there." By this Christ means that it was good for them that he was not there since his power would have been less obvious if he had helped Lazarus at once. The closer God's deeds approximate to the normal course of nature, the more they are despised and their glory is diminished. We experience this daily. If God stretches out his hand at once, we are not conscious that he is helping us. So if the disciples are to acknowledge the resurrection of Lazarus as a truly divine work, it had to be delayed, so that it might be very different from a human remedy.

However, we should remember what I said before — that in Christ's person, God's fatherly kindness is reflected to us. When God allows us to be overwhelmed with distress and to collapse under this for a long time, we should recall that through all this God is concerned about our salvation. During these times we naturally groan in anxiety and sadness, but the Lord rejoices for our good. He shows us a double kindness in not only pardoning our sins, but joyfully devising ways of correcting them.

". . . so that you may believe." He does not mean that this was the first feeble start of faith in them, but that it was the confirmation of faith already begun, though still very meager and weak. But he hints that if God's hand had not been openly displayed, they would not have believed.

16. Then Thomas . . . Up to this point the disciples had tried to dissuade Christ. Thomas is now ready to follow, but without any confidence. At any rate, he does now strengthen himself with Christ's promise and follows him cheerfully and calmly.

"Let us also go, that we may die with him." This is the language of despair, for they should not have been worried about their own life. The relative phrase **"with him"** may refer to either Christ or Lazarus. If you take it as referring to Lazarus, it will be ironical, as if he said, "What is the point of going there? Unless this is the only way we can do our duty as friends and die with him!" But I prefer the other meaning; Thomas does not refuse to die with Christ. Nevertheless, as I have said, this comes from mindless enthusiasm. He should rather have taken heart from faith in the promise.

Verses 17–27

18. Bethany was less than two miles from Jerusalem. The evangelist carefully describes everything that contributes to the veracity of the story. He relates how **Bethany was less than two miles from Jerusalem**, in case anyone should be surprised that many friends came to comfort the sisters from there, whom God meant to be witnesses of the miracle. For although they were moved by neighborly duty, they were really gathered together there through the secret counsel of God for another purpose — that Lazarus' resurrection would not be obscure or that the witnesses might not be only his own family. This is convincing proof of the base ingratitude of the nation and a striking demonstration of divine power at a well-known place, before a huge crowd and near the city gates — as if it were performed in a theatre which instantly vanishes from everyone's eyes. What is more, the Jews maliciously close their eyes and refuse to see what is in front of them. Nor is it new or unusual that people who too incessantly stare at miracles are quite dull and stupid in thinking about them.

The distance between the two places was **less than two miles**, for the stadium or furlong is six hundred feet — that is, one hundred and twenty-five Roman yards.

19. . . . to comfort them in the loss of their brother. This was their purpose; but God had another aim, as we have said. It is clear from this that the house of Lazarus and his sisters were greatly respected and honored. Again, as it is natural that the death of their own friends should bring grief and mourning to people, this duty that the evangelist mentions is not to be blamed except in that sinful excess which prevails in this as in other parts of life and corrupts what is not in itself sinful.

20. When Martha heard that Jesus was coming . . . Martha goes outside the village, as we shall see later, not only perhaps because of her reverence for Christ, but so that she might meet him more privately. The danger Christ was in was fresh in Martha's mind. The anger of his enemies, though it had cooled down a little after Christ went into Galilee, had not really died down and could break out again more violently when they learned of his arrival.

21-22. "Lord . . . if you had been here . . ." Martha begins by complaining, though in doing so she quietly makes her desire known. It is as if she had said, "You could by your presence have saved my brother from death; and even now you can do it, for God will not deny you anything." But by speaking like this, she gives way to her feelings rather than restraining them under the rule of faith. I agree that her words do partly stem from her faith, but I believe that uncontrolled desires were mixed with them and carried her beyond the correct bounds. For when she tells herself that her brother would not have died had Christ been present, what basis does she have for her confidence? It did not arise from any promise of Christ.

Therefore, the only conclusion is that she thoughtlessly gives way to her desires instead of subjecting herself to Christ. When she ascribes to Christ power and supreme goodness this proceeds from faith; but when she convinces herself about more than she had heard from Christ, this does not come from faith. We should always see that the Word and faith are in agreement with each other, in case anyone should make up something which does not have the authority of God's Word. Moreover, Martha was unduly influenced by Christ's bodily presence. So her faith, mixed up and entangled with unchecked desires, and even not completely free from superstition, could not shine with full brightness, so that we can see only a few sparks of it in these words.

23. "Your brother will rise again." Christ's friendliness is wonderful. He forgives Martha's faults which we have touched on and of his own accord promises her more than she had dared to ask for plainly and directly.

24. "I know he will rise again." Martha's excessive timidity is apparent here as she waters down what Christ has said. We said that she went further than she had a right to do when she manufactured for herself a hope out of her own imagination. She now falls into the opposite mistake of doing nothing, as if she were frightened when Christ extended his hand to her. We must be on our guard against both these errors. On the one hand, we must not drink in empty hopes which will prove to be nothing but wind; and on the other hand, we must not close our hearts firmly when the Lord speaks. Again, in her reply Martha wanted to find out more than she dared hope from Christ's words, as if she had said, "If you mean the last resurrection, I do not doubt that my brother will be raised at the last day, and I comfort myself with this trust. But I do not know if you are pointing me to something greater."

25. "I am the resurrection and the life." First of all Christ says that he is **"the resurrection and the life."** Then he explains each part of the statement separately and distinctly. First, Christ calls himself **"the resurrection,"** because the restoration from death to life naturally precedes the state of life. But the whole human race is plunged in death. Therefore, no one will possess life unless he is first risen from the dead. So Christ is here teaching that he is the start of life. Later he adds that the continuity of life is also the work of his grace.

The explanation which follows clearly shows that Christ is speaking about spiritual life: **"He who believes in me will live, even though he dies."** So, in what way is Christ **"the resurrection"**? By his resurrection he regenerates the sons of Adam, who by their sin were alienated from God, so that they begin to live a new life. Away with those who idly say that people are prepared for receiving the grace of God by the movement of nature. They might as well say that the dead walk! Since no part or faculty of the soul is not corrupted and turned aside from what is right, the fact that men live and breathe and are endowed with sense, understanding, and will tends to their destruction. This is how death reigns everywhere, for the death of the soul is alienation from God. So people who believe in Christ, although they had been once dead, begin to live; for faith is a spiritual resurrection of the soul and, as it were, brings the soul alive, that it may live for God. As it was said earlier, "The dead will hear the voice of the Son of God and those who hear will live" (5:25).

This is indeed a strong commendation of faith, which conveys to us the life of Christ and thus liberates us from death.

26. "And whoever lives and believes in me . . ." Christ now explains the second clause, about how Christ is **"the life"** — because he will never allow the life to be lost which he has once given, but keeps it to the end. What would become of people, as they are so inherently frail, if when they have obtained life they are then left to themselves? The ongoing life must, therefore, also rest on Christ's power, so that he may complete what he has started.

". . . will never die." It is said that believers **"will never die"** because their souls, in that they are born again "not of perishable seed" (1 Peter 1:23), have Christ living in them, through whom they are continually brought to life. Although "your body is dead because of sin, yet your spirit is alive because of righteousness" (Romans 8:10). The fact that day by day "outwardly [they] are wasting away" does not take anything away from their true life, but in fact helps their progress since "inwardly [they] are being renewed day by day" (2 Corinthians 4:16). What is more, death is itself a sort of liberation from the slavery of death.

"Do you believe this?" At first it appears that Christ is speaking about spiritual life in order to distract Martha from her present desire. Martha wanted her brother to be restored to life. Christ replies that he is the author of a better life, because he brings alive the souls of believers with a heavenly power. Yet I have no doubt that Christ intended to include both graces. So he describes in general that spiritual life which he gives to everyone who belongs to him; but he also wants to offer Martha a taste of the power which he would soon show in raising Lazarus.

27. "Yes, Lord." To show that Martha believes what she had heard about Christ — that he is **"the resurrection and the life"** — she replies that she believes he is **"the Christ"** and **"the Son of God."** This knowledge includes all of God's blessings, for we must recall the reason why the Messiah was promised and the duty the prophets ascribe to him. When Martha confesses that he was the One who was to come into the world, she strengthens her faith by the predictions of the prophets. From this it follows that the full restoration of everything and perfect happiness are to be found in Christ and, in summary, that he was sent to set up and prepare the true and perfect kingdom of God.

Verses 28–38

28. She . . . called her sister aside. It was probably at Martha's request that Christ stayed outside the village and did not enter into the large crowd. She was afraid of the danger, since Christ had only recently barely escaped from being killed. So she tells her sister privately, so that the news of his arrival would not spread.

"The Teacher is here." The word "Teacher" reveals the esteem in which these godly women held Christ. Although they had not benefitted as much as they should have, it was still a great thing that Christ was honored in that house in an exceptional way. Although people used to throw themselves on the ground before kings and leaders, Christ, so far as his human life was concerned, had nothing royal or magnificent about him, and yet Mary **fell at his feet** (verse 32) for a different reason. She would not have done so had she not been persuaded that he was the Son of God.

32. "Lord, if you had been here . . ." She seems to be speaking reverently to Christ, but she should not have limited Christ's power, which filled heaven and earth, to his bodily presence.

33. He was deeply moved in spirit. Had Christ not been sad for their unhappiness, he would have remained unmoved. He voluntarily empathizes with the mourners, even to the point of crying with them. I think that the evangelist shows the reason for this emotion when he records, **When Jesus saw her weeping, and the Jews who had come along with her also weeping . . .** But I have no doubt that Christ was looking higher — namely, at the common misery of the human race. He remembered what he had been commanded by the Father and why he had been sent into the world — to free us from all ills. This very thing Christ has done, and he wants to show us that he has done it with earnestness and feeling. Accordingly, when he is about to raise Lazarus, before he gives the cure or helps, he is seen to be deeply moved in spirit and to be troubled and to cry, because he is as much moved by our ills as if he had suffered with them himself.

But how can being **deeply moved in spirit** and being **troubled** be part of the Son of God? Some people find it absurd when we say that Christ, like other people, was subject to human feelings; they think that the only way he was sad or happy was when he took to heart other people's emotions, when he thought it was right, through some secret dispensation. It is in this sense, Augustine thinks, that the evangelist says that Christ was deeply moved in the spirit, because other people are swept along by their feelings, which dominate them and so they become troubled. Therefore, he thinks that the meaning here is that Christ, who was otherwise calm and free from all passion, brought groaning and grief on himself of his own accord. But I think it is more in keeping with Scripture if we make the simple statement that when the Son of God put on our flesh he also, of his own accord, experienced our human feelings, so that he did not differ in any way from his brothers, except that he never sinned. In this way we take none of Christ's glory away from him when we say that it was only a voluntary submission by which it came to pass that he was like us in the emotions of the soul. Because he was submissive from the beginning, we must not imagine that he was free and exempt from them. In this way he showed that he was our brother, so that we might know that we have a Mediator who willingly pardons us and is prepared to help our weaknesses which he himself experienced.

If anyone objects that men's passions are sinful and so it is inconsistent that they should be shared by the Son of God, my answer is that there is a great difference between us and Christ. Our feelings are sinful because they rush on without any restraint and know no bounds; but in Christ they were composed and regulated in obedience to God and were completely free of sin. Men's feelings are sinful and perverse on two accounts: first, because they are carried away by impetuous emotion and are not regulated by the true rule of modesty; and, second, because they do not always arise from a legitimate cause, or at least are not directed to a legitimate end. I say that there is excess because no one rejoices or grieves only sufficiently or as God permits, and many people even shake off all restraint. Our vain minds make us sorrow or grieve over trifles or for no reason at all, because we are too devoted to the world. Nothing like this was found in Christ. No passion of his ever went beyond its proper bounds. He had none that were improper or not founded on reason and sound judgment.

To make this even clearer, it is important that we make the distinction between man's first nature, as it was formed by God, and this degenerate nature which is corrupt because of sin. When God created mankind, he implanted emotions in him, but these emotions were obedient and submissive to reason. The fact that these emotions are unruly and rebellious is an accidental fault, as this does not stem from the Creator, but through some other cause. When Christ took human emotions on himself, he did so without any disorder. He who obeys the passions of the flesh is not obeying God. Christ was indeed **troubled** and greatly upset, but in such a way that he kept himself in his Father's will. In summary, if you compare Christ's compassions with ours, they are as different as pure, clear water flowing in a gentle river and muddy, dirty foam.

Christ's example alone should be sufficient for rejecting the unbending hardness of the Stoics, for where should we seek for the rule of supreme perfection but in Christ? We should try to correct and tame that obstinacy which pervades our affections because of Adam's sin, so that we may follow Christ our leader and so that he may bring us into subjection. But Paul does not demand a hardened senselessness from us, but tells us to grieve in moderation: "We do not want you to . . . grieve like the rest of men, who have no hope" (1 Thessalonians 4:13). Christ took our emotions into himself, so that by his power we may subdue whatever is sinful in them.

36. "See how he loved him!" John now describes two different opinions about Christ. The first people, who said, **"See how he loved him!"** think less highly of Christ than they ought to have done, for they ascribe to him nothing but what is human. Nevertheless, they speak about him with greater frankness and humility than the others, who maliciously decry him for not having prevented Lazarus from dying. Although they applaud Christ's power, about which the former are silent, yet in doing so they reproach Christ. It is clear enough from this that the miracles which Christ had done were not unknown to them. But their ingratitude is so bad that they do not hesitate to complain because on this one occasion he did nothing. Men have always been grateful to God in this way, and continue to be. If Christ does not satisfy our wishes, we at once start complaining, "He has been used to helping me up to now; why does he now desert me and disappoint me?" There is a double disease here. We thoughtlessly desire what is not expedient for us, and we want to subject God to the perverse desires of our flesh. Again, we make inappropriate demands and our vigorous impatience carries us forward before the proper time.

38. Jesus, once more deeply moved . . . Christ does not come to the tomb as an idle spectator, but like a wrestler preparing for the contest. So it is no wonder that he groans again, for the violent tyranny of death which he had to overcome stands in front of his eyes. Some say this groan arose out of indignation, because he was offended at the unbelief we have spoken about. But I prefer a much more plausible reason — that Christ was thinking about the event itself rather than the people. Various details follow which show more fully Christ's power in raising Lazarus. These include the length of time — **"four days"** (verse 39), during which the tomb had been secured by a **stone** (verse 41), which Christ commands should be taken away in everyone's presence.

Verses 39–44

39. "By this time there is a bad odor." This is a sign of distrust, for Martha expects less from Christ's power than she should have. The root of this evil lies in her comparing God's infinite and incomprehensible power with her human reasoning. Since there is nothing so inconsistent with life than putrefaction and stench, Martha infers that no cure can be effected here. When our minds are ruled by a wrong way of thinking we, as it were, banish God from us so that he cannot do his work in us. Certainly it was no thanks to Martha that her brother did not forever lie in the grave, for she cuts off the hope of life for him and at the same time tries to stop Christ from raising him. Weakness of faith causes this. Pulled this way and that, we fight ourselves; as we stretch out one hand for God's help, we put away that readily offered assistance with our other hand. It is true that Martha was not lying when she said, **"I know that even now God will give you whatever you ask"** (verse 22); but a confused faith is of little help unless it can be made to work when we come to a concrete situation.

Further, in Martha we see how many defects there are in even the best person's faith. She was the first person to go and meet Christ, which showed her extraordinary example of piety. And yet she keeps on putting difficulties in Christ's path. So, in order that Christ's grace may come to us, we must learn to give it far greater power than our senses can grasp. And if the first and single promise of God is not strong enough for us, we must at any rate, like Martha, give way when Christ confirms us a second and third time.

40. "Did I not tell you . . . ?" Christ reproves Martha's distrust in not having a sufficiently strong hope from the promise which she had heard. This passage clearly shows that more was said to Martha than John records, though, as I have suggested, that is what Christ meant when he said that he was **"the resurrection and the life"** (verse 25). Therefore, Martha is condemned for not expecting a divine work.

". . . if you believed." This is said not only because faith opens our eyes to be able to see God's glory shining in his deeds, but because our faith smooths the way for God's power and goodness to be displayed to us. As the psalmist says, "Open wide your mouth and I will fill it" (Psalm 81:10). Again, unbelief blocks God's way and, as it were, keeps his hands closed. For this reason it is said elsewhere, "And he did not do many miracles there because of their lack of faith" (Matthew 13:58). This does not mean that God's power is limited by men's will, but because, as far as they can, their malice opposes it, and therefore they do not deserve it to be shown to them. It often happens that God overcomes such obstacles. But whenever he withdraws his hand and does not help unbelievers, it is because they are enclosed within the constraints of their unbelief and will not allow it to enter.

". . . see the glory of God." Observe that a miracle is called **"the glory of God,"** because God, by displaying in it the power of his hand, glorifies his name. Martha, satisfied with Christ's second declaration, allows the stone to be removed. As yet she says nothing; but when she hears the Son of God give this order with a good reason, she gladly relies on his order alone.

41. Then Jesus looked up. Here is the sign of a mind truly prepared for prayer. For anyone to call on God in the right way, he must be linked with him, and this cannot happen unless he is raised above the earth and ascends to heaven. True, this is not always visible. Hypocrites, plunged in the deep filth of the flesh, seem to bring heaven down to them by their stern looks. But what they pretend to do, the children of God must really do. The person who raises his eyes to heaven must not mentally shut God up in heaven, for he is present everywhere. As the prophet says, "Do I not fill heaven and earth?" (Jeremiah 23:24). But since men's minds can never free themselves from their evil ideas and imagine something base and earthly about God unless they are raised above the world, Scripture sends them to heaven and declares that "Heaven is my throne" (Isaiah 66:1).

So far as lifting up the eyes are concerned, it is not a constant activity without which no prayer can ever take place, for the tax collector prayed with his face bent to the ground, and his prayer still ascended to heaven through his faith. It is, however, a useful practice because through it men are encouraged to seek God. In addition to this, the fervor of prayer often affects the body in such a way that the body unwittingly follows the mind by itself. We certainly cannot doubt that when Christ raised his eyes to heaven he was carried there with tremendous strength. Besides, as he was completely one with the Father, he wanted to bring others to the Father with him.

"**Father, I thank you.**" Although he had not asked for anything, Christ begins with thanksgiving. In fact, there can be no doubt that although the evangelist does not say that Christ's prayer used formal words, a prayer had preceded this, as otherwise it could not have been "**heard.**" Christ probably prayed in the middle of those groanings which the evangelist mentions. Nothing could be more absurd than that Christ was greatly upset in himself, as stupid people are liable to be. Having gained Lazarus' life, Christ now thanks the Father. By saying that he received his power from the Father and not claiming it for himself, Christ merely acknowledges that he is the minister of the Father. By accommodating himself to the limits of man's understanding, Christ at one moment asserts his divinity and claims for himself whatever belongs to God, and at another moment will be content to bear a human character and give all the glory of divinity to the Father. The evangelist brings both ideas together when he says that the Father "**heard**" Christ, but that Christ gives thanks so that men will know that he was sent by the Father and will acknowledge him to be the Son of God. Since Christ's majesty cannot be conceived in its true greatness, the power of God, which was seen in his flesh, gradually elevated men's evil and dull senses to that height. Christ wanted to be completely ours, and we should not be surprised if he accommodates himself to us in various ways. If he even allowed himself to be "made . . . nothing" (Philippian 2:7), there is nothing absurd in saying that he abases himself on our account.

42. "I knew that you always hear me." This is to stop anyone from thinking that Christ did not stand high enough in God's favor to be able to perform as many miracles as he pleased. Therefore, Christ means that they are in such close agreement that the Father denies him nothing — and even that he had no need to pray, since he only performed what he knew the Father had commanded him. But Christ called on the name of the Father so that men should be more fully assured that this was truly a divine work. If anyone raises the objection, "Why, then, did he not raise everyone from the dead?" the answer is easy. God had planned that only a certain number of miracles would take place, just sufficient to witness to the Gospel.

43. Jesus called in a loud voice. Christ's power is more clearly seen by the fact that he did not touch the body with his hand but only called out, using his voice. At the same time Christ commends to us the secret and wonderful efficacy of his Word. For how did Christ restore life to the dead but through his Word? So in the raising of Lazarus Christ shows us a visible sign of his spiritual grace which we daily experience through the perception of faith, for Christ shows that his voice brings life.

44. . . . his hands and feet wrapped with strips of linen. The evangelist takes pains to refer to the cloth around Lazarus' face and to the strips of linen, to indicate to us that Lazarus came out of the tomb just as he had been laid in it. This way of burying the dead is still used by the Jews. They cover the body with linen and wrap the head separately in a cloth.

"Take off the grave clothes and let him go." To emphasize the wonder of the wonder of the miracle, all that remained was for the Jews to touch with their hands the divine deed which they had seen with their eyes. Christ could have shaken off the grave clothes which bound Lazarus, or made them disappear. But Christ wants to use the hands of the spectators as his witnesses. This order was given to the Jews in order to take away every trace of doubt.

Verses 45–52

45. Therefore many of the Jews . . . put their faith in him. Christ did not allow this miracle to go by without bearing fruit, for through it some people were drawn to faith. We have to understand that miracles have two purposes. They either prepare us for faith or they confirm us in faith. Here the evangelist points to the former. He means that those people he is talking about admired and revered Christ's divine power, so that they submitted to him as his disciples. Otherwise just the miracle would not have been enough to produce faith. So the words **put their faith in him** only indicated a willingness to accept Christ's teaching.

46. But some of them went to the Pharisees. In those who accuse Christ we see detestable ingratitude, or rather horrible anger, which shows the blindness and insanity of their unbelief. The resurrection of Lazarus should definitely have softened even their stony hearts. But the bitter poison of ungodliness will infect and corrupt any work of God. So before men can benefit from miracles, their hearts have to be purified. Those who do not reverence God in their lives, even should they see heaven and earth come together, will always reject sound teaching through their obstinate ingratitude.

In our own day you will see many enemies of the Gospel fighting fanatically against the obvious and visible hand of God. They demand miracles from us, but only to show that they are monsters of men in their stubborn resistance. The Jews reported Christ to the Pharisees because the more hypocritical they were, the more they opposed the Gospel. For the same reason, the evangelist soon mentions them by name when he says that the council assembled. They were part of the priesthood, but he mentions them specifically because they were the bellows which kindled the anger of the whole council.

47. The chief priests and the Pharisees called a meeting of the Sanhedrin. The priests' blindness, described here, is no less monstrous. If they had not been totally brutish and stupid, they would have been touched with at least some reverence for Christ, after such a remarkable display of his divine power. They now meet with the deliberate and definite aim of burying God's glory, which they could not help being astonished at. True, they do not openly boast that they want to make war on God. But since they cannot put out Christ's light without overturning God's power, they are fighting against it openly and definitely through their presumptuous sacrilege. Unbelief is always proud and despises God. But when people have been struggling against God for a long time, their final action, which is completely devoid of any fear of God, is to ascend above heaven like the Titans. They acknowledge that Christ was **performing many miraculous signs.** But where does his great power come from? So they publicly prepare to prevent God's power from shining out of Christ's miracles. But God does not stand idly by. Although he ignores them at that moment, he scorns their foolish arrogance until the time he will execute his wrath, as Psalm 2:4, 12 says.

"What are we accomplishing?" Here they are blaming their sloth, as if they were saying that it is because of their inactivity that Christ makes gradual headway, and if they actively exerted themselves his progress would be stopped. This is how confident wicked people are. They claim everything for themselves, as if it were in their power to do what they like, and as if even the result of the work depended on their will. If anyone thinks about this correctly, they are putting their own energy against God's power, as if by persevering they could be stronger than God in the end.

48. "If we let him go on like this . . ." What would happen if they left him alone? Quite clearly, as we have already said, they have no doubt that they have the power to block Christ's path and to impede his progress just by strongly opposing him. If Christ had been an imposter it would, indeed, have been their duty to interfere, in case he led the sheep away from the Lord's flock. But when they acknowledge Christ's miracles, they make it quite plain that they could not care less about God, whose power they so boldly and disdainfully despise.

"The Romans will come." They cloak their wickedness with a plausible disguise — namely, their zeal for the public good. Their main worry and fear was that their tyranny would be destroyed; but they pretend to care about the temple and the worship of God, about the reputation of their nation and the condition of the people. And what is the object of all this? They are not seeking these sort of pretenses in order to deceive anyone. They are not haranguing the people, but are holding in secrecy a private consultation among themselves. They are all aware of their common treachery. Why do they not bring forward their plans and ideas openly? Because impiety, no matter how evil and clear-cut it is, is nearly always accompanied by hypocrisy. So it wraps itself up in indirect evasions or shadows, to deceive under the guise of virtue.

Indeed, their main aim was to appear to be serious, moderate, and prudent, so that they could deceive other people. But it is likely that when they pretended to have a just reason for persecuting Christ, they were themselves deceived by that poor disguise. Hypocrites may be inwardly reproved by their consciences, but they are later drunk with their vain ideas, and when they sin, appear to be innocent. Yet, quite clearly, they contradict themselves. To start with, they said that Christ did many miracles. Now they fear the Romans, as if there were not more than enough protection in God's power, which showed itself present in these signs.

"The Romans will come." Here the evangelist means that the main object of their deliberation was to guard against the impending danger. They are saying, "If the Romans know that any changes are being made in public affairs they would, we fear, send in an army to destroy our nation along with the temple and the worship of God." But it is wicked to deliberate about guarding against dangers which we can avoid only by deciding to leave the right path. First of all, we should ask what God commands and wants to be done. We ought to abide by this, whatever the consequences are for us. These men, however, are determined to remove Christ, so that there will be no trouble from allowing him to continue as he started off. But what if he had been sent by God? Should they reject God's prophet in order to buy peace with the Romans? Such are the ploys of those who do not truly and sincerely fear God. They are not worried about what is right and lawful, for they are only interested in the consequences.

But here is the only godly and holy way to behave. We should, first of all, find out what pleases God. Then we should follow boldly whatever he commands and not be discouraged by any fear, even if we are surrounded by a thousand deaths. Our actions must not be dependent on the prevailing winds but constantly on God's Word alone. The person who boldly ignores dangers, or at least rises above fearing them, and just obeys God will be successful in the end. Against all expectations, God blesses the constancy which is based on obedience to his Word.

Unbelievers, however, are so far from benefitting from their caution that the more timid they are, the more snares they are caught up in.

In this story the form and character of our own age is graphically portrayed. People who want to be thought of as prudent and cautious have this song constantly on their lips: "We must take care about the public quiet; the reformation we are attempting is not without many dangers." After they have raised this unfair odium against us, they can find no better way to counteract disturbances than by burying Christ, as if such ungodly contempt for God's grace could really be successful when they work out the remedy of abolishing the teaching of salvation so as to allay disturbances. On the contrary, what wicked men dread, will happen. Even if they achieve their ends, a most unworthy reward comes from appeasing the world by offending God.

"The Romans will come and take away both our place and our nation." It is not clear whether they mean the temple or the land. They believed that their salvation depended on both. If the temple was destroyed, sacrifices and public worship of God and calling on his name would cease. So they could not help being worried about the temple if they had any concern about religion. It was also very important in upholding the state of the church, so that they would not be taken away into exile again. They still remembered the Babylonian captivity, which was a most severe vengeance of God. They also had a well-known proverb, frequently found in the law, that it was a kind of disowning if the Lord threw them out of the land. So they concluded that the church would not be safe unless Christ was destroyed.

49. Then one of them, named Caiaphas . . . They had a brief consultation because Caiaphas did not hesitate for long. He says that there is only one way to be safe: to kill an innocent man. How wicked men become when, free from any reverence for God, they plan according to the judgment of the flesh and not according to God's Word and are confident that what the author of all good does not allow is nevertheless good for them. It is as if Caiaphas were saying that they had to provoke God's wrath if they were to do well and prosper. So let us learn never to separate what is useful from what is lawful, since we must not expect anything good or pleasing except from God's blessing. This is promised not to the wicked and rebellious, who ask for the devil's help, but to believers who sincerely walk in his ways. This was, however, a plausible argument, as the good of the public should always be put first. But a people are not better protected through the unjust death of an innocent man than a man's whole body is protected when you only cut his throat or run him through with a sword.

. . . who was high priest that year. John does not call him the high priest of that year, as if the office were only an annual one, but because it was a gift that could be bought with money and was given to different people contrary to the law's commands. God intended this dignity to be terminated only by death, but when things were troubled and confused, the Romans frequently changed the priests at will.

51. He did not say this on his own. Here the evangelist does not mean that Caiaphas, like a madman or a fanatic, said what he did not understand, for he spoke what he himself believed. The evangelist means that a higher impulse guided his tongue, because God intended that he should make known through his mouth something loftier than came into his mind. It might be said that Caiaphas spoke with two tongues. He vomited out the ungodly and cruel plan of killing Christ which he had conceived in his own mind; but God turned his tongue to a different purpose, so that using words ambiguously, he also uttered a prophecy. God intended that the heavenly oracle should flow from the high priest's throne, so the Jews might have less excuse. No one in the whole assembly had his conscience pricked, and yet they later saw that their insensibility did not deserve pardon. Nor did Caiaphas' wickedness prevent his tongue from being used by the Holy Spirit, for God took notice of the priesthood he himself had instituted rather than this man's position. In the same way, God intended to bless his people through the mouth of Balaam, to whom had been given the spirit of prophecy.

It is quite ridiculous for Roman Catholics to infer from this that we should regard as an oracle whatever the Roman pontiff sees fit to pronounce. First, even granting (which is not true) that the high priest is always a prophet, they still have to prove that the Roman pontiff is appointed at God's command. For the priesthood was abolished at the coming of one man, who was Christ, and nowhere do we read that God later commanded that any one person should rule the whole church. Secondly, if you did grant them that the right and dignity of high priest was transferred to the Bishop of Rome, we must see what good it did the priests to embrace Caiaphas' prophecy. In line with his judgment, they conspire to put Christ to death. But far be it from us to have that sort of obedience that drives us into the horrible apostasy of denying the Son of God. With the same voice Caiaphas blasphemes and also prophesies. Those who follow his declaration despise the prophecy and adopt the blasphemy. We must take care that the same thing does not happen to us if we listen to the Caiaphas of Rome, or else the comparison would be defective.

In addition to this, I ask, because Caiaphas prophesied once, does that mean that his every word will then be prophetic? Soon after this he condemned as blasphemy (see Matthew 26:65) the most important article of our faith. So we conclude that what the evangelist now relates was a most unusual event, and it would be foolish to follow it as an example.

Jesus would die. First, the evangelist shows that our whole salvation consists of this, that Christ brings us into being one flock; for in this way he reconciles us to the Father, in whom is "the fountain of life" (see Psalm 36:9). From this we also conclude that the whole human race is dispersed and alienated from God until God's children are united under Christ as their head. Therefore, the communion of saints is a preparation for eternal life, since everyone whom Christ does not gather to the Father remains in death, as we will see again in chapter 17. This is also why Paul teaches that Christ was sent to gather together all things in heaven and earth (see Ephesians 1:10). So, in order to enjoy Christ's salvation, discord must be removed, and we must become one with God and the angels and among ourselves. The cause and pledge of this unity was Christ's death, through which he drew all things to himself; and we are gathered into Christ's fold daily by the Gospel.

52. . . . and not only for that nation. The evangelist means that the reconciliation effected by Christ is extended to the Gentiles also. But how is it that those who are called God's children, because they were miserably scattered and wandered about, became God's enemies? My answer, which I have already stated, is that there were in the heart of God children who in themselves were wandering and lost sheep, or rather were not sheep at all, but rather wolves and wild beasts. Hence it is through election that he reckons as God's children, even before they are called, those who at last begin to be manifested by faith both to themselves and to others.

Verses 53–57

53. They plotted to take his life. The evangelist relates that Christ fled again, knowing that his enemies sought him in their anger (verse 54). But we must remember that he did not flee in such a way that he departed from his Father's calling. His only intention was to offer himself to undergo a voluntary death at the divinely appointed time. The consultation that the evangelist mentions was not so much for slaying Christ as for finding some way to put him down. They had already decided to put him to death. It only remained to agree on how to carry out their resolve.

54. A village called Ephraim. As far as the name of the town which we read about here is concerned, I think that it was either pronounced wrongly then, or it was completely new. We know how much the language changed after the Babylonian exile, and also how different the country looked. So it is not surprising that some places are mentioned which are unknown in antiquity.

Where he stayed with his disciples. John refers to the disciples of Christ — not those who had received his teaching, but his constant companions, who used to live with him in the same house.

55. Many went up from the country to Jerusalem. There was no precise instruction that they should purify themselves before sacrificing the Passover. So the evangelist does not say that everyone, but only **many**, came. Of course, no one who was unclean was allowed to eat the Passover. But I believe that this sanctification was undertaken voluntarily and from personal inclination. Other people were not forbidden to eat, even though they had not been prepared by such a ceremony before the feast day.

57. ... if anyone found out where Jesus was. The evangelist's purpose is to show how well-known Christ was throughout Judea, for those who assemble in the temple, wherever they come from, are mainly set on seeking Christ and arguing about him among themselves. True, they seek him in a human way; but yet, through seeking him they show that it is the priests' tyranny which prevents Christ from appearing openly.

John
Chapter 12

Verses 1–8

1. Jesus arrived at Bethany. We see that the people who thought that Christ would not go to the feast were making hasty judgments. This warns us not to be rash, but to wait patiently and quietly until the right time, which is unknown to us, comes. Christ went to Bethany first, so that he might go on from there to Jerusalem three days later. Meanwhile, he wanted to give Judas a suitable moment and place to betray him — so that he might present himself a victim prepared for the sacrifice at the appointed hour. Christ is not ignorant about what will take place but comes to his moment of sacrifice voluntarily.

As Jesus had come to Bethany **six days before the Passover**, it can be worked out from Matthew and Mark that Christ remained there four days. John does not say on which day the supper was prepared for Christ, when he was anointed by Mary. But it seems likely that it was not long after his arrival. People who think that the anointing mentioned by Matthew (26:7) and Mark (14:3) is different from this one are mistaken. The time factor has misled them, for the two evangelists mention two days before relating that Christ was anointed. But the solution is easy and may be given in two ways. John does not say that Christ was anointed on the first day of his arrival; so it could have taken place even when he was preparing to depart. Yet, as I have said, the other conjecture is the more probable, that Christ was anointed at least one or two days before his departure. Judas had certainly made a bargain with the priests before Christ sent two of his disciples to prepare the Passover. At least one day must have elapsed between these two events. The evangelists add that Judas looked for a convenient moment to betray Christ after he had received the bribe. And so when, after mentioning two days, the evangelists add the story of the anointing, they narrate last what happened first. The reason is that when they have related the words of Christ, "As you know, the Passover is two days away — and the Son of Man will be handed over to be crucified" (Matthew 26:2), they now put in what they had omitted — the manner and the occasion on which he was betrayed by his disciple. There is thus sufficient agreement that he was anointed at Bethany.

2. Here a dinner was given in Jesus' honor. Matthew (26:7) and Mark (14:3) say that on this occasion Christ was dining with Simon the leper. John does not name the house, but hints plainly enough that he was not dining in the house of Lazarus and Martha, for he says that **Lazarus was among those reclining at the table with him** — a fellow guest with Christ. Nor do Matthew and Mark in any way contradict John when they say that Christ's head was anointed, while our author says it was his feet. The usual practice was to anoint the head, and because of this Pliny thought it extravagant when some ankles were anointed. The three agree that Mary did not anoint Christ sparingly,but poured a large quantity of ointment on him. John's reference to Christ's **feet** (verse 3) is equivalent to his saying that Christ's whole body was anointed down to the feet. The word **feet** amplifies the sense, as appears better in what follows, when he adds that Mary wiped Christ's **feet** with her hair.

3. And the house was filled with the fragrance of the perfume. This was not a simple liquid extracted from nard but a compound of many scented substances. It is hardly surprising that the whole house was filled with the fragrance.

4. But one of his disciples, Judas Iscariot . . . objected. Judas' grumbling follows, which Matthew ascribes to the disciples in general and Mark to some of them. But it is common in Scripture to apply to many what applies to a few. However, I believe that it is likely that the murmuring originated with Judas and that the rest were moved to support him. Murmurings are like bellows, which kindle in us all kinds of dispositions; especially where we are prone to make unfavorable judgments, slanders are readily embraced by us. But the credulity which God's Spirit reproves in the apostles is a warning to us not to be too facile and credulous in listening to malicious words.

5. "Why wasn't this perfume sold . . . ? . . . It was worth a year's wages" [NIV footnote: "Greek three hundred denarii"]. Pliny tells us that a pound of common ointment cost no more than ten denarii. But he also says that the highest price of the best ointment was three hundred and ten denarii. The evangelists agree that this was very special ointment, and Judas is correct in saying that a pound of it was worth three hundred denarii. Moreover, since almost all luxuries involve excess and superfluity, the greater the expense, the more plausible reason Judas had for grumbling. It was as if he said, "If Mary had spent only a little, she would have had some excuse. But she has wasted a vast sum of money for nothing; has she not done harm to the poor, who might have been greatly helped with such a sum? Therefore her action is unforgivable."

6. Because he was a thief. The rest of the apostles condemn Mary thoughtlessly and not from any ill will. But Judas takes up a plausible position for his wickedness when he puts forward the poor, for whom he cared nothing. From this we learn what a repulsive monster the desire for possessing is. It is the loss which Judas thinks he has sustained by this chance of stealing being taken away that stirs him to such a rage that he does not hesitate to betray Christ. And probably he was not only lying to others about the poor having been defrauded, but was even flattering himself inwardly, as hypocrites do, as if Christ's betrayal was a small matter through which he would receive compensation for his loss. He really only had one reason for betraying Christ — to somehow regain the loot which had slipped through his hands. This indignation over what he had lost drove him to the idea of betraying Christ.

It is surprising that Christ should have chosen as treasurer a man whom he knew to be a thief. Wasn't it like offering him a rope to hang himself? Mortal man's only reply can be that the judgments of God are a profound abyss. Yet Christ's actions should not be made an ordinary rule for committing the care of the poor or any sacred fund to a worthless and wicked man. God has laid down a law about who should be called to govern in the church and in other offices, and we are not at liberty to break this law. It was different with Christ, as in the eternal wisdom of God he gave a place for his secret predestination in the person of Judas.

7. **"Leave her alone."** When Christ tells them to leave Mary alone, he is showing that people who disturb their neighbors without reason and stir up quarrels about nothing are behaving wickedly and unjustly. The other evangelists record that Christ gives a longer answer, although the substance is the same. The anointing which Judas complains about is defended on the ground that it is for Christ's burial. So Christ does not approve of it as an ordinary service or one which should be commonly used in the church; for if he had wanted some office of this sort to be performed daily, he could have said something else instead of applying it to his burial. God certainly does not care for external display. On the contrary, he sees that man's mind is too prone to unspiritual observances and frequently commands us to be sparing and sober in the use of them. They are absurd interpreters, therefore, who infer from Christ's reply that costly and splendid worship is pleasing to God. In fact, Christ excuses Mary on the grounds that she had given him an extraordinary office which should not be thought of as a perpetual norm for worshiping God.

". . . for the day of my burial." When Christ says that the ointment had been saved, he means that it was not poured out at the wrong time but at the correct time. Something is said to be saved when it is kept in store to be brought out at the right moment. It is certain that if anyone had earlier laden him with costly delicacies, he would not have allowed it. But Christ says that Mary did this not as something ordinary, but as her last duty towards Christ. Moreover, the anointing of bodies was a spiritual symbol then, not an empty rite. It set before them the hope of resurrection. The promises were still obscure, and Christ, rightly called "the firstfruits of those who have fallen asleep" (1 Corinthians 15:20), was not yet risen. Therefore, believers needed aids such as these which directed them to Christ who was still absent. Accordingly, the anointing of Christ was not superfluous then; for he was soon to be buried, and was anointed as if to be laid in the tomb.

The disciples did not know this yet; and undoubtedly Mary was suddenly moved by the directing of the Spirit to do something she had not thought of before. But Christ applies what they disapproved of to the hope of his resurrection, so that this use of it might recall them from their wicked bad temper. God wanted the childhood of his ancient people to be ruled by such exercises; but it would be foolish to try to do the same today — and, indeed, it could not be done without injury to Christ, who has dispelled such shadows by the brightness of his coming. Since, however, his resurrection had not yet brought the end of the shadows of the law, his burial had to be adorned with an outward ceremony. The scent of his resurrection is now strong enough of itself to bring life to the whole world without spikenard and ointments. And we must remember that when we judge men's actions we must abide by Christ's verdict alone, for we must one day stand before his judgment-seat.

8. "You will always have the poor among you." We must observe what I have already pointed out — that a distinction is expressly drawn here between Mary's extraordinary action and the daily service due to Christ. Those people who want to worship Christ with splendid and costly trappings are apes, not imitators. Christ approved what was done that once but forbade its repetition.

"But you will not always have me." When Christ says that he will not always be with his disciples, this saying should be referred to the kind of presence to which carnal worship and extravagant honors are suitable. His presence with us by the grace and power of his Spirit, his dwelling in us, and his feeding in us with his flesh and blood have nothing to do with bodily observances. So all the pomp that the Roman Catholics have invented for worshiping Christ is offered to him in vain, for he openly rejects it. When he says that the poor will always be with us, he is, it is true, reproving the hypocrisy of Judas; but we may learn from it the valuable lesson that gifts of money for meeting the needs of the poor are sacrifices and are a sweet savor to God.

Verses 9–15

9. Meanwhile a large crowd of Jews found out . . . The nearer the time of Christ's death approached, the more necessary it was that his name should be made known everywhere, as a preparation for a fuller faith after his death. In particular, the evangelist relates that the recent miracle of the resurrection of Lazarus became very widely known. Since Christ had shown in it a striking proof of his divinity, God wanted it to have many witnesses. When he says that they came not only because of Jesus, but also on account of Lazarus, he does not mean that they came as an act of courtesy to Lazarus, as if they were honoring him in particular, but that they might see the wonderful example of Christ's power in Lazarus.

10. So the chief priests made plans. What insane anger — to try to kill someone who had clearly been raised from the dead by divine power! But Satan torments the wicked with such a spirit of giddiness that there is no end to their madness, even if God should set heaven and earth and sea against them. This wicked council meeting is described in this way to show us that Christ's enemies were brought to their great obstinacy not by error or folly, but by furious wickedness, so that they were not even afraid to make war on God. It also tells us that God's power in the raising of Lazarus was not obscure, for the only way in which ungodliness could wipe it out was by basely and shockingly doing away with an innocent man. Moreover, Satan tries his hardest to bury altogether, or to some extent to obscure, the works of God, and therefore it is our duty to devote ourselves diligently to continual meditation on them.

12. The next day the great crowd . . . Christ's entry into Jerusalem is related more fully by the other evangelists (Matthew 21:1ff.; Mark 11:1ff.; Luke 19:29ff.), but here our author gives a complete summary. In the first place we must remember Christ's purpose. He came to Jerusalem of his own accord to offer himself up to death. His death had to be voluntary because God's wrath against us could only be appeased by a sacrifice of obedience. And the outcome was not hidden from him. But before Christ is dragged to the cross, he wants to be received by the people as their king in a solemn ceremony. In fact, Christ openly acknowledges that his reign is inaugurated by his marching to death. But although his arrival was acclaimed by a great crowd of people, he remained unknown to his enemies until he proved that he was the true Messiah by fulfilling the prophecies, as we will see later. He did not want to omit anything that would help confirm our faith substantially.

The great crowd that had come for the Feast. Foreigners were far more ready to pay homage to the Son of God than were the citizens of Jerusalem, who should have been an example to everyone else. They had daily sacrifices; the temple was ever before them and should have kindled in their hearts a desire to seek God; the chief teachers of the church were there, and there too was the sanctuary of the divine light. Their ingratitude was therefore utterly base; they had been steeped in these practices from their childhood, and yet they reject and neglect the Redeemer promised to them. But it is a fault common to nearly every age that the closer and more familiarly God has shown himself to men, the more audaciously have they despised him. There was a much greater zeal in these others who had left their own lands and came together to celebrate the Feast. They eagerly ask about Christ, and when they hear that he is coming to the city, they go out and rejoice with him. But there is no doubt they were aroused by a secret impulse of the Spirit to go to him. We do not read of this being done. But as earthly princes summon their subjects by the sound of a trumpet or the voice of a herald when they enter to possess their kingdom, so Christ assembled this people through a secret movement of the Spirit to acclaim him as king.

When the crowds wanted to make Christ king in the wilderness (6:15), he withdrew to the mountain in secret; for the only kingdom they thought of then was one in which they could be well-fattened like cattle. Christ could not allow and agree with their foolish and absurd desire without denying himself and renouncing the office placed on him by the Father. But now he claims for himself the kind of kingdom which he received from the Father. I confess that the people who went out to meet him did not really understand the nature of this kingdom. But Christ looked to the future. In the meanwhile he did not allow anything to be done that was inconsistent with his spiritual kingdom.

13. They took palm branches. The palm was a symbol of victory and peace in antiquity. But it was also normal to use branches of palm trees when they conferred kingship on anyone or when they humbly asked pardon of a conqueror. But these men seem to have taken up branches of palm trees as a sign of joyfulness and happiness at welcoming a new king.

. . . shouting, "Hosanna!" The use of this expression indicates that they recognized Christ as the Messiah promised from long ago to the fathers and from whom redemption and salvation were to be looked for. Psalm 118:25-26, from which the acclamation is taken, was written about the Messiah, so that all the saints might ardently long for his coming with an unceasing desire and, when he was manifested, welcome him most reverently. It is therefore likely — in fact, it can be inferred with certainty — that this prayer was common among all the Jews and therefore was on everyone's lips. So the Spirit of God supplied words for these men to wish Christ well; and he chose them as heralds to bear witness that the Messiah had come.

The word **Hosanna** is made up of two Hebrew words and is equivalent to "Save!" or "Make safe, I beg you!" The Hebrews pronounce it differently: "Hosiah-na." But it is quite usual for pronunciation to be corrupted when words are taken over into a foreign language. Although the evangelists wrote in Greek, they deliberately kept the Hebrew word in order to show more clearly that the crowds of people used the established form of prayer which had been first delivered by David and had from age to age been received uninterruptedly among God's people and was now specially consecrated to bless Christ's kingdom. The words which immediately followed were used for the same reason: **"Blessed is he who comes in the name of the Lord!"** This is a joyful prayer for the happiness and prosperity of that kingdom on which the restoration and blessedness of the church of God depended.

But David seems to speak about himself rather than about Christ in that psalm. This difficulty must therefore be solved first. The answer is easy. We know that the kingdom was given to David, and his line was to be a kind of prelude of the eternal kingdom which was to be manifested in its own time. It was not right that David should keep this to himself, for the Lord often, through his prophets, directs the eyes of all the godly to another. So everything that David sang about himself is correctly referred to the King who, it was promised, should spring from his descendants as the Redeemer.

We can learn a useful lesson from this. If we are members of the church, the Lord stirs us up today to cherish the same desire in common with believers under the law. We ought to desire wholeheartedly that Christ's kingdom will flourish and prosper; moreover, our prayers should show this. We should note that he gives the words to us so that there might be more spirit in our praying. Woe then in our laziness if through our coldness we extinguish, or by our lukewarmness we quench, that heat which God kindles! So we must know that the prayers we conceive by the leading and teaching of God will not be in vain. If only we are not lazy or become weary in asking, Christ will be a faithful guardian of his kingdom and will defend it through his invincible power and protection. It is true that even if we remain slack, his majesty will continue to stand. But as often it does not flourish as magnificently as it should, or even collapses — as we see today a terrible scattering and desolation — we are definitely to blame. When the restoration is small or negligible, or at least is slow in advancing, we must blame our own laziness. Daily we ask from God that his kingdom may come, but hardly one person in a hundred earnestly desires it. We are justly deprived of that blessing from God which is too much trouble to ask.

We also learn from this expression that it is God alone who saves and defends the church. He does not claim for himself or command us to give him anything that is not his. Therefore, as he guides our tongues, we pray that he may save Christ's kingdom, and we acknowledge that God is the only author of the safety that keeps this kingdom strong. God uses the activities of men to this end, but they are men whom his own hand has prepared. Moreover, he makes use of men for advancing or upholding the kingdom of Christ in such a way that he alone begins and completes everything through them by the power of his Spirit.

". . . who comes in the name of the Lord." We must first understand the meaning of **"comes in the name of the Lord."** The person who **"comes"** in God's **"name"** does not rashly thrust himself forward or falsely assume the honor; but because he is correctly called, he has God as the leader and author of his actions. This title belongs to all true ministers of God. A prophet comes in God's name who, directed by the Holy Spirit, honestly gives to men the teaching he has received from heaven. A king comes in the same name through whose hand God governs his people. But because the Spirit of the Lord rested on Christ and he is the head of all things, so that all who have ever been ordained to rule the church are under his command — or rather, are streams flowing from the fountain — Christ is correctly said to have come in the **"name"** of God. And it is not only that he surpasses all others in the high rank of his authority, but God manifests himself to us fully in him. For as Paul says, "In Christ all the fullness of the deity lives in bodily form" (Colossians 2:9), and he is "the radiance of God's glory" (Hebrews 1:3); in summary, he is the true "Immanuel" (Matthew 1:23). It is therefore by special right that he is said to have come **"in the name of the Lord,"** since through him God has shown himself completely and not partially as formerly in the prophets. Therefore, we ought to begin with him as the head when we want to bless the servants of God.

Now, since false prophets arrogantly claim the name of God and parade themselves under this false pretense (although in fact they are carried away by the impulse of the devil to destroy the church), we should add an antithesis to this prayer: that the Lord may scatter and annihilate them. Thus we cannot bless Christ without at the same time cursing the Pope and the sacrilegious tyranny he has erected against Christ. He hurls his anathemas at us so strongly, like thunderbolts; but we can safely despise them as hot air. By implication, Christ once gave this authority to children when he approved of their calling out in the temple area, "Hosanna to the Son of David" (Matthew 21:15).

14. Jesus found a young donkey. The other evangelists narrate this part of the story in greater detail. They tell us that Christ sent two of his disciples to collect the ass. John, writing last of all, thought it sufficient to note briefly the substance of what the others had said. That is why he leaves out many details. An apparent contradiction which many people puzzle over is easily resolved. When Matthew says that Christ sat on a she-ass and her foal, we should view this as an expression which supplies the whole for a part, or a part for the whole. Some people think that Christ first sat on the ass and then on the foal. From this conjecture they allegorize that he sat first on the Jewish people who had long ago been broken in by bearing the yoke of the law and later tamed the Gentiles like a wild and fresh colt. But the simple truth is that Christ rode on an ass which had been brought with its mother. This agrees with the words of the prophet Zechariah who expressed the same thing twice in different words by a repetition common enough among the Hebrews. "On an ass," he says, "and on its colt which was under the yoke." Our evangelist, who tries to be brief, leaves out the former clause, quoting only the latter.

15. The Jews themselves are forced to explain the prophecy of Zechariah (9:9) which was then fulfilled, a prophecy of the Messiah. But at the same time they laugh at us for being deceived by a mere trifle into giving the honor of Messiah to the son of Mary. But our faith rests on very different testimonies. When we say that Jesus is the Christ, we do not start out from his entry into Jerusalem sitting on an ass. For in him such a glory which belonged to the Son of God was visible, as we have seen in chapter 1 of this Gospel. But it was in his resurrection that his divine power especially shone forth. Yet we should not despise this confirmation, that by his wonderful providence God showed in that entry, as in a theatre, the fulfillment of Zechariah's prophecy.

"Do not be afraid." In the prophet's statement, as the evangelist quotes it, we ought to observe that our minds are quietly calm, and fear and trembling are banished from them, only when we know that Christ reigns among us. The prophet's actual words are different. He exhorts believers to exercise joy and jubilation. But our evangelist expressed how our minds exult with true joy. It is when that fear is removed with which all must be tormented until they are reconciled to God and obtain the peace which is born of faith (Romans 5:1). Therefore, we receive through Christ the benefit that, since we are freed from the tyranny of Satan, the yoke of sin is broken, guilt is canceled and death abolished, and we safely glory, relying on the protection of our king, since those who are put under his protection have no need to fear any danger. Not that we are free from fear so long as we live in the world; but the trust which rests on Christ is above all fear. Though Christ was still far away, the prophet told the godly men of that age to be joyful and happy because he was to come. **"Do not be afraid . . . your king is coming."** Now that he has arrived so that we can enjoy his presence, we should resist fear more strongly, so that, delivered from our enemies, we may peacefully and joyfully honor our king.

"O Daughter of Zion." The prophet addressed Zion in his own time because the habitation and seat of the church were there. Now God had collected for himself a church out of the whole world; but this promise is directed especially to believers who submit to Christ so that he may reign in them. When he is described as riding on an ass, he means that his kingdom will be quite different from the pomp, splendor, wealth, and power of the world, and it is right that this should be made known through an outward appearance, so that everyone can be fully aware that it is spiritual.

Verses 16–19

16. At first his disciples did not understand all this. Just as the seed does not germinate as soon as it is thrown onto the earth, so the fruit of God's deeds do not appear immediately. The apostles are God's servants in fulfilling the prophecy; but they do not understand what they are doing. They hear the shout of the crowd as definitely welcoming Christ the King and not as a confused noise. Even so, they do not see the point of it or what it means. So to them it is an empty show until the Lord opens their eyes.

When the evangelist says that they eventually realized that **these things had been written about him,** he indicates just how ignorant they were before they came to understand. This happened because they did not have the Scripture as their guide and master to direct their minds to right and pure thinking. We are blind unless God's Word leads the way. Nor is it even enough that the Word of God should shine on us, unless the Spirit in his turn enlightens our eyes, which would otherwise be blind to the brightest lights. Christ honored his disciples with this grace after his resurrection, because the time was not ripe for the Spirit to pour out his riches with a liberal hand until he was received into the heavenly glory (see 7:39). From this example we learn to make our judgments about everything that relates to Christ not through our own unspiritual feelings, but from the Scriptures. We must also understand that it is a special grace of the Spirit to educate us gradually out of our dullness in considering God's works.

. . . that these things had been written about him and that they had done these things to him. I explain this in the following way. For the first time it dawned on the disciples' minds that Christ had not done these things thoughtlessly, and that the men were not just playing a meaningless game, but that the whole affair had been governed by God's providence, because it was necessary to fulfill all that had been written. So it should be understood as, "they did these things to Christ, just as had been written about him."

17. The crowd . . . continued to spread the word. John again repeats his statement that many people had by the report of a great miracle been aroused to come to meet Christ. They go out in their crowds because the rumor of Lazarus' restoration to life had spread everywhere. They had good reason therefore for ascribing to the son of Mary the office of Christ, since his most remarkable power had been made known to them.

19. "See, this is getting us nowhere." With these words the Pharisees whip themselves up into a greater rage. It is a kind of reproach of their laziness — as if they had said that the reason why the people went over to following Christ was their own excessive slowness and cowardice.

This is how desperate people talk when they prepare to make their last effort. And if God's enemies are so pertinacious in evil, we ought to be far more steady in a righteous undertaking.

Verses 20–26

20. Now there were some Greeks . . . I do not think that they were Gentiles or uncircumcised, for it follows at once that they had come to worship. Now it was strictly prohibited by Roman law and severely punished by the proconsuls and other magistrates if any person was found to have left the worship of his own land and gone over to Judaism. But Jews who were dispersed throughout Asia and Greece were allowed to cross the sea to offer sacrifice in the temple. Moreover, the Jews were not allowed to associate with Gentiles in the solemn worship of God, because they thought that they themselves, the temple, and the sacrifices would in that way be defiled. But though they were the descendants of Jews, yet as they lived far across the sea, it is not surprising that the evangelist introduces them as foreigners and as people who were not familiar with what was then happening in Jerusalem and round about. Therefore, the significance of this is that Christ was welcomed as king not only by the inhabitants of Judea, who had come from villages and towns to the Feast, but the report had also gone out to men who lived beyond the sea and who had come from distant lands.

. . . to worship. They could have done this in their own country. But John is here describing the solemn **worship** associated with sacrifices. Although religion and godliness were not confined to the temple, they were nowhere else allowed to offer sacrifices to God, nor had they anywhere else the Ark of the Testimony, the symbol of the divine presence. Every person worshiped God daily at home spiritually. But the saints under the law were expected to make an outward profession of worship, such as was prescribed by Moses, by appearing in the temple in the presence of God. The feasts were appointed for this purpose. And if these men embarked on such an expensive journey, with considerable inconvenience and much risk, so that they would not neglect the outward profession of their piety, what excuse can we offer today unless we show that we worship the true God in our own land? Certainly the worship of the law has come to an end. But the Lord has left to his church baptism, the holy Supper, and the rite of public prayer for believers to practice. If we neglect them, it shows that our desire for godliness is very cold.

21. They came to Philip. It is a sign of reverence that they do not force themselves on Christ but wish to obtain access through Philip; for reverence always results in modesty. But when the Roman Catholics draw from this that we should call on departed saints, that they may be our advocates with Christ and the Father, it is too ridiculous to need refutation. The Greeks speak to Philip who is present. How, I ask, is this like calling on the dead from whom one is separated? But such are the fruits of human presumption after it has once let itself wander outside the limits of the Word of God.

23. "The hour has come." Many interpret this as referring to Christ's death, because it showed his glory. So according to them, Christ now declares that the time of his death is at hand. But I think it refers to the proclamation of the Gospel, as if he had said that soon the knowledge of him would be spread throughout every region of the world. In this way Christ wanted to counter the dismay into which his death might throw the disciples; for he shows that there is no reason why their courage should fail, for the teaching of the Gospel will be proclaimed throughout the whole world. Again, in case this contemplation of his glory should quickly vanish when he was condemned to death, hung on the cross, and then buried, Christ anticipates and warns them in good time that the ignominy of his death does not obstruct his glory. To this end he uses a very appropriate simile.

24. "Unless a kernel of wheat falls to the ground and dies, it remains only a single seed. But if it dies, it produces many seeds." Christ compares his death with sowing seed, which appears to lead to the destruction of the wheat but is nevertheless the cause of an abundant increase. Although this warning was especially necessary then, it is of continual use in the church. We should start with the head. That dreadful appearance of ignominy and malediction which is seen in the death of Christ not only obscures his glory but removes it altogether from our sight. We must not, then, hold to his death alone but must also consider the fruit which his resurrection bears. In this way nothing will prevent his glory from shining everywhere. From him we must then come to his members. For not only do we think that in death we perish, but even our life is a sort of continual death (see Colossians 3:3). It is all up with us then unless that consolation which Paul sets up helps us: "Though outwardly we are wasting away, yet inwardly we are being renewed day by day" (2 Corinthians 4:16). The godly are distressed by various afflictions; they are hard-pressed by the difficulties of their situation; they suffer hunger or nakedness or disease; they are worried by reproaches; they seem every moment to be almost swallowed up by death. They should always meditate on the fact that this is a sowing which will yield fruit in its season.

25. "The man who loves his life will lose it." Christ adds an exhortation to his teaching. If to bear fruit we must die, we should patiently allow God to put us to death. But since Christ contrasts the love and the hatred of life, we must understand what it is to love and to hate life. The person who is under the influence of immoderate desire for this present life and cannot leave the world without coercion is said to love life. But the person who despises this life and advances courageously to death is said to hate life. Not that we should hate life completely, for it is rightly thought of as one of God's highest blessings. But believers should lay it down cheerfully when it hinders their access to Christ. They should be like the person who wishes to do anything quickly and who shakes off a heavy and inconvenient burden from his shoulders.

In summary, it is not wrong in itself to love this life, provided we only journey in it as foreigners, always mindful of where we are traveling to. The true way to love life is when we remain in it as long as God pleases and are prepared to change our home as soon as he tells us — or, to put it in a word, when we, as it were, carry it in our hands and offer it to God as a sacrifice. Whoever is too attached to this present life loses his life; that is, he throws it to everlasting ruin. For to lose does not mean to abandon or to suffer the loss of something valuable, but to give it over to destruction.

It is quite common for the word "soul" to be used for life. Some people think that in this passage "life" means the center of the affections — as if Christ had said, "Anyone who indulges the desires of the flesh loses his soul." But this is too forced, and the other is more natural — that he who neglects his life is going the best way about enjoying it eternally.

"... this world ..." To underline the meaning, the phrase "this world," used only once, ought to be repeated, so that the sense may be: "Those who love their life in this world do not have its best interests at heart. On the other hand, those who despise their life in this world truly know how to preserve it." Indeed, anyone who is attached to this world deprives himself, of his own accord, of the heavenly life, of which we can only be heirs by being lodgers and guests in the world. The result is that the more anxious people are about their own safety, the further they remove themselves from God's kingdom — that is, from the true life.

"The man who hates his life ..." I have already suggested that this expression is used comparatively, in that we ought to despise life so far as it hinders us from living for God. If meditation on the heavenly life held full sway in our hearts, the world would have no power to hold us back. This is the solution to a potential problem. Many people, through despair or from other reasons, and especially from weariness of life, commit suicide. But we cannot say that they provide for their own safety. Other people are swept away to death by ambition, who also throw themselves into ruin. But here Christ is speaking specifically about the hatred or contempt for this fleeting life which believers have because of their desire for a better life. So anyone who has not learned to look to heaven has not yet learned how life is to be saved. Moreover, Christ added this latter clause to frighten those who desire the earthly life too much; for if we are overwhelmed by the love of the world so that it is not easy to forget it, it is impossible for us to go to heaven. But since Christ arouses us so forcefully, it would be madness to sleep the sleep of death.

26. "Whoever serves me . . ." That death may be less bitter and disagreeable to us, Christ invites us by his example to submit to it cheerfully. This certainly makes us ashamed of refusing the honor of being his disciples. But Christ only admits us into that number on the condition that we follow the path that he points out. He goes on ahead of us and encounters death. So the bitterness of death is mitigated and, in a way, sweetened when we experience it with the Son of God. So far from shrinking from Christ because of the cross, we should rather desire death in order to please him. The next statement has the same purpose in mind.

"And where I am, my servant also will be." Christ insists that his servants should not refuse to submit to death, to which they see him going before them. It is not right that the **"servant"** should have anything different from his Lord. The future tense in the phrase **"also will be"** is used instead of the imperative "let him be," as was normal in Hebrew. Some people view this as a consolation, as if Christ had promised to those who were not unwilling to die with him that they should share in his resurrection. But as I said, the former view is more probable. For later Christ adds the consolation that the Father will not leave Christ's servants unrewarded when they have been his inseparable companions in life and death.

Verses 27–33

27. "Now my heart is troubled." This statement, at first sight, seems to be at odds with the rest of his discourse. Christ had shown extraordinary courage in exhorting his disciples not only to suffer death but to desire it willingly and eagerly whenever the circumstances demanded. Yet now, by shrinking from death, he confesses his weakness. But we do not read anything here that is at all inconsistent, as every believer knows from his own experience. It is not surprising if scornful men laugh at it, for it can only be understood by practice.

Moreover, it was useful and even necessary for our salvation that the Son of God should be so affected. The main thing to consider about his death is his atonement, through which he appeased the wrath and curse of God, which he could not have done without taking upon himself our guilt. The death which he went through had to be full of horror, since he could not perform the satisfaction for us without experiencing for himself God's dreadful judgment. From this we understand the enormity of sin, for which the Heavenly Father exacted so terrible a punishment from his one and only Son. So we must learn that death was no game or amusement to Christ, but that he was thrown into the severest torments for our sake.

Nor was it inappropriate that the Son of God should be troubled in this way. For his divinity was hidden, and it did not show its power and in a sense rested so that an opportunity might be given to make expiation. But Christ himself put on not only our flesh but also human feelings. It is true that in him these feelings were voluntary. He feared, not because he was forced to, but because of his own accord he had subjected himself to fear. Yet we must believe that it was not in pretense but in reality that he feared. But he differed from other people in that he kept all his feelings ruled by obedience to God's righteousness, as we have said elsewhere.

There is also another advantage that Christ's death brings us. If the dread of death had not upset Christ, which of us would have thought that his example concerned us? For we must all meet death with feelings of regret. But when we realize that even Christ did not have within him a hardness like stone or iron, we take courage and follow him; the weakness of the flesh, which makes us tremble at death, does not stop us from becoming the companions of our leader in struggling with it.

"What shall I say?" Here we see, as if it were in front of our eyes, how much our salvation cost the Son of God, for he was reduced to such straits that he found no words to express the intensity of his sorrow. He flees to prayer, which alone remains for him, and asks to be delivered from death. And also, seeing that he had been appointed by the eternal purpose of God to be a sacrifice for sins, he quickly corrects that wish which his great sadness had expressed and, as it were, puts out his hand to pull himself back, that he may acquiesce entirely to his Father's will.

In this passage there are five steps to note. First stands the complaint which breaks forth out of infinite sorrow. Secondly, he feels that he needs a remedy, and in case he would be overwhelmed by fear he asks himself what he should do. Thirdly, he goes to the Father and begs him to deliver him. Fourthly, he retracts the wish, which he knows to be against his calling, and chooses instead to suffer anything than not to fulfill what his Father had told him to do. Last of all, Christ is satisfied with the glory of God alone, forgets all the rest, and deems them nothing.

But it may be thought to be unbecoming that the Son of God should express a wish which he immediately retracts so he can obey his Father. I quite agree that this is the folly of the cross, which is an offense to proud people. But the more the Lord of glory humbled himself, the plainer proof we have of his infinite love for us. Moreover, we must remember, as I have already said, that the human feelings from which Christ was not immune were pure and uncontaminated by sin. The reason is that they were composed and regulated to the obedience of God, for there is nothing to prevent Christ from having a natural fear of death and yet desiring to obey God. So Christ corrects himself in the next sentence.

"No, it was for this very reason that I came to this hour." Although he may legitimately dread death, yet when he considers why he was sent and what his office of Mediator demands, he offers to his Father the dread conceived in his natural senses, that it might be subdued; or rather, having subdued it, he prepares freely and willingly to execute God's command. Now, if Christ's feelings, which were completely free from sin, needed to be restrained for him, so that he would obey his Father, how earnest we should be in this, for the numerous affections springing from our flesh are so many inner enemies. We must also observe that we ought to bridle not only those affections which are diametrically opposed to the will of God, but also those which hinder the course of our calling, even though in other respects they are not wicked or sinful. To make this clearer, we should put God's will first. Secondly comes the pure and complete will of man, such as God gave to Adam and such as was in Christ. Then lastly, our own, which is infected by sin. The will of God is the rule to which everything inferior to it should be subjected. Now the pure will of nature will not of itself rebel against God. But man, even if he were completely righteous, would still face many obstacles unless he subjected his affections to God. Christ had only one battle to fight — to cease fearing what he naturally feared as soon as he knew that God's will was otherwise. But we have a double battle, for we have to struggle with the obstinacy of our flesh. Consequently, the bravest wrestlers never win without a wound.

"Father, save me . . . ?" The rule we should observe whenever we are either upset by fear or oppressed with grief is to raise our hearts to God at once. There is nothing worse or more harmful than inwardly brooding over what torments us. Most people in the world have hidden worries gnawing at them. This is the just punishment for apathy in everyone who will not rise up to God so that they can receive relief.

28. "Father, glorify your name!" Christ testifies, through these words, that he puts the glory of the Father before everything else and disregards and neglects even his own life. The true regulating of our desires is so to seek God's glory that everything else gives way to this. We should regard it as abundant reward that we may with a quiet mind bear everything that is troublesome and irksome.

"I have glorified it." This is equivalent to Christ saying, "I will complete what I have begun," for "God does not leave the work of his hands defective" (see Psalm 138:8). But since God's purpose was to forestall the offense of the cross, he not only promises that Christ's death will be glorious, but also commends the many ornaments with which he had already adorned it.

29. . . . said it had thundered. It was a dreadful thing that the crowd was unmoved by so evident a miracle. Some were deaf and caught what God had pronounced distinctly only as a confused sound. Others were less dull, but yet detracted greatly from the majesty of the divine voice by pretending that its author was an angel. But the same thing is common today. God speaks plainly enough in the Gospel, in which there is also displayed a power and energy of the Spirit which should shake heaven and earth. But many are as cold towards the teaching as if it came only from a mortal man, and others think God's Word is confused and barbarous stammering, as if it were nothing but thunder.

But the question arises: did that voice sound from heaven in vain and without being at all beneficial? My answer is that what the evangelist here ascribes to the whole crowd only applies to part of it. Besides the apostles, there were some who interpreted it more correctly. But the evangelist wanted to indicate briefly what commonly happens in the world — that the majority, although they hear God speaking clearly and loudly, do not in fact hear him.

30. "This voice was for your benefit, not mine." Had Christ no need of being strengthened, or did the Father care less about Christ than about us? We must hold on to this principle: because Christ clothed himself with flesh for our sake, all the blessings he received from the Father were given for our sake. Again, it is true that the voice came from heaven for the people's sake, for he did not need an outward miracle. Moreover, there is a tacit reproof here: the Jews were stone-deaf to God's voice, for since God spoke for their sake, their ingratitude in not listening was inexcusable.

31. "Now is the time for judgment on this world." As if he had already finished the fight, the Lord now rejoices at the victory not only over the fear but also over death. He proclaims magnificently the fruit of his death, which might have been a cause of consternation to his disciples. The word **"judgment"** is taken as "reformation" by some and "condemnation" by others. I agree with the former, who explain it to mean that the **"world"** must be restored to its proper order. For the Hebrew word *mishpat*, which is translated "judgment," means "a well-ordered society." Now we know that outside Christ there is nothing but confusion in the world. And although Christ had already begun to set up God's kingdom, it was his death that was the true beginning of a correctly ordered state and the complete restoration of the world.

We must also note, however, that this correct ordering cannot be set up in the world until Satan's kingdom is first of all wiped out and until the flesh and whatever is against God's righteousness is annihilated. Finally, the renewing of the world must be preceded by a mortification. And so Christ declares that **"the prince of this world"** is to be cast out. Confusion and deformity arise because while Satan exercises his tyranny, iniquity is spread abroad. Therefore, when Satan has been thrown out, the **"world"** is called back from its revolt against God's rule. If anyone asks how Satan was thrown out by Christ's death, since he does not cease to go on making war, my answer is that this throwing out is not to be limited to any short period of time, but that it describes the amazing effect of Christ's death which appears daily.

32. "When I am lifted up . . ." The way the judgment is to be decided now follows. When Christ is lifted up on the cross, he will gather all men to himself to raise them from earth to heaven. The evangelist says that Christ indicated how he would die. Therefore, the meaning is not in doubt that the cross will be a sort of carriage in which Christ will exalt everyone along with himself to his Father. It might have been thought Christ was then carried away from the earth so as to have nothing in common with men any longer. But he proclaims that his departure will be very different, for he will draw to himself those who were fixed on the earth. Although Christ refers to the form of his death, he means in general that it will not be a parting to separate him from men but a new way of drawing earth up to heaven.

"I . . . will draw all men to myself." When Christ says, **"all"** he must be referring to the children of God, who are his flock. Yet I agree with Chrysostom, who says that Christ used the universal word because the church was to be gathered from Gentiles and Jews alike, according to the saying, "There shall be one flock and one shepherd" (10:16). The Vulgate has, "I will draw all things to me," and Augustine maintains that it should be read in that way. But the consent of all the Greek manuscripts should weigh more with us.

Verses 34–36

34. "We have heard from the Law . . ." Without doubt they just intended to carp maliciously at Christ's words. And their malice blinds them so that in the middle of bright light they see nothing. They say that Jesus was not to be thought of as the Christ, because he said that he would die whereas the law ascribes eternity to the Messiah. As if the law had not definitely declared both sides — that Christ will die and that his kingdom will flourish to the end of the world. But they seize on the second clause as an excuse for calumny. The source of their error was that they judged the splendor of the Messiah's kingdom from their unspiritual senses. Hence they reject Christ because he does not correspond to their ideas. Under the phrase **"the Law"** they include the prophets; and the present tense **"abideth"** (KJV) is used for the future **"will remain,"** after the Hebrew idiom.

"Who is this 'Son of Man'?" This is a mocking question, as if Christ had been defeated by that little refutation. This shows how arrogant ignorance is. It is as if they said, "Go on, boast that you are the Christ, when your own confession proves that you have no affinity with him."

35. "Just a little while longer." The Lord gently rebukes them in his reply and at the same time pricks them sharply. He accuses them of being blind to the light and threatens that **"the light"** will soon be taken away from them. When Christ says that some **"light"** remains for **"just a little while longer,"** he confirms what he had already said about his death. Although **"the light"** does not mean his bodily presence but rather his Gospel, he nevertheless refers to his departure, as if he is saying, "I shall not cease to be **the light** when I have gone away, and so nothing in me will be diminished by your darkness." When he says, **"You are going to have the light just a little while longer,"** Christ is indirectly reproving them for closing their eyes and shutting out **"the light."** Hence he means that they do not deserve an answer to their objection, because they deliberately look for opportunities to fall into error.

"Walk while you have the light." This statement, that **"the light"** will not continue to shine on them except for **"a little while longer,"** applies equally to all unbelievers. Scripture promises God's children that the sun of righteousness (see Malachi 4:2) will rise and never set. "The sun will no more be your light by day, nor will the brightness of the moon shine on you, for the Lord will be your everlasting light" (Isaiah 60:19). Everyone should walk carefully, for darkness will follow if one is contemptuous of **"the light."** The reason that such a thick and murky night lay over the world for many centuries before this was that so few troubled to go into the brightness of heavenly wisdom. Christ enlightens us by his Gospel, that we may follow the way of salvation which he shows us. Therefore, those who make no use of God's grace extinguish, as far as they can, **"the light"** offered to them.

"The man who walks in the dark does not know where he is going." To instill more fear into them, Christ issues this warning about how wretched is the state of those who are destitute of **"light"** and do nothing but go astray in the whole direction of their life, for they cannot take one step without the risk of slipping or even falling down. But now Christ declares that we are in darkness unless he shines on us. From this you can gather what the human mind is worth when it is its own leader and master apart from Christ.

36. "Put your trust in the light." Christ exhorts them to keep hold of **"the light"** by faith, for he calls people children of **"light"** who are the genuine heirs who persevere to the end.

When he had finished speaking . . . It might seem surprising that Christ withdrew from those who were so eager to welcome him. But we can easily gather from the other evangelists that this is a reference to his enemies, who were eaten up with envy at the godly zeal of these good and sincere people. For the strangers who had gone out to meet Christ followed him to the temple, where he met with the saints and with the people who lived in the town.

Verses 37–41

37. Even after Jesus had done all these miraculous signs . . . In case anyone should be disturbed or perplexed at seeing that Christ was despised by the Jews, the evangelist removes this stumbling block by showing that he was supported with clear and definite testimonies which gave authority to him and his teaching. But God's glory and power, which shone brightly in his miracles, were not displayed to the blind. Therefore, we must first of all understand that it was not Christ's fault that the Jews did not believe in him. He abundantly testified who he was through his many miracles; and therefore it was unjust and extremely unreasonable that their unbelief should diminish his authority. But since many might become anxious and worried about why the Jews were so stupid that the visible power of God did not move them at all, John goes further and says that faith is not born in the ordinary human faculties but is a unique and rare gift of God. And it was once foretold of Christ that very few would believe the Gospel.

38. . . . the word of Isaiah the prophet . . . John does not mean that this prediction imposed a necessity on the Jews, for Isaiah spoke nothing but what the Lord revealed to him from the secret treasures of his counsel. Indeed, this would have happened even if the prophet had remained silent. But since no one would have known what was going to happen if God had not testified through the mouth of the prophet, in the prediction the evangelist sets before their eyes as in a mirror what otherwise would have been obscure and incredible to men.

"Lord, who has believed our message?" This sentence has two clauses. Isaiah has already begun to speak about Christ, and when he foresees that everything that will afterwards be preached by the apostles will be everywhere rejected by the Jews, he first exclaims, as if amazed at some evil monstrosity, **"Lord, who has believed our message?"**

". . . to whom has the arm of the Lord been revealed?" In the second clause Isaiah says why there are so few people — because men do not reach this by their own efforts, and God does not enlighten everyone indiscriminately, but honors a few people with the grace of his Spirit. If the obstinate unbelief of a few Jews should not have been an obstacle to believers, however few they were, the same reasoning should convince us today not to be ashamed of the Gospel even if it has only a few disciples. But we should, first of all, note the reason which is added here — that it is not their own acumen but God's revelation that makes them believers. The word **"arm,"** as is well-known, denotes power. The prophet declares that God's **"arm,"** which is contained in the teaching of the Gospel, is hidden until it is revealed; and at the same time he says that everyone will not share in this revelation indiscriminately. From this it follows that many people are left in their blindness, without inner light, because "'though hearing, they do not hear or understand'" (Matthew 13:13).

39. For this reason they could not believe. This is much harsher, for as the words were taken at face value, the way was shut up against the Jews, and the power to believe was taken from them by the prophet, dooming them to blindness before they had made a choice either way. My answer is that there is nothing absurd in this if nothing can happen other than what God has foreseen. But we must note that the mere foreknowledge of God is not in itself the reason for things happening. We are, however, not so much concerned with God's foreknowledge here as with his judgment and vengeance. God declares not what he sees from heaven that men will do, but what he himself will do; that is, he will strike the ungodly with stupidity and dizziness, that he may take vengeance on their malice. In this passage he points out the near and inferior reason why God intends his Word, by nature salutary, to be destructive and deadly to the Jews. Their malice deserved it.

It was impossible for them to escape the punishment, for God had determined to give them over to a reprobate mind and to change the light of his Word into darkness for them. This prophecy differs from the former in that there the prophet says that no one believes except those whom God of his free grace enlightens in his own good pleasure, the reason for which is not apparent. Since everyone is equally ruined, God of his mere goodness distinguishes from the rest some as it seems good to him. But in this passage he speaks of the hardness with which God punished the malice of an ungrateful people. Those who do not notice these steps misunderstand the scriptural passages, which are quite different from each other.

40. "He has blinded their eyes and deadened their hearts." This passage, from Isaiah 6:9-10, is where the Lord forewarns the prophet that his work in teaching will have no other result than to make the people worse. First, he says, "Go and say to this people, Hearing, hear and do not hear" — as if he were saying, "I send you to speak to the deaf." Later he adds, **"He has . . . deadened their hearts."** Through these words he intends his Word to be a punishment to the reprobates, that it may make their blindness worse and plunge them into deeper darkness. It is indeed a terrifying judgment of God when he so overwhelms men's minds by the light of teaching as to deprive them of all understanding, and when, even through what is their only light, he brings darkness on them.

We should note, moreover, that it is a side effect of the Word of God that it blinds people. For there is nothing less reasonable than that truth should not differ from falsehood, that the bread of life should become a deadly poison, and that medicine should make an illness worse. But men's wickedness is to blame, as it is this which turns life into death. We should also note that the Lord himself sometimes blinds men's minds by depriving them of judgment and understanding — either by Satan and false prophets when through impostures Christ sends them out of their minds, or by his ministers when the preaching of salvation is harmful and deadly to them. So long as the prophets devote themselves faithfully to the task of teaching and entrust the fruit of their work to the Lord, they should not give up or waver, even if the result is less than they had hoped. Instead, they should be content with knowing that God approves of the labor, though it is useless to men, and that "we are . . . the aroma of Christ among those who are being saved and those who are perishing" (2 Corinthians 2:15), as Paul testifies.

In Scripture the "heart" is sometimes seen as the center of the affections. But here, as in many other places, it means the so-called intellectual part of the soul. Moses speaks in this way: "the Lord has not given you a mind that understands" (Deuteronomy 29:4).

". . . so they can neither see with their eyes . . ." We must remember that the prophet is speaking about unbelievers here, who have already rejected God's grace. It is clear that everyone would continue to be like this by nature if the Lord did not bring people to obey him whom he had elected. So to start with, the state of mankind is equal and the same. But when reprobate men have of their own accord and by their own malice rebelled against God, they make room for this vengeance, that they may be given over to a reprobate mind and rush even more and more to their own destruction. It is their own fault if God does not want to convert them, for they were the authors of their own hopelessness. These words of the prophet briefly teach us what is the start of our conversion to God — when he enlightens hearts which were necessarily turned from him so long as they were possessed by the darkness of Satan. Yet such is the power of divine light that it attracts us to itself and transforms us into God's image.

". . . and I would heal them." Isaiah adds that healing would be the result of conversion. By this word the prophet means God's blessing and a prosperous condition, as well as deliverance from all the miseries which spring from the wrath of God. Now if this happens to the reprobate, contrary to the nature of the Word, we should note the contrast implied in its opposite use; namely, that the purpose for which God's Word is preached to us is to enlighten us in the true knowledge of God, to turn us to God, and to reconcile us to him that we may be blessed and happy.

41. Isaiah said this because he saw Jesus' glory. In case readers should think that this prediction was inappropriately quoted, John specifically says that the prophet was not sent as a teacher just to one age, but rather that the glory of Christ was shown to him so that he might witness the things which should occur during Christ's reign. The evangelist takes for granted that Isaiah saw Christ's **glory**; and from this he infers that Isaiah accommodates his teaching to the future state of Christ's kingdom.

312

Verses 42–46

42. Yet at the same time many ... When the Jews in uproar and ferocity rejected Christ, it might have appeared that they all conspired against him to a man. But the evangelist says that in the middle of the general madness of the nation many people retained their sanity — a remarkable example indeed of God's grace; for when ungodliness has once gained the upper hand, it is a sort of universal pestilence which infects every part of the body. Therefore, it is a remarkable gift of God that among such corrupt people some remained untainted. In today's world we have the same grace of God. Although ungodliness and contempt for God are everywhere, and many people strive furiously to exterminate the Gospel's teaching altogether, it always finds some places of retreat, so that faith has, as it were, its havens that it may not be banished completely from the world.

The word **yet** is emphatic, for in the ranks of the rulers there was such an aggressive and dangerous hatred of the Gospel that it was incredible that a single believer could be found among them. So much the greater admiration was due to the power of God's Spirit, which penetrated where no opening was made. It was not a vice which belonged only to that age that rulers were obstinate and disobeyed Christ. Honor, wealth, and rank are usually accompanied by pride. The result is that people who are swollen with pride and barely acknowledge that they are men are not easily subdued by voluntary humility. Whoever, then, is exalted in the world will mistrust his rank if he is wise, in case it should be an obstacle to him. When he says that there were **many** it must not be understood as if they were the majority or even half, for compared with the huge crowd of the rest they were few; but they were many when viewed in themselves.

... because of the Pharisees ... John seems to speak incorrectly when he separates faith from confession. "For it is with your heart that you believe and are justified, and it is with your mouth that you confess and are saved" (Romans 10:10). It is impossible that the faith which has been kindled in the heart will not produce its flame. My answer is that John was showing here how weak faith was in lukewarm people, or rather in cold people. In summary, John means that they embraced Christ's teaching because they knew it had come from God. But their faith was neither so living nor so strong as it should have been. Christ does not give his own a spirit of fear but of constancy, that they may dare boldly and fearlessly to confess what they have learned from him. I do not think they were completely silent; but as their confession was not frank, the evangelist simply, to my mind, denies that they professed their faith. Their true profession would have been to ally themselves openly to Christ. Therefore, no one should flatter himself who in any way conceals or dissembles his faith in case he should incur men's hatred. However hateful Christ's name may be, the cowardice is inexcusable which makes us swerve, in even the smallest degree, from confessing him.

We should also notice that **the leaders** have less courage and firmness because ambition nearly always holds sway in them, and there is nothing more servile than that. To put it in a word, earthly honors may be called golden chains which bind men so that they cannot freely do their duty. That is why less well-known and poorer people ought to bear their lot with greater patience, for they are at least free from many dangerous traps. Yet the great and noble ought to struggle against their high rank, in case it hinders them from submitting to Christ.

John says that these **leaders** were afraid of **the Pharisees.** Not that the other teachers of the law and priests allowed anyone with impunity to call himself a disciple of Christ, but because in these men cruelty (under the guise of zeal) burned with greater violence. Zeal in defending religion is certainly an excellent virtue. But when hypocrisy is added to it, there is no more dangerous plague. So we should all the more earnestly ask the Lord to guide us through the unerring rule of his Spirit.

. . . for fear they would be put out of the synagogue. It was the fear of disgrace that hindered them, for they would have been **put out of the synagogue.** Here we observe how great man's depravity is, for it not only corrupts and debases the best of God's ordinances, but turns them into destructive tyrannies. Excommunication should have been the nerve of holy discipline, so that punishment might be prompt in anyone who despised the church. But it was now used in such a way that anyone who confessed that he belonged to Christ was banished from the fellowship of the faithful.

43. For they loved praise from men. The evangelist specifically says that these men were not inspired by some superstition, but were only avoiding being thought little of by men. If ambition weighed more with them than the fear of God, it follows that they were free of vain scruples of conscience. Readers can now observe what great ignominy is incurred before God through the cowardice of people who, out of fear of being hated, cloak their faith in front of men. And what is even more foolish, not to say brutish, than choosing the paltry approval of men over the judgment of God? John declares that everyone who shrinks from unpopularity among men when the pure faith ought to be confessed are full of this kind of madness. And this is right, for the apostle, when praising the unshakable steadiness of Moses, says that "he persevered because he saw him who is invisible" (Hebrews 11:27). By this he means that when anyone has his eyes trained on God, his resolve will be unbreakable and immovable.

The softness which makes us give way to treacherous pretense comes from our senses being blunted at the sight of the world. A true sight of God would immediately scatter all the mists of wealth and honor. Away with those who see the indirect denial of Christ as something trivial! The Spirit declares, on the contrary, that this monstrosity is more horrible than if heaven and earth were confused.

. . . **loved praise from men.** This means here to desire to be well thought of among men. Therefore, the evangelist says that they were so devoted to the world that they preferred to please men rather than God. Moreover, when he accuses people who denied Christ of this crime, he shows at the same time that the excommunication which the priests abused, contrary to divine and human law, was empty and worthless. So we must realize then that all the anathemas which the Pope mutters against us today are mere scarecrows.

44. Then Jesus cried out . . . Christ's declaration aims at encouraging his people to a right and unshakable constancy of faith. But it also contains an implicit rebuke, in which Christ wanted to correct their perverse fear. The shout suggests vehemence, for it is not a simple lesson but an exhortation in order to excite them more keenly. The statement amounts to this, that faith in Christ does not rely on any mortal man, but on God; for it finds in Christ nothing except what is divine, or rather it beholds God in his face. So he concludes that it is foolish and unworthy for faith to waver or doubt, for it is impossible to do a greater injustice to God than to be dissatisfied with his truth. So a person has duly benefitted from the Gospel if he relies on believing in God, and not in men, and firmly and quietly stands firm against all the devices of Satan. Therefore, to give God honor, we must learn to stand firm in faith, not only though the world were shaken, but even if Satan disturbed and overthrew everything under heaven.

"When a man believes in me, he does not believe in me only, but in the one who sent me." Believers are said "not to believe in Christ" when they do not give all their attention to Christ's human appearance. Christ compares himself with the Father and tells us to look at God's power, for the weakness of the flesh has no strength in itself. When he later exhorts the disciples to belief in him, the sense will be different. In that passage God is not contrasted to man, but Christ is put forward with all his gifts, and this should be enough to strengthen our faith.

45. "When he looks at me . . ." The word **"looks"** here should be understood as "knowledge." So that our consciences can be really and thoroughly at peace, which otherwise would have been continually liable to all sorts of disturbances, Christ sends us to the Father. The stability of faith is sure because it transcends the world. When Christ is truly known, the glory of God shines in him, so that we may know for certain that our faith does not depend on man but is founded on the eternal God, for it passes on from Christ's flesh to his divinity. Because this is so, it must not only be fixed forever in our hearts but also show itself boldly in our tongues when necessary.

46. "I have come into the world as a light." To make his disciples bolder and more persevering, Christ goes further in proclaiming the certainty of faith. First, he testifies that he came into the world to be **"a light"** through which men could be delivered from darkness and errors. At the same time Christ shows how we receive so great a blessing when he says that **"no one who believes in me should stay in darkness."** Moreover, Christ accuses everyone of ingratitude who does not separate from unbelievers even after they have been taught by the Gospel. For the more excellent this blessing of being called from darkness into **light** is, the less excuse they have who through laziness or neglect quench the **"light"** that had been kindled in them.

The words **"I have come into the world as a light"** are very emphatic. Although Christ was **"a light"** from the beginning, he has every reason to apply this title to himself because he came to be this **"light."** So that we may keep the various steps distinct he tells us, first, that he is **"a light"** for others rather than for himself; secondly, not only for angels but for men also; thirdly, that he was manifested in the flesh to shine with full brightness.

The words **"no one"** seem to have been put in deliberately, partly to show that all believers without exception might enjoy this benefit in common, and partly to show that unbelievers perish in darkness because they flee from the **"light"** on their own accord. Now, if all the wisdom of the world was gathered together in one mass, not a spark of true **"light"** would be found in that vast heap. On the contrary, it would be a confused chaos, for it belongs to Christ alone to deliver us from darkness.

Verses 47–50

47. "As for the person who hears my words . . ." When Christ had spoken about his grace and exhorted his disciples to steadfast faith, he then began to hit out at the rebels. Yet even here Christ softened the severity deserved by the ungodliness of those who, as it were, set themselves to reject God. Christ delayed pronouncing judgment on them because he had come rather for everyone's salvation. We must understand that Christ was not speaking here about unbelievers in general, but about those who wittingly or voluntarily reject the preaching of the Gospel which is shown to them. So why does Christ choose not to condemn them? It is because he sets to one side, for a time, his role as Judge and offers salvation to everyone indiscriminately and stretches out his arms to embrace everyone, so that everyone can be encouraged to repent. He emphasizes through an important detail the crime of rejecting an invitation so kind and gracious, for it is as if he had said, "See, I have come to call everyone; and forgetting the role of Judge, my one aim is to attract and rescue from destruction those who already seem ruined twice over." No one, therefore, is condemned because he despises the Gospel, except for those who spurn the lovely news of salvation and deliberately decide to bring destruction upon themselves.

The word **"judge,"** as is clear from its antithesis **"save,"** is used here for the word "condemn." This should be understood as referring to the proper and genuine office of Christ. The Gospel condemns, as it were, accidentally, because condemnation does not spring from its nature, as we have said elsewhere.

48. ". . . the one who rejects me." In case the ungodly should flatter themselves that their reckless disobedience to Christ would pass unpunished, he adds the dreadful threat that even if he did nothing in this matter, his teaching would be enough to condemn them. He says elsewhere that no other judge would be needed but Moses in whom they boasted (see 5:45). So the meaning here is: "Because I burn with a great desire for your salvation, I refrain from my right of condemning you and am entirely given over to saving those who were lost. But do not imagine that you have slipped out of God's hands; for even should I be totally silent, the Word, which you have despised, is of itself your fit judge."

". . . and does not accept my words." This explains the previous clause. Since hypocrisy is innate in people, nothing comes easier to them than to boast in words that they are ready to receive Christ; and we see how common this boasting is, even among the worst men. We must therefore keep to this definition, that we reject Christ when we do not embrace the pure teaching of the Gospel. The Roman Catholics shout aloud Christ's name; but as soon as his pure truth is put forward, nothing is more hateful to them. This is how Judas kissed Christ (see Matthew 26:49). So we must learn to receive Christ along with his Word and to give him the worship of obedience that he demands as his sole right.

". . . that very word which I spoke." It is impossible to give a nobler or more magnificent title to the Gospel than to grant it the power of judging. For according to this, the last judgment will be simply the approbation or ratification of the teaching of the Gospel. Certainly Christ will himself mount the judgment-seat, but he declares that he will pronounce judgment from the Word which is now preached. This threat ought to terrify the ungodly, since they cannot escape the judgment of his teaching which they now despise so proudly.

But when Christ mentions the last judgment, he hints that they are now without understanding. He reminds them that the punishment which is now a joke to them will then be made public. On the other hand, it gives the godly an inestimable consolation that however much they may now be condemned by the world, they do not doubt that they are already absolved in heaven. For wherever the faith of the Gospel has its abode, the judgment-seat of God is set up to save.

49. "For I did not speak of my own accord." In case the outward appearance of the man should detract from the majesty of God, Christ frequently sends us to **"the Father."** This is why he so often mentions **"the Father."** And indeed, just as it would be wrong to transfer to another person any spark of divine glory, the Word, to which judgment is granted, must have proceeded from God. Christ here makes a distinction between himself and his **"Father"** — not simply about his divine person, but rather about his flesh, in case his teaching should be judged humanly and therefore have less weight. If consciences were subject to human laws and teaching, Christ's argument would not apply. "My Word," he says, "will judge because it has not come from man." This is in accord with the saying, "There is only one Lawgiver and Judge, the one who is able to save and destroy" (James 4:12).

50. "His command leads to eternal life." He again praises the fruit of his teaching, that all may more willingly yield to it. It is only fair that the ungodly should feel God's vengeance, whom they now refuse to have as the author of life.

John
Chapter 13

Verses 1–7

1. It was just before the Passover Feast. John deliberately omits many things which he knew had been narrated by Matthew and the others. He undertakes to explain those details which they had left out, like the story of the washing of the feet. And although later he does explain more fully why Christ washed his disciples' feet, he prefaces this with the saying that he testified by this same sign that the love with which he first embraced them was eternal, so that when they should be deprived of his presence they might still be convinced that even death would not quench this love. This conviction should be now fixed in our hearts as well.

It says that Christ **loved his own who were in the world.** Why does he use this circumlocution to describe the apostles, except to inform us that they, like us, were struggling in a dangerous and difficult warfare, in which Christ took greater care of them? And so although we appear to be very distant from Christ, we must realize that he is thinking about us, for he loves **his own** who are **in the world.** And there is no doubt that he still has the same attitude now which he had at the moment of his death.

The time had come for him to leave this world and go to the Father. This should be noted carefully, for it refers to Christ's knowledge that his death was a passing on to the heavenly kingdom of God. And if while he was hurrying there he did not cease to love his own as before, we have no reason to think that his attitude has changed. Now, since he is the firstborn from the dead, this definition of death applies to the whole body of the church — that is, it is passing on to God, from whom believers are now absent.

2. The evening meal was being served. Later we will deal more fully with Christ's reason for washing his disciples' feet and the value of this narrative. For now we concentrate on the actual words. John says that it was done when Judas had already made up his mind to betray Christ — not only to show Christ's wonderful patience, that he could bear to wash the feet of such a wicked and treacherous apostate, but also because he purposely chose the time when he was near death to perform what may be thought of as the last act of his life.

The devil had already prompted Judas Iscariot . . . to betray Jesus. When John says that Judas' decision to betray Christ had been motivated by the devil, this shows the enormity of the crime. It was a dreadful and most tragic wickedness, in which Satan's power was openly displayed. Certainly all the wickedness which men do is incited by Satan; but the more revolting and execrable the crime, the more should we see in it the fury of the devil, who drives God-forsaken men here and there. But although men's passion is inflamed by Satan's bellows, it does not cease to be a furnace in itself. It has the fire burning within itself, and it greedily receives the draught of the bellows; and so the wicked are left without any excuse.

3. Jesus knew that the Father had put all things under his power. I believe that this was added to tell us the source of Christ's quiet, composed thinking. As he had already gained the victory over death, he raised his mind to the glorious triumph which was quickly to follow. Men in the grip of fear are usually most upset. The evangelist is indicating that Christ experienced no such agitation because although he was soon to be betrayed by Judas, he knew that the Father **had put all things under his power.** It may be asked why Christ was reduced to such a grief that he sweat blood. My answer is that both were necessary. He had to have a dread of death, while he nevertheless fearlessly discharged everything that belonged to the office of Mediator.

5. . . . and began to wash his disciples' feet. These words explain Christ's purpose, rather than his outward action; the evangelist adds that he began with Peter.

6. "Lord, are you going to wash my feet?" This question expresses a strong dislike for something that was foolish and unsuitable. By asking Christ what he was doing, Peter is, as it were, pushing him away with his hand. This humility would have been praiseworthy if obedience was not of greater value in Christ's sight than any kind of service or honor; or rather, if it were not the true and only rule of humility to submit in obedience to God and have all our senses devoted to his good pleasure, so that everything God declares to be in line with his will will be approved by us, without any argument. Therefore, above everything else we should keep this rule of serving God correctly, so that we may be always ready to agree without delay, whenever and whatever he commands.

7. "What I am doing . . ." These words teach us that we should simply obey Christ, even though it is not clear to us why he wants this or that thing done. In a well-organized house the decisions are taken by one person, the head of the family; and the servants have to use their hands and feet for him. Thus the man who refuses God's commands because he does not know the reason for it is too haughty. But this warning has an even wider application. We should not worry that we are ignorant about the things that God wants to be hidden from us for a time. This kind of ignorance is more learned than any other kind of knowledge, for we are letting God be wiser than we are.

Verses 8–11

8. "You shall never wash my feet." Up to now Peter's modesty was excusable, even though it was not entirely blameless. But now he sins more seriously, because he does not give in when he is corrected. Indeed, it is a common fault that obstinacy goes with error. It is doubtless a plausible excuse that the refusal arises from reverence, but because he does not simply obey the word, the very desire to honor Christ loses all its goodness. The true wisdom of faith is to approve and embrace with reverence whatever comes from God, knowing that it is done rightly and properly. There is no other way in which Christ's name can be sanctified by us. For if we do not decide that whatever God does is done for the best reason, our naturally stubborn flesh will continually grumble and will not give him his due honor unless forced to. In summary, until a man renounces his freedom to pass judgments on God's deeds, no matter how much he may try to honor God, pride will always lurk disguised as humility.

"Unless I wash you . . ." Christ's reply still not does say why he has decided to wash the disciples' feet. But with a comparison drawn from the soul to the body, Christ shows that in washing the disciples' feet he does nothing unusual or inconsistent with his role. Meanwhile Christ shows the folly of Peter's wisdom. The same thing will always happen to us whenever the Lord begins to contend with us. So long as he remains silent, men imagine that they have a good reason to differ with him. But nothing is easier than for him to refute with a word all their plausible arguments. Since Christ is his Lord and Master, it seems absurd to Peter that Christ should wash his feet. But in refusing such a service, Peter rejects the principal part of his own salvation. The statement also contains a general lesson. In the sight of God we are all filthy and polluted until Christ washes away our stains. Now, since he claims the office of washing, everyone must offer himself to be cleansed from his pollution, so that he may obtain a place among the children of God.

But before going on, we must understand the meaning of the word **"wash."** Some people think it refers to the free pardon of sins; others to newness of life; while others apply it to both — and I concur with this last view. Christ washes us when he wipes out our sins by the expiation of his sacrifice, that we may not come into God's judgment. On

321

the other hand, Christ washes us when by his Spirit he takes away the depraved and vicious desires of the flesh.

9. "Not just my feet . . ." When Peter heard that he was lost unless he accepted the cleansing Christ offered him, this necessity proved, eventually, to be a sufficient instructor to tame him. Peter, therefore, lets go of his opposition and gives way and wants to be washed all over, acknowledging that, as far as he is concerned, he is through nature altogether covered with pollution, and so it is no good for just a part of him to be washed. Even here he errs through thoughtlessness, in treating as valueless the benefit he had already received. He speaks as if he had not been given any pardon of sins or any sanctification by the Spirit. For this reason Christ justly reproves him, for he reminds him of what he had earlier bestowed on him. At the same time he reminds all his disciples, through the person of this one man, that they should not only remember the grace they had received but also consider what they still need for the future.

10. "A person who has had a bath needs only to wash his feet; his whole body is clean." First Christ says that believers are completely "clean." Not that they are pure in every part, so that there no longer remains in them any stain, but they are cleansed in their chief part; that is, the reign of sin is destroyed, so that the righteousness of God is in command — just as if we were to say that a body is altogether healthy because it was not infected in general with any disease. We must declare ourselves to be Christ's disciples by newness of life, for he says that he is the author of purity in all his followers.

Moreover, the other comparison was also applied to the present instance, so that Peter might not reject the washing of the feet as foolish. As Christ washes from head to foot those whom he admits to be his disciples, so the lower part has to be cleansed daily in those whom he has cleansed. God's children are not totally regenerated on the first day so that they only live a heavenly life. On the contrary, the remnants of the flesh remain in them, and they have a constant struggle all through their lives. **"Feet,"** therefore, is a metaphor for all the passions and cares by which we are brought into contact with the world. For if the Spirit occupied every part of us, we should no longer have anything to do with the pollutions of the world. But as it is, in the part in which we are carnal we crawl on the ground, or at least our feet stick in the mire and we are to that extent unclean. Therefore Christ always finds something in us to cleanse. Moreover, what is spoken of here is not the forgiveness of sins, but the renewal by which Christ gradually and continually delivers his followers completely from the desires of the flesh.

"You are clean, though not every one of you." This proposition is, as it were, the minor in the syllogism, and hence it follows that the washing of the feet belongs properly to them. But an exception is added, so that they may all examine themselves, and to see if perhaps Judas might be touched with a feeling of repentance. Yet Christ's intention was to fortify the rest of the disciples in time, in case they should be worried by the atrocity of the crime which was soon to be manifested. Yet Christ deliberately refrains from naming him, in case he should shut the gate of repentance against him. But since he was beyond hope, the warning served only to aggravate his guilt. But it was of great advantage to the other disciples, for through it Christ's divinity was made known to them more fully, and they also perceived that purity is no common gift of the Spirit.

Verses 12–17

12. **When he had finished washing . . .** Now at last Christ explains his intention in washing his disciples' feet, for what he had interjected about spiritual washing was a sort of digression from his aim. Had it not been for Peter's opposition, Christ would not have said a word about it. Now he unfolds the reason for what he had done. He who is the Master and Lord of all gave an example to be followed by all the godly, that no one might think it a burden to stoop to a service, however mean and low, to his brothers and fellows. The reason love is despised is that everyone elevates himself too much and despises almost everyone else. Nor did Christ intend merely to teach modesty, but also to lay down this rule of love, that they should serve one another. There is no love where there is not a willing slavery in assisting a neighbor.

"**Do you understand what I have done for you?**" We see that for a little while Christ kept his disciples in the dark, so that he might test their obedience; and then at the right time he revealed to them what it had not been expedient for them to know earlier. Nor does he wait until they ask, but he anticipates their question of his own accord. We shall experience the same thing, provided we let ourselves be guided by his hand even through unknown ways.

14. "**Now that I, your Lord and Teacher . . .**" Here is an argument from the greater to the lesser. Pride hinders us from fostering the equality which ought to flourish among us. But Christ, who is far exalted above all, humbles himself that he may shame the proud men who forget their station and rank and exempt themselves from brotherly fellowship. What does a mortal man think he is when he refuses to bear his brothers' burdens in order to fit in with their customs and, in summary, to perform the duties by which the unity of the church is upheld? Briefly, the man who does not think of associating with weak brothers on the basis of submitting in a kindly and friendly way to services which seem low has too high an opinion of himself.

15. "**I have set you an example.**" We should now note that Christ

says that he has set us "an example." It is not right to take all his actions indiscriminately as objects of imitation. The Roman Catholics boast that they follow Christ's example in keeping the Lenten fast. But we must first see whether or not Christ intended to put forward "an example" as a norm for disciples to conform to. We read nothing of this sort. Therefore, the imitation of it is no less wicked than if they tried to fly up to heaven. Besides, whereas they ought to have followed Christ, they were aping rather than imitating him. Every year they hold a theatrical foot-washing, and when they have discharged this empty and bare ceremony, they think they have done their duty well and are then free to despise their brothers. But what is far worse, when they have washed twelve men's feet they cruelly torture all Christ's members and thus spit in the face of Christ himself. This ceremonial comedy is nothing but a shameful mockery of Christ. At any rate, Christ does not enjoin an annual ceremony here, but tells us to be ready through our life to wash the feet of our brothers.

16. "I tell you the truth . . ." These are proverbial sayings with a wider reference, though they should also be applied to the case in hand. In my opinion, those who take them to have a general application are mistaken, as if Christ were now exhorting his disciples to bear the cross. It is more correct to say that he was using the sayings to serve his purpose.

17. "Now that you know these things . . ." Christ adds that they are "blessed" if they know and do these things. Knowledge does not deserve to be called true unless it leads believers to conform themselves to their head. On the contrary, to look on Christ and the things that belong to him as outside ourselves is a vain imagination. Infer from this that until a man has learned to give way to his brothers he does not know whether Christ is his Master. Since no one devotes himself to his brothers in every respect, and there are many who are slow and cold in the duties of love, it shows us how far we still are from the full light of faith.

Verses 18–20

18. "I am not referring to all of you." Christ again declares that among the disciples is one who is in reality anything but a disciple. And he does so partly on Judas' account, to make him more inexcusable, and partly for the sake of the others, that they might not be shaken by Judas' downfall. Not only does Christ encourage them to persevere in their calling in spite of Judas' fall, but because the happiness he mentions is not common to everyone, he tells them to seek it more eagerly and remain in it more firmly.

"I know those I have chosen." The very fact that they will persevere, he ascribes to their election. The frail strength of men would sway before every breeze and would be brought down by the lightest movement unless the Lord upheld it by his hand. But since he guides those whom he has elected, all the schemes that Satan can use will not stop them from persevering to the end with unshaken constancy. And he ascribes to election not only their perseverance but also the beginning of their godliness. What is the cause of one man rather than another devoting himself to the Word of God? Because he has been elected. Again, what is the reason for this man to continue, unless it is God's steadfast purpose to complete the work which his hand began?

In summary, the source of the distinction between the children of God and unbelievers is that the former are drawn to salvation by the Spirit of adoption, while the others are carried away to destruction by their flesh, unrestrained by any bridle. Otherwise Christ would have said, "I know what kind of person each of you will be." But he sets before them that free election on which they are founded, that they may claim nothing for themselves but, on the contrary, may acknowledge that they differ from Judas by grace alone and not by their own virtue. Let us therefore learn that every part of our salvation depends on this.

When elsewhere (see 6:70) Christ includes Judas in the number of the elect, the expression is different, and not contradictory. For there a temporal election is meant, by which God appoints us to any particular work — like Saul, who was elected king, but yet was reprobate. But here Christ is speaking about eternal election, by which we are made God's children and by which God predestined us to life before the creation of the world. And, indeed, the reprobate are sometimes adorned by God with the gifts of the Spirit, to carry out the office with which he invests them. Thus, regal virtues shone forth for a time in Saul, and Judas also was distinguished by outstanding gifts befitting an apostle of Christ. But this is very different from the sanctification of the Spirit with which the Lord honors only his own children. He renews them in mind and heart that they may be holy and blameless in his sight. Besides, there is a deep root in them which cannot be torn up, because God does not repent of his adoption. Meanwhile, it is settled that it is the gift of the divine election when, having embraced the teaching of Christ by faith, we also follow it in our life; and that this is the only reason for our happiness by which we are distinguished from the reprobate. They perish miserably, for they are destitute of the grace of the Spirit; but we have Christ for our guardian, guiding us by his hand and upholding us by his power.

Moreover, Christ here gives a clear witness to his divinity: firstly, by declaring that he does not judge in a human way; and secondly, by making himself the author of election. For when he says, **"I know,"** the knowledge he speaks about is special to God. But the second proof is the more powerful, for he testifies that those who were chosen before the creation of the world were chosen by himself. Such a remarkable demonstration of his divine power should affect us more deeply than if the Scripture had called him God a hundred times.

"But this is to fulfill the scripture . . ." It might have been thought wrong that a man should be elected to such an honorable position who was not imbued with true piety. It could easily have been objected, why did not Christ elect one whom he intended to admit as an apostle? Or rather, why did he appoint a man to be an apostle who, as he well knew, would become so wicked? He says that this must have happened because it was foretold — or at least, it was not new, for David had experienced the same thing. Some think that the prediction quoted applied correctly to Christ. To others it seems merely a comparison: as David was basely betrayed by an enemy in his own house, so a similar state awaits the Son of God. According to this, the meaning would be, "The fact that one of my disciples wickedly betrays his Master is not the first treachery to happen in the world. On the contrary, we now experience what Scripture says happened in ancient times." But since in David there was outlined what was afterwards to be seen more fully in Christ, I readily agree with the former, who expound this as strictly the fulfillment of what David had foretold by the Spirit of prophecy (see Psalm 41:9). Some think that the words are broken off and need the principal verb to be supplied. But if you read it continuously, **"But this is to fulfill the scripture: 'He who shares my bread has lifted up his heel against me,'"** there will be nothing lacking.

". . . lifted up his heel against me.'" This is a metaphor which means to attack anyone treacherously, under the pretense of friendship, in order to overcome him, when he is unprepared. Now, what Christ our head and pattern suffered, we who are his members should endure patiently. And, indeed, it has usually happened in the church in nearly every age that it has had no enemies more dangerous than its own household. Therefore, lest believers should be troubled by such shamefulness, let them get used to putting up with traitors in good time.

19. "I am telling you now before it happens." In this statement Christ tells his disciples that when one reprobate forsakes their company, it is far from being a good reason for them to be discouraged. It ought, rather, to confirm their faith. If we did not see before our eyes in the church what has been foretold about her distresses and struggles, the doubt might rise in our minds, where are the prophecies? But when the truth of Scripture agrees with our experience, we perceive more clearly that God takes care of us and that we are guided by his providence.

". . . so that when it does happen you may believe that I am he." This phrase means that Christ is the promised Messiah. It does not mean that Judas' treachery began to lead the disciples to faith; rather, their faith made greater progress when they came to experience what they had heard about before, from Christ's lips. This can be explained in two ways: either that Christ says they will believe after the event, because nothing was hidden from him; or that there will be nothing lacking in him about everything that the Scriptures testify concerning Christ. As the two interpretations agree well enough, I leave readers free to choose between them.

20. "I tell you the truth . . ." Either he describes a new discourse, which is broken and imperfect, or Christ was forestalling the offense which would arise from the crime of Judas. The evangelists do not always link up Christ's discourses but sometimes assemble various statements in fragments. However, it is more probable that Christ wanted to provide something to combat this scandal. Quite clearly, we are open to being hurt by bad examples. So the failure of one person inflicts a deadly wound on two hundred other people, extinguishing their faith, whereas the steadiness of ten or twenty godly men hardly edifies a single person. This is why when Christ was setting such a monstrosity before their eyes, it was also necessary that he should stretch out his hand to his disciples, in case, struck by this new thing, they should collapse. Nor was Christ thinking only about these disciples, but of those disciples who would come later. Otherwise the memory of Judas might even today harm us seriously. When the devil cannot alienate us from Christ by hatred of his teaching, he excites either boredom or else contempt of the ministers.

Now this admonition of Christ shows that it is unreasonable that the ungodliness of any whose conduct is wicked or unbecoming their office should diminish the apostolic authority in any way. The reason for this is that we should think about God, the author of the ministry, in whom we find nothing worthy of contempt. And then we should contemplate Christ himself who, appointed by the Father to be the sole teacher, speaks through his apostles. Whoever, therefore, does not deign to receive the ministers of the Gospel rejects Christ in them and God in Christ.

The Roman Catholics are foolish when they turn this into praise for themselves. In the first place they adorn themselves with strange and borrowed feathers which have no link with Christ's apostles. Secondly, even granting they are apostles, nothing was further from Christ's mind in this passage than to transfer his own right to men — for what else is it to receive those whom Christ sends but to give to them, that they may fulfill the office committed to them?

Verses 21–29

21. After he had said this . . . The holiness and excellence of the apostolic office makes Judas' treachery even more base and detestable. Such a hateful monstrosity struck even Christ with horror when he saw the incredible wickedness of one man polluting the sacred order where God's majesty ought to have shone. To the same end the evangelist adds that he **testified.** He means that the thing was so monstrous that at first hearing it was absolutely unbelievable.

. . . troubled in spirit. Here **spirit** denotes the mind or the soul. I disagree with those who explain it as if Christ were driven by a violent impulse of the Spirit to break out into these words. I readily acknowledge that all Christ's affections were guided by the Spirit; but the evangelist means something different, that Christ's suffering was inward and genuine. And it is very important for us to know this, for Christ's zeal is held out for us to imitate, that we may be deeply horrified by those monstrosities which overturn the sacred order of God and his church.

22. His disciples stared at one another. Those who are unconscious of any evil in themselves are made uneasy by Christ's saying. Here Judas alone is so senseless in his malice that he is untouched. Christ had such great authority among the disciples that they were quite convinced that he never said anything without good reason. But Satan had sifted all reverence from Judas' heart, so that it was harder than a rocky cliff and rejected every admonition. Although Christ seems to be unkind in inflicting this torture, for a time, on the innocent, this sort of anxiety was beneficial to them, and Christ did them no harm. It is correct that when the children of God have heard the judgment on the ungodly, they should also be tortured, that they may sift themselves and guard against hypocrisy; for this gives them an opportunity of examining themselves and their life.

The passage also teaches us that we should sometimes not point out the ungodly at once but wait until God has dragged them into the light by his own hand. It often happens that there are secret diseases in the church which we must not disguise. And yet the wickedness of the men concerned is not ripe enough for discovery. In such cases we should take this middle path.

23. . . . whom Jesus loved. The special love which Christ had for John clearly shows that it is not always inconsistent with Christian love if we love some people more than others. But everything depends on our love being directed towards God and on our loving every man in the proportion that he excels in God's gifts. Christ never swerved in the slightest from this goal. But with us it is a very different matter, for such is the vanity of our mind that there are few who come nearer to God when they love people. But the love of people for one another will never be properly regulated unless it is directed to God.

. . . was reclining next to him. What John records here may seem to be improper today. But this is how they sat at meals. They did not sit at a table as we do, but when they had taken off their shoes, they lay half-stretched out, leaning on couches.

26. ". . . when I have dipped it in the dish." If you ask what the point was in offering the piece of bread which had been dipped in the dish to identify the traitor when Christ could have openly named him if he had wanted him to be known, my answer is that the sign was given in such a way that it meant that Judas was known about to only one person and Christ did not immediately expose him to everyone. But it was advantageous that John should witness this fact, so that he might later reveal it to the others at the right moment. Christ deliberately delayed the unmasking of Judas, so that we might be more patient with hypocrites being hidden until they are dragged out into the light. We see Judas sitting among the others and yet condemned by the mouth of the Judge. Those who have a position among God's children are no better off than any other people.

27. Satan entered into him. It is certain that Judas conceived such a crime only through the instigation of Satan. So why is it said only now that Satan entered into him, when he had already held sway in his heart? Just as those who are more fully confirmed in the faith which they had before are often said to believe, so that the increase of their faith is called faith, so now that Judas is entirely given over to Satan and is carried away by a wild impetuosity to extremes, Satan is said to have entered into him. Just as the saints gradually progress and in proportion as they increase with new gifts are said to be filled with the Holy Spirit, so in proportion as the ungodly provoke God's anger against themselves by their ingratitude, the Lord strips them of his Spirit, of all light of reason, and indeed of all human feelings and delivers them to Satan. It is a terrifying judgment of God when men are given over to a reprobate mind, so that they are hardly any different from the animals and indeed rush into vices from which the animals shrink. Therefore, we must walk carefully in the fear of the Lord, in case we overcome his goodness by our evil, and he should eventually deliver us to Satan.

By handing **the bread** Christ was not giving an opportunity for Satan. Rather, Judas delivered himself entirely to Satan when he had taken **the bread.** It was the occasion, not the cause. His heart ought to have been softened by Christ's great kindness, but it was harder than iron. And so his desperate and incurable obstinacy deserved that God should, by his righteous judgment, harden his heart still more through Satan. When by kindness to our enemies we heap burning coals on their heads (Romans 12:20) if they resist, they are the more incurable and are burnt up to their destruction. And yet our kindness is not at fault, for their hearts should have been influenced to love us.

Augustine was wrong in thinking that this **bread** was a symbol of Christ's body, for it was given to Judas apart from the celebration of the Supper. Moreover, those who imagine that the devil entered essentially, as they say, into Judas are absurd. The evangelist is only speaking of his power and efficacy. By this example we are warned of the dreadful punishment which awaits all those who profane the benefits of the Lord by abusing them.

"What you are about to do, do quickly." Christ does not speak to

Judas in such a way that he can be thought of as egging him on. Rather, it expresses his detestation. Up to now, Christ had tried to call him back in various ways but in vain. Now he speaks to him as a man beyond hopes: "Perish, since you are determined to perish." In this, Christ executes his role of Judge, who condemns to death not those whom he wants to ruin, but those who have already ruined themselves, through their own fault. In summary, Christ does not lay on Judas the necessity of perishing, but declares him to be what in fact he had been all along.

28. But no one at the meal understood. Either John had not yet told the others what he had heard from Christ, or they were so upset by it that they lost their presence of mind. Indeed, it is probable that John himself was almost out of his mind. But we can often see the same thing happening in the church that happened to the disciples — few believers discern the hypocrites whom the Lord condemns with a clear voice.

29. ... or to give something to the poor. Christ's great poverty is well-known from other places. Yet from his little he gave something to the poor, so as to lay down a principle for us. For the apostles would not have guessed that he was speaking about the poor unless it had been their custom to help the poor.

Verses 30-35

31. "Now is the Son of Man glorified." The last hour was at hand. Christ knew how weak-minded the disciples were, and he wanted to support them in every possible way, so that they might not fail. Even today, the very thought of the cross of Christ would make us tremble if we were not immediately met by the consolation that on the cross he triumphed, victorious over Satan, sin, and death. What then might have happened to the apostles when they saw the Lord soon carried off to the cross, laden with every kind of insult? Might not a sight so sad and ugly have overwhelmed them a hundred times? Christ therefore forestalls this danger and recalls them from the external aspect of his death and points to its spiritual fruit. So whatever ignominy appears in the cross which could bewilder believers, Christ testifies that the same cross brings him honor and glory.

"God is glorified in him." This clause, which immediately follows the other, is added for confirmation. It was a paradox that the glory of **"the Son of Man"** arose from a death humanly ignominious and even accursed in God's eyes. Christ therefore shows how he would win glory from such a death — because he glorifies God the Father. In the cross of Christ, as in a splendid theatre, the incomparable goodness of God is set before the whole world. Indeed, God's glory shines in all creatures on high and below, but never more brightly than in the cross, in which there was a wonderful change of things. There the condemnation of all men was manifested, sin blotted out, salvation restored to men; in summary, the whole world was renewed and all things restored to order.

". . . in him." Although the preposition *in* is often used for the Hebrew word which in such instances is equivalent to "through," I have preferred to translate it as "God is glorified *in* the Son of Man," because that phrase seemed more emphatic. When Christ says, **"God is glorified,"** I take it to mean, "for God is glorified."

32. "If God is glorified . . ." Christ concludes that he will win a glorious triumph by his death, because his sole aim in it is to glorify his Father. For the Father did not seek his glory from the death of the Son without making the Son share in that same glory. Therefore, God promises that when the ignominy which Christ will endure for a time has been wiped out, a sublime glory will shine in his death. And this was accomplished, for the death of the cross which Christ suffered, so far from obscuring his honor, there shines brightest, since there his incredible love for mankind, his infinite righteousness in atoning for sin and appeasing the wrath of God, his wonderful power in overcoming death, subduing Satan, and, indeed, opening up heaven, put forth its full brightness. This truth is now open for all of us, for though the whole world should conspire to disgrace us, yet if we sincerely and honestly strive to promote God's glory, we should not doubt that God will also glorify us.

". . . and will glorify him at once." Christ increases the consolation by referring to the short length of time, promising that it will happen at once. And although this glory began on the day of his resurrection, yet here Christ especially describes its extension, which immediately followed, when raising the dead by the power of the Gospel and by his Spirit he created a new people for himself. The special glory of the death of Christ is the fruit which sprang from it for mankind's salvation.

33. "My children, I will be with you only a little longer." Because the disciples could not help feeling the profoundest sorrow at their Master's departure, he tells them in good time that he will no longer be with them at the same time as he exhorts them to be patient. Finally, to remove any untimely eagerness of desire, Christ says that they cannot immediately follow him. In calling them, lovingly, **"my children,"** Christ teaches them that he is not going away from them because he cares little about their salvation, for he loves them most tenderly. It is true that he put on our flesh in order to be our brother; but by this other name he expresses more strongly the ardor of his love.

". . . as I told the Jews." When Christ says that he is repeating to them what he had already told the Jews, it is true so far as the words go, but the meaning is different. It was so that they may endure patiently his temporary absence that Christ declares that they cannot follow him. He, as it were, puts a check on them, that they may remain at their post until they have finished their earthly warfare. He does not therefore exclude them forever from God's kingdom, like the Jews, but only tells them to wait quietly until he brings them, along with himself, into the kingdom of heaven.

34. "A new commandment I give you." To the consolation he adds this exhortation, that they should **"love one another."** It is as if he was saying, "While I am absent from you in body, testify by your mutual **love** that you have not been taught by me in vain. Let this be your constant study, your chief meditation." There is no general agreement on why Christ calls it **"a new commandment."** Some think it is because whereas whatever was commanded in the law about **"love"** was literal and external, Christ wrote it anew by his Spirit in the hearts of believers. So according to them, the law is **"new"** because Christ made it known in a **"new"** way, that it might be totally vigorous. Others explain it to mean that the law calls us to **"love,"** and yet because in it the teaching of **"love"** is bound up with so many ceremonies and additions, it does not appear so clearly; whereas perfection in **"love"** is set forth in the Gospel without any shadows.

I myself, without rejecting this interpretation out of hand, consider Christ's meaning to be simpler. We know that laws start off by being kept very carefully but gradually slip out of men's minds until at last they become obsolete. Therefore, in order to impress more deeply on the minds of his disciples the teaching of brotherly **"love,"** Christ presents it as something **"new."** It is as if he said, "I want you to remember this commandment always, as if it were a law recently made."

In summary, we see that Christ's purpose in this passage was to exhort his disciples to **"love,"** that they might never let themselves be drawn away from the pursuit of it, or the truth of it to slip away from them. How necessary this admonition was we learn from daily experience. Since it is hard to maintain brotherly **"love,"** people put it on one side and contrive for themselves new methods of worshiping God, and Satan suggests many ways in which they may occupy themselves. Thus, by their own affairs it comes about that they vainly try to mock God, but they deceive themselves. Meanwhile, we must know that this **"love"** is called **"new"** because it now began, for the first time, to please God, since it is elsewhere called "the fulfillment of the law" (Romans 13:10)

"You must love one another." Brotherly **"love"** is indeed extended to strangers, for we are all of the same flesh and are all created in God's image. But because God's image shines more brightly in the regenerate, it is right that the bond of **"love"** should be much closer among Christ's disciples. **"Love"** seeks its cause in God; from him it has its root; to him it is directed. Thus, as it recognizes anyone as a child of God, it embraces him with greater zeal and warmth. Moreover, the mutual attitude of **"love"** can only exist in those who are ruled by the same Spirit. Christ here speaks of the highest degree of **"love"**; but we ought to believe, on the other hand, that just as the goodness of God extends to and is shed on the whole world, so we ought to "**love**" all, even those who hate us. And Christ holds out his own example — not because we can reach it, for he is infinitely ahead of us, but that we may at any rate aim at the same target.

35. "All men will know . . ." Christ again confirms his earlier saying that those who "**love one another**" have not been taught in his school in vain. It is as if he said, "Not only will you know that you are my disciples, but your profession will also be approved of by others as true." Since through this mark Christ distinguishes his own from strangers, those who discard "**love**" and adopt new and fabricated worship labor in vain. Nor is it superfluous that Christ insists on this so earnestly. The love of ourselves and of our neighbor no more agree than do fire and water. Self-love keeps all our senses bound in such a way that "**love**" is altogether banished. And yet all the time we think that we have acquitted ourselves well, for Satan has many attractions to deceive us with. Whoever, then, desires truly to belong to Christ and to be acknowledged by God must mold and direct his whole life to loving his brothers and must stir himself up to this diligently.

Verses 36–38

36. "Lord, where are you going?" This question depends on Christ's saying in verse 33, "**Where I am going, you cannot come.**" It is clear from this how ignorant Peter was. After he had been so frequently warned about Christ's departure, he was worried as if it was news to him. But we are also like him in this. We hear daily from Christ's mouth everything that is in line with a useful life and all that we need to know; but when we come to it, we are as surprised as newcomers to whom nothing has been told. Peter also reveals that he is in the grip of an overwhelming desire for Christ's bodily presence, for he thinks it absurd that he could remain and that Christ could go elsewhere.

"Where I am going . . ." With these words Christ restrains Peter's excessive desire. Christ speaks briefly, as is right for a teacher, but immediately softens the severity of his statement. He says that he will be separated from his own disciples only temporarily. This passage teaches us to subject all our desires to God, that they may not go beyond their bounds; and if ever they become extravagant and foolish, we must submit them to this bridle. Besides, in case we should be disheartened, a consolation is immediately put in to help us when Christ promises that we shall one day be gathered to him.

"But you will follow later." Christ means that Peter is not yet ready to bear the cross but, like corn still in the blade, must grow and be strengthened as time passes, so that he may follow. We must therefore pray to God that he will increase and improve what he has begun in us. Meanwhile, we must crawl until we are enabled to run more swiftly. Now as Christ bears with us while we are soft and tender, so we must learn not to despise the weak brethren who are still very far from the goal. It is, of course, desirable that everyone should run with the greatest earnestness, and we all should quicken our pace; but if there are any people who proceed more slowly, we ought to wish them well, so long as they keep going.

37. "Lord, why can't I follow you now?" In this question Peter reveals his dissatisfaction with Christ's reply. He understands that he has been warned about his own weakness and therefore concludes that he is to blame for not following Christ at once. Yet he remains unconvinced, for men are by nature puffed up with confidence in their own strength. Peter's expression reflects our innate opinion in attributing too much to our own strength. Consequently, those who are powerless try to attempt everything without begging for God's help.

38. "Will you really lay down your life for me?" Christ did not choose to argue with Peter, but wanted him to become wise through his own experience, like fools who never become wise until they have undergone some misfortune. Peter promises unshakable firmness and, indeed, speaks out of sincere conviction; but his confidence is full of rashness, for he does not consider what has been given him. Since this an example for us all, we should each examine our own defects, that we may not be swollen with a vain confidence. We cannot promise too much about God's grace; but what is reproved here is the careless presumption of the flesh, for faith produces fear and anxiety.

"Before the rooster crows . . ." Since temerity and rashness come from self-ignorance, Peter is blamed for pretending to be a valiant soldier while he is out of range of being shot at. For he had not yet had his strength tested, and so thinks he can do anything. Later he was punished for his arrogance as he deserved. We must learn to distrust our own strength and go quickly to the Lord, that he may support us by his power.

John
Chapter 14

Verses 1–7

1. "Do not let your hearts be troubled." Christ speaks at length to strengthen his disciples, and not without reason, for an arduous and terrible struggle lay ahead of them. It was an extraordinary temptation that soon they would see him hanging on the cross, a sight that would cause them nothing but despair. The hour of deepest distress was very near, and so he shows them the solution, so that they may not be defeated and overwhelmed. He does not simply encourage and exhort them to be steadfast, but teaches them where they must look for courage — faith in him; he who has in himself sufficient strength to hold up the salvation of his followers is acknowledged to be the Son of God.

We should always notice the time when these words were spoken; Christ wanted his disciples to stay brave and courageous when everything seemed in utter confusion. And so we ought to use the same shield to ward off such attacks. It is, of course, impossible for us to avoid feeling these various emotions; but though we may be shaken, we must not fall. Thus it is said that believers are not **"troubled"**; although they are weighed down with very great difficulties, yet, relying on God's Word, they hold their ground, upright and steady.

"Trust in God" [KJV, "ye believe in God"]. This could also be read as an imperative: "Believe in God, and believe in me." But the former fits in better and is the more commonly received. Here, as I have said, Christ points out how to stand steadfast — by faith, resting in Christ and only thinking of him as present and stretching out his hand to help us. But it is surprising that faith in the Father is here put first. For Christ could have told his disciples that they should believe in God because they had believed in Christ. For since Christ is the exact image of the Father, we should first look to him. And this is also why Christ comes down to us, so that our faith may begin with him and rise up to God. But Christ had a different objective. Everyone acknowledges that we should believe in God; it is, indeed, a settled axiom to which everyone assents without

335

dissent. But there is hardly one person in a hundred who *really* believes; not only because the uncovered majesty of God is too distant from us, but also because Satan intrudes all kinds of clouds to block our sight of God. The consequence is that our faith, seeking God in his heavenly glory and inaccessible light, comes to nothing. Moreover, the flesh suggests of its own accord a thousand ideas which turn us away from the right view of God.

Therefore, Christ offers himself as the object of our faith and as the way to our faith's resting-place. He is the true Immanuel who, as soon as we seek him by faith, responds within us. It is one of the leading articles of our life in Christ that our faith should be directed to Christ alone, and not wander through long, roundabout ways, and that it should be fixed on him so that it does not waver in temptations. The true proof of faith is when we never let ourselves be torn away from Christ and from the promises given to us in him. People who are taught by men's ideas will be shaken by the slightest breeze. Proud men are ashamed of Christ's humiliation and therefore fly to God's incomprehensible divinity. But faith will never reach heaven unless it submits to Christ, who appears as a lowly God, and it will never be firm unless it seeks a foundation in Christ's weakness.

2. "In my Father's house are many rooms." As Christ's absence caused them grief, he tells them that he is not going away in such a way as to remain separate from them, since there is room for them too in the heavenly kingdom. It was right for him to remove their idea that when Christ ascended to the Father, he would leave his disciples on earth without taking any more notice of them. This passage has been wrongly interpreted to mean that Christ taught that there are various degrees of honor in the heavenly kingdom, for he says that there are *"many* **rooms"** — not that they are different or unlike each other, but that there are enough of them for a great many people — as if he were saying that there is room not only for himself but also for his disciples.

"I am going there to prepare a place for you." Here commentators differ. Some read these words as closely linked with what goes before: "If the rooms had not been prepared already, I would have said that I am going before you to prepare them." But I agree rather with those who render it: "If the heavenly glory was awaiting only me, I would not have deceived you. I would have told you that there was no room for anyone but myself in my Father's house. But the case is far different, for I am going before you to prepare a place for you." The context, in my opinion, demands that we read it this way, for there immediately follows, **"If I go and prepare a place for you . . ."** By these words Christ lets us know that the purpose of his leaving his disciples is to **"prepare a place"** for them. In a word, Christ, did not ascend to heaven privately for himself, to live there alone, but rather that it might be the common inheritance of all godly people, and that in this way the head might be united to the members.

But a question arises: what was the state of the fathers after death, before Christ ascended into heaven? The conclusion usually drawn is that believing souls were shut up in an intermediate state of prison, because Christ says that by his ascension into heaven the place will be prepared. But the answer is straightforward. This **"place"** is said to be prepared for the day of resurrection. For by nature the human race is banished from the kingdom of God; but the Son, who is the only heir of heaven, took possession of it in their name, so that through him we may too may enter. For in his person we already possess heaven by hope, as Paul tells us in Ephesians 1:3. Still, we shall not enjoy this great blessing until he comes from heaven again. The state of the fathers after death, therefore, is not here distinguished from ours; Christ has prepared a **"place"** both for them and for us, into which he will receive us all at the last day. Before we were reconciled, believing souls were, so to speak, placed on a watch-tower, looking for the promised redemption, and now they enjoy a blessed rest until the redemption is completed.

3. "And if I go . . ." The conditional **"if"** should be interpreted as an adverb of time, like saying: "After I have gone, I will return to you." This return is not to be understood as referring to the Holy Spirit, as if Christ had shown his disciples some new presence of himself in the Spirit. It is certainly true that Christ lives with us and in us by his Spirit, but here he is speaking about the last day of judgment, when he will finally come to gather his own people. And, indeed, if we consider the whole body of the church, he is preparing a place for us every day. It follows from this that the right day for us to enter heaven has not yet come.

4. Because we need an extraordinary fortitude to endure our long separation from Christ patiently, he adds another confirmation — that the disciples **"know"** that his death is not annihilation but is a passing to the Father; and they **"know the way"** they must follow to arrive at the communion of the same glory. Both clauses should be noted carefully. First, we must see Christ, by the eyes of faith, in his heavenly glory and blessed immortality. Second, we must understand that he is the firstfruits of our life, and that he has opened **"the way"** which was closed against us.

5. Thomas said to him . . . At first sight Thomas's question seems to contradict what Christ had said, though he did not mean to disbelieve his Master. I reply: the saints' knowledge is sometimes confused because they do not understand how or why the things explained to them are certain. For example, the prophets foretold the calling of the Gentiles with a true perception of faith, and yet Paul declares that it was a "mystery" hidden from them (see Ephesians 3:2-4). Similarly, when the apostles believed that Christ was departing to the Father, and yet did not know how he would obtain the kingdom, Thomas says, fairly enough, that they **"don't know where"** he is going. Hence he concludes that **"the way"** is even more obscure, for before we start along a road we must know where we are going.

6. "I am the way." Though Christ does not give a direct reply to the question put to him, he omits nothing that is useful to know. It was right for Thomas's curiosity to be checked, and so Christ does not explain what his state would be when he leaves the world to go to the Father, but instead emphasizes a more necessary subject. Thomas would gladly have heard what Christ intended to do in heaven, for we never weary of such subtle speculations; but it is more important for us to study and labor at another question — namely, how we may share in the blessed resurrection. His saying comes to this, that whoever obtains Christ needs nothing else; and therefore whoever is not satisfied with Christ alone is striving after something beyond absolute perfection.

". . . the way and the truth and the life." He lays down three steps, as if saying that he is the beginning, the middle, and the end. From this it follows that we should begin with him, continue in him, and end in him. We certainly should seek no higher wisdom than that which leads us to eternal **"life,"** and he declares that this is to be found in him. Now, the method of obtaining **"life"** is by becoming new creatures. He declares that we should not seek it anywhere else, and at the same time reminds us that he is **"the way"** by which alone we can reach it. So that he may not fail us in any respect, he reaches out to those who are going astray and stoops low enough to guide the sucking child. Presenting himself as a leader, he does not leave his people in the middle of the race, but makes them share in **"the truth."** Finally he makes them enjoy the fruit of it, which is the most excellent and delightful thing that can be imagined.

As Christ is **"the way,"** weak and ignorant people have no reason to complain that they are abandoned by him; and as he is **"the truth and the life,"** he also has in himself what will satisfy most perfectly. In short, Christ now declares about blessedness what I have recently said about the object of faith. Everyone believes and acknowledges that human happiness lies in God alone, but then they go wrong in seeking God elsewhere than in Christ. They tear him, so to speak, from his true and solid divinity.

". . . the truth." Some people think this means here the saving light of heavenly wisdom; others think it is the substance of **"life"** and of all spiritual blessings, in contrast to shadows and images, as it says in 1:17, "Grace and truth came through Jesus Christ." I think **"the truth"** here means the perfection of faith, just as **"the way"** means its beginning and rudiments. The whole may be summed up like this: "If anyone turns aside from Christ, he will do nothing but go astray; if anyone does not rest on him, he will find no food, but wind and vanity; if anyone is not satisfied with him alone and wants to go further, he will find death instead of life."

"No one comes to the Father . . ." This explains the previous statement. He is "the way" because he leads us "to the Father," and he is "the truth and the life" because we see "the Father" in him. As for calling on God, it may truly be said that prayers are heard only through Christ's intercession; but as Christ is not now talking about prayer, we should simply understand the meaning to be that people invent real mazes for themselves whenever they abandon Christ and try to come to God. Christ proves that he is "the life" because God, with whom is "the fountain of life" (Psalm 36:9), cannot be enjoyed in any other way than by Christ. So all theology, when separated from Christ, is not only empty and confused but also mad, deceitful, and spurious; for although philosophers sometimes come up with excellent sayings, they contain nothing but what is ephemeral, and even mixed up with perverse errors.

7. "If you really knew me . . ." He confirms what we have just said, that it is a foolish and pernicious curiosity when people are not satisfied with him and try to go to God by indirect paths. They admit that there is nothing better than the knowledge of God, but when he is near them and speaks to them intimately, they wander through their own speculations and seek above the clouds him whom they do not deign to acknowledge when he is present. Christ therefore blames the disciples for not acknowledging that the fullness of the Godhead was revealed in him. He says: "I see that up till now you have not known me properly, because you do not yet acknowledge the living image of the Father which is expressed in me."

"From now on, you do know him and have seen him." He adds this not only to soften the severity of the rebuke, but also to accuse them of ingratitude and laziness if they do not consider and ponder what has been given to them, for he says this to commend his teaching rather than to praise their faith. The meaning therefore is that God is now clearly revealed to them if they would but open their eyes. The word "see" expresses the certainty of faith.

Verses 8–14

8. "Show us the Father." It seems quite absurd the way apostles continually argue with the Lord; for why did he speak at all except to teach them what Philip was asking about? Yet there is not one of their faults described here that we do not share with them. We profess to be enthusiastic in seeking God, and yet when he presents himself before our eyes we are blind.

9. "Even after I have been among you such a long time . . ." Christ rightly rebukes Philip for not having the clear eyes of faith. He had God

present in Christ, and yet he did not see him. What was stopping him but his own ingratitude? So today, those who are not content with Christ but rush into foolish speculations to find God make little progress in the Gospel. This foolish desire springs from a contempt of Christ's lowliness, and this is very wrong, for by that humiliation he reveals the infinite goodness of God.

10. ". . . that I am in the Father, and that the Father is in me?" I do not see these words as referring to Christ's divine essence, but to the method of the revelation; for as far as his hidden divinity is concerned, Christ is no better known to us than "the Father." But he is said to be the express image of God, because in him God has entirely revealed himself; his infinite goodness, wisdom, and power are seen in him substantially. And yet the ancient writers are not wrong when they take this as a proof of Christ's divinity; but as Christ does not simply inquire what he is in himself, but what we ought to acknowledge him to be, this description applies to his power rather than to his essence. "The Father," therefore, is said to be "in" Christ, because full divinity resides in him and displays its power. And Christ, in his turn, is said to be "in the Father," because by his divine power he shows that he is one with "the Father."

"The words I say to you . . ." He proves from the effect that we should not seek God anywhere else than in him, for he maintains that his teaching, being heavenly and truly divine, is a proof and a bright mirror of the presence of God. If it is objected that all the prophets should be counted as sons of God because they speak divinely from the Spirit's inspiration and because God was the author of their teaching, the answer is straightforward. We should consider what their teaching contains, for the prophets direct their disciples to someone else; but Christ leads them to himself. Besides, we should remember what Hebrews 12:25 says — namely, that now God "warns us from heaven" by the mouth of his Son, and that when he spoke through Moses, he spoke, as it were, "on earth."

"The words I say to you are not just my own." That is, they are not given in a merely human way, because "the Father," displaying the power of his Spirit in Christ's teaching, wishes his divinity to be recognized in him.

"It is the Father . . . who is doing his work." This must not be restricted to miracles, for it is rather a continuation of the previous statement that God's majesty is clearly revealed in Christ's teaching. It is like saying that his teaching is truly a work of God from which it may be known with certainty that God lives in him. By "his work," therefore, I understand an example of God's power.

11. "Believe me when I say that I am in the Father." First he demands that the disciples believe him when he tells them that he is the Son of God. But as they had been too lazy up till now, he indirectly

reproves their indolence. "If my assertion does not produce faith," he says, "and if you have so low an opinion of me that you do not think you should believe my words, at least consider that power which is a visible image of the presence of God." It is quite absurd of them not to believe Christ's words entirely, since they should have accepted without hesitation everything that he expressed, even by a single word. But here Christ is reproving his disciples for having made so little progress although they had received so many lessons on this same subject. He is not explaining the nature of faith, but is declaring that he has what is enough to convince unbelievers.

His repetition — "I am in the Father and the Father in me" — is not superfluous, for we know too well from experience that our nature prompts us to foolish curiosity. As soon as we have gone out of Christ, we have nothing but the idols we have formed. But in Christ there is nothing but what is divine and keeps us in God.

12. "I tell you the truth . . ." Everything he had told his disciples about himself hitherto, so far as it was relevant to them, was temporary. The consolation would not have been complete if he had not added this clause, particularly as our memory is so short when we think about God's gifts. We do not need to look elsewhere for examples of this, for when God has loaded us with every kind of blessings, if he pauses for fourteen days we imagine he is no longer alive. This is why Christ not only mentions his present power, which the apostles were seeing at that time with their eyes, but promises a continual sense of it in the future. And, indeed, not only was his divinity attested while he was living on earth, but believers experienced vivid instances of it after he had gone to the Father. But either our stupidity or our malice prevents us from considering God in his works and Christ in God's works.

"He will do even greater things than these." Many people are perplexed by this statement. Ignoring the other answers which have usually been given, I content myself with this one. First, we must understand what Christ means. The power by which he proves himself to be the Son of God is so far from being confined to his bodily presence that it will certainly be clearly demonstrated by many striking proofs when he is absent. Christ's ascension was soon followed by the wonderful conversion of the world, in which Christ's divinity was more powerfully displayed than while he was living among men. Thus we see that the proof of his divinity was not confined to his person, but was spread through the whole body of the church.

". . . because I am going to the Father." The reason why the disciples will do greater things than Christ himself is because when he has taken possession of his kingdom he will demonstrate his power more fully from heaven. Hence it is clear that his glory is in no way diminished, because after his departure the apostles, who were only his instruments, performed more excellent works. Moreover, it became clear in this way that he is sitting at the Father's right hand, "that at the name of Jesus every knee should bow" (Philippians 2:10).

13. "**I will do whatever you ask in my name.**" By these words he plainly declares that he will be the author of everything the apostles do. But, you may ask, was he not even then the Mediator in whose name people should pray to the Father? I reply that he discharged the office of Mediator more clearly after he entered the heavenly sanctuary, as we shall repeat later at the appropriate place.

"**. . . so that the Son may bring glory to the Father.**" This passage agrees with what Paul says, that "every tongue [should] confess that Jesus Christ is Lord, to the glory of God the Father" (Philippians 2:11). The aim of everything is the sanctification of God's name. But here is declared the true way of sanctifying it — in the Son and by the Son. For although the majesty of God in itself is hidden from us, it shines in Christ; although his hand is concealed, it is visible to us in Christ. Consequently, in the benefits which the Father gives us, we have no right to separate the Son from him: "He who does not honor the Son does not honor the Father, who sent him" (5:23).

14. This is no mere repetition. All people perceive and feel that they are unworthy to approach God, and yet most people burst forward as if they were out of their senses and address God rashly and arrogantly. Afterwards, when they remember the unworthiness I have mentioned, everyone works out some justification for himself. But when God invites us to himself he offers us only one Mediator by whom he is entreated and gracious. But here again the wickedness of the human mind breaks out, for most people do not stop leaving the road and pursuing many circuitous detours. The reason they do so is that they have a poor idea of God's power and goodness in Christ. Then there is a second error: we do not stop to think that we are rightly excluded from approaching God until he calls us, and that we are only called through the Son. And if one passage is not enough for us, let us know that when Christ repeats that we must pray to the Father in his name, he is, as it were, putting his hand on us, so that we do not waste our effort in vainly seeking other intercessors.

Verses 15–18

15. "**If you love me . . .**" The disciples' "**love**" for Christ was true and sincere, and yet there was some superstition mixed with it, as is frequently the case with ourselves; for it was very foolish of them to want to keep him in the world. To correct this fault, he tells them to direct their love to another end, by keeping the commandments which he had given them. This is undoubtedly useful teaching, for very few of those who seem to love Christ honor him properly. On the contrary, when they have done the most trivial things they stop bothering. But true "love" for Christ is regulated by observing his teaching as our only rule. But we are also reminded how sinful our affections are, since even our love for Christ is not without fault if it is not joined with pure obedience.

16. "And I will ask the Father . . ." Christ gave this as a remedy to soothe the grief which they might feel at his absence. But at the same time, he promises that he will give them strength to keep his commandments, for otherwise the exhortation would have had little effect. So he loses no time in telling them that though he is absent from them in body, he will never let them remain without help; for he will be with them by his Spirit.

Here he calls the Spirit the gift of "the Father," but a gift which he will obtain by his prayers. In another passage he promises that he will give the Spirit himself: "If I go, I will send him to you" (16:7). Both statements are true and appropriate, for insofar as Christ is our Mediator and intercessor, he obtains from the Father the grace of the Spirit; but insofar as he is God, he gives that grace from himself. The meaning of this passage therefore is: "I was given to you by the Father to be a Counselor, but only for a time; now, having discharged my office, I will pray to him to give you another Counselor, who will not be with you for a short time but will remain with you always."

"He will give you another Counselor." The word "Counselor" is here applied to both Christ and the Spirit, and rightly so, for the task of comforting and exhorting us, and guarding us by their protection, belongs to both of them equally. Christ was the protector of his disciples while he lived in the world, and afterwards he committed them to the protection and guardianship of the Spirit. It may be asked, are we not still under Christ's protection? The answer is straightforward. Christ is a continual protector but not in a visible way. While he lived in the world, he openly revealed himself as their protector; but now he guards us by his Spirit.

He calls the Spirit "*another* Counselor" because of the difference between the blessings which we obtain from each of them. Christ's special work was to appease God's wrath by atoning for the sins of the world, to redeem people from death, to obtain righteousness and life; and the Spirit's special work is to make us share not only in Christ himself, but in all his blessings. And yet there would be nothing wrong in inferring from this passage a distinction of persons, for there must be some way in which the Spirit differs from the Son so as to be "another" than the Son.

17. ". . . the Spirit of truth." Christ gives the "Spirit" another title — that he is the teacher "of truth." From this it follows that until we have been inwardly instructed by him, all our minds are seized with vanity and falsehood.

"**The world cannot accept him.**" This contrast shows the special excellence of that grace which God gives only to his elect, for he means that it is no ordinary gift that the world is deprived of. In this sense, too, Isaiah 60:2 says: "See, darkness covers the earth and thick darkness is over the peoples, but the Lord rises upon you." God's mercy to the church deserves all the more praise when he exalts the church above the world by a unique privilege. And yet Christ exhorts the disciples not to be puffed up, as the world usually is by the outlook of the sinful nature, and so drive away the Spirit's grace. All that Scripture tells us about the Holy Spirit is only a dream to earthly people, because they trust in their own reason and despise illumination from heaven. This pride is everywhere, and as far as possible it extinguishes the light of the Holy Spirit; yet we should be aware of our own poverty and recognize that whatever belongs to sound understanding comes from no other source. Yet Christ's words show that nothing which relates to the Holy Spirit can be learned by human reason, but that he is known only by the experience of faith.

"**The world,**" he says, "**cannot accept him, because it neither sees him nor knows him. But you know him, for he lives with you and will be in you.**" Therefore, it is only the Spirit who by living in us makes himself known by us; for otherwise he is unknown and incomprehensible.

18. "I will not leave you as orphans." This passage shows what people are and what they can do without the protection of the Spirit. They are orphans, exposed to every kind of fraud and injustice, incapable of governing themselves, and in short unable of themselves to do anything. The only remedy for such a great weakness is for Christ to rule us by his Spirit, which he promises to do. First, then, the disciples are reminded of their weakness, so that they distrust themselves and rely only on Christ's protection. Second, having promised a remedy, he raises their hopes, for he says that he will never leave them. When he says, "**I will come to you,**" he is showing how he will live in his people and how he fills everything. This is by the power of his Spirit, and so it is clear that the grace of the Spirit is striking proof of his divinity.

Verses 19–20

19. "Before long . . ." He continues to commend this special grace, which should have been enough to alleviate and even remove the disciples' grief. "When I have withdrawn from the world's sight," he says, "I shall still be present with you." In order to enjoy this secret sight of Christ, we must not judge his presence or absence by physical perception, but must look hard at his power with the eyes of faith. In this way believers always have Christ present by his Spirit and see him although they are physically distant from him.

"**Because I live . . .**" This may be explained in two ways. Either it confirms the previous clause or it may be read separately, and then the meaning will be, "**because I live, you will live.**" I willingly take the former option, though we may infer the other doctrine from it, that Christ's life is the cause of our life. He begins by indicating the reason for the distinction between his being seen by his disciples and not by "**the world.**" It is because Christ can only be seen by the spiritual life, which "**the world**" lacks. "**The world**" does not see Christ, but this is not surprising, because blindness is the cause; but as soon as anyone begins to live by the Spirit, he is immediately given eyes to see Christ. This is because our life is closely linked with Christ's and flows from it as from a spring. In ourselves we are dead, and the life we flatter ourselves we have is the worst death. So when it is a question of how to obtain life, we must look to Christ, and his life must be conveyed to us by faith, that our consciences may be fully convinced that while Christ lives we are free from all danger of destruction; for it is an undoubted truth that his life would be nothing if his members were dead.

20. "**On that day . . .**" Many people refer this to the day of Pentecost; but it rather denotes the uninterrupted course of a single day, so to speak, from the time when Christ exerted the power of his Spirit until the final resurrection. From that time they began to "**realize**"; but it was a sort of feeble beginning, because the Spirit had not yet worked so powerfully in them. The gist of these words is to show that we cannot know by idle speculation what is the sacred and mystic union between us and him, and again, between him and the "**Father**"; the only way of knowing it is when he pours his life into us by the secret working of the Spirit. This is the experience of faith, which I mentioned just now.

The Arians used to abuse this passage to prove that Christ is God only by participation and grace, but their sophistry is easily refuted. For Christ is not just speaking about his eternal essence, but about the divine power which was revealed in him. As the "**Father**" has put all fullness of blessings in the Son, so in turn the Son has given himself entirely to us. He is said to be "**in**" us because, by the working of his Spirit, he clearly shows that he is the author and the cause of our life.

Verses 21–24

21. "**Whoever has my commands . . .**" He repeats his earlier statement that the sure proof of our love for him lies in our obeying his "**commands.**" He reminds the disciples of this frequently so that they do not turn aside from this goal, for there is nothing we are more prone to than to slide into a sinful attitude and to love something other than Christ under the name of Christ. This is also what Paul says: "From now on we

regard no one from a worldly point of view. Though we once regarded Christ in this way, we do so no longer. Therefore, if anyone is in Christ, he is a new creation" (2 Corinthians 5:16-17). To "have" his commands means to be properly instructed in them; to "obey" his commands is to mold ourselves and our life by their rule.

"**He who loves me will be loved by my Father.**" Christ speaks as if people loved God before he loved them — which is absurd, for "when we were God's enemies, we were reconciled to him" (Romans 5:10); and John's words are well-known — "not that we loved God, but that he loved us" (1 John 4:10). But there is no debate here about cause or effect, and therefore there is no basis for the inference that the love with which we love Christ precedes God's love to us. Christ only meant that all who love him will be happy because they will also be loved by him and by the Father — not that God begins to love them, but because they have a testimony of his fatherly love to them impressed on their hearts. The clause which follows next has the same purport.

"**And I . . . will . . . show myself to him.**" Knowledge undoubtedly precedes love; but Christ meant, "I will enable people who keep my teaching purely to make daily progress in faith"; that is, "I will make them approach me more closely and intimately." From this we should infer that the fruit of godliness is progress in the knowledge of Christ. He who promises to give to the person who has such godliness rejects hypocrites and causes people to make progress in faith when they wholeheartedly accept the Gospel teaching and mold themselves entirely in obedience to it. And this is why many people fall back, and why we see hardly one person in ten proceed in the right course; for the majority do not deserve for him to manifest himself to them. It should also be noticed that a fuller knowledge of Christ is represented here as a reward for our love to Christ; and from this it follows that it is an invaluable treasure.

22. Then Judas (not Judas Iscariot) said . . . Not unreasonably, he asks why Christ confines his light to only a few people, for he is "the sun of righteousness" (Malachi 4:2) by whom the whole world should be enlightened. Therefore, it seems wrong that he should only shine on a few people and not shed his light everywhere indiscriminately. Christ's reply does not solve the whole problem, for it makes no mention of the first cause why Christ, showing himself to a few, conceals himself from the majority of people. Certainly he finds everyone alike at first — that is, entirely alienated from him. Therefore, he cannot choose anyone who loves him, but he chooses from among his enemies those whose hearts he inclines to love him. But he did not intend, at present, to deal with that distinction, which was far from his purpose. He meant to exhort his disciples to study godliness earnestly, so that they might make greater progress in faith; and therefore he is satisfied with distinguishing them from the world by this mark of obeying the Gospel teaching.

Now this mark comes after the beginning of faith, for it is the effect of their calling. Elsewhere Christ had told the disciples that they were called by free grace, and he will remind them of it later. But now he is only commanding them to obey his teaching and to apply themselves to godliness. By these words Christ shows how the Gospel is obeyed properly: it is when our duties and outward actions proceed from the love of Christ. The arms and feet and whole body labor in vain if the love of God does not reign in the heart to govern the external parts. And since it is certain that we only obey Christ's commands insofar as we love him, it follows that a perfect love of him can be found nowhere in the world, because there is no one who obeys his commands perfectly. But God is pleased with the obedience of those who sincerely aim at this goal.

23. "My Father will love him." We have already explained that God's love to us is not put in second place, as if it followed our godliness as the cause of our love, but that believers may be quite sure that their obedience to the Gospel pleases God, and that they may continually expect fresh gifts from him.

"And we will come to him" — to those who love him; that is, they will feel that God's grace lives in them, and they will daily increase more and more in the gifts of God. He is, therefore, speaking not of that eternal love with which he loved us before we were born and even before the world was created, but of the love with which he seals our hearts by making us share his adoption. Nor does he even mean the first illumination, but those steps of faith by which believers must continually advance, as it is said that "whoever has will be given more" (Matthew 13:12).

The Roman Catholics are therefore wrong to infer from this passage that our love for God is twofold. They imagine that we love God naturally before he regenerates us by his Spirit, and also that by this preparation we merit the grace of regeneration — as if Scripture did not everywhere teach, and our experience loudly proclaim, that we are altogether alienated from God and that we are infected and filled with hatred of him until he changes our hearts. We must therefore keep to Christ's meaning, that he and the Father will come to confirm believers in continual trust in his grace.

24. "He who does not love me . . ." As believers are mixed with unbelievers in the world, and as they must be tossed by various storms as in a troubled sea, Christ again confirms them by this warning not to be drawn away by bad examples. It is as if he said, "Do not look to the world and depend on it, for there will always be people who despise me and my doctrine; but as for you, preserve constantly to the end the grace you have once received." Yet he also suggests that the world is rightly punished for its ingratitude when it perishes in its blindness, for by despising true righteousness, it shows a wicked hatred against Christ.

". . . these words you hear . . ." Lest the disciples should be discouraged or waver because of the world's obstinacy, he again claims authority for his teaching by testifying that it is from God and was not of human, earthly invention. And, indeed, the strength of our faith consists in our knowing that God is our leader, and that we are founded on nothing but his eternal truth. So whatever the world's shameless rage, let us follow Christ's teaching, which transcends heaven and earth. When he says that the words are not his, he is accommodating himself to his disciples; it is like saying that they are not human words, because he teaches faithfully what the Father has given him. Yet we know that as he is the eternal wisdom of God, he is the only source of all teaching, and all the prophets who have been from the beginning spoke by his Spirit.

Verses 25–28

25. "All this I have spoken . . ." He adds this so that they do not despair, though they may have profited less than they should; for he was then sowing a seed of doctrine which lay hidden, as it were, in the disciples. So he urges them to remain hopeful until fruit is yielded by the teaching which now seems to be useless. In short, he affirms that in the teaching which they had heard they have plenty of consolation, and they should not seek it anywhere else. And if they do not see it immediately, he tells them to be of good courage until the Spirit, the interior teacher, speaks the same thing in their hearts. This admonition is very useful to everyone, for if we do not immediately understand what Christ teaches, pride overcomes us, and we cannot be bothered to spend unprofitable labor on what is obscure. But we must bring an eager desire to be taught; we must listen and pay attention if we want to become proficient in God's school; and especially we need patience until the Holy Spirit enables us to understand what we thought we had often read or heard to no avail.

26. "The Holy Spirit . . . will remind you of everything I have said to you." So that our desire for learning may not become weak, and so that we do not fall into despair when we do not immediately perceive the meaning of what Christ says to us, let us know that this is spoken to us all. Isaiah certainly threatened unbelievers with the message that the Word of God would be "nothing but words sealed in a scroll" (Isaiah 29:11); but the Lord also frequently humbles his people in this way. Therefore we should wait patiently and calmly for the time of revelation and must not reject the Word because of that. Again, when Christ declares that it is the Holy Spirit's special role to teach the apostles what they had already learned from his mouth, it follows that the outward preaching will be vain and useless if it is not accompanied by the Spirit's teaching. God therefore has two ways of teaching: first, he sounds in our ears by human speech; and second, he addresses us inwardly by his

Spirit. He does this either simultaneously or at different times, as he thinks fit.

But observe what all these things are which he promises the Spirit will teach. He **"will remind you of** *everything I have said to you."* From this it follows that he will not be a builder of new revelations. By these words we may refute all the inventions which Satan has brought into the church from the beginning, claiming they come from the Spirit. Muhammad and the Pope both hold as a principle that Scripture does not contain teaching that is complete, but that something higher has been revealed by the Spirit. In our own day the Anabaptists and Libertines have drawn their mad ideas from the same pit. But the spirit that introduces any new idea apart from the Gospel is a deceiving spirit, and not the Spirit of Christ. Christ promises the Spirit who will confirm the Gospel teaching as if he were signing it. I have already explained what is meant by the Spirit being sent by the Father in Christ's name.

27. "Peace I leave with you." By the word **"peace"** he means the prosperity which people wish one another when they meet or part. This is what the word means in Hebrew. He is therefore alluding to the ordinary custom of his country, as if he were saying, "I leave you my farewell." But he immediately adds that this **"peace"** is far more than what is usually found among people, who generally only use the word **"peace"** as a cold formality; or if they sincerely wish anyone **"peace,"** they cannot actually give it to them. But Christ reminds them that his **"peace"** does not consist in an empty and unavailing wish, but is accompanied by its effect. In short, he says that he is going away from them in body, but his **"peace"** remains with the disciples; that is, they will always be happy through his blessing.

"Do not let your hearts be troubled." Again he corrects the disciples' alarm at his departure. It is no cause for alarm, he tells them, for they lack only his bodily presence, but they will enjoy his actual presence through the Spirit. Let us learn to be always satisfied with this kind of presence, and let us not give free rein to the flesh, which always binds God by its external inventions.

28. "If you loved me . . ." The disciples unquestionably **"loved"** Christ, but not as they ought to have done, for some physical affection was mixed with their love so that they could not bear to be separated from him. But if they had **"loved"** him spiritually, they would have desired nothing more deeply than his return to the Father.

"For the Father is greater than I." This passage has been twisted in various ways. The Arians, in order to prove that Christ is some sort of inferior God, argued that he is less than **"the Father."** To remove any excuse for such a false accusation, the orthodox Fathers said that this should be taken as referring to his human nature. Although the Arians had wickedly abused this testimony, the Fathers' reply was neither correct nor appropriate. Christ is not speaking here either about his human nature or about his eternal divinity, but for the sake of our weakness he places himself between God and us. Indeed, it has not been granted to us to reach the height of God, so Christ came down to us, that he might raise us to it. "You should have been glad," he says, "that I am going to the Father, for this should be your ultimate aim." By these words he shows not how he differs in himself from the Father, but why he came down to us, which was to unite us to God. For until we have reached that point, we stand as it were in the middle of the course. We also imagine a half-Christ, an incomplete Christ, if he does not lead us to God.

There is a similar passage in Paul's writings, where he says that Christ will hand over "the kingdom to God the Father . . . so that God may be all in all" (1 Corinthians 15:24, 28). Christ certainly reigns not only in human nature, but as God revealed in flesh. In what way, therefore, will he lay aside the kingdom? It is because the divinity we now see only in Christ's face will then be openly visible in him. The only difference is that Paul there describes the highest perfection of the divine brightness, whose rays began to shine from the time when Christ ascended to heaven.

To make the matter clearer, we must speak still more plainly. Christ is not here comparing the Father's divinity with his own, nor his own human nature with the Father's divine essence, but rather his present state with the heavenly glory to which he was soon going to be received. It is like saying, "You want to keep me in the world, but it is better for me to ascend to heaven." Let us therefore learn to see Christ humbled in the flesh, so that he may lead us to the source of blessed immortality; for he was not appointed to be our guide merely to raise us to the sphere of the moon or the sun, but to make us one with God the Father.

Verses 29-31

29. "I have told you now . . ." It was right that the disciples should be warned about this frequently, for it was a secret far beyond all human grasp. He declares that he foretells what will happen, so that when it happens they may **"believe."** It was a useful confirmation of their faith when they recalled Christ's predictions and saw happening before their eyes what they had previously heard from his mouth. Yet it seems to be a sort of concession, as if Christ had said, "Because you are not yet able to comprehend such a deep mystery, I bear with you till the event has happened, which will be an interpreter to explain this teaching." Although at the time he seemed to be speaking to the deaf, afterwards it became apparent that his words had not been scattered in vain or (so to speak) in the air, but that they were seed sown in the ground. Now as Christ here speaks about his Word and what will happen, so his death and resurrection and ascension to heaven combined with his teaching to produce faith in us.

30. **"I will not speak with you much longer."** By saying this he intended to fix the disciples' attention on himself and impress his doctrine more deeply on their minds, for when we have plenty we often lose our appetite; we desire more eagerly what we have not got, and we are more avid for what is about to be taken away from us. So, to make them want to hear his teaching, he threatens that he will go away very soon. Although Christ never stops teaching us in our lifetime, we may learn from this statement, for since our life is short we ought to seize the present opportunity.

"For the prince of this world is coming." He could have said directly that he would soon die, and that the time was close at hand for him to die, but he uses a paraphrase to fortify their minds beforehand, lest they should be terrified by such a hideous and terrible kind of death and become faint. First, he says that this power will be given to Satan; and next, he adds that he will go away not because he is forced to do so but in order to obey the Father.

The devil is called **"the prince of this world"** not because he has some kingdom separate from God (as the Manichees imagined), but because by God's permission he exercises his tyranny over the world. Therefore, whenever we hear this name given to the devil, let us be ashamed of our miserable lot. However proud we may be, we are the devil's possession until we are regenerated by Christ's Spirit, for the **"world"** here includes the whole human race. There is only one deliverer who frees and rescues us from this dreadful slavery. Now, since this punishment was inflicted because of the sin of the first man, and since it grows worse every day because of new sins, let us learn to hate both ourselves and our sins. We are held captives under Satan's dominion, but still this slavery does not excuse us, for it is voluntary. It ought also to be observed that what is done by wicked people is here ascribed to the devil; since Satan motivates them, all that they do is rightly regarded as his work.

"He has no hold on me." Because of Adam's sin, Satan holds the dominion over death, and therefore he could not touch Christ, who is pure from all pollution by sin, if he had not voluntarily subjected himself. And yet I think that these words have a wider meaning than the one they are usually given; for the ordinary interpretation is, "Satan has found nothing in Christ, for there is nothing in him that deserves death, because he is pure from every stain of sin." But I think Christ is asserting here not only his own purity, but also his divine power, which was not subject to death; for it was right to assure the disciples that he was not yielding through weakness, in case they thought less highly of his power. But in this general statement the former is also included, that in enduring death he was not compelled by Satan. From this we gather that he was substituted in our place when he submitted to death.

31. "But that the world may know . . ." (KJV). Some people think these words should be read as closely linked with the words **"Come now; let us leave,"** as a single sentence. Other people read the first part of the verse separately and suppose that it breaks off abruptly. As it makes no great difference to the meaning, I leave it to you to choose whichever of these views you prefer. What is to be especially noticed is that God's decree is here put in the highest place, in case we should imagine that Christ was dragged to death by Satan's violence, in such a way that something happened contrary to God's purpose. It was God who appointed his Son to be the reconciler and who decided that the sins of the world should be expiated by his death. To achieve this, he permitted Satan to triumph over Christ for a while, as if victorious. Therefore Christ, to obey his Father's decree, offers no resistance to Satan, and so he can offer his obedience as the ransom for our righteousness.

"Come now; let us leave." Some people think that Christ, after saying these things, moved to a different place, and that what follows was spoken by him on the road. But as John later adds that Christ went away with his disciples, it seems more likely that he wanted to exhort them to give God the same obedience they saw so outstandingly exemplified in him, and not that he led them away at that moment.

John
Chapter 15

Verses 1–6

1. "I am the true vine." The essence of this comparison is that by nature we are barren and dry except insofar as we have been grafted into Christ and draw a new power from him, from outside ourselves. As the Greek word translated **"branches"** sometimes means "vines," and the Greek word translated **"vine"** sometimes means "vineyard," I am more inclined to think that Christ is comparing himself with a field planted with vines, and comparing us to the plants themselves. However, I will not quarrel with anyone about this. I would only advise the reader to follow what seems more probable from the context.

First, remember the rule which should be observed in all parables. We should not examine minutely every property of **"the vine,"** but only consider generally Christ's purpose in the comparison. There are three main parts. First, we have no power to do good except what comes from himself. Second, we have our root in him, but the Father cultivates us by pruning. Third, he removes unfruitful **"branches"** so that they can be thrown onto the fire and burned.

Almost everyone is ashamed to deny that all the good he has comes from God. But then they imagine that universal grace has been given to them, as if it had been implanted in them naturally. But Christ chiefly insists that the vital sap flows only from himself. It follows that human nature is unfruitful and totally lacking in anything good, for no one has the nature of a vine until he is implanted in him. But this is given to the elect alone by special grace. So the Father is the first author of all blessings and plants us with his hand; but the life begins in Christ, in that we begin to take root in him. When he calls himself **"the true vine,"** he means, "I am *truly* the vine, and people who seek strength anywhere else are working in vain. Useful fruit will come only from the branches produced by me."

2. "He cuts off every branch in me that bears no fruit." Some people corrupt God's grace; some suppress it maliciously; others choke it by laziness. Here Christ wants to stir us up to anxiety. But you may ask, can anyone grafted into Christ be unfruitful? My reply is that many people are thought to be in **"the vine"** who in fact have no root in **"the vine."** Thus, in the prophets the Lord calls the people of Israel his "vine" because by outward profession they were supposed to be the church.

". . . while every branch that does bear fruit he trims clean." Here he shows that believers need constant attention, to prevent them from degenerating, and that they produce nothing good unless God is continually caring for them. It will not be enough that we were once made partakers of adoption if God does not continue the work of his grace in us. He speaks about pruning because our sinful nature abounds in superfluities and harmful vices and is too fertile in producing them, and because they grow and put out new shoots endlessly if we are not pruned by God's hand. When he says that vines are trimmed or pruned so that they **"will be even more fruitful,"** he is telling us what progress the godly should make in godliness.

3. "You are already clean because of the word." He reminds them that they have already experienced in themselves what he had said. They have been planted in him and also cleaned or pruned. He points out the means of pruning — namely, teaching. He is undoubtedly speaking about external preaching, because he specifically mentions "the word I have spoken to you." Not that words spoken by humans have such a great effect, but when Christ works in the heart by the Spirit, **"the word"** itself is the instrument of cleaning. Yet Christ does not mean that the apostles are free from all sin, but he reminds them of their experience so that they may learn from it how necessary it is to continue in grace. He also commends to them the teaching of the Gospel from the fruit which it produces, so that they may be more powerfully moved to meditate on it continually, since it is like the vine-dresser's knife for pruning what is bad.

4. "Remain in me." Again he exhorts them to be diligent and careful in keeping the grace which they had been given. And, indeed, Christ has no other purpose in mind than to keep us as a hen keeps her chicks under her wings (see Matthew 23:37), lest we be carried away by our indifference and fly to our destruction. Therefore, to prove that he did not begin the work of our salvation only to leave it interrupted midway, he promises that his Spirit will always be effective in us as long as we do not prevent him. "Remain in me," he says, "for I am prepared to remain in you." And again (verse 5), **"If a man remains in me and I in him, he will bear much fruit."** By these words he declares that all who have a living root in him are fruitful branches.

5. "Apart from me you can do nothing." This is the conclusion and application of the whole parable. As long as we are separate from him, we bear no fruit that is good and pleasing to God, for we are unable to do anything good. The Roman Catholics not only weaken this statement but destroy it completely — and, indeed, they evade it altogether. Although they acknowledge in words that we can do nothing without Christ, they foolishly imagine that we possess some power which, though not enough by itself, with the help of God's grace cooperates with him. They cannot bear man to be so emptied that he can do nothing of himself. But these words of Christ are too plain to be evaded so easily. The Roman Catholics imagine that we can do nothing without Christ, but that when we are helped by him we have something of ourselves in addition to his grace. But Christ, on the contrary, declares that we can do nothing of ourselves. **"No branch can bear fruit by itself,"** he says (verse 4). Therefore, he is saying not only that we need the cooperation of his grace, but that we have no power at all other than what he gives us.

Then follows another quibble: they argue that the branch has something by nature, for if a fruitful branch is grafted into the vine it will produce something. But this is easily answered: Christ does not explain what the branch has by nature, before it is joined to the vine, but rather means that we begin to become **"branches"** when we are united to him. Indeed, Scripture shows us elsewhere that we are useless, dry wood before we are in him.

6. "If anyone does not remain in me . . ." Again he lays before them the punishment of ingratitude and by doing so rouses and urges them to perseverance. This is indeed a gift from God, but he needed to tell us to fear or our irrepressible sinful nature might uproot us.

". . . withers." Those who are cut off from Christ are said to **"wither"** like a dead branch. Just as our strength begins in him, so it is sustained in him. Not that any of the elect is ever cut off, but there are many hypocrites who apparently flourish and are green for a time, but who afterwards, when they should yield fruit, disappoint the Lord's hope.

Verses 7–11

7. "If you remain in me . . ." Believers often feel they are starved and very far from the rich fatness which can produce abundant fruit. Therefore Christ specifically adds that whatever those who are in him may need, there is relief for their poverty as soon as they ask God. This is a very useful admonition, for the Lord often lets us go hungry in order to train us to pray earnestly. If we fly to him, we shall never lack what we ask; he will supply us with everything we need, from his inexhaustible abundance (1 Corinthians 1:5).

"If . . . my words remain in you . . ." He means that we take root in him by faith, for as soon as we have left the Gospel teaching we are looking for Christ outside himself.

"Ask whatever you wish, and it will be given you." He is not giving us permission to indulge ourselves. It would be a bad way of helping our salvation if God gave in to us so readily and indulgently, for we know what foolish and extravagant desires people have. But here he limits his people's wishes to praying aright; this subjects all our desires to God's judgment. This is confirmed by the context, for he means that his people do not desire riches, honor, etc., which the sinful nature foolishly desires; rather, they want the vital sap of the Holy Spirit, which enables them to bear fruit.

8. **"This is to my Father's glory."** This confirms the previous statement, for he shows that we should not doubt that God will listen to the prayers of his people when they want to be made fruitful; this contributes greatly to his glory. But by this end or effect he also kindles in them the desire to do good, for there is nothing we should value more highly than to glorify God's name.

". . . that you bear much fruit, showing yourselves to be my disciples." This next clause is to the same effect, for he says that he has no one in his flock who does not bear fruit to the glory of God.

9. **"As the Father has loved me . . ."** He wanted to express something far greater than is usually imagined. Those who think he is here speaking about the secret love which God the Father always had for his Son are speculating irrelevantly. Rather, Christ was wanting to lay in our hearts, so to speak, a sure pledge of God's love to us. Therefore this passage has nothing to do with the over-subtle question of how the Father always loved himself in the Son. The love mentioned here must be understood to refer to us, because Christ says that the Father loves him as the head of the church. This is very necessary for us, for whoever seeks to be loved by God without a Mediator gets involved in a maze where he will find neither the right way nor the exit. We should therefore look to Christ, in whom will be found the pledge of God's love. The love of God was poured out on him so that it might flow from him to his members. He is distinguished by the title of "my Son, whom I love," in whom the Father's will is satisfied (see Matthew 3:17). But we must note the purpose, which is that God may be pleased with us. We may therefore see in him, as in a mirror, God's Fatherly love to all of us, since he is not loved separately or for his own sake alone, but so that he may unite us with him to the Father.

"Remain in my love." Some people explain this as meaning that Christ demands a return of love from his disciples. Others better understand it as Christ's love to us. He means for us to enjoy continually the love he had for us, and so he warns us to be careful not to deprive ourselves of it. Many people reject the grace which is offered to them, and many throw away what they once had in their hands. Therefore, once we have been received into Christ's grace, we must see that we do not fall from it by our own fault. What some people infer from these words — that God's grace is ineffective unless it is helped by our constancy — is frivolous. I cannot agree that the Spirit demands from us no more than what we can do. Rather, he shows us what we ought to do: if we have not enough strength, we should seek it elsewhere. Similarly, when in this passage Christ exhorts us to persevere, we must not rely on our own efforts and battles, but must pray to him who commands us in order to confirm us in his love.

10. "If you obey my commands . . ." He shows us the way to persevere: by following wherever he calls. So Paul refers to "those who are in Christ Jesus . . . who do not live according to the sinful nature but according to the Spirit" (Romans 8:1, 4). The faith which grasps the free love of Christ is forever joined with a good conscience and newness of life. Indeed, Christ does not reconcile believers to the Father for them to live licentiously with impunity, but so that he may keep them under his Father's rule and dominion, governing them by his Spirit. Hence it follows that Christ's love is rejected by those who do not prove by true obedience that they are his disciples.

If anyone objects that the safety of our salvation then depends on ourselves, I reply that it is wrong to give this meaning to Christ's words; the obedience which believers give him is not the cause of his continuing love to us but is the effect of his love. For why is it that they answer to their calling except that they are led by the Spirit of free adoption?

But it may seem too hard that the condition imposed on us is to obey Christ's commands, which contain the absolute perfection of righteousness — a perfection far above what we can manage; it would seem that Christ's love will be useless if we are not granted angelic purity. The solution is easy: when Christ speaks about the desire to live a good and holy life, he includes the main point of his teaching — namely, our being freely credited with righteousness; and hence, by his forgiveness our service pleases God even though in itself it deserves to be rejected as imperfect and impure. Believers, therefore, are regarded as obeying Christ's commands when they apply themselves to them, even though they fall far short of the mark, for they are set free from the rigor of the law which says, "Cursed is the man who does not uphold the words of this law by carrying them out" (Deuteronomy 27:26).

". . . just as I have obeyed my Father's commands." As we have been elected in Christ, so the living picture of our calling is displayed in him. And so he justly offers himself to us as a pattern which all godly people should follow. He says: "The likeness of what I demand from you shines in me, for you see how sincerely I am devoted to obeying my Father, and how I persevere in this. My Father has loved me, too — not for a moment or for a short time but constantly." This conformity between the head and the members is always before our eyes, and so believers must try to follow the example of Christ and confidently hope that his Spirit will renew them every day, making them better and better so that they walk in newness of life to the end.

11. "I have told you this . . ." He adds that his love is far from being unknown to the godly, but that it is perceived by faith, so that they enjoy blessed peace of conscience. The joy which he mentions comes from that peace with God which is possessed by all who have been justified by free grace. Therefore, as often as God's fatherly love to us is proclaimed, let us know that we are given the basis for true joy and that with calm consciences we can be sure of our salvation.

"My joy . . . your joy." It is called Christ's **"joy"** and ours in different respects. It is Christ's because he gives it to us, for he is both its author and its cause. I say that he is its cause because we were freed from guilt when the punishment that brought us peace was upon him (see Isaiah 53:5). I also call him its author because by his Spirit he drives fear and anxiety away from our hearts, and then we become serenely happy. It is said to be ours for a different reason: we enjoy it because it has been given to us. Now, as Christ says that he told them this so that his **"joy"** might be in them, we conclude that all who have learned from this speech have something they can rest on.

". . . that my joy may be in you" (KJV, "remain in you"). By the word **"abide"** (KJV) in this passage he means that it is not a fleeting or temporary **"joy"** that he is talking about, but a **"joy"** which never fails or passes away. Therefore, let us learn that we should seek to trust for our salvation in Christ's teaching, which flourishes both in life and in death.

". . . that your joy may be complete." He adds that this **"joy"** will be solid and full — not that believers will be entirely free from all sadness, but that the ground for **"joy"** will be far greater, so that no fear, no anxiety, no grief will ever swallow them up. Neither life nor death nor any miseries will stop people from triumphing over sadness if they have been allowed to glory in Christ.

Verses 12-15

12. "My command is this . . ." Since it is right for us to regulate our life according to Christ's **"command,"** we must first understand what he wants or commands. Therefore he repeats here what he has already said, that he wants above all else that believers should cultivate mutual love among themselves. True love and reverence for God come first in order, but he dwells chiefly on love to our neighbor because this is the true proof of it. Besides, as he previously offered himself as a pattern for keeping the teaching generally, he now offers himself as a pattern in a particular instance, for he loved all his people, that they might love each other.

13. "Greater love has no one than this . . ." Christ sometimes tells us how greatly he loves us in order to confirm our confidence in our salvation; but now he goes further, to inflame us by his example to love our brothers. Yet he joins both together: he wants us to experience by faith how immeasurably sweet is his goodness, and then he entices us for this reason to work at loving each other. Thus Paul writes, "Live a life of love, just as Christ loved us and gave himself up for us as a fragrant offering and sacrifice to God" (Ephesians 5:2). God could have redeemed us by a word or a wish, but another way seemed better to him for our benefit: that, not sparing his own much-loved Son, he might testify in his person how much he cares for our salvation. Our hearts must be harder than stone or iron if they are not softened by the immeasurable sweetness of God's love.

It may be asked how Christ died for his friends, since we were enemies before he reconciled us (see Romans 5:10). He destroyed the enmity between God and us by expiating our sins through his sacrificial death. The answer to this question will be found in the comment on chapter 3, that we are at variance with God until our sins are blotted out by the death of Christ; but the cause of this grace, which has been revealed in Christ, was the perpetual love of God, with which he loved even those who were his enemies. Similarly, Christ laid down his life for strangers, but he still loved them or he would not have died for them.

14. "You are my friends." He does not mean that we obtain such a great honor by our own merit, but is only reminding them of the condition on which he receives us into favor and deigns to count us as **"friends."** As he said earlier, **"If you obey my commands, you will remain in my love"** (verse 10). "For the grace of God that brings salvation has appeared to all men" (Titus 2:11). But ungodly people, opposed to Christ through wicked contempt of the Gospel, renounce his friendship.

15. "I no longer call you servants." He shows his love for the disciples in another way, by opening his mind fully to them, for there is intimate communion between friends. "I have given in to you far more than any mortal usually does to his servants," he says. "May this be a pledge of my love for you, then, that I have in a kind and friendly way explained the secrets of heavenly wisdom to you which I heard from the Father." It is indeed a wonderful commendation of the Gospel that in it we find the heart of Christ opened, so to speak, so that we can no longer find it doubtful or obscure. We need not ascend above the clouds or descend into the deep to be sure of our salvation (see Romans 10:6-7). Let us be satisfied with this testimony of his love towards us which is contained in the Gospel, for it will never deceive us. Moses said to the people long ago, "What other nation is so great as to have their gods near them the way the Lord our God is near us whenever we pray to him?" (Deuteronomy 4:7). But God has given us a far higher distinction, by giving himself to us entirely, in his Son. So much the greater is people's ingratitude and perversity when they are dissatisfied with the wonderful wisdom of the Gospel and eagerly, proudly fly to new speculations.

"... everything that I learned." The disciples certainly did not know everything that Christ knew, and indeed it was impossible for them to reach such a height. Though God's wisdom is incomprehensible, he gave them each a certain amount of knowledge, as much as he thought they needed. Why then does he say that he revealed "everything"? My reply is that this was limited to the person and office of the Mediator. He puts himself between God and us, having received from God's secret sanctuary the things he was to deliver to us by hand, so to speak. Therefore, when Christ taught the disciples, he did not leave out anything relating to our salvation which it was important for us to know. Appointed as the church's unique teacher and Master, he heard nothing from the Father which he did not faithfully teach his people. Just let us humbly want and be ready to learn and we shall feel that Paul has good reason to say that "we proclaim him, admonishing and teaching everyone with all wisdom" (Colossians 1:28).

Verses 16–21

16. "You did not choose me." He expresses even more clearly that their attaining such great honor is not by their own merit but by his grace. It is as if he had said that whatever they had was not obtained by their own skill or hard work. People generally think that God's grace and human will are combined, but the contrast — "You did not choose me, but I chose you" — firmly claims for Christ alone what is usually divided between Christ and man. It is as if he had said that a man is not moved of his own accord to seek Christ until he has been sought by him.

True, this does not refer to the ordinary election of believers, by which they are adopted to be the children of God, but to the special election by which he appointed his disciples to the office of preaching the Gospel. But still, if they were chosen for the apostolic office by free gift and not by their own merit, it is all the more certainly of free grace that we are chosen to become heirs of eternal life, delivered from being children of wrath and a cursed seed. Besides, in this passage Christ so commends his grace in choosing them as apostles that he joins it to that earlier election by which they had been grafted into the body of the church. He includes in these words all the dignity and honor which he had given them. Yet I agree that he is talking specifically about the apostolate; his intention is to move the disciples to perform their office diligently.

He takes as the basis of his exhortation the free favor he has honored them with. For the more we owe to the Lord, the more earnest we should be in doing what he commands; otherwise we cannot escape the charge of base ingratitude. So it is clear that there is nothing that should kindle in us the longing after a holy and godly life more than when we acknowledge that we owe everything to God and that we have nothing of our own; that the beginning of our salvation, and all the parts which follow from it, flow from his free mercy. Besides, the truth of this statement of Christ's may be clearly seen by the fact that he chose as his apostles those who might have been thought to be the most unfit of all. Yet he wanted them to be a lasting monument to his grace. As Paul says in 2 Corinthians 2:16, what mortal is able to represent God's person? It is Christ alone who makes them fit by his election. So Paul ascribes his apostleship to grace (Romans 1:5) and says that God set him apart from birth (Galatians 1:15). Moreover, since we are altogether unworthy servants, those who appear to be the most excellent of all will not be fit for the least job till they have been chosen. But the higher the honor to which anyone has been raised, the greater his debt to God; let him remember this.

"I chose you." Election is hidden until it is actually made known, when someone receives the position to which he has been destined. Paul, in the passage quoted above, after he has declared that he was separated from birth, adds that he was created an apostle because it so pleased God. Similarly the Lord says in Jeremiah 1:5 that he knew Jeremiah before he was in his mother's womb, though he calls him at last to become a prophet in God's own good time. It may happen that someone properly qualified begins to teach; in the church it is the rule that no one is called until he is prepared and has the necessary gifts. That Christ says he is the author of both is not surprising, since it is only by him that God acts, and he acts with the Father. So election and ordination belong equally to both.

"... to go ..." He now shows why he mentioned his grace: it was to make them apply themselves more earnestly to the work. The office of apostle was not an honorary one; they had to face the greatest difficulties. Therefore Christ adds this stimulus, that they should not shrink from work, annoyance, or danger. This is argued from their aim, but Christ reasons from the effect when he says **"and bear fruit,"** for it is hardly possible for anyone to devote himself earnestly and diligently to the task unless he expects the work to bring some results. Therefore Christ tells them that their efforts will not be useless or unsuccessful, as long as they are ready to obey. He not only tells the apostles what their calling involves and demands but also promises them success, so that they do not grow cold or listless.

It is almost impossible to tell the value of this consolation against the many temptations which afflict Christ's ministers every day. So whenever we seem to be working in vain, let us remember that Christ will in the end prevent our efforts from being worthless or useless. This promise is most helpful when no fruit appears. Today's wits, and those who seem wise to the world, ridicule our efforts as unconsidered and a vain attempt to mix heaven and earth. The fruit does not yet match our wishes. But since Christ, on the contrary, has promised that the result of the work, though hidden for a while, will follow, let us work diligently to do our duty while the world mocks on.

". . . fruit that will last." Why does Christ say this "fruit" will be everlasting? As the Gospel teaching wins souls to Christ for eternal salvation, many people think this is the everlasting "fruit." But I would apply the statement much more widely, as meaning that the church will last to the very end of the world. For the apostles' work bears "fruit" even today, and our preaching is not just for one age but will enlarge the church so that new "fruit" will appear after our death.

When he says "your fruit," he speaks as if it had been obtained by their own work, though Paul teaches that those who water or plant are nothing (1 Corinthians 3:7). Indeed, the creation of the church is so excellent a work of God that its glory cannot be ascribed to mankind. But as the Lord displays his power through men, he transfers to them even what is properly his, so that they may not labor in vain. But let us remember that when he so graciously honors his disciples, it is to encourage them and not to puff them up.

"Then the Father will give you whatever you ask in my name." This clause was not put in without reference to the context, as many people might think. Since the job of teaching is far beyond human power, it suffers innumerable attacks by Satan, and these could never be warded off without God's power. So that the apostles may not be discouraged, Christ meets them with the best sort of help — as if he were saying, "If the work given to you is so difficult that you cannot do it, my Father will not leave you, for I have appointed you to be ministers of the Gospel with the assurance that my Father will have his hand stretched out to help you whenever you pray to him in my name." And, indeed, the fact that most teachers either droop through laziness or utterly give way through despair comes about simply because they are sluggish in the duty of prayer.

Christ's promise, therefore, urges us to call on God, for whoever acknowledges that the outcome of his work depends on God alone will offer that work to him with fear and trembling. On the other hand, if anyone relies on his own efforts and neglects God's assistance, he will either throw away his spear and shield when he comes to the trial, or he will be very busy but have nothing to show for it. Here we must beware of two faults — pride and distrust, for as God's help is blithely ignored by those who think the matter is already in their power, so there are many people who give in to difficulties because they do not stop to think that they are fighting through the power and protection of God, under whose banner they go to war.

17. "This is my command . . ." This, too, was added appropriately, so that the apostles would know that mutual love among ministers is demanded above everything else, so that they build the church with one accord. There is no greater hindrance than when everyone works on his own and they do not work for the common good. Therefore, if ministers do not foster brotherly fellowship with each other, they may erect some mounds, but these will be separate, and no church will be built.

18. "If the world hates you . . ." Having armed the apostles for battle, Christ exhorts them to be patient, for the Gospel cannot be proclaimed without the world immediately raging against it. Consequently, it will never be possible for godly teachers to avoid the world's hatred. Christ gives them plenty of warning of this, in case they should suffer the usual fate of raw recruits who, lacking experience, are courageous before they have seen the enemy, but are terrified when the battle begins. And not only does Christ forewarn his disciples, so that nothing new and unexpected happens to them, but he also strengthens them by his own example. For it is not right for him to be hated by the world and we who represent him to enjoy the favor of the world.

"Keep in mind that it hated me first." I have translated the verb in the indicative mood — "you know"; but if anyone prefers to translate it in the imperative — "know that . . ." — I have no objection, for it makes no difference to the meaning. The next phrase is more difficult: the Greek means "before you," and when he says that he is **"before"** (KJV) the disciples, this may be either **"before"** in time or **"before"** in rank. The former has been more widely accepted: that Christ was hated by the world earlier in time than the apostles were. But I prefer the second interpretation: that Christ, who is far above them, was not exempt from the world's hatred, and therefore his ministers should not refuse the same state. The phrase is the same as the one we have seen twice before, in 1:27 and 1:30: "A man who comes after me . . . was before me."

19. "If you belonged to the world . . ." Here is another consolation — that the reason they are hated by the world is that they have been separated from it. This is their true happiness and glory, for this is how they have been rescued from destruction.

"But I have chosen you out of the world." To "choose" here means to "separate." Now, if they were **"chosen . . . out of the world,"** it follows that they were a part of **"the world,"** and that it is only by God's mercy that they are distinguished from the rest, who perished. Again, by the term **"the world,"** Christ here describes all who have not been regenerated by God's Spirit; as we shall see more fully under chapter 17, he contrasts the church with the world. But this teaching does not contradict Paul's exhortation, "as far as it depends on you, live at peace with everyone" (Romans 12:18). The exception is equivalent to saying that we should see what is right and proper for us, and thus no one should try to please the world and yield to its corruptions.

But yet another objection may be raised. We see that it is common for the wicked, who are "**of the world,**" to be not only "**hated**" but cursed. In this respect it is true that "**the world**" does *not* love them "**as its own.**" My answer is that earthly people, who are ruled by their sinful nature, never have a true hatred of sin, but only hate it when it suits their own convenience or harm. Christ did not mean to deny that "**the world**" foams and rages within itself with internal divisions. He only meant to show that "**the world**" hates nothing in believers except what is of God. Hence, too, it is clear how foolishly the Anabaptists rave, as they infer from this one argument that they are God's servants just because they displease most people. For it is easy to reply that many who are "**of the world**" favor their teaching because they are delighted at the thought of having everything in shameful confusion. Many who are "**out of the world**" hate it because they do not want the political order to break down.

20. "Remember the words . . ." This might also be read in the indicative mood, "You remember the words," but the meaning is not very different. I think it is better to read it as an imperative. It confirms what Christ has said immediately beforehand, when he said that he was hated by "**the world**" although he was far more excellent than his disciples. It is not right that the servant's condition should be better than that of "**his master.**"

"If they obeyed my teaching, they will obey yours also." Having spoken about people, he now talks about doctrine. Nothing gives greater uneasiness to the godly than to see God's teaching haughtily despised by people. It is truly shocking and dreadful, and the sight might shake the stoutest heart. But when, on the other hand, we remember that resistance no less obstinate was shown to the Son of God himself, we need not be surprised that people have so little reverence for God's teaching. When he calls it his "**teaching**" and theirs, he is referring to the ministry. Christ is the only teacher of the church, but he meant that his doctrine, of which he was the first teacher, would be preached afterwards by the apostles.

21. "They will treat you this way . . ." As the world's fury is monstrous when it rages against the preaching of its own salvation, Christ says that this is because it is carried away by blind ignorance to its own destruction; for no one would deliberately engage in battle against God. Therefore, it is blindness and ignorance of God that carries the world away, so that it does not hesitate to make war on Christ. We must always observe the reason for this conduct; true consolation comes only with the testimony of a good conscience. Our minds should also be made grateful for God giving us his light, while the world perishes in its blindness. But we must understand that hatred of Christ arises from stupidity of mind in not knowing God; for, as I have often said, unbelief is blind — not that the wicked do not understand or know, but because the knowledge they have is confused and quickly vanishes away. I have dealt with this subject more fully elsewhere.

Verses 22–27

22. "If I had not come . . ." He has said that the Jews hated the Gospel because they did not know God. In case anyone should think that this tended to lessen their guilt, he adds that it is through malice that they are blind, just like someone shutting his eyes so that he does not have to see the light. Otherwise it might have been objected against Christ, "If they do not know your Father, how is it that you do not cure their ignorance? Why do you not at any rate test whether they were quite unteachable or not?" He replies that he has performed the duty of a good and faithful teacher, but without success because their malice would not let them become sound in mind. In the person of those men, he wanted to strike terror into all who reject the truth of God when it is offered to them or who choose to fight against it when it is known. Though God's dreadful vengeance awaits them, Christ here looks rather to his own disciples and encourages them by giving them reason to be confident of victory; otherwise they might at any time give way to the malice of the wicked. When we learn that this will be the outcome, we can triumph already, as if we were in the midst of the battle.

". . . they would not be guilty of sin." It may seem that by these words Christ was suggesting that there is no sin except unbelief; and some people do think this. Augustine speaks more carefully, but he comes near to that opinion: since faith forgives and blots out all sins, he says, the only sin that damns anybody is unbelief. This is true inasmuch as unbelief not only hinders people from being delivered from the condemnation of death but is the source and cause of all evils. But all that reasoning has nothing to do with the present passage, for the word **"sin"** is not used in a general sense but relates to the subject now under consideration — as if Christ had said that their ignorance is utterly inexcusable because in his person they were maliciously rejecting God. It is as if we were to call someone innocent, just, and pure when we simply wanted to acquit him of a single crime he has been accused of. Christ acquits them only of one kind of sin, because it removes from the Jews the excuse of ignorance in despising and hating the Gospel.

But yet another question arises: was unbelief not enough to condemn people before Christ came? Some fanatics wrongly deduce from this passage that everyone who died before Christ came died without faith and remained in a state of doubt and suspense until Christ revealed himself to them — as if there were not many passages of Scripture which show that their conscience alone was enough to condemn them. Paul says, "Death reigned from the time of Adam to the time of Moses" (Romans 5:14), and, "All who sin apart from the law will also perish apart from the law" (Romans 2:12).

So what does Christ mean? Undoubtedly an admission is made in these words that the Jews have no more to offer in extenuation of their guilt since they knowingly and willfully rejected the life offered to them. Thus, the excuse which he allows them does not free them from all blame but only lessens the heinousness of their crime, as if he was saying, "The servant who knows his master's will, and despises it, will be punished more severely" (compare Luke 12:47). Christ was not here promising pardon to anyone but was convicting his enemies, who had obstinately rejected God's grace, so that it would be clear that they were unworthy of all pardon and mercy.

"If I had not come and spoken to them . . ." It should be observed that he does not speak of his coming by itself but connects it with his teaching; for they would not have been held guilty of such a great crime just because of his bodily presence. It was contempt of his teaching that made them utterly inexcusable.

23. This noteworthy passage teaches that no one can hate the Gospel teaching without showing his impiety against God. There are many people, certainly, who profess differently in words, for although they loathe the Gospel they still want to be thought very good servants of God; but they are worthless, for contempt of God is hidden inside them. In this way Christ reveals the hypocrisy of many people by the light of his teaching. We have spoken more fully on this subject under 3:20 and 5:23.

24. "If I had not done among them what no one else did . . ." I think he includes all the instances which he gave of his divine glory, for he clearly proved by miracles and by the Holy Spirit's power and by other examples that he was the Son of God, so that the majesty of the one and only was plainly seen in him (see 1:14). It is often objected that Christ did not perform more or greater miracles than Moses or the prophets. The explanation is well-known: Christ's miracles were more excellent in that he was not merely a minister like the rest but was actually their author, for when he performed miracles he used his own authority and his own power. But as I have said, he includes all the evidences of heavenly and spiritual power by which his divinity was displayed.

"They have seen these miracles, and yet they have hated . . ." He concludes that his enemies cannot get out of this, for they despise his power, which was clearly altogether divine. God had openly revealed his divinity in the Son, and therefore it would be in vain for them to say that they were only concerned with a mortal man. This passage warns us to consider God's works carefully, for in them he displays his power so that we may offer him the honor which is his due. Consequently, all those who obscure God's gifts or overlook them in contempt are ungrateful to God and malicious.

25. "But this is to fulfill what is written." What is contrary to nature seems incredible. But nothing is more contrary to reason than to hate God; therefore, Christ says that their minds were infected with such a great malice that **"'They hated me without reason.'"** Christ is quoting from Psalm 35:19, which he says is now fulfilled. Not that the same thing had not already happened to David, but Christ wants to reprove the nation for their obstinate malice, which prevailed continually from age to age, being forever passed from grandfathers to grandchildren. It is as if he had said that they were no better than their forefathers who had hated David for no reason.

By the word **"Law"** he means the Psalms, for the whole teaching of the prophets was simply an appendix to the law, and we know that Moses' ministry lasted until the time of Christ. He calls it **"their Law"** not to express honor for them but to wound them more deeply by a familiar title, as if he had said, "They have a law handed down to them by hereditary right, and in it they see their behavior graphically portrayed."

26. "When the Counselor comes . . ." Christ has explained to the apostles that they should not value the Gospel less because it has many enemies, even within the church itself. Now by the witness of the Spirit he opposes their wicked fury, and if this witness supports his followers' consciences they will never give way. It is as if he had said, "The world will indeed rage against you; some people will make fun of you, and others will curse your teaching, but none of their attacks will be so violent as to shake your faith when the Holy Spirit has been given to you to strengthen you by his witness." Indeed, when the world rages all around, our one protection is that God's truth, sealed by the Holy Spirit in our hearts, despises all that is in the world. If it were subject to human judgment, our faith would be overwhelmed a hundred times a day.

We should therefore note carefully how we should stand among so many tempests. It is because "we have not received the spirit of the world but the Spirit who is from God, that we may understand what God has freely given us" (1 Corinthians 2:12). This one testimony is able to drive away, scatter, and overturn whatever the world sets up to obscure or destroy God's truth. Whoever is endowed with this Spirit is so far from the danger of despairing over the hatred or contempt of the world that he will be victorious over the whole world. Yet we must beware of relying on the respect of men; for as long as our faith wanders like this, or rather as soon as it leaves God's sanctuary, it must waver miserably. It must therefore be recalled to the inner, secret witness of the Spirit, which believers know has been given to them from heaven.

The Spirit is said to **"testify about"** Christ because he keeps and settles our faith in him alone, so that we do not look for any part of our salvation anywhere else. And he calls him the **"Counselor,"** so that we may rely on his protection and never be afraid. By using this title, Christ wanted to strengthen our faith, so that it should not yield to any temptations. Also, when he calls him **"the Spirit of truth,"** it is to be applied to present circumstances. People who do not have this witness get carried away all over the place and have no firm resting-place; but wherever the Spirit speaks, he sets people's minds free from all doubt and fear of being deceived.

When he says that he will **"send"** him **"from the Father,"** and again that he **"goes out from the Father,"** he does so in order to increase the weight of his authority. Unless we were convinced that he had come from God, the witness of the Spirit would not be sufficient against such powerful attacks and so many fierce devices. So it is Christ who sends the Spirit, but from the heavenly glory, so that we may know it is not a human gift but a sure pledge of God's grace. From this it is clear how idle was the Greeks' subtlety when they denied that the Spirit comes from the Son, for Christ, as usual, names the Father here in order to raise our eyes to contemplate his divinity.

27. "But you also must testify." Christ means that the Spirit's testimony will not be such that the apostles will have it to themselves, or that they alone will enjoy it, but that it will be widely broadcast by them because they will be the Spirit's instruments, as if he spoke by their lips. We see how "faith comes from hearing" (Romans 10:17) and yet derives its certainty from the seal and deposit of the Spirit (see Ephesians 1:13-14). Those who are not aware enough of the darkness of the human mind think that faith is formed naturally, just by preaching. On the other hand, there are fanatics who scorn external preaching and wonderfully breathe secret revelations and "enthusiasm." But we see that Christ joins these two together. Therefore, although there is no faith until God's Spirit enlightens our minds and seals our hearts, we must still not try and look for visions or oracles from the clouds; but the Word, which is near us, in our mouth and heart (see Deuteronomy 30:14; Romans 10:8), must keep all our senses bound and fixed on itself, as Isaiah 59:21 beautifully says: "My Spirit, who is on you, and my words that I have put in your mouth will not depart from your mouth, or from the mouths of your children, or from the mouths of their descendants from this time on and forever."

"For you have been with me from the beginning." This was put in to tell us that all the more credit is due to the apostles because they were eyewitnesses of what they proclaim. As 1 John 1:1 puts it: "That . . . which we have heard, which we have seen with our eyes, which we have looked at and our hands have touched." Thus the Lord wanted to provide for our welfare in every possible way, so that nothing might be lacking for the complete confirmation of the Gospel.

John
Chapter 16

Verses 1–7

1. "All this I have told you . . ." Again he says that nothing he has said is superfluous: wars and struggles await them, so they must be provided with the necessary weapons beforehand. But he also means that if they meditate deeply on his teaching, they will be ready to resist. Let us also remember that what he said then to his disciples is said to us.

First, we must understand that Christ does not send his followers into the arena unarmed, and therefore no one can fail in this warfare except through his own laziness. But we must not wait until we are in the midst of the battle, but must try to get to know these words of Christ and let them become familiar to our minds, so that we can engage in the battle when necessary. We must not doubt that the victory is in our hands as long as those warnings of Christ are deeply impressed on our minds. For when he says, **"so that you will not go astray,"** he means that there is no danger of anything forcing us aside from the right course. But how few learn this doctrine properly is clear from the fact that those who seem to know it by heart when they are out of range give way as soon as they actually have to start fighting, as if they are completely ignorant and had never received any instruction. Let us therefore familiarize ourselves with these weapons so that we never forget how to use them.

2. "They will put you out of the synagogue." It was no little obstacle to their minds that they were to be banished like criminals from the assembly of the godly, or at least from those who boasted that they were God's people and rejoiced in the title of "the church." For believers are subject not only to persecutions but also to reproach and ignominy, as Paul tells us (1 Corinthians 4:11-13). But Christ commands them to stand firm against this attack because though they may be banished from the synagogue, they still remain in God's kingdom. In short, we should not be crushed by people's perverse judgments, but should endure boldly the reproach of Christ's cross and be content with this one thought: our cause may be wickedly condemned by other people, but God approves of it.

Moreover, we gather from this that the ministers of the Gospel are not only ill-treated by the avowed enemies of the faith, but sometimes endure the greatest reproaches from those who are apparently members, even pillars, of the church. The teachers of the law and the priests, who condemned the apostles, boasted that God had appointed them to govern the church; and, indeed, the ordinary government of the church was in their hands, and their office as rulers was divine and not human. But by their tyranny they corrupted the whole order which God had instituted. Consequently, the power which had been given to them for building up was nothing but a monstrous oppression of God's servants; and excommunication, which should have been a medicine to purge the church, was used in the opposite way, to drive out the fear of God.

Since the apostles had experienced this in their own age, we have no reason to be greatly alarmed at the Pope's anathemas which he thunders against us because of the Gospel witness; for we should not fear that they will hurt us any more than the early ones hurt the apostles. In fact, nothing is more desirable than to be driven out of any assembly from which Christ is banished. Yet let us note that though excommunication was so greatly abused, it still did not manage to destroy the discipline which God had appointed in his church from the beginning; for although Satan tries his hardest to corrupt all God's ordinances, we must not give in to him by letting corruption take away what God consecrated forever. Therefore excommunication, just as much as baptism and the Lord's Supper, must be brought back to its correct and lawful use by correcting its abuses.

"In fact, a time is coming . . ." Christ emphasizes this stumbling block, that the Gospel's enemies claim such authority that they think they are offering holy sacrifices to God when they kill believers. It is hard enough for innocent people to be cruelly tormented, but it is far more bitter and distressing that the outrages which the wicked commit against the children of God should be regarded as proper punishment for their crimes. But we should be so certain of the protection of a good conscience that we can patiently bear being oppressed for a time until Christ appears from heaven to defend his cause and ours.

However, it is surprising that the enemies of the truth, although aware of their own evil, not only deceive people but even claim before God to deserve praise for their unjust cruelty. I reply that hypocrites, although their consciences accuse them, always turn to flattery to deceive themselves. They are ambitious, cruel, and proud; but they cover all these vices with a cloak of zeal, so that they may indulge in them with impunity. To this is added a wild sort of drunkenness after they are steeped in the blood of the martyrs.

3. "They will do such things . . ." Not for nothing, Christ frequently reminds the apostles that unbelievers rage against them so much only because they do not know God. This is not said to lessen their guilt, but so that the apostles may boldly despise their blind fury. The authority of the ungodly, and the splendor which shines in them, often shake modest and godly minds. Christ, on the other hand, tells his followers to rise up and with holy sublimity despise their enemies, who are only motivated by error and blindness. This is our strong wall, when we are convinced that God is on our side and those who oppose us are destitute of reason. Again, these words warn us what a serious evil ignorance of God is; it even leads people who have murdered their own parents to look for praise and applause for their crime.

4. "... so that when the time comes you will remember that I warned you." He repeats what he has already said: this is not an academic philosophy, but one suitable for practice and use. Now he talks about these matters so that they may show in practice that they have not been taught in vain. First, he tells them to store in their minds what they have heard; second, to remember them when they need to be used; and third, he says that it is important that he foretells things to come.

"I did not tell you this at first." Because the apostles were still delicate and weak as long as Christ was with them in the flesh, their most good and kind Master spared them and would not let them be pressed beyond what they were able to bear. Therefore, they had no great need of being strengthened while they were given leisure and freedom from persecution. Now he warns them that they must change their outlook; as a new stage awaits them, he urges them to prepare for a struggle.

5. "Now I am going to him who sent me." With the best of consolations, he reduces the grief which they might feel at his leaving them. This was very necessary. Up to now they had been pampered, but in the future they were to face severe and hard battles. What would have become of them if they had not known that Christ, the guardian of their salvation, was in heaven? For going to the Father is nothing but being received into the heavenly glory so as to possess the highest authority. So this is offered to them as a solace and remedy for grief: Christ, though absent in body, sits at the right hand of the Father to protect believers by his power.

Here Christ reproves the apostles for two faults: they were too much attached to the visible presence of his flesh, and when this had been taken away they were overcome by grief (verse 6) and did not raise their eyes. The same thing happens to us, for we always restrict Christ to our senses, and then, if he does not appear as we desire, we make it a matter of despair.

It may seem a false charge against the apostles that they did not ask where their Master was going, for they had asked him about this earlier. But the explanation is easy: when they asked, they did not raise their minds to trust, as they should have done most of all. And so the meaning is: "As soon as you hear of my departure, you become alarmed and do not stop to think where or why I am going."

7. "But I tell you the truth . . ." He tells them that his absence will be useful and uses a sort of oath, so that they may give up wanting to have him visibly present. Because we are sinful, nothing is harder than to tear from our minds this foolish attitude by which we drag Christ down from heaven to us. He explains what the advantage is by saying that the Holy Spirit could not be given to them in any other way than by his leaving the world. But he offers himself to us through the grace and power of his Spirit, and this is far more useful and desirable than if we could see him. And we must now ask whether Christ could not have drawn down the Holy Spirit while he dwelt on earth. Christ takes for granted everything that the Father has decreed. And, indeed, when once the Lord has shown us what he wishes to be done, it is foolish and harmful to argue about what is possible.

Verses 8–15

8. "When he comes . . ." Leaving aside the variety of expositions which have been produced by the obscurity of this passage, I will state only what seems to me to be Christ's true meaning. He had promised his Spirit to the disciples. He now shows the excellence of this gift by its effects, for not only will the Spirit rule, sustain, and protect them individually, but his effect and power will be felt more widely.

"He will convict the world." That is, "He will not remain shut up in you, but his power will go out from you to be shown to the whole world." He therefore promises them a Spirit who will be the Judge of the world, and by whom their preaching will become so alive and effective that it will bring to order people who were running riot in unbridled licentiousness and were not restrained by any fear or reverence.

It should be noted that Christ is not here speaking about secret revelations, but about the power of the Spirit, which appears in the external teaching of the Gospel and in human speech. How can someone's voice penetrate minds, take root there, and eventually produce fruit, making hearts of stone into hearts of flesh and renewing the people themselves, unless the Spirit of Christ makes the Word alive? Otherwise it would be a dead letter and an empty sound, as Paul so beautifully teaches in 2 Corinthians 3:6, where he boasts of being a minister of the Spirit in that God worked powerfully in his teaching. Therefore, the meaning is that since the apostles had been given the Spirit, they would be given a heavenly and divine power by which they would exercise jurisdiction over the whole world. This is ascribed to the Spirit rather than to themselves, because they will have no power of their own but will only be ministers and instruments; the Spirit alone will preside over them.

I think that the word **"world"** includes both those who were to be truly converted to Christ and hypocrites and reprobates. For the Spirit convicts people in two ways in the preaching of the Gospel. Some people are deeply moved and humble themselves of their own accord; they agree willingly with the judgment which condemns them. Others, although they are convinced of guilt and cannot escape, do not sincerely yield or submit to the Spirit's authority and control. On the contrary, when they are subdued they groan inwardly, and although they are beaten they still do not stop cherishing an inner obstinacy.

We now understand how the Spirit was to **"convict"** the world through the apostles. It was because God revealed his judgment in the Gospel, by which their consciences were struck and they began to see what was wrong with them and how gracious God is. What Paul says in 1 Corinthians 14:24 will shed no little light on this passage: "If an unbeliever or someone who does not understand comes in while everybody is prophesying, he will be convinced by all that he is a sinner and will be judged by all." There Paul is speaking particularly about one kind of conviction — that is, when the Lord leads his elect to repentance by the Gospel. But this clearly shows how God's Spirit, through the sound of a human voice, leads people who were previously unused to his yoke to acknowledge and submit to his rule.

It may now be asked why Christ said this. Some people think he is showing the cause of the hatred which he had mentioned, as if he had said that they will be hated by the world because the Spirit for his part will urge **"the world"** through them. But I agree rather with those who say that Christ's purpose was different, as I intimated at the beginning of my comment on this verse. It was very important for the apostles to know that the gift of the Spirit which was promised to them was no ordinary thing. He therefore describes its unique excellence by saying that in this way God will set up his judgment-seat to judge the whole world.

9. ". . . in regard to sin . . ." It now remains to be seen what it is to **"convict"** people of **"sin."** Christ seems to make unbelief the only cause of sin; and this is twisted by commentators in various ways. But as I have already said, I shall not refer to what individuals teach or think. First, it is to be noted that the judgment of the Spirit begins with the demonstration of **"sin."** The beginning of spiritual teaching is that people born in sin have in them nothing but the material of sin. Again Christ mentions unbelief, to show what human nature is in itself. Since faith is the bond by which he unites himself to us, we are outside him and separated from him until we believe in him. It is as if he had said, "When the Spirit comes, he will show and convince you that outside me sin reigns in the world." Unbelief is mentioned here because it separates us from Christ; consequently, nothing is left to us but **"sin."** In short, by these words he condemns the corruption and depravity of human nature, so that we should not think there is a single drop of uprightness in us without Christ.

10. "... in regard to righteousness ..." We must keep to the series of steps which Christ lays down. He now says that the world must be convicted of **"righteousness,"** for people will never hunger and thirst after righteousness, but on the contrary will contemptuously reject everything that is said about it unless they have felt convicted of **"sin."** We must understand that believers, in particular, cannot progress in the Gospel till they have first been humbled, and this cannot happen until they are aware of their sins. Certainly it is the particular task of the law to summon consciences to God's judgment-seat and to strike them with terror; but the Gospel cannot be preached properly without leading from **"sin"** to **"righteousness"** and from death to life. Therefore it is necessary to borrow from the law that first clause of which Christ spoke.

"Righteousness" here means that which is communicated to us by Christ's grace. Christ associates this with his ascension to the Father — and with good reason. Just as Paul declares that "he was ... raised to life for our justification" (Romans 4:25), so now Christ sits at the Father's right hand in such a way as to exercise all the authority that has been given to him and to "fill the whole universe" (Ephesians 4:10). In short, from his heavenly glory he fills the world with the sweet smell of his **"righteousness."** Now the Spirit proclaims by the Gospel that this is the only way in which we are accounted righteous. The next step after the conviction of **"sin"** is for the Spirit to convince the world what true **"righteousness"** is — namely, that Christ by his ascension into heaven has established the kingdom of life and now sits at the Father's right hand to confirm true **"righteousness."**

11. "... in regard to judgment ..." Those who understand the word "judgment" as meaning "condemnation" are not being unreasonable, for Christ immediately adds that **the prince of this world now stands condemned."** But it seems to me that a different sense fits better: now that the light of the Gospel has been kindled, the Spirit reveals that the world has been ordered and set to rights by Christ's victory, in which he overthrew Satan's rule. It is as if he had said that it is a true restoration by which everything is reformed, when Christ alone holds the kingdom, having subdued and triumphed over Satan. **"Judgment,"** therefore, is contrasted with what is confused and disordered; or, to put it briefly, it is the opposite of confusion. Or we might say it is "uprightness," a sense it often bears in Scripture. The meaning, therefore, is that Satan, as long as he holds power, mixes and stirs everything up, so that there is a horrible and deformed confusion in God's works. But when Christ strips him of his tyranny, the world is restored, and a well-tempered order appears. Thus the Spirit convicts the world in regard to **"judgment"**;

that is, having overcome the prince of wickedness, Christ restores to order what was previously collapsed and broken.

12. "I have much more to say to you." Christ's sermon could not have so much influence over his disciples as to stop their ignorance from keeping them puzzled about **"many things"** (KJV). Indeed, they hardly had a taste of what should have renewed them completely if it were not for the weakness of their flesh. Awareness of their poverty, therefore, could not but oppress them with fear and anxiety; but Christ counters this by saying that when they receive the Spirit they will be new and very different men.

". . . more than you can now bear." When he says that they would not be able to **"bear"** it if he now told them more, or more exalted, things, his purpose is to encourage them with the hope of greater progress, so that they do not lose heart. They should not estimate the grace he was to give them by their present feelings, since they were so far from heaven. In short, he tells them to be cheerful and courageous however weak they may be at present. Moreover, as they had nothing but his teaching to rely on, Christ tells them that he has accommodated it to their capacity; but they may soon hope for something higher and richer. It is as though he were saying, "If what you have heard from me is not yet enough to make you firm, be patient for a while. Before long, when the Spirit has taught you, you will need nothing more. He will remove all your present ignorance."

Now it may be asked what those things were which the apostles were not yet able to learn. The Roman Catholics, who put forward their own inventions as the oracles of God, wickedly abuse this passage. "Christ," they tell us, "promised the apostles new revelations, and therefore we must not stop at the Scripture, for here he promises his followers something beyond Scripture." First, if they want to talk with Augustine, the solution will be found easily, for he says, "Since Christ is silent, which of us is to say it was this or that? Or if someone does dare to say, how will he prove it? Who is so boastful and impudent, even if what he says is true, as to affirm without any divine testimony that those are the things which the Lord did not wish to say at that time?" But there is a surer way of refuting them, in Christ's own words which follow.

13. "But when he, the Spirit of truth, comes . . ." Here **"the Spirit"** whom Christ promised to the apostles is said to be the perfect teacher of **"truth."** And why was he promised, but for them to pass on the wisdom which they had received from him? This was given to them by the Spirit, by whose leading they discharged the office to which they had been appointed.

"He will guide you into all truth." The same Spirit led them into **"all truth"** when they wrote down the substance of their teaching. Whoever thinks that anything ought to be added to their teaching, as if it were imperfect and incomplete, not only accuses the apostles of dishonesty but blasphemes against the Spirit. If the teaching they committed to writing had come from mere learners or novices, it would have needed adding to; but as their writings may be regarded as permanent records of the revelation promised and given to them, nothing can be added to them without terrible injustice to the Spirit.

When they come to establish what those things actually were, the Roman Catholics are quite ridiculous, for they define those mysteries which the apostles were unable to bear as certain childish nonsense, the most absurd and stupid things imaginable. Did the Spirit have to come down from heaven for the apostles to learn what by what ceremony to consecrate cups and altars, baptize church bells, bless holy water, and celebrate Mass? So how do fools and children learn when they understand all those things so precisely? It is perfectly clear that the Roman Catholics are mocking God when they claim that those things came from heaven; they are as like the mysteries of Ceres or Proserpine as they are unlike the pure wisdom of the Spirit.

If we do not want to be ungrateful to God, let us be satisfied with the teaching which the apostles say they wrote, since the highest perfection of heavenly wisdom is revealed in that teaching which makes the man of God complete (compare 2 Timothy 3:17). We must not think ourselves free to go beyond this, for our height and breadth and depth consist in knowing the love of God which is revealed to us in Christ (see Ephesians 3:18). This knowledge, as Paul tells us, surpasses knowledge (compare Ephesians 3:19); and when he declares that "all the treasures of wisdom and knowledge" are hidden in Christ (Colossians 2:3), he is not inventing some unknown Christ but one he pictured in his preaching, so that, as he says in Galatians 3:1, "Before your very eyes Jesus Christ was clearly portrayed as crucified." But to remove all ambiguity, Christ himself later explains in his own words what the things were which the apostles were not yet able to bear.

"He will tell you what is yet to come." Some people limit this to the Spirit of prophecy, but in my opinion it means the future state of his spiritual kingdom, which the apostles saw soon after his resurrection, but were then quite unable to comprehend. So he is not promising them predictions of things that would happen after their death, but only means that his kingdom would be very different and its glory much greater than their minds are now able to conceive. Paul, in Ephesians 1 — 4, explains the treasures of this hidden wisdom, which even the angels in heaven learn with amazement through the church (see Ephesians 3:10). So there is no need to look for them in the papal archives or repositories.

"He will not speak on his own." This confirms the clause **"he will guide you into all truth."** We know that God is the source of **"truth"** and that outside him nothing is sure or solid. So Christ declares that the oracles of the Spirit will be divine, and the apostles may put their full trust in them. It is as if he were saying that whatever the Spirit brings comes from God himself. And yet these words do not diminish the Spirit's majesty, as if he were not God or were inferior to the Father; but they are adapted to our understanding. His divinity is explicitly stated since, because of the veil that is between us, we do not properly understand how reverently we should receive what the Spirit reveals to us. Elsewhere he is called the "deposit" by which God guarantees our salvation and the "seal" by which he endorses its certainty (see Ephesians 1:13-14). In short, Christ wanted to tell us that the teaching of the Spirit would not be of this world, as if it were produced in the air, but would come from the secret places of his heavenly sanctuary.

14. "He will bring glory to me." Christ now tells them that the Spirit will not come to set up any new kingdom, but rather will confirm the **"glory"** given to him by the Father. Many people imagine that Christ taught only the rudiments and then sent the disciples to a higher school. Thus they make the Gospel no more than the law, which was "put in charge to lead us to Christ" (Galatians 3:24).

This error is followed by another just as intolerable, that having said good-bye to Christ's law, as if his reign had come to an end and he was nothing at all, they substitute the Spirit in his place. From this source come the sacrileges of Roman Catholicism and Islam, for although these differ from each other in many respects, they have a common starting point — that in the Gospel we are initiated into the true faith, but we must look elsewhere for the full teaching to make us perfect. If Scripture is quoted against the Pope, he denies that we should confine ourselves to it, because the Spirit has come and has carried us beyond Scripture by many additional things. Muhammad claims that without his Koran people always remain children. Thus, by falsely claiming the Spirit, the world has been bewitched to leave the simple purity of Christ; for as soon as the Spirit is separated from the Word of Christ, the door is open to all sorts of madness and impostures. In our own day, many fanatics have tried a similar method of deceiving. The written teaching seems to them to be of the letter, and so they have chosen to make up a new theology based on revelations.

We now see that Christ's instruction that he would be glorified by the Spirit whom he was going to send is not superfluous. It was intended to teach us that the role of the Holy Spirit was simply to establish Christ's kingdom and to maintain and confirm forever everything the Father had given him. What then is the purpose of the Spirit's teaching? It is not to withdraw us from the school of Christ, but rather to ratify that word by which we are commanded to listen to him; otherwise he would diminish Christ's **"glory."** Then Christ adds the reason.

". . . by taking from what is mine." By these words Christ means that we receive the Spirit in order to enjoy Christ's benefits. What does he give us? Washing in Christ's blood; sin being blotted out in us by his death; our old self being crucified; his resurrection being effective in reforming us to newness of life; and, in short, coming to share in his blessing. Therefore, the Spirit gives us nothing apart from Christ; he takes from Christ what he gives us. We should think the same about his teaching, for in enlightening us he does not lead us away from Christ in the slightest, but fulfills what Paul says: Christ "has become for us wisdom from God" (1 Corinthians 1:30) and displays the "treasures of wisdom and knowledge" which are hidden in Christ (see Colossians 2:3). In a word, the Spirit gives us only the riches of Christ, that in everything he may display his **"glory."**

15. "All that belongs to the Father is mine." As it might seem that Christ takes away from the Father what he claimed for himself, he acknowledges that he has received from the Father everything that he communicates to us by his Spirit. He speaks as the Mediator, for we must receive from his fullness. He always thinks of us, as we have said. But on the other hand, we see that most people deceive themselves, for they pass Christ by and seek God by circuitous ways.

Others explain these words as meaning that **"all that belongs to the Father"** belongs equally to the Son, because he is the same God. But he is not speaking here about his hidden and, so to speak, intrinsic power so much as about the task which he has been given with relation to us. In short, he tells of his riches so that he may invite us to enjoy them, and he counts the Spirit among the gifts which we receive from the Father by his hand.

Verses 16–20

16. "In a little while you will see me no more." Christ had often forewarned the apostles of his departure, partly so that they might bear it with greater courage and partly so that they might more ardently long for the grace of the Spirit, for which they had no great desire while they had Christ with them physically. We must therefore beware of getting tired of reading what Christ, not without cause, insists on. First, he tells them that he will soon be taken away from them, so that they may remain firm when they lose his presence, on which alone they were relying. Next, he promises them help in his absence; indeed, he declares that soon after he has been taken away, he will be restored to them, but in a different way — that is, by the presence of the Holy Spirit.

"And then after a little while you will see me." Some people explain this second clause differently: "You will see me when I have risen from the dead, but only for a short time; for I shall soon be received into heaven." But I do not think the words will allow this interpretation. On the contrary, he relieves and soothes their sorrow over his absence by the consoling assurance that it will not last long. And so he commends the grace of the Spirit, by which he will be present with them forever. It is as though he was promising that after a little while he would return and they would not be without him for long.

Nor should we think it odd that he says he is *seen* when he lives in the disciples by the Spirit; for although he is not seen with the eyes, his presence is known by the sure experience of faith. What Paul teaches us is indeed true — that believers, as long as they remain on earth, are away from the Lord, because they live by faith and not by sight (see 2 Corinthians 5:6-7). But it is equally true that, meanwhile, they can justly glory that they have Christ living in them by faith, that they are joined to him as parts of the body to the head, that by hope they possess heaven along with him. So the grace of the Spirit is a mirror in which Christ wants to be seen by us. As Paul says, "Though we once regarded Christ [from a worldly point of view], we do so no longer. Therefore, if anyone is in Christ, he is a new creation" (2 Corinthians 5:16-17).

17. "Because I am going to the Father." Some people explain these words as meaning that Christ will no longer be seen by the disciples because he will be in heaven and they on earth. I would rather refer it to the second clause: "You will soon see me, for my death is not a destruction which will separate me from you, but a passing to the heavenly glory, from which my divine power will spread to you." So in my opinion, he wanted to teach them about his state after death, so that they might be content with his spiritual presence and not regard it as a loss to them that he no longer dwelt with them as a mortal man.

19. Jesus saw . . . Though sometimes the Lord seems to be speaking to the deaf, he at last comes to the help of his disciples' ignorance, so that his teaching may not be useless. We must strive that our slowness is not accompanied by pride or laziness, but that we show ourselves on the contrary to be humble and willing to learn.

20. "You will weep and mourn." He shows why he told them that his departure was close at hand, and at the same time adds a promise about his prompt return. This was so that they might understand better how much they needed the help of the Spirit. He says: "A hard and severe temptation awaits you, for when I am taken away from you by death, the world will triumph over you. You will feel the deepest sorrow. The world will think itself happy and you miserable. I have therefore determined to give you the weapons you need for this warfare." He describes the time between his death and the day when the Spirit is sent, for it was then that their faith lay, so to speak, overwhelmed.

"Your grief will turn to joy." He means the "joy" they would have when they had received the Spirit — not that they would be free from all sorrow after that, but all the sorrow which they would endure would be swallowed up by spiritual "joy." We know that the apostles fought a hard battle as long as they lived, that they endured shameful reproaches, that they had many reasons for weeping. But, renewed by the Spirit, they put off their previous feeling of weakness, so that with lofty hero-ism they easily trampled underfoot all the evils that they experienced. Here their present weakness is compared with the power of the Spirit which was soon to be given to them; for although they were almost overwhelmed for a time, they afterwards not only fought bravely, but won a glorious victory in the midst of their wars. Yet it should also be noted that Christ points out not only the interval between his resurrec-tion and the death of the apostles, but also the period which followed afterwards — as if he were saying, "You will lie prostrate, as it were, for a short time; but when the Spirit has raised you, a new joy will begin and will continue to increase until you are received into the heavenly glory, and then you will have perfect joy."

Verses 21–24

21. **"A woman giving birth to a child . . ."** He uses a metaphor to confirm the statement he has just made. Or rather, he expresses his meaning more clearly: not only will their sorrow be turned into **"joy,"** but it bears within itself the matter and ground of **"joy."** It often hap-pens that when prosperity follows adversity people forget their earlier grief and give themselves up completely to joy, and yet the earlier grief is not the cause of the joy. But Christ means that the sorrow they will endure for the Gospel's sake will be fruitful. Indeed, the result of all griefs can only be unhappy unless they are blessed in Christ. But as the cross of Christ always contains in itself the victory, he justly compares the sorrow arising from it with the sorrow of a woman in labor, which is rewarded when she is cheered by the child's birth. The image would not fit if sorrow did not produce **"joy"** in Christ's members when they share in his suffering, just as the woman's labor causes the birth. The image must also be applied in that although the woman's sorrow is very severe, it quickly passes away. It was no small relief to the apostles, therefore, when they heard that their sorrow would not last long.

We must now apply this teaching to ourselves. Having been regener-ated by the Spirit of Christ, we should have such a **"joy"** flourishing in us that all feeling of our ills will vanish. We should be like women in labor, for whom the mere sight of the baby so moves them that their pain no longer hurts. But as we have received only the firstfruits, and these are very tenuous, we hardly feel more than a few drops of that spiritual gladness which is sprinkled on our pain and soothes its bitterness. And yet that small amount clearly shows that those who contemplate Christ by faith are so far from ever being overwhelmed by sorrow that in their worst sufferings they rejoice with great **"joy."**

But since all creatures are required to labor till the final day of redemption, let us know that we too must groan until we are set free from the unending miseries of the present life and see clearly the fruit of our faith. To sum up, believers are like women in labor because when they are born again in Christ they have already entered into the heavenly kingdom of God and the blessed life. They are like pregnant women in labor because they are still held captive in the prison of the flesh while they long for that happy state which lies hidden under hope.

22. "And no one will take away your joy." The value of the **"joy"** is greatly increased because it is forever. It follows that the sufferings are light, and we should endure them calmly because they only last a short time. By these words Christ tells us what true **"joy"** is like. The world inevitably loses its joys quickly, for it seeks them only in things that fade. Therefore we must come to Christ's resurrection, in which there is eternal stability.

"I will see you again." Here he means that he will visit them again by the grace of his Spirit, and they will enjoy his presence forever.

23. "You will no longer ask me anything." When Christ has promised the disciples **"joy"** from their unshaken firmness and courage, he talks about another grace of the Spirit which will be given to them. They will receive such a light of understanding that they will be raised to heavenly mysteries. At the time they were so slow that the slightest difficulty of any kind made them hesitate; as children learning the alphabet cannot read a single line without many pauses, so the disciples stumbled at almost everything Christ said. But a little later, when they had been enlightened by the Holy Spirit, they no longer suffered any delay in becoming familiar and acquainted with the wisdom of God, so as to progress among the mysteries of God without stumbling.

Certainly the apostles did not cease to inquire of Christ, even when they had been raised to the highest degree of wisdom, but this is only a comparison between the two states, as if Christ had said that their ignorance would be corrected so that, instead of being stopped by the least thing as they were now, they would penetrate the most sublime mysteries with ease. So we read in Jeremiah 31:34, "'No longer will a man teach his neighbor, or a man his brother, saying, "Know the Lord," because they will all know me, from the least of them to the greatest,' declares the Lord." The prophet is not taking away or abolishing teaching, which must flourish most in Christ's kingdom; but he says that when everyone is taught by God, there will be no room left for the gross ignorance which rules people's minds until Christ, the sun of righteousness, enlightens them by the rays of his Spirit. Besides, although the apostles were very like children and, indeed, were more like blocks of wood than men, we know well what they became when they had been taught by the Spirit.

"My Father will give you whatever you ask in my name." He tells them where they will get this new ability. They will be able to draw freely as much as they need from God, the fount of wisdom — as if he had said, "You must not fear that you will lack the gift of understanding, for **my Father** will be ready with all the abundance of blessings to enrich you bountifully." Moreover, he is warning them by these words that the Spirit is not promised in such a way that those to whom he is promised may wait for him lazing about and snoring, but that they must on the contrary be earnest in seeking the grace offered. In short, he tells them that he will then fulfill the role of Mediator in such a way as to obtain for them from the Father whatever they ask for.

But here arises a difficult question. Was this the first time that people used the name of Christ to call on God, who could never be favorable to anybody except for the sake of the Mediator? Christ is describing the future, when the **Father** will give the disciples whatever they ask in his name. If this is a new and unusual favor, it would seem that we may infer that while he lived on earth, he did not exercise the office of advocate through whom believers' prayers became acceptable to God. This is still more clearly expressed by what immediately follows.

24. "Until now you have not asked for anything in my name." The apostles probably observed the rule of prayer laid down in the law, but we know that the fathers were not used to praying without a mediator. God had trained them by many exercises to use such a form of prayer. They saw the high priest enter the holy place in the name of the whole people. They saw sacrifices offered every day, that the prayers of the church might be acceptable to God. It was therefore one of the principles of faith that to call on God without a mediator would be rash and useless. Christ had already told his disciples plainly enough that he was the Mediator, but their knowledge was so obscure that they could not yet form their prayers properly in his name.

Nor is it silly to say that they prayed to God trusting in the Mediator, as the law demanded, without clearly and fully understanding what that meant. The veil of the temple was still drawn across; God's majesty was still concealed underneath the cherubim; the true High Priest had not yet entered the heavenly sanctuary to intercede for his people and had not yet consecrated the way by his blood. It is therefore not surprising if he was not acknowledged as the Mediator, as he is now that he appears in heaven for us before the Father, reconciling him to us by his boldness. For indeed, after Christ had expiated our sin and been received into heaven, he openly showed himself to be the Mediator.

We should note the frequent repetition of the phrase that we must pray in Christ's **"name."** We learn from this that it is a wicked profanation of God's name when anyone ventures to present himself at God's judgment-seat without going through Christ. If we are deeply convinced that God will bountifully give us whatever we **"ask"** in the **"name"** of his Son, we shall not go here and there for advocates to help us, but will be content with the One who so often and so kindly offers us his labors.

We are said to pray "in the name of Christ" when we take him as our advocate to reconcile us to his Father's favor, even though we may not explicitly mention his name with our lips.

"Ask and you will receive." This refers to the time when he was to be revealed, shortly afterwards. People who obscure this teaching today by claiming the protection of the saints are all the less excusable. Previously people had to turn their eyes to the high priest (who foreshadowed Christ) and to the sacrificial animals whenever they wanted to pray. We are more than ungrateful if we do not keep our senses fixed on the true High Priest who is displayed to us as our propitiator, through whom we may have free and ready access to the throne of God's glory.

"And your joy will be complete." By this he means that nothing will be lacking for the perfect abundance of all blessings, provided that we ask God for whatever we need in his name.

Verses 25–28

25. "Though I have been speaking figuratively . . ." Christ's purpose is to encourage his disciples, so that they may hope to make better progress and may not think that the teaching they now hear is useless — even though they may not understand much of it. They might begin to think Christ did not want to be understood and that he was deliberately keeping them in suspense; so he tells them that they will soon see the fruit of this teaching, which they might not care for because of its obscurity. The Hebrew word *mashal* sometimes means "proverb," but as proverbs usually contain figures of speech the Hebrew word *meshalim* is used for allegories or remarkable sayings, which the Greek call *apophthegmata* — containing something ambiguous or obscure. The meaning therefore is, "I seem to you to be speaking figuratively now, and not simply or plainly; but I will soon speak to you in a more familiar way, so that there may be nothing perplexing or difficult for you in my teaching."

Here we see what I mentioned above: the disciples are encouraged with the hope of further progress, so that they may not reject the teaching because they do not yet understand what it means. Unless we are excited by the hope of making headway, our desire to learn will inevitably cool. However, this fact clearly shows that Christ was not speaking allegorically but was using a simple and even elementary way of speaking to his disciples; but they were so ignorant that they listened to him with astonishment. The obscurity therefore lay not so much in the teaching as in their minds. And, indeed, the same thing happens to us today, for God's Word is called our light, and not without reason. But its brightness is so clouded by our darkness that we think we are listening to mere allegories. God threatens through the prophet that he will not be understood by unbelievers or the reprobate, as if he had a stammer (see Isaiah 28:11), and Paul says that the Gospel is hidden from such people because Satan has blinded their minds (2 Corinthians 4:4). Similarly, weak and ignorant people find that it sounds so confused that they cannot understand it, for although their minds are not completely darkened, like those of unbelievers, they are still, so to speak, enveloped by mists. So the Lord permits us to be stupefied for a while, to humble us by a conviction of our own poverty. But when he enlightens people by his Spirit, they make such progress that his Word is familiar and known to them.

That is the meaning of the next clause, **"a time is coming"** — that is, will soon come — **"when I will no longer use this kind of language."** The Holy Spirit certainly did not teach the apostles anything other than what they had heard from the mouth of Christ himself; but by shining into their hearts, he lit up their darkness, and they heard Christ speak in a new and different way and easily understood what he meant.

". . . but will tell you plainly about my Father." In these words he reminds us that the purpose of his teaching is to lead us to God, in whom solid happiness lies. But another question remains: why does he say elsewhere that the knowledge of the secrets of the kingdom of heaven has been given to the disciples (Matthew 13:11)? Here he acknowledges that he has spoken to them allegorically, but there he makes a distinction between them and the rest of the people, to whom he spoke in parables. I reply: the apostles' ignorance was not so great that they did not have at least a slight taste of what their Master meant, and so it is not without cause that he separated them from the blind. He now says that his Word has until now been allegorical in comparison with the clear light of understanding which he would soon give them by the grace of his Spirit. Both statements are therefore true — that the disciples were far above those who had no taste for the Word of the Gospel, and yet they were still like children learning their ABCs, compared with the new wisdom which the Spirit would give them.

26. "In that day . . ." He repeats the reason why the heavenly treasures were to be so liberally opened up. It is because they would ask for whatever they need in the **"name"** of Christ. God will refuse nothing that is asked in the **"name"** of his Son. But there seems to be a contradiction in the words, for Christ immediately adds that it will not be necessary for him to pray to **"the Father."** Now what is the point of praying in his name if he does not act as intercessor? Elsewhere John calls him our advocate (1 John 2:1), and Paul says that Christ is now interceding for us (Romans 8:34); the same thing is confirmed by Hebrews 7:25. I reply: Christ does not actually say in this passage that he will not be our intercessor, but only that the Father will be so favorably disposed towards the disciples that he will freely give them whatever they ask, without any difficulty. What Christ is saying is, "The Father will meet you and, because of his great love for you, will anticipate the intercessor who otherwise would speak on your behalf."

When it says that Christ intercedes with **"the Father"** for us, we should not imagine anything physical is meant, as if he were on his knees before **"the Father"** offering humble supplication for us. But the virtue of his sacrifice by which he pacified God's wrath towards us is always powerful and effective. The blood by which he atoned for our sins, his obedience, is a continual intercession for us. This remarkable passage teaches us that we have the heart of God as soon as we place before him the **"name"** of his Son.

27. "Because you have loved me . . ." These words tell us that the only bond of our union with God is that of being united with Christ, and we are united to him by an unfeigned faith which springs from the sincere attitude which he calls love. No one believes sincerely in Christ if he does not embrace him in his heart; so Christ has expressed the power and nature of faith well by using this word. But if God only begins to love us when we have loved Christ, it follows that the beginning of salvation is from ourselves, because we have anticipated the grace of God. But many passages of Scripture contradict this idea. God promises, "I will cause them to love me," and John says, "not that we loved God" (1 John 4:10). It would be superfluous to collect many passages, for nothing is more certain than this doctrine, that the Lord "calls things that are not" (Romans 4:17), raises the dead, joins with strangers, forms hearts of flesh out of stones, reveals himself to those who are not seeking him. I reply: God loves people in a secret way before they are called if they are among the elect, for he loves all his own people before they are created. But as they are not yet reconciled, they are rightly called God's "enemies," as Paul says in Romans 5:10. This is why the Word says that we are loved by God when we love Christ; although previously we trembled before him as our hostile Judge, we now have the pledge of his Fatherly love.

28. "I came from the Father." This expression draws our attention to Christ's divine power. Our faith in him would not be firm if it did not grasp his divine power. His death and resurrection, the two pillars of faith, would be little help to us if heavenly power were not joined with them. We now understand how we ought to love Christ. Our love should be such that our faith contemplates the purpose and power of God, by whose hand Christ is offered to us. We must not receive coldly the statement that he came from God, but must also understand why he came — namely, that he might be "for us wisdom from God — that is, our righteousness, holiness and redemption" (1 Corinthians 1:30).

"Now I am leaving the world and going back to the Father." By this second clause he points out that this power is perpetual, for the disciples might have thought that it was a temporary blessing that he was sent into the world as Redeemer. He therefore says that he is returning to **"the Father,"** so that they may be assured that none of the blessings which he brought will be lost by his departure, because from his heavenly glory he sheds on the world the power and effectiveness of his death and resurrection. Therefore, he left the world when, laying aside our infirmities, he was received into heaven. But his grace towards us still flourishes just the same, for he is seated at the right hand of **"the Father"** so that he may have dominion over the whole world.

Verses 29–33

29. Jesus' disciples said . . . This verse shows how effective Christ's consolation was, for it suddenly brought great cheerfulness to those who had been cast down and broken. And yet the disciples certainly did not yet understand fully what Christ had been saying; but although they were not yet capable of this, the mere scent of it refreshed them. When they exclaim that their Master is speaking **"clearly and without figures of speech,"** they are certainly going too far; yet they are stating honestly what they feel. We have the same experience today, for anyone who has tasted just a little of the Gospel teaching is more excited and feels much greater energy in that small measure of faith than if he had been acquainted with all of Plato's writings. Indeed, the groans that God's Spirit arouses in the hearts of the godly prove that God works in a secret way beyond their understanding, or Paul would not call them "groans that words cannot express" (Romans 8:26).

So we should understand that the apostles felt they had made some progress — they could say with truth that Christ's words were not completely enigmatic. But they were deceived in that they thought they were wiser than they were. Their mistake came from not knowing what the gift of the Holy Spirit would be. Therefore they rejoiced before the time, just like someone thinking himself to be rich with a single gold coin. From certain signs they concluded that Christ came from God, and they gloried in it as if nothing else were needed. Yet they were still far from that knowledge while they did not understand what Christ would be to them in the future.

31. "You believe at last!" (KJV, "Do ye now believe?"). Since the disciples were too pleased with themselves, Christ reminds them that, remembering their weakness, they should rather keep themselves within the little they are capable of. But we are never fully aware of what we lack and of our great distance from the fullness of faith until we come to some serious experience, for then the event shows how weak our faith was, which we imagined to be full. Christ reminds the disciples of this and tells them that they will soon forsake him (verse 32). For persecution is a touchstone to test our faith, and when its smallness becomes evident, those who were previously swollen with pride begin to tremble and draw back.

Christ's question therefore was ironical — as if he had said, "Do you boast as if you were full of faith? The trial is close at hand which will show up your emptiness." So we should restrain our foolish self-assurance when it becomes over-exultant. But it might seem that either the disciples had no faith at all, or it was extinguished when they left Christ and were scattered about. I reply that although their faith was weakened and had almost given way, still something was left for new shoots to grow from later on.

32. "Yet I am not alone." This correction is added in order to teach us that when Christ is forsaken by men, nothing is taken from him. Since his truth and his glory are founded on himself and do not depend on the world's faith, if he is forsaken by the whole world he is in no way diminished, because he is God and needs no help from others.

"For my Father is with me." God will be on his side, so that he will have no need to borrow anything from men. Whoever meditates on this properly will stand firm, even if the whole world wavers; the failure of everyone else will not overturn his faith. We do not give God due honor if we are not satisfied with him alone.

33. "I have told you these things . . ." Again he insists how necessary those consolations are which he had addressed to them, and he proves it by pointing out that many distresses and tribulations await them in the world. Therefore, we should notice first this warning that all godly people should be convinced that their life is subject to many afflictions, so that they may be prepared to endure. Since, therefore, the world is like a rough sea, true **"peace"** will be found nowhere but in Christ. Next, we must note how that **"peace"** is enjoyed, as he describes it here. He says that they will have **"peace"** if they make progress in his teaching. Do we want to have minds calm and easy in the midst of afflictions? Let us pay attention to this discourse of Christ, which in itself will give us **"peace."**

"Take heart!" Although our sluggishness has to be corrected by various afflictions, and we must be stirred to look for a remedy for our ills, the Lord still does not want our minds to be broken but wants us to fight keenly — which is impossible unless we are sure of success. If we have to fight while we are uncertain about the result, all our enthusiasm will quickly fail. Therefore, when Christ calls us to the battle, he arms us with the certainty that we shall win, though we must still work hard at it.

"I have overcome the world." As there is always good reason for us to tremble, he teaches us to be confident, for he has won the victory over **"the world,"** not just for himself but for our sake. So although we ourselves are almost overwhelmed, if we look at that magnificent glory to which our head has been exalted, we may boldly despise all the evils which hang over us. If we want to be Christians, we must not seek to be free from the cross, but must be content with the fact that while we fight under Christ's banner we are out of danger even in the midst of the battle. In **"the world"** Christ includes everything that is opposed to the salvation of the godly, and especially all the corruptions which Satan uses to lay snares for us.

John
Chapter 17

Verses 1–5

1. After Jesus said this . . . When the Lord had preached to the disciples about bearing the cross, he showed them the consolations they could rely on to enable them to persevere. Having promised the coming of the Spirit, he raised their hopes and talked to them about the splendor and glory of his kingdom. Now he devotes himself to prayer — as is proper, for teaching is cold unless God gives it efficacy. He therefore gives teachers an example, that they should not only spend their time sowing the Word, but also mix their prayers with it and thus implore God's help, that his blessing may make their work fruitful. In short, this prayer of Christ is, as it were, the seal of the preceding teaching, both to ratify it in itself and to give it full authority with the disciples.

He looked toward heaven. This was a sign of unusual ardor and vehemence, for by this attitude Christ was witnessing that in his mind he was in heaven rather than on earth, so that he left people behind him and talked intimately with God. He **looked toward *heaven*,** not because God (who also fills the earth) is shut up there, but because it is there chiefly that his majesty appears. Another reason is that we are reminded that the majesty of God is exalted far above all creatures. Lifting up the hands in prayer makes the same point, for people are lazy and slow by nature, and their earthly spirit pulls them downwards; they need to be stirred up like this — they need vehicles to raise them to God.

Besides, if we truly want to imitate Christ, we must take care that outward gestures do not express more than is in our minds, but that the inward feeling directs our eyes, hands, tongue, and everything else. The tax collector with downcast eyes prayed aright (Luke 18:13), but that is not inconsistent with this statement; for although he was confused because of his sins, and humbled himself, this humbling did not stop him from seeking pardon confidently. But it was right for Christ to pray in a different way, for he had nothing to be ashamed of. And it is certain that

David himself prayed now in one posture, now in another, according to his circumstances.

"Father, the time has come." Christ asks that his kingdom may be glorified, so that he in turn might **"glorify"** the Father. He says that **"the time has come"** because although he has been revealed as God's Son by miracles and all sorts of signs, his spiritual kingdom was still obscure; soon afterwards it shone brightly. It may be objected that nothing could be less glorious than Christ's death, which was then close at hand. I reply that in that death we see a boundless glory which is concealed from the ungodly. In his death we see that the world has been reconciled to God by the expiation of sins; the curse has been blotted out and Satan vanquished.

Christ also prays that his death may, by the power of the Heavenly Spirit, bear such fruit as had been decreed by God's eternal purpose. For he says that **"the time has come"** — not a time decided by human will, but one which God appointed. And yet the prayer is not superfluous because while Christ depends on God's will, he knows that he should desire what God promised would certainly take place. True, God will do whatever he has decreed, not only despite the whole world sleeping, but even if it were opposed to him; but it is our duty to ask from him whatever he has promised, because the purpose of promises is to provoke us to prayer.

"... that your Son may glorify you." He means that the shining of his glory and his Father's go together. Why is Christ revealed if not to lead us to the Father? It follows from this that all the honor which is given to Christ, so far from diminishing the Father's honor, confirms it. We must always bear in mind that Christ in this passage is speaking not as eternally divine, but as God revealed in the flesh, and as Mediator.

2. **"You granted him ..."** Again he says that he is asking nothing but what accords with the Father's will. It is a general rule of prayer not to ask more than God would freely give, for nothing is more unreasonable than bringing before him whatever we like.

"... authority over all people" means the authority given to Christ when the Father appointed him King and head. But we must not miss the purpose, which is **"that he might give eternal life"** to all his people. Therefore Christ receives **"authority"** not so much for himself as for our salvation. And so we should submit to Christ not only so that we may obey God, but because there is nothing more lovely than that subjection, since it is the cause of our eternal life.

"... to all those you have given him." Christ does not say that he has been put in command over the whole world in order to give life indiscriminately, but he restricts this grace to **"those you have given him."** But how were they **"given"**? For the Father has also subjected the reprobate to him. I reply: only the elect belong to his own flock, which he has undertaken to guard as a shepherd. So the kingdom of Christ

ex
th
hi

it
nc
ab
w
by
an
an
no
us
by
ad

lvation to the elect, who follow
ly compels the others to obey
with his iron rod.
w describes how he gives life:
rue knowledge of God. He is
life that we hope for, but only
understand this verse properly,
death until we are enlightened
hone, we possess him by faith
is why knowing him is truly
ord here is important, for it is
ut only that which transforms
eed, it is the same as the faith
and made to share the divine

... that they may know you, the only true God, and Jesus Christ, whom you have sent.” God is known only in the face of **“Jesus Christ,”** who is his exact and living image. Christ here puts the Father first, not with reference to faith (as if our minds came down from the knowledge of God to Christ) but because God is known by the intervention of the Mediator.

The two adjectives **“only”** and **“true”** are added because, first, faith must distinguish between God and empty human imaginings and embrace him with unswerving and unwavering confidence; and second, faith must be content with him alone, deciding that there is nothing defective or imperfect in him. Some people explain it as meaning, “That they may know you who alone are God,” but this is weak. The meaning is, “That they may know you alone to be the true God.”

But Christ may seem to be disclaiming the right and title of divinity. The name of God applies to Christ as it does to the Father, but then the same question might be raised about the Holy Spirit. For if only the Father and the Son are one God, the Holy Spirit is excluded, which is just as absurd. The answer is easy if we note the way Christ speaks throughout John’s Gospel (which I have reminded my readers about so often that they ought to be used to it by now). Christ appears in the form of a man and describes God’s power, essence, and majesty as “the Father.” So Christ’s Father is **“the only true God”**; that is, he is the God who previously promised the world a Redeemer. But in Christ will be found the unity and truth of the Godhead, because he was humbled to raise us on high. When we have reached this point, his divine majesty is seen, and we learn that he is wholly in the Father and the Father wholly in him. In short, whoever separates Christ from the divinity of the Father does not yet know him who is **“the only true God,”** but rather is inventing a strange God for himself. This is why we are told to know

God, and Christ whom he **sent,** by whom he invites us to himself as if by stretching out his hand.

Some people believe it would be unfair for people to perish merely because of their ignorance of God, but this comes from their not recognizing that there is no source of life other than in God alone, and that everyone who is alienated from him is deprived of life. Now, if there is no approaching God except by faith, we are forced to conclude that unbelief keeps us in a state of death. You may object that people who are otherwise righteous and innocent are treated unfairly if they are condemned, but it is obvious that nothing right or sincere is found in people as long as they remain in their own nature. But Paul says that believers are "renewed in knowledge in the image" of God (Colossians 3:10).

It is now worth summarizing those three points.

1. The kingdom of Christ brings life and salvation.

2. Not everyone receives life from him, nor is it Christ's task to give life to everyone, but only to the elect, whom the Father has committed to his care.

3. This life consists in faith, and Christ gives it to those whom he enlightens in the faith of the Gospel.

From this we learn that the gift of illumination and heavenly wisdom is not common to everyone, but is special to the elect. It is undoubtedly true that the Gospel is offered to everyone, but here Christ is speaking about the secret and effective way of teaching by which God's children alone are drawn to faith.

4. **"I have brought you glory."** He said this because God had been known to the world by Christ's teaching and miracles. God's **"glory"** is when we know what he is. When Christ adds, **"by completing the work you gave me to do,"** he means that he has finished the whole course of his calling, for the time was now right for him to be received into the heavenly **"glory."** He is speaking not just about his task of teaching, but also includes the other parts of his ministry. The chief part was still to come, the sacrifice of his death by which he was to expiate the sin of us all; but since the time of his death had already come, he speaks of it as if he had already endured it. What he is asking, therefore, is that the Father will send him to take possession of the kingdom. He has completed his course, and nothing is left for him to do but to display by the power of the Spirit the fruit and effectiveness of all that he had done on earth by his Father's command. As Paul puts it, he "made himself nothing, taking the very nature of a servant. . . . Therefore God exalted him to the highest place and gave him the name . . ." (Philippians 2:7, 9).

5. **". . . the glory I had with you . . ."** He wants to be glorified **"with"** the Father, not so that the Father may glorify him secretly, without any witnesses, but so that, having been received into heaven, he may magnificently display his greatness and power, so that every knee may bow to him (see Philippians 2:10). So this is contrasted with earthly, fading

glory, just as Paul expresses the blessed immortality of Christ by saying that "he died to sin once" but now "lives to God" (see Romans 6:10).

Next he declares that he desires nothing that does not belong to him, but only that he may appear, in the flesh, as he was before the creation of the world. Or to put it more clearly, that the divine majesty which he always had may now shine in the person of the Mediator and in the human flesh which he has put on. This notable passage teaches us that Christ is not a new or temporary God, for if his **"glory"** was eternal, he too has always existed. Moreover, a clear distinction is made here between Christ's person and the Father's person; we infer that he is not only the eternal God, but also that he is the eternal Word of God, begotten by the Father before all ages.

Verses 6–11

6. "I have revealed you." Here Christ begins to pray to the Father for his disciples; and with the same feeling of love with which he was at once to suffer death for them, he now pleads for their salvation. The first argument he employs is that they have embraced the teaching which actually makes people children of God. Christ did not lack faith or diligence in calling everyone to God, but his labor was only profitable and effective in the elect. His preaching, which revealed the name of God, was open to everyone, and he never ceased to assert his **"glory"** even among those who were obstinate. So why does he say that he only revealed it to a few people, if it is not that only the elect profit from the Spirit's inner teaching? So we must infer that not everyone to whom the teaching is offered is truly and effectively taught, but only those whose minds are enlightened. Christ ascribes the cause to God's election, for the only reason he gives for having revealed the Father to some people and passed over others is that they were given to him. So it follows that faith comes from God's eternal predestination; it is not given indiscriminately to everyone, since not everyone belongs to Christ.

"They were yours; you gave them to me." First he points out the eternity of election, and then how we should think of it. Christ says that the elect always belonged to God. God therefore distinguishes them from the reprobate, not by faith, nor by any merit, but by pure grace; for while they are far away from him, he regards them in secret as his own. The certainty is in his committing everyone he has chosen to the guardianship of his Son, that they may not perish. That is where we must look if we are to be certain that we are among God's children. In itself the predestination of God is hidden, but in Christ alone it is revealed to us.

"They have obeyed your word." This is the third step. The first is free election, and the second is the gift by which we enter into Christ's care. We are received by Christ and gathered into the fold by faith. God's Word slips away from the reprobate but takes root in the elect, and so they are said to obey it.

7. Here he expresses the chief thing in faith: we should so believe in Christ that our faith is not satisfied with seeing his flesh but sees his divine power. This verse means that believers feel that all they have is heavenly and divine. Indeed, unless we lay hold on God in Christ, we shall remain continually vacillating.

8. "And they accepted them [Christ's words]." He expresses the mode of this knowledge: they received the doctrine which he taught them. But lest anyone should regard his doctrine as human or of earthly origin, he declares that God is its author: **"I gave them the words you gave me."** He speaks, as he usually does, as the Mediator or Servant of God, saying that he taught only what he had received from the Father. Since his own condition was still in humble flesh, his divine majesty hidden under the form of a servant, by "the Father" he simply means God. Yet we must keep to John's witness at the beginning of his Gospel, that insofar as Christ was the eternal Word of God, he was always one God with the Father. Therefore, the meaning is that Christ was a faithful witness of God to the disciples, so that their faith was based on nothing but God's truth, since the Father himself spoke in the Son. The "accepting" that he speaks about came from his effectively revealing to them the name of his Father through the Holy Spirit.

"They knew with certainty . . ." He now repeats in other words what he had mentioned before: that Christ **"came from"** the Father and was **"sent"** by him mean the same as what was said earlier, that all that Christ has is from the Father. The sum of it is that faith should look directly at Christ, yet so as to know nothing earthly or contemptible about him, but to be carried upwards to his divine power, so as to be convinced that he is God, and all that is of God, perfectly in himself.

"And they believed." Note also that in the first clause he uses the verb "know," and now he uses the verb "believe." Thus he shows that nothing can be known about God correctly except by faith, but in faith there is such certainty that it is right to call it knowledge.

9. "I pray for them." Up to this point Christ has presented what would win favor with the Father for the disciples. Now he frames the prayer itself and shows that he is asking nothing but what agrees with the Father's will, because he is pleading with the Father only for people whom the Father himself willingly loves. He openly declares that he is **"not praying for the world,"** for he is only looking after his own flock which he received from the Father's hand. Perhaps this seems absurd, for no better rule of prayer can be found than to follow Christ as our guide and teacher, and yet we are commanded to pray for everyone, and Christ himself afterwards prayed for everyone indiscriminately: "Father, forgive them, for they do not know what they are doing" (Luke 23:34).

My reply is that the prayers which we utter for everyone are still limited to God's elect. We ought to pray that this person and that person and everyone may be saved and so include the whole human race, because we cannot yet distinguish the elect from the reprobate. And yet by desiring the coming of God's kingdom we pray at the same time that he may destroy his enemies. The only difference is that we pray for the salvation of everyone we know to have been created in God's image and with the same nature as ourselves; and we leave to God's judgment those whom he knows to be reprobate. But in the prayer related here there was a certain special reason which should not be taken as an example. Christ is not praying simply from an attitude of faith and love but enters into the heavenly sanctuary and holds before his eyes the secret judgments of the Father, which are hidden from us as long as we walk by faith.

We also learn from these words that God chooses out of the world those he thinks fit to choose to be heirs of life, and this distinction is not made according to people's merits but depends entirely on his good pleasure. Those who think the cause of election lies in people have to begin with faith, but Christ explicitly states that those who are given to him belong to the Father, and it is certain that they are given so that they may believe, and that faith comes from this giving. If the origin of faith is this giving, and if election precedes it in order and time, what is left but to acknowledge that those God wishes to be saved out of the world are elected by free grace? Now, since Christ prayed only for the elect, belief in election is necessary for us if we want him to plead with the Father for our salvation. Therefore, people who try to blot out the knowledge of election from believers' hearts do them great harm, for they deprive them of Christ's support. These words also show up the false stupidity of those who under the excuse of election surrender to laziness, whereas it should rather stir us up to earnest prayer, as Christ teaches us by his example.

10. "All I have is yours." The former clause suggests that the Father will certainly listen to him. He says, "I do not plead with you for anyone but those you acknowledge to be **yours**; for I possess nothing separate from you, and therefore I shall not be refused." In the following clause, **"and all you have is mine,"** he shows that he has good reason for caring about the elect: they are his because they are the Father's. All these things are spoken to confirm our faith. We must not seek salvation anywhere other than in Christ. But we shall not be satisfied with having Christ unless we know that in him we possess God. We must therefore believe that there is a unity between the Father and the Son which means they have nothing separate from each other.

"And glory has come to me through them." This is connected with the second clause of the verse, for it follows that it is reasonable for him, on his part, to promote their salvation. And this is the best teaching for confirming our faith, that Christ will never neglect our salvation if he is glorified in us.

11. "I will remain in the world no longer." He gives another reason why he prays so diligently for the disciples — because they were soon to be deprived of his physical presence, under which they had rested till now. While he was living among them he cherished them under his wing as a hen does her chickens (see Matthew 23:37). But now that he is about to leave, he asks the Father to cover them with his protection. And he does so for their sake, for he provides a remedy for their fear, that they may rest on God himself, into whose hands, as it were, he now commits them. It is no little consolation to us when we hear the Son of God caring all the more for the salvation of his people when he leaves them bodily, for we may infer from it that from his heavenly glory he can help us.

"Holy Father . . ." The whole prayer is that the disciples should not lose heart as if they were in a worse state on account of the bodily absence of their Master. Christ was given by the Father to be their guardian for a time, and now that he has discharged the duties of that office, he gives them back, as it were, into his Father's hands, that from now on they may enjoy his protection and may be held up by his power. It amounts therefore to this, that when the disciples were deprived of Christ's bodily presence they were suffering no loss, because God receives them under his guardianship, and his power is everlasting.

". . . so that they may be one." He shows how they will be kept, for those the Heavenly Father has decreed to **"protect"** he brings together into a holy unity of faith and the Spirit. But because it is not enough for people to agree in general, he adds the phrase **"as we are one."** Our unity will be truly happy when it bears the image of God the Father and of Christ, just as the wax receives the form of the seal impressed on it. But in what way the Father and Christ are **"one"** I shall explain shortly.

Verses 12–13

12. Christ says that he kept the disciples in the Father's **"name."** He represents himself as only a servant, doing nothing but by the power and under the authority of God. He means, therefore, that it would be inconsistent if they perished now, as if by his departure God's power were extinguished or dead. But it may seem absurd that Christ should surrender to God the task of keeping them, as if, after completing the course of his life, he ceased to be the guardian of his people. The reply is clear: he is speaking here only about visible guardianship, ending at his death. While he was living on earth he had no need to borrow power from elsewhere to keep his disciples; but all this relates to the person of the Mediator, who appeared for a time under the form of a servant. But now he tells the disciples to lift their minds directly to heaven as soon as they begin to lose their outward help. From this we conclude that Christ keeps believers today no less than before, but in a different way, because divine majesty is displayed openly in him.

Again he uses the same argument: that it would be quite wrong for the Father to reject those whom his Son at his command had kept to the very end of his ministry. It was as if he had said, "What you gave me to do, I have faithfully carried out, and I took care that nothing in my hands should perish. When you now receive what you entrusted to me, it is up to you to see that it continues safe."

He makes an exception of Judas, and with good reason, for although he was not one of the elect or of God's true flock, still the dignity of his office made him seem like one of them. Nor indeed would anyone have thought otherwise of him while he held that distinguished rank. If we think about it, Christ had to speak like this in the way ordinary people would. But in case anyone should think that God's eternal election was overthrown by Judas' destruction, he immediately adds that he was **"the one doomed to destruction"** — meaning that his ruin, which to human view was sudden, had long been known to God.

". . . so that Scripture would be fulfilled." This relates to the previous clause. Judas fell so that the **Scripture** might be **"fulfilled."** But it would be wrong for anyone to infer from this that Judas' fall should be ascribed to God rather than to himself because the prophecy made him do it. The course of events should not be ascribed to prophecies just because it was predicted in them. And, indeed, the prophets only threatened what would have happened even if they had not mentioned it. The cause of things must not, therefore, be sought in them. I acknowledge that nothing happens but what has been ordained by God, but the only question now is whether their being foretold or prophesied makes people do things, and I have already shown this is not so.

Nor did Christ mean to transfer the cause of Judas' ruin to **Scripture.** He only wanted to remove the occasion of stumbling which might shake weak minds. Now he removes it by showing that God's Spirit had long ago testified that it would happen, for we are nearly always afraid of what is new and sudden. This is a very useful warning and has wide application. Why is it that most people today give way to offenses? It is just because they do not remember the testimonies of Scripture by which God has well-armed his people and foretold all the evils and distresses which they would see.

13. "I say these things while I am still in the world." Here Christ shows that he was so careful in praying to the Father for his disciples not because he was anxious about their future state but to provide a remedy for their anxiety. We know how our minds depend on external aids, and if these present themselves we seize them eagerly and are not easily torn from them. Therefore Christ prays to his Father in the presence of the disciples, not because he needed words, but to remove all doubt from them. He speaks while he is still in their hearing, that their hearts may be calm. For their salvation was already safe, having been placed by Christ in the hands of God.

". . . that they may have the full measure of my joy within them." He calls it his **"joy"** because the disciples had to receive it from him; or, more briefly, because he is its author, cause, and pledge. There is nothing but fear and unease in us; in Christ alone there is peace and joy.

Verses 14–19

14. "I have given them your word." He now pleads with the Father for the disciples in a different way. They needed his help because of the world's hatred. At the same time, he says that the cause of this hatred is that they have embraced God's Word, which the world cannot bear. It is as if he had said, "It is for you to protect those who are hated by the world because of your Word." We must now bear in mind what we have just heard, that the point of this prayer is that Christ's **"joy"** may be fulfilled in us. Therefore, as often as the world's rage is kindled against us so that we seem on the brink of destruction, let us learn at once to ward it off with this shield, that God will never abandon those who labor for the Gospel.

"For they are not of the world." He says this because those he regenerates by his Spirit are separated from **"the world."** God will not let his sheep wander among wolves, but will show himself to be their Shepherd.

15. "My prayer is not that you take them out of the world." He teaches what the safety of the godly consists in. It is not that they are free from all vexations and live in ease and pleasure, but that in the midst of danger they remain safe by God's help. For he does not tell the Father what is expedient but rather cares for their weakness, that they may restrain their desires (which are inclined to go too far) in the way he lays down. In short, he does not promise his disciples the grace of the Father to relieve them of all anxiety and labor, but to give them unconquerable strength against their enemies and not to let them be overwhelmed by the many battles they will have to endure. So if we want to be kept by the rule which Christ laid down, we must not wish to be exempt from evils or pray to God to take us straight into blessed rest, but must rather be content with the assurance of victory. Meanwhile we must bravely resist all the evils Christ prayed to his Father to deliver us from. In short, God does not take his people out of the world, because he does not want them to be lazy and delicate; but he delivers them from evil, that they may not be overwhelmed. He wants them to fight, but he does not let them be mortally wounded.

16. "They are not of the world." Again he says that the whole **"world"** hates them, to remind them that the Heavenly Father will help them by his kindness; and at the same time he says that this hatred is not their fault, but is because **"the world"** hates God and Christ.

17. "Sanctify them." This sanctification includes God's kingdom and his righteousness; that is, God renews us by his Spirit and confirms in us the grace of renewal and continues it to the end. First of all, therefore, he asks the Father to **"sanctify"** the disciples, or in other words to consecrate them entirely to himself and to defend them as his sacred property. Next, he describes the means of sanctification, and not without reason; for there are fanatics who chatter emptily about sanctification but neglect God's **"truth,"** by which he consecrates us to himself. Again, as there are others who talk a lot of nonsense about **"the truth"** and yet neglect the Word, Christ explicitly says that **"the truth"** by which God sanctifies his sons exists nowhere but in the Word.

"Your word is truth." Here **"word"** means the Gospel teaching, which the apostles had already heard from the mouth of their Master and which they were later to preach to others. In this sense Paul says that the church has been cleansed "by the washing with water through the word" (Ephesians 5:26). True, it is God alone who sanctifies, but as the Gospel is "the power of God for the salvation of everyone who believes" (Romans 1:16), whoever departs from it as the means must become more and more defiled.

"Truth" is here taken as the light of heavenly wisdom in which God reveals himself to us so that he may mold us in his image. It is true that the outward preaching of the Word does not itself effect this, for the reprobate wickedly profane it. But let us remember that Christ is speaking about the elect, whom the Holy Spirit effectively regenerates by the Word. Now, as the apostles were not altogether lacking in this grace, we should infer from Christ's words that sanctification is not instantly completed in us on the first day, but that we make progress in it throughout the whole of our life until at last God puts off our flesh and fills us with his righteousness.

18. "As you sent me . . ." He confirms his prayer by another argument — namely, that the calling of Christ and of the apostles is the same calling. He says, "I now appoint them to an office which I have so far held by your command. Therefore, they need to be equipped with the power of your Spirit, so that they may be able to bear the burden."

19. "For them I sanctify myself." By these words he explains more clearly the source of the sanctification which is completed in us by the Gospel teaching. He consecrated himself to the Father, so that his holiness might come to us; for as the blessing on the firstfruits is spread to the whole harvest, so the Spirit of God cleanses us by Christ's holiness and makes us share it. This is not just by imputation; he is said to have become our "wisdom," but also he is said to have become our "holiness" (1 Corinthians 1:30) because he has, so to speak, presented us to his Father in his own person, that we may be renewed to true holiness by his Spirit. Although this sanctification belongs to the whole life of Christ, it shone brightest in the sacrifice of his death, for then he showed himself to be the true High Priest, consecrating the temple, the altar, all the vessels, and the people by the power of his Spirit.

Verses 20–23

20. "My prayer is not for them alone." Up till now his prayer had included only the apostles; now he extends it to all the disciples the Gospel will have until the end of the world. This is indeed a remarkable basis for confidence. If we believe in Christ through the Gospel teaching, we should not doubt at all that we are already gathered with the apostles into his faithful protection, so that not one of us will perish. This prayer of Christ is a safe harbor, and whoever retreats into it is safe from all danger of shipwreck; Christ has solemnly sworn that he will devote himself to caring and working for our salvation.

He began with his apostles so that their salvation, which we know to be certain, might make us more certain of our own salvation; and therefore, whenever Satan attacks us, let us learn to resist him with this shield. Then it will not be in vain that Christ united us with the apostles, so that everyone's salvation was bound up, as it were, in the same bundle. Therefore, there is nothing that should more powerfully stir us to accept the Gospel. It is an inestimable blessing that we are presented to God by the hand of Christ, to be preserved from destruction, and so we really ought to love it and care for it above all else. In this respect the world's madness is monstrous. Everyone wants salvation; Christ teaches us a way to obtain it, and there is no good hope for anyone who turns aside from this way, and yet scarcely one person in a hundred deigns to receive what was offered so graciously.

". . . for those who will believe in me." By these words Christ reminds us of what we have said more than once already: our faith should be directed to him. The phrase which comes next, **"through their message,"** expresses admirably the power and nature of faith and at the same time is a familiar confirmation to us who know that our faith is founded on the Gospel taught by the apostles. Let the world condemn us a thousand times; it should be enough for us that Christ acknowledges us to be his own and pleads with the Father for us.

Let us remember that the Son of God, who alone is competent to judge, approves only that faith which is drawn from the apostles' teaching. Moreover, the sure witness to this will be found only in their writings.

We must also note the saying, **"believe in me through their message."** This means that faith comes from hearing, because the outward preaching of men is the instrument by which God draws us to faith. Hence it follows that God is, strictly speaking, the author of faith, and men are servants through whom people come to believe (1 Corinthians 3:5).

21. ". . . that all of them may be one." He again rightly says that the purpose of our happiness consists in unity. The ruin of the human race is that, alienated from God, it is also broken and scattered in itself. Conversely, its restoration consists in its being properly united in one body. Paul describes the perfection of the church as consisting in believers being joined together in one Spirit and says that apostles, prophets, evangelists, and pastors are given to restore and build up the body of Christ until we all reach unity in the faith. So he exhorts believers to "grow up into him who is the Head, that is, Christ. From him the whole body, joined and held together by every supporting ligament, grows and builds itself up in love, as each part does its work" (Ephesians 4:3, 11-16). So whenever Christ speaks about unity, let us remember how foul and horrible is the world when it is scattered apart from him. Next let us learn that a blessed life begins when we are all governed and live by the one Spirit of Christ.

Again, we must learn that whenever Christ says in this chapter that he is **"one"** with the Father, he is not speaking simply of his divine essence, but he is called **"one"** as Mediator and as our head. Many of the Fathers interpreted these words in an absolute sense, as meaning that Christ is **"one"** with the Father because he is the eternal God. But the controversy with the Arians led them to seize on isolated passages and twist them out of their natural meaning. But Christ's intention was very different from raising us to mere speculation about his divinity, for he reasons from the end that we ought to be one because otherwise the unity he has with the Father would be empty and barren.

To understand rightly what it means that Christ and the Father are **"one,"** we must take care not to deprive Christ of being Mediator. We should think of him rather as the head of the church and join him to the parts of his body. Then the connection will be preserved best; that is, if the unity of the Son with the Father is not to be fruitless and useless, its power must be spread through the whole body of believers. From this, too, we infer that we are **"one"** with Christ — not because he transfuses his substance into us, but because by his Spirit's power he communicates his life to us, with all the blessings he has received from the Father.

". . . so that the world may believe." Some people interpret **"the world"** as meaning the elect, who were still dispersed at that time. But since in the whole of this chapter the word denotes the reprobate, I am more inclined to take a different view. It happens that immediately afterwards he draws a distinction between all his people and the same **"world"** which he mentions here.

The verb "to believe" was used imprecisely by the evangelist for "to know" — that is, when unbelievers are convicted by their own experience and perceive the heavenly and divine glory of Christ. Consequently, believing, they do not believe, because this feeling does not penetrate into the inner attitude of the heart. And it is a just vengeance of God that the splendor of the divine glory dazzles the eyes of the reprobate, because they do not deserve to have a genuine and clear view of it. Later he uses the verb "to know" in the same sense.

22. "I have given them the glory that you gave me." Notice that such a pattern of perfect happiness was expressed in Christ that he kept nothing for himself alone but rather was rich in order to enrich his believers. Our happiness lies in having the image of God restored and re-formed in us, when it had been blotted out by sin. Christ is not only, as the eternal Word of God, his living image, but the Father's **"glory"** has also been imprinted on his human nature (which he has in common with us), so that he may transform his members to it. Paul also teaches us this: "we, who with unveiled faces all reflect the Lord's glory, are being transformed into his likeness" (2 Corinthians 3:18). It follows from this that no one is to be counted among Christ's disciples unless God's **"glory"** is seen to be impressed on him by the likeness of Christ, as by the seal of a ring. The words that follow say the same thing.

23. "I in them and you in me." He wants to teach that in him lies all the fullness of blessings and that what was hidden in God is now made plain in him, so that he may pass it on to his people, as water flows from a fountain through various channels to water the fields everywhere.

". . . and have loved them." He means that this is a most striking sign and excellent pledge of God's love towards the godly, which **"the world"** is forced to feel whether it chooses to or not, when the heavenly Spirit who lives in them sends out rays of righteousness and holiness. There are, indeed, many other ways in which God daily testifies to how he loves us, but the mark of adoption is better than any of them. So he also adds, **"and have loved them even as you have loved me."** By these words he wanted to point out the cause and origin of his love, for the particle **"as"** means "because": "*because* you loved me." The title of "Beloved" belongs to Christ alone. But the Heavenly Father has the same love for all the members as he does for the head, so that he loves only those who are in Christ.

There seems to be a contradiction here, however: Christ, as we have seen elsewhere, declares that God's infinite love for the world was the reason why he gave his "one and only Son" (see John 3:16). If the cause must precede the effect, we infer that God the Father loved people outside Christ — that is, before he was appointed the Redeemer. I reply that in that and similar passages "love" means the mercy by which God was moved towards those who were unworthy, and even towards his enemies, before he reconciled them to himself. It is a wonderful goodness of God, and incomprehensible to the human mind, that he was benevolent to people he could not but hate and removed the cause of the hatred so that there might be nothing in the way of his love. And, indeed, Paul tells us that we are loved in Christ in two senses. First, because "he chose us in him before the creation of the world" (Ephesians 1:4). Second, because in Christ God has reconciled us to himself and shown that he is gracious to us (Romans 5:10). Thus we are at once both enemies and friends until atonement has been made for our sins and we are restored to God's favor.

But when we are justified by faith, we begin properly to be loved by God as children are loved by a father. The love by which Christ was appointed as the person in whom we were to be freely chosen before we were born, and while we were still ruined in Adam, is hidden in God's heart and far exceeds human understanding. No one will ever feel that God is favorable to him unless he sees that God is appeased in Christ. But as all hunger for God's love vanishes when we are grafted into his body, there is no danger that we shall be cut off from God's love, for this foundation cannot be shaken — that we are loved because the Father has loved him.

Verses 24–26

24. "I want those you have given me to be with me where I am." This expresses not a command but a request. But it may be understood in two ways: either that he wishes the disciples to enjoy his external presence, or that God will at last take them into the heavenly kingdom to which he is going before them.

". . . to see my glory." Some people interpret this as meaning sharing in Christ's "glory." Others explain it as knowing by the experience of faith what Christ is and how great his majesty is. After careful consideration, I think that Christ is speaking about the perfect happiness of the godly, as if he had said that his desire would not be satisfied till they have been received into heaven. At that time they saw Christ's "glory" as someone shut up in the dark sees a feeble and glimmering light through small cracks. Christ now wants them to go on to enjoy the full brightness of heaven. In short, he asks that the Father will lead them by uninterrupted progress to the full view of his "glory."

"Because you loved me." This also fits Christ as Mediator much better than Christ as God alone. Christ was undoubtedly speaking as the head of the church when, earlier, he prayed that the apostles might be joined with him and might see the **"glory"** of his kingdom. Now he says that the Father's love is its cause; and so it follows that he was loved inasmuch as he was appointed as the world's Redeemer. The Father embraced him with that love "before the creation of the world," so that he might be the one in whom the Father would love his chosen people.

25. "Righteous Father . . ." He contrasts his disciples with "the world" so as to describe more fully the Father's approval and favor of them. For it is right that only those who know the God the world rejects should be singled out. And Christ rightly pleads with special feeling for those who acknowledged God despite the world's unbelief. By calling him "Righteous Father," Christ triumphs over "the world" and its malice. It was like saying, "However proudly the world may despise or reject God, it takes nothing from him and cannot prevent the honor of his righteousness from remaining sound." Thus he declares that the faith of godly people should be founded on God, so that it will never fail even if the whole "world" attacks it.

"I know you, and they know that you have sent me." Christ does not just say that God was known by the disciples, but gives two steps: first, that he himself had known the Father; and second, that the disciples knew that he was "sent" by the Father. But as he immediately adds that he has revealed to them the name of the Father, he praises them, as I have said, for the knowledge of God which differentiates them from the rest of "the world." Yet we must note the order of faith, as it is described here. Strictly speaking, only the Son who came from the Father's heart knows the Father. Therefore, everyone who wants to approach God must go to Christ, who meets them, and they must devote themselves to him. And when he has been known by the disciples, he will at last raise them to God the Father.

26. "I have made you known to them, and will continue to make you known." Christ acted as teacher, but in order to make the Father "known" he used the secret revelation of the Spirit and not just the sound of his voice. He therefore means that he taught the apostles effectively. Moreover, as their faith up till then was very weak, he promises greater progress in the future and so prepares them to hope for more abundant grace of the Spirit. Although he is speaking about the apostles, we should draw a general exhortation from this, to concentrate on making constant progress, and not to think that we have run so well that we do not still have a long journey ahead of us while we are surrounded by the flesh.

". . . in order that the love you have for me may be in them." That is, "that you may love them in me," or "that the love with which you have loved me may be shed on them." Strictly speaking, the love God has for us is none other than that which he had for his Son from the beginning, and so it makes us acceptable too, and lovable to him in Christ. Indeed, as we said above, as far as we are concerned and apart from Christ, we are hated by God; he only begins to love us when we are united to the body of his beloved Son. It is an inestimable privilege of faith that we know that Christ was loved by the Father for our sake, that we might share the same love forever.

"... and that I myself may be in them." This teaches us that the only way we are included in the love which he is talking about is by Christ living in us. For as the Father cannot look at his Son without at the same time having his whole body before his eyes, we must be truly parts of Christ's body if we want to be seen by him.

John
Chapter 18

Verses 1–6

1. When he had finished praying . . . In this story John leaves out many things which the other three evangelists relate, and he does so on purpose, as his intention was to collect many things worth recording, about which they say nothing. Therefore the reader should go to the other evangelists for what is lacking here.

. . . crossed the Kidron Valley. In the original Greek there is an article before **Kidron**, which seems to suggest that the brook takes its name from the cedars, but this is probably an error which has crept into the text, for the **Kidron Valley** or brook is often mentioned in Scripture. The place was so called from its being dark, for it was an overhung, shady valley. On that point, however, I am not arguing but only stating what is more probable.

The chief thing is the evangelist's intention in saying where the place was. He wanted to show that Christ went to his death willingly. He came into a place which he knew was well-known to Judas (verse 2). Why did he do this but to present himself, of his own accord, to the traitor and the enemies? Nor did he make a mistake through thoughtlessness, for he already knew everything that was going to happen. John afterwards adds that he went forward to meet them. He was therefore not coerced to death but bore it willingly, so that he might be a voluntary sacrifice. Without obedience, atonement would not have been gained for us.

Moreover, he entered the garden not to seek a hiding-place, but to have a better opportunity and more time for prayer. His praying three times to be delivered from death is not inconsistent with the voluntary obedience we have mentioned, for it was necessary for him to fight against difficulties so that he should be victorious. Now, having subdued the fear of death, he goes forward freely and willingly to death.

3. So Judas came . . . guiding a detachment of soldiers. That Judas came accompanied by soldiers and such a large guard is a sign of a bad conscience, which is always needlessly afraid. It is certain that the

detachment of soldiers was borrowed from the governor, who also sent a captain in command of a thousand soldiers, for a garrison was stationed in the city in case of sudden mutinies, and the governor himself kept a bodyguard wherever he went. The rest were servants of the priests. But John mentions the **Pharisees** separately because they were more enraged than all the rest, as if they cared more about religion.

4. Jesus, knowing . . . The evangelist states more clearly how readily Christ went forward to death; but at the same time he describes the great power which he exercised by a single word, in order to inform us that wicked men had no power over him except insofar as he gave permission.

5. "I am he." He replies mildly that he is the person they are looking for, and yet he lays them prostrate on the ground, as though they had been struck down by a violent tempest, or rather by lightning. He did not lack the power, then, to restrain them if he had thought it right; but he wished to obey his Father, by whose decree he knew that he was called to die.

We may infer from this how dreadful and terrifying to the ungodly Christ's voice will be when he ascends his throne to judge the world. Then he stood as a lamb prepared for sacrifice, and his majesty was apparently all gone; and yet when he speaks just one word, his armed and determined enemies fall down. And what was the word? He does not pronounce any dread curse against them but only replies, **"I am he."** So what will happen when he comes, not to be judged by man, but to be the Judge of the living and the dead — not in that low and contemptible state, but shining in heavenly glory and with his angels? Then, he wanted to give an example of the effectiveness which Isaiah ascribes to his voice. Among other mighty works of Christ, the prophet declares that "he will strike the earth with the rod of his mouth; with the breath of his lips he will slay the wicked" (Isaiah 11:4). True, Paul puts the fulfillment of this prophecy at the end of the world (2 Thessalonians 2:8), but we see the ungodly every day with all their rage and pride struck down at Christ's voice. When those men fell down who had come to bind Christ, it was a visible symbol of the fear which all the ungodly feel within themselves, whether they want to or not, when Christ speaks through his ministers. Moreover, as this was to some extent accidental to the voice of Christ, whose property it is to raise people lying in death, he will undoubtedly display toward us such power as to raise us right to heaven.

Verses 7–9

7. Again he asked them . . . From this we see how strong the blindness is with which God strikes the minds of the ungodly, and how dreadful their stupidity is when through God's just judgment they are bewitched by Satan. Cattle and asses show some kind of feeling if they fall down; but those people, when they have had Christ's divine power openly displayed, carry on as fearlessly as if they had not seen in him even the shadow of a man. Indeed, Judas himself is unmoved. Therefore, let us learn to fear God's judgment by which the reprobate, delivered into Satan's hands, become more stupid than brute beasts. Nor can it be doubted that Satan hurried them on with wild fury to this reckless daring; for there is no insanity that drives people with such violence as this kind of blindness. Ungodly people are given over to a depraved mind (see Romans 1:28) and then rush against God as though they were dealing with a fly. They feel his power, certainly, but not so as to yield. They would sooner be broken a hundred times than give in. In short, their malice is a veil to stop them from noticing God's light, and their obstinacy makes them harder than stones, so that they never let themselves be tamed.

8. "I told you that I am he." Here we see how God's Son not only submits voluntarily to death, so that he may blot out our transgressions by his obedience, but also how he fulfills the task of a good shepherd in protecting his flock. He sees the wolves attack and does not wait till they come to the sheep which have been committed to his care, but immediately goes forward to guard them. So whenever wicked people or devils attack us, let us not doubt that he is at hand to help us in the same way. Yet by his example Christ has given shepherds a rule to follow if they want to fulfill their task properly.

9. "I have not lost one." This passage seems to be quoted inappropriately, as it relates to their souls rather than to their bodies. Christ did not keep the apostles safe to the last, but amidst endless dangers and even in the midst of death he did secure their eternal salvation. I reply that the evangelist is not just speaking about their bodily life, but rather means that Christ, by sparing them for a time, made provision for their eternal salvation. Consider how weak they were; what do we think they would have done if they had been on trial for their life? So while Christ did not want them to be tried beyond the strength which he had given them, he rescued them from eternal destruction.

And from this we may deduce a general doctrine, that even if Christ tests our faith with many temptations, still he will never allow us to come into the ultimate danger without also supplying us with strength to overcome. And, indeed, we see how he continually bears with our weakness when he comes forward to repel so many attacks by Satan and ungodly people, because he sees that we are not yet able or prepared for them. In short, he never brings his people into the field of battle until they have been well trained, so that even in perishing they do not perish, because they can gain both in death and in life.

Verses 10–14

10. Then Simon Peter, who had a sword, drew it. The evangelist now describes Peter's foolish zeal in trying to defend his Master unlawfully. He is bold and courageous and runs great risk for Christ, but as he does not think about what his calling demands and what God permits, his action is far from praiseworthy, and indeed he is severely reprimanded by Christ. But let us learn that in Peter Christ is condemning everything that people dare to attempt arbitrarily. This doctrine is especially worth noticing, for nothing is more common than, under the cloak of zeal, to defend everything we do as if it did not matter whether God approved or not. People may think something is right, but this is based on mere vanity.

Even if we saw nothing blameworthy in Peter's zeal, we should still be dissatisfied for this one reason, that Christ declares that he is displeased. But we see that it was not because of Peter that Christ was not kept from death, and also that his name was not perpetually disgraced. For in offering violence to the captain and the soldiers, he acts like a highwayman because he resists the power which God has ordained. Christ was already hated more than enough by the world, and this single act might have given his enemies some substance for all their false accusations. Besides, it was exceedingly thoughtless of Peter to try to prove his faith with his sword when he could not do so with his tongue. When he is later called to confess his Master, he denies him; but now he raises a riot without his Master's authority.

Let us be warned by this striking example to moderate our zeal; and as our unrestrained sinful nature is always eager to attempt more than God commands, let us learn that our zeal will turn out badly whenever we try and do anything contrary to God's Word. Sometimes the beginning promises much, but in the end we shall be punished for our rashness. Let obedience be the basis of everything we undertake. We are also warned that those whose task is to plead Christ's cause do not always behave so skilfully that they commit no fault; and therefore we should be all the more earnest in asking the Lord to guide us by the spirit of prudence in every action.

11. "Put your sword away!" By this command Christ reproves Peter's action. But we must pay attention to the reason, which is that a private individual was not permitted to rise against those who had been invested with public authority. This can be inferred from the other three evangelists, who tell of Christ's general statement, "All who draw the sword will die by the sword" (Matthew 26:52). We too must be sure not to resist our enemies by force or arms, even when they provoke us unjustly, except so far as legal and social rights permit. Whoever goes beyond the bounds of his calling, even if he wins the whole world's applause, will never have his action approved by God.

"Shall I not drink the cup the Father has given me?" This seems to be a special reason why Christ had to be silent: that he might be led like a lamb to the slaughter. But it serves as an example, for the same patience is demanded from all of us. Scripture compares afflictions to drinking medicine. As the master of a house distributes food and drink to his children and servants, so God has this right over us, that he treats each one as seems good to him; and as he cheers us by prosperity or humbles us by adversity, he is said to give a sweet or bitter drink. The drink reserved for Christ was to suffer the death of the cross in order to reconcile the world. Therefore he says that he must **"drink the cup"** which his Father measured out and gave to him.

Similarly, we should be prepared to endure the cross. And yet we should not take any notice of the fanatics who assert that we must not seek remedies for sicknesses or any other kinds of affliction lest we reject **"the cup"** which God presents to us. We know that we must "die once" (Hebrews 9:27), and so we should be ready for death; but because we do not know when we shall die, the Lord permits us to defend our life with the aids which he himself has appointed. We must endure diseases patiently, however grievous they may be to our bodies; and while they do not seem to be fatal, we should try to alleviate them; only we must be careful not to attempt anything but what God's Word permits. In short, provided we always determine that the Lord's will must be done, we are not failing to drink **"the cup"** he has given us even when we seek deliverance from the evils which press upon us.

12. The detachment of soldiers with its commander . . . It might seem odd that Christ, who prostrated the soldiers by his voice, now lets himself be **arrested.** If he meant to surrender to his enemies in the end, why did he need to perform that miracle? There were two benefits of this demonstration of God's power. First, it removes the stumbling block of thinking that Christ yielded as if he had been overcome through weakness; and second, it proves that he suffered death entirely voluntarily. So he asserted his power over his enemies as far as was useful, but when he had to obey his Father, he restrained himself, so that he might become a victim. Let us remember that the body of the Son of God was bound in order that our souls might be set free from the bonds of sin and Satan.

13. . . . and brought him first to Annas. The other evangelists omit this, because it does not add much to the substance of the story. Nothing worth recording was done there. Perhaps the place was convenient, and they therefore kept Christ in Annas' house until the high priest called the council.

. . . the high priest that year . . . He does not mean that the office of high priest was annual, as many people have wrongly thought, but that Caiaphas was high priest at that time, as Josephus makes clear. The law made this honor a perpetual one, ending only with the holder's death; but ambition and internal revolts caused Roman governors at will to depose one high priest and substitute another who could prevail by money or favor. Thus Vitellius later deposed Caiaphas and appointed Jonathan the son of Annas as his successor.

14. . . . who had advised the Jews. The evangelist repeats Caiaphas' statement which we heard earlier, for God used the unclean mouth of a treacherous and wicked high priest to utter a prophecy (11:50), just as he guided Balaam's tongue contrary to his intentions, so that he was made to bless the people when he wanted to curse them as a favor to King Balak (Numbers 24:5).

Verses 15–18

15. . . . and another disciple . . . A weak conjecture has deceived some people into thinking that this disciple was John, because he normally speaks of himself anonymously. But how could John, a lowly fisherman, have been friendly with an elevated high priest? And how was it possible for him, one of Christ's household, to frequent the house of the high priest? It is more likely that he was not one of the twelve, but is called a **disciple** because he had embraced the teaching of the Son of God.

John does not arrange the events very precisely, being satisfied with a brief summary. After telling us that Peter denied Christ once, he mixes other things and later returns to the other two denials. Inattentive readers were led by this to conclude that the first denial took place in the house of Annas. But these words do not say this, but rather state clearly that it was the high priest's maid who led Peter to deny Christ. We must therefore understand that when Christ was brought before the high priest, not just anyone was allowed in, but the **disciple** who was known to the high priest asked for Peter to be admitted, as a favor. There is no reason to doubt that godly zeal was the motive for both of them to follow Christ, but since Christ had particularly said that he spared Peter and the others, it would have been far better for him who was so weak to groan and pray in some dark corner than to mix with people. He now eagerly undertakes the duty from which Christ had released him. When it comes to confessing his faith, which he ought to have maintained to the death, his courage fails. We should always see what the Lord requires of us, so that those who are weak may not undertake what is unnecessary.

17. . . . the girl at the door asked Peter. Peter is let into the high priest's hall, but it costs him very dearly, for as soon as he sets foot inside he is led to deny Christ. When he stumbles so disgracefully at the first step, the emptiness of his boasting is exposed. He had boasted that he would prove a valiant champion, able to face death resolutely; and now, at the voice of just one girl, and without any threatening, he is beaten and throws down his weapons. This is a true specimen of human strength. Certainly all the strength that seems to be in us is mere smoke which is immediately blown away with a puff of wind. Away from the battle, our spirits are high, without cause; but experience shows how foolish and empty our boasting is. Even when Satan is not attacking, we invent empty terrors for ourselves, and we are shaken before we need be.

The voice of a mere woman terrified Peter. What about us? Do we not sometimes jump at the sound of a leaf falling? The false appearance of a danger which was out of range made Peter tremble; are we not led away from Christ every day by childish absurdities? In short, our courage is such that it fails all by itself when there is no enemy. And in this way God punishes human arrogance, by reducing fierce minds to weakness. A man filled not with bravery but with wind promises that he will easily beat the whole world, and yet he is terrified at the shadow of a thistle. Let us therefore learn to be brave only in the Lord.

"I am not." This does not seem to be an absolute denial of Christ; but when Peter is afraid to confess that he is one of his disciples, it is equivalent to denying that he has anything to do with him. We should note this carefully, in case anyone thinks he has escaped by acting speciously when he denies his faith only indirectly.

18. When the evangelist adds that Peter was standing near the fire with the officers and servants, it helps to connect the various parts of the narrative, as we shall see. But it shows how stupid Peter was, that he carelessly warmed himself along with a crowd of wicked men after denying his Master — though it is possible he may have been restrained by fear lest, in leaving the high priest's house, he should fall into another similar danger.

Verses 19–24

19. The high priest interrogates Christ as if he were some troublemaker who had split the church into parties by collecting disciples; and he interrogates Christ as if he were a false prophet who had tried to corrupt the purity of the faith by new and perverse teaching. Christ had completed his task of teaching and does not begin a new defense; but, so as not to abandon the cause of truth, he shows that he is ready to defend all that he had taught. But he reproves the high priest's shamelessness in asking about what was well-known, as if it were doubtful. Not satisfied with having rejected the Redeemer offered, together with the salvation promised to them, they also condemn all his exposition of the law.

20. "I have spoken openly to the world." Some people have fallen into a childish error of thinking that Christ's reply condemns those who expound the Word of God in their own rooms when the tyranny of the ungodly stops them from expounding it publicly. But Christ is not discussing what is or is not lawful; he simply intended to put down the shameless malice of Caiaphas.

This passage seems to conflict with another of Christ's sayings, where he tells the disciples that it is not given to everyone to hear the secrets of the kingdom of heaven and that he therefore confers this grace only on the twelve (see Matthew 13:11). I answer that when in the present passage he says, **"I said nothing in secret,"** this refers to the substance, which was always the same, though the form of teaching varied. He did not speak differently among the disciples to teach them anything different; nor did he act cunningly, as if he deliberately intended to conceal from the people what he spoke to a few people indoors. Therefore, he could testify with a clear conscience that he had openly declared and honestly proclaimed the substance of his teaching.

22. This is added to tell us how furious Christ's enemies were and how tyrannical their rule was; and secondly, what sort of discipline existed among the priests. They sit as judges, but they are as cruel as wild beasts. A council is assembled, where the utmost gravity should have prevailed; yet **one of the officials** is so presumptuous that, in the middle of the trial and in the presence of the judges, he strikes the accused, who had not been found guilty in any way. It is not surprising, then, that Christ's teaching is condemned by such a barbarous assembly, from which all justice, even all humanity and decency, are banished.

23. "If I said something wrong . . ." That is, "If I have sinned, accuse me, and then when the case has been tried I can be punished according to the offense. For this is not a lawful way of proceeding; a quite different order and moderation should be followed in court." Christ therefore claims that he has been done a grievous injury if he has not sinned, and that even if he had sinned they ought to act lawfully and not with violence.

But here Christ seems not to observe the rule which he elsewhere lays down for his followers: he does not turn the other cheek (see Matthew 5:39). The answer is that in Christian patience it is not always the duty of someone who has been struck to swallow the injury without a word. First, he should bear it calmly; then he should give up all thought of revenge and try to overcome evil with good. The spirit of Satan already urges wicked people too powerfully to do evil without anybody provoking them. Therefore, it is foolish to expound Christ's words as commanding us to provoke those who are already too set on mischief. He simply means that each of us should be more ready to bear a second injury than to take revenge for the first. There is nothing to stop a Christian from expostulating when he has been treated unfairly, so long as his mind is free from anger and his hand clean from vindictiveness.

24. This sentence is to be read as a parenthesis. John says that Christ was taken to Annas' house and then continues the story as if the meeting of the priests had been held there. Now he reminds us that Christ was taken from Annas' house to the high priest's. As the tense of the Greek verb has deceived many people, I prefer to translate it by the pluperfect, "he *had* sent."

Verses 25–27

25. He denied it. How shocking is Peter's stupidity! He has denied his Master and not only has no feeling of repentance but hardens himself by his freedom in sinning! If each of them in turn had asked him, he would not have hesitated to deny his Master a thousand times. This is how Satan carries wretched men away after he has shifted them. We must also notice the detail which the other evangelists narrate, that he "swore" he did not know Christ (see Matthew 26:74; Mark 14:71). It happens like this with many people every day. At first the fault will not be so very great; then it becomes a habit; and in the end, when the conscience has been put to sleep, he who has got used to despising God will think nothing unlawful for himself but will dare to commit extreme sins. The best thing is for us to be on our guard in good time, so that if we are tempted by Satan while we are still uncorrupted we do not allow ourselves the slightest indulgence.

27. At that moment a rooster began to crow. The evangelist mentions the crowing of the rooster to tell us that Peter was warned by God at that moment. This is why the others say that he then "remembered" the Lord's words (Matthew 26:75; Mark 14:72), though according to Luke the mere crowing of the cock did not affect Peter until Christ looked at him (Luke 22:61). Thus, when a person has begun to fall through Satan's suggestions, no voice, no sign, no warning will recall him until the Lord himself looks at him.

Verses 28–32

28. Then the Jews led Jesus . . . The trial which the evangelist mentions took place before dawn. Yet there is no doubt that they were active throughout the city to inflame the people. Thus the rage of the people was suddenly kindled, as if with one consent they all demanded Christ's death. The trial was conducted by the priests — not that it was in their power to sentence him; but when they had crushed him by their initial decision, they could deliver him to be judged as if everything was known about him. The Romans called both the governor's house and the judgment-seat where he tried cases the "praetorium."

They wanted to be able to eat the Passover. They abstained from all defilement so that they would be purified according to the law's commands and could eat the Lord's **Passover.** So we may approve of their religion, but there are two faults, both of them gross. First, they do not stop to think that they carry more pollution within themselves than they can contract from entering any place, however profane; and second, they carry their attention to detail to excess and neglect the most important things. Paul says that "to those who are corrupted and do not believe, nothing is pure" (Titus 1:15). But these hypocrites are so full of malice, ambition, deceit, cruelty, and greed that they almost infect heaven and earth with their stench; and they only fear external pollution. This is an intolerable mockery: they expect to please God as long as they do not become defiled from contact with something unclean, though they have forgotten true purity.

Hypocrisy has another fault: it is careful to perform ceremonies but happily neglects the most important things. God commanded the Jews to perform the ceremonies contained in the law simply to accustom them to love and zeal for true holiness. Besides, nothing in the law forbade them to enter the house of a Gentile. This was just a precaution derived from the tradition of the fathers, to prevent anyone's accidentally becoming unclean from an impure house. But those fine interpreters of the law "swallow a camel" while they carefully "strain out a gnat" (see Matthew 23:24). Hypocrites usually think it a greater crime to kill a flea than to kill a man. This fault is closely linked to the other one, of greatly preferring human traditions to the sacred commandments of God. They want to keep themselves pure in order to **eat the Passover** properly; but they think uncleanness is restricted to the governor's house, and they do not hesitate to pursue an innocent person to death, witnessed by heaven and earth. In short, they observe the shadow of a **Passover** with feigned and false reverence, and yet not only do they violate the true **Passover** with sacrilegious hands but try as far as they can to overwhelm it in eternal ruin.

29. So Pilate came out to them. This irreligious man is willing to permit a superstition which he ridicules and despises; but in the most important matter he performs the duty of a good judge, ordering them to bring forward any accusation they have. The priests, however, not having enough authority to condemn someone they declare guilty, merely reply that he ought to abide by their existing judgment.

30. They indirectly complain of Pilate that he does not respect their integrity enough. "Why do you not take it on yourself to agree that the person we have accused is worthy of death?" they ask. This is how the ungodly, whom God has raised to a high degree of honor, are, as it were, blinded by their own greatness and allow themselves to do whatever they like. How people get drunk on pride! They want Christ to be counted as a criminal just because of their accusation. But if we look at the facts, what criminal acts do we find in him except that he has cured every kind of disease, has driven evil spirits out of people, made paralytics and the lame walk, and restored sight to the blind, hearing to the deaf, and life to the dead? These were the facts, and those men knew them perfectly well. But as I just said, when people are drunk with pride, nothing is harder than to rouse them to judge soundly and fairly.

31. ". . . by your own law." Undoubtedly Pilate is offended at their barbarism and violence and is reproaching them when he says that this form of condemnation which they were eager to carry out was against the common law of all nations and human feelings. At the same time, he censures them for boasting that they had a **"law"** given to them by God.

"Take him yourselves." This is said ironically, for he would not have allowed them to pronounce the death sentence. It is like saying, "If he were in your power, he would be executed right away, without being heard in his own defense. Is this how your law judges people, condemning them without any crime?" This is how ungodly people falsely take God's name as an excuse and expose his holy teaching to the reproach of enemies; and the world eagerly seizes on it as an occasion of slander.

"We have no right." People who think that the Jews are here refusing an offer which Pilate had made to them are mistaken. Rather, they knew he had mocked them by saying, **"Take him yourselves,"** and they reply, "You would not allow it; and since you are the judge, do your duty."

32. . . . so that the words Jesus had spoken . . . would be fulfilled. Finally the evangelist adds that it was necessary for this to be done in order that the prediction which Christ had uttered should be fulfilled: "They will . . . turn him over to the Gentiles" (Matthew 20:18-19). If we want to profit from the story of Christ's death, the main thing is to think about God's eternal purpose. The Son of God is put before a tribunal of a mortal man. If we think that this is done by human will and do not raise our eyes to God, our faith will necessarily be put to shame and defeated. But when we see that our condemnation before God is blotted out by the condemnation of Christ, because it pleased the Heavenly Father to reconcile mankind to himself in this way, this single thought will raise us high, and we shall glory even in Christ's ignominy, boldly and without shame. So let us learn, in each part of this narrative, to turn our eyes to God as the author of our redemption.

Verses 33–36

33. Pilate then went back inside the palace. We can draw this conclusion from the other Gospels: probably the evangelist leaves out many things which were said on both sides. But John dwells chiefly on a single point, that Pilate carefully inquired whether Christ was being accused justly or not. In front of the people, who were inflamed with sedition, everything was in an uproar. Therefore he goes **back inside the palace.** He intends to acquit Christ, but Christ offers himself to be condemned, in order that he may obey his Father. This is why he is so sparing in his replies. Having a judge who was favorable and who would willingly have listened to him, it was not difficult for him to plead his own cause; but he considers the purpose of his coming into the world and what his Father is now calling him to do. Therefore he chooses to be silent, that he may not escape death.

"Are you the king of the Jews?" It would never have occurred to Pilate to ask about the kingdom if the Jews had not brought this charge against Christ. Pilate takes up the most serious point, so that he may dispose of it and acquit the prisoner. Christ's answer suggests that there is no basis for that accusation. It contains an indirect refutation, as if he had said, "It is absurd to bring that charge against me, for not even the slightest suspicion of it can fall on me."

Pilate seems to have taken it amiss that Christ asked him why he suspected him. Therefore he angrily reproaches him that all the evil comes from his own nation. "I sit here as a judge," he says. "It is not foreigners but your own countrymen who are accusing you. There is no reason therefore to involve me in your quarrels. I and the Romans would let you live in peace, but you make trouble among yourselves, and I am reluctantly compelled to take a part in it."

36. "My kingdom is not of this world." In these words Christ acknowledges that he is a king, but so far as was necessary to prove his innocence, he clears himself of the false accusation by saying that there is no disagreement between his kingdom and political order. It is like saying, "I am falsely accused, as if I had attempted to produce a disturbance or to overturn the state. I have preached about the **kingdom** of God, but that is spiritual, and therefore you have no right to suspect me of aspiring to kingly power." This was Christ's defense before Pilate; but the same teaching is useful to believers to the end of the world, for if the kingdom of Christ were earthly, it would be unstable and changeable, because "this world in its present form is passing away" (1 Corinthians 7:31). But since it is called heavenly, this assures us of its perpetuity. Thus, if the whole world were overturned, provided our consciences are always directed to the **"kingdom"** of Christ, we will still remain firm amidst shakings and convulsions, and even amidst dreadful ruin and destruction. If we are treated cruelly by ungodly people, still our salvation is secured by the **"kingdom"** of Christ, which is not subject to human will. In short, though the world is constantly tossed by innumerable storms, the **"kingdom"** of Christ, in which we should seek tranquillity, is separated from them.

We are also taught the nature of this **"kingdom."** If it made us happy after the flesh and brought us riches, luxuries, and all that is desirable for our present life, it would smell of the earth and of the world; but as it is, our condition seems to be wretched, but our true happiness remains unimpaired. We also learn who belongs to this **"kingdom"**: those who, having been renewed by God's Spirit, practice the heavenly life in holiness and righteousness. Yet we should also notice that it does not say that the **"kingdom"** of Christ is not *in* **"this world,"** for we know that it has its seat in our hearts. As Christ says elsewhere, "The kingdom of God is within you" (Luke 17:21). But strictly speaking the **"kingdom"** of God, while it lives in us, is a stranger to the world, because its condition is totally different.

"My servants would fight." He shows that he was not aiming at an earthly kingdom, because no one is incited, no one takes up arms. If a private individual claims royal authority, he has to gain power by seditious men. Nothing of this kind is seen in Christ, and it therefore follows that he is not an earthly king.

But here a question arises: is it lawful to defend the **"kingdom"** of Christ by arms? When earthly rulers are commanded to "kiss the Son" (Psalm 2:10-12), they are urged not only to submit to his authority as private individuals, but also to use all the power they possess in defending the church and maintaining godliness. The answer is:

1. Those who draw the conclusion that the Gospel teaching and the pure worship of God are not to be defended by arms are wrong and ignorant. Christ is only saying that in the present case the Jews' false accusations against him were frivolous.

2. Godly kings may defend Christ's **"kingdom"** by the sword, but it is not done in the way worldly kingdoms are defended; for Christ's **"kingdom"** is spiritual and must be founded on the teaching and power of the Spirit. It must be built up in the same way, for neither human laws and edicts nor human punishments reach the conscience. Yet this does not stop rulers from defending Christ's **"kingdom"** incidentally, partly by establishing external discipline and partly by lending their protection to the church against the ungodly. However, the depravity of **"this world"** causes Christ's **"kingdom"** to be established more by the blood of martyrs than by force of arms.

Verses 37–40

37. "You are right in saying I am a king." Although Pilate had already learned from the previous answer that Christ claims some sort of **"kingdom"** for himself, Christ now asserts this more definitely; and, not satisfied with this, he makes another statement which, as it were, seals what he had said. From this we infer that the teaching about Christ's "kingdom" is especially important, since he thought it worthy of such strong affirmation.

"For this reason I was born . . . to testify to the truth." This is, no doubt, a general statement, but it must be viewed in relation to the context. The words mean that it is natural for Christ to be truthful; moreover, it was **"for this reason"** the Father sent him, and so this is his particular task. There is no danger, therefore, that our trust in him will be deceived, for it is impossible for him to teach what is untrue when his divine commission and natural disposition are to maintain **"the truth."**

"Everyone on the side of truth . . ." Christ added this not so much to exhort Pilate (for he knew that he would not gain anything by doing so) as to defend his teaching against the base reproaches which had been cast on it. It was like saying, "I am charged with asserting that **I am a king**, as if it were a crime, and yet this is an unquestionable truth, which is received with reverence and without argument by all who have right judgment and sound understanding." When he says that they are **"on the side of truth,"** he does not mean that they naturally know **"the truth,"** but that they are ruled by God's Spirit.

38. "What is truth?" Some people think Pilate asks this question out of curiosity, as irreligious people sometimes are eager to learn something new and yet do not know why they wish it, for they intend only to gratify their ears. For my own part, I rather think it is an expression of disdain, for Pilate thought himself highly insulted that Christ should make out that he lacked all knowledge of **"the truth."** Here we see in Pilate a disease which is common among men. We are all aware of our ignorance, but few of us are willing to admit it. Consequently, most people reject true teaching. Afterwards, the Lord, who is the teacher of the humble, blinds proud people and thus inflicts on them the punishment they deserve. From the same pride arises such disdain that they do not choose to submit to learn, because everyone claims to be wise and intelligent. **"Truth"** is believed to be a common thing; but God declares, on the contrary, that it lies far beyond the reach of human understanding.

The same thing happens in other matters. The principal matters of theology are: the curse pronounced on the human race; the corruption of nature; the mortification of the sinful self; the renewal of life; the free reconciliation brought about by the unique sacrifice; the imputation of righteousness, by which a sinner is accepted by God; and the illumination of the Holy Spirit. These things are paradoxes, and so they are contemptuously rejected by ordinary human understanding. Therefore, few people make progress in God's school, because hardly one in ten pays attention to the rudiments. And why is this but because they measure God's secret wisdom by their own understanding?

But it is evident that Pilate spoke mockingly, for he at once goes out. In short, he is angry with Christ for boasting that he is bringing forward **"the truth,"** which previously lay hidden in darkness. Yet Pilate's indignation shows that wicked people never reject the Gospel teaching so spitefully that they are not moved by it a little. Although Pilate did not go as far as to become humble and teachable, he is made to feel some inner compunction.

39. "But it is your custom . . ." Pilate was wondering all the time how he might save Christ's life, but the people were so furious that he tried to keep to a middle path, in order to allay their anger. He thought it would be enough if Christ were dismissed as a criminal and marked with perpetual disgrace. He therefore chooses Barabbas above all others, so that by comparison with him their hatred for Christ might be softened, for Barabbas was strongly detested by everyone because of his atrocious crimes. Indeed, what is more detestable than a robber? But Luke tells us that in addition to this he was guilty of other crimes (see Luke 23:19).

That the Jews preferred him to Christ only happened by a singular intervention by God's providence, for it would have been most unsuitable for the Son of God to be rescued by so unworthy a price. Yet by his death he was thrown into the deepest ignominy, so that in consequence of the release of Barabbas he was crucified between two robbers. He had taken upon himself the sins of all, which could not be expiated in any other way; and the glory of his resurrection, which quickly followed, made his death itself a splendid triumph.

This **custom**, by which the Roman governor gave some criminal up to the Jews every year at the Passover, involved a gross and base abuse. No doubt it was done in honor of the day, but it was in reality nothing but a shameful profanation of it. For Scripture declares that "acquitting the guilty and condemning the innocent — the Lord detests them both" (Proverbs 17:15), and therefore the Lord is far from taking delight in that perverted sort of pardon. Let us learn from this example that nothing is more perverted than to try and serve God by our own inventions. As soon as people begin to follow their own imaginations, there will be no end until they fall into extreme madness and openly mock God. The rule for the worship of God, therefore, should be derived only from what he himself ordains.

John
Chapter 19

Verses 1–6

1. Then Pilate took Jesus . . . Pilate sticks to his original purpose, but he adds a second ignominy, hoping that after Christ has been scourged the Jews will be satisfied with this lesser punishment. When he tries so hard and unsuccessfully, we see the decree by which Christ was appointed to die. Yet Christ's innocence is often asserted in the judge's testimony, to assure us that he was free from all sin. He took the place of a guilty person and bore the punishment due to other people's sins. In Pilate we also see a remarkable example of a trembling conscience. He acquits Christ with his mouth and acknowledges that he finds **"no basis for a charge against him"** (verse 4), and yet punishes him as if he were guilty. Thus, those who have not enough courage to defend with unshaken constancy what is right must be driven here and there and forced to adopt opposite and conflicting opinions.

We all condemn Pilate, and yet, shameful to say, there are so many Pilates in the world who flog Christ — not only in his followers, but also in his teaching. There are many people who, for the purpose of saving the life of those who are persecuted for the sake of the Gospel, constrain them to a wicked denial of Christ. What is this but to expose Christ to ridicule, that Christ may lead a dishonorable life? Others select only particular parts of the Gospel and tear the whole Gospel to pieces. They think that they have done exceedingly well if they correct a few bad abuses. It would be better for the teaching to be buried for a while than for it to be flogged in this way, for it would come to life again in spite of the devil and tyrants. But nothing is more difficult than to restore it to its purity once it has been corrupted.

2. The soldiers twisted together a crown of thorns. This was undoubtedly done on Pilate's authority, to brand the Son of God with the mark of the crime which made him king and to placate the anger of the Jews, as if he had been convinced that the accusations which they brought against Christ were well founded. However, the wickedness and insolence of the soldiers is indulged in more freely than the judge had ordered, as ungodly men seize the opportunity to do evil whenever they can. But we see here the amazing cruelty of the Jewish nation, whose mind is not moved to compassion by such a sad sight. But all this is directed by God in order to reconcile the world to himself by the death of his Son.

6. "You take him." Pilate did not wish to give Christ into their hands or to abandon him to their anger, but he declares that he will not be their executioner. This is clear from the reason he immediately adds when he says, **"I find no basis for a charge against him."** It is as if he had said that he will never be persuaded to shed innocent blood for their gratification. That it is only the priests and officers who demand that he shall be crucified is evident from the fact that there was less rage among the people except so far as it was stirred up by the troublemakers.

Verses 7–11

7. "We have a law." They mean that they are prosecuting Christ with the **"law"** on their side and are not motivated by hatred or sinful passion, for they saw that Pilate had indirectly reproved them. They speak as if they were in the presence of a man who was ignorant of the **"law,"** as if they had said, "We are permitted to live in our own way, and our religion does not allow anyone to boast of being the Son of God." Nor was this accusation totally without plausibility, but they erred grievously in applying it. The overall teaching was undoubtedly true, that it was not lawful for men to assume any honor which belonged to God, and that anyone who claimed for himself what belongs only to God must die. But their error came from their view of who Christ was, because they did not reflect on the titles given in Scripture to the Messiah, from which they would easily have seen that he was the Son of God. They did not even deign to inquire whether or not Jesus was the Messiah promised by God.

So we see how they drew a false conclusion from a true principle because they reasoned badly. This example warns us to distinguish carefully between a general doctrine and its application. There are many ignorant and weak people who reject the very principles of Scripture, for they have been deceived by the semblance of truth. Such licentiousness progresses too much in the world today. Therefore, let us remember that we should be on our guard against error, so that principles which are true may hold sway and that the authority of Scripture may not be diminished.

On the other hand, we can easily answer wicked men in this way when they falsely and improperly allege the testimony of Scripture, and the principles which they draw from it, to support their evil ideas. In the same way the Roman Catholics, when they extol in elevated terms the authority of the church, put forward nothing except what all the children of God are agreed on. They maintain that the church is the mother of believers, that she is the pillar of truth, that she ought to be listened to, and that she is guided by the Holy Spirit. All this we agree with, but when they want to appropriate to themselves all the authority which belongs to the church, they wickedly, and with sacrilegious presumption, seize what does not at all belong to them. We must examine the basis of what they assume to be true, that they deserve the title of The Church, in which matter they completely fail. People who are satisfied with general principles and do not look at the details imagine that the Roman Catholics are right in attacking us. But when the matter is investigated, smoke which deceives the simple quickly disperses.

8. He was even more afraid. These words can be explained in two ways. First, Pilate was afraid that some blame might be attached to him if a demonstration arose because he had not condemned Christ. Second, once he heard about the name of the Son of God, his mind was touched by religion. This second view is confirmed by what immediately follows.

9. He went back inside the palace. "Where do you come from?" he asked Jesus. Clearly, Pilate was perplexed and worried, because he was afraid that he would be punished for sacrilege if he laid his hand on the Son of God. It should be noted that when he asks, **"Where do you come from?"** he is not asking which country he comes from but, "Are you a man who was born on earth, or are you some god?" Therefore, my interpretation of this passage is that Pilate was struck with the fear of God. He did not know what to do. On the one hand, he saw an impending uprising, and on the other hand, his conscience obliged him not to offend God just to avoid danger.

This example is most noteworthy. Christ's countenance was greatly disfigured; and yet as soon as Pilate hears God's name, fear of violating the majesty of God grips him, even though he was completely mean and despicable. If reverence for God had so much influence on an irreligious man, is he not worse than the reprobates who now judge divine things with levity and carelessness and without any fear? Pilate shows that men have an innate sense of religion which does not allow them to rush fearlessly in any direction they choose when the question relates to divine things. This is why I say that those who, in dealing with the teaching of Scripture, are not more impressed with the majesty of God than if they had been arguing over the shadow of an ass are given over to "a depraved mind" (Romans 1:28). Nevertheless, one day they will feel to their destruction what veneration is due to God's name, which they now mock so disdainfully and outrageously.

But Jesus gave him no answer. We should not think it odd that Jesus gives **no answer** if we keep in mind what I have said before, that Christ did not stand before Pilate to plead his own cause — as is customary with accused people who want to be acquitted — but rather to suffer condemnation. For he had to be condemned in order to take our place. This is why he makes no defense. Christ's silence is consistent with Paul's words, "Christ Jesus, who while testifying before Pontius Pilate made the good confession" (1 Timothy 6:13). Christ maintained the faith of the Gospel, insofar as this was necessary, and his death was nothing other than the sealing of the teaching he delivered. Christ did not fail to make a legitimate confession, but he kept silent rather than ask for an acquittal. Moreover, there was some danger that Pilate would acquit Christ as one of the fictitious gods, just as Tiberius wanted to place him among the gods of the Romans. Therefore Christ refuted this foolish superstition by keeping silent.

10. This shows that Pilate's sudden fear was temporary and had no solid foundation. For now, forgetting all fear, he bounds into haughty and dreadful contempt for God. He threatens Christ, as if there were no Judge in heaven. This always happens with irreligious people, who shake off the fear of God and then quickly return to their natural disposition. So we also infer that it is said with good reason that "the heart of man is deceitful" (Jeremiah 17:9); for though some fear of God lives in men, godlessness also comes from them. Whoever, then, is not born again by the Spirit of God, though he feigns for a time to reverence the majesty of God, will quickly show, by the contrast of his actions, that this fear was phony.

Again, we see in Pilate an example of a proud man who is driven to madness by his ambition. When he wants to increase his power, he deprives himself of all praise and reputation for justice. He acknowledges that Christ is innocent, and therefore he makes himself no better than a robber when he boasts that he has power to cut his throat! Thus evil consciences, in which faith and the true knowledge of God do not rule, must be woken up, and there must be within them various feelings of the flesh which fight with each other. This is how God avenges himself against men's pride when they overstep themselves, claiming for themselves infinite power. By condemning themselves of injustice, they stamp themselves with the worst reproach and disgrace. No blindness, therefore, is greater than pride. This should not surprise us, since pride feels the hand of God, which it strikes against as an avenger. We must therefore remember that we should not rashly indulge in foolish boastings, lest we expose ourselves to ridicule. People who do not hold a high rank should take special care to conduct themselves modestly and not be ashamed of being subject to God and to his laws.

11. "You would have no power . . ." Some people explain this in a general way, that nothing happens in the world except by God's permission. It is as if Christ had said that Pilate, though he thinks that he can do all things, will do nothing more than God permits. The statement is undoubtedly true that this world is governed by God and that, whatever evil men do, they still cannot even move a finger without the hidden power of God. But I prefer the opinion of those who confine this passage to the office of the magistrate. Through these words Christ rebukes the foolish boasting of Pilate in extolling himself, as if his power had not been from God. It is as if he said: "You claim everything for yourself, as if you will not have to give an account to God one day. You were not made a judge without his permission. Consider, then, that his heavenly throne is far superior to yours." It is impossible to find any more suitable admonition to repress the insolence of those who rule over others, that they may not abuse their authority. The father thinks that he may do what he likes to his children, the husband to his wife, the master to his servants, the prince to his people, unless they look to God, who wants them to be ruled by a definite law.

"Therefore the one who handed me over to you . . ." Some think that this makes the Jews more guilty than Pilate because with wicked hatred and malicious treachery they show anger against an innocent man — that is, the private individuals, and not those people invested with lawful authority. I think that this makes the Jewish leaders more guilty, and less excusable on any other ground, since they use a divinely appointed government to comply with their lawless desires. It is a dreadful sacrilege to pervert a holy ordinance in order to do evil. The robber who with his own hand cuts the throat of any poor traveler is justly abhorred. But the person who under the guise of a judicial trial puts to death an innocent man is much more wicked. Yet Christ does not emphasize their guilt in order to acquit Pilate, for he does not compare them but rather condemns them all because they equally pollute a holy power. The only difference is this, that he makes a direct attack on the Jews but indirectly censures Pilate, who complies with their wicked desire.

Verses 12–16

12. From then on, Pilate tried to set Jesus free. Though Pilate does not conduct himself conscientiously and is motivated more by ambition than respect for justice, and for that reason is wretchedly irresolute, his modesty is nevertheless commendable because when he is severely reproved by Christ, he does not fly into a rage but on the contrary wants to release him the more. He is a judge, and yet he humbly allows the accused person to reprove him. Hardly one person in a hundred will be found who receives a reproof so humbly, even from one who is his equal.

"You are no friend of Caesar." By using threats they force Pilate to condemn Christ, for they could do nothing that was more hateful or more likely to produce fear than to accuse him of disloyalty to Caesar. "You show," they say, "that you do not care about Caesar's authority if you acquit Christ, who has tried to cause a state of confusion." This wickedness at last breaks down Pilate's resolution, who up till then had only been shaken by their furious cries. The evangelist has good reason for carefully examining the details of those circumstances, for it is very important for us to know that Pilate did not condemn Christ before he himself had acquitted him several times, so that we may know that it was for our sins that he was condemned, and not for his own. We also see from this how Christ offered to die of his own volition when he declined to avail himself of the judgment in his favor; and, indeed, it was this obedience that made his death "a fragrant offering" (Ephesians 5:2) for blotting out all sins.

13. . . . sat down on the judge's seat. Hence we see what conflicting thoughts passed through Pilate's mind, as if he had been acting two characters on stage. He ascends **the judge's seat** in order to pronounce solemnly the death sentence on Christ, and in the usual way. Nevertheless he openly declares that he does so reluctantly and against his conscience. When he calls Christ **"king"** (verse 14), he is speaking ironically, meaning that the Jews only had a trivial charge against him. He checks their anger and warns them that it would bring disgrace on the whole nation if a report were spread everywhere that one of their own people had been given the death sentence for aspiring to be **"king."**

. . . at a place known as the Stone Pavement. When the evangelist says that **Gabbatha** was the name of the place in Hebrew, he refers to the Aramaic or Syriac language, which was then in common use, for in Hebrew *Gabah* means "elevated." It was right, therefore, that Christ should be condemned from a high place, so that he, coming from heaven as the supreme Judge, may acquit us at the last day.

14. . . . about the sixth hour. The evangelists appear to differ, and even to contradict each other, in calculating the time. The other three evangelists say that "darkness" came on **about the sixth hour**, while Christ was hanging on the cross (Matthew 27:45; Mark 15:33; Luke 23:44). Mark, too, specifically says that it was "the third hour" when the sentence was pronounced on him (Mark 15:25). But this may be easily explained. It is clear enough from other passages that the day was at that time divided into four times, as the night also contained four watches. So the evangelists sometimes allot not more than four "hours" to each day and extend each hour to three. At the same time they reckon the space of an hour which was drawing to a close as belonging to the next. According to this calculation, John relates that Christ was condemned **about the sixth hour** because the time of the day was drawing towards **the sixth hour**, or towards the second part of the day. Hence we infer that Christ was crucified at or about **the sixth hour**; for as the evangelist afterwards mentions, **the place . . . was near the city** (verse 20). The "darkness" began between the sixth and ninth hour and lasted until the ninth hour, at which time Christ died.

15. "We have no king but Caesar." Here is a shocking display, that the priests, who ought to have been well-acquainted with the law, reject Christ, in whom the salvation of the people completely rested, on whom all the promises depended, and in whom the whole of their religion was founded. By rejecting Christ, they deprived themselves of the grace of God and of every blessing. We see, then, what madness had gripped them. Let us suppose that Jesus was not the Christ. They still have no excuse for acknowledging **"no king but Caesar."** For, first, they rebel against the spiritual kingdom of God; and, second, they prefer the tyranny of the Roman Empire, which they hated greatly, to a just government, such as God had promised them. Thus ungodly men, in order to run away from Christ, not only deprive themselves of eternal life but bring down on their heads every kind of misery. On the other hand, the sole happiness of the godly is to be subject to the royal authority of Christ, whether, in the flesh, they are placed under a just and lawful government or under the oppression of tyrants.

16. Finally Pilate handed him over to them to be crucified. Doubtless Pilate was constrained by their inability to hand Christ over; and yet this was not done in a chaotic way, but he was solemnly condemned in the ordinary way, because there were also two robbers who, after having been tried, were at the same time condemned to be crucified. But John uses this expression in order to make it even clearer that Christ, though he had not been convicted of any crime, was given up to the insatiable cruelty of the people.

Verses 17–22

17. He went out to the Place of the Skull. The details related here help greatly not only to show the truth of the narrative, but also to build up our faith. We must look for righteousness in the satisfaction for sin made by Christ. To show that he is the sacrifice for our sins, he wanted to be led out of the city, to be hanged on a tree. For the custom was, complying with the injunction of the law, that the sacrifices, the blood of which was shed for sin, were carried out of the camp (Leviticus 6:30 and 16:27), and the same law declares that "anyone who is hung on a tree is under God's curse" (Deuteronomy 21:23). Both of these were fulfilled in Christ, so that we might be completely certain that atonement has been made for our sins by his sacrificial death, that "Christ redeemed us from the curse of the law by becoming a curse for us" (Galatians 3:13), and that "God made him who had no sin to be sin for us, so that in him we might become the righteousness of God" (2 Corinthians 5:21); he was led out of the city in order that he might carry with him, and take away, our defilements which were laid on him (see Hebrews 13:12).

18. As if the severity of the punishment was not enough in itself, Christ is hanged **in the middle**, between two robbers, as if he not only had deserved to be classed with other robbers, but had been the most wicked and the most detestable of them all. We ought always to remember that Christ's evil executioners did nothing but what had been determined by the hand and design of God, for God did not surrender his Son to their lawless passions but determined that, according to his own will and good pleasure, he should be offered as a sacrifice. And if there were good reasons for the counsel of God in all those things which he willed his Son to suffer, we should consider, on the one hand, the dreadful weight of his anger against sin and, on the other hand, his infinite goodness towards us. In no other way could our guilt be removed but by the Son of God becoming a curse for us. We see him driven out into an accursed place, as if he had been polluted by a mass of all sorts of evil, that there he might appear to be accursed before God and men. We are really stupid if we do not clearly see in this mirror how much God hates sin; and we are harder than stones if we do not tremble at this judgment.

When, on the other hand, God declares that our salvation was so dear to him that he did not spare his one and only Son, what abundant goodness and what astonishing grace do we see! Whoever, then, takes a correct view of the reasons for the death of Christ, together with the benefit it brings us, will not, like the Greeks, regard the teaching of the cross as "foolishness," nor, like the Jews, will he regard it as "a stumbling block" (see 1 Corinthians 1:23), but rather as an invaluable token and pledge of the power, wisdom, righteousness, and goodness of God.

When John says that the name of the place was **Golgotha** (verse 17), he takes it from the Aramaic or Syriac language. The name is derived from *Galgal*, which means "to roll"; a **skull** is round like a ball or a globe.

19. Pilate had a notice prepared. The evangelist relates a memorable action of Pilate, after having pronounced the sentence. It is perhaps true that it was customary to place notices when criminals were executed, so that everyone might know the reason for the punishment as a deterrent. But in Christ's case there is this extraordinary detail, that the **notice** which is put above him implies no disgrace, for Pilate's intention was to avenge himself indirectly on the Jews (who by their obstinacy had extorted from him an unjust sentence of death on an innocent man) and in the person of Christ to throw blame on the whole nation. Thus he does not accuse Christ of any crime.

But the providence of God, which guided the pen of Pilate, had a higher objective. It did not, indeed, occur to Pilate to praise Christ as the author of salvation and the King of a chosen people. But God dictated to him this commendation of the Gospel, although he did not know the meaning of what he wrote. It was the same hidden guidance of the Spirit that caused the **notice** to be written in three languages. Most probably this was not an ordinary practice, but the Lord showed by this careful planning that the time was now ready for the name of his Son to be made known throughout the world.

21. The chief priests of the Jews protested to Pilate. They feel that they are sharply rebuked; and therefore they want the **notice** to be changed, so as not to disgrace the nation but to rather throw the whole blame on Christ. They do not conceal their deep hatred of the truth, since the tiniest spark of truth is more than they can endure. Thus Satan always prompts his servants to put out, or at least to choke by their own darkness, God's light as soon as it shines even slightly.

22. "What I have written, I have written." Pilate's firmness must be put down to God's overruling. There can be no doubt that they attempted, in various ways, to change his mind. So we know that he was held by a divine hand, and he remained unmoved. Pilate did not yield to the cries of the priests and did not allow himself to be corrupted by them. God testified through his mouth the strength of his Son's kingdom. And if in Pilate's example Christ's kingdom was shown to be unshakable against the attacks of its enemies, what value should we give to the testimonies of the prophets, whose tongues and hands God consecrated to his service?

The example of Pilate reminds us, also, that it is our duty to remain steadfast in defending the truth. A heathen refuses to retract what he has written truly about Christ, even though he did not understand what he was doing. How great, then, our shame if we are terrified by threats or dangers and we stop following his teaching which God has sealed in our hearts by his Spirit! Moreover, it should be noted how detestable is the Roman Catholics' tyranny, which forbids the reading of the Gospel, and the whole of the Scripture, by ordinary people. Pilate, though he was a reprobate man and in other respects an instrument of Satan, was nevertheless, through hidden guidance, appointed to be a herald of the Gospel, that he might write a short summary of it in three languages. What do we do with those who do all that they can to suppress its knowledge, since they show that they are worse than Pilate?

Verses 23–24

23. The other evangelists also mention that "they divided up his clothes" (Matthew 27:35; Mark 15:24; Luke 23:34). There were **four** soldiers who divided among themselves all **his clothes**, except **the undergarment**, which, being **seamless**, could not be divided, and therefore they decided **by lot** (verse 24) who would get it. To concentrate our minds on God's purpose, the evangelists remind us that in this event also there was a fulfillment of Scripture. It may be thought, however, that the passage which they quote from Psalm 22:18 is inappropriately applied to the subject in hand. Although David complains in it that he was exposed as a prey to his enemies, he makes use of the word **clothing** to denote metaphorically all his property — as if he had said, in a single word, that "he had been stripped naked and bare by wicked men." When the evangelists ignore the metaphor, they depart from the natural meaning of the passage. But we ought to remember, in the first place, that the psalm ought not to be restricted to David, as is evident from many parts of it, and especially from a clause in which it is written, "I will declare your name to my brothers" (Psalm 22:22), which must be seen as referring to Christ. Therefore, we should not be surprised if what was faintly outlined in David is seen in Christ with all that superior clarity the truth ought to have when compared with its figurative representation.

We must also learn that Christ was stripped of his **clothes** so that he might clothe us with righteousness — that his naked body was exposed to the insults of men so that we may appear in glory before the judgment-seat of God. As for the allegorical interpretation which some people have twisted out of this passage, by making it mean that heretics tear Scripture in pieces, this is too far-fetched. However, I would not object to the following comparison: that, as the **clothes** of Christ were once divided by ungodly **soldiers**, so today there are perverse men who through strange ideas tear the whole of the Scripture with which Christ is clothed in order that he may be revealed to us.

The Roman Catholics tell us that Scripture is torn in pieces by heretics but that **the undergarment** — that is, the church — remains untorn. In this way they try to prove, without paying any attention to the authority of Scripture, that the unity of the church is itself founded on something other than the authority of Scripture. When, therefore, they separate faith from Scripture, so that it may continue to be attached to the church alone, they not only strip Christ of his **clothes** but tear his body in pieces in a shocking sacrilege. Even if we agree with them when they say that the words **this garment was seamless** are a metaphor for the church, they are still far from proving their argument, for it still remains to be proved that the church is placed under their authority, about which they offer no evidence.

Verses 25–27

25. Near the cross of Jesus stood his mother. The evangelist mentions here incidentally that while Christ obeyed God the Father, he did not fail to perform the duty which he owed, as a son, towards **his mother.** It is true that Christ forgot himself so he could obey his Father. But once he had carried out that duty, he did not neglect **his mother.** So we learn how we should carry out our duty towards God and towards men. It often happens that, when God calls us to do his will, our parents or wife or children draw us in the opposite direction, so that we cannot give equal attention to everything. If we place men in the same category as God, we judge wrongly. Therefore we must give the priority to the command, the worship, and the service of God; after that, insofar as we can, we must give to men what is their due.

And yet the commands on the two tablets of stone never clash with each other, though at first sight they appear to. We must start with the worship of God, and after that put men in a secondary place. This is the teaching of the following statements: "Anyone who loves his father or mother more than me is not worthy of me" (Matthew 10:37); and, "If anyone comes to me and does not hate his father and mother, his wife and children, his brothers and sisters — yes, even his own life — he cannot be my disciple" (Luke 14:26). Therefore we should devote ourselves to the interests of men, as long as they do not interfere with the worship and obedience which we owe to God. When we have obeyed God, it will then be the right time to think about parents and wife and children. Christ looks after **his mother**, but this is after he is on the cross, to which he has been called by his Father's command.

If we note the time and place when these things happened, Christ's care for **his mother** was worthy of admiration. I will say nothing about his severe bodily tortures, and I will say nothing about the reproaches which he suffered. Even though horrible blasphemies against God filled his mind with inconceivable grief, and though he fought a dreadful battle with eternal death and with the devil, yet none of these things prevents him from being concerned about **his mother**. We also learn from this passage how God, through his law, commands us to honor our parents (see Ephesians 6:1-2). Christ appoints **the disciple** (verse 26) to take his place and commands him to support and take care of **his mother**. From this it follows that the honor that is due to parents consists not in mere veneration, but in all necessary duties.

On the other hand, we should consider the faith of those holy women. It is true that in following Christ to the cross they showed no common affection; but if they had not been supported by faith, they could never have been present on this stage. As for John himself, we infer that although his faith was smothered for a short while, it was not completely extinguished. It is shameful if fear of the cross deters us from following Christ, even when the glory of his resurrection is set before our eyes; the women saw nothing but the disgrace and cursing of the cross.

Mary the wife of Clopas, and Mary of Magda. He calls her either **the wife** or the "daughter" of Clopas. I prefer the latter interpretation. He says that she was **his mother's sister**, according to the Hebrew idiom which includes cousins and other relatives in the word "brothers." We see that it was not in vain that **Mary of Magda** had "seven demons" driven out of her (Mark 16:9), since she showed herself to the end to be such a faithful disciple of Christ.

26. "Dear woman, here is your son." It is as if Christ had said, "From now on I shall not live on the earth and be able to discharge to you my filial duties; therefore, I put this man in my place, that he may perform my duty." He means the same thing when he says to John, **"Here is your mother"** (verse 27). By these words he commands him to treat her as a **mother** and to care for her as if she had been his own **mother.**

In refraining from mentioning his mother's name, and in simply calling her **"Dear woman,"** some think that he did so in order not to pierce her heart with a deeper wound. I do not object to this view; but there is another conjecture which is equally probable, that Christ intended to show that having completed the course of human life, he lays down the condition in which he had lived and enters into the heavenly kingdom, where he will exercise dominion over angels and men. For we know that Christ was always accustomed to guard believers against looking at the flesh, and it was especially necessary that this should be done at his death.

27. This disciple took her into his home. It is a token of the reverence due by a **disciple** to his Master that John so readily obeys the command of Christ. Hence also it is evident that the apostles had their families, for John could not have exercised hospitality towards the mother of Christ or have taken her **into his home** if he had not had a house and a regular way of living. Those men, therefore, are fools who think that the apostles relinquished their property and came to Christ naked and empty; they are worse than fools who make perfection to consist in beggary.

Verses 28–30

28. Later, knowing that all was now completed . . . John purposely passes over many things which the other three evangelists relate. He now describes the last act, which was of the greatest importance.

When John says that **a jar of wine vinegar was there** (verse 29), he speaks as if it were usual. There has been much controversy about this subject, but I agree with those who think that it was a kind of drink usually given to accelerate death when the wretched criminals had been tortured enough. It should be noted that Christ does not ask for anything to drink until **all was now completed**; and thus he testifies to his infinite love for us and the inestimable care for our salvation. No words can express adequately the bitterness of the sorrows which he endured; and yet he does not want to be freed from them until God's justice has been satisfied and until he has made perfect atonement.

How can he say that everything has been **completed** when the chief part was still lacking (that is, his death)? Moreover, does not his resurrection contribute to the completion of our salvation? I reply: John includes what was soon to follow. Christ had not yet died and had not yet risen again, but he saw that there was nothing to prevent him from advancing to his death and resurrection. And so, by his own example Christ teaches us to be perfectly obedient, that it may not be hard to live according to his will, even though we must languish in the middle of the most excruciating pains.

. . . so that the Scripture would be fulfilled. From what is stated by the other evangelists (Matthew 27:48; Mark 15:23, 36; Luke 23:36), it may readily be concluded that the passage referred to is Psalm 69:21, "They put gall in my food and gave me vinegar for my thirst." This is undoubtedly a metaphorical expression, and by it David means not only that they denied him the help he needed, but that they cruelly increased his troubles. But there is no inconsistency in saying that what had been dimly outlined in David was more clearly exhibited in Christ. For from it we perceive more fully the difference between truth and figures, when the things which David suffered only figuratively appear openly and, as it were, in substance in Christ. To show that he was the person whom David represented, Christ chose to drink **vinegar** in order to strengthen our faith.

"I am thirsty." Those who invent an allegorical meaning for the word **"thirsty,"** as if he meant that instead of a pleasant drink they gave him a bitter drink, care more for ingenuity than true edification; and the evangelist specifically refutes them when he says that Christ asked for vinegar when he was near death.

29. When he says that they **put the sponge on a stalk of the hyssop plant**, it means that they attached it to the end of a bunch of **hyssop** so that it might be lifted up to Christ's mouth, for in that country hyssops grow as large as small shrubs.

30. "It is finished." John repeats the same word which he had recently used. The word Christ uses deserves our close attention, for it shows that our salvation was completely accomplished by his death. We have already said that his resurrection is not separate from his death; but Christ only intends to keep our faith fixed on himself alone, and not to allow it to deviate in any other direction. The meaning, therefore, is that everything which contributes to man's salvation is in Christ and is not to be sought elsewhere; or — it amounts to the same thing — the perfection of salvation is contained in him.

There is also an implied contrast here, for Christ contrasts his death with the ancient sacrifices and all the figures, as if he said, "But of all that was practiced under the law, there was nothing that had any power in itself to make atonement for sins, to appease God's wrath, and to obtain justification. But now the true salvation is exhibited and shown to the world." This doctrine is the basis for the abolition of all the ceremonies of the law. It would be absurd to follow shadows when we have the reality in Christ.

If we give our assent to this word which Christ pronounced, we should be satisfied with his death alone for salvation, and we do not have the freedom to look elsewhere. For Christ was sent by the Heavenly Father to obtain for us a complete acquittal and to accomplish our redemption. He knew well what belonged to his office and did not fail in what he knew to be demanded of him. It was chiefly for the purpose of giving peace and tranquillity to our consciences that he said, **"It is finished."** We must stop here, therefore, if we do not want to be deprived of the salvation which he has procured for us.

But the whole Roman Catholic religion aims at leading men to think up for themselves innumerable ways of seeking salvation. Hence we infer that it is brimming over with abominable sacrileges. More especially, this word from Christ condemns the abomination of the Mass. All the sacrifices of the law must have stopped, for the salvation of mankind has been completed by the one sacrifice of the death of Christ. What right, then, have the Roman Catholics, or what plausible excuse can they have for saying, that they are authorized to set up a new sacrifice to reconcile God to men? They reply that it is not a new sacrifice but the same sacrifice which Christ offered. But this is easily refuted. In the first place, they have been given no instruction to offer it; and, second, once Christ completed, by a single oblation, all that was necessary to be done, he declared from the cross that everything **"is finished."** They are worse than forgers, therefore, for they wickedly corrupt and falsify the covenant sealed by the precious blood of the Son of God.

He . . . gave up his spirit. All the evangelists take great care in relating Christ's death, and not without cause, for from it comes our gift of life, as well as a fearless triumphing over death, since the Son of God has endured it in our place and, fighting against it, has been victorious. But we must note the phraseology which John uses and which teaches us that all believers who die with Christ peacefully commit their souls to God's protection. For God is faithful and will not allow what he has undertaken to preserve to perish. The children of God, as well as the reprobate, die; but the difference between them is that the reprobate give up the soul without knowing where it goes or what becomes of it, while the children of God commit it as a precious trust into God's protection, and he will faithfully guard it until the day of the resurrection. The word **"spirit"** is clearly used here to denote the immortal soul.

Verses 31–37

31. Now it was the day of Preparation. This narrative also builds up our faith. First, because it shows that what had been foretold in Scripture is fulfilled in the person of Christ; and second, because it contains a mystery of no ordinary value. The evangelist says that the Jews asked for the bodies to be taken down from the crosses. This had undoubtedly been laid down in God's law. However, the Jews, as is usually the case with hypocrites, direct their whole attention to small matters and pass over the greatest crimes without hesitation. To observe their Sabbath strictly, they are careful to avoid outward pollution, and yet they do not think how terrible a crime it is to take an innocent life. Thus we saw a little earlier that **to avoid ceremonial uncleanness the Jews did not enter the palace** (18:28), while the whole country was polluted by their wickedness. Yet by them the Lord carries out what was of the greatest importance for our salvation, so that by a wonderful arrangement the body of Christ remains uninjured, and **blood and water** flow out of his side (verse 34).

The next day was to be a special Sabbath. Another reading which is more generally approved says, "and that Sabbath day was great"; but the reading which I have adopted is supported by many manuscripts that are ancient and of great authority. Let the reader choose for himself. If "that" is in the genitive, the word **Sabbath** will mean "the week." It is as if the evangelist had said that the festival of that week was very solemn, on account of the Passover. Now, the evangelist speaks of the following day, which began at sunset, and they were the more scrupulous about leaving the bodies still hanging. But if we take the nominative reading, "and that Sabbath day was a high day," the meaning is similar, with very little variation of words. It means that the impending Passover would make the **Sabbath** more holy.

33. But when they came to Jesus and found that he was already dead . . . The fact that they broke the legs of the two robbers and then found that Christ was already dead, and therefore did not touch his body, is an extraordinary work of God's providence. Ungodly men will doubtless say that it happens naturally that one man dies sooner than another. But if we examine carefully the whole narrative, we shall be forced to ascribe this to God's hidden purpose, that Christ's death happened much more quickly than people expected, so there was no need to **break his legs.**

34. Instead, one of the soldiers pierced Jesus' side with a spear. The soldier **pierced** Christ's **side** with his **spear** to find out if he was dead; but God had a higher purpose in mind, as we will now see.

. . . bringing a sudden flow of blood and water. Some people have deceived themselves by imagining that this was a miracle. It is natural that the **blood**, when it is congealed, should lose its red color and resemble **water.** It is well-known also that **water** is contained in the membrane which immediately adjoins the intestines. They were led astray because the evangelist takes great pains to explain that **blood** flowed with the **water**, as if he were relating something unusual and different to nature. But his intention was quite different. He wanted to fit his narrative in with the passages of Scripture which he immediately adds, and more especially with what believers might infer from it when he says elsewhere that Christ came "by water and blood" (1 John 5:6). By these words he means that Christ brought the true atonement and the true washing. Forgiveness of sins and justification, as well as the sanctification of the soul, were prefigured in the law by those two symbols of sacrifices and ablutions for appeasing God's wrath. Ablutions were the tokens of true holiness, remedies for purging uncleanness and removing the stains of the flesh.

That faith may no longer rest on these factors, John declares that the fulfillment of both of these graces is in Christ; and here he gives us a visible token of the same fact. The sacraments which Christ left with his church have the same purpose: the purification and sanctification of the soul, which consists of "a new life" (Romans 6:4) and which is highlighted in our baptism and which is in the Lord's Supper the pledge of a perfect atonement. But these are very different from the ancient figures of the law, for they show Christ as present, whereas the figures of the law pointed to him as still absent and at a distance. For this reason I do not object to what Augustine says, that our sacraments have flowed from Christ's side; for when baptism and the Lord's Supper lead us to Christ's side to draw from it, as from a well which they represent, then we are truly washed from our pollutions and are renewed to a holy life and live before God, redeemed from death and delivered from condemnation.

36. "Not one of his bones will be broken." This quotation is taken from Exodus 12:46 and Numbers 9:12, where Moses refers to the paschal lamb. John takes it for granted that that lamb was a figure of the true and only sacrifice through which the church was to be redeemed. This is consistent with the fact that it was sacrificed as the memorial of a redemption which had been already made. As God intended it to celebrate the former favor, he also intended that it should show the spiritual deliverance of the church, which was still in the future. So Paul without any hesitation applies to Christ the rule which Moses lays down about eating the lamb: "For Christ, our Passover lamb, has been sacrificed. Therefore let us keep the Festival, not with old yeast, the yeast of malice and wickedness, but with bread without yeast, the bread of sincerity and truth" (1 Corinthians 5:7-8).

From this analogy, or similarity, faith derives great benefit, since in all the ceremonies of the law it views the salvation which has been displayed in Christ. This is the purpose of the evangelist John when he says that Christ was not only the pledge of our redemption but also its price, in that we see accomplished in him what was formerly seen by the ancient people under the figure of the Passover. In this way the Jews are also reminded that they ought to seek in Christ the substance of everything that the law prefigured but did not actually accomplish.

37. "They will look on the one they have pierced." This passage is violently distorted by those who try to interpret it literally as referring to Christ. This is not the evangelist's purpose in quoting it. Rather, he shows that Christ is that God who had complained, through Zechariah, that the Jews had pierced his heart (Zechariah 12:10). God speaks there in a human way, declaring that he is wounded by the sins of his people, and especially by their obstinate contempt of his Word, just as a mortal man receives a deadly wound when his heart is pierced. He says elsewhere that his spirit was deeply grieved (see Matthew 26:38).

Now, as Christ is God and "appeared in a body" (1 Timothy 3:16), John says that in his visible body was clearly fulfilled what his divine majesty had suffered from the Jews, so far as it was capable of suffering. Not that God is at all affected by the outrages of men or that the reproaches which are thrown at him from the earth ever reach him, but by this expression he wanted to declare the great sacrilege which the wickedness of men is guilty of when it rebels against heaven. What was done through the hand of a Roman soldier the evangelist John justly imputes to the Jews; thus they are elsewhere accused, "whom you crucified, both Lord and Christ" (Acts 2:36), even though they did not lay a finger on his body.

So now we ask whether God promises the Jews repentance to salvation or threatens that he will come as an avenger. For my own part, when I study the passage carefully I think that it includes both; namely, that out of a worthless and unprincipled nation God will gather a remnant for salvation, and that through his awesome vengeance he will show to despisers whom they are dealing with; for we know that they were inclined to treat the prophets as insolently as if the prophets had told nothing but stories and had received no commission from God. God declares that they will not pass unpunished, for he will in the end maintain his cause.

Verses 38–42

38. Joseph of Arimathea asked Pilate ... John now relates who buried Christ and where and with what honor. He mentions two people who buried Christ — namely, **Joseph** and **Nicodemus** (verse 39), the former of whom asked Pilate to give him the dead body, which would otherwise have been exposed to the lawless violence of the soldiers. Matthew (27:57) says that Joseph was "a rich man," and Luke (23:50) says that he was "a member of the Council" — that is, he held the rank of a senator. As for Nicodemus, we have seen in chapter 3 that he held an honorable position among his own countrymen. That he was also rich may be inferred from the great expense which he went to in procuring the mixed **spices** (verse 40).

Until then, riches had prevented them from professing to be Christ's disciples, and this could afterwards have hindered them no less from making a profession so hated and disgraced. The evangelist expressly says that Joseph had formerly been held back by this fear from venturing to declare openly that he was a disciple of Christ. About Nicodemus, he repeats what we have already seen, that he came to Jesus secretly and **at night** (see 3:2 and 7:50). From where do they suddenly derive such heroic courage, so that when things are at their worst they boldly come out into the open? I pass over the evident danger which they must have incurred; the most important point is that they did not hesitate to engage in perpetual war against their own nation. It is therefore certain that this was carried out by a heavenly impulse, so that they who were afraid to give him due honor while he was alive now run to his dead body as if they had become new men.

They bring their **spices** to embalm Christ's body; but they would never have done so if they had not been sprinkled with the sweet scent of his death. This shows the truth of what Christ had said, that "unless a kernel of wheat falls to the ground and dies, it remains only a single seed. But if it dies, it produces many seeds" (12:24). Here we have striking proof that his death was more life-giving than his life; so great was the efficacy of that sweet savor which Christ's death breathed into the minds of those two men that it quickly extinguished all their human passions. So long as ambition and the love of money reigned in them, the grace of Christ had no effect on them. Now they cease to relish the whole world.

Moreover, we must learn from their example what duty we owe to Christ. Those two men, as a testimony of their faith, not only took Christ down from the cross in great danger, but boldly carried him to the grave. Our slothfulness will be base and shameful if, now that he reigns in the heavenly glory, we withhold from him the confession of our faith. So much the less excusable is the wickedness of those who, though they now deny Christ by base hypocrisy, plead in his behalf the example of Nicodemus. In one thing, I admit, they resemble him, that they endeavor, as far as lies in their power, to bury Christ; but the time for burying is past, since he has ascended to the Father's right hand, that he may reign gloriously over angels and men and that every tongue may proclaim his dominion (Philippians 2:9-11).

. . . secretly because he feared the Jews. As this fear is contrasted with the holy boldness which the Spirit of the Lord wrought in the heart of Joseph, there is reason to believe that it was not free from blame. Not that all fear, by which believers guard against tyrants and enemies of the church, is faulty, but because weakness of faith is manifested whenever the confession of faith is withheld through fear. We ought always to consider what the Lord commands and how far he bids us advance. He who stops in the middle of the course shows that he does not trust in God, and he who sets a higher value on his own life than on the command of God is without excuse.

A disciple of Jesus. When we perceive that the evangelist bestows on Joseph the honorable designation of **a disciple** at a time when he was excessively timid and did not venture to profess his faith before the world, we learn how graciously God acts towards his people, and with what fatherly kindness he forgives their offenses. And yet the false Nicodemites have no right to flatter themselves, who not only keep their faith concealed within their own breast but, by pretending to give their consent to wicked superstitions, do all that is in their power to deny that they are disciples of Christ.

40. This was in accordance with Jewish burial customs. When Christ had endured extreme ignominy on the cross, God determined that his burial should be honorable, that it might serve as a preparation for the glory of his resurrection. The money expended on it by Nicodemus and Joseph is very great and may be thought by some to be superfluous; but we ought to consider the design of God, who led them, by his Spirit, to render this honor to his own Son, that the sweet savor of his grave might take away our dread of the cross. But those things which are out of the ordinary course ought not to be regarded as an example.

Besides, the evangelist expressly states that he was buried according to the **Jewish burial customs.** By these words he informs us that this was one of the ceremonies of the law, for the ancient people, who did not receive so clear a revelation of the resurrection and who had not such a demonstration and pledge of it as we have in Christ, needed such aids to support them, that they might firmly believe and expect the coming of the Mediator. We ought, therefore, to attend to the distinction between us, who have been enlightened by the brightness of the Gospel, and the fathers, to whom the figures supplied the absence of Christ. This is the reason why allowance could then be made for a greater pomp of ceremonies, which at the present day would not be free from blame; for those who now bury the dead at so great an expense do not, strictly speaking, bury dead men, but rather, as far as lies in their power, draw down from heaven Christ himself, the King of life, and lay him in the tomb, for his glorious resurrection abolished those ancient ceremonies.

Among the heathen, too, there was great anxiety and ceremony in burying the dead, which unquestionably derived its origin from the ancient fathers of the Jews, in the same way as sacrifices; but as no hope of the resurrection existed among them, they were not imitators of the fathers but apes of them; for the promise and Word of God is, as it were, the soul which gives life to ceremonies. Take away the Word, and all the ceremonies which men observe, though outwardly they may resemble the worship of godly persons, are nothing else than foolish or mad superstition. For our part, as we have said, we ought now to maintain sobriety and moderation in this matter, for immoderate expense quenches the sweet savor of Christ's resurrection.

41. At the place where Jesus was crucified, there was a garden. This is the third point which ought to be observed in the story of the burial.

It is related by the evangelist for various reasons. In the first place, it did not happen by accident, but by an undoubted providence of God, that the body of Christ was buried in **a new tomb**; for although he died as all other men die, still, as he was to be "the firstborn from among the dead" (Colossians 1:18) and "the firstfruits of those who have fallen asleep" (1 Corinthians 15:20), he had **a new tomb, in which no one had ever been laid.** True, Nicodemus and Joseph had a different purpose in mind, for, in consequence of the short time that now remained till sunset, which was the beginning of the Sabbath, they looked to the convenience of the place; but contrary to their intention, God provided for his own Son **a new tomb** which had not yet been used. The good men were merely gratified "since the tomb was nearby" (verse 42), so that they would not violate the Sabbath; but God offers them what they did not seek, so that the burial of his Son might have some token to distinguish him from the rank of other men. The local situation served also to prove the truth of his resurrection and to throw no small light on the narrative which is contained in the following chapter.

John
Chapter 20

Verses 1–9

1. Early on the first day of the week . . . As the resurrection of Christ is the most important article of our faith, and without it the hope of eternal life is extinguished, for this reason the evangelists are the more careful to prove it, as John here collects many proofs in order to assure us that Christ is risen from the dead. It may be thought strange, however, that he does not produce more competent witnesses, for he begins with a woman; but thus the saying is fulfilled that "God chose the foolish things of the world to shame the wise; God chose the weak things of the world to shame the strong" (1 Corinthians 1:27). There certainly was nothing more of earthly grandeur in the disciples than in the women who followed Christ; but as Christ was pleased to reckon them the principal witnesses of his resurrection, on this single ground their testimony is entitled to the greatest deference and is not liable to any objection. As to the priests and teachers of the law, and the whole people, even Pilate, nothing but gross and willful blindness prevented them from firmly believing that Christ was risen. All of them, therefore, deserved that seeing they should not see; yet Christ revealed himself to the little flock.

Before proceeding farther, however, it is necessary to show how the evangelists agree with each other, for at first sight there appears to be some contradiction in their words. John only mentions one woman, **Mary of Magdala**; Matthew (28:1) mentions two, "Mary Magdalene and the other Mary"; Mark (16:1) mentions three, "Mary Magdalene, Mary the mother of James, and Salome"; Luke (24:10, 22) does not fix the number, but only tells us that it was women who had followed Christ from Galilee. But the difficulty is easily resolved. Matthew inserts the names of two well-known women, particularly well-known among the disciples; so John satisfies himself with mentioning the name of Mary Magdalene alone, but without excluding the others. Indeed, it is evident from looking at the context of his words that she was not alone, for shortly afterwards Mary says, using the plural, **"We don't know where**

they have put him" (verse 2). So although John says nothing about her companions, his narrative does not contradict the other evangelists, who tell us that there were others as well.

The discrepancy concerning the time may also be resolved easily. When John says that they came before dawn, we must understand that they set out on their journey during the darkness of the night, that before they came to the sepulchre the day had dawned, and that they had bought the spices in the evening, after sunset, when the Sabbath was over. This is how the narrative of the other evangelists should be reconciled.

There seems to be another contradiction in John's stating that Mary spoke only to himself and Peter, while Luke tells us that she came to the eleven apostles and that "their words seemed to them like nonsense" (Luke 24:11). But this is easily explained, for John intentionally left out the rest of the apostles, because only he and Peter came to the tomb. As for Luke mentioning only Peter, it is for the same reason that we have just given about Mary Magdalene and the rest of the women. Probably the other nine disciples were held back by fear of being too easily noticed if they went in a body. This is also consistent with what Luke seems to suggest — namely, that they despised Mary's words, for he at once adds that Peter "ran" (Luke 24:12). He therefore means simply that when they first heard it they seemed astonished, but that at length Peter took courage and followed her to see for himself.

When Luke tells us that Christ appeared to Mary before she had told the disciples the grave was empty, the order of events is reversed. This is clear from the context, for he adds what he says happened before she saw Jesus; nor is there anything strange in this, for the Hebrew writers frequently put first what actually happened later.

The evangelists do not tell us when or how Christ rose: they were content to explain when and to whom his resurrection was made known. Therefore, John says that Mary came — as the Hebrew may be literally translated — "on one day of the Sabbath." The Hebrew custom is to use the word *ehad*, "one," instead of "first," because in counting we begin with one. Now, as every seventh day was dedicated to rest, they called the whole week a "Sabbath," honoring the holiness of the day by naming the rest of the time for it. The women, therefore, came to the tomb on the first day after the Sabbath, having bought spices after the sunset of the Sabbath day. Afterwards they left the city secretly, during the darkness of the night, as people do when they are afraid. Now, it was the first day of the Sabbath with respect to the following Sabbath, because it was the beginning of the week which ended with the Sabbath.

3. As there was so little faith, or rather almost no faith, both in the disciples and in the women, it is astonishing that they had so much zeal. Indeed, it must have been piety that drew them to seek Christ. Some seed of faith, then, remained in their hearts, though smothered for a time, so that they were not aware of possessing what they did possess. Thus God's Spirit often works in the elect in a hidden way. In short, we must believe that there was some hidden root from which we see fruit coming. Although their feeling of piety was confused and mingled with much superstition, I still call it faith (though imprecisely), because it was produced only by the Gospel teaching and led only to Christ. In the end a true and sincere faith sprang from this seed, left the tomb, and ascended to Christ's heavenly glory.

When Scripture speaks of the rudiments of faith, it says that Christ is born in us and that we, conversely, are born in him; but the disciples must be placed almost below infancy while they are ignorant of Christ's resurrection; yet the Lord nourishes them as a mother nourishes the child in her womb. Previously they were like children and had made a little progress, but Christ's death had made them so weak that they had to be conceived and formed again. As Paul says: "My dear children, for whom I am again in the pains of childbirth until Christ is formed in you . . ." (Galatians 4:19).

When we read that Peter ran more slowly but was the first to enter the tomb, we may learn that many people are given more in the end than appears at the beginning. Indeed, we sometimes see many people who were most enthusiastic to begin with but give up when it comes to the battle; others, who appeared to be slow and lazy, gain fresh courage when danger is near.

5. Here **the strips of linen** might be thought of as a slough intended to lead to belief in Christ's resurrection, for it was unlikely that his body had been stripped naked in order to be taken somewhere else. This would not have been done by a friend, or even by an enemy.

7. . . . the burial cloth that had been around Jesus' head. This contradicts the falsehood of the Roman Catholics, who claim that the whole body was sewn up in one linen cloth, which they show to the wretched people, calling it the Holy Shroud — to say nothing of their gross ignorance of Latin, which led them to suppose that the word translated "burial cloth" (which denotes what was used to wipe the sweat from the face) signified a covering for the whole body — or their impudence in boasting that they have this very cloth in five or six different places. But this gross falsehood is intolerable, because it openly contradicts the Gospel story. To this is added a fabulous miracle which they have made up, that the image of Christ's body remained visible in the linen cloth. I ask you, if such a miracle had been performed, would nothing have been said about it by the evangelist, who is so careful to tell us about less important things? Let us be satisfied with this simple view of the matter, that Christ, by laying aside the tokens of death, meant to testify that he had clothed himself with a blessed and immortal life.

8. He saw and believed. It is a poor exposition which some people give of these words, that John **believed** what he had heard Mary say —

namely, that Christ's body had been carried away; there is no passage in which the word "believe" carries this meaning, especially when it is used simply and on its own. Nor is this inconsistent with the fact that Peter and John return home while they are still doubtful and perplexed, for John has used this phraseology in some passages when he wanted to describe the increase of faith. Besides, Luke (24:12) tells us that Peter wondered at seeing the tomb in such good order — meaning that Peter was thinking of something greater and more exalted than what Mary had told him.

9. They had often heard from Christ's lips what they now saw with their eyes, but this came from their hearts. Alerted now by the sight of something new, they begin to think of Christ's divinity, though they are still far from having a clear and accurate knowledge of him. John, therefore, accuses himself when he acknowledges that the first time he believed was when he saw the proofs of Christ's resurrection.

Moreover, he amplifies his own and Peter's guilt by adding that they had not only forgotten Christ's words, but they did not believe the **Scripture**; he says this is the reason for their deficient faith. From this, too, we may usefully learn to ascribe it to our laziness when we are ignorant of what we ought to know about Christ, because we have not profited as we ought from the **Scripture**, which clearly reveals Christ's power.

Without going any further for an example of this, it may seem that Christ's resurrection is only taught obscurely and metaphorically in the Scriptures; but the attentive reader will find clear enough testimonies. Paul proves (Acts 13:34) that Christ must have risen from the dead because God declares through the prophet Isaiah (55:3) that under his reign the mercy promised to David would be sure. An unlearned person might imagine that what Paul quotes is not at all relevant; but those who believe the principles of faith and are well-acquainted with the Scriptures have no difficulty in perceiving the force of this argument, for in order that Christ may obtain the grace of God for us forever, Christ himself must live forever.

There are many such passages, and we do not need to collect them now. Let us therefore be satisfied with the three following. Psalm 16:10 says, "You will not . . . let your Holy One see decay." Peter and Paul explain this prediction as referring to Christ (Acts 2:27 and 13:35), and rightly so, for there is not one of all the sons of Adam who is not in himself subject to corruption. Consequently, Christ's immortality is asserted here. Similarly, it is beyond doubt that Psalm 110:1 refers to Christ: "The Lord says to my Lord: 'Sit at my right hand until I make your enemies a footstool for your feet.'" Now, death will not be destroyed until the last day. So the kingdom is given to Christ till the end of the world, and this kingdom cannot exist without his life. But Isaiah speaks more clearly than all the rest when, after foretelling the death of Christ, he immediately adds, "Who shall declare his generation?" (Isaiah 53:8, KJV; compare NIV, "Who can speak of his descendants?"). In short, we ought to believe that the teaching of Scripture is so full and complete in every respect that whatever is defective in our faith ought by rights to be attributed to ignorance of it.

Verses 10–15

10. It is possible that the disciples' minds were still doubtful and uncertain when they returned home. For although John says that they believed, their faith was not strong but was only some confused memory of the miracle; it was like a trance until they received more confirmation. And, indeed, a strong faith could not be produced merely by what they had seen. Besides, Christ did not show himself to them until they had been more fully awakened from the stupor of their sinful nature. Certainly they had shown their zeal in a praiseworthy manner by hurrying to the tomb, but Christ hid himself from them because they were looking for him too superstitiously.

11. But Mary stood outside the tomb. The evangelist now begins to describe how Christ appeared both to the women and to the disciples, to testify to his resurrection. Although he mentions only one woman, **Mary,** I think it likely that the other women were there too, for it is unreasonable to suppose (as some have done) that the women fainted from fear. Those writers are trying to avoid a contradiction, but I have already shown that no such contradiction exists.

As for the women remaining at **the tomb** while the disciples return to the city, they do not deserve special praise for this. The disciples take comfort and joy with them, but the women are filled with idle and useless weeping. In short, it is only superstition, together with the feelings of the sinful nature, that keeps them near **the tomb.**

12. . . . and saw two angels. What amazing forbearance our Lord shows when he overlooks so many faults in Mary and her companions! For it is no small honor that he confers on them by sending his **angels** and, at length, making himself known to them, which he had not done for the apostles. Although the apostles and the women were suffering the same disease, the apostles' stupidity was less excusable because they had profited so little by their thorough and careful teaching. Certainly one purpose Christ had when he chose to reveal himself to the women first was to fill the apostles with shame.

. . . in white. Whether Mary knew them to be **angels** or thought they were men is uncertain. We know that white clothes were a sign of the heavenly glory, as we find that Christ was clothed in "white" when he was transfigured on the mountain and showed his glorious majesty to the three apostles (Matthew 17:2). Luke tells us that the angel who appeared to Cornelius was "in shining clothes" (Acts 10:30). I do not deny that linen clothes were common in the East, but in the angels' dress God was pointing out something remarkable and uncommon, marking them out, as it were, to distinguish them from ordinary people. Besides, Matthew (28:3) compares the appearance of the angel who talked to the women to "lightning." Still, it is possible that their fear arose solely from their minds being struck with wonder, for it seems that they stood astonished.

Again, whenever we read that "angels" appeared in the visible form of men, clothed "in white," this was done for the sake of human ignorance. For my part, I have no doubt that they were sometimes clothed with real bodies; but whether or not those **two angels** just had what looked like bodies would be a pointless inquiry, and so I will leave it undecided. To me it is enough that the Lord gave them a human shape so that the women could see and hear them, while the magnificent and unusual clothing they wore distinguished them from ordinary people and indicated something divine and heavenly.

. . . one at the head and the other at the foot. Only one angel is mentioned by Matthew (28:2). This, however, does not contradict John's narrative, for both angels did not address Mary at the same time, but only the one who had a commission to speak. There is no good reason for Augustine's allegory that the position of the angels indicated that the Gospel would be preached from the east to the west. It is more worth noticing that Christ initiated the glory of his kingdom by such preliminaries, for the honor which the angels give to the tomb not only removes the ignominy of the cross but makes Christ's heavenly majesty shine.

13. "Woman, why are you crying?" From what the other Gospels say, we may readily conclude that the angel held a long conversation; but John gives a brief summary because this was enough to prove the resurrection of Christ. The conversation consists of reproof mixed with comfort. The angel reproves Mary for her excessive weeping, but at the same time mingles joy with it when he says that there is no reason to weep, since Christ has risen.

14. . . . and saw Jesus standing there. It may be asked how Mary made the mistake of not recognizing Jesus, when she must have known him extremely well. Some people think that he appeared in a different form, but I think that the fault lay rather in the eyes of the women, as Luke 24:16 says of the two disciples that "they were kept from recognizing him." We will not say, therefore, that Christ was continually assuming new shapes, like Proteus, but that it is in the power of God, who gave men eyes, to make their vision less sharp whenever he thinks proper, that "seeing, they may not see."

In Mary we have an example of the mistakes into which the human mind frequently falls. Although Christ offers himself to our sight, we imagine that he assumes various shapes, so that our senses conceive anything rather than the true Christ. Not only are our powers of understanding liable to be deceived, but they are also bewitched by the world and by Satan, so that we do not discern the truth.

15. "Sir, if you have carried him away . . ." She calls him **"Sir,"** after the custom of her people, for the Hebrews use the same word (Greek, *kyrie*) in addressing laborers and other people of low rank. We see that Mary is only thinking of earthly matters. She only wants to obtain Christ's dead body so she can keep it hidden in the tomb; but she leaves out the most important matter: aspiring to the divine power of his resurrection. It is not surprising, therefore, if such groveling places a veil before her eyes.

Verses 16–18

16. "Mary." That Christ allowed Mary for a while to fall into a mistake was useful for confirming her faith; but now he corrects her with a single word. He had spoken to her before, but it was as if he was someone unknown to her. Now he assumes the character of the Master and addresses his disciple by name. We saw earlier that the Good Shepherd calls by name every sheep of his flock (see 10:3). That shepherd-voice, therefore, enters into Mary's heart, opens her eyes, awakens all her senses, and affects her in such a way that she immediately surrenders herself to Christ.

Thus in Mary we have a living image of our calling; for the only way in which we are admitted to the true knowledge of Christ is when he first knows us and then familiarly invites us to himself, not by that ordinary voice which sounds in the ears of everyone alike, but by the voice with which he especially calls the sheep which the Father has given him. Thus Paul says, "Now that you know God — or rather are known by God" (Galatians 4:9).

"Rabboni!" The effectiveness of the word is evident from this detail, that Mary immediately gives Christ the honor which is due to him, for the word **Rabboni** is not only respectful but contains a profession of obedience. Mary is therefore declaring that she is a disciple of Christ and devotes herself to him as her **Teacher.** This is a secret and wonderful change of the human understanding, when God, enlightening her by his Spirit, makes her clearsighted when she had previously been slow to understand and, indeed, completely blind. Moreover, the example of Mary should serve to exhort all those whom Christ invites to himself to respond to him at once.

The word **Rabboni** is Aramaic. The meaning is the same as if we were to say, "My Lord" or "Master." In Christ's time it had become the usual practice to say "Rabbi" or **"Rabboni."**

17. "Do not hold on to me." This seems to disagree with Matthew's narrative, for he explicitly says that the women "clasped his feet and worshiped him" (Matthew 28:9). Now, since he allowed himself to be touched by some, why should he forbid Mary to hold on to him? The answer is straightforward, provided we remember that the women were not repelled from touching Christ until they held on to him too much; for, as far as was necessary for removing doubt, he unquestionably did not forbid them to touch him, but seeing that they were concentrating too much on embracing his feet, he restrained and corrected their thoughtless zeal. They concentrated on his bodily presence and did not understand any other way of enjoying him than by conversing with him on earth. And so we should conclude that they were not forbidden to hold on to him until Christ saw that, by their foolish and unreasonable desire, they wanted to keep him in the world.

"For I have not yet returned to the Father." We should notice this reason which he adds, for by these words he tells the women to restrain their feelings until he is received into the heavenly glory. In short, he showed the purpose of his resurrection. It was not what they had imagined — that he would return to life and then triumph in the world — but rather, by his ascension to heaven he would take possession of the kingdom which had been promised to him and, seated at the Father's right hand, would govern the church by the power of his Spirit. The words therefore mean that the state of his resurrection would not be full and complete in every respect until he sat down in heaven at the Father's right hand; and therefore the women were wrong to be content with having nothing more than half of his resurrection and wanting to enjoy his presence in the world.

This teaching is useful in two ways. The first is that those who want to succeed in their search for Christ must raise their minds aloft; and the second is that all who try to go to him must get rid of the earthly affections of the flesh. As Paul exhorts: "Since, then, you have been raised with Christ, set your hearts on things above, where Christ is seated at the right hand of God" (Colossians 3:1).

"Go instead to my brothers." Some people limit the word **"brothers"** to Christ's relatives, but in my opinion wrongly — for why should he have sent the women to them rather than to the disciples? They reply, because John 7:5 says that they were unbelievers. But I do not think it likely that Christ conferred such a great honor on those mentioned there. They must also admit that Mary obeyed Christ's command. But it follows straightaway that she came to the disciples. We conclude that Christ was speaking about them.

Besides, Christ knew that the disciples were assembled in one place; and it would have been quite absurd for him to attend to all sorts of people and ignore the disciples, who were assembled in one place and were tossed between hope and fear. Also, Christ seems to have borrowed this expression from Psalm 22:22, where we find these words: "I will declare your name to my brothers." It is beyond all controversy that this passage contains the fulfillment of that prophecy.

I therefore conclude that Mary was sent to the disciples in general; and I consider that this was done by way of reproach, because they had been so slow and sluggish to believe. And, indeed, they deserve to have not only women for their teachers, but even oxen and asses, for the Son of God had been teaching them long and laboriously. Yet this is a mild punishment when Christ has his disciples learn from the women, so that through them he may bring them back to himself. Here we also see Christ's inconceivable kindness in choosing and appointing women to be the witnesses of his resurrection to the apostles, for the commission which is given to them is the only foundation of our salvation and contains the chief point of heavenly wisdom.

We should also, however, notice that this event was extraordinary — we might almost say accidental. They are commanded to announce to the apostles what they were later to proclaim to the whole world, performing the task they were given. But in doing so they are not acting like apostles; and therefore it is wrong to derive a law from this command of Christ and to allow women to perform baptisms. Let us be satisfied that Christ displayed the boundless treasures of his grace in them when on one occasion he made them teachers of the apostles; he did not intend this unique privilege to be seen as an example. This is especially apparent in Mary Magdalene having previously been possessed by seven demons (Mark 16:9; Luke 8:2), for it amounted to this, that Christ had brought her out of the lowest hell in order to raise her to heaven.

If anyone objects that there was no reason for Christ to prefer the women to the apostles, since they were no less worldly and stupid, I reply that it is not up to us but to the Judge to discriminate between them. But I would go further and say that the apostles deserved to be more severely censured because they had not only been better instructed than anyone else, but had been appointed teachers of the whole world and had been called "the light of the world" (Matthew 5:14) and "the salt of the earth" (Matthew 5:13), and yet they defaulted so basely. Yet it pleased the Lord to show a proof of his power by means of those weak and contemptible vessels.

"I am returning to my Father" (KJV, "I ascend unto my Father"). By the word **"ascend"** he confirms the teaching I have just explained, that he rose from the dead not for the purpose of remaining on earth any longer, but in order to enter the heavenly life and draw believers with him. In short, by this term he forbids the apostles to think only of his resurrection by itself, but tells them to go further, until they come to the spiritual kingdom, to the heavenly glory, to God himself. There is great emphasis on the word **"ascend,"** for Christ stretches out his hand to his disciples so that they will not seek their happiness anywhere but in heaven. For where our treasure is, there also our heart must be (see Matthew 6:21). Christ states that he is ascending on high, and therefore we must ascend if we do not wish to be separated from him.

When he adds that he is ascending **"to my Father,"** he quickly dispels the grief and anxiety which the apostles might feel at his departure; for he means that he will always be present with his disciples by divine power. True, the word **"ascend"** implies distance of places, but though Christ is absent in body, he is with God, and so his power, which is felt everywhere, shows his spiritual presence clearly. Why did he ascend to God but that, seated at his right hand, he might reign both in heaven and on earth? In short, he used this expression to impress on the disciples' minds the divine power of his kingdom, that they might not be hurt by his bodily absence.

". . . to my Father and your Father, to my God and your God." The fruit and effect of the brotherly union which we have mentioned is expressed when Christ makes God the **"Father"** common to both himself and us. "I am ascending," he says, "to my Father, who is also your Father." Elsewhere we learn that we are made to share in all Christ's blessings; but the foundation of this privilege is that he shares with us the very source of blessings. It is unquestionably an invaluable blessing that believers can safely and firmly believe that Christ's God is also their God and Christ's **"Father"** is their **"Father."** Nor need we fear that this is a rash confidence, since it is founded on Christ; or that it is proud boasting, since Christ himself has dictated it to us with his own mouth.

Christ calls him **"my God"** inasmuch as by "taking the very nature of a servant" he humbled himself (see Philippians 2:7). Therefore this belongs to his human nature, but it is applied to his whole person because of his unity — he is both God and man. As for the other phrase — **"my Father and your Father"** — there is also a difference between him and us, for he is God's Son by nature, while we are his sons only by adoption. But the grace we obtain through him is so firmly based that it cannot be shaken by any efforts of the devil, so as to hinder us from always calling him our **"Father"** who has adopted us through his one and only Son.

Verses 19–23

19. On the evening . . . The evangelist now tells us that Christ's resurrection was proved to the disciples by their seeing him. God provided that they were assembled in one place, so that the event might be more certain and trustworthy. It is notable how gently Christ acted towards them, not keeping them in suspense any longer than that evening. Moreover, he enlightened them by bringing the pledge of new life while darkness was spreading over the world.

... **when the disciples were together.** It was a sign of faith, or at least of a godly attitude, that they had all assembled. It is true that keeping themselves behind locked doors was some proof of their weakness; but although the strongest and boldest minds are sometimes overcome by fear, it is easy to see that the apostles were then frightened in a way that showed their faith. This example is worth noticing, for although they are less courageous than they should have been, they still do not give way to their weakness. True, they seek concealment to escape danger, but they gather courage enough to remain together; otherwise they would have been scattered, and none of them would have dared look at anyone else.

Similarly, we too should struggle against the weakness of our flesh and not give way to fear, which tempts us to apostasize. Christ also blesses their zeal when he appears to them while they are together, though Thomas is rightly deprived of the grace given to all his brothers because, like a wandering soldier, he had deserted from the banner of union. Here is a lesson for those who are excessively timid: they must learn to discipline themselves and take it on themselves to correct their sinful fear. In particular, they should beware lest fear scatters them.

... **with the doors locked.** This detail was added deliberately, because it contains a clear proof of Christ's divine power. Some think that the doors were unlocked by someone and that Christ entered in the usual way, but this is completely contrary to the evangelist's meaning. We must understand that Christ entered by a miracle, in order to give proof of his divinity and make his disciples more attentive. Yet I am far from admitting what the Roman Catholics say, that Christ's body passed through the locked doors. They maintain this in order to make Christ's glorious body not only like a spirit, but also infinite and not confined to any one place. But the words do not convey this meaning. The evangelist does not say that he entered through the locked doors, but that he suddenly **came and stood among them,** although the doors had been locked and had not been opened to him by anyone. We know that Peter went out of a prison which was locked (Acts 12:10). Must we therefore say that he passed through iron and planks? Away, then, with that childish sophistry which has nothing substantial and contains many absurdities! Let it be enough for us that Christ wanted to confirm the authority of his resurrection for his disciples by a remarkable miracle.

"Peace be with you!" This is the ordinary Hebrew greeting. The word **"peace"** denotes all the happiness and prosperity usually desired for a happy life. Therefore the phrase means, "May you be well and happy!" I say this because there are some people who enter into unnecessary discussions about **"peace"** and harmony, though Christ intended simply to wish his disciples well.

20. He showed them his hands and side. This confirmation had to be added so that by all these means they might know that Christ was risen. If anyone thinks it strange and unworthy of Christ's glory that he should bear the wounds even after his resurrection, let him consider, first, that Christ rose not so much for himself as for us; and second, whatever is for our salvation is glorious to him. When he humbled himself for a time, it took nothing away from his majesty; and now, since the wounds we are speaking about serve to illuminate the authority of his resurrection, they do not detract at all from his glory. But if anyone should infer from this that Christ still has the wounded **side** and pierced **hands**, that would be absurd, for it is certain that the use of the wounds was temporary, until the apostles were fully convinced that he was risen from the dead.

The disciples were overjoyed when they saw the Lord. This means that all the grief which Christ's death had caused them was dispelled by his new life.

21. Again Jesus said, "Peace be with you!" The only purpose of this second greeting seems to me to be that the Lord should make them concentrate on the great and important subjects he was about to speak of.

"As the Father has sent me . . ." By these words Christ, as it were, installs the apostles in the office to which he had already appointed them. True, they had already been sent throughout Judea, but only as heralds commanding people to listen to their supreme teacher, not as apostles exercising a permanent office of teaching. But now the Lord ordains them to be his ambassadors, to establish his kingdom in the world. Let us therefore be sure that the apostles were now for the first time appointed to be ordinary ministers of the Gospel.

His words amount to saying that hitherto he has discharged the office of teacher and that, having finished his course, he commits it to them. He means that the Father appointed him a teacher on condition that he should lead the rest for a while, but afterwards should put them in his place. This is why Paul says that "he gave some to be apostles, some to be prophets, some to be evangelists, and some to be pastors and teachers" (Ephesians 4:11). Christ therefore says, first, that although he held a temporary teaching office, the preaching of the Gospel is not temporary but permanent. Again, so that his teaching may not have less authority in the mouths of the apostles, he commands them to succeed to the same task which he had received from the Father; he puts them in his role and gives them the same authority. It was right that their ministry should be confirmed in this way, for they were obscure and ordinary men. Moreover, even if they had had the highest rank and magnificence, we know that anything human is far beneath faith.

Therefore, Christ had to communicate to his apostles the authority he had received from the Father, so that in this way he might declare that the preaching of the Gospel was committed to him not by human authority but by God's command. But he is not putting them in his place in such a way as to relinquish the supreme teaching office which the Father chose to give him alone. He therefore remains, and will always remain, the only teacher of the church, with the sole difference that while he lived on earth he spoke with his mouth, but now he speaks through the apostles. The succession therefore is such that it takes nothing from Christ; his authority remains whole and complete and his honor entire. The decree by which we are commanded to listen to him and no one else is inviolable (see Matthew 17:5). In short, Christ here meant to adorn not men but the Gospel teaching.

Moreover, we should note that the only subject which is dealt with in this passage is the preaching of the Gospel. Christ does not send his apostles to atone for sins or to obtain righteousness, as he was sent by the Father to do. Consequently, he does not refer in this passage to anything which is his alone; he only appointed ministers and pastors to govern the church, and it is on the condition that he alone keeps possession of the whole power, while they claim for themselves nothing but the ministry.

22. He breathed on them. No mortal is qualified to discharge such a difficult office, and so Christ prepares the apostles by the grace of his Spirit. And, indeed, to govern the church of God, to carry the embassy of eternal salvation, to build the kingdom of God on earth, and to raise people to heaven is far beyond human capacity. Therefore, it is not surprising if no one is found fit unless he is inspired by the Holy Spirit. No one can speak one word about Christ unless the Spirit governs his tongue (see 1 Corinthians 12:3); that is how far it is from the truth that anyone is able to discharge faithfully and sincerely all the duties of such an excellent office. Again, it is Christ's glory alone to form those whom he appoints to be teachers of the church, for the fullness of the Spirit was poured out on him, so that he might give a certain measure of it to each one.

"Receive the Holy Spirit." Although he remains the only shepherd of his church, he has to display the power of his Spirit in the ministers through whom he works. This also he testified to by an outward symbol when he **breathed** on the apostles, for it would be meaningless if the Spirit did not proceed from him. Moreover, Christ not only communicates to his disciples the Spirit he has received, but he gives this Spirit as his own, as the Spirit which he has in common with the Father.

Note that those Christ calls to pastoral office he also adorns with the necessary gifts, so that they may be equal to their duty, or at least may not come to it empty and naked. A sure criterion is given here for judging the calling of those who govern God's church — if we see the gifts of the Holy Spirit.

Christ particularly wanted to uphold the dignity of the order of apostles, for it was reasonable that those who had been chosen to be the earliest and most distinguished preachers of the Gospel should possess unique authority. But if Christ then gave his Spirit to the apostles by breathing, it might seem superfluous to send the Spirit afterwards. My reply is that the Spirit was given to the apostles on this occasion in such a way that they were only sprinkled with his grace and not saturated with full power. When the Spirit appeared on them in tongues of fire (Acts 2:3), they were completely renewed. And, indeed, Christ did not appoint them to be heralds of his Gospel so as to send them out to the work immediately, but ordered them to wait quietly, as we read in Luke 24:49. If we consider everything properly, we shall conclude not that he gives them the gifts necessary for the present, but that he makes them the instruments of his Spirit in the future. This breathing should therefore be referred and extended especially to that magnificent sending of the Spirit which he had so often promised.

Although Christ could have given grace to his apostles by a secret inspiration, he chose to add a visible breathing in order to confirm them more fully. Christ took this symbol from the common way of speaking in the Scriptures, where the Spirit is often compared to wind — a comparison which we explained briefly in commenting on chapter 3. But note that with the outward and visible symbol is also joined the Word, for this is the source of the sacraments' power; not that the efficacy of the Holy Spirit is contained in the word which sounds in our ears, but because the effect of everything that believers gain from the sacraments depends on the testimony of the Word. Christ breathes on the apostles, and they receive not only the breathing but also the Spirit. And why is this if it is not because Christ promises him to them?

Similarly, in baptism we clothe ourselves with Christ (see Galatians 3:27), we are washed by his blood (Revelation 1:5), and our old self is crucified (Romans 6:6), in order that God's righteousness may reign in us. In the Holy Supper we are spiritually fed with Christ's body and blood. Where does their great power come from but from the promise of Christ, who does and achieves by his Spirit what he declares by his Word? Let us therefore learn that sacraments of human invention are nothing but absolute mockeries or frivolous games, because signs can have no truth unless the Word of the Lord is in them. Since we never play with sacred things like this without wickedly insulting God and ruining souls, we should be most careful to guard against these tricks of Satan.

If anyone objects that the Roman Catholic bishops are not to blame when they consecrate their priests by breathing, because the Word of Christ accompanies the sign, the answer is obvious. First, Christ did not speak to the apostles so as to appoint a permanent sacrament in the church, but wanted to declare once what we said just now, that the Spirit proceeds only from himself. Second, he never appoints men to an office without at the same time giving his ministers strength and ability. Besides which, in Roman Catholicism the priests are made for a very different, even contrary, purpose — namely, to sacrifice Christ to death daily, whereas the disciples were made apostles to sacrifice men with the sword of the Gospel. We should also believe that Christ alone gives all the blessings which he represents and promises by outward signs, for he does not tell the apostles to **"receive the Holy Spirit"** from the external breathing but from himself.

23. "If you forgive anyone his sins . . ." Here without doubt our Lord has encapsulated the whole Gospel, for we must not separate this power to **"forgive . . . sins"** from the teaching office with which it is closely linked in this passage. A little before, Christ said, **"As the Father has sent me, I am sending you"** (see 6:57 and 20:21). Now he shows what this sending means and demands, but he interweaves with that declaration what is necessary: that he gives them his Holy Spirit so that they might do nothing of themselves.

The chief purpose of preaching the Gospel is that people may be reconciled to God; and this is done by the free pardon of sins, as Paul also tells us when he calls the Gospel, for this reason, "the ministry of reconciliation" (2 Corinthians 5:18). Many other things are contained in the Gospel, but the main thing God intends is to receive people into grace by not imputing their sins. Therefore, if we wish to show ourselves faithful ministers of the Gospel, we must apply ourselves most earnestly to this. The chief difference between the Gospel and secular philosophy is that it makes our salvation consist in the forgiveness of sins through free grace. This is the source of the other blessings God gives, such as enlightening and regenerating us by his Spirit, molding us in his image, and arming us with unshaken courage against the world and Satan. Thus the whole doctrine of godliness and the spiritual building of the church rest on this foundation — that God has acquitted us of all sins and adopts us as his children by free grace.

When Christ tells the apostles to **"forgive"** sins, he is not conveying to them what is uniquely his. It belongs to him to **"forgive . . . sins."** So far as this honor is unique to him, he does not give it to the apostles; but he tells them to declare the forgiveness of sins in his name, that he may reconcile people to God through them. In short, strictly speaking it is he alone who forgives sins through his apostles.

But since he appoints them only to be witnesses or heralds of this blessing and not authors of it, why does he praise their power in such lofty terms? I reply that he does so in order to confirm our faith. Nothing is more important for us than to be able to believe firmly that God does not remember our sins. Zechariah, in his song, calls this "the knowledge of salvation" (Luke 1:77); and since God uses human witnesses to prove it, consciences will never be at rest unless they know God himself is speaking in their person. So Paul says, "We implore you on Christ's behalf: Be reconciled to God" (2 Corinthians 5:20).

We now see why Christ uses such magnificent language to commend and adorn the ministry which he is giving the apostles. He does so in order that believers may be fully convinced that what they hear about the forgiveness of sins is confirmed, and that people may not think less of the reconciliation offered by human voices than if God himself had stretched out his hand from heaven. Every day the church receives the most abundant fruit of this teaching, when she realizes that her pastors are divinely ordained to be sureties of eternal salvation and that the forgiveness of sin which is committed to them is not to be sought afar off.

Nor should we think less highly of this invaluable treasure because it is displayed in earthen vessels. We have reason to thank God, who has conferred on people so high an honor as to represent his person and his Son in declaring the forgiveness of sins. There are fanatics who despise this mission, but they trample the blood of Christ underfoot.

The Roman Catholics are absurd to twist this passage to support their magical absolutions. If someone does not confess his sins in the ear of a priest, they think that he cannot hope for forgiveness, for Christ intended sins to be forgiven through the apostles; but they cannot absolve without hearing the case, and so confession is necessary. But they are rambling ridiculously when they neglect the most important point — that this right was granted to the apostles in order to maintain the authority of the Gospel which they had been commissioned to preach. Christ is not here appointing confessors to inquire into the details of each sin but preachers of the Gospel who will cause their voice to be heard and will seal on believers' hearts the grace of the atonement obtained through Christ. We must therefore concentrate on the mode of forgiving sins to know what power the apostles have been given.

"If you do not forgive them . . ." Christ adds this second clause to terrify people who despise his Gospel, that they may know they will not escape punishment for this pride. As the message of salvation and eternal life has been committed to the apostles, they were also armed with vengeance against all the ungodly who reject the salvation offered to them, as Paul teaches (2 Corinthians 10:6). But Christ places this last because the true and real purpose in preaching the Gospel had to be shown first. It is the nature of the Gospel that we are reconciled to God; it is incidental that unbelievers are judged to eternal death. That is why Paul, in the passage just cited, threatens vengeance against unbelievers and then adds, "once your obedience is complete." He means that it is proper to the Gospel to invite everyone to salvation; it is incidental that it brings destruction on anyone.

Note, however, that everyone who hears the voice of the Gospel is liable to eternal damnation if he does not accept the forgiveness of sins which it promises. As it is "the fragrance of life" to the children of God, it is "the smell of death" to those who are perishing (see 2 Corinthians 2:16). Not that the preaching of the Gospel is necessary for the condemnation of the reprobate, for by nature we are all lost, and in addition to the hereditary curse everyone brings on himself fresh causes of death; the obstinacy of those who knowingly and willingly despise the Son of God deserves much more severe punishment.

Verses 24–29

24. We are told about Thomas's unbelief so that the faith of the godly might be more fully confirmed. He was not only slow and reluctant to believe — he was also plainly obstinate. His hardness was the reason Christ allowed them to see and to touch him again. Thus a new help testifying to Christ's resurrection was given, not only to Thomas, but to us. Moreover, Thomas's obstinacy is evidence that this wickedness is innate in almost everyone; they hinder themselves of their own accord when the way to faith is open to them.

25. **"Unless I see . . ."** This indicates that the source of the fault is that everyone wants to be wise from his own understanding and flatters himself too much. The words come nowhere near faith but are what might be called a sensual judgment. The same thing happens with all who are so devoted to themselves that they leave no room for the Word of God. It does not matter whether you read "the place" or "the shape" or "the print" of the nails, for scribes may have altered the Greek slightly, but it does not change the meaning. Choose whichever you prefer.

27. **"Put your finger here."** We have already spoken once about how Christ entered and the form of his greeting. When he so readily yields to Thomas's wrong request and of his own accord invites him to **"reach out"** and touch his side, we see how he longed for Thomas and us to believe — for it was not just to Thomas, but to us too that he looked, that there might be nothing lacking to confirm our faith.

Thomas's stupidity was astonishing and monstrous; he was not satisfied with just seeing Christ but wanted to have his hands also witness Christ's resurrection. Thus he was not only obstinate but also proud and insulting towards Christ. At least now, when he saw Christ, he ought to be overwhelmed with shame and amazement; but on the contrary he stretches out his hand boldly and fearlessly as if unconscious that he was in the wrong. We may readily infer from the evangelist's words that he did not come to his senses until he had been convinced by touching. When we give God's Word less honor than is due to it, a growing obstinacy comes over us unawares, bringing with it a contempt of the Word and shaking off all reverence for it. We should work all the harder to restrain the wantonness of our mind, so that none of us extinguishes the sense of godliness, so to speak, by wrongly contradicting — or we may shut the gate of faith against ourselves.

28. **"My Lord and my God!"** At last Thomas wakes up and exclaims in wonder, as people often do when they have been out of their minds and then come to themselves. The abruptness of the language is most vehement; doubtless it was shame that made him break out into this expression in order to condemn his own stupidity. Besides, such a sudden exclamation shows that faith was not completely extinguished in him, though it had been smothered; for he is not handling Christ's divinity when he touches his hands or side, but he infers from those signs much more than they showed. How is this except that he comes to himself after forgetfulness and sleep? It therefore shows the truth of what I have already said, that the faith which seemed to be destroyed was, as it were, hidden and buried in his heart.

The same thing happens with many people: they grow wanton for a time, as if they had cast off all fear of God, and no faith appears in them; but as soon as God has punished them with a rod, the rebellion of their sinful nature is subdued, and they return to their right senses. It is certain that disease would not of itself be sufficient to teach godliness; so we infer that when the obstructions have been removed, the good seed, which had been lying smothered, springs up. There is a striking instance of this in David. As long as he is given up to his lust, we see him indulging without restraint. Everyone would have thought that faith was then completely wiped out of his mind, and yet a brief warning by the prophet recalls him so suddenly that we may easily infer that some spark still remained in his mind, though it was smothered, and now it quickly bursts into flame. As far as these men themselves are concerned, they are as guilty as if they had renounced faith and all the grace of the Holy Spirit. But God's boundless goodness prevents the elect from rushing headlong into complete alienation from God. We should therefore be most careful lest we fall from faith. Yet we must believe that God keeps his elect by a secret bridle, that they may not fall to their destruction, and that he always cherishes miraculously in their hearts some sparks of faith, which he afterwards, at the proper time, rekindles by the breath of his Spirit.

There are two clauses in this confession. Thomas acknowledges Christ as his **"Lord"** and then goes further and also calls him **"God."** We know the sense in which Scripture gives Christ the title of "Lord": the Father made him the chief governor to hold everything under his rule, that every knee may bow before him; in short, that he may be the Father's delegate in governing the world. Thus the name "Lord" properly belongs to him, inasmuch as he is the Mediator revealed in the flesh and is head of the church. But Thomas, having acknowledged him to be **"Lord,"** is at once, and rightly, carried on to Christ's eternal divinity; for the reason Christ descended to us and was first humbled, and was then placed at the Father's right hand and given dominion over heaven and earth, was so that he could raise us to his own divine glory and the Father's. Therefore, if our faith is to arrive at Christ's eternal divinity, we must begin with the knowledge which is nearer and more easily acquired. Some people have rightly said that by the Christ-Man we are led to the Christ-God, because our faith progresses gradually: we see Christ on earth, born in a stable, and hanging on a cross, and then he rises to the glory of his resurrection, and at last to his eternal life and power, in which shines his divine majesty.

Yet we should understand that we cannot know Christ properly as our **Lord** without the knowledge of his divinity immediately following. Nor is there any doubt that this confession should be common to all believers, for we see that it is approved by Christ. He would certainly never have allowed the Father to be robbed of any honor due to him or such honor to be wrongly transferred to himself. But he clearly ratifies what Thomas said; and this passage is therefore quite sufficient to refute the madness of Arius, for it is unlawful to imagine two Gods. The unity of person in Christ is also expressed here, for the same Christ is called **"Lord"** and **"God."** Thomas twice emphatically calls him his own, showing that he is speaking from a lively and earnest feeling of faith.

29. "Because you have seen me . . ." The only thing Christ blames in Thomas is that he was so slow to believe that he needed to be drawn violently to faith by the experience of his senses, which is altogether inconsistent with the nature of faith. If anyone objects that nothing is more unsuitable than to say that faith is a conviction based on touching and seeing, the answer is easily derived from what I have already said. It was not simply by touching and seeing that Thomas was brought to believe that Christ is God; but, being awakened from sleep, he recalled the teaching which he had almost forgotten. Faith cannot come from the mere experience of things, but must have its origin in the Word of God. Christ therefore blames Thomas for giving less honor to the Word of God than he should have done, and for having regarded faith as linked to the senses, when it springs from hearing and ought to be completely fixed on the Word.

"Blessed are those who have not seen and yet have believed." Here Christ commends faith because it acquiesces in the mere Word and does not depend at all on the sense and reason of the sinful nature. He therefore includes, in a short definition, the power and nature of faith — that it is not content with the immediate exercise of sight but penetrates to heaven, so as to believe what is hidden from human senses. And, indeed, we should give God this honor, that his truth is worthy of being believed on its own account without any other proof.

Faith does indeed have its own sight, but it is one which does not stop at the world and earthly objects. That is why it is called "being . . . certain of what we do not see" (Hebrews 11:1). Paul contrasts it with "sight" (2 Corinthians 5:7), meaning that it is not content with looking at the condition of present objects and does not look about in all directions to the things that are visible in the world, but depends on the mouth of God and, relying on his Word, rises above the whole world to fix its anchor in heaven. In short, there is no true faith but that which is founded on God's Word and rises to the invisible kingdom of God so as to go beyond all human understanding.

You may object that this saying of Christ is inconsistent with another of his sayings, where he states that the "eyes" which "see" him are "blessed" (Matthew 13:16). But I reply that Christ is not just speaking of physical sight there, as he is in this passage, but of revelation, which is common to all believers from the time the Redeemer appeared in the world. In Matthew 13:17 he compares the apostles with the prophets and righteous men who had been kept under the obscure shadows of the Mosaic law. He says that the condition of believers now is much more desirable, because a brighter light is shining on them, or rather because the substance and truth of the images is revealed to them. There were many unbelievers at that time who saw Christ with their physical eyes and yet were no more blessed by it; but we who have never seen Christ physically enjoy the blessedness which Christ commands. It follows that he calls **"blessed"** the eyes which see in him spiritually what is heavenly and divine.

Today we see Christ in the Gospel in the same way as if he were standing with us. In this sense Paul says to the Galatians, "Before your very eyes Jesus Christ was clearly portrayed as crucified" (Galatians 3:1). Therefore, if we want to see in Christ what will make us happy and **"blessed,"** let us learn to believe when we do not see. To these words of Christ corresponds what is said in 1 Peter 1:8: "Though you have not seen him, you love him; and even though you do not see him now, you believe in him and are filled with an inexpressible and glorious joy."

It is absurd how the Roman Catholics distort these words to prove their doctrine of transubstantiation. That we may be **"blessed,"** they tell us to believe that Christ is present in the likeness of bread. But we know that nothing was farther from Christ's thoughts than to subject faith to human inventions; and as soon as it passes in the slightest degree beyond the limits of the Word, it ceases to be faith straightaway. If we have to believe uncritically all that we do not see, then every monstrous thing that people may like to invent, every fable they may make up, will imprison our faith. If this saying of Christ is to apply to the case in hand, we must first prove from the Word of God the very point in question. They bring forward the Word of God in support of their transubstantiation, but when the Word is expounded properly it does not support their view.

Verses 30–31

30. Jesus did many other miraculous signs. If the evangelist had not warned his readers by saying this, they might have thought that he had not left out any of the miracles that Christ performed and had given a full and complete account. John therefore declares that he has only written some things out of a large number — not that the others were unworthy of being included, but because these were enough to build up faith. And yet it does not follow that the others were performed in vain, for they were of benefit to that age. Secondly, although they are unknown to us today, we must not deduce that it is of little importance for us to know that the Gospel was sealed by a large number of miracles.

31. But these are written that you may believe . . . By these words he means that he committed to writing what ought to satisfy us, because it is quite sufficient to confirm our faith. He wanted to reply to people's empty curiosity, which is insatiable and allows itself excessive indulgence. Besides, John was well aware of what the other evangelists had written, and as nothing was farther from his intention than to supersede their writings, he certainly does not separate their narrative from his own.

It may seem absurd, however, that faith is based on such miracles when it ought to be devoted exclusively to God's promises and Word. I reply: no other use is here assigned to miracles than to be aids and supports of faith. They serve to prepare people's minds, so that they may give greater reverence to the Word of God. We know how cold and sluggish our attention is if we are not excited by something external. Besides, it adds no small authority to the teaching already received when, to support it, he stretches out his mighty hand from heaven — just as Mark says that the apostles taught, "and the Lord worked with them and confirmed his word by the signs that accompanied it" (Mark 16:20). Therefore, although faith properly rests on the Word of God and looks to the Word as its only object, the addition of miracles is not superfluous, provided they are related to the Word and direct faith to it. We have already explained why miracles are called **signs.** It is because by them the Lord prompts people to contemplate his power when he displays anything strange and unusual.

. . . that Jesus is the Christ. He means **the Christ** as he had been promised in the Law and the Prophets — the Mediator between God and men, the Father's supreme ambassador, the only restorer of the world, and the author of perfect happiness. John was not seizing on a bare and empty title to adorn **the Son of God** but included in the name of **Christ** all the offices which the prophets ascribe to him. Therefore, we must contemplate him as he is described there. This shows more clearly what was said a little while ago, that faith does not restrict its view to miracles but carries us direct to the Word. It is as if John had said that what the prophets had taught in words had been proved in miracles. And, indeed, we see that the evangelists themselves do not stop at describing the miracles but dwell more on the teaching, for miracles by themselves would produce nothing but a confused wonder. Therefore, the words mean that these things were **written** so that we might **believe,** as far as faith can be helped by signs.

... **the Son of God.** He adds this because not one of the ordinary rank of men could have been found fit to perform such great things — to reconcile the Father to us, to atone for the sins of the world, to abolish death, to destroy Satan's kingdom, to bring us true righteousness and salvation. Moreover, as the name of **Son** belongs only to Christ, it follows that he is a **Son** by nature and not by adoption. Therefore, this name contains Christ's eternal divinity. And, indeed, anyone who does not realize, through such shining proofs as are in the Gospel, that Christ is God is not even worthy to look at the sun and the earth, for he is blind in clear light.

... **that by believing you may have life.** This effect of faith was added to restrain human desire, so that we may not desire to know more than is sufficient for obtaining **life.** What wickedness it was to not be satisfied with eternal salvation and to want to go beyond the bounds of the heavenly kingdom! John here repeats the most important point of his teaching, that we obtain eternal **life** by faith, because outside Christ we are dead, and we are restored to **life** only by his grace. We have spoken fully enough about this in commenting on chapters 3 and 5.

... **in his name.** As to John's saying **his name** rather than just **Christ,** the reason has been explained in commenting on 1:12.

John
Chapter 21

Verses 1–14

1. Afterwards Jesus appeared again. The evangelist is still working to prove Christ's resurrection, and he tells us that Christ appeared to seven disciples, among whom he mentions Thomas, not out of respect to him but because his witness is the more credible in view of his obstinate unbelief. The evangelist gives sufficient detail, for he carefully collects all the evidence which substantiates the story.

3. "I'm going out to fish." Peter gave his attention to fishing, and this should not be thought of as being inconsistent with his office. When Jesus **breathed on** him (20:22), he had ordained him to be an apostle, as we saw a little earlier. But Peter refrained from exercising the office of apostleship for a short time, until he was clothed with new power. For he had not yet been told to appear in public to carry out his office of teaching, but had only been reminded of his future calling, so that he, and the others, might understand that they had not in vain been chosen from the beginning. Meanwhile, they did what they were used to doing, and what men do in private life. It is true that Paul, in the middle of his preaching work, earned a living by using his own hands, but this was for a different reason. His time was so organized that his manual labors did not interfere with his teaching. Peter and his companions, on the other hand, gave themselves up entirely to fishing, because they were not engaged in any public duties.

But that night they caught nothing. God permitted them to work hard for no reward throughout the whole **night**, in order to demonstrate the truth of the miracle. Had they caught any fish, what followed immediately afterwards would not have demonstrated the power of Christ so clearly. But when they work to no avail throughout the night, and then are suddenly favored with a huge catch of fish, they have good reason for acknowledging the goodness of the Lord. In the same way, God often tests believers, so that he may lead them to value his blessing more highly. If we were always prosperous whenever we started our work, hardly anyone would attribute the success of his labors to God's blessing. Everyone would boast about their work and congratulate himself. But when they sometimes work and toil without any results, and then later are successful, they are bound to acknowledge something out of the ordinary. This results in their beginning to praise God's goodness for their prosperity and success.

6. "Throw your net on the right side of the boat." Christ does not command with authority and power as Master and Lord but advises like one of the people. The disciples, who are at a loss about what to do, readily obey him, even though they do not realize who he is. If anything like this had been said to them before they started fishing, they would not have obeyed so quickly. I mention this so that no one may think that they were so submissive, for they had already been worn out by long and useless toil. Yet it demonstrated great patience and perseverance that, though they had labored unsuccessfully throughout the night, they continue their toil after daybreak. If we want to allow an opportunity for the blessing of God to come on us, we should constantly expect it, for nothing is more unreasonable than to stop working immediately if it does not promise to be successful.

That Simon Peter was naked proves that the disciples had worked earnestly. Yet they do not hesitate to throw **the net** again — to try once more, so that they may not miss any opportunity. Their obedience to Christ's command cannot be ascribed to faith, since they listened to him as a person who was unknown to them. If we dislike our calling because the work which we engage in seems to be unproductive, we should still take courage when the Lord exhorts us to steadfast perseverance. In the end we shall receive a happy result, but it will come at the right time.

They were unable to haul the net in. Here Christ demonstrated two examples of his divine power. The first consisted in their taking such a large catch of fish; secondly, despite his hidden power, he kept **the net** whole, which would otherwise have been torn to shreds. Other details are mentioned also — namely, that the disciples find burning coals on the shore, that the fish are laid on them, and that bread is also prepared. As far as the number of the fish is concerned, we should not look for any deep mystery here. Augustine gives ingenious ideas about the number of fish and says that it denotes the law and the Gospel, but if we examine the matter carefully, we shall find that this is childish trifling.

7. Then the disciple whom Jesus loved said to Peter . . . The evangelist shows, through his example, that it is our duty to raise our hearts to God whenever we succeed in anything beyond our expectation, for we should instantly remember that this act of kindness has flowed from the grace of him who is the author of every blessing. That holy recognition of the grace of God which lived in John's heart also led him to the knowledge of Christ. For he does not perceive Christ with his eyes but, being convinced that the great multitude of fishes had been brought to him by God's hand, he concludes that it was Christ who had guided his hands. But as John has faith before Peter, so Peter excels him in zeal after him, when he disregards personal danger and jumps into the water. The rest follow in the ship. It is true that they all come to Christ in the end, but Peter is motivated by a special zeal in comparison with the others. Whether he reached the shore by walking or by swimming is uncertain. It is enough for us to know that the act of leaving the ship and going to the shore was not a foolish or rash action, but showed that he had made more progress than the others in zeal.

10. **"Bring some of the fish you have just caught."** Although the net was filled in a moment, without any great effort on their part, this catch is now attributed to the disciples by Christ. Thus, we call the bread which we daily eat, "*our* bread," and yet, by asking that it may be given to us, we acknowledge that it comes from the blessing of God (Matthew 6:11).

12. **None of the disciples dared ask him . . .** It may be asked, what stopped them? Was it shame arising from reverence, or was it something else? But if Christ saw that they were uncertain, he should have removed their doubt, as he had done on many other occasions. I reply: the disciples did not ask Christ because they were afraid of wronging him, so clearly did he show himself to them through his signs.

14. **The third time.** The number three refers to the space of time. Christ had already appeared to his disciples more than seven times, but all that had happened in one day and is counted as one appearance. Therefore the evangelist means that Christ had been seen by the disciples at intervals, in order to confirm their belief in his resurrection.

Verses 15–19

15. **When they had finished eating . . .** The evangelist now relates how Peter was restored to the rank of honor from which he had fallen. This treacherous denial, which has been previously described, had undoubtedly made him unworthy of being an apostle. How could he be able to instruct others in the faith, considering he had rebelled against it so badly? He had been made an apostle, but so had Judas. From the time that Peter had abandoned his post, he had been deprived of the honor of apostleship. Now both the liberty and the authority to teach, both of which he had lost through his own fault, are restored to him. So that the degree of his apostasy might not stand in his way, Christ blots out and destroys its memory. This kind of restoration was necessary, both for Peter and for his hearers. Peter needed it so that he might carry out the duties of his office more boldly once he was reassured that he had been called by Christ and was reinstated. His hearers needed to know

that Peter was restored, so that the blot on his personality might not be a reason to despise the Gospel. For us today, it is very important indeed that Peter emerges for us as a new man, no longer in disgrace, so that his authority is not diminished.

"Simon son of John, do you truly love me more than these?" Through these words Christ shows that no one can serve the church faithfully and manage to feed the flock unless he looks beyond men. First, the office of feeding is in itself hard work and full of difficulties, for nothing is more difficult than keeping men under God's yoke. Many of these people are weak, others are evil and unsteady, others are dull and sluggish, and others are slow and unteachable. Satan advances all the stumbling blocks he can, in order to destroy or weaken the courage of a good pastor.

In addition to this, we must bear in mind many people's dismay. So, no one will steadfastly persevere in carrying out this office unless Christ's love rules in his heart in such a way that he forgets himself and devotes himself entirely to Christ and overcomes every obstacle. Paul declares that he felt like this when he says, "For Christ's love compels us, because we are convinced that one died for all, and therefore all died" (2 Corinthians 5:14). Although he means the love with which Christ loved us, and of which he shows us proof in his death, yet he links with this the mutual love which springs from the experience of having received so great a blessing. On the other hand, ungodly and false teachers are identified by him in another passage as "anyone" who "does not love the Lord" (1 Corinthians 16:22).

Therefore, those who are called to govern the church should remember that if they wish to discharge their office correctly and faithfully, they must start with the love of Christ. Meanwhile, Christ testifies clearly how highly he values their salvation when he uses such earnest and striking language. He also declares that if the salvation of their flock is the aim of their earnest efforts, he will see it as proof of the strength of their love for himself. Indeed, nothing better could have been said that was more appropriate for encouraging the ministers of the Gospel than to tell them that no service can be more pleasing to Christ than that which is spent on feeding his flock. All believers should take special comfort from this. They are taught that they are so dear and so precious in the sight of the Son of God that he substitutes the pastors, as it were, for himself. This same teaching should also frighten false teachers who corrupt and overturn the government of the church, for Christ, who declares that he is insulted by them, will inflict on them dreadful punishment.

"Feed my lambs." The word **"feed"** is metaphorically applied by Scripture to any kind of governing; since the subject in hand is the spiritual government of the church, it is important to note in what the office of pastor or shepherd consists. No meaningless position is described here to us; nor does Christ bestow on a mortal man any government to be exercised by him in a muddled way just as he pleases. In the explanation of chapter 10, we have seen that Christ is the only pastor or shepherd of the church. We have seen also why he applies this name to himself. It is because he feeds — that is, governs — his sheep, because he is the only true food of the soul. But because he uses men to preach this doctrine, he also gives them his own name, or at least shares it with them. Therefore, these men are seen as pastors in God's sight as they govern the church through the ministry of the Word, under Christ, who is their head. Hence we may easily understand what burden Christ lays on Peter, and on what condition he appoints him to govern his flock.

This enables us to refute clearly the Church of Rome, which twists this passage to support the Popery. "To Peter," they tell us, "in preference to others, it is said, '**Feed my lambs.**'" We have already explained the reason why this was said to him rather than to the others; namely, so that, being free from every disgraceful blot, he might boldly preach the Gospel. Christ three times appoints him to be pastor so that the three denials through which Peter had brought on himself everlasting shame may be set aside and thus may form no barrier to his apostleship. This has been judiciously observed by Chrysostom, Augustine, Cyril, and most of the other commentators. Besides, nothing was given to Peter through these words that is not also given to all the ministers of the Gospel.

Therefore, it is in vain for the Roman Catholics to maintain that Peter holds the highest position since he alone is specially spoken to. While I agree that some special honor was conferred on him, I ask, how will they prove from this that he has been elevated to the primacy? Though he was the most important among the apostles, does it follow from this that he was the universal bishop of the whole world? On what ground does the Pope claim to be Peter's heir? Can anyone with sound understanding agree that Christ bestows on him here any hereditary right? As Christ gave Peter the duty of teaching, but did not intend to erect a throne through which some could miserably oppress the church, so he says briefly what kind of church government he approves of. This unmasks all the mitered bishops who, satisfied with a mere theatrical display and an empty title, claim for themselves episcopal authority.

16. "Take care of my sheep." Christ does not give to Peter and others the office of feeding every kind of person, but only his **"sheep"** or his **"lambs"** (verse 15). Elsewhere he describes those whom he reckons belong to his flock. **"My sheep,"** he says in effect, "hear my voice, and follow me; they do not recognize a stranger's voice" (see 10:5, 27). True, faithful teachers must try to bring everyone to Christ. Since they cannot distinguish between **"sheep"** and wild beasts, they should try by every possible way to tame those who resemble wolves rather than **"sheep."** But having done their very best, their labor will be no good to anyone except for the elect **"sheep."** For docility and faith come when the Heavenly Father gives those individuals to his Son, so that they may obey him. These are the people he elected before the creation of the world. Again, this passage teaches us that no one can be "fed" to salvation by the teaching of the Gospel except those who are humble and teachable; Christ has a good reason for comparing his disciples to **"lambs"** (verse 15) and **"sheep."** However, it must also be noted that the Spirit of God tames those who by nature were bears or lions.

17. Peter was hurt. Peter undoubtedly did not understand why Christ kept on asking the same question, and so he thinks he is being obliquely blamed for not replying sincerely to Christ. But we have already shown that this repetition was not superfluous. Besides, Peter was not yet sufficiently aware how deeply Christ's love must be engraved on the hearts of those who have to struggle against innumerable difficulties. He later learned through long experience that such a trial was not wasted. Leaders in church government are also taught, through Peter, that they should not examine themselves superficially, so that they will not shrink or faint in the middle of their work. Likewise, we are taught that we should patiently and humbly submit if the Lord ever subjects us to a severe trial, because he has good reasons for doing so, although these are generally unknown to us.

18. "I tell you the truth ..." Having exhorted Peter to feed his sheep, Christ also equips him for the impending warfare. Thus he demands from him not only faithfulness and diligence, but invincible courage in danger and steadfastness in bearing the cross. In short, he tells him to be prepared to die whenever this becomes necessary. Although all pastors are not in the same situation, this warning applies to them all to a certain extent. The Lord spares many and does not shed their blood, but is simply satisfied that they devote themselves to him sincerely and unreservedly all their lives. But as Satan continually makes many new attacks, anyone who takes on the office of feeding must be prepared for death since they must not only look after the **"sheep"** but also cope with the wolves. So far as this relates to Peter, Christ wanted to forewarn him about his death, so that he might always remember that the teaching of which he was a minister must eventually be sealed with his own blood. However, it seems that in these words Christ was not thinking only of Peter, but that he honored him with the title of *martyr* in company with the others, as if to say that Peter would be a very different kind of fighter from what he had previously shown himself to be.

"When you were younger ..." Old age seems to be set aside for tranquillity and rest; so old men are usually relieved of public duties, and soldiers are discharged from the army. Thus Peter might have contemplated a peaceful old age. But Christ declares that the order of nature will be reversed, so that he who had lived at his ease when he was young will be ruled by someone else when he is old and even endure violent subjection.

In Peter we have a striking image of our own situation. Many have an easy and pleasant life before Christ calls them; but as soon as they confess his name and are welcomed as his disciples, or at least sometime later, they are drawn into tough struggles, to a life full of troubles, to great dangers, and sometimes to death itself. This situation, though hard, must be patiently endured. Yet the Lord softens the cross through which he likes to test his servants, so that he spares them for a little time until their fortitude has returned. For the Lord is well aware of their weakness and does not push them beyond their limit. Thus he put up with Peter while he remained feeble and weak. So we must devote ourselves to him with every breath, so long as he continues to give us strength.

In this respect the base ingratitude of many people is apparent. For the more gently the Lord deals with us, the more completely we live a soft life. So we can hardly find one person in a hundred who does not complain if after a lengthy period of endeavor he is treated harshly in some way. What we should do is reflect on God's goodness in sparing us for any length of time. So Christ says that while he lived on earth he talked cheerfully with his disciples, as if he had been at a marriage, but that later fasting and tears were in store for them (see Matthew 9:15).

18. "Someone else will dress you." Many people think that this refers to the kind of death which Peter would suffer, meaning that he was hanged with his arms stretched out. But I think the word **"dress"** simply denotes all the outward actions which govern a man's whole life. **"You dressed yourself"** means, "you were used to wearing the kind of clothes you chose." But now "this freedom of choice in your dress will be taken from you." It is better to remain ignorant about the way in which Peter was killed than to trust unreliable stories.

". . . and lead you where you do not want to go." This means that Peter did not die a natural death, but a violent one with the sword. It may seem strange that Christ should say that Peter's death will not be voluntary. This must refer to the struggle between the flesh and the Spirit, which believers experience within themselves. For we never obey God in a free and unrestricted way, but are rather dragged, as if by ropes, in the opposite direction, by the world and the flesh. Hence Paul complains, "What I do is not the good I want to do; no, the evil I do not want to do — this I keep on doing" (Romans 7:19). In addition to this, we note that the fear of death is naturally implanted in us, for to desire to leave the body is repugnant to nature. Thus Christ, although he was prepared to obey God with his whole heart, prayed that he might be delivered from death. Moreover, Christ feared the cross because of men's cruelty, and therefore we need not be surprised if to some extent he shrank from the prospect of death. But this revealed more clearly his obedience to God. Although he would have happily avoided death left

469

to himself, he did nevertheless endure it voluntarily, because he knew that this was God's will. Had there not been a mental struggle, there would have been no need for patience.

It is very beneficial to know about this teaching; it urges us to prayer, because we would never be able, without God's extraordinary help, to conquer the fear of death. So nothing remains for us except to present ourselves humbly to God and to submit to his rule. This teaching also serves to sustain our minds, that we may not completely collapse if persecutions ever make us tremble with fear. People who imagine that the martyrs were unaffected by fear make their own fear a reason for despair. But there is no reason why our weakness should deter us from following their example, since their fear was similar to ours, and they could only triumph over the enemies of truth by battling against themselves.

19. . . . to indicate the kind of death by which Peter would glorify God. This circumlocution is very emphatic. The goal set before all believers should be to glorify God, both by their life and by their death. However, John wanted to especially honor those who died using their blood to seal the Gospel of Christ and glorify his name, as Paul teaches us (Philippians 1:20). We now have a duty to reap the fruit which Peter's death has produced. If our faith is not strengthened by this, and if we do not keep the same goal in view — that God's glory may be seen in us, this can only be put down to our own laziness.

Jesus said this . . . Here Christ explains why he predicted this violent death. It was so that Peter might be prepared to endure it, as if he had said, "Since you must endure death after my example, follow your leader." To help Peter to be more willing to obey God who calls us to the cross, Christ offers himself as the leader. This is not a general exhortation in which he invites Peter to imitate him, as he is just speaking about the kind of death he would undergo. This one thought greatly soothes all the bitterness of death, since the Son of God comes before us with his blessed resurrection, which is our triumph over death.

Verses 20–25

20. Peter turned . . . Peter is an illustration of how our curiosity can be not only superfluous but even harmful when we are distracted from our duty by looking at other people. We find that it comes almost naturally to us to examine the way other people live rather than to examine our own way of living as we put the blame on them for no good reason. We willingly deceive ourselves with this pretense of an apology — that other people are no better than we are, as if their laziness exonerated us. Hardly one person in a hundred considers the impact of Paul's words,

"For each one should carry his own load" (Galatians 6:5). Therefore, in the person of this one man there is a general reproof of all who look around in every direction to see how other people behave, while paying no attention to the duties which God has laid on them. Above all, they are seriously mistaken in neglecting and overlooking what everyone's calling demands.

God may choose just one person in ten to test with weighty calamities or with massive labors, and he might allow the other nine to remain in their ease, or at least test them only lightly. In any case, God does not treat everyone in the same way but tests everyone as he thinks suitable. As there are different kinds of Christian warfare, each person should learn to keep his own position and not make inquiries like busybodies about other people when the heavenly captain commands each one of us; we ought to be so humble in serving him that we forget everything else.

. . . whom Jesus loved. This circumlocution was inserted to tell us why Peter asked the question here related. He thought it strange that he alone should be called, and that John, whom Christ had always **loved** so warmly, should be overlooked. So Peter thought he had a good reason for asking why John was not mentioned, as if Christ had changed his attitude towards him. Yet Christ cuts short his curiosity and tells him to obey God's calling, and that he has no right to inquire what happens to other people.

22. "If I want him to remain . . ." This sentence has often been shortened, and the former clause read affirmatively, in this way: "I want him to remain alive until I return." But this has been done through the ignorance of transcribers, not through the mistake of the translator. For a translator could not make such a mistake about the Greek word, while a single letter could easily creep into the Latin version and so alter the whole meaning. Therefore the whole sentence is a question and ought to be read as one thought; Christ intended to put his hand on his disciple in order to keep him within the limits of his calling. "It is no concern of yours," he says, "and you have no right to inquire what happens to your companion; leave that to me. Be concerned only about yourself, and be ready to follow where you are called." Not that all concern for fellow-Christians should be abandoned, but it should have some limits put on it, so that it may be concern and not curiosity that occupies our attention. So each one should look to his neighbors' concern if this enables him to draw them, in any way, with him to Christ. However, stumbling blocks in other people should not hinder anyone's progress.

23. Because of this, the rumor spread . . . The evangelist says that the disciples believed that John **would not die**, but they misunderstood Christ's words. The evangelist is referring to those who were present at this conversation — that is, the apostles. The name **brothers** was not exclusive to them, but they were the firstfruits, as it were, of that holy fellowship. It is also possible that in addition to the eleven, he refers to others who were with them then. Then the phrase **the rumor spread** refers to this mistake being spread everywhere. But it probably did not last long and only stayed with them until they were enlightened by the Holy Spirit. They thought more purely and more correctly about the kingdom of Christ once they had set aside unspiritual and foolish ideas.

What John says about the apostle happens every day, and we should not be surprised by it. If Christ's disciples, who belonged to his family and were so close to him, were so badly mistaken, how much more are people who have not been so well instructed in Christ's school likely to make mistakes! But we must also note how this mistake arises. It is obvious that Christ's teaching is useful, and it builds us up; but we obscure the light by bringing in wicked ideas of our own making. Christ did not mean to declare anything definite about John, just that he had complete power over his life and death. So the teaching is simple and useful in itself, but the disciples imagine and contrive more than they had been told. To avoid this danger, we must learn to be wise and to think soberly. But the human mind is so evil that it rushes headlong into foolishness. The result was that this very error, against which the evangelist had specifically warned them to be on their guard, still continued to spread in the world. There was a story that John ordered a grave to be dug for him, which he went into, and the next day it was found empty. So we see that we shall never cease to make mistakes unless we unreservedly receive what the Lord has taught us and reject all human inventions.

24. This is the disciple . . . Until now John refers to himself in the third person, but now he declares that it is himself, so that greater weight may be attached to the statements of an eyewitness and to one who had known all about what he writes about.

25. Jesus did many other things as well. In case anyone should suspect his account, as if it had been written with partiality because Jesus loved him, he anticipates this objection and says that he has left out more than he has written. He does not record every single deed of Christ but only those which relate to his public office. We should not imagine that this hyperbole is absurd, when we accept the numerous similar figures of speech in heathen authors. We should not only take into account the number of Christ's deeds, but we should also consider their importance and magnitude. Christ's majesty, because it is infinite, swallowed up (so to speak) both human understanding and heaven and earth as it demonstrated a miraculous display of its own splendor in those deeds. If the evangelist, looking at Christ's brightness, exclaims in astonishment that even the whole world does not have room for a complete narrative, who can be surprised? Nor is he at all at fault when he uses an ordinary figure of speech to commend the excellence of Christ's deeds. For we know how God accommodates himself to our normal way of speaking because of our ignorance.

But we should remember what I have already stated, that the summary which the evangelists have written down is enough both to regulate faith and to bring salvation. Anyone who has really benefitted from such teachers will be truly wise. They were appointed by God to witness to us, and they have faithfully carried out their duty. However, our duty is to rely completely on their testimony and to want nothing more than what they have handed down to us. This is especially the case because they wrote under God's guidance and reliable providence, so that they would not burden us with a limitless mass of narratives and yet, in their selection, would make known to us everything that God knew would be necessary for us. He alone is wise, and the only source of wisdom; to him be praise and glory forever. Amen.

Contemporary Romance
Miami Nights
Miami Inferno
Miami Blaze, Coming Soon

SEAL Team Phantom Series
Delta Salvation
Delta Recon
Delta Rogue, Coming Soon

11-18

DISCARD

CPSIA information can be obtained
at www.ICGtesting.com
Printed in the USA
LVHW080511311018
595357LV00010BA/667/P

9 781537 521275